# Portrait Sculpting

## *Anatomy & Expressions in Clay*

Philippe & Charisse Faraut

On the front cover: *The Fisherman's Daughter*, Philippe Faraut, 2002.
On the back cover: *Creating the Skin of the Neck*, Philippe Faraut. 2003.
*Creating the Wrinkles of the Eyes*, Philippe Faraut. 2003.
*Mask of a Smile*, Philippe Faraut. 2003.
*Mask of Disgust*, Philippe Faraut. 2003.
*Mask of Fear*, Philippe Faraut. 2003.
On the title page: *Mutiny*, in progress, Philippe Faraut. 2004.


First published in 2004 by PCF Studios, Inc.



**Library of Congress Control Number**: 2004093850

**Publisher's Cataloging-in-Publication**
***(Provided by Quality Books, Inc.)***

Faraut, Philippe.
Portrait sculpting : anatomy & expressions in clay / Philippe & Charisse Faraut. -- 1st ed.
p. cm.
Includes bibliographical references and index.
LCCN 2004093850
ISBN-10: 0-9755065-0-1
ISBN-13: 978-0-9755065-0-9

1. Head in art. 2. Modeling. 3. Sculpture--Technique. I. Faraut, Charisse. II. Title.
NB1932.F37 2004 731'.74
QB104-200263

First Edition, 2004
Printed and bound in the United States of America on acid-free paper
*Fourth Printing, 2010*

Visit us at www.pcfstudios.com for information on seminars and supplies for artists.

**Attention colleges and universities**: Quantity discounts are available on bulk purchases of this book for educational purposes. For information, please contact:

PCF
STUDIOS, INC.
PO Box 722 • Honeoye, NY 14471
585-229-2976 • 585-229-2865 fax
info@pcfstudios.com • www.pcfstudios.com

# PORTRAIT SCULPTING

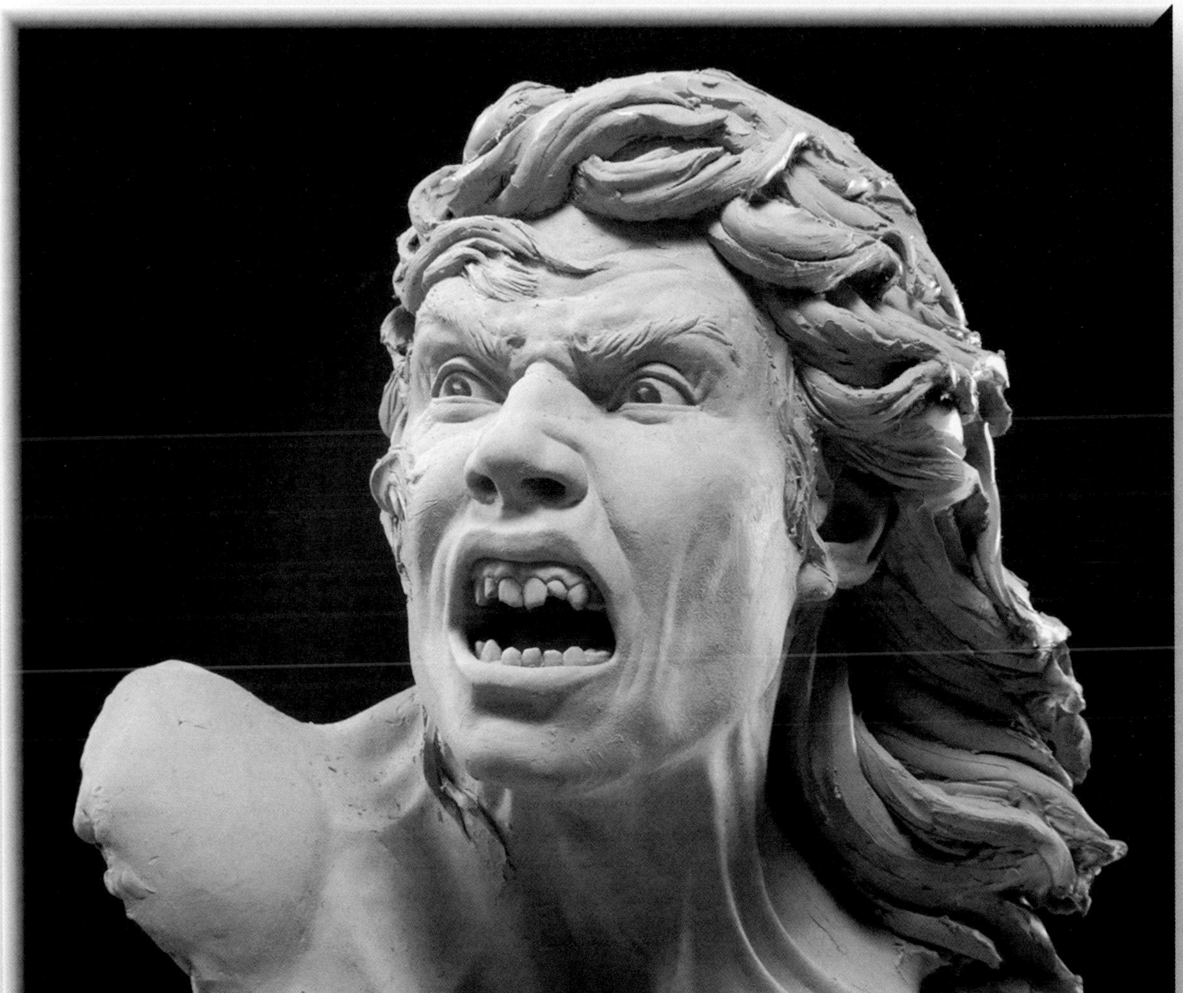

## *Anatomy & Expressions in Clay*

PHILIPPE & CHARISSE FARAUT

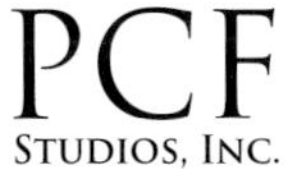

# Foreword

## Is it Genetic?

Buried somewhere deep in the human genome must be a gene for the making of figurative art. People seem to have a built-in urge to produce human images. How else might we explain their persistence in the arts of painting and sculpture? The impulse appears almost as strong as the impulse to produce living offspring. Are the two somehow related? Is there something in mankind's genes that compels us to continually make objects in our own image (including those depicting the various gods)? For whatever reason – and despite a sometimes-inhospitable art world – the human figure has certainly demonstrated its staying power.

In "The Use and Abuse of Art" Jaques Barzun showed that each new wave of 20th century art has regularly been destroyed by the following wave. "Destruction by novelty," Barzun noted, "becomes an incessant function of art." This has been a hallmark of 20th century art. Upheavals by an avant garde, always seeking new ground, have constantly bulldozed the art scene, clearing it of fading shibboleths in preparation for the next new stunner. One theme has consistently resisted whatever the fashion in vogue, however. The human figure in art – under almost continuous attack in the past century – has gone underground when necessary yet continues as a powerful 21$^{st}$ century force.

Inertia has allowed our art schools to continue the convention of offering drawing from life. Such classes, felt vaguely as being necessary, are routinely designated as the preliminary courses from which students are expected to advance onward and upward to yet more important modern pursuits. However rudimentary, these life-drawing courses often trigger the figurative-gene latent in the impressionable young. A few older artists have also felt the representational urge long after their student days have passed. Even those working abstractly are still in danger of falling victim to this figurative gene. Their symptoms may manifest themselves in irrational urges. The stricken sufferer may abandon his notion of novelty or abstraction and return to art school seeking instruction in anatomy, or in advanced drawing, or in figure sculpture. Alternatively he or she may hire a model and plunge headlong into an active program of working directly from life.

Early cultures have all made wonderful figurative objects. Paleolothic peoples have produced "fertility" figures at Willendorf, Lespugue and other places. Egyptian artists have created large and small figures in wood, stone, faience and bronze. The figurative gene, running especially rampant in ancient Greece, has produced bronze and marble figures whose beauty rival nature itself. The Renaissance saw the human figure in art reach its full flower. Seeds from that flower were dispersed in a wide and deep swath. Efforts of modern critics and museums have failed to stamp them out. Those pesky genes will not be inactivated. The figure will continue in art. There's just no stopping it.

Richard McDermott Miller
*(1922-2004)*

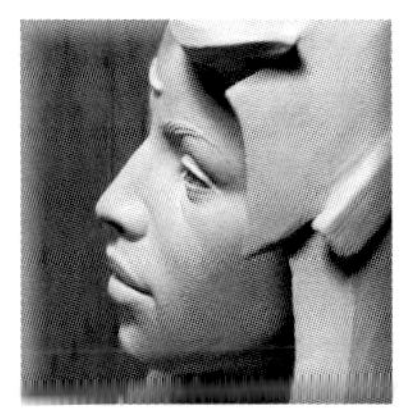

# INTRODUCTION

*All people have the same anatomical structures and number of facial features — cranium, mandible, eyes, mouth, to name a few. Yet, there is infinite variation in these features giving us our individuality. These differences, whether pronounced or subtle, make the face the most challenging part of the human form to sculpt. This is complicated by the fact that most of us have little knowledge of the real shape of the features of the face. Therefore, sculpting it requires not only practice, but also more importantly, the ability to analyze form and the patience to study anatomy. One of the first goals we must have is to learn how to see. It is this ability to observe and analyze what is in front of us that enables us to translate it into clay. A good translation is possible only with the acquisition of good mechanical skills. Thus, both our physical and mental abilities must evolve together through simultaneously practicing the physical act of sculpting, the study of anatomy and the "art of seeing."*

*It is not difficult to take a piece of clay and model something that resembles a face, but to capture a likeness, an expression or even the subtle shape of a mouth, requires the study of bone structure, muscles and some anatomical rules that can rarely be broken. It does not, however, have to be tedious. One does not have to learn the name of every muscle and bone in the human body. If, upon encountering an unfamiliar volume, line or fold, a reference book is required, it may be surprising how rapid an understanding of anatomy can be gained.*

*The goal of this text is to give sculptors of all levels the opportunity to explore portraiture from the inside out. The reader is guided by a series of exercises from building bone structure, through the addition of muscle masses to the subtleties of feature construction. Several unique methods for modeling the head in clay are introduced. These structured approaches encourage the artist to first understand anatomy and volumes, and then in-depth studies of expression, aging and surface textures provide additional tools for mastering advanced portraiture.*

*The number of samples presented offers the opportunity to study a variety of portraits expressing a wide range of emotions. All of the sculptures and illustrations in the following pages are original works of art completed by the authors.*

To Pascal, *Sacwé tonnèw* -P.F.

To my teacher Marie Berg LoParco and my friend Cheri -C.F.

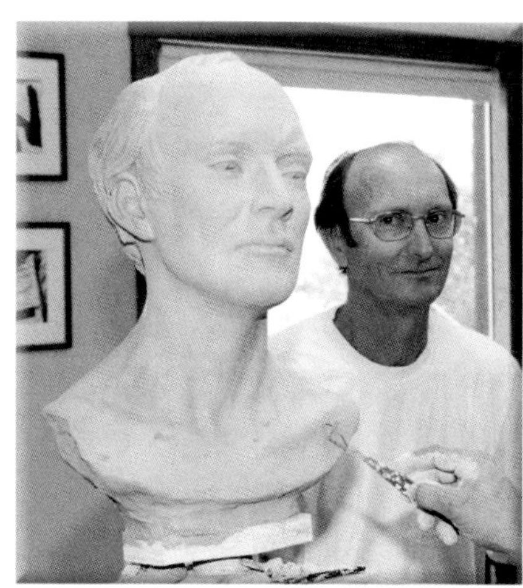

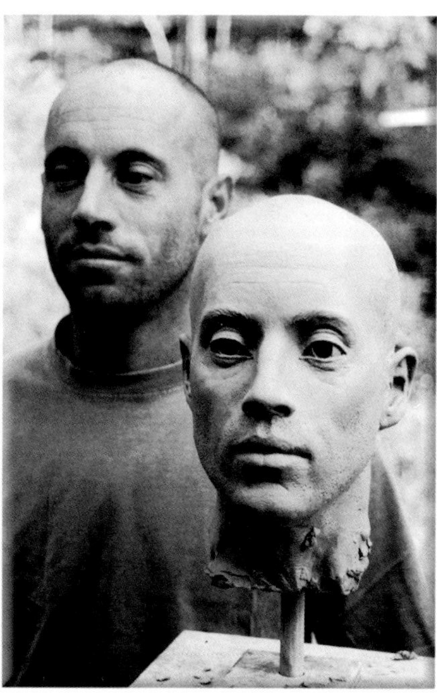

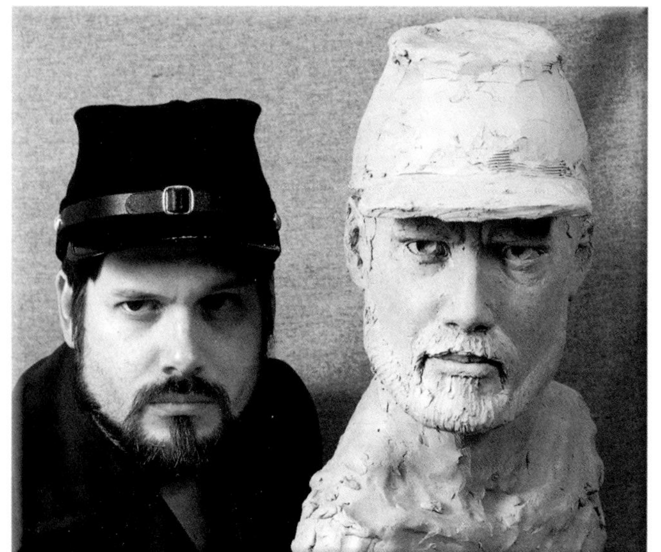

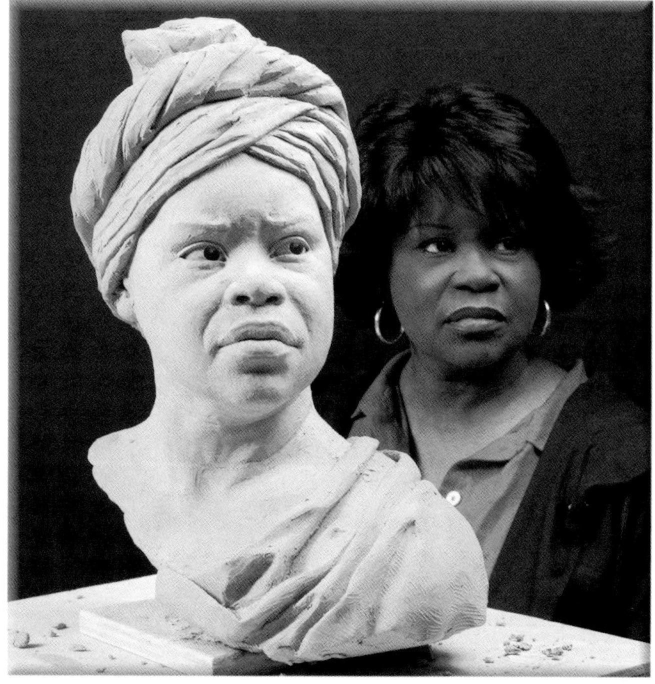

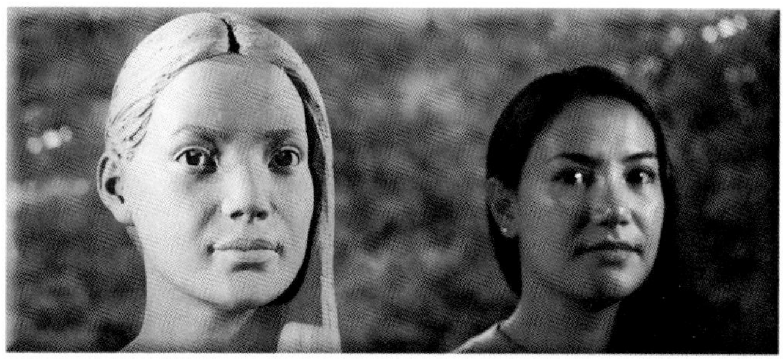

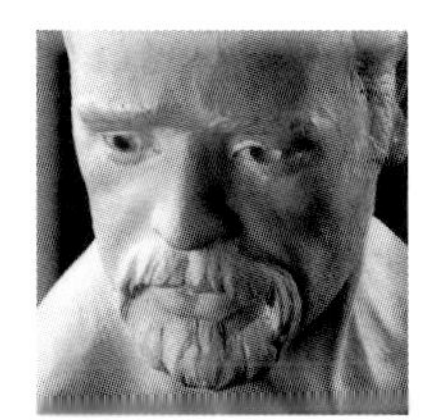

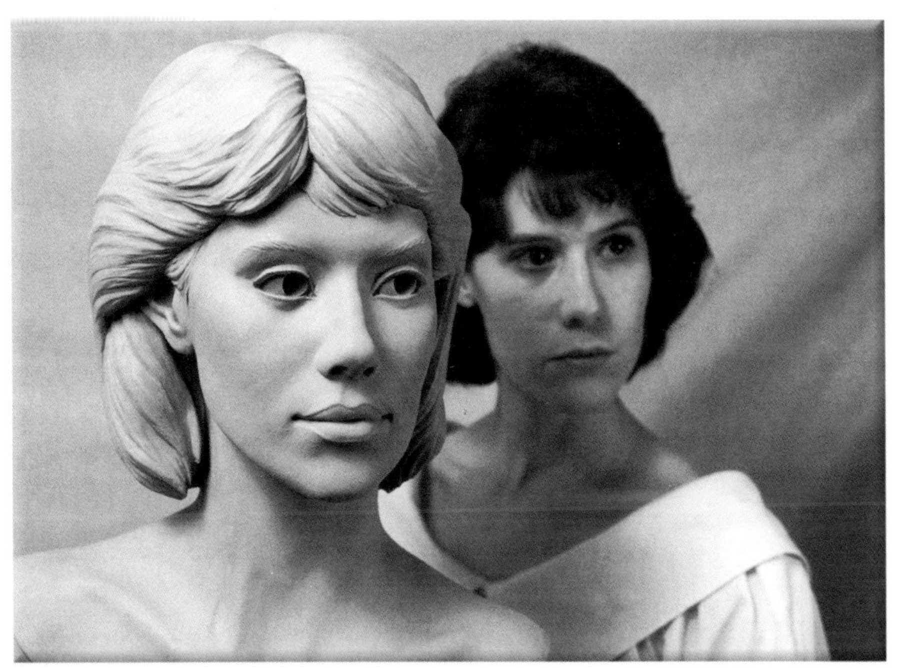

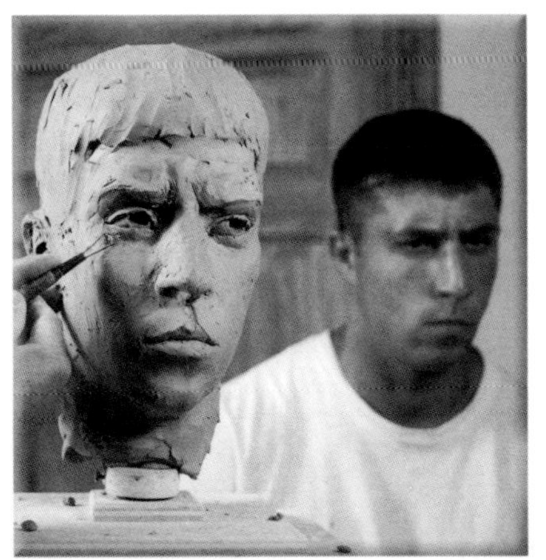

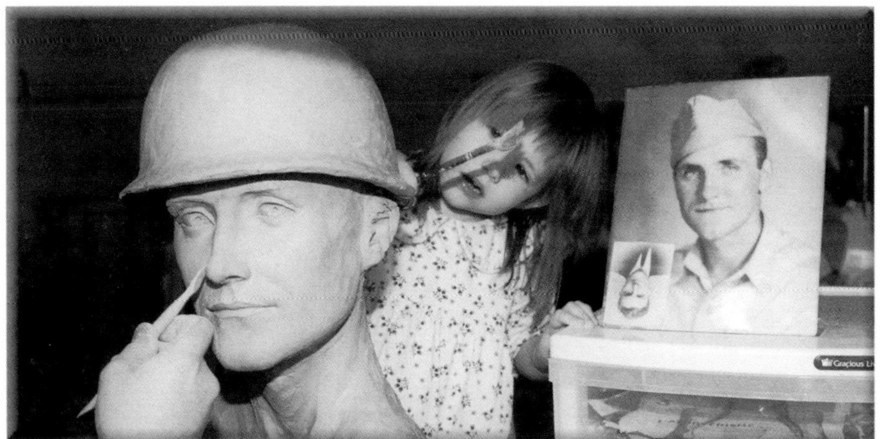

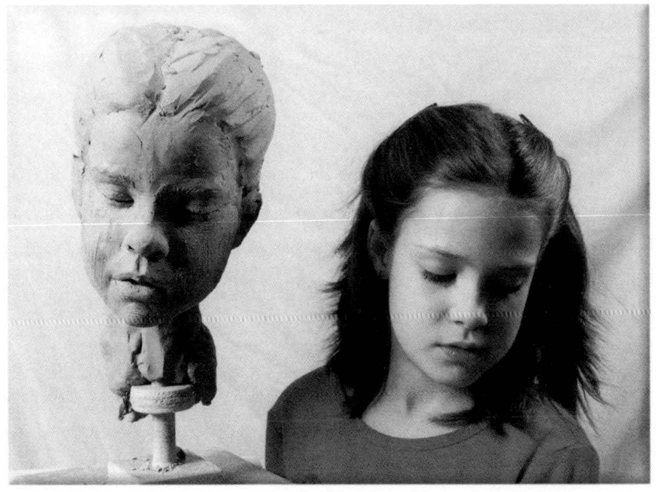

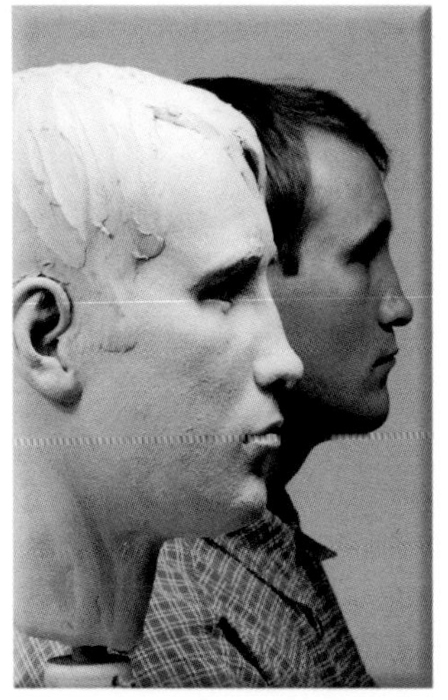

# Table of Contents

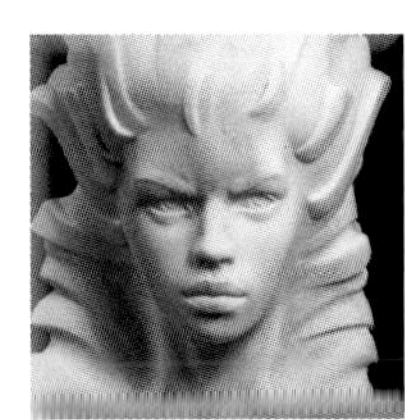



## CHAPTER 8



## CHAPTER 9



**List of Illustrations**

Chapter 1

# Materials, Tools & Lighting

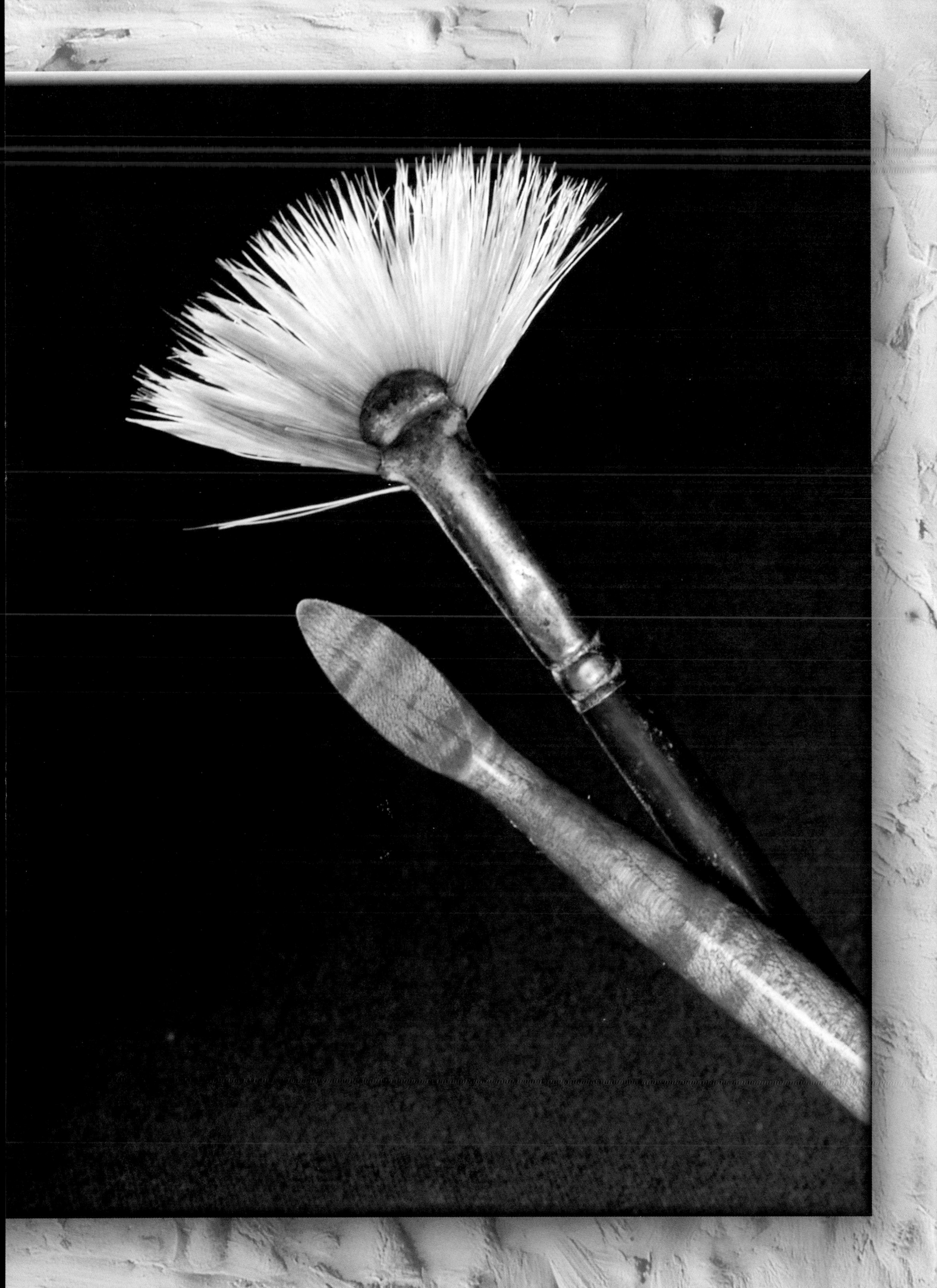

## Clay

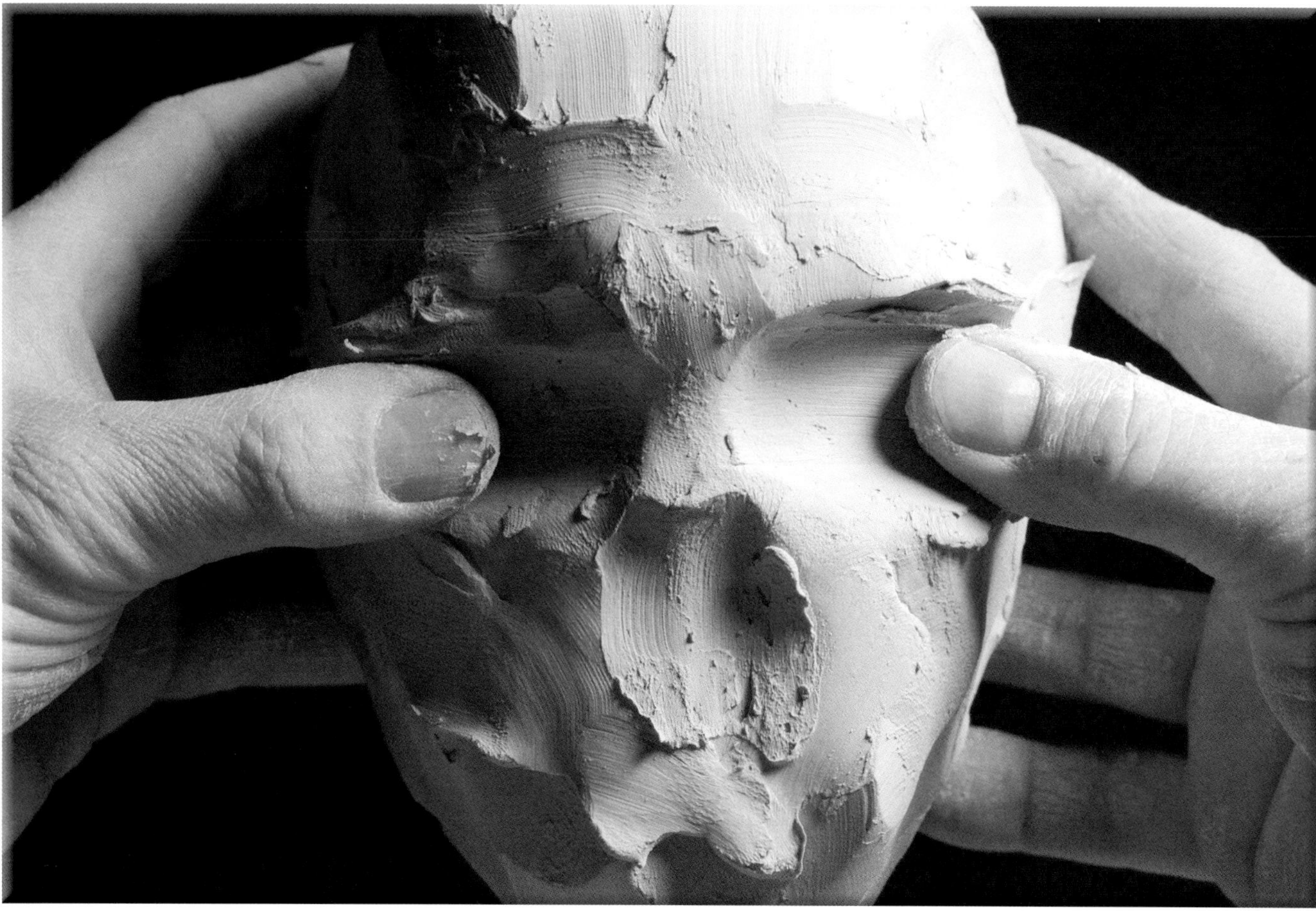

Clay is the natural product of millions of years of gradual weathering of pegmatite rocks such as granite. It is found in sedimentary deposits where it is mined. It is then dried, pulverized, sifted and can either be combined with a mixture of oil and wax to form what is referred to as oil-based clay or hydrated to form water-based clay.

There are three main types of water-based clay: stoneware, porcelain and earthenware. Stoneware is fired at a high temperature resulting in a nonporous material, most commonly used for pottery. Porcelain clay is the most refined, best used for miniature work due to its tendency to sag and crack when used for large pieces. The clay used throughout this book is a low-fire, white earthenware without grog (clay that has been fired, ground and mixed into the clay to reduce shrinkage and give it more body). It is available through ceramic supply stores in 25 pound bags. White refers to the color of the clay once fired. Depending on its origin, it may vary from light gray to almost black when taken from the bag. There is a great variety of other color choices in earthenware ranging from buff to deep red depending on the iron-oxide content. The red colors have the disadvantage of staining both skin and work surfaces.

The main advantage of water-based clay is its range of consistency from very soft and pliable when taken from the bag (which allows rapid build-up of the initial shape) to very firm when dry (which facilitates the refining process). Additionally, it is possible to control the consistency. A piece that has become too dry can be wrapped in wet towels. Conversely, a piece that is too wet will dry if left uncovered. Lastly, any sculpture modeled in wet clay can be fired and kept as a one-of-a-kind piece without going through the steps of mold making. The disadvantage of using water-based clay is the necessity of keeping the piece moist and covered between sessions.

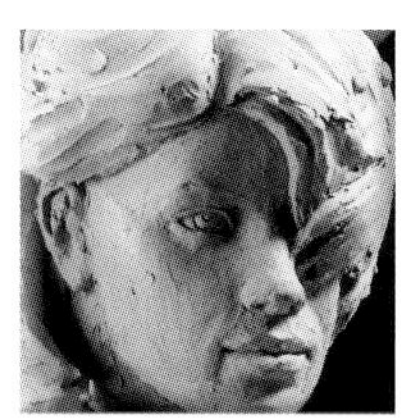

## Stands

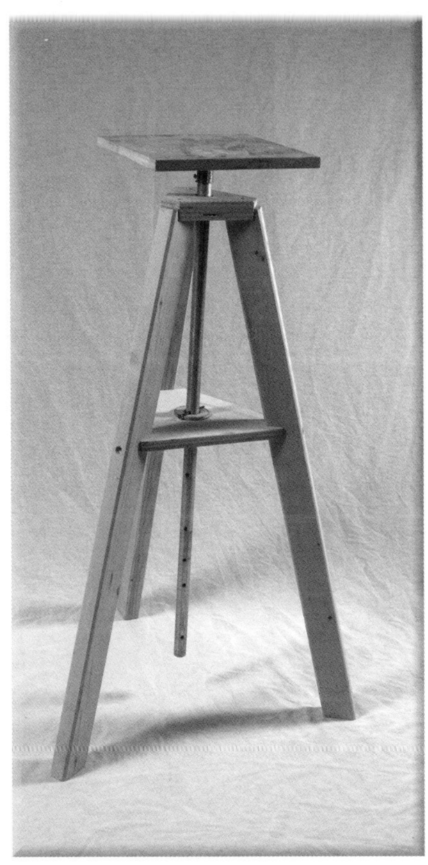

There are several modeling stands on the market. Most of these are very sturdy and often have castors. The design shown above has the advantages of being lightweight, easily broken down for storage and convenient to transport to client locations.

## Armatures

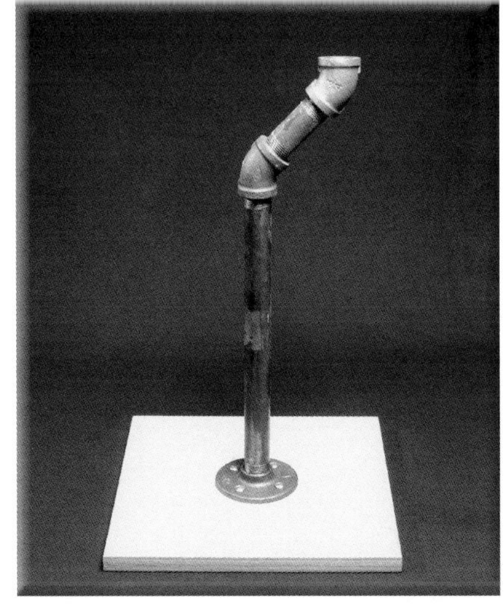

When the position and attitude of the head and shoulders are known at the beginning of a project, this sturdy armature made from metal pipes can be used. All the components are available at hardware stores.

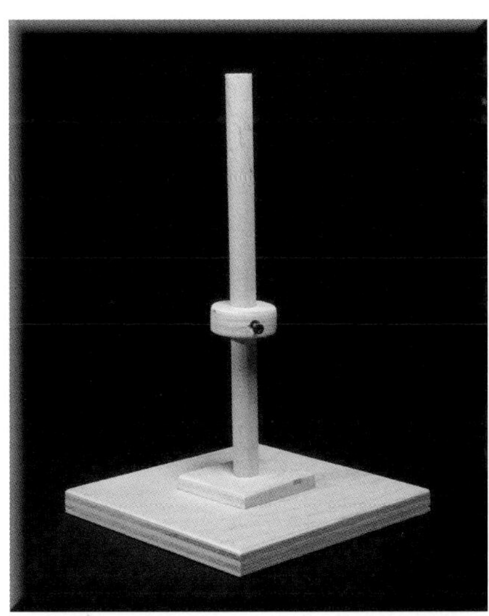

This armature is made of a 10" x 10" piece of plywood and a ¾" dowel with an adjustable plywood washer that prevents the clay, when still very soft, from sagging. Since the dowel is straight, it allows the position and attitude of the head to be changed at any point during the modeling process by sliding the entire sculpture upward and manipulating it in any direction. The washer can then be readjusted to support the new position.

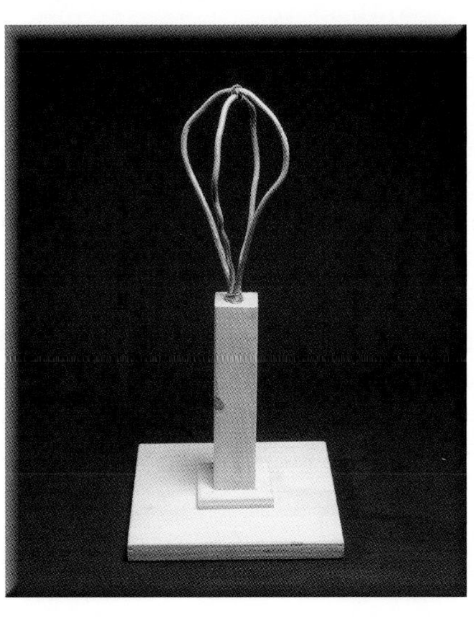

An armature that can be purchased through sculpture supply stores or made at home uses aluminum wires and wood. It is not designed for the piece to be removed for hollowing, as the clay is fully entrapped within the wires. A mold would need to be made from the piece while still on the armature. The sculpture would be destroyed if removed from the armature.

## Tools

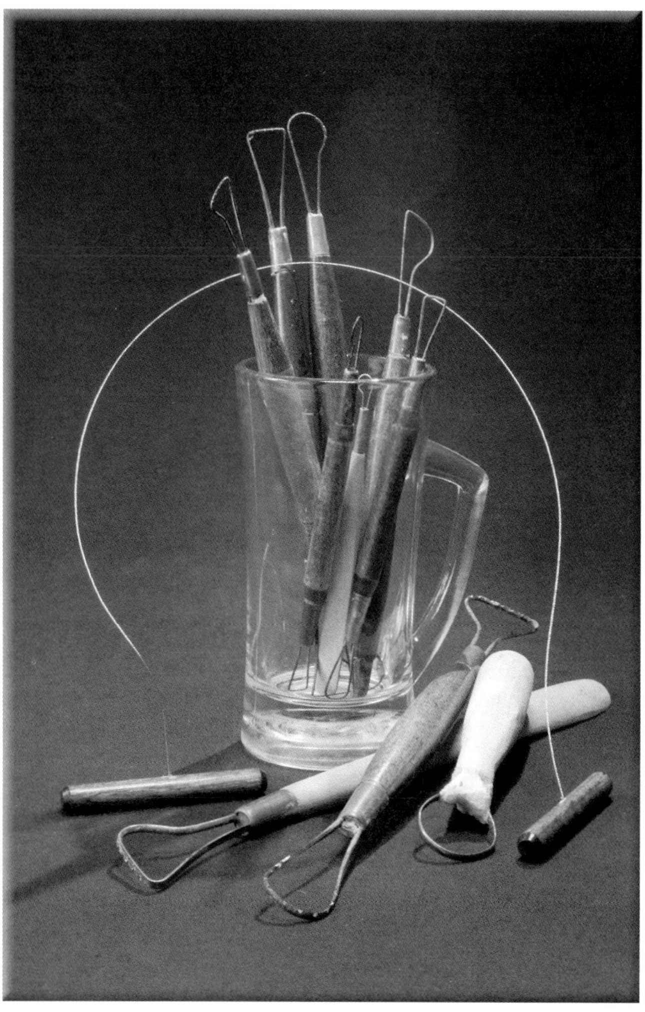

The tools used for modeling clay can be very simple. Most can be hand-made or bought through sculpture supply catalogs and craft stores. Wire tools of different dimensions including one wire clay cutter and ribbon modeling tools with and without teeth are shown above.

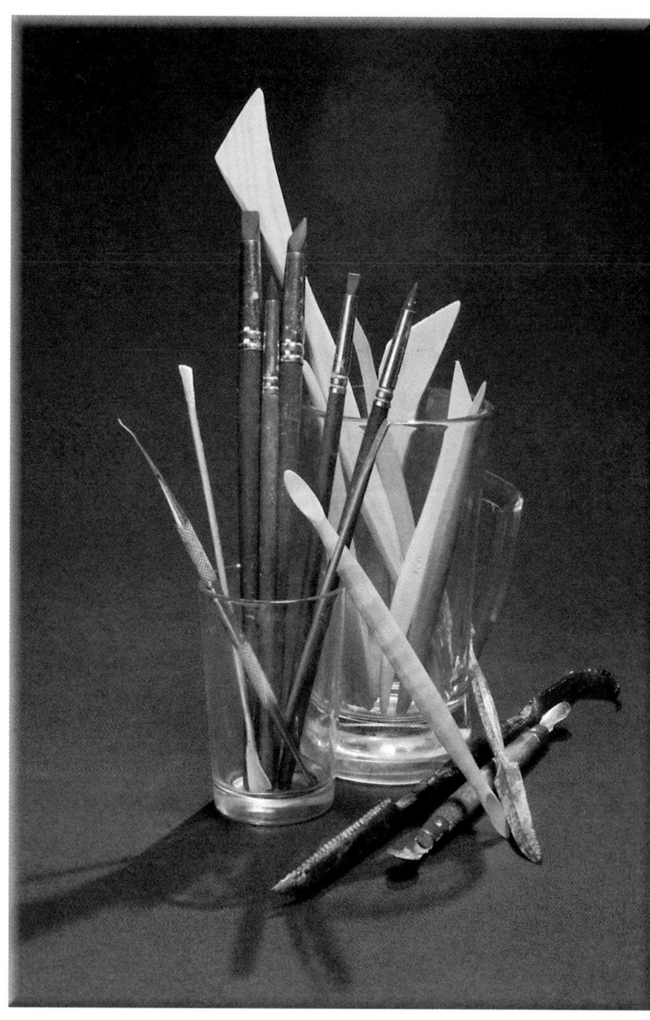

A variety of wooden modeling tools, some purchased and some hand-made are invaluable. Dental tools, silicone tipped tools, plaster modeling and carving tools are useful at different stages.

Scrapers come in a variety of shapes and materials: wood, metal, rubber and plastic.

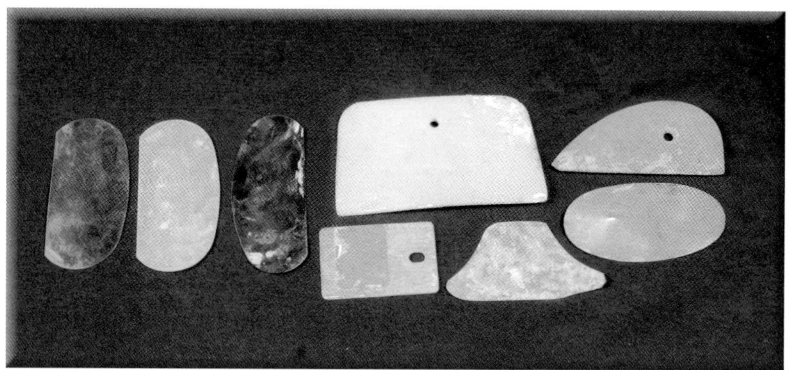

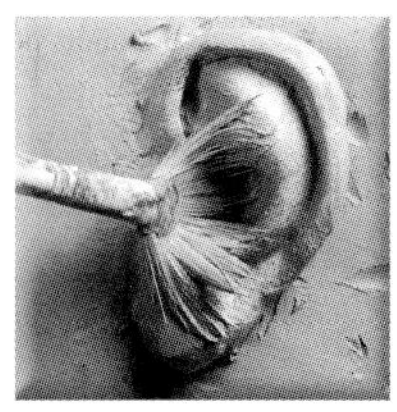

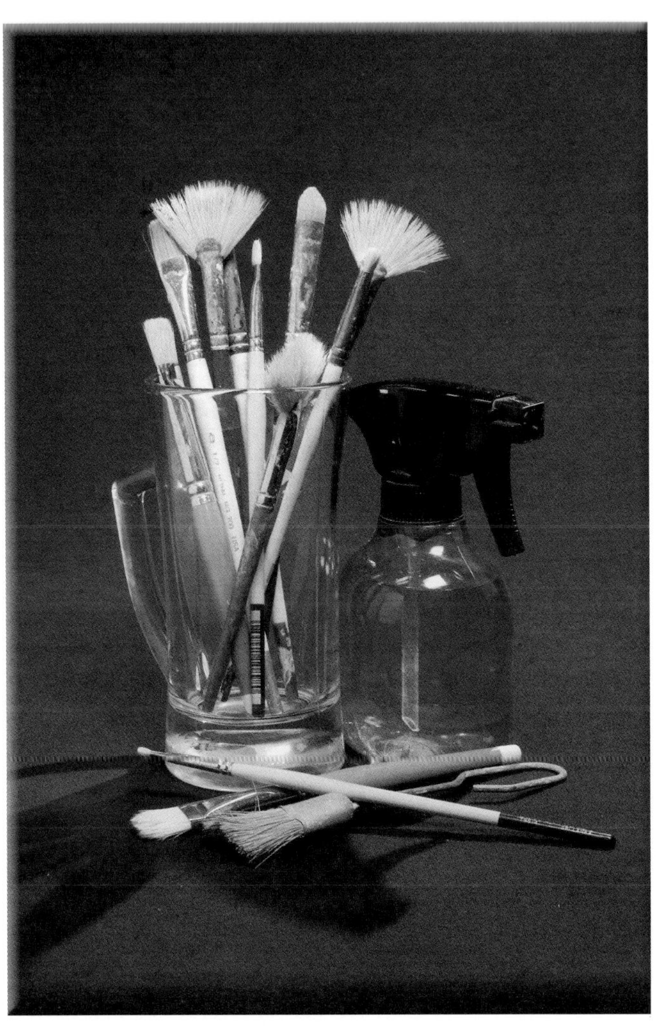

Brushes of different shapes, sizes and stiffness can be used both wet and dry. Of the many varieties available, fan, filbert, flat tipped and even basting brushes can be utilized.

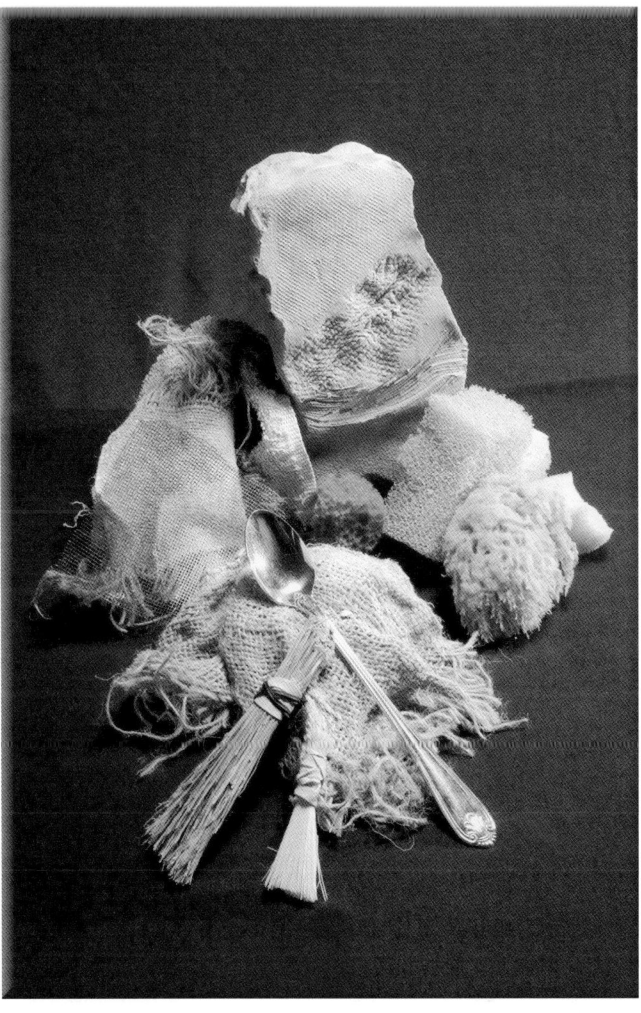

Textures are achieved through the use of many found objects such as sponges, burlap, kitchen utensils, and broom bristles bound with rubber bands.

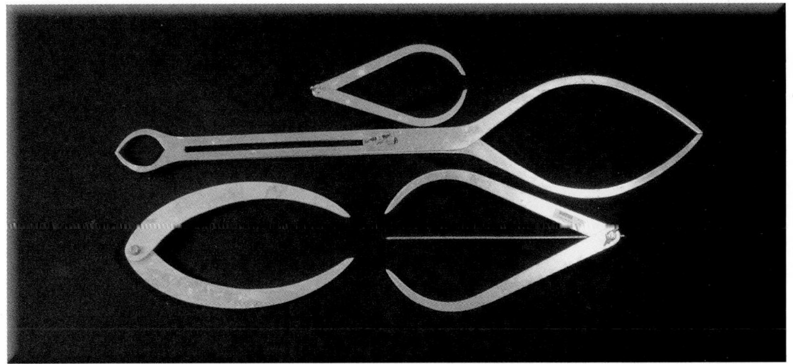

Calipers of different sizes are used to take measurements from the model and apply them to the clay. Proportional calipers are used for enlarging or reducing.

## Reference

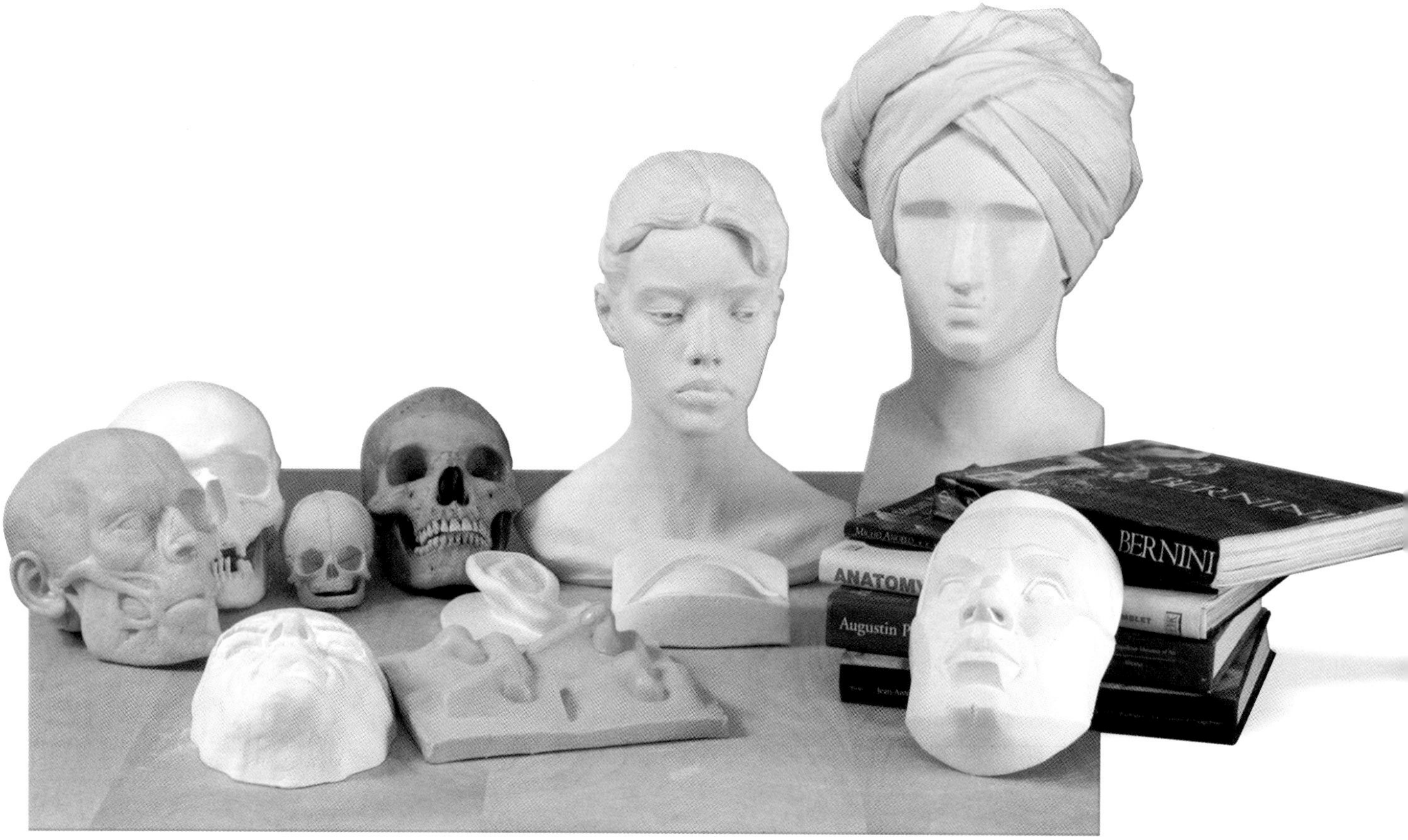

Working from a live model or a three-dimensional cast is a necessity for the figurative sculptor. Knowledge of the underlying structure of the human face is acquired by the observation of nature and the study of anatomy. Plaster casts of masterpieces or good quality busts are also a source of reference.

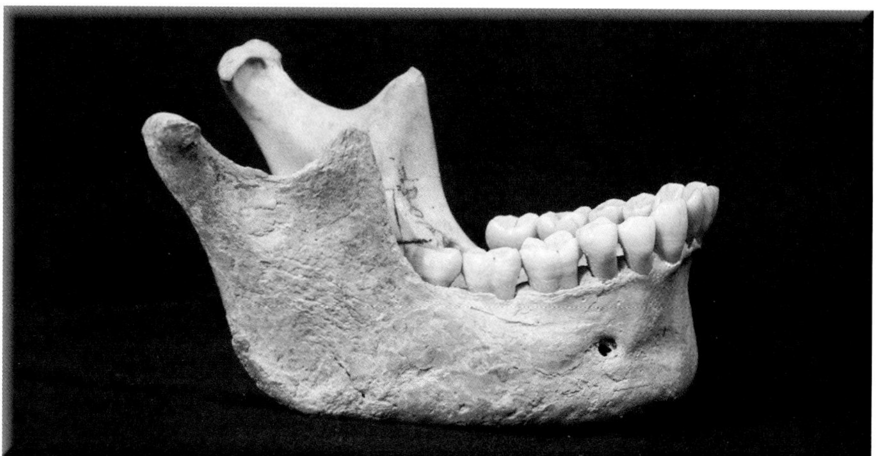

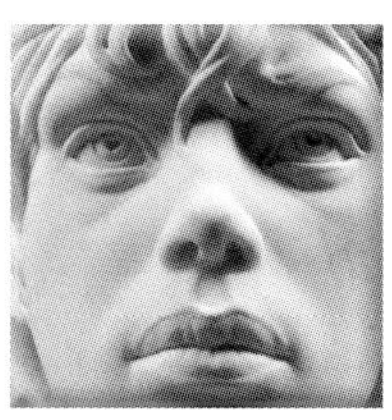

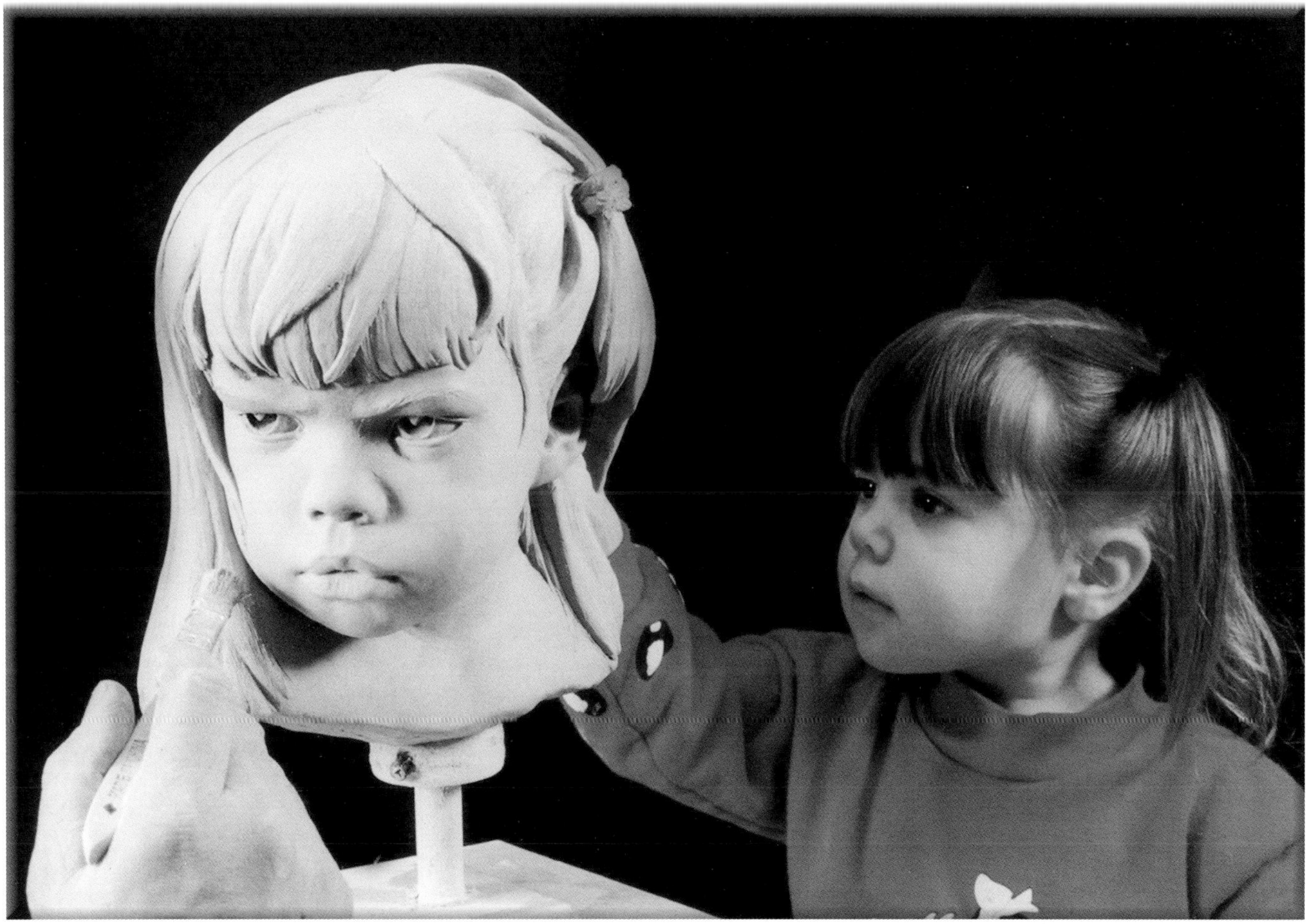

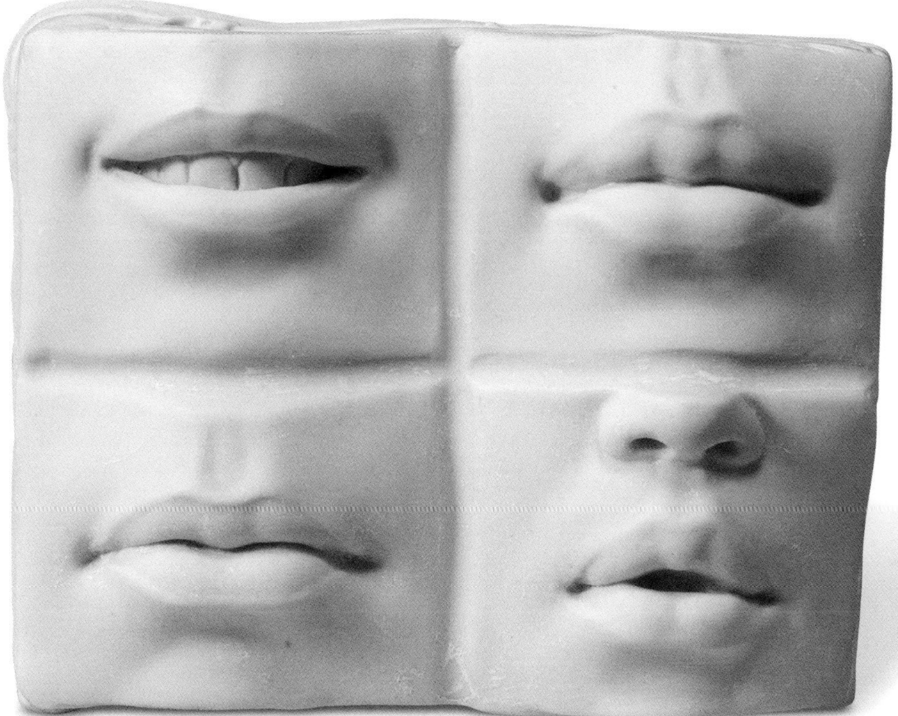

When working with models, it will help the process for all involved to respect their comfort. Adults may be able to pose comfortably for 30 minutes or more; however, a good book or a game of chess may entice them to sit longer. With children, especially, it is not uncommon for them to be unable to hold a pose without something distracting them. A large dose of patience along with the willingness to allow the back of the piece to be temporarily "modified" can entertain even some of the most active subjects.

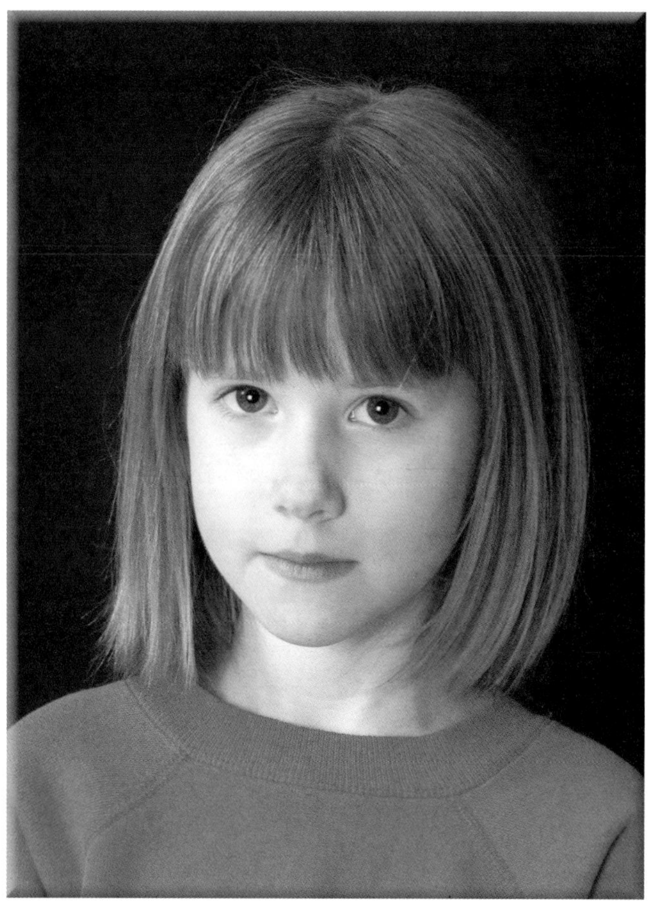

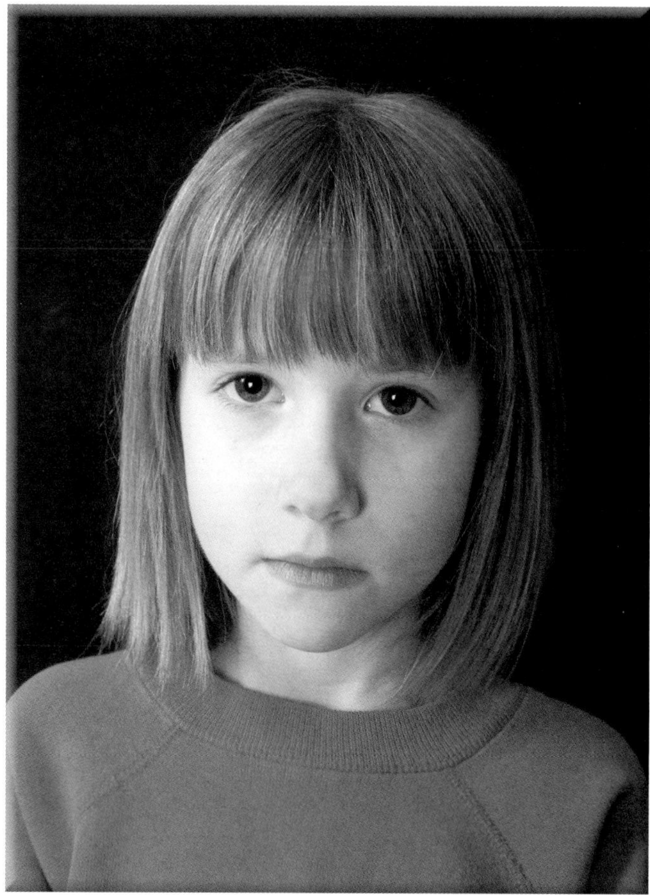

Photographs can be used, but preferably as supplemental reference once there is a firm understanding of anatomy. Care must be taken to use controlled lighting and a 100mm lens. The photo above was shot correctly while the image to the right, taken with a 28mm lens, clearly shows perspective distortion. Color is an unnecessary distraction, therefore, when this is the only available reference, images should be converted to black and white. This process is available at any quick print shop or by scanning photos and using a computer to convert them to grayscale. Various angles including views from all sides and above will give valuable information about the subject's form.

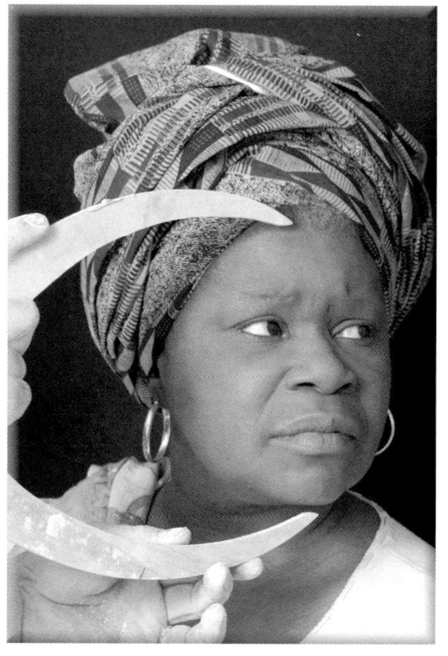

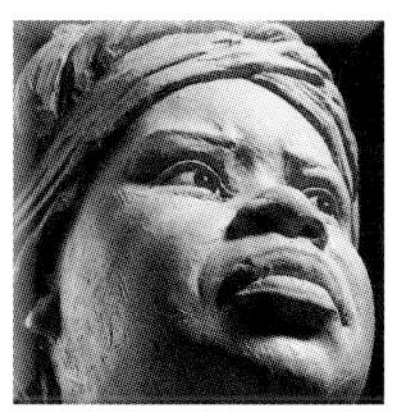

## Lighting

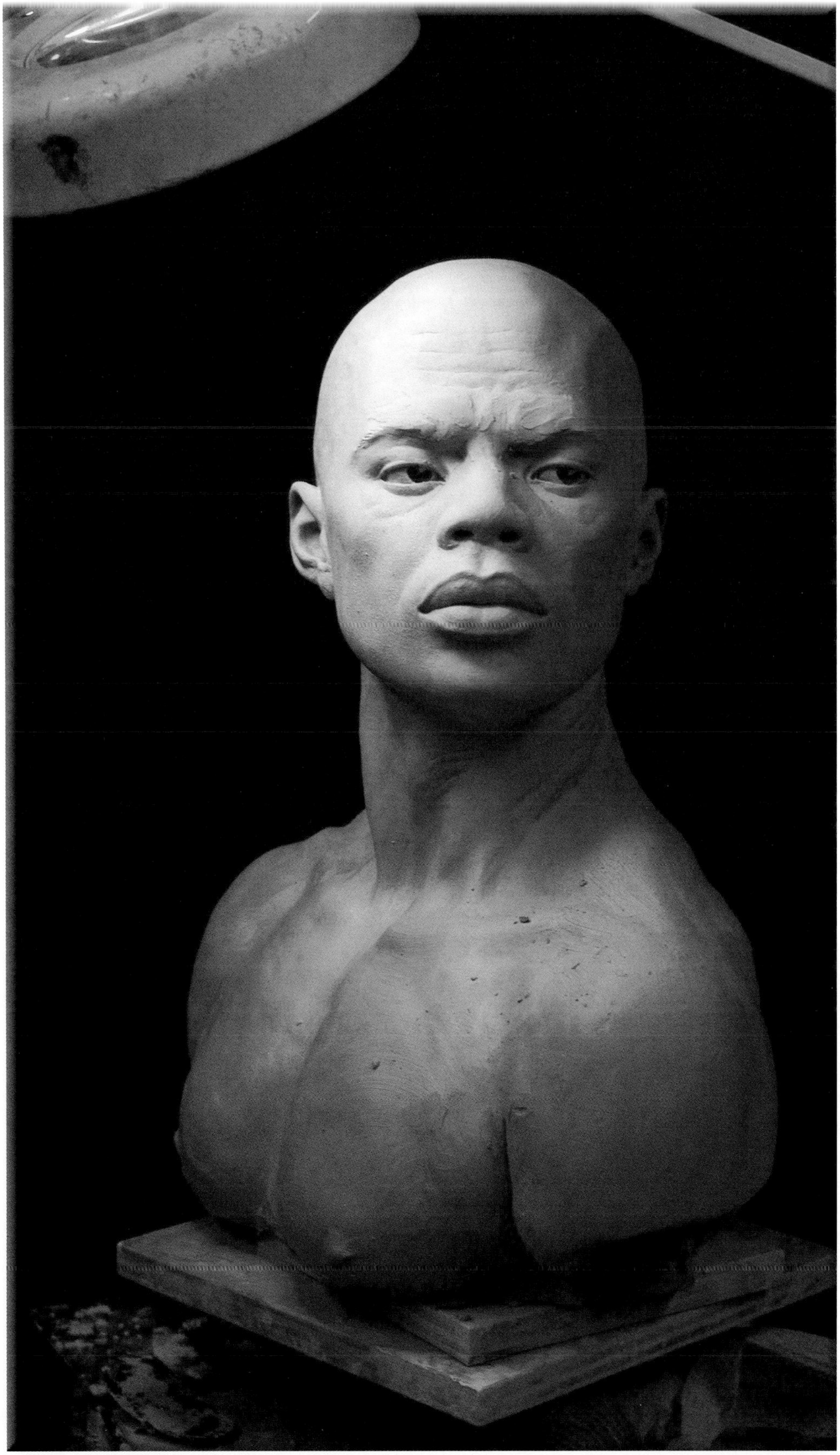

When used thoughtfully, light is itself a tool. Studio lighting should be pleasing and comfortable. The sculptor should not have to strain his or her eyes in order to see the volumes since it is light and shadows reflected on forms that define their volumes.

The intensity and source of the light should be the same for both the model and the sculpture in order to be able to duplicate the volumes accurately. The best source of light is a large, high, north-facing window. If not available, large fluorescent lights give a satisfactory result.

During a sculpting session, the work, as well as the model, must be turned frequently to change the effect of light and shadows. A small, movable fluorescent lamp (as seen in the photo to the left) is very useful to control the ability to see the volumes and final texture when used in an otherwise dark room. It should be free standing to allow the sculptor to move about and evaluate sharpened shadows created by this more focused light.

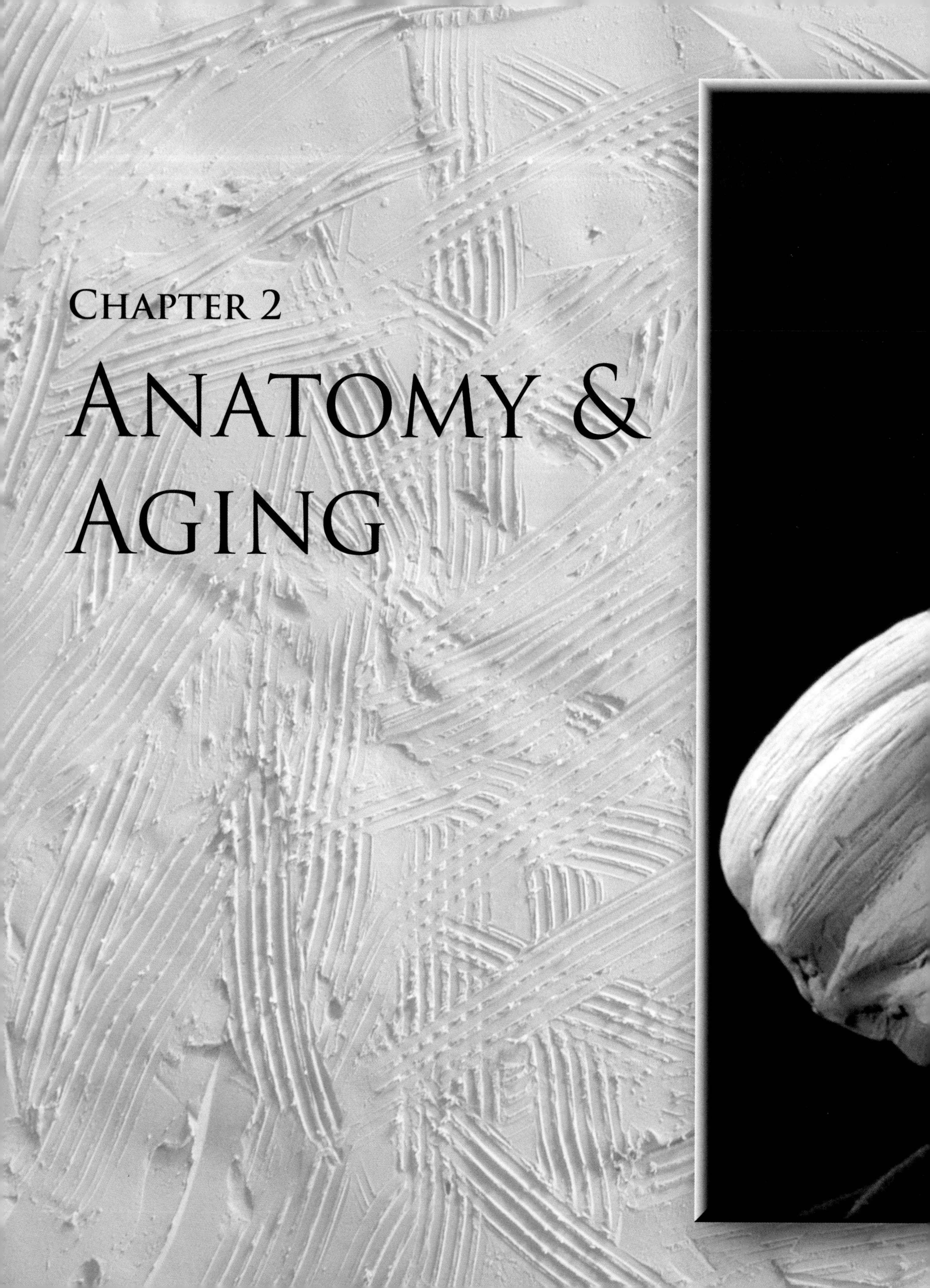

Chapter 2

# Anatomy & Aging

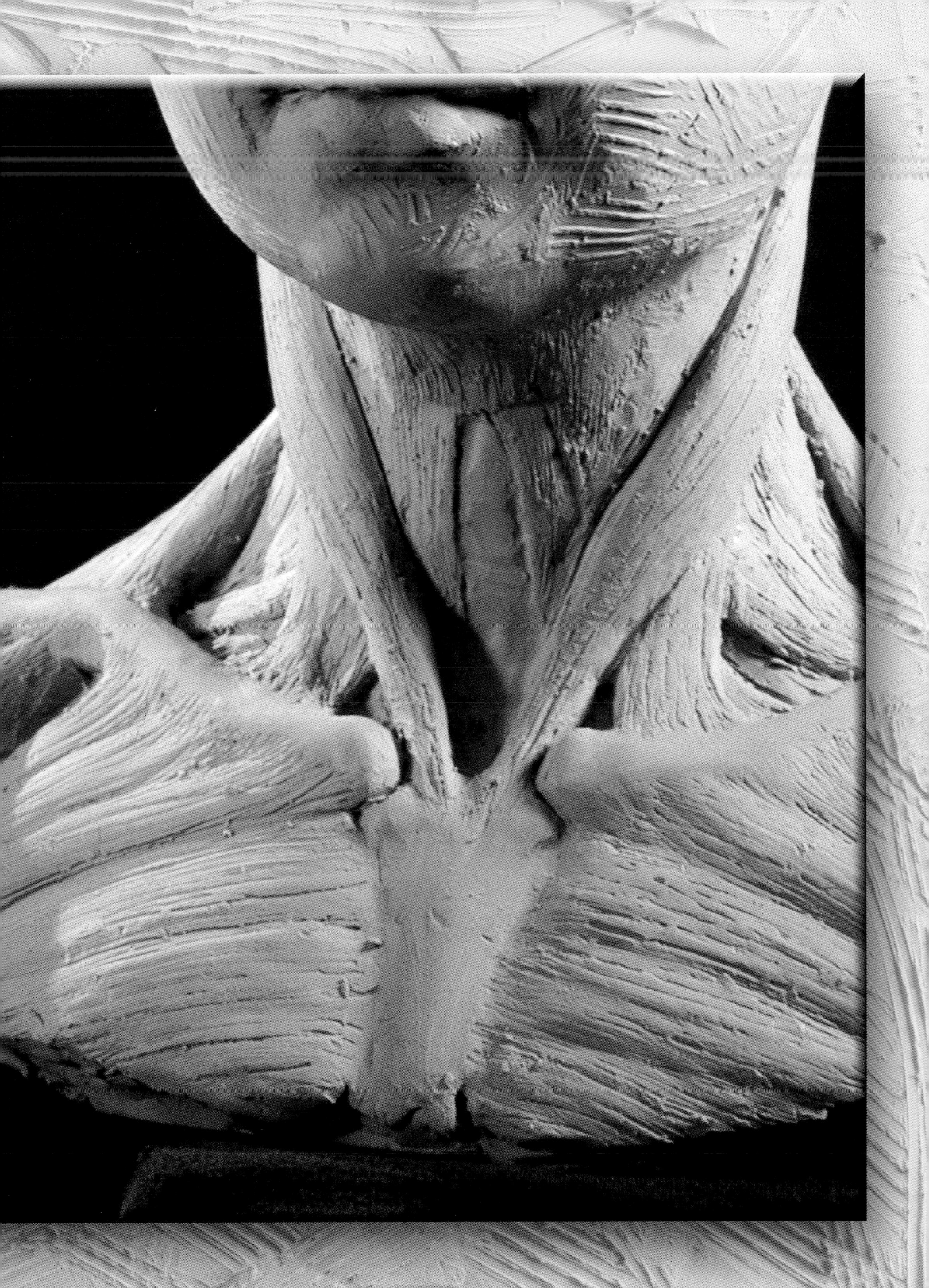

## The Skull

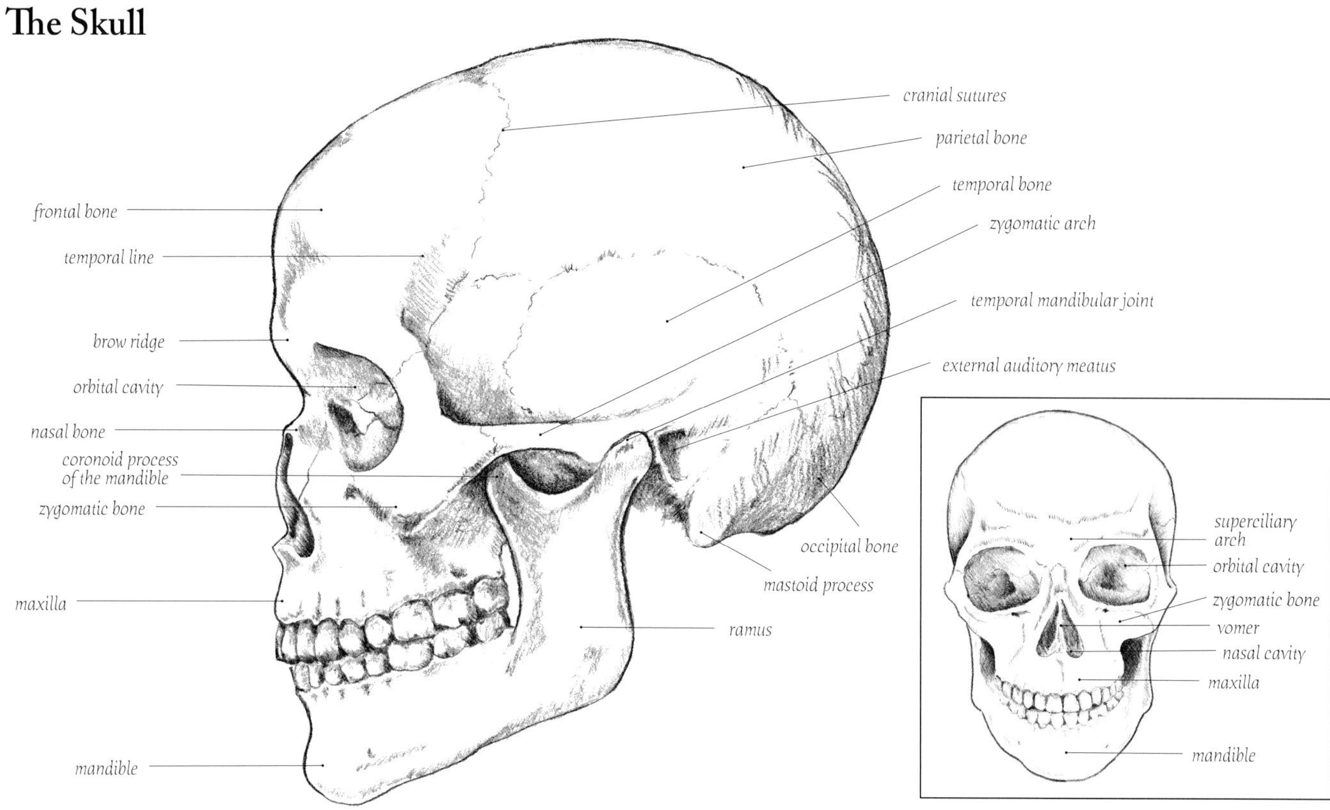


**Bones of the Skull**

An understanding of the bone structure and muscle masses of the human head is the foundation of portrait sculpture. There are tremendous differences between skulls, depending on gender, age and race. In general the male skull is larger than the female skull; the jaw is squarer; the chin, more pronounced; the brow ridge, more prominent; and the forehead, more sloping. Male teeth are often a bit larger. Some of these differences can easily be seen in the diagram below which compares a male and a female skull. The photos on the facing page illustrate the surprising diversity found in skulls from various regions.

Recognizing these differences and examining three-dimensional models with this in mind facilitates comparative study and the refinement of observational skills required to successfully capture the shape and features of the sculpted model.

The actual sculpting of different skulls reinforces this knowledge and develops the ability to build volumes based on observation only and is highly recommended. This chapter focuses on this type of exercise.

The less familiar we are with a shape, the easier it is to duplicate it in three-dimension. This is because we are forced to focus on form and volumes themselves rather than on preconceived ideas of what the shape should be. For the majority of us, the intricate shapes of a skull, when observed closely, are surprisingly unfamiliar, making this exercise a very productive experience. To take full advantage of this exercise, a three-dimensional and anatomically correct model is needed in order to accurately see every nuance of the skull – something a photo or a drawing cannot provide. Casts of human skulls are available to purchase. Suppliers are listed in Appendix B at the end of this book.

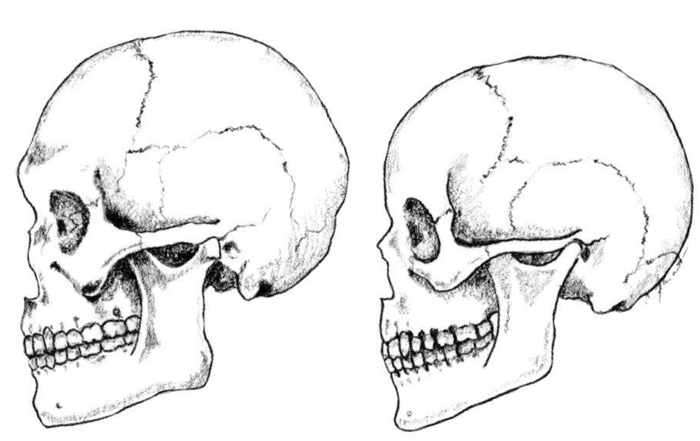

**Male and Female Skull Comparison**

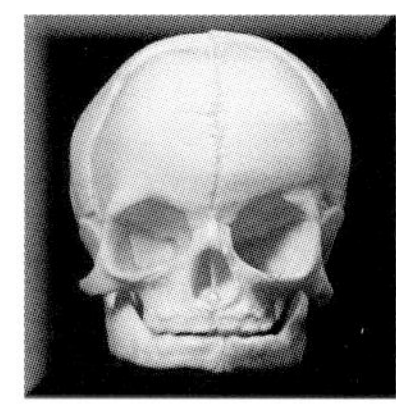

Peruvian Male Skull

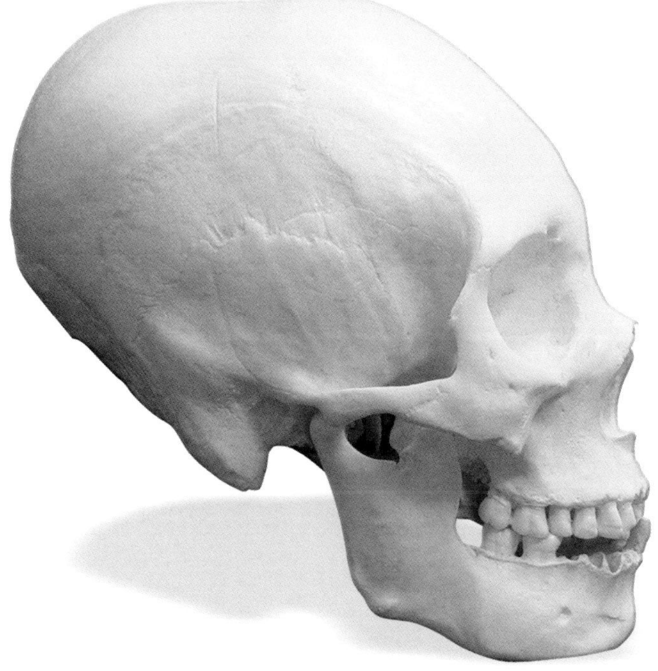

Australian Male Skull

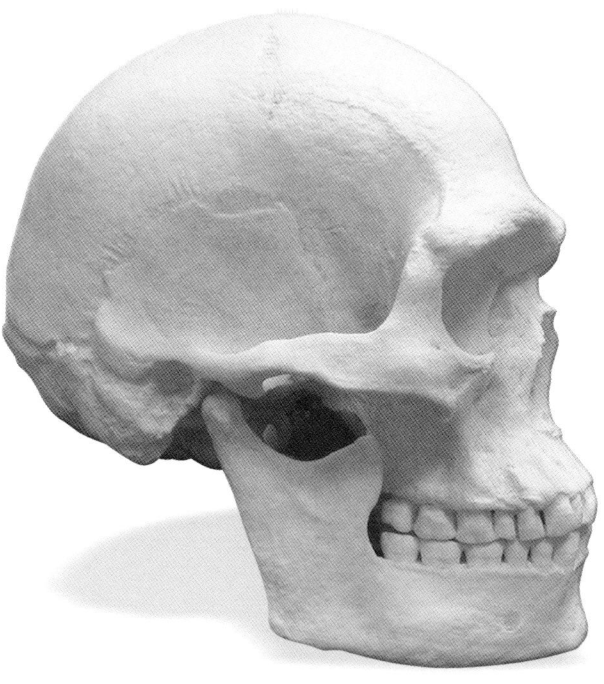

African Male Skull

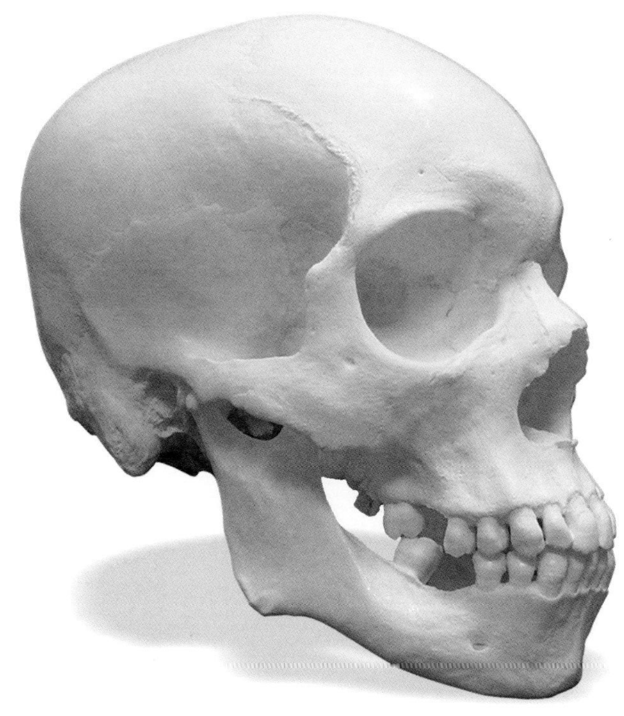

European Female Skull

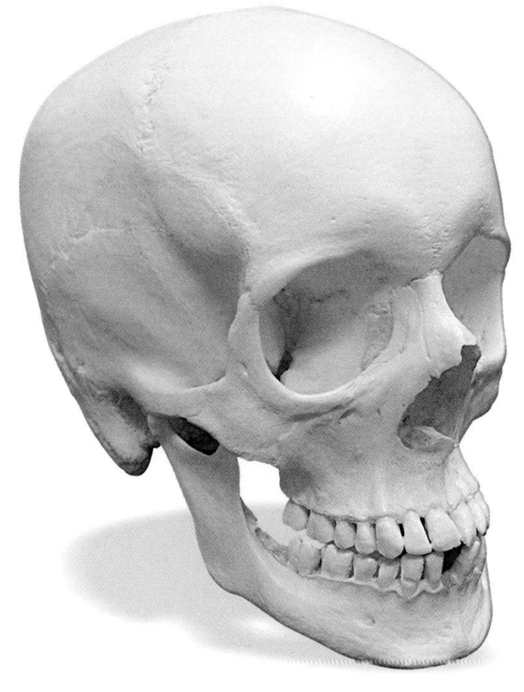

## Demonstration 1: Modeling a Skull

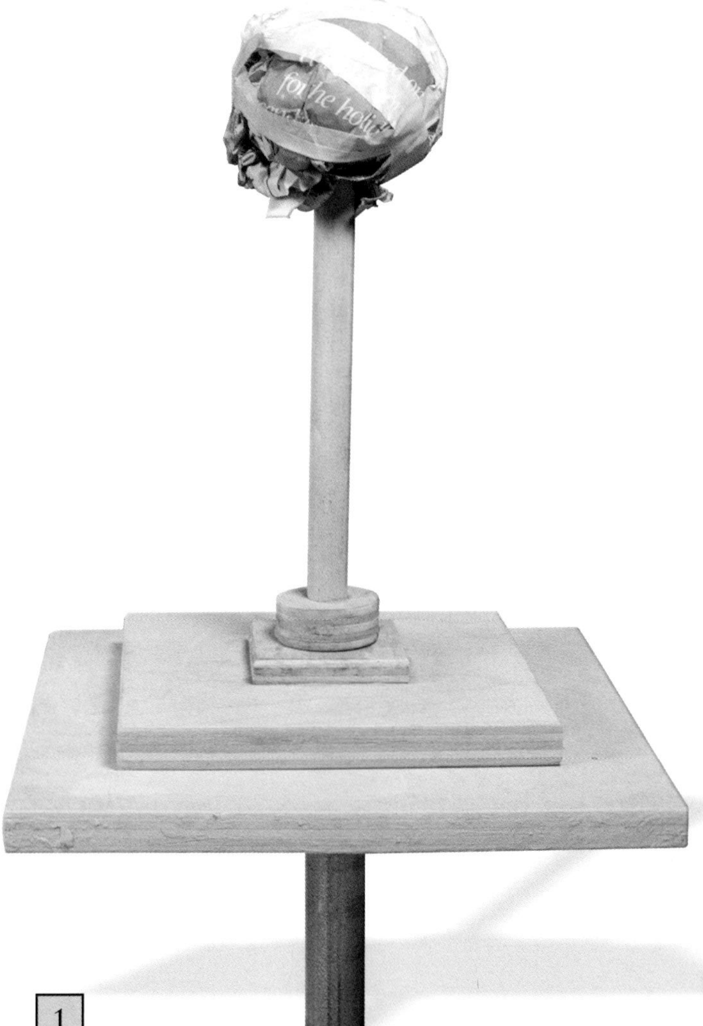

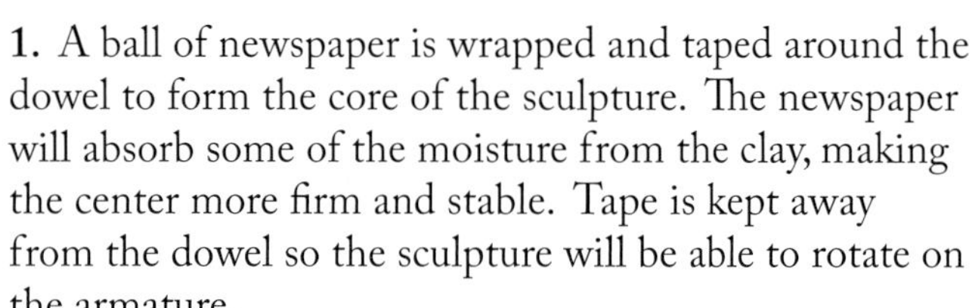


1. A ball of newspaper is wrapped and taped around the dowel to form the core of the sculpture. The newspaper will absorb some of the moisture from the clay, making the center more firm and stable. Tape is kept away from the dowel so the sculpture will be able to rotate on the armature.

2. An even layer of clay is built around the paper.

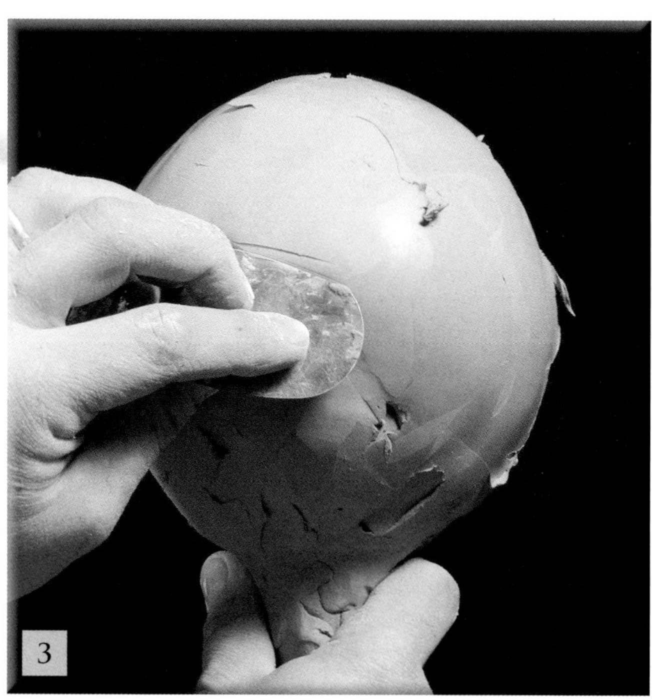


3. The ball is rounded with a metal scraper.

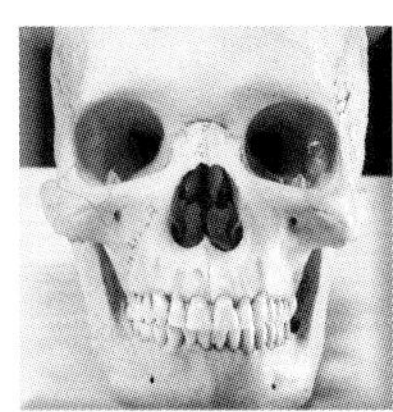

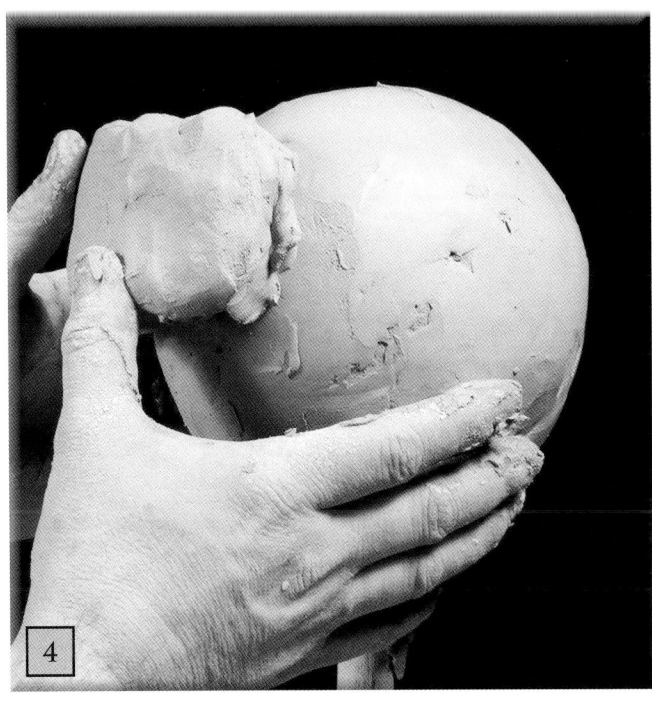


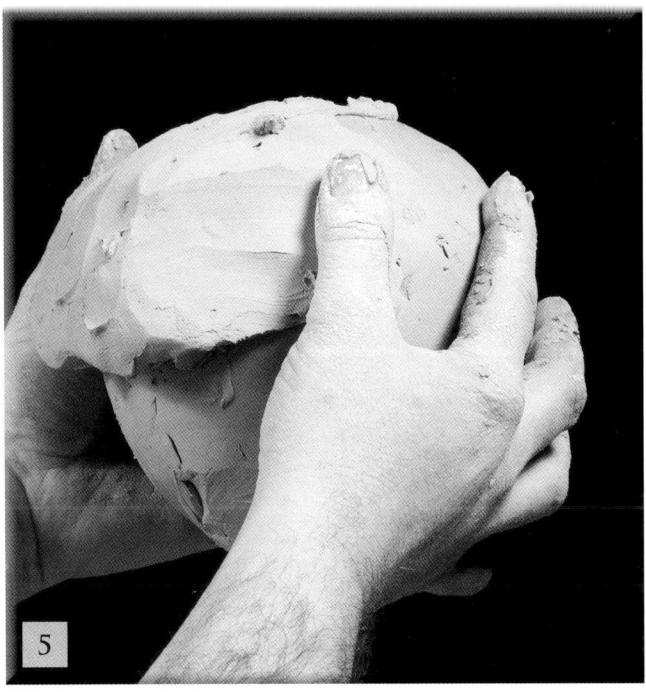


4. A rectangular piece of clay is positioned to create the volume of the forehead.

5. The clay is then pulled back on each side to form the temporal planes.

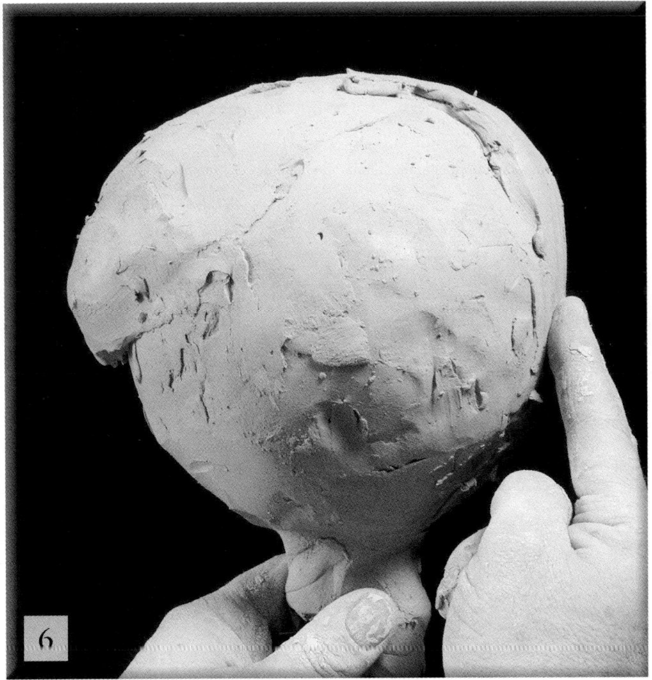


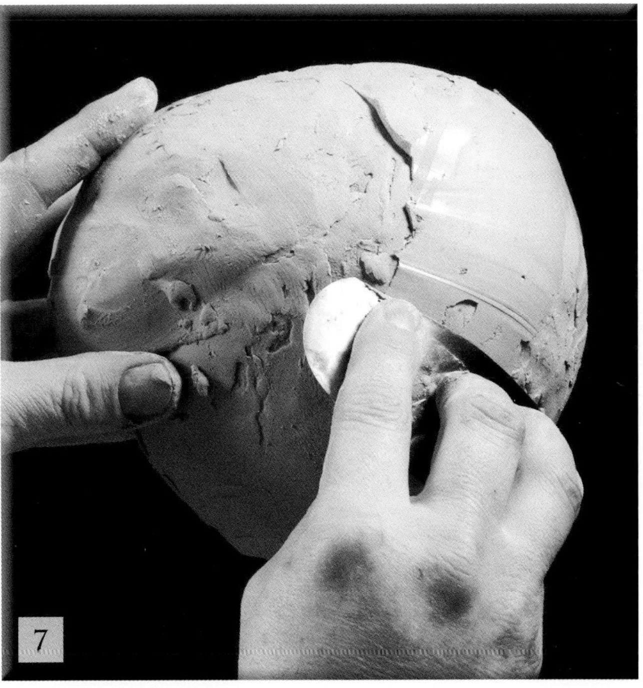


6. A coil of clay is applied on the top of the head and shaped to define the profile of the cranium.

7. Volume is then built on each side.

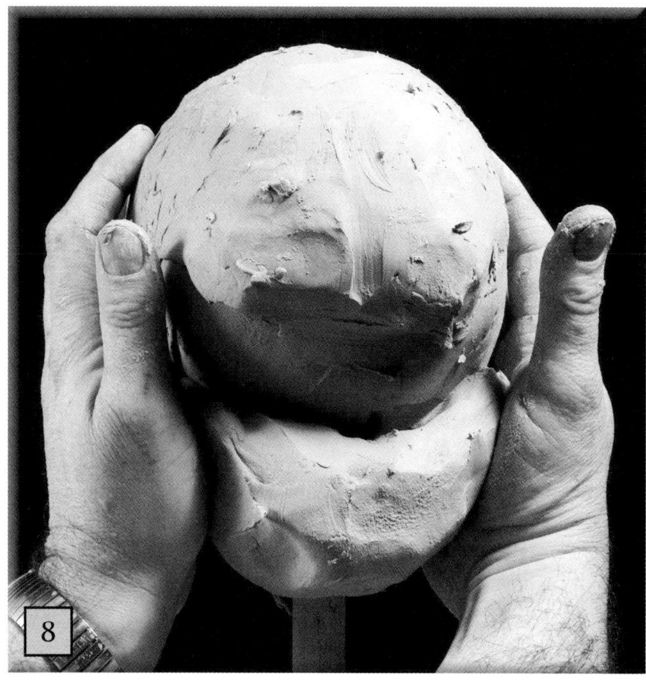


**8.** To build the volume of the mandible, a horseshoe-shaped piece of clay is wrapped around the base and flattened on each side to form the planes of the ramus.

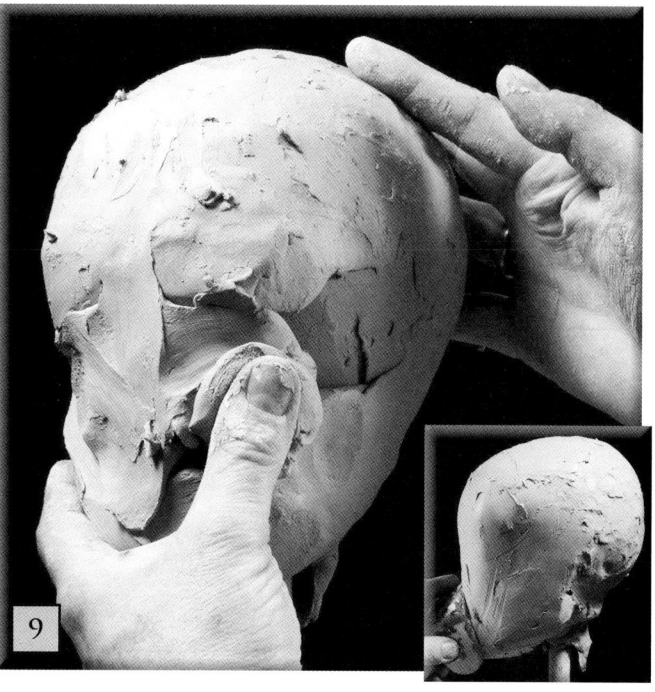


**9.** The depression between the mandible and the foundation is filled and smoothed, preparing the volume for the maxilla.

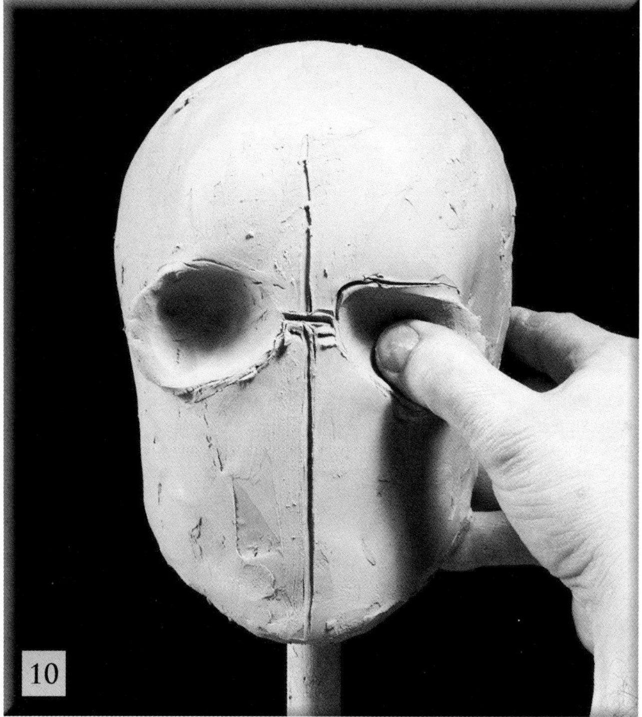


**10.** The orbital cavities' location is determined by observation of the model and measurement with calipers.

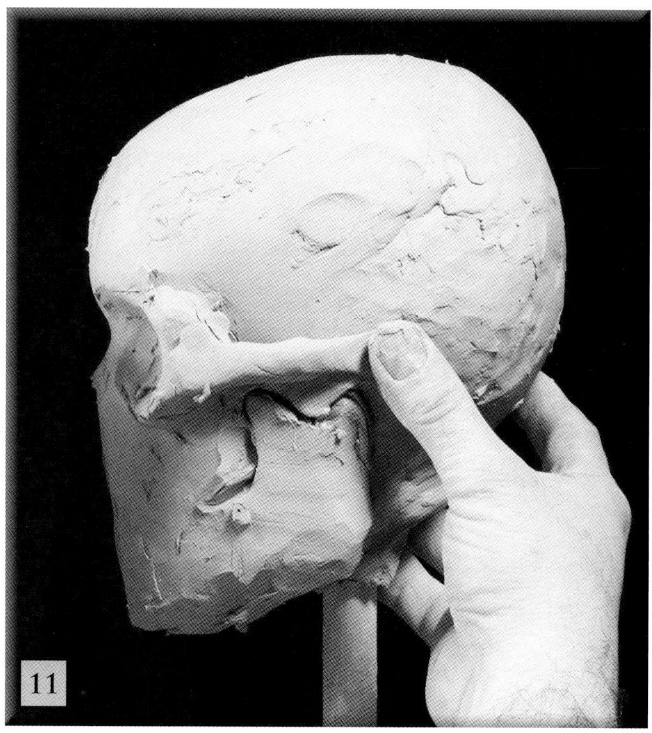


**11.** The zygomatic arch is a bone originating from the edges of the orbital cavity, stretching to the external auditory meatus.

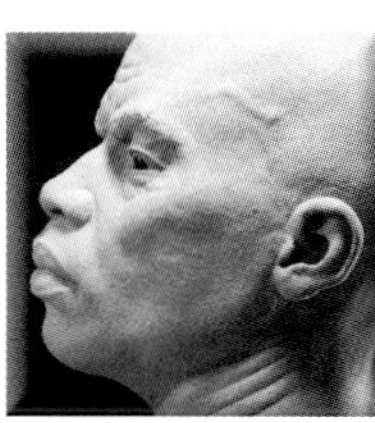

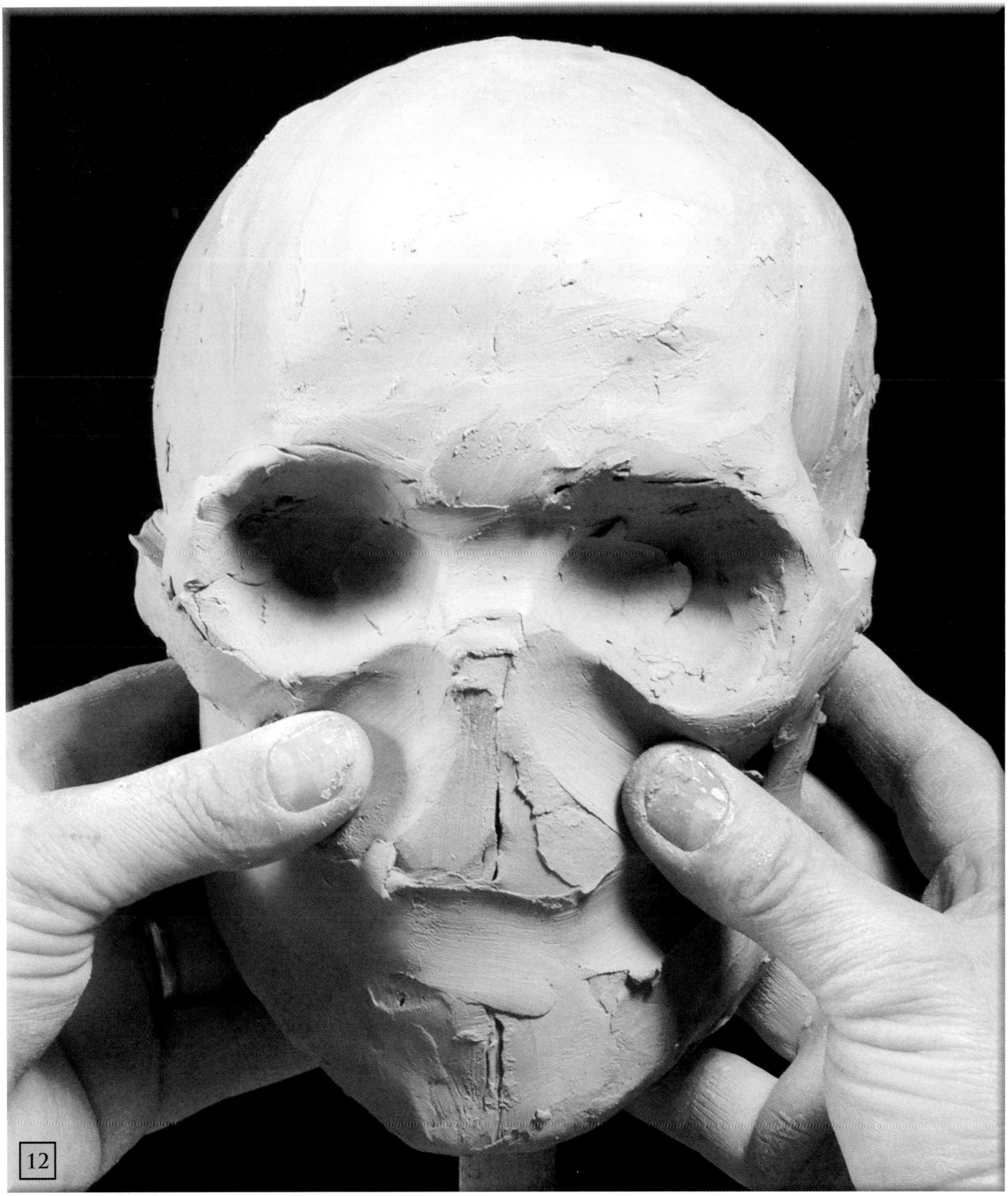

**12.** To define the zygomatic bone (cheekbone) and the upper part of the maxilla, a depression is created under the orbital cavity.

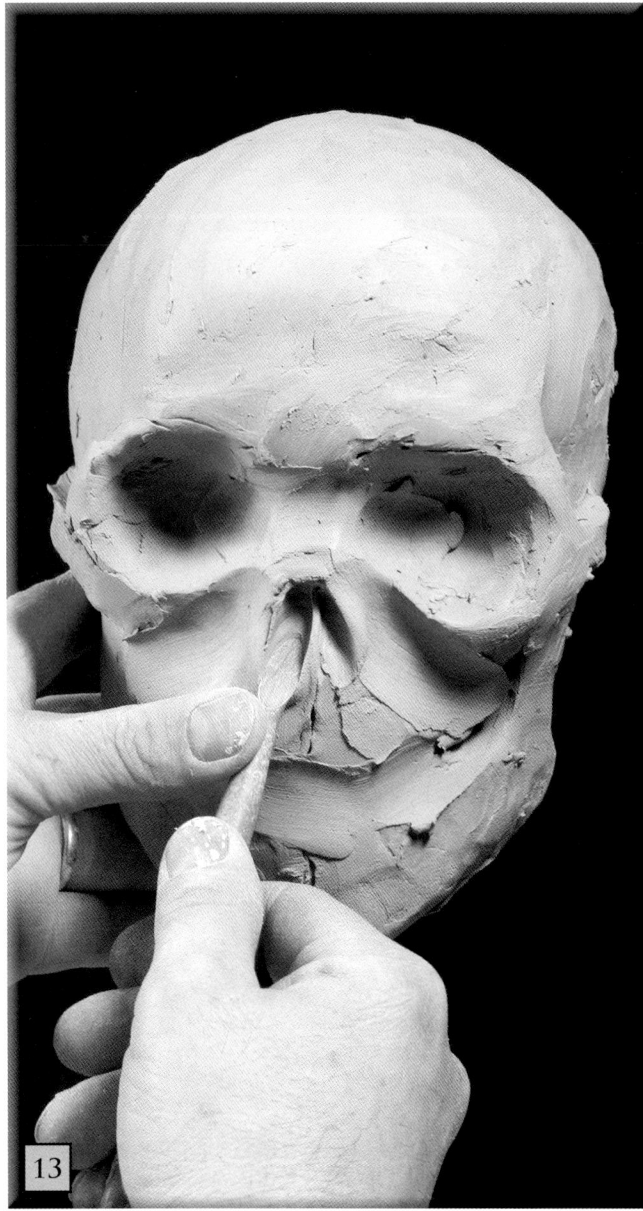

13. The nasal cavity is carved out with a wooden tool, leaving a ridge at the center called the vomer.

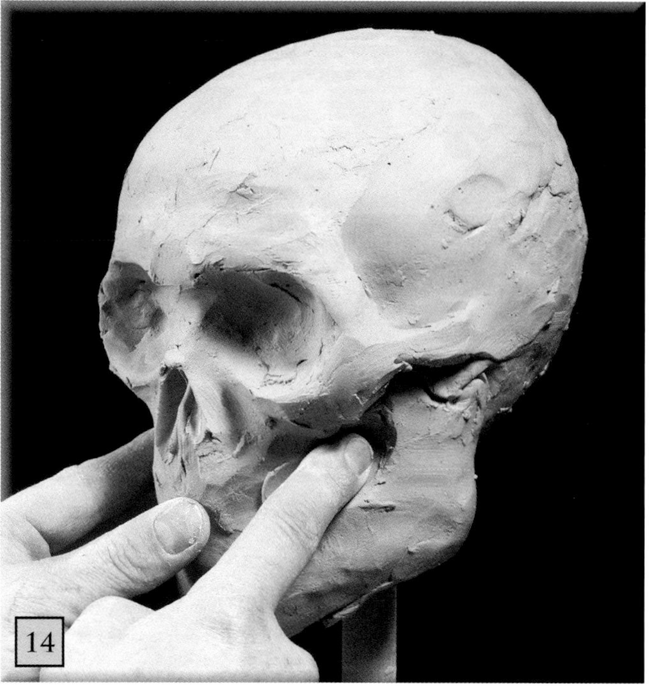

14. The width of the ramus needs to be measured and indicated before pushing in the clay on both sides to define the volume in the back of the maxilla.

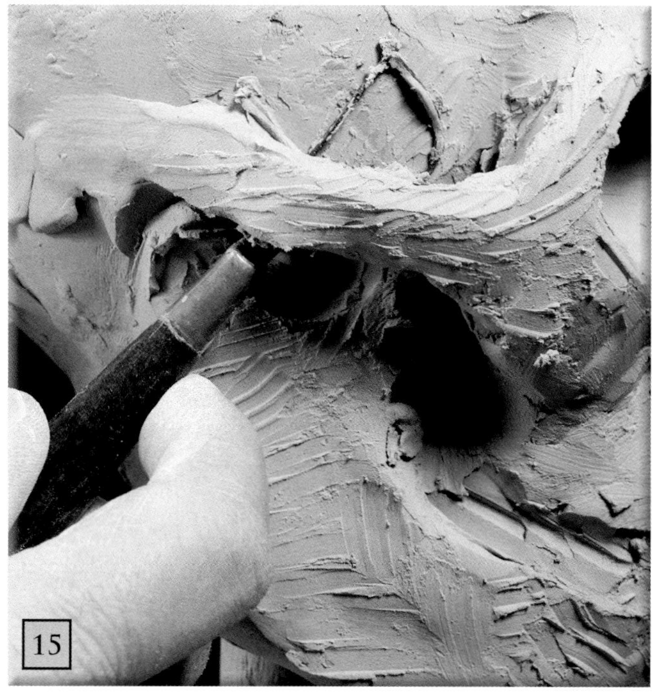

15. The zygomatic arch is suspended in its center, leaving space for the temporalis which covers the temporal bone and connects with the coronoid process of the mandible.

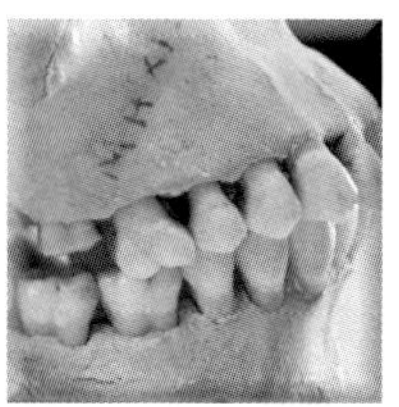

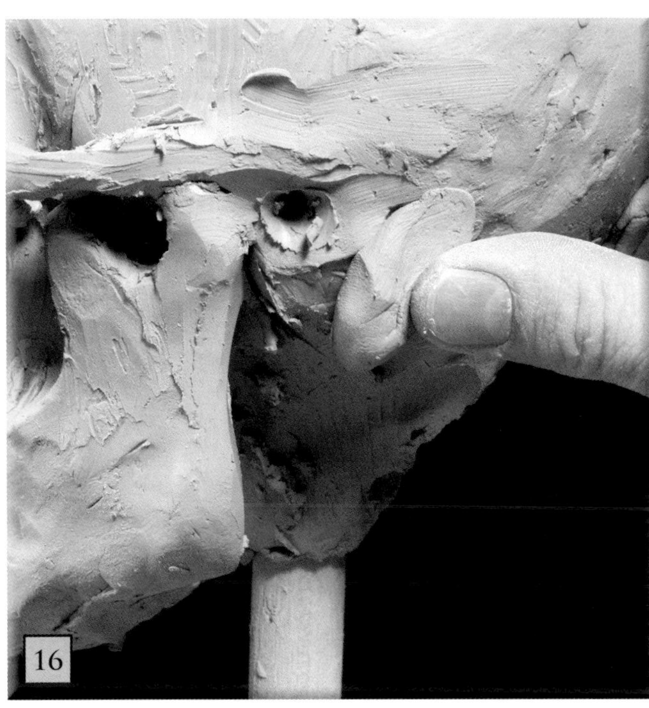

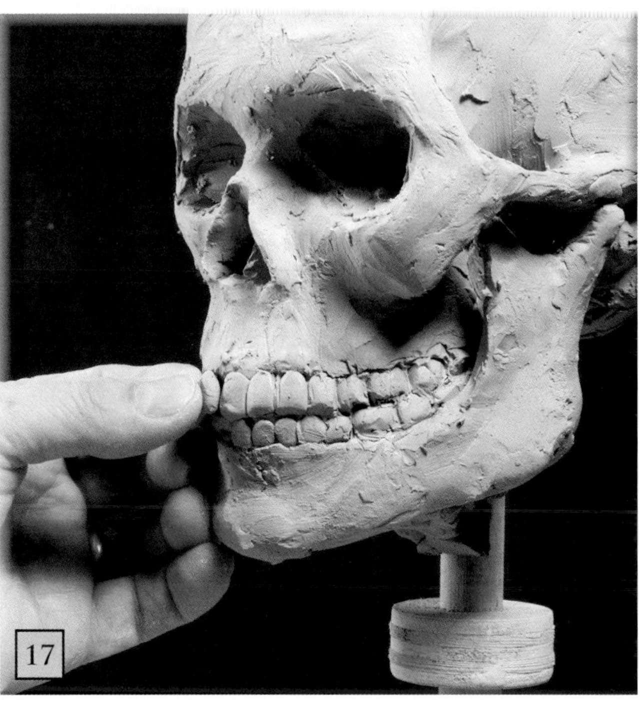

16. The mastoid process is a projection of bone behind the ear. It begins to form only after the age of two. The external auditory meatus is a hole in the bone just behind the temporal mandibular joint.

17. The teeth are added one at a time paying special attention to their symmetry.

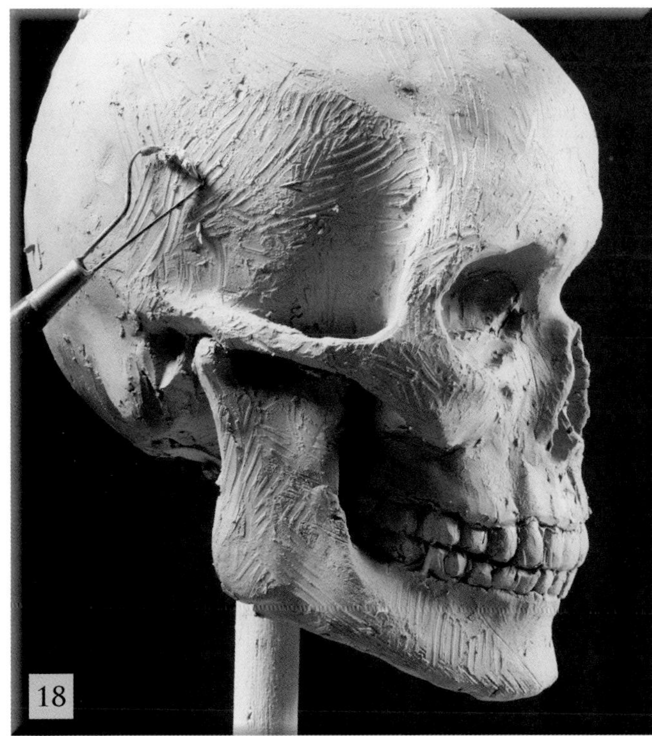

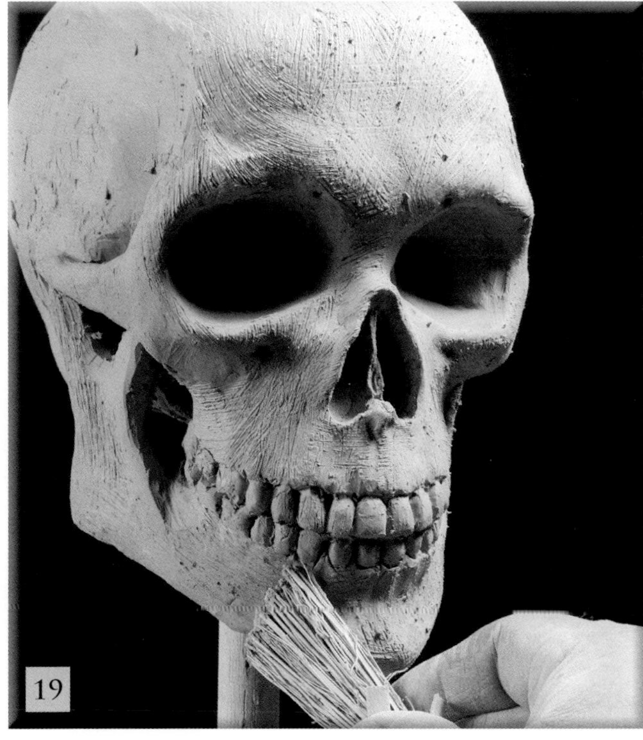

18. The planes of the temporal bone are refined. These also define the temporal lines.

19. After refining all the volumes with loop tools, a bristle brush is used to blend them together.

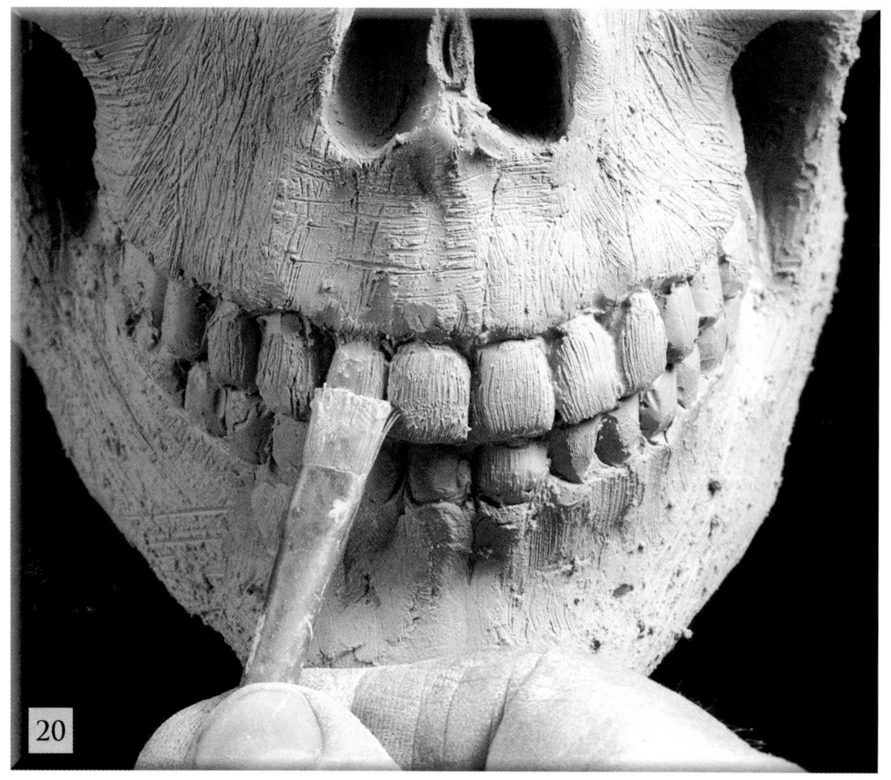

20. The teeth are first refined with a stiff brush. A soft brush is used for the final texture.

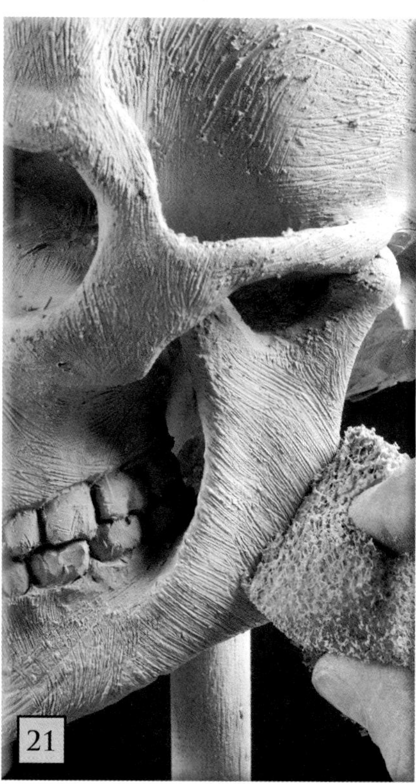

21. A coarse sponge is used to refine the final shape.

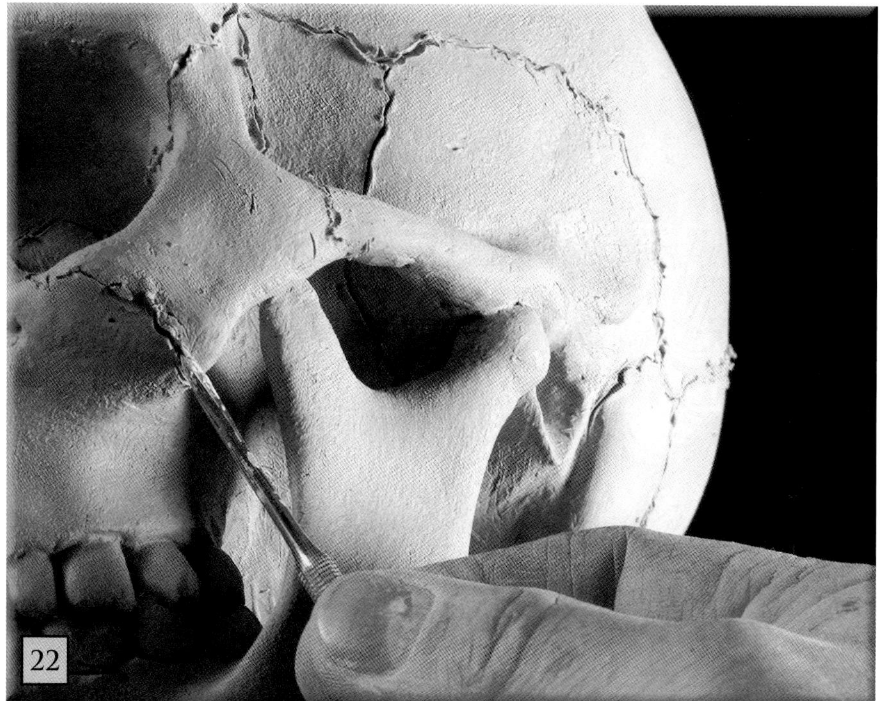

22. A soft sponge is used to create the surface texture. The cranial sutures are engraved with a thin metal tool.

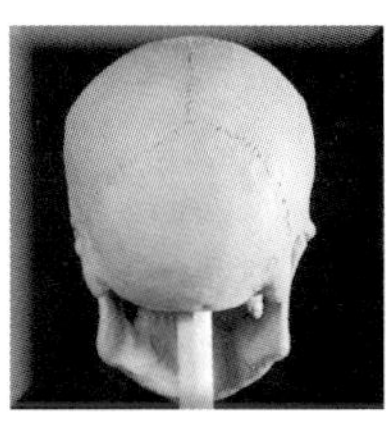

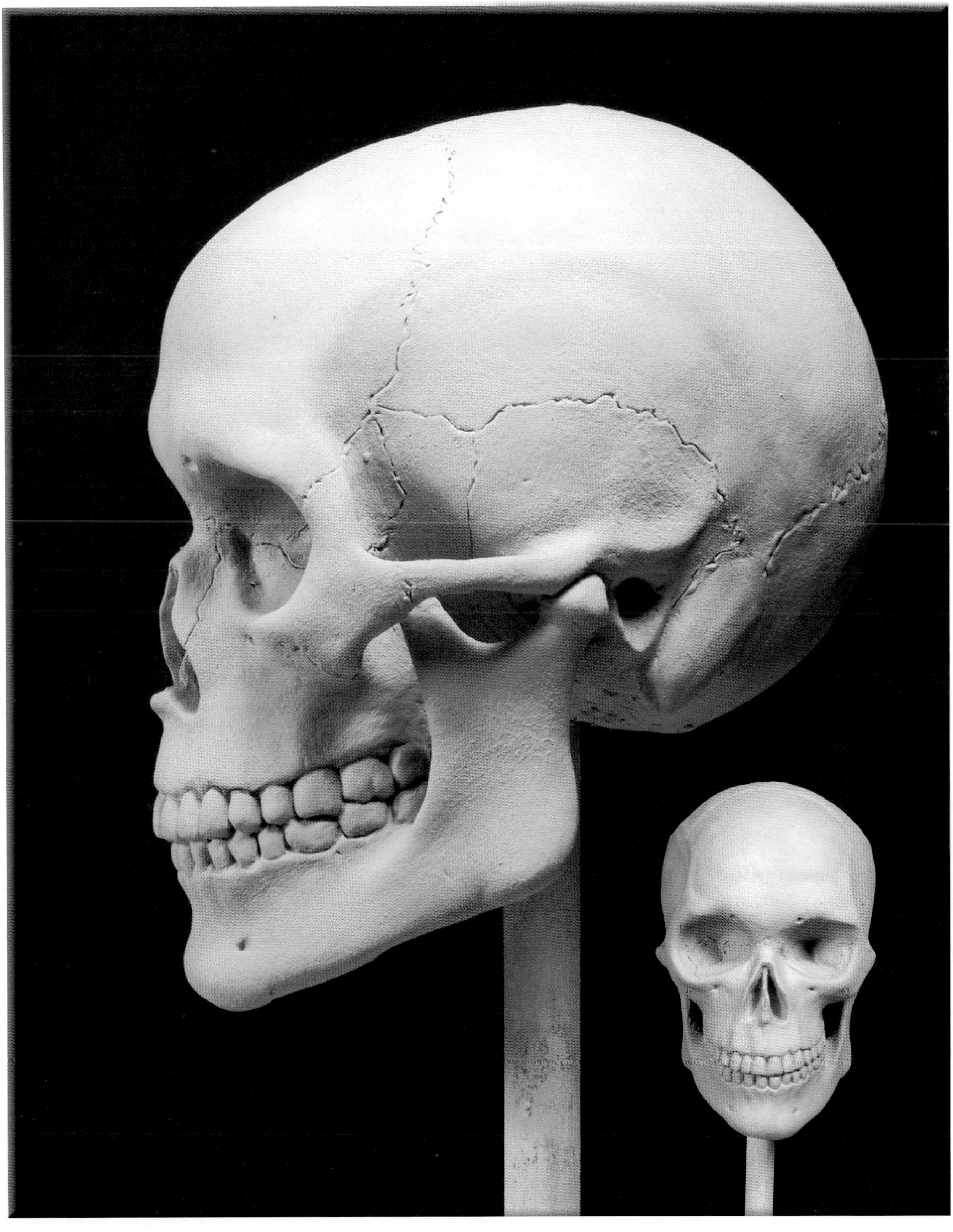

## The Muscles

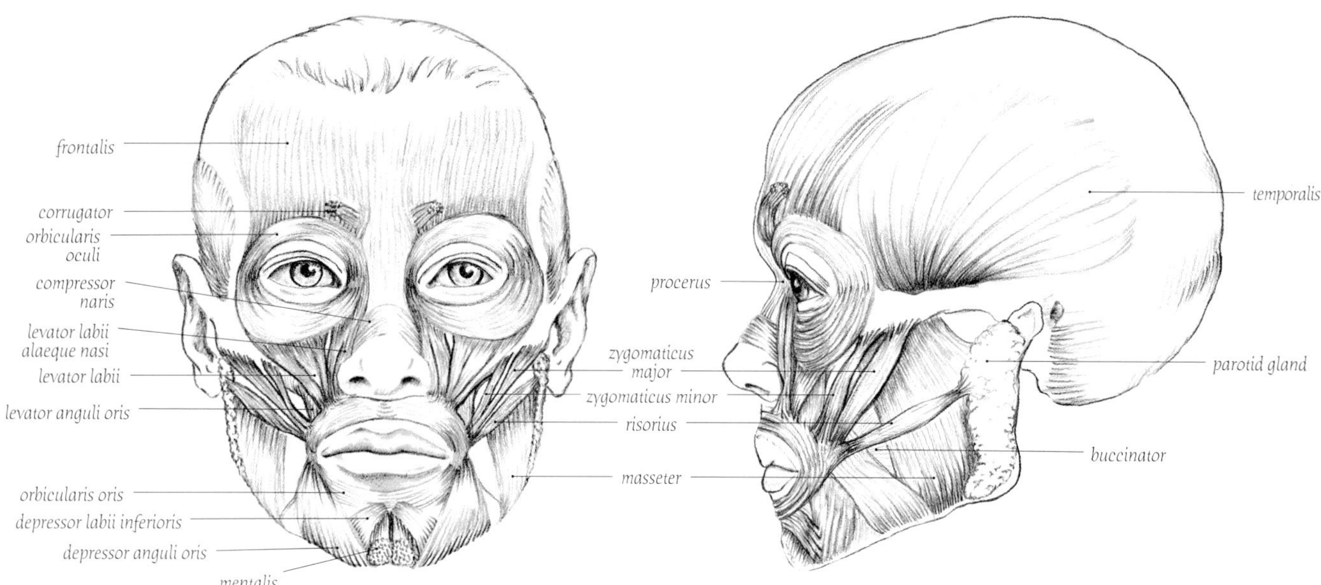


MUSCLES OF THE FACE

The function of the muscles throughout the body is always to contract, or pull, usually one bone toward another, creating for example, a movement of rotation around a joint. With the exception of the masseter and the temporalis, most of the muscles of the face have the peculiarity of not connecting one bone to another. Instead, they attach at one end, directly or indirectly, to the skull, and at the other, into the skin or into another muscle connected to the skin. Facial muscle functions are discussed in more detail in Chapter 7.

In the face, the pulling action from a fixed origin to an area very close to the skin creates depressions and folds that are the signatures of different expressions. Furthermore, the repeated action of some muscles is partly responsible for slow, permanent changes to both the surface of the skin and the shape of underlying bone. For example, a person with the habit of chewing on only one side of the mouth will have a strengthening of the masseter on that side, giving it more volume. It will also, over time, create some degree of distortion in the mandible, pulling it toward the same side. Careful observation will also reveal thickening of the temporalis.

The next demonstration is designed to illustrate the origin and placement of the major facial muscles. Facial muscles, having very little mass, can be applied without the help of a three-dimensional model if none is available, because they closely follow the shape of the skull. A good anatomy book can be sufficient.

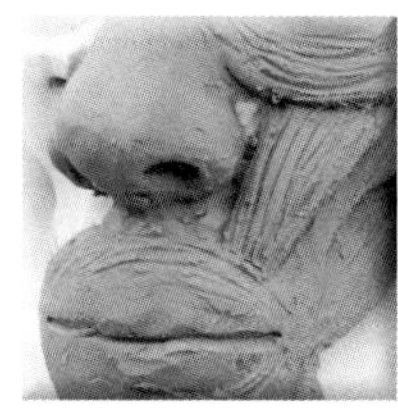

## Demonstration 2: Modeling Facial Muscles

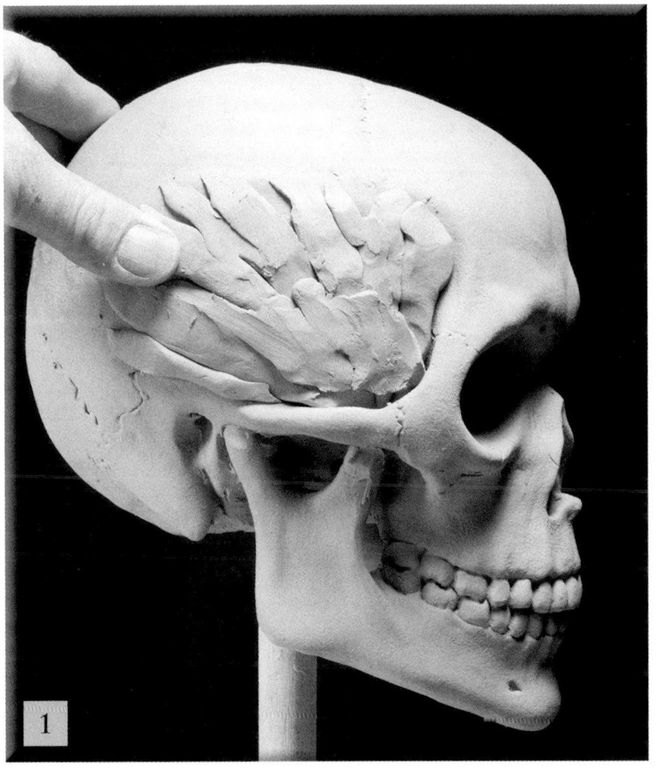

1. The fan shaped temporalis muscle attaches to the temporal bone of the cranium, passes under the zygomatic arch, and connects to the coronoid process of the mandible. Thin coils of clay following the direction of the fibers are applied and then flattened.

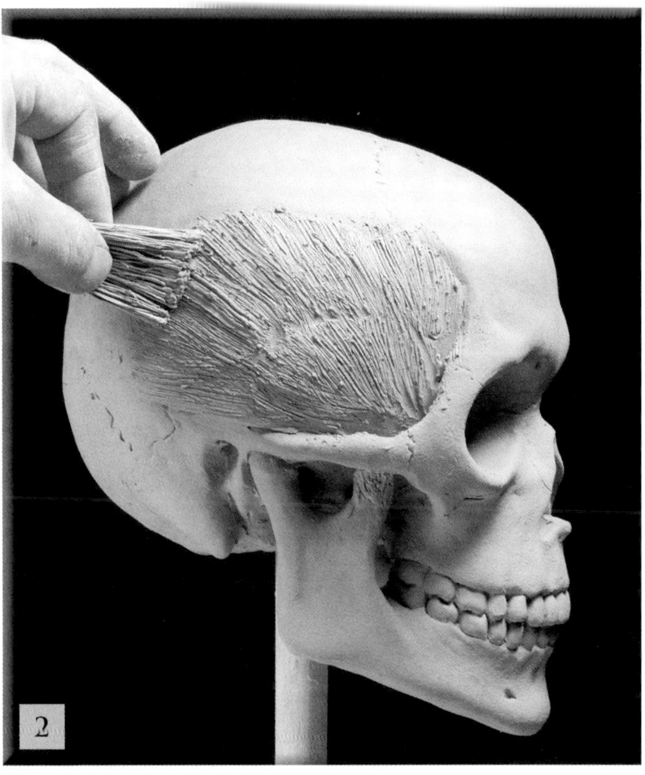

2. The fibrous texture of the muscle is rendered with a bristle brush.

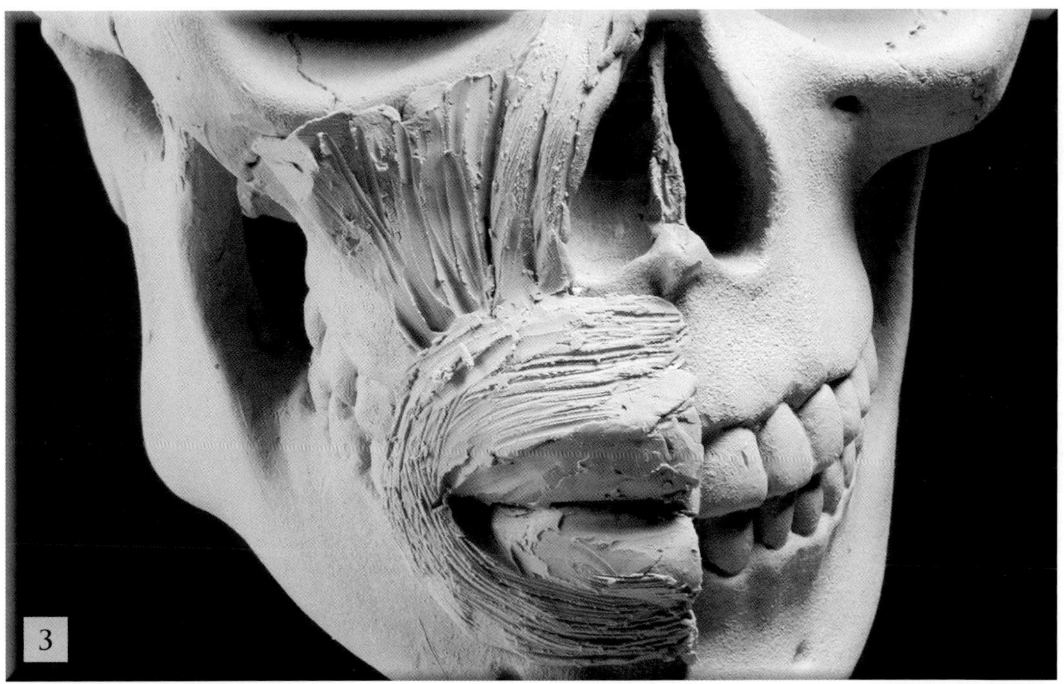

3. Other muscles are applied one at a time in the following order: levator anguli oris, levator labii alaeque nasi, levator labii and the orbicularis oris.

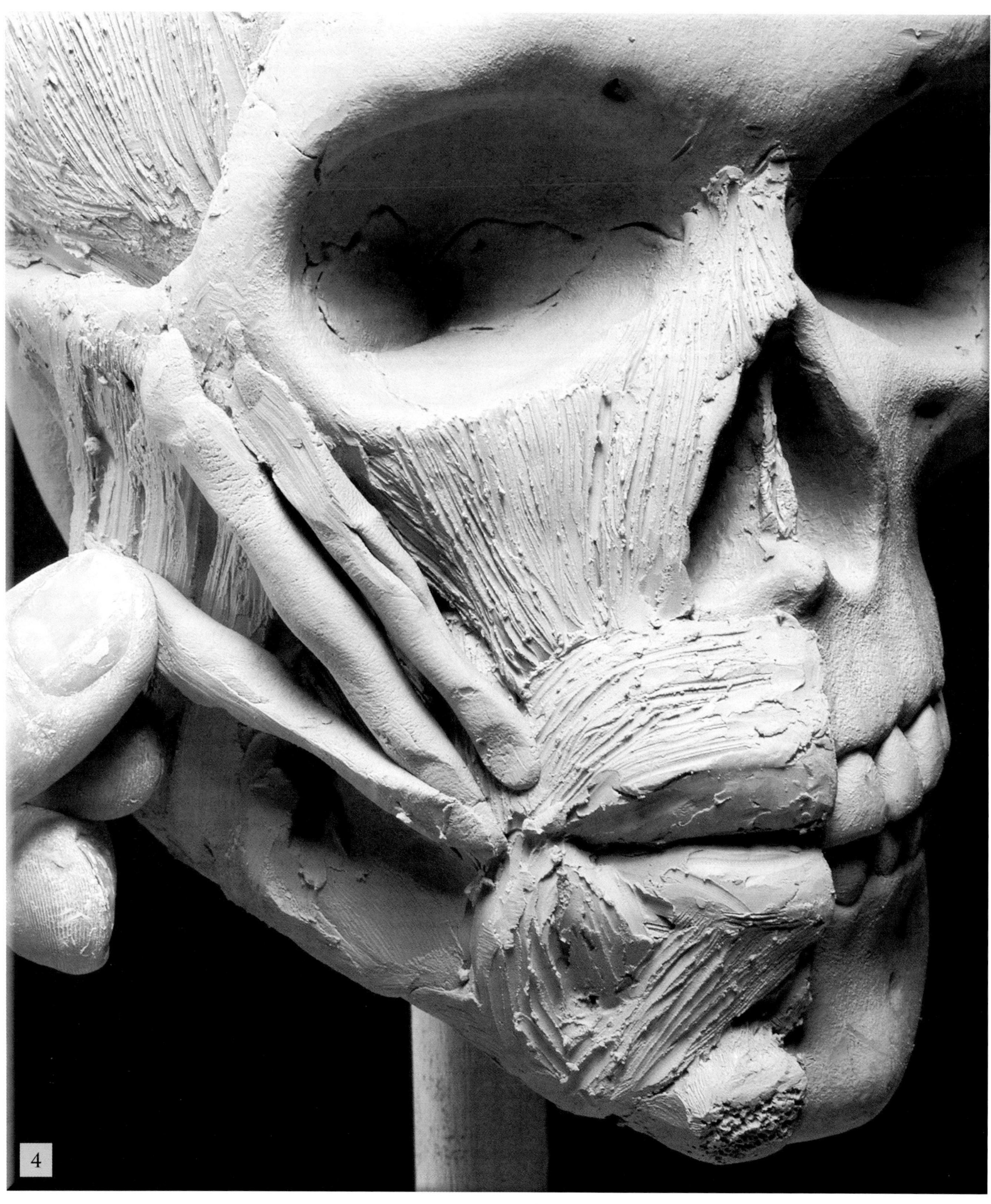


**4.** Next, the mentalis, depressor anguli oris, depressor labii, buccinator, masseter, zygomaticus minor, zygomaticus major and risorius are added.

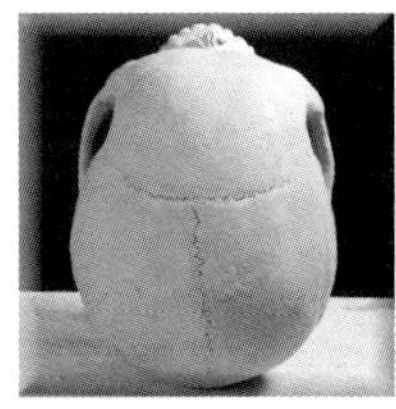

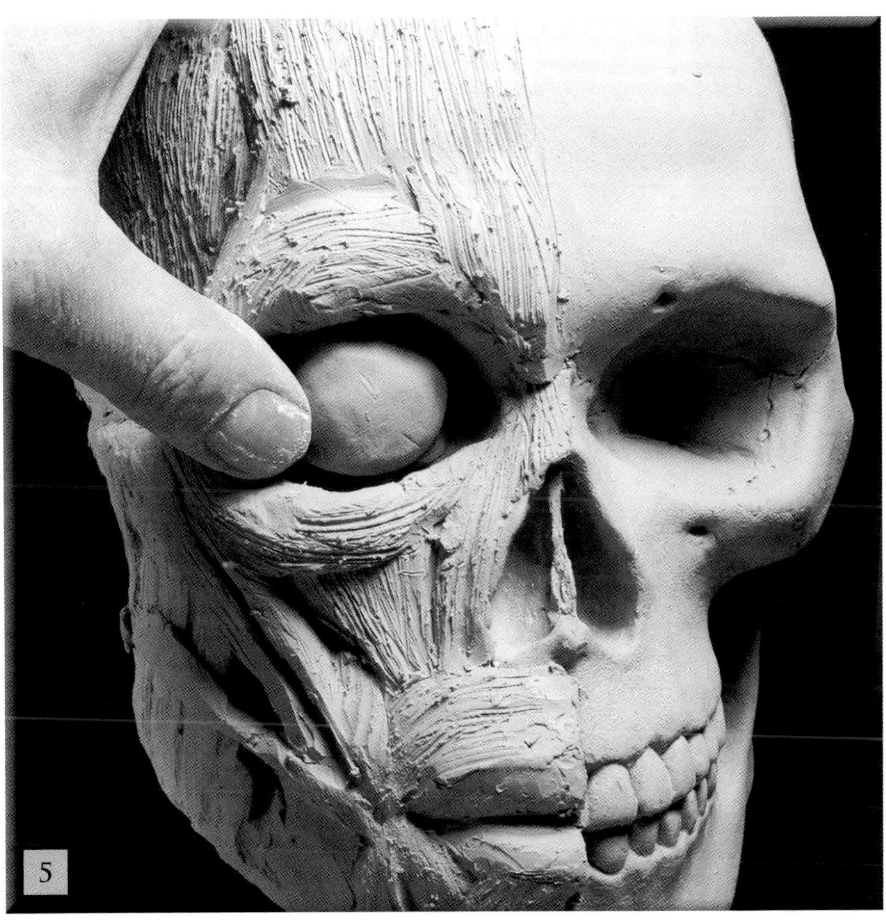


5. The frontalis, orbicularis oculi and eyeball are placed.

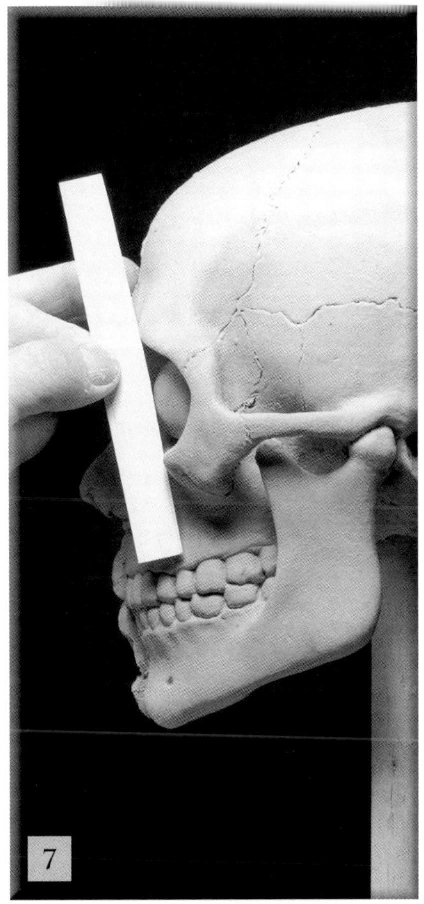


7. The eyeball is an average of twenty-five millimeters in diameter and is centered in the orbital cavity. The outer point of the cornea is tangent to a line drawn from the center of the superior and inferior edges of the orbit.

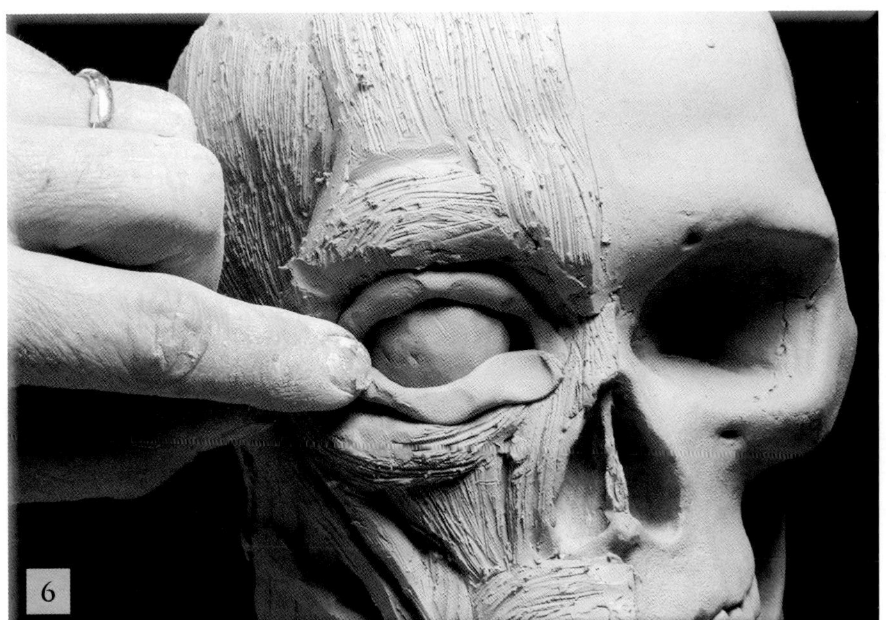


6. Small coils of clay create the volumes of the eyelids.

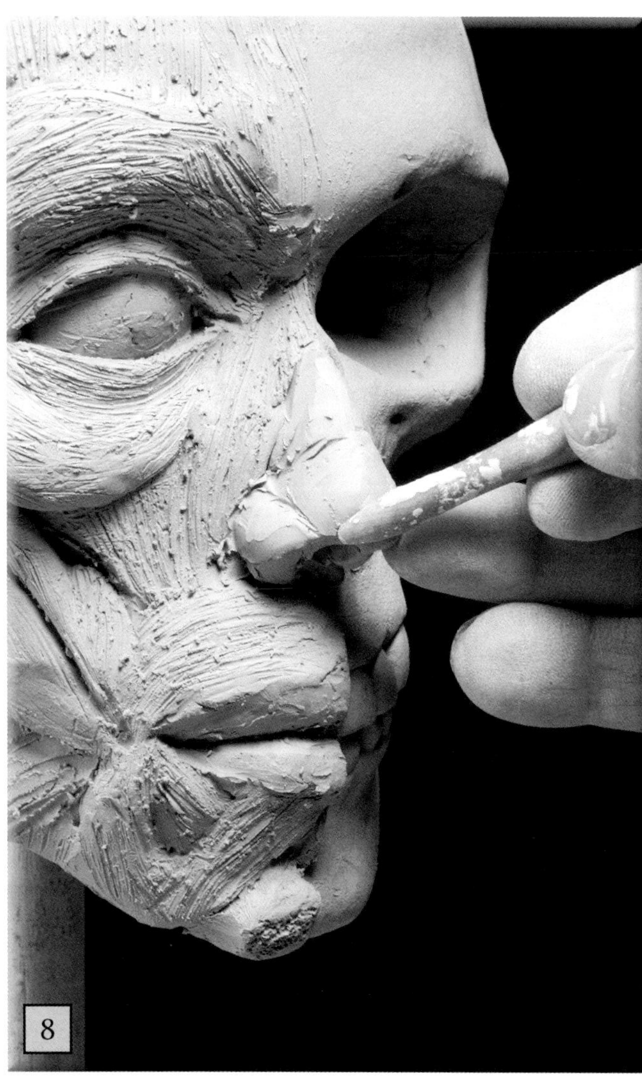

8. The placement of the corrugator, building of the cartilage of the nose, and the addition of the compressor naris and procerus are shown above.

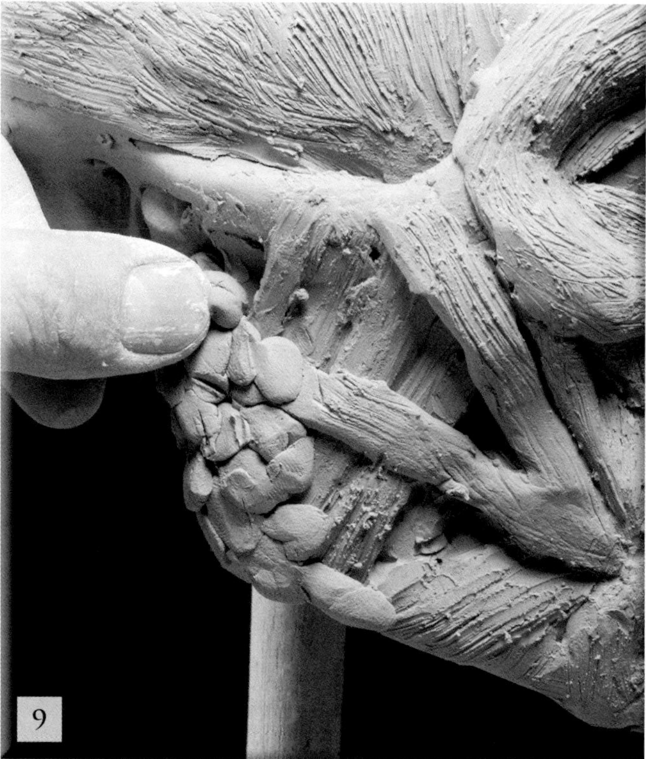

9. The parotid gland folds around the ramus.

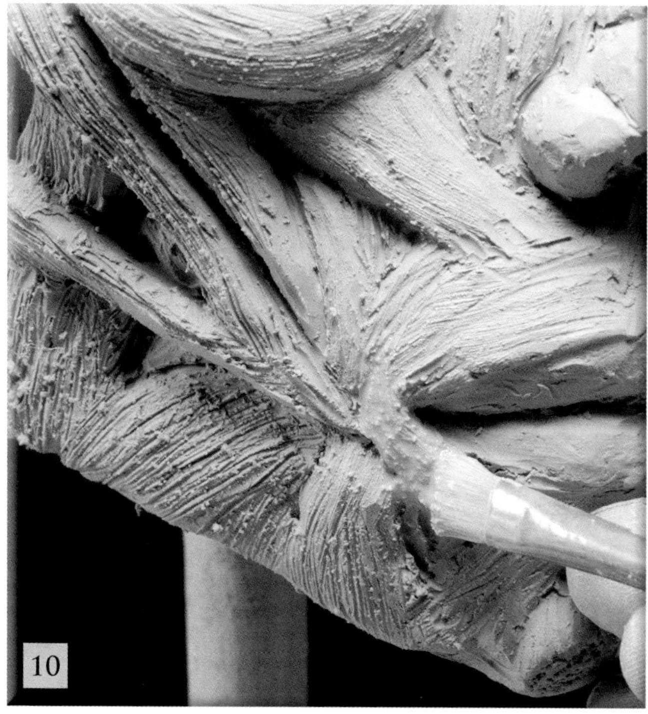

10. The insertion of one muscle into others is defined with a stiff brush.

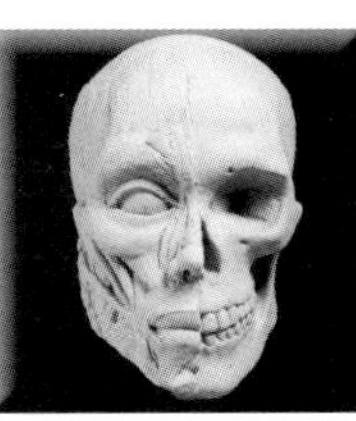

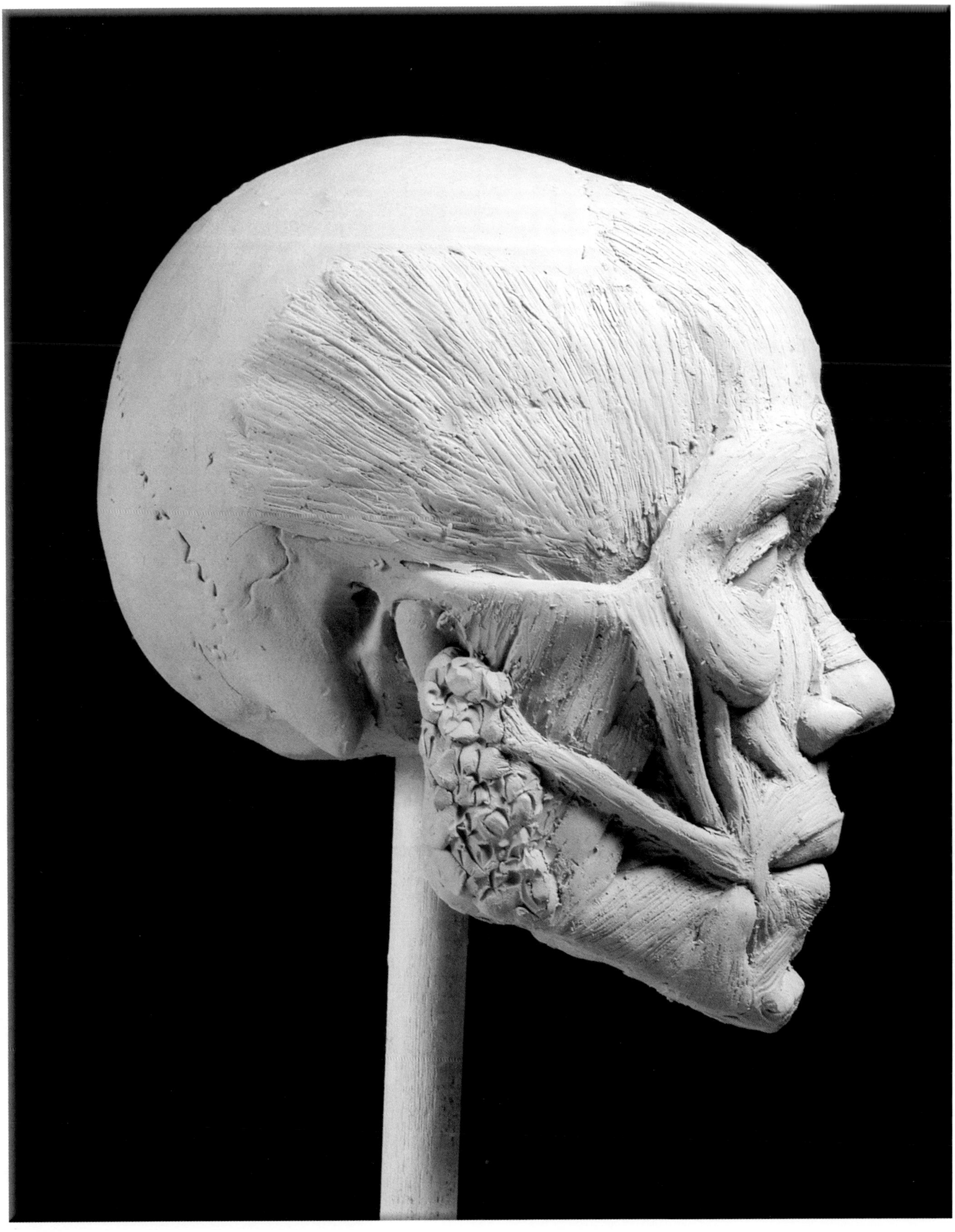

## The Neck

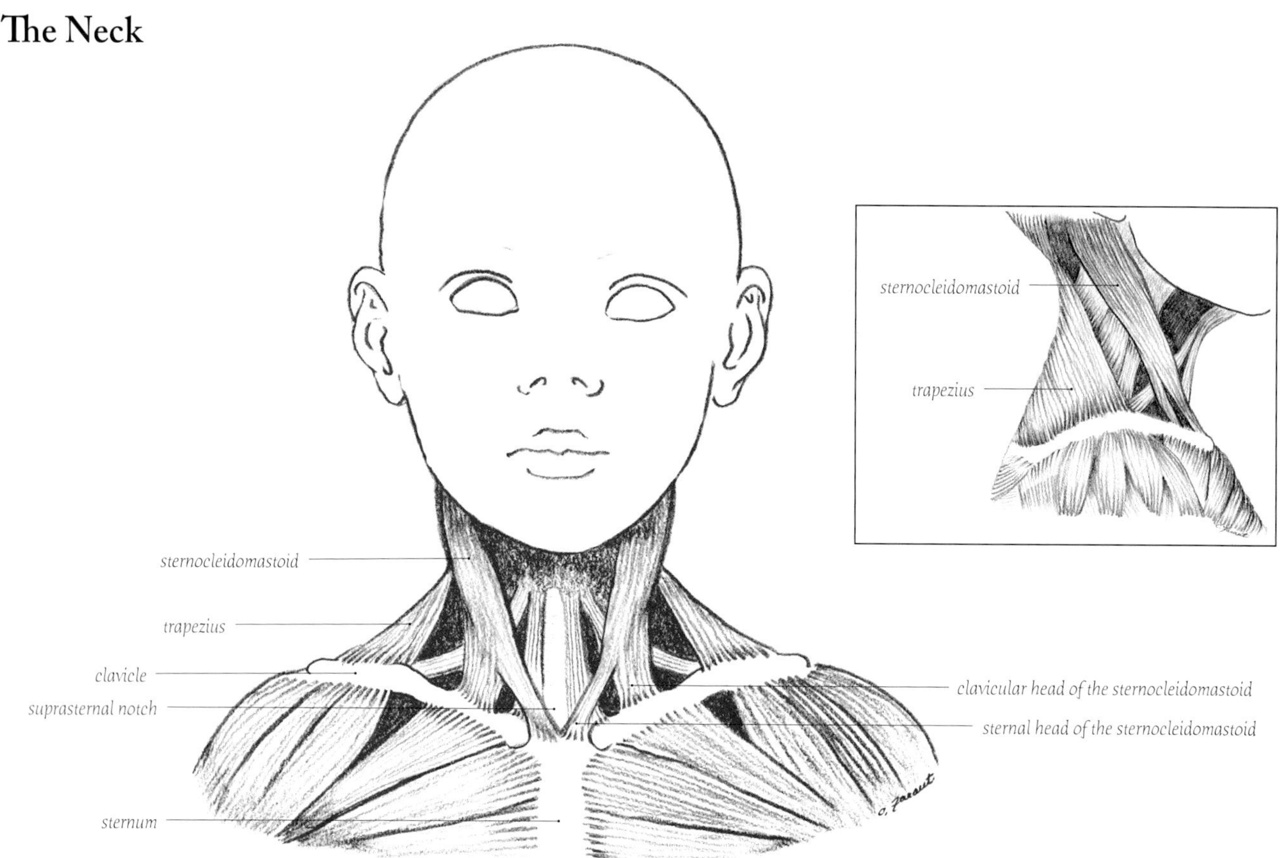


MUSCLES OF THE NECK

The most visible bones of the neck are the clavicle and the sternum in the front. The scapula, the seventh cervical vertebra, and the first thoracic vertebra are the most visible bones of the upper back.

The most prominent muscles of the neck are the sternocleidomastoid and the trapezius. The sternocleidomastoid originates from the sternum and from the medial third of the clavicle and inserts into the mastoid process and the superior nuchal line of the occipital bone. The tendons of the sternal attachment of the sternocleidomastoid form the two lateral ridges of the suprasternal notch.

The trapezius is a large muscle that covers the shoulder, the upper part of the back and the back of the neck. It originates from the superior nuchal line at the base of the skull, from the ligamentum nuchea and from the spines of the twelve thoracic vertebrae. It inserts into the lateral third of the clavicle and the upper border of the spine of the scapula.

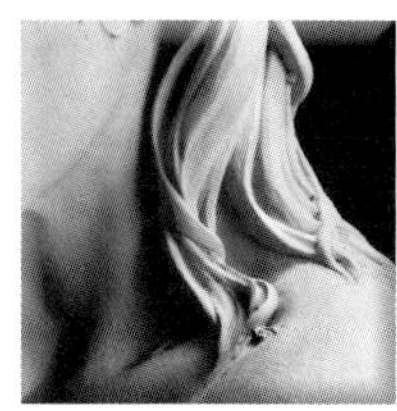

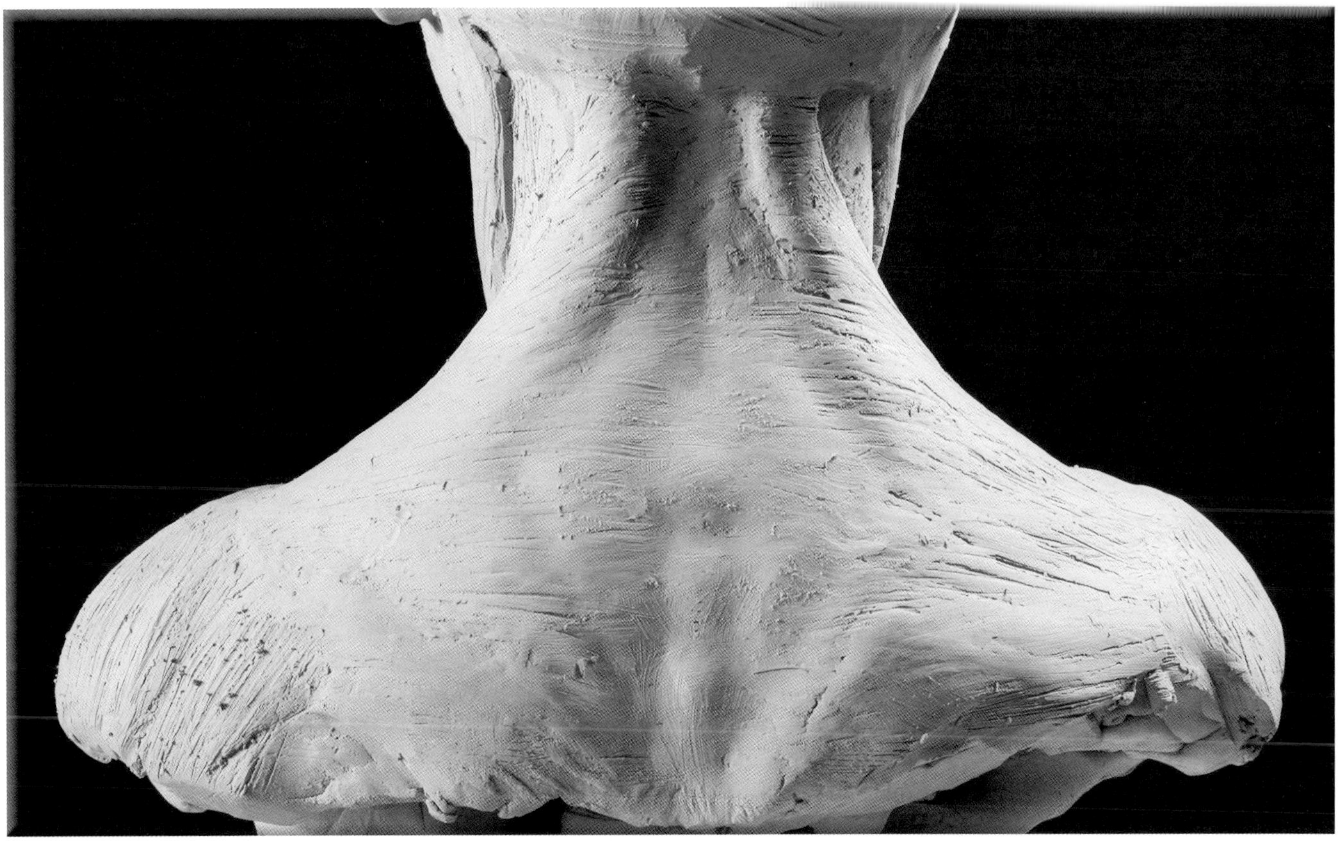

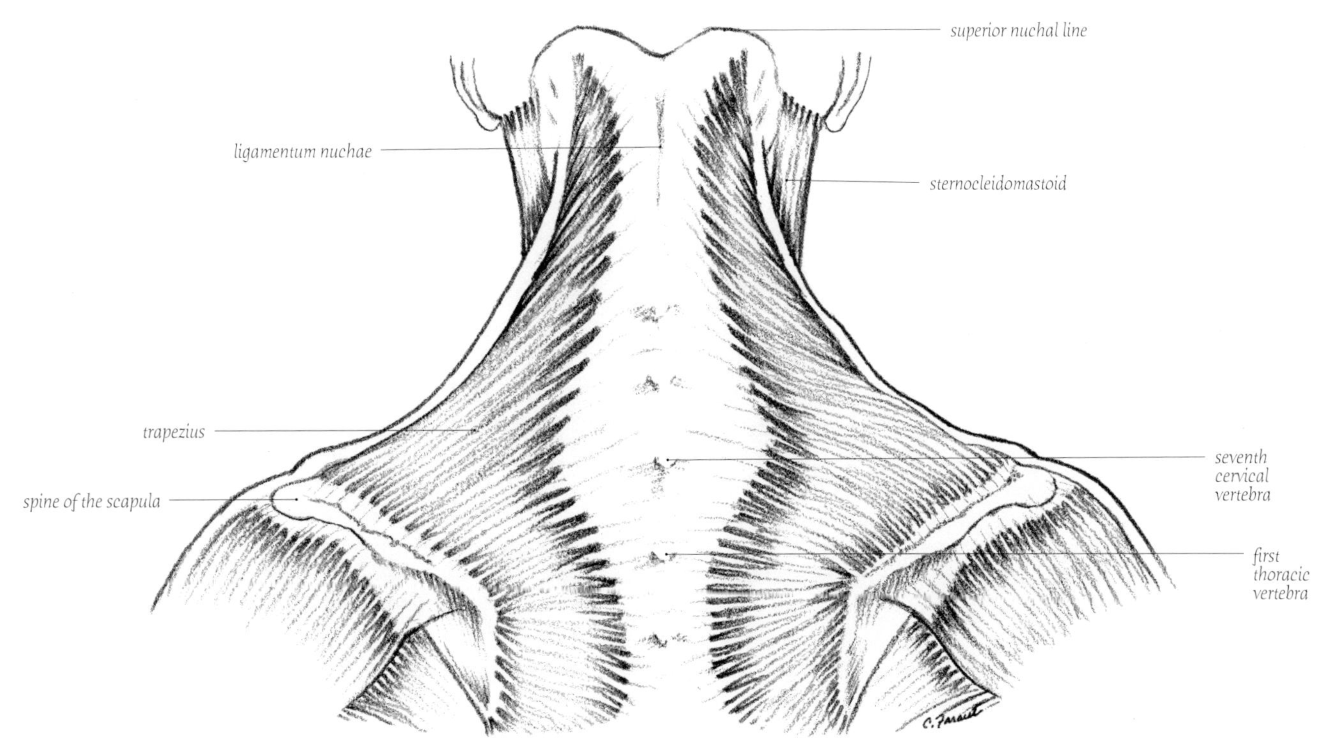


MUSCLES OF THE UPPER BACK

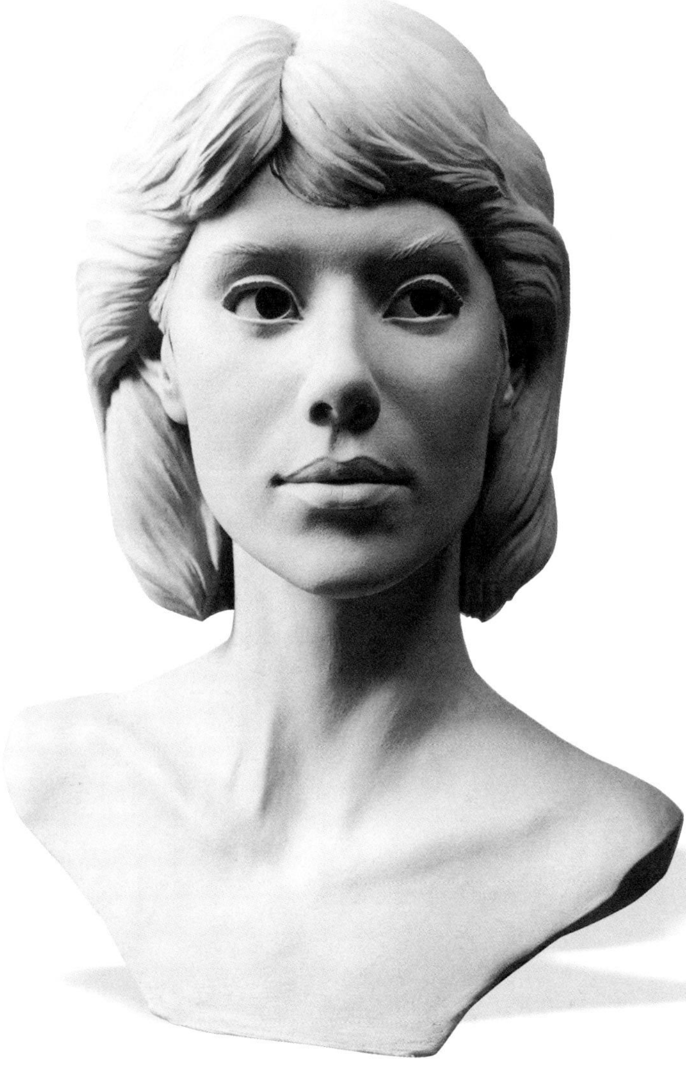

When the head is rotated to one side, the sternal head of the opposite sternocleidomastoid becomes very visible and almost vertical. The clavicular head is also often visible.

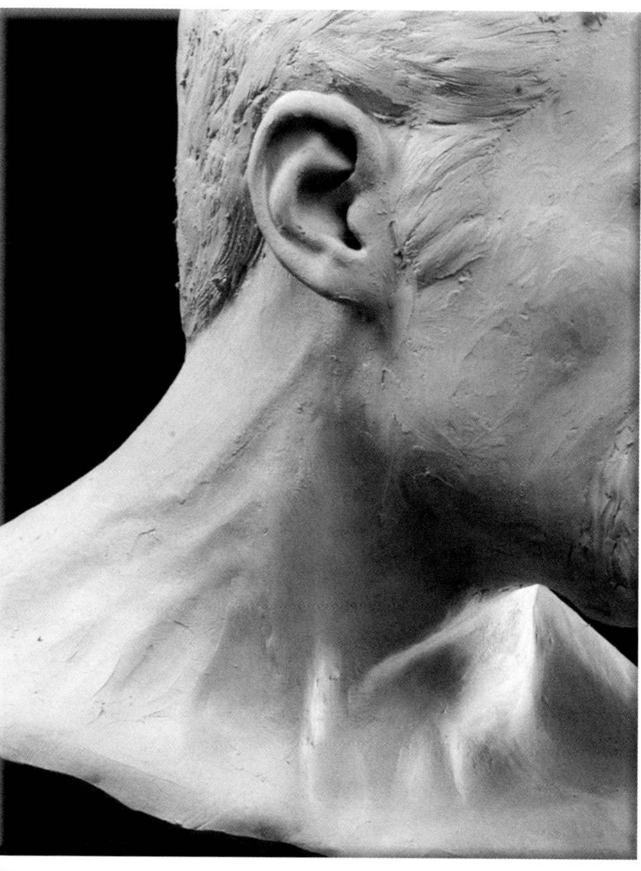

The neck is considered to have an anterior and posterior triangle on either side. The posterior triangle has fine muscles that can sometimes be seen running diagonally through it when the neck is stretched to the opposite side.

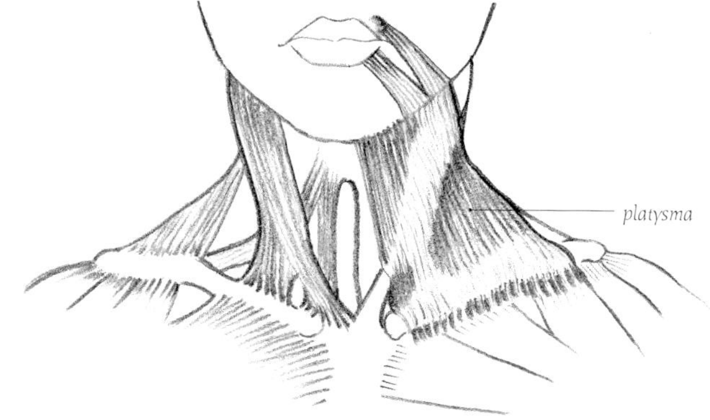


## The Platysma

The platysma is a large, thin muscular sheet with edges that become visible when tensed. This is illustrated in the photo on the opposite page by the raised ridges running downward from the jaw to the clavicle.

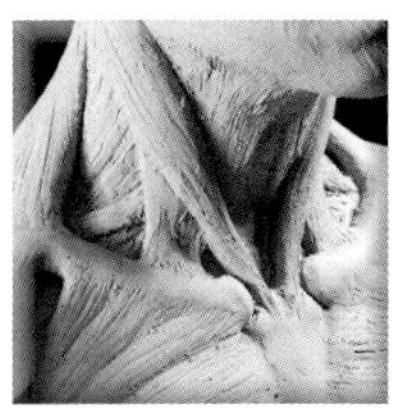

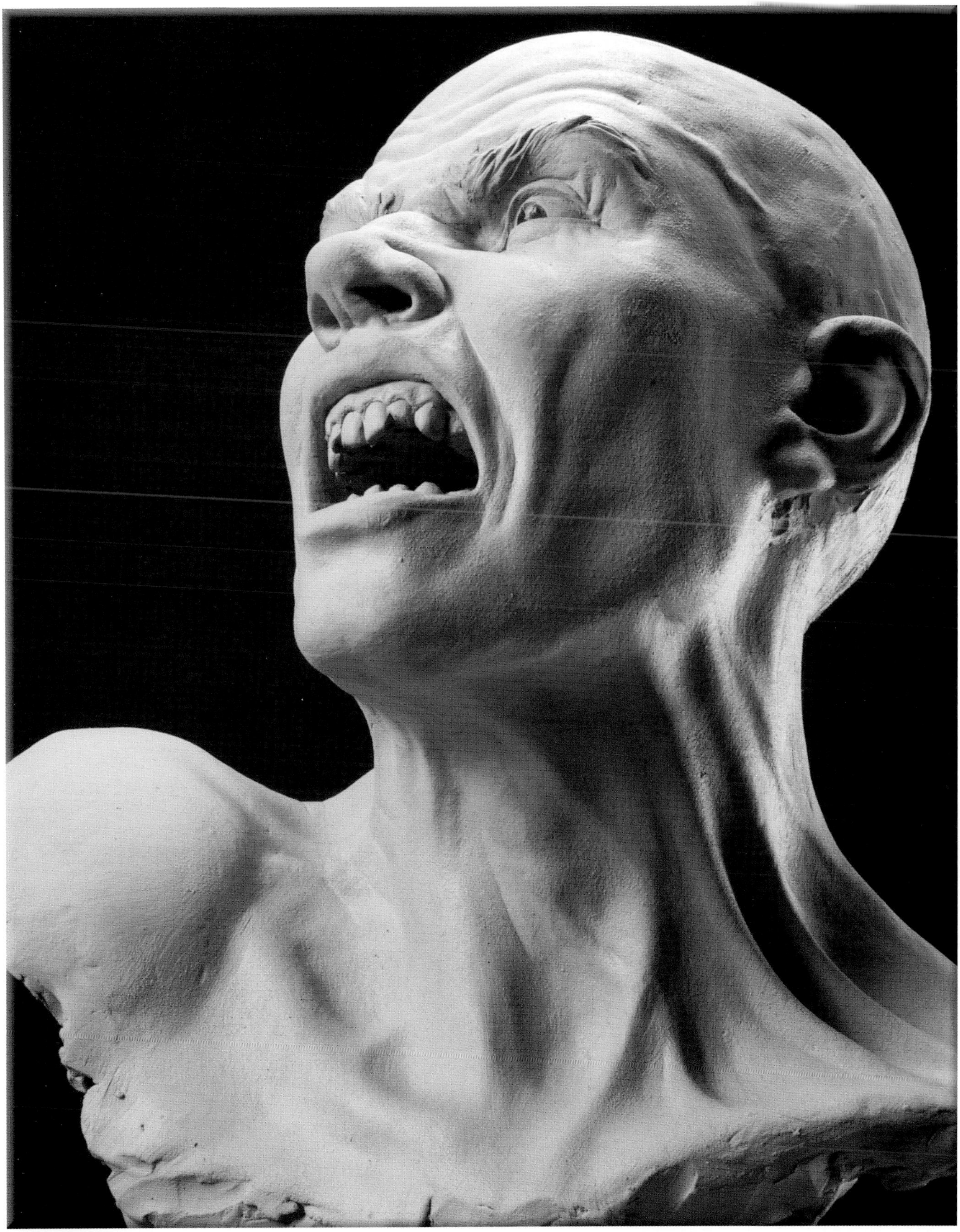

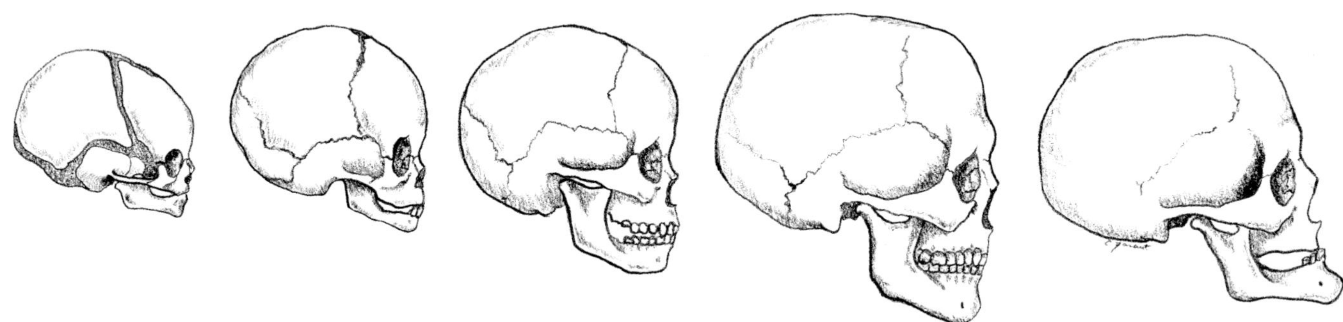

## AGE PROGRESSION OF THE SKULL

This diagram shows the growth of the skull of a Caucasian male from infant to elder.

At birth the head is mostly cranium. The face comprises slightly less than one quarter of its total volume. The jaw is nearly horizontal and the bones of the skull are not completely developed. As the brain grows, the cranium enlarges, with ossification completed around age twenty-five. In the early years, the upper and lower jaws increase in size and rapidly change shape. Changes in the mandible are very noticeable due to the lengthening of the ramus caused by the presence and growth of teeth. The orbital cavities change from being round to being more rectangular. In an elderly person, the loss of back teeth causes the angle of the mandible to widen and rise forward, and the cranial sutures nearly disappear.

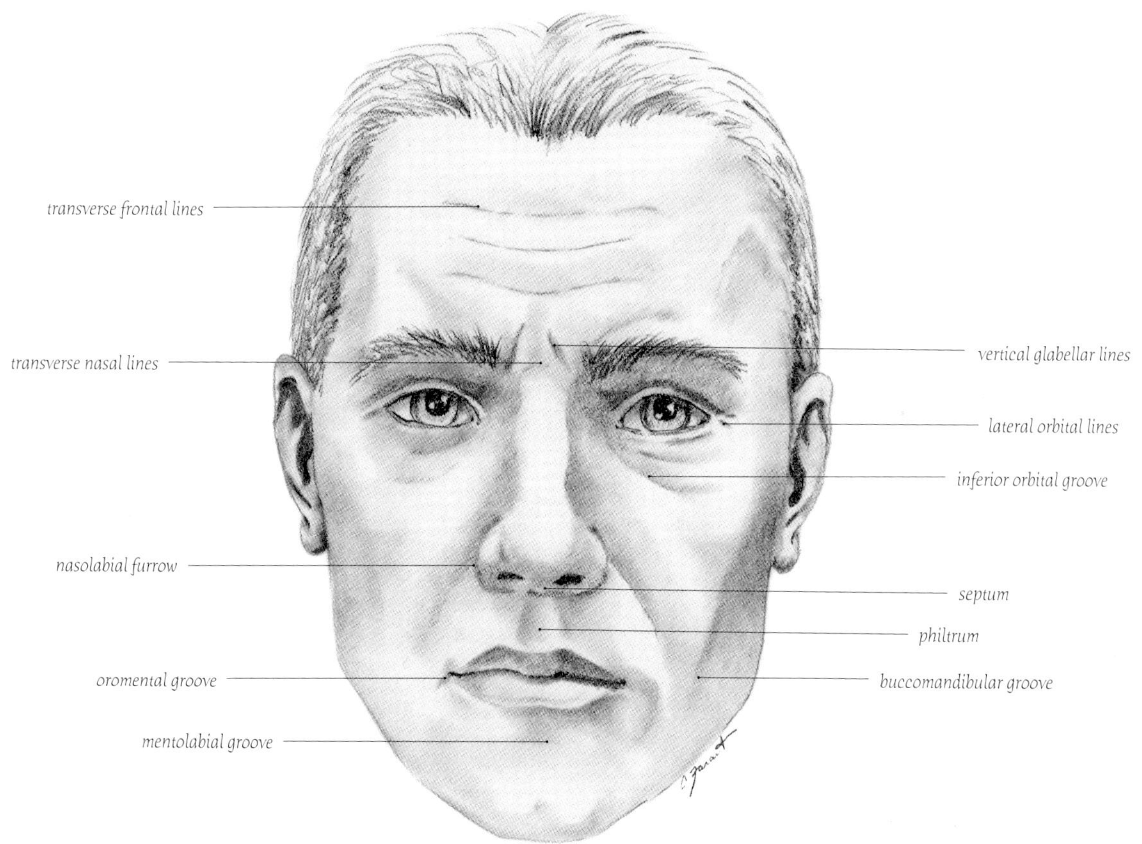


## FACIAL GROOVES AND LINES

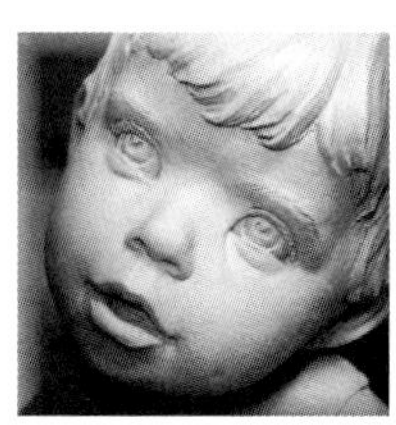

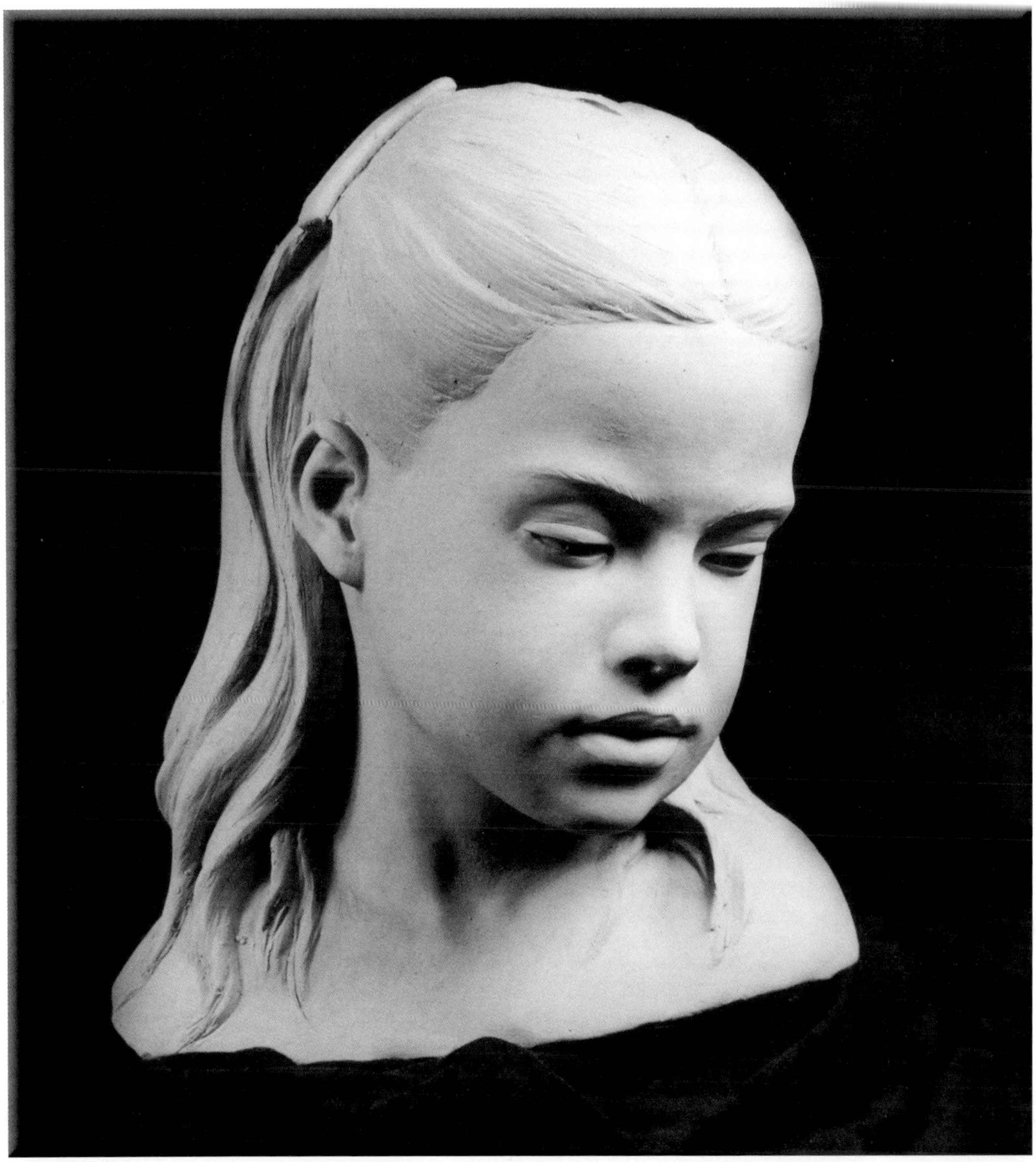

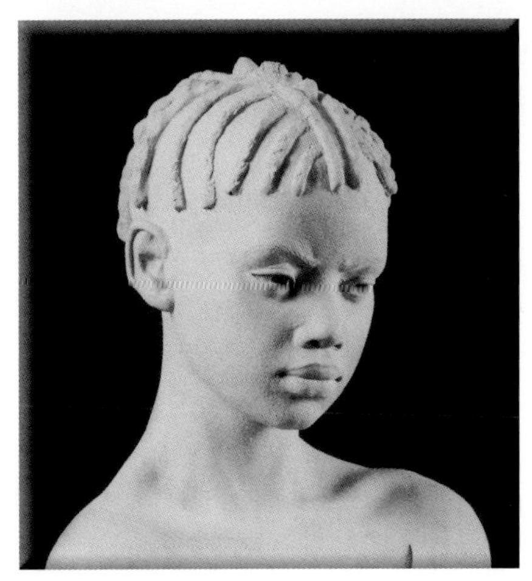

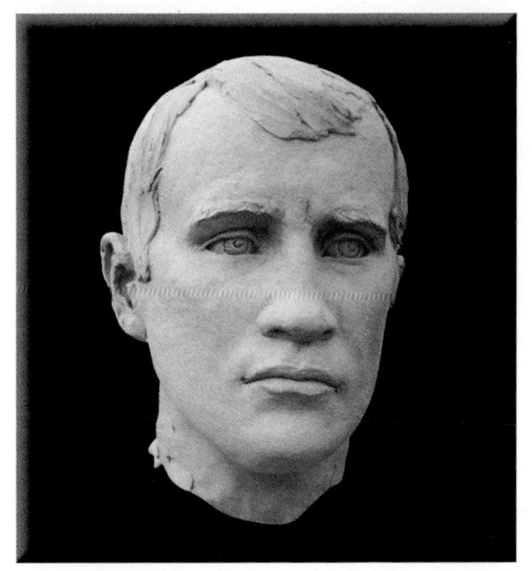

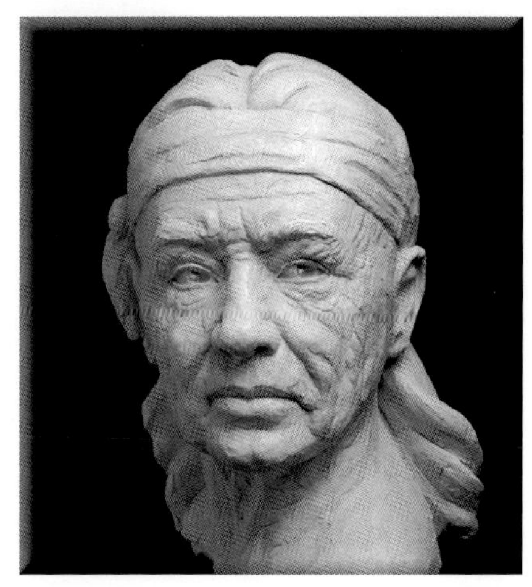

## Aging

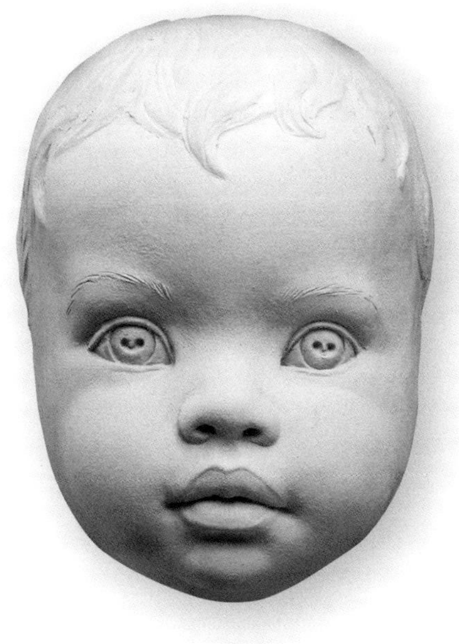

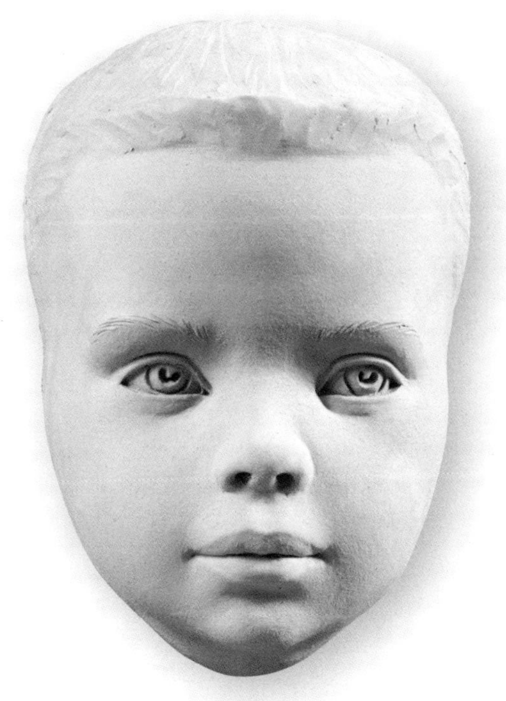

The greatest transformations in the face during the first twenty years are produced by the underlying growth of the skull. Facial changes occurring after this are primarily due to changes in the soft tissues – muscle and skin.

During the natural aging process, the upper half of the face usually shows the first wrinkles – transverse frontal lines, vertical glabellar lines, transverse nasal lines and lateral orbital lines. Later, wrinkles appear on the face in a predictable pattern. The inferior orbital groove, nasolabial furrow, oromental groove, philtrum, buccomandibular groove and surface wrinkles in general all deepen and become more pronounced.

The eyes especially show the effects of aging. The excess of upper lid skin hides some of the eyelid and the under eye pouch is more pronounced. The sagging of the outer edge of the eyebrow can give a sad look, while a tired look is created by a uniform sagging of the brows. Additionally, these effects give the appearance of smaller, deeper set eyes.

In old age, the chin becomes more prominent, the lips are thinner and small wrinkles appear over the entire skin surface.

The most important thing to remember when rendering wrinkles is that they occur perpendicular to the stretch of the underlying muscle's fibers.

The masks shown here illustrate the hypothetical aging process of an individual.

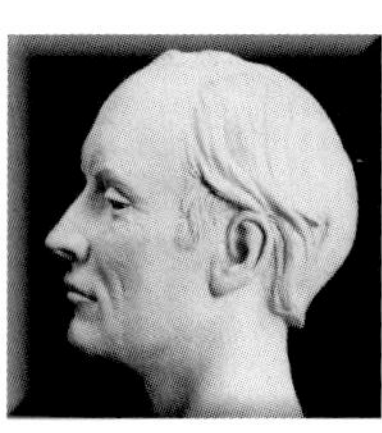

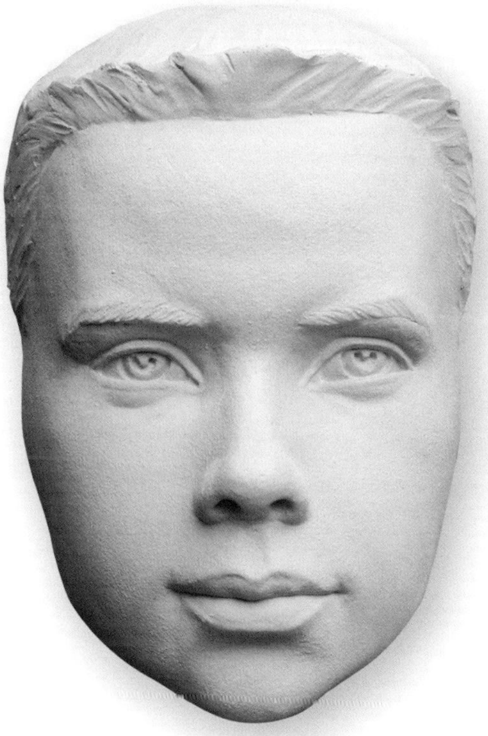

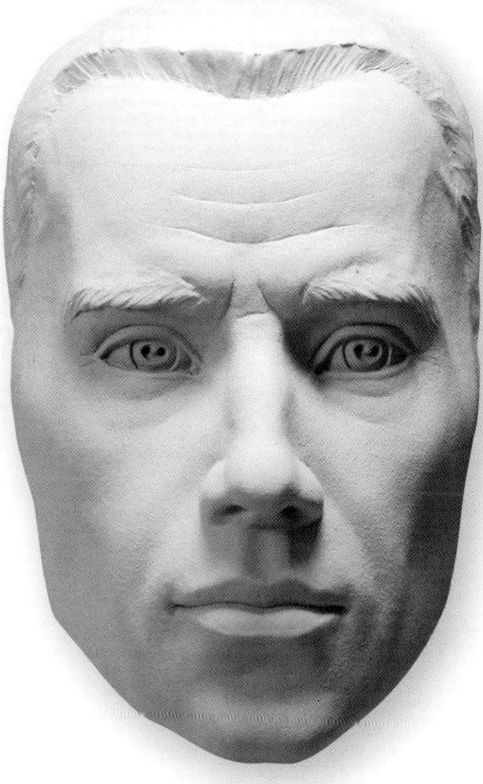

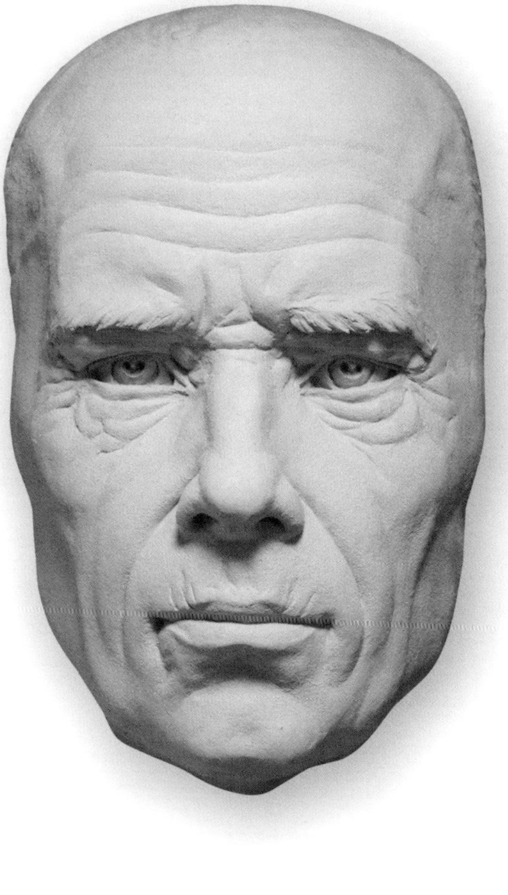

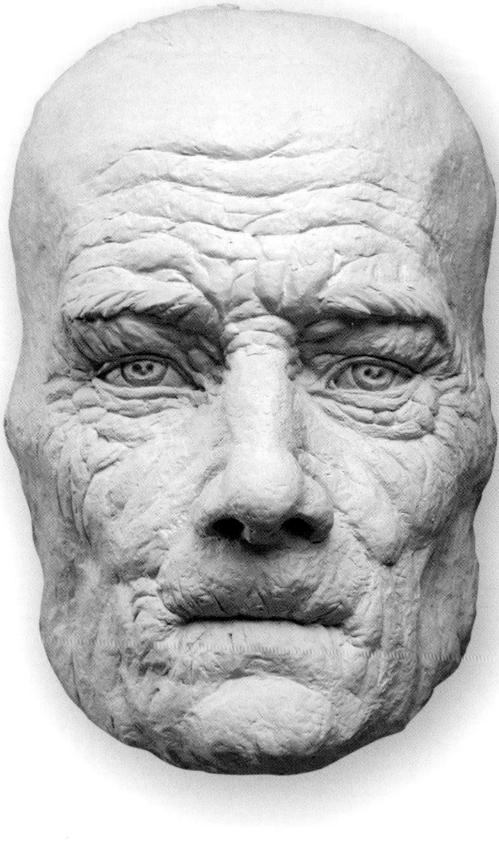

Chapter 3

# Features & Hair

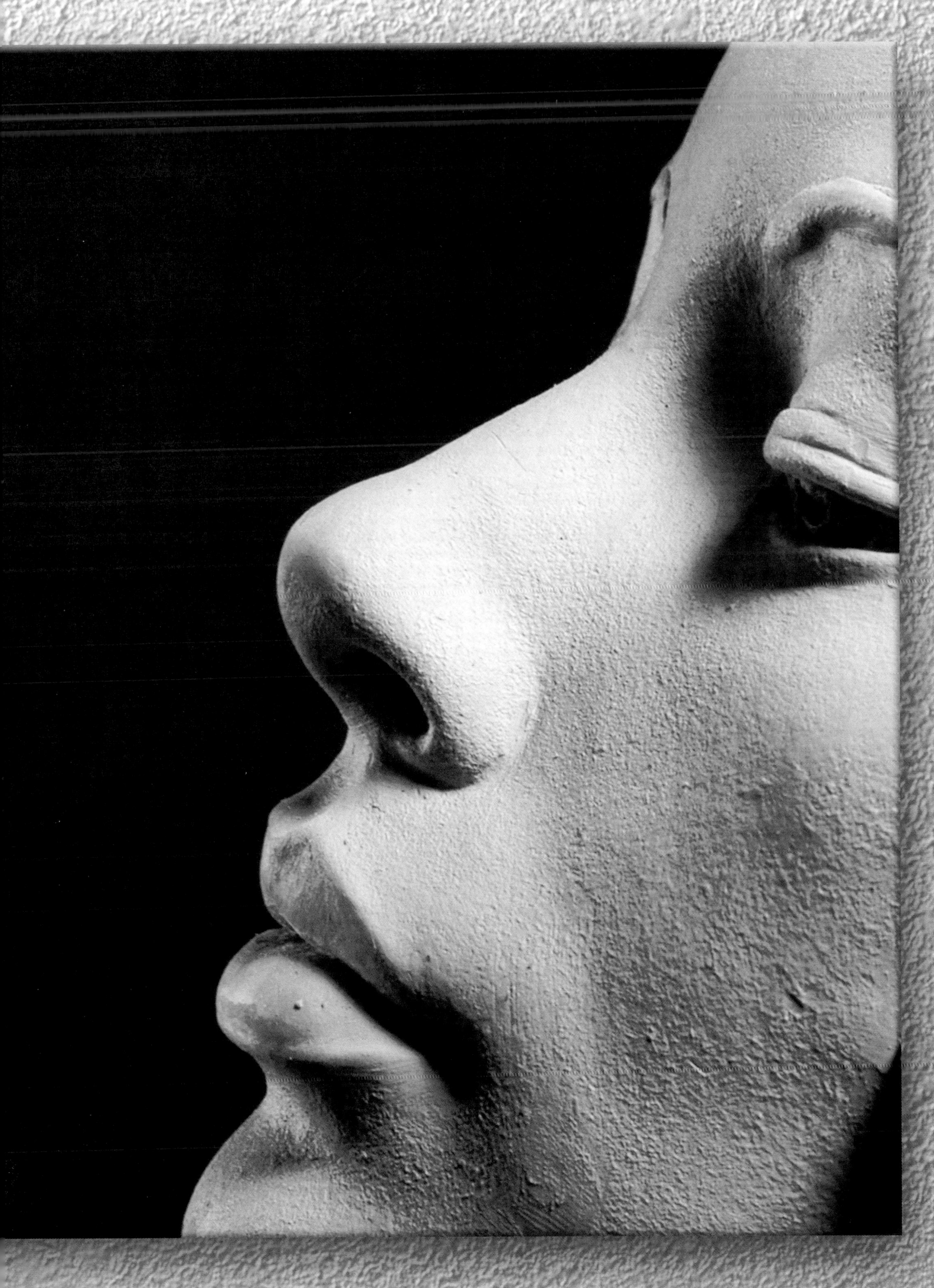

Before attempting to sculpt a complete head, it is best to study and understand the complexity, form and volumes of the individual features. A good approach is to model them one by one on a board independently of the rest of the face. It is more productive and less overwhelming to focus only on a nose or an ear rather than the entire head. Only when we master the modeling of these features can we hope to be able to bring them together on the planes of the head.

In order to study and model the individual features of the face, it is necessary to have a three dimensional model or a plaster cast to copy. We cannot assume that we know by instinct the complexities of these shapes. While it is true that each feature infinitely varies from person to person they have common structures and can be rendered in clay by following common rules of construction.

The following demonstrations should be practiced often and with different models.

## The Nose

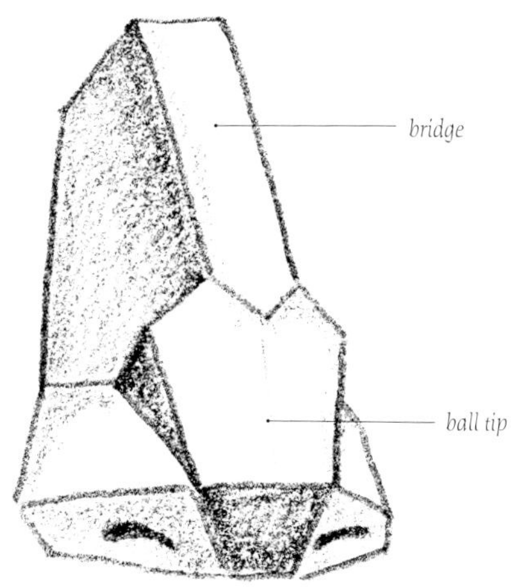


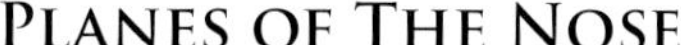
PLANES OF THE NOSE

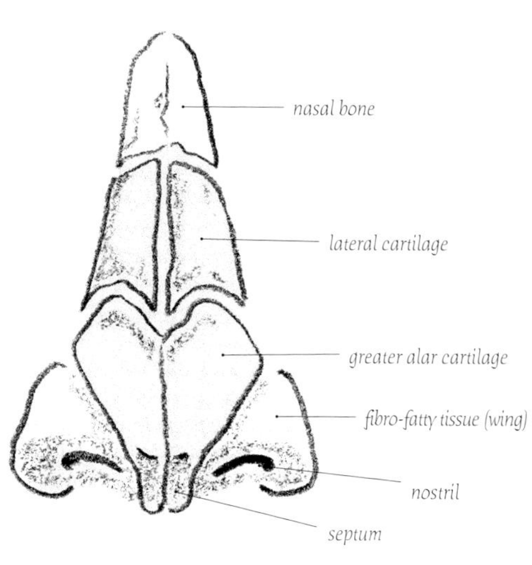


1/2 1/2

The nose is made up of bone, cartilage, and fatty tissue. The widest part of the bridge of the nose is where the nasal bone and cartilage meet and form the bump of the nose when seen in profile. The tip of the nose is composed of the paired greater alar cartilages. These cartilages are always visible, but not always easy to see without a strong sidelight. They can be rounded or pointed at the tip. From the side view, the septum is visible because it descends lower than the wing of the nose where it meets the upper lip. An intermediary small plane separates the septum and the upper lip.

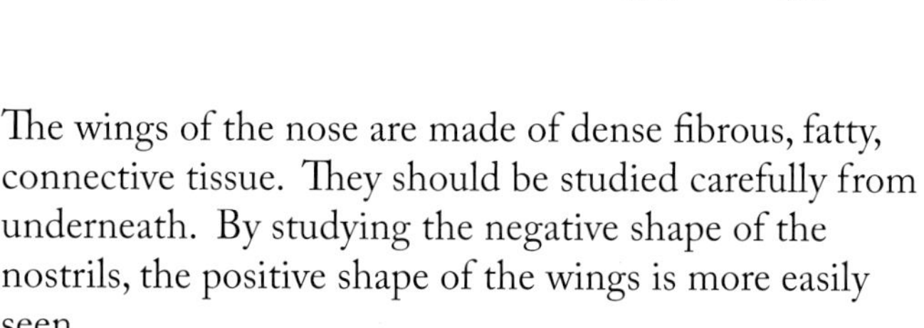

The wings of the nose are made of dense fibrous, fatty, connective tissue. They should be studied carefully from underneath. By studying the negative shape of the nostrils, the positive shape of the wings is more easily seen.

A good rule of thumb to remember is that when the nose is viewed in profile, half of it is on the face, as defined by a line running vertically from the point of connection between the septum and the upper lip, and the other half is off the face (see above diagram).

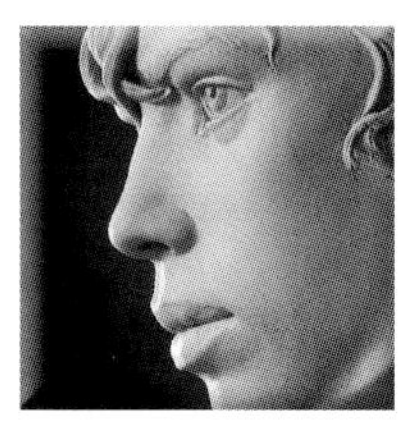

## Demonstration 3: Modeling the Adult Nose

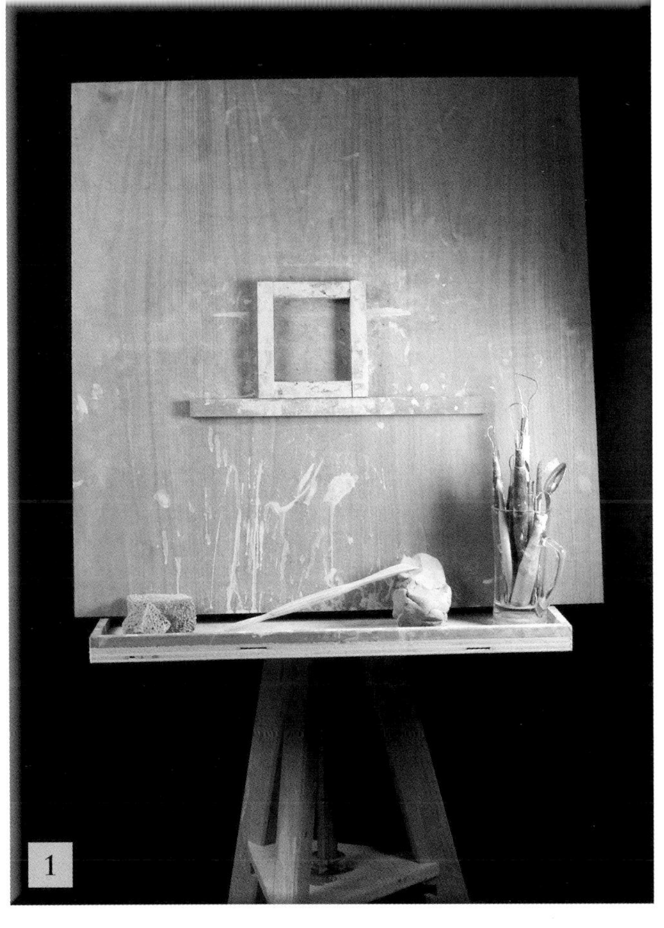


1. A nearly vertical board is set up and a wooden frame nailed at eye level to form a base for the sculpture.

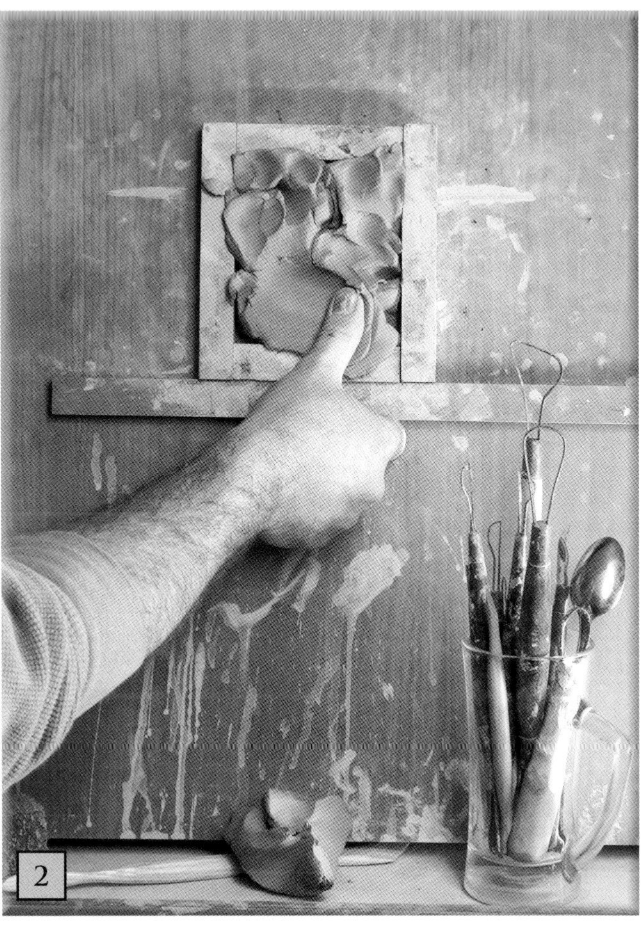


2. The inside of the frame is filled with clay and the surface smoothed.

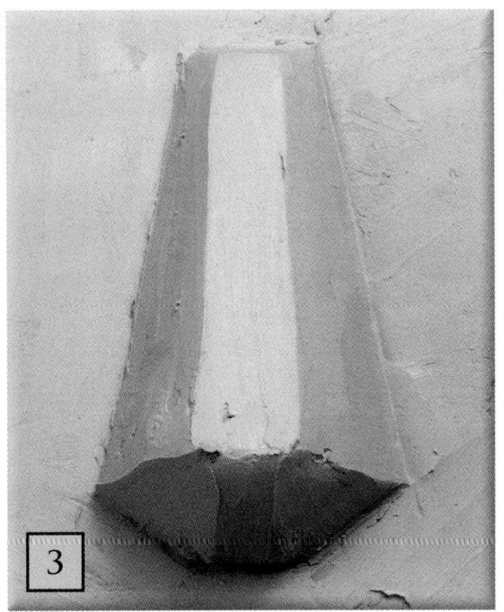


3. A symmetrical shape is built composed of six planes as shown.

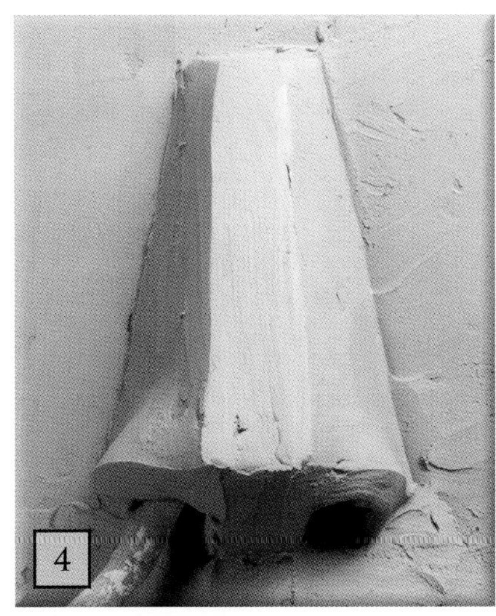


4. The wings of the nose are pulled from the inside.

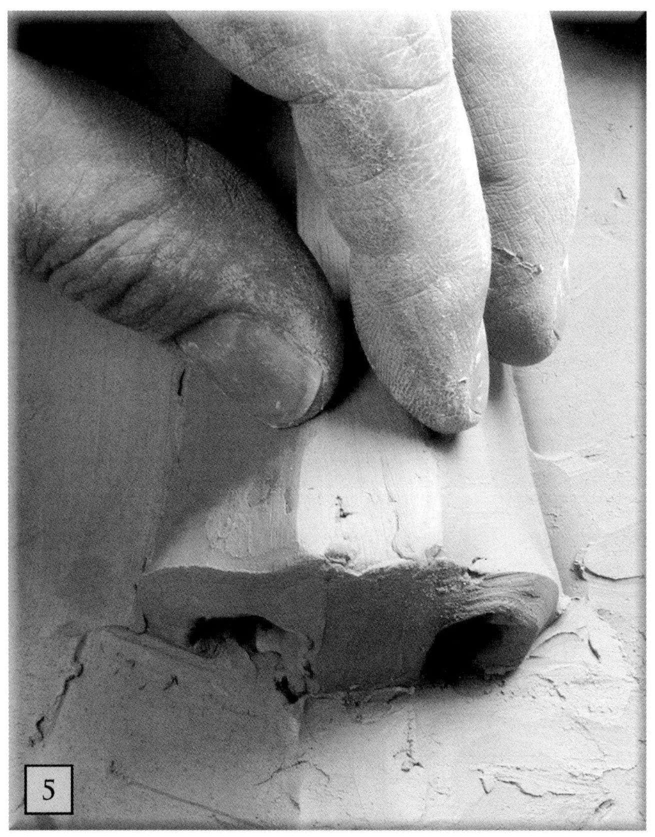


5. The greater alar cartilages are defined. In this woman's nose they are very subtle.

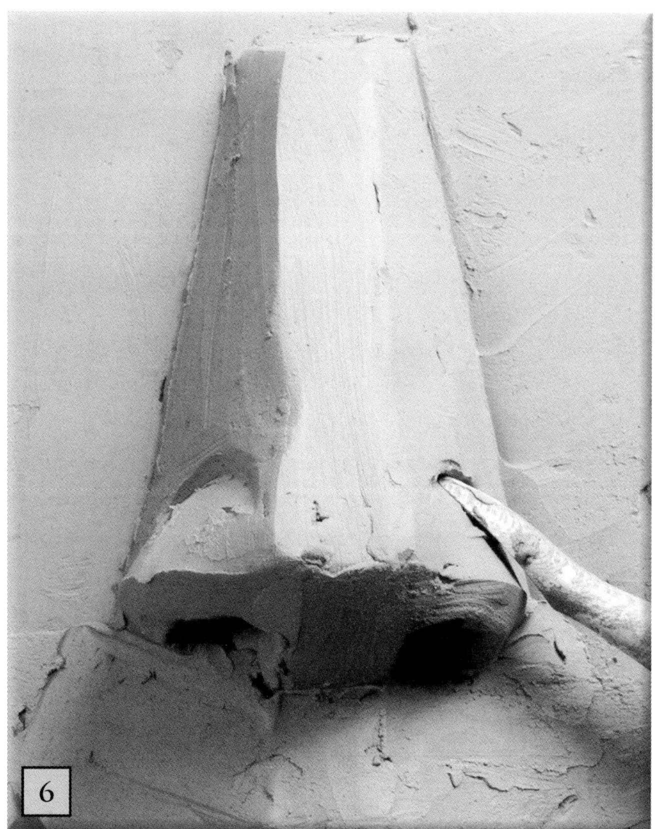


6. The planes on the upper part of the wing are indicated with a wooden tool.

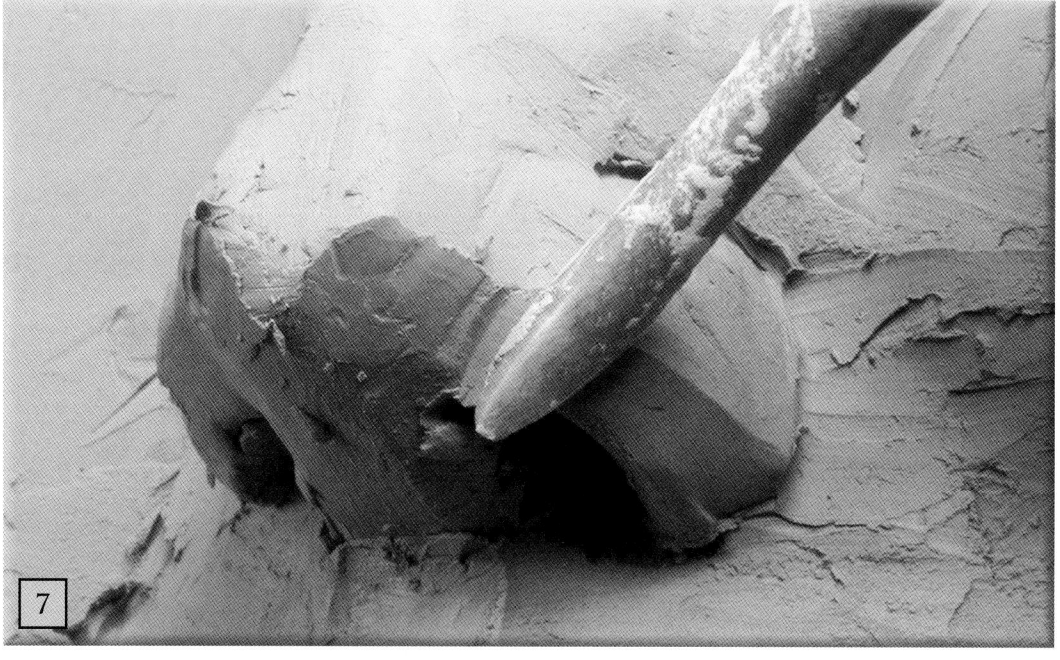


7. The lower planes of the wings are defined. They project along the sides of the septum to form a V-shape all the way to the tip of the nose.

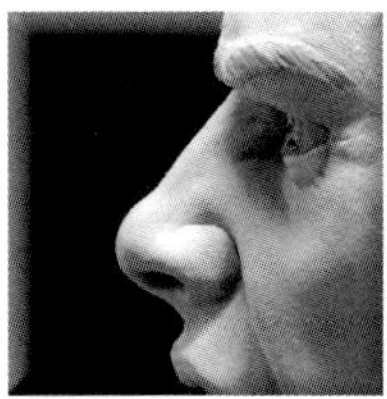

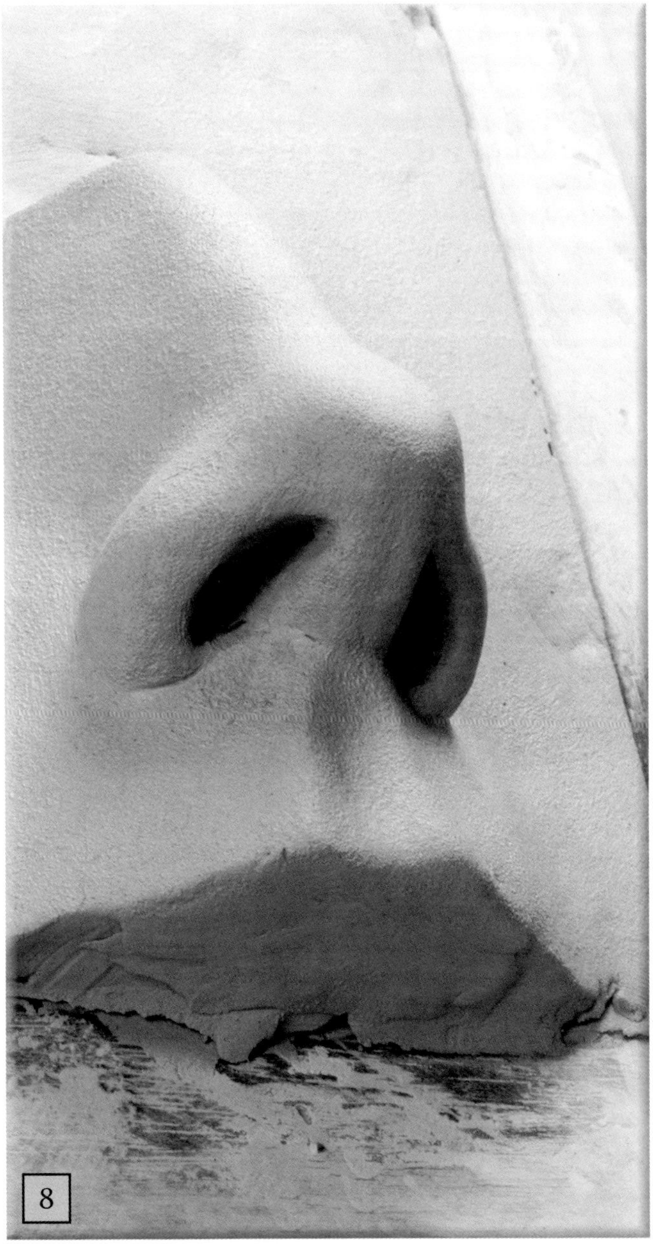

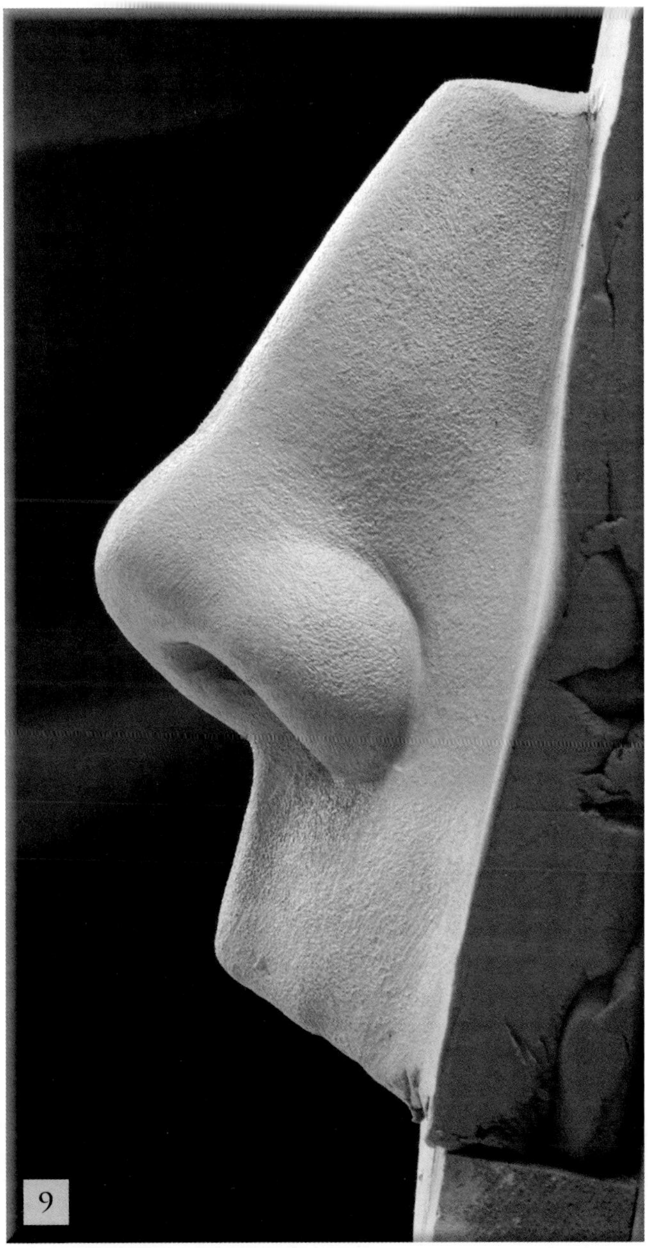

8

9

**8, 9.** Once the planes are in place, it is easy to bring the volumes to a smooth transition between one another using a variety of brushes and sponges (see pages 159-161). The above images show a woman's finished nose.

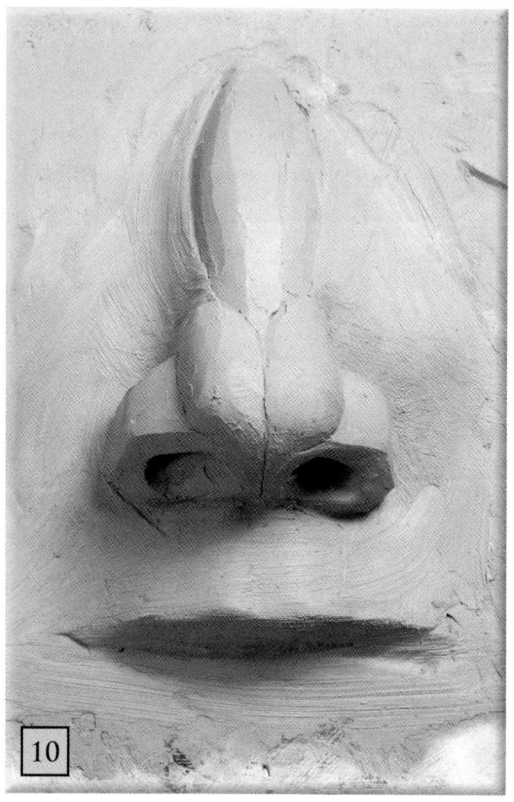

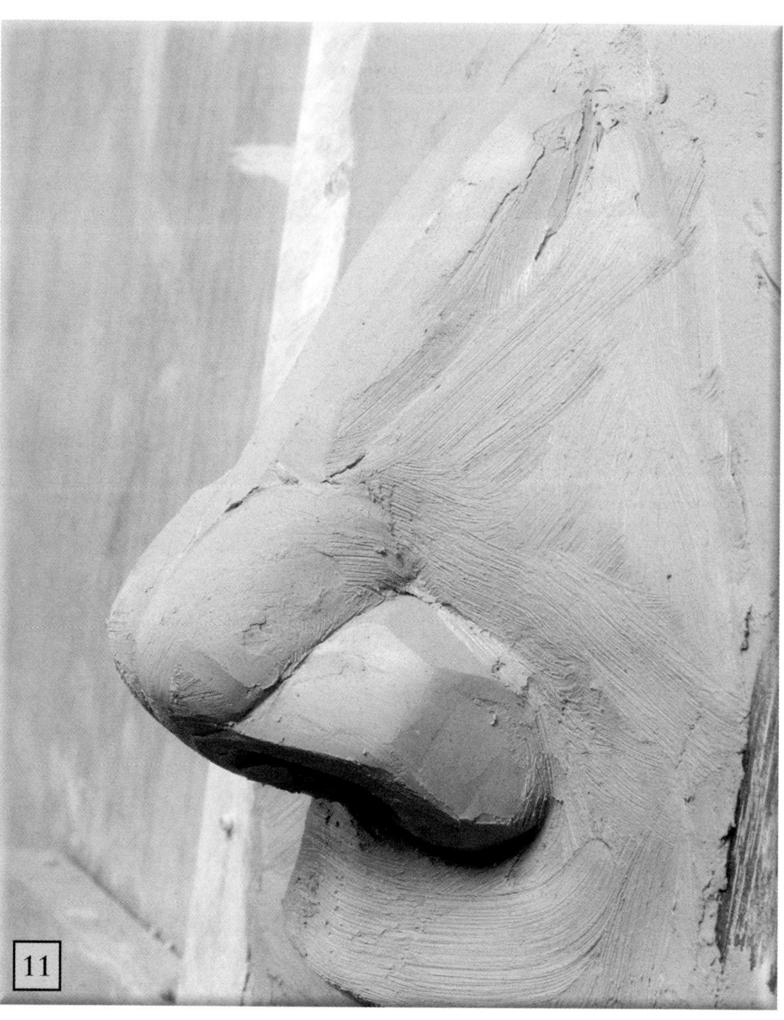

**10, 11, 12.** Practice on a man's nose where the planes are more defined. Use the same technique as above adjusting for the proper volumes.

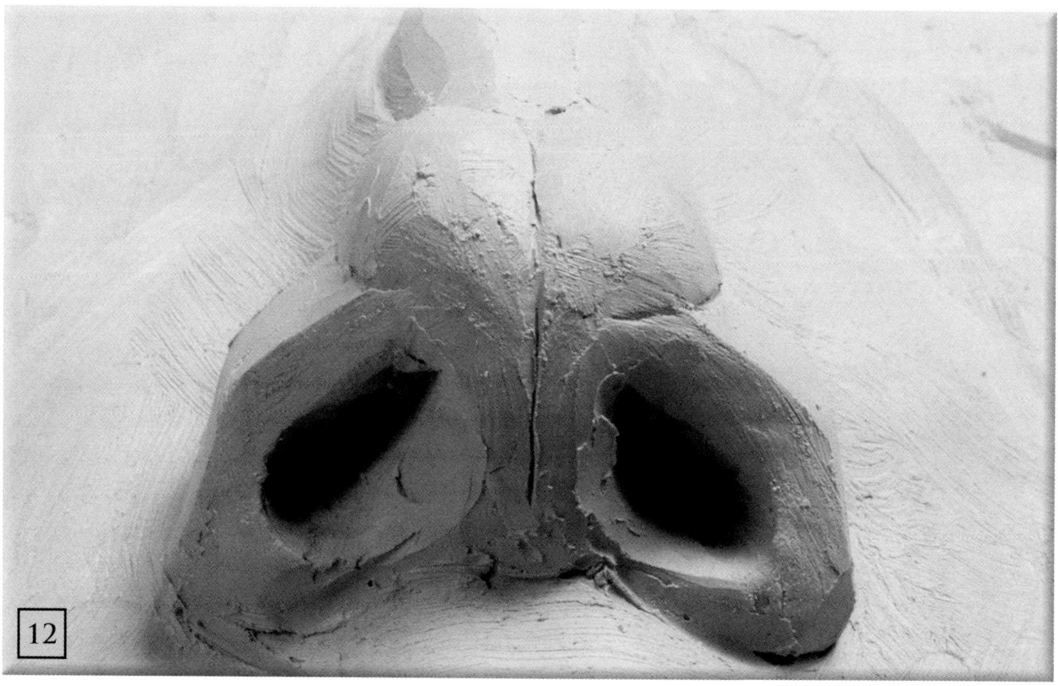

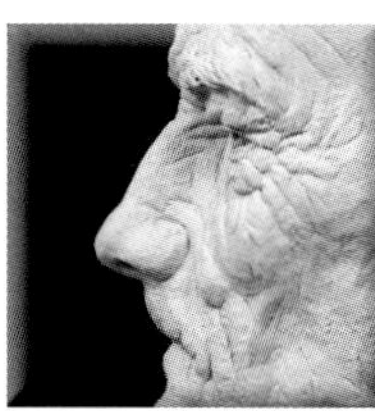

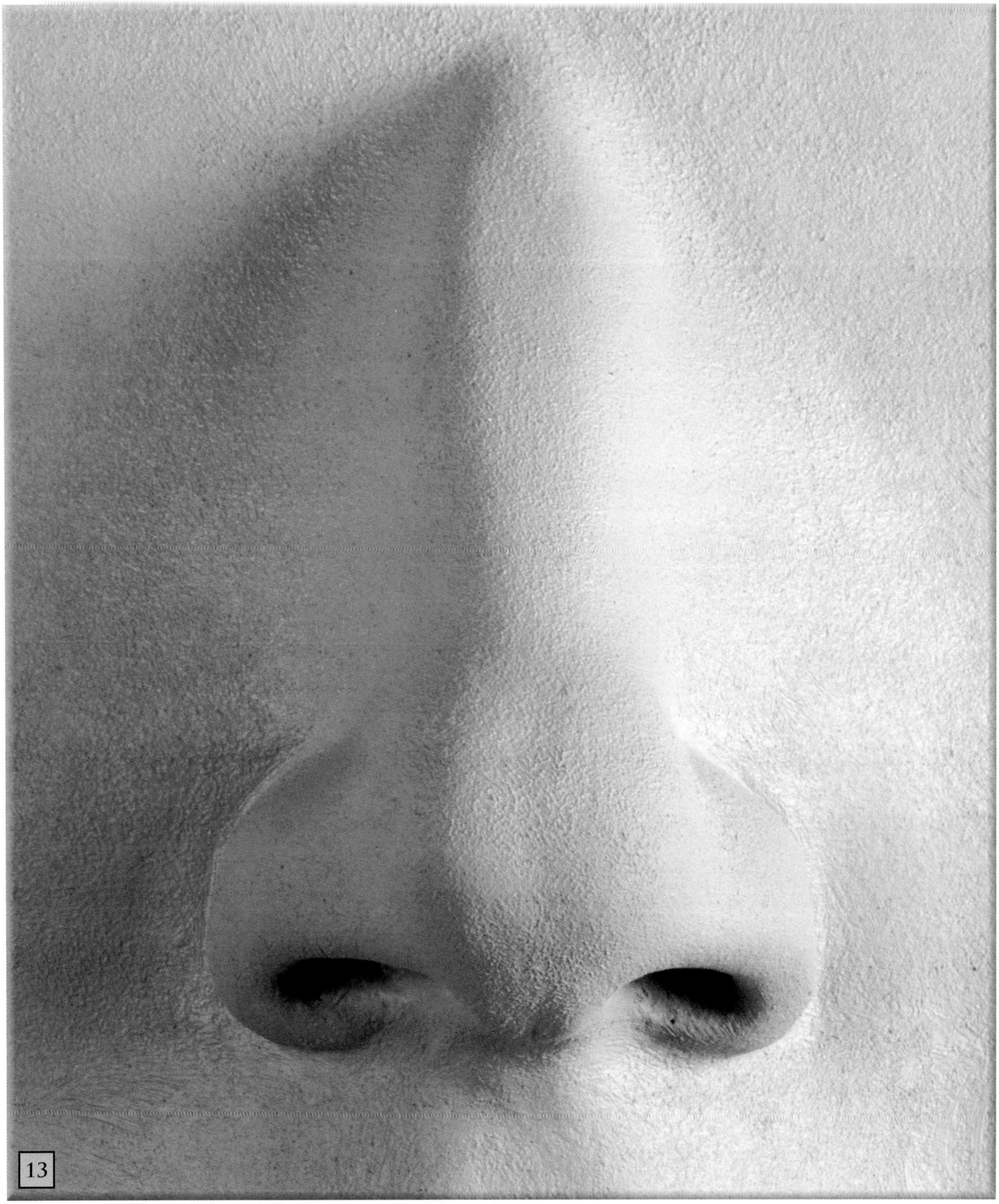

13

13. After refining and texturing the surface, the planes are still visible.

## Demonstration 4: A Child's Nose

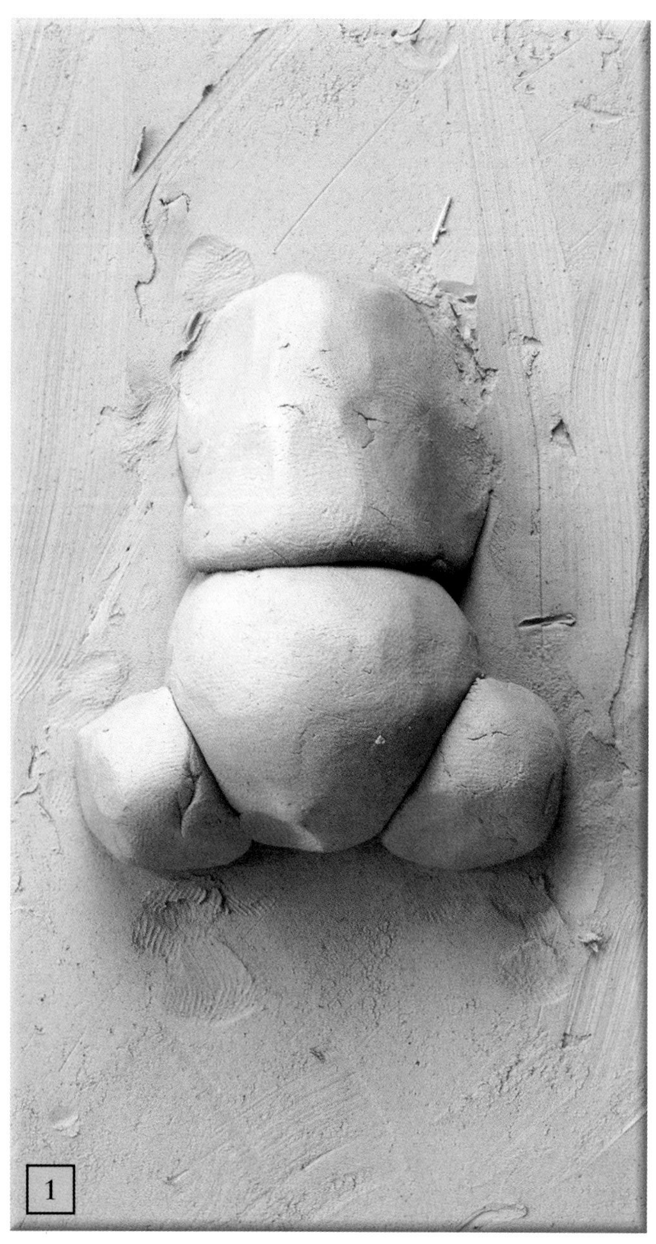


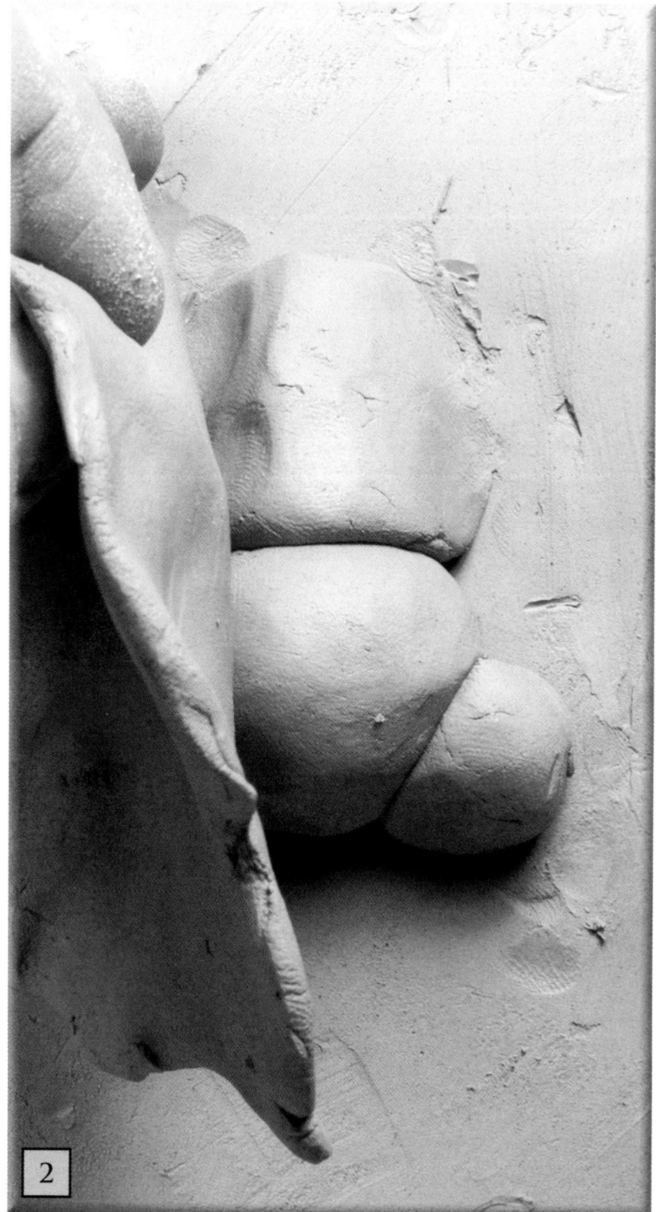


**1.** A baby's nose is composed of a rounded tip, nostrils and a somewhat flattened bridge.

**2.** A thin piece of clay is applied over the volumes.

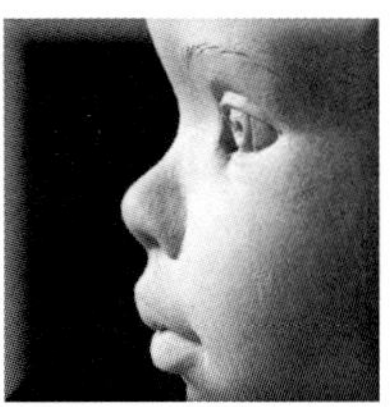

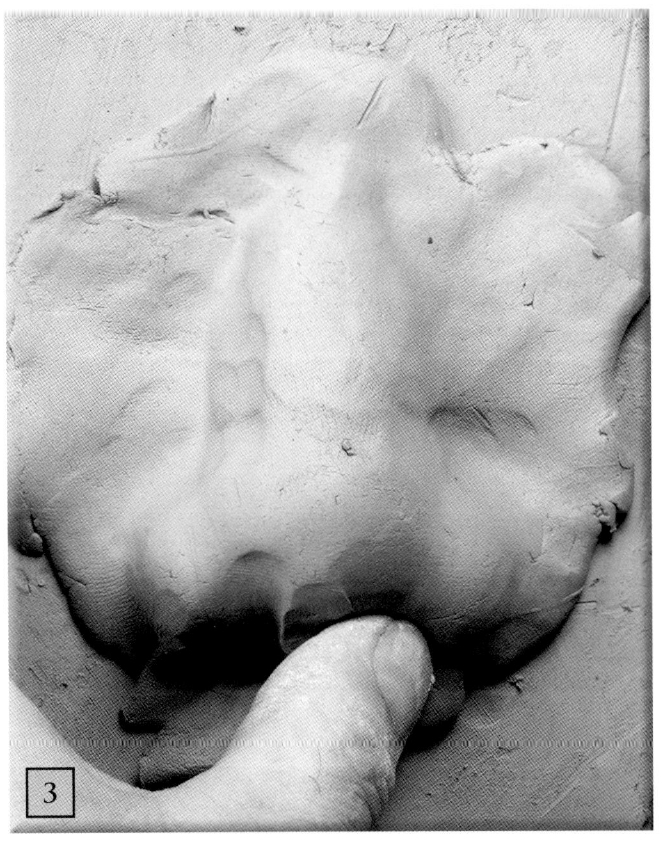

3. The clay is gently pressed following the shape underneath.

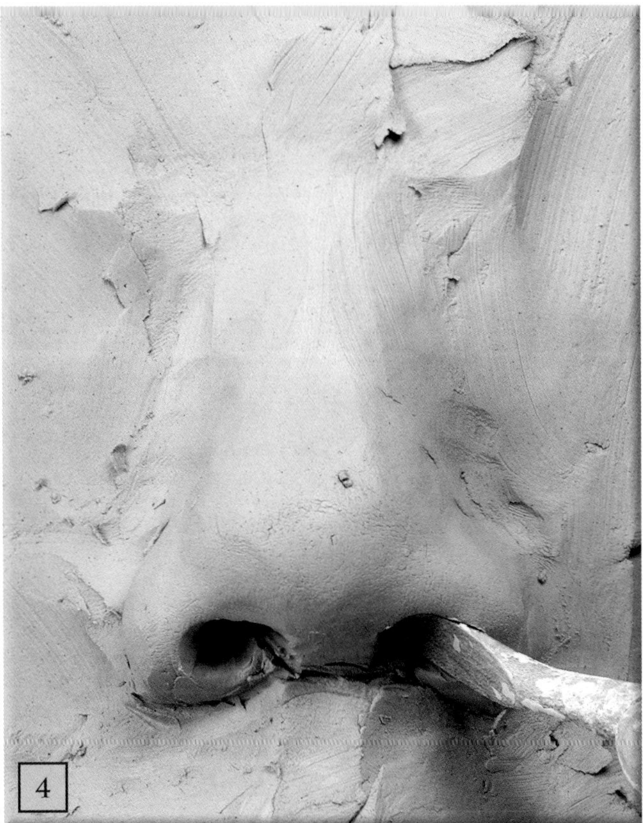

4. In a baby, the nostrils are round or even elongated in a direction parallel to the front of the face as opposed to the adult where they are almost perpendicular.

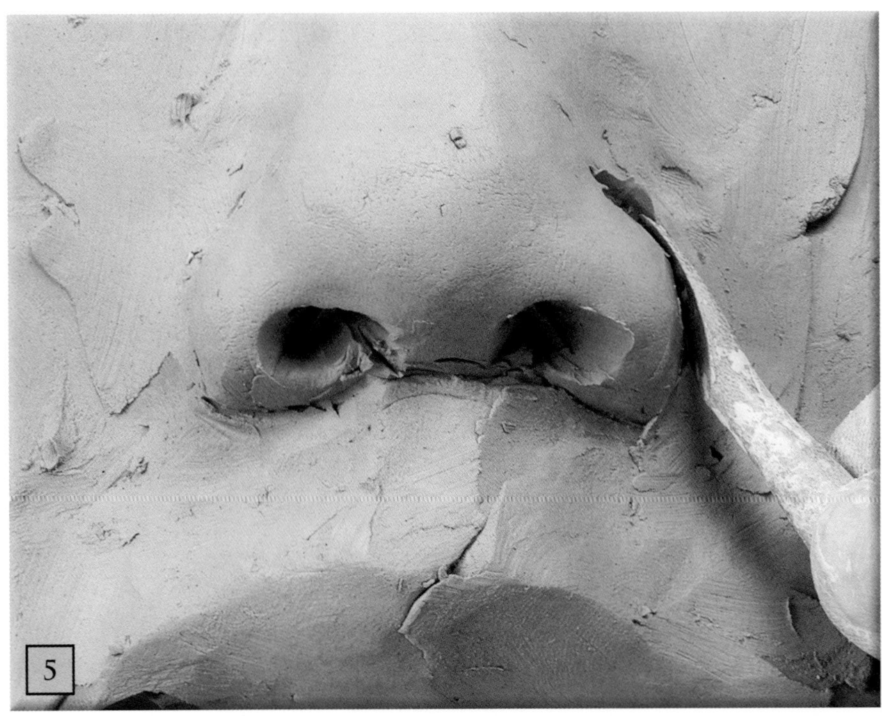

5. Adding the volume of the upper lip helps determine the shape of the nostrils. The wings are defined with a wooden tool.

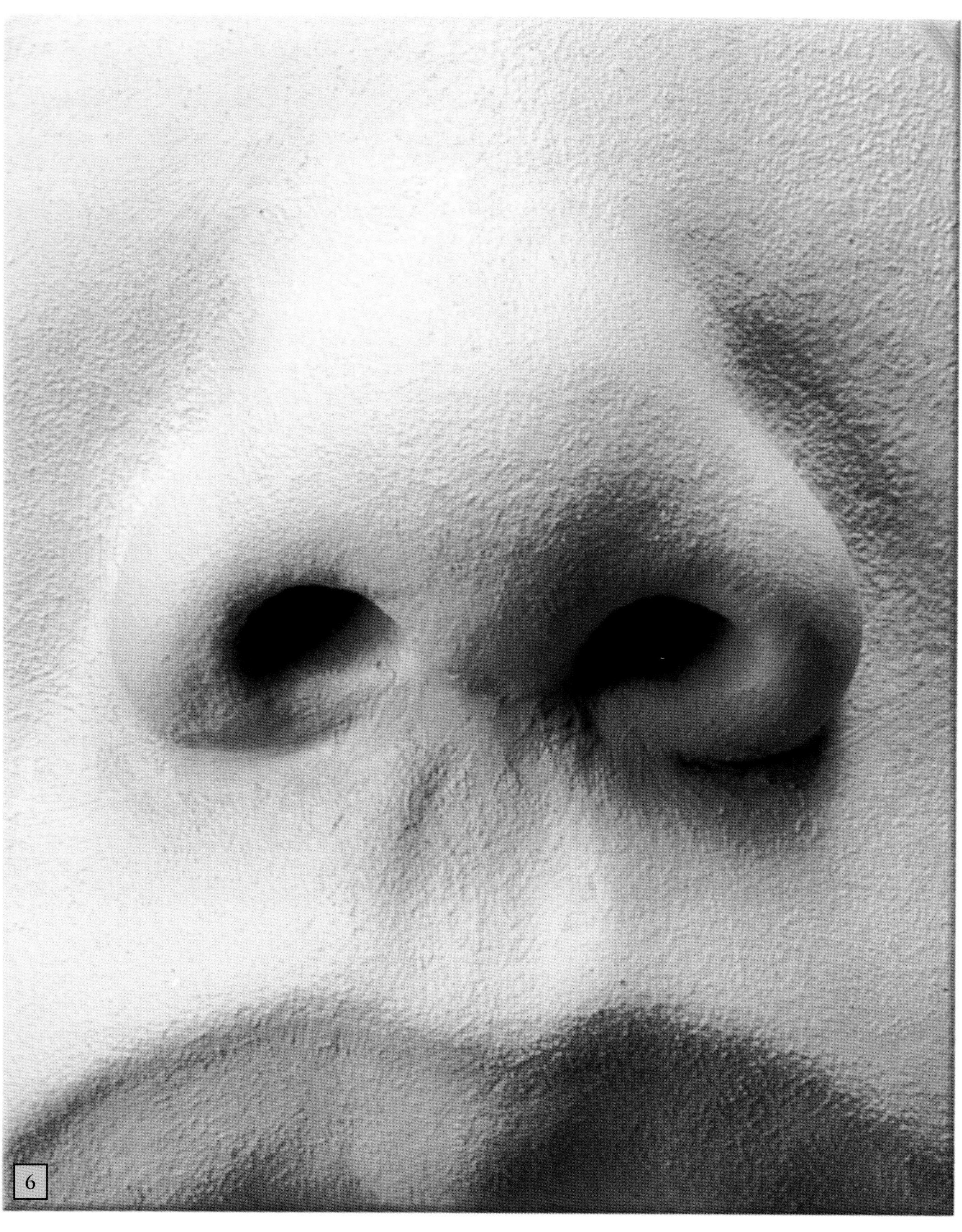
6

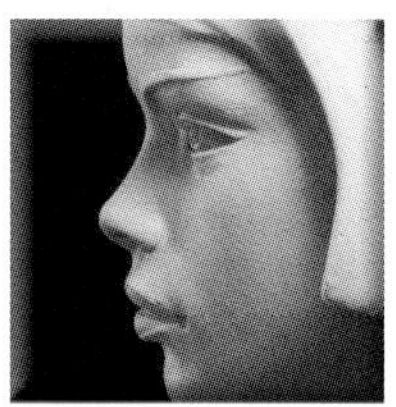

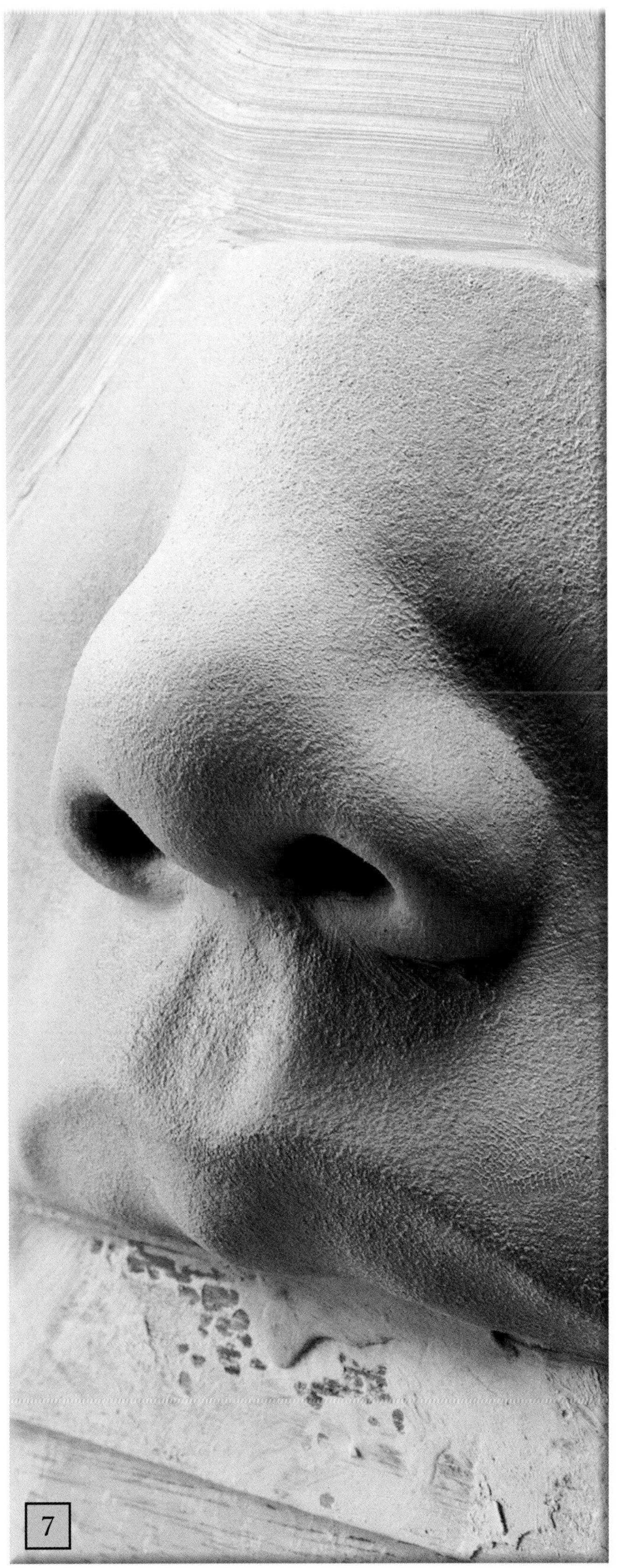

7

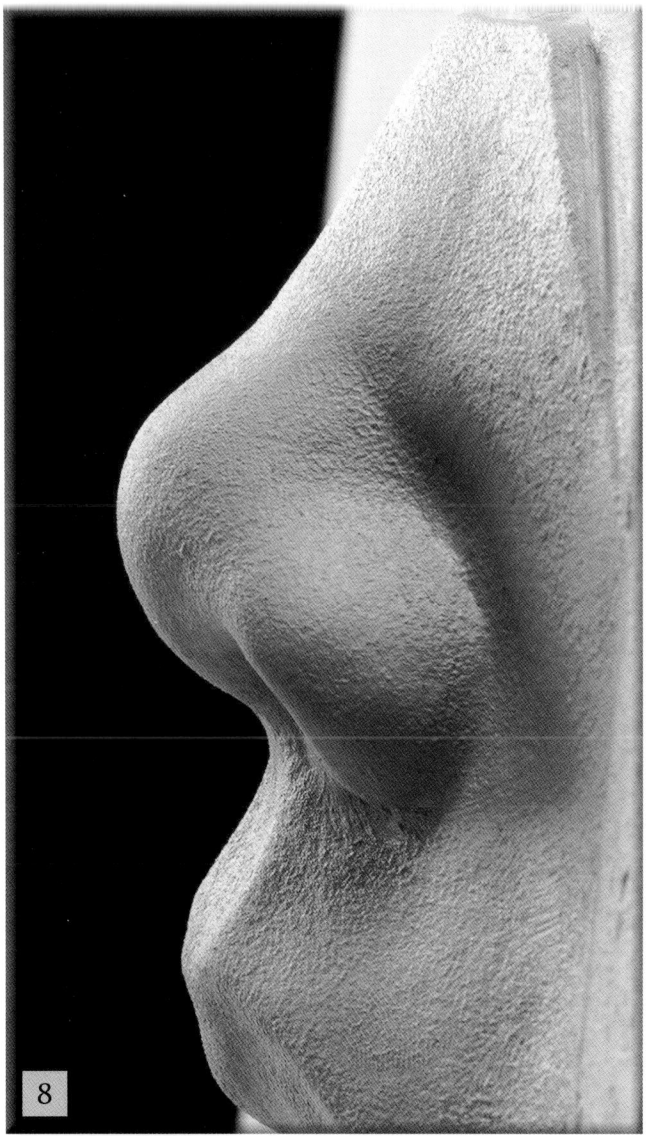

8

**6, 7, 8.** Notice that the fullness of the volumes on each side of the bridge accentuates the creases of the upper part of the wings. The bottom of these creases should be formed by soft curves rather than sharp wrinkles.

## The Eyes

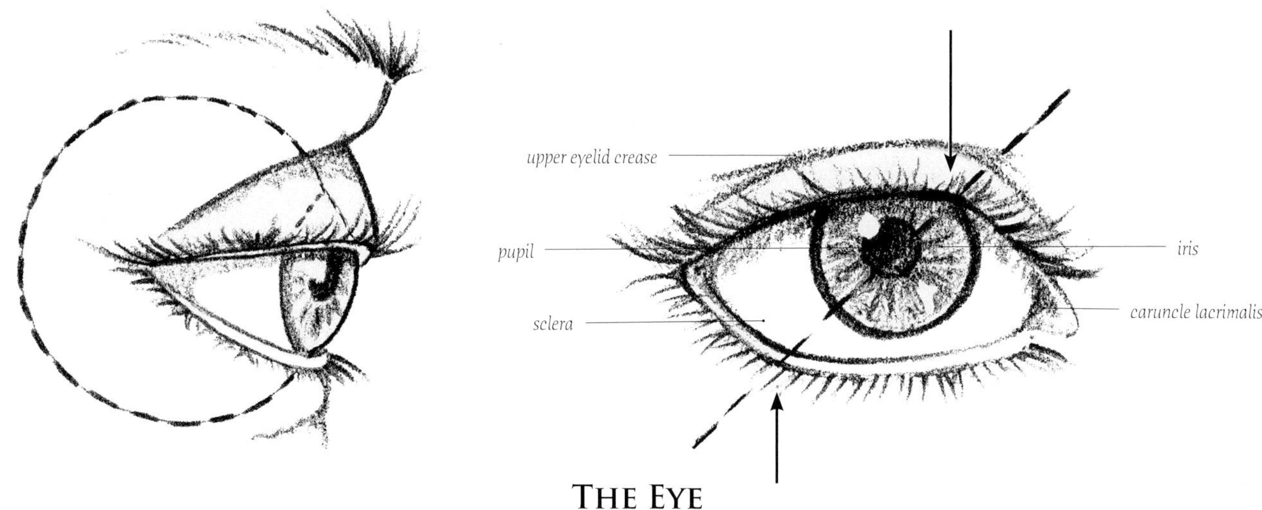


THE EYE

The eyes are the focal point of attention and perhaps the most difficult features to model successfully to achieve a likeness. It is critical that their height, width and depth be accurate. When sculpting a portrait, it is necessary to take precise measurements to confirm the correct location of the eyes. The eyeball is a sphere approximately 25mm in diameter protected within a cone of bone called the orbital cavity. It has a transparent dome sitting on its anterior surface called the cornea. Behind the cornea is a flat disc called the iris with a contractile, round aperture in the center called the pupil. The iris is on average 12mm in diameter and can be of many different colors. These colors need to be represented in terms of light and dark shading in monochromatic mediums such as clay. For example, brown eyes should be represented by dark shading and blue eyes by light shading. This effect is achieved by varying the amount of clay removed from the iris.

The eyelids are folds of skin shielding the eyeball. The upper eyelid is large and movable and can cover the eye. The lower lid motion is negligible, but will puff up during a smile. The upper eyelid is longer than the lower eyelid on the horizontal plane and protrudes farther from the face than the lower eyelid as seen in profile (see diagram). The thickness of the rim of the both eyelids is relatively consistent from the outer corner to inner corner where a U-shaped pit (the caruncle lacrimalis) is formed at the junction of the two lids.

The open, visible eye is not a simple oval. The upper lid has a high point about one-third of the way from the inner corner and the lower lid has a low point about one-third of the way from the outer corner. The inner corner of the eye is always lower than the outer corner.

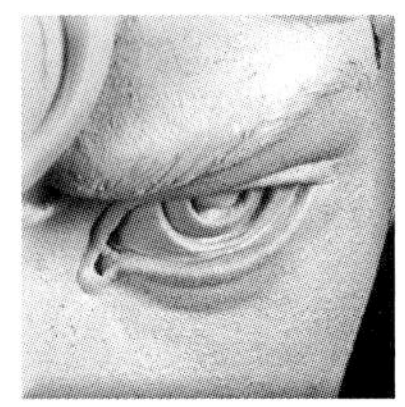

## Demonstration 5: Modeling the Eyes

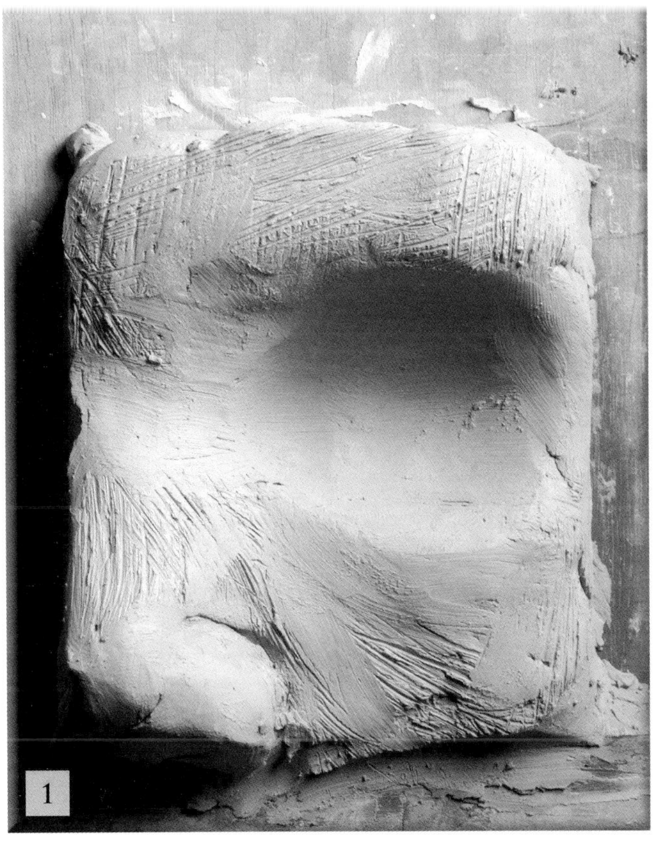

1. A rectangle of clay is modeled to the basic shape of the orbital cavity, though not as deep as it would be in reality. A baby's nose is sketched in as a reference point.

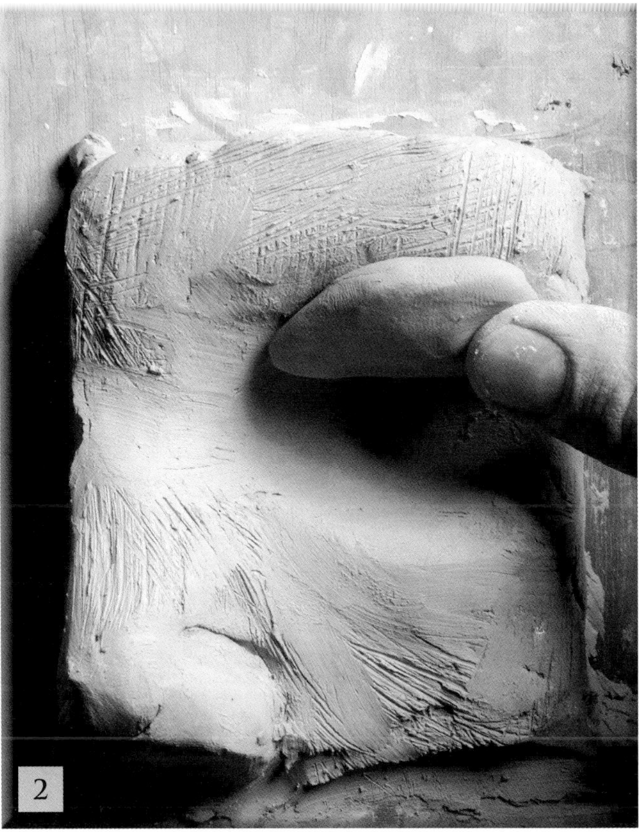

2. A teardrop-shaped piece of clay is applied with the narrow end toward the nose and the wider part above the outer corner of the eye, forming a bulge.

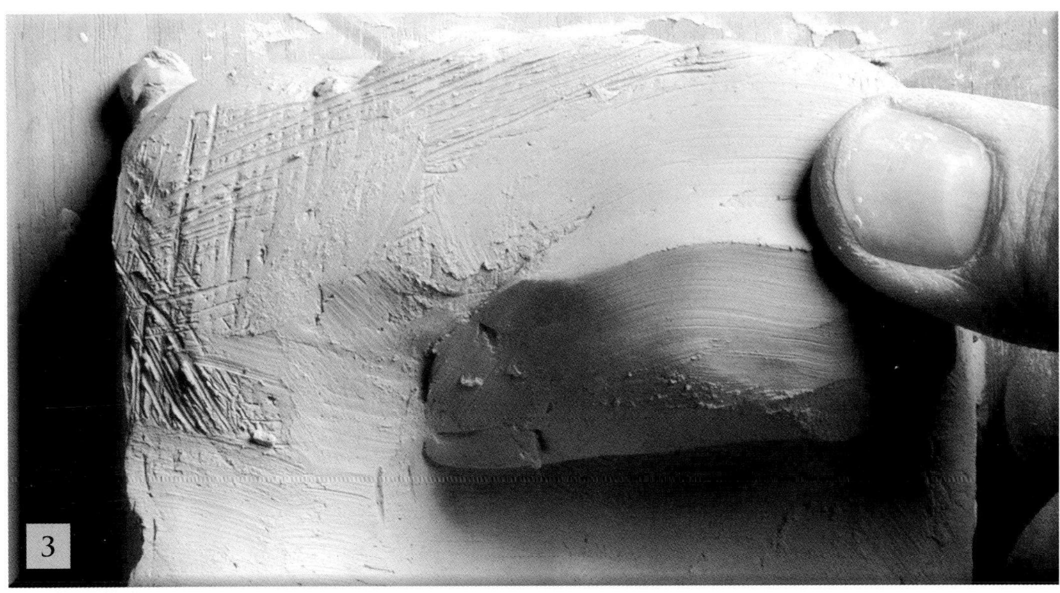

3. The ridge of the eyebrow is shaped by dragging the thumb above and below the edge of the brow ridge.

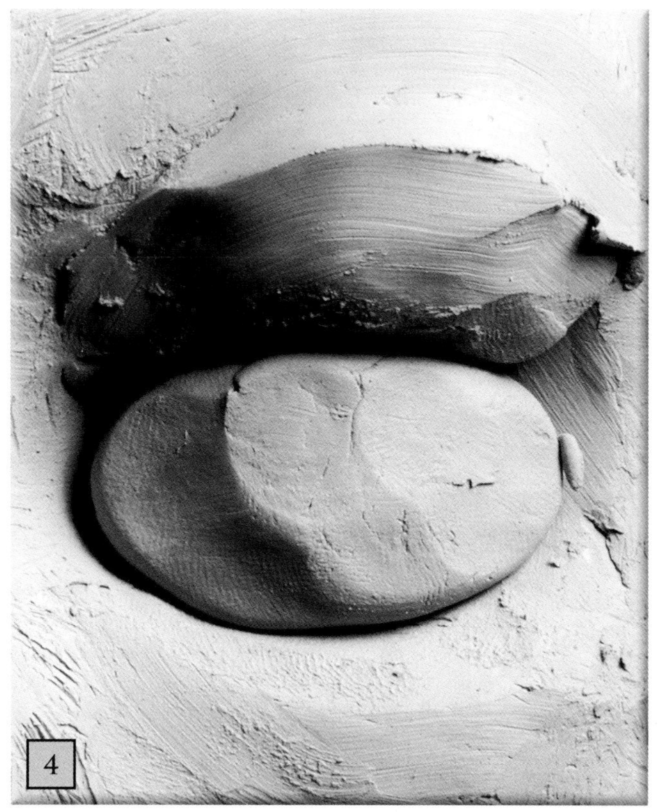


4. An olive-shaped volume is pressed into the cavity.

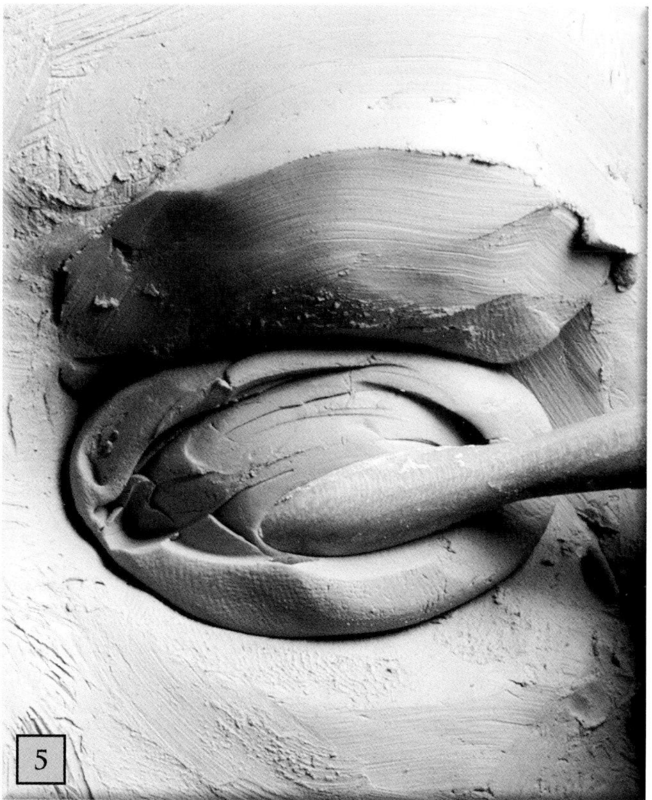


5. A spoon-shaped tool is used to form the visible part of the eyeball.

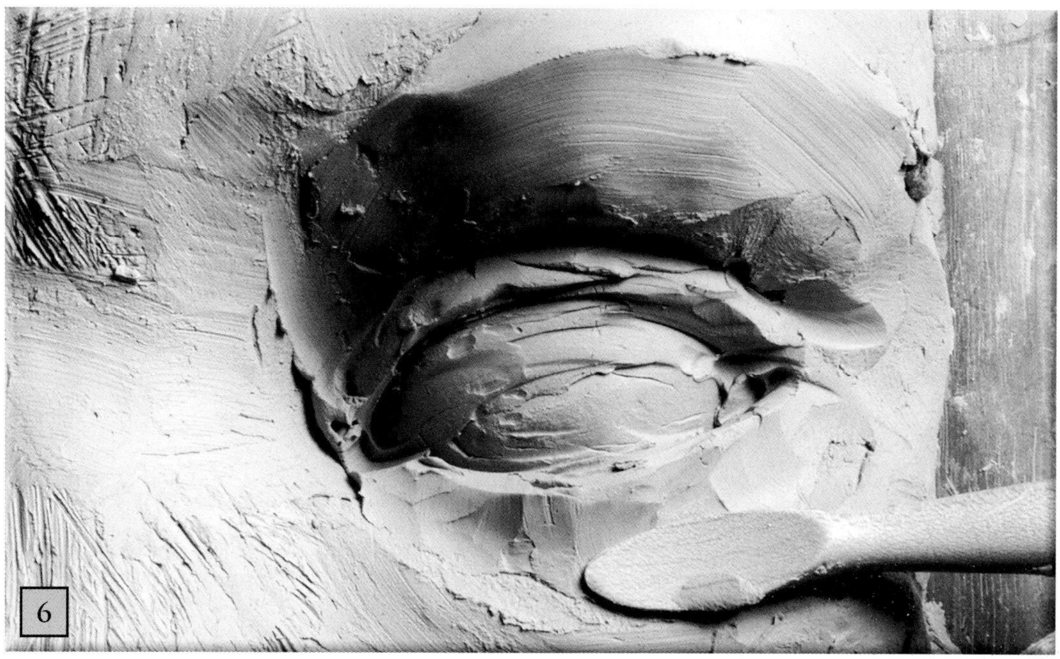


6. The upper eyelid is refined with the concave side of the spoon tool. The lower eyelid is blended with the other side of the tool.

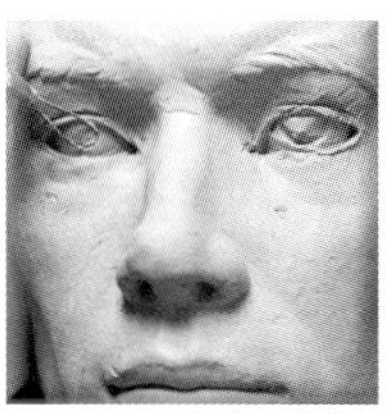

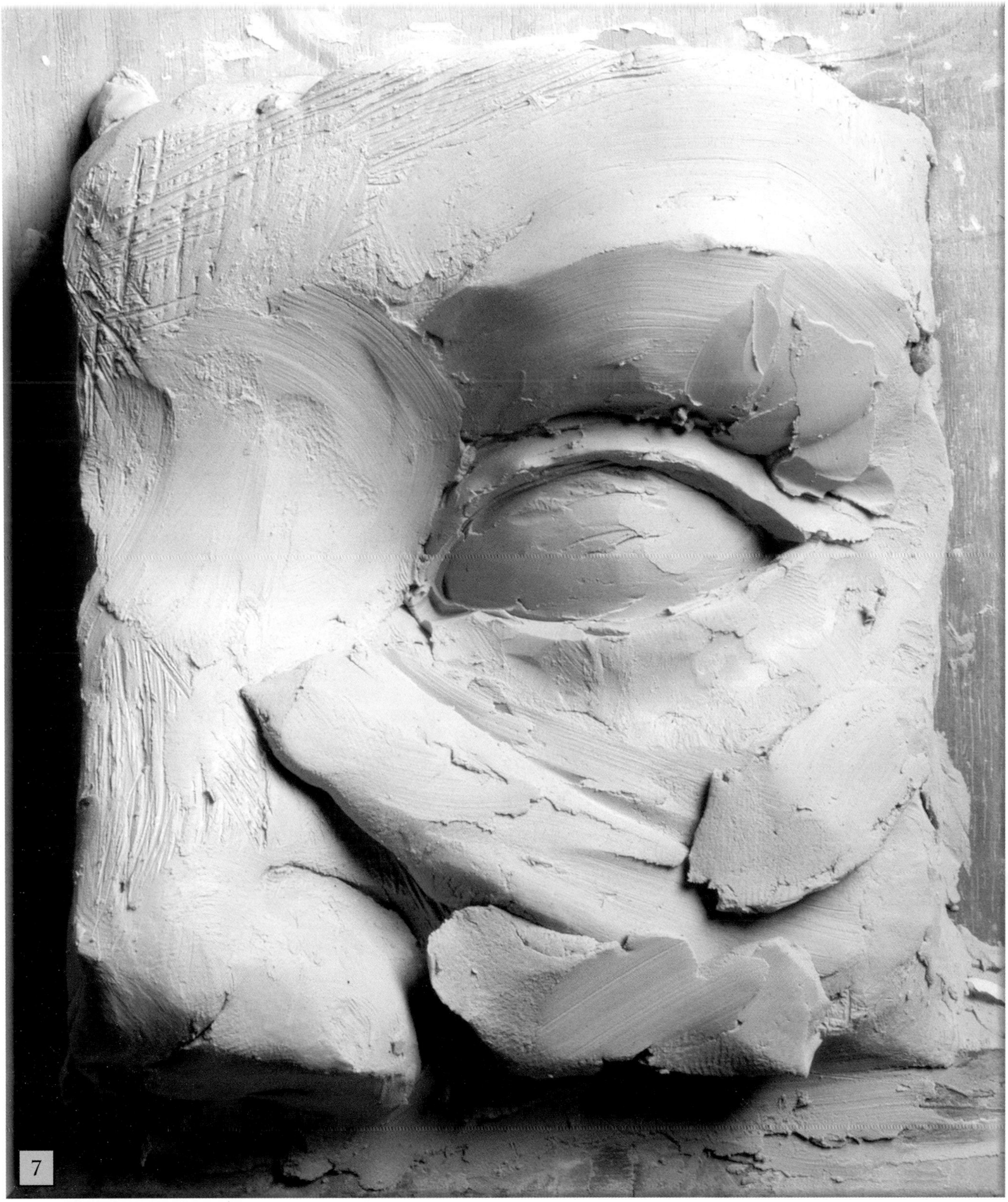

7. Clay is added to form the volumes of the upper cheeks, nose, bridge, and cheekbone.

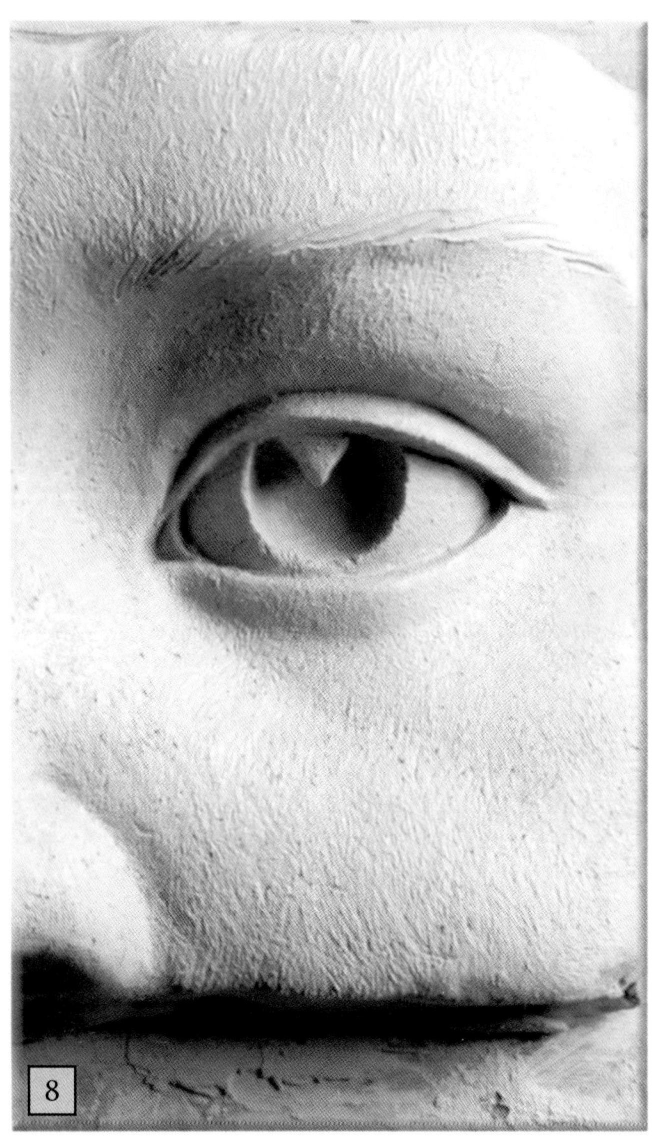


8. The illusion of a dark colored eye is achieved by deeply hollowing out the iris.

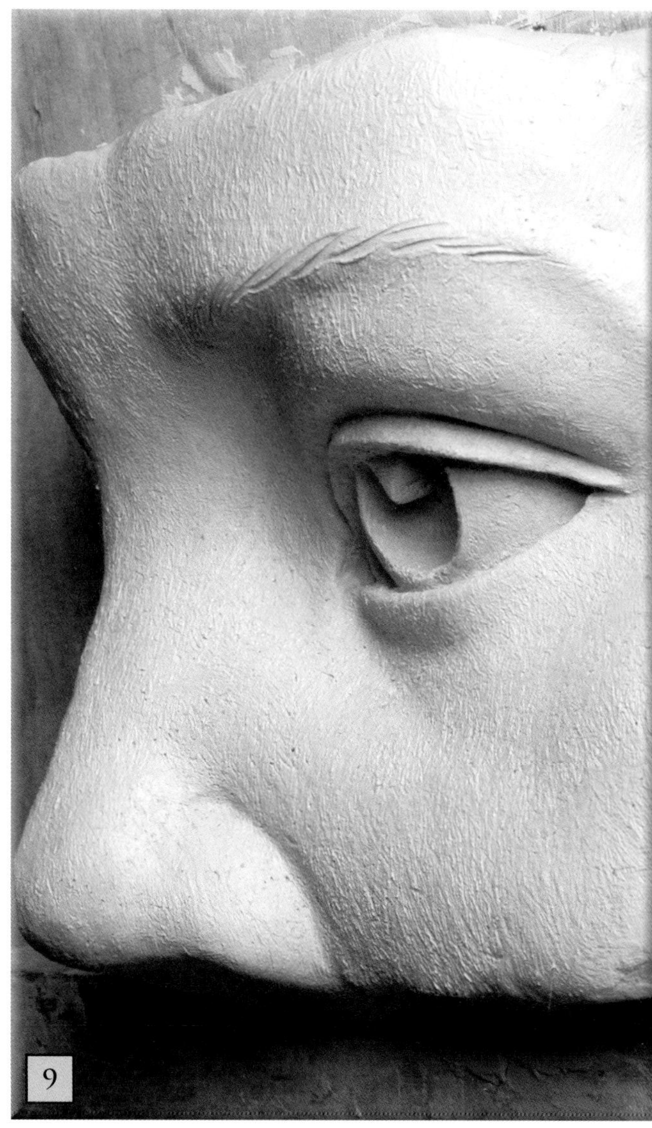


9. A triangle of clay is left inside the cavity of the iris to create a highlight.

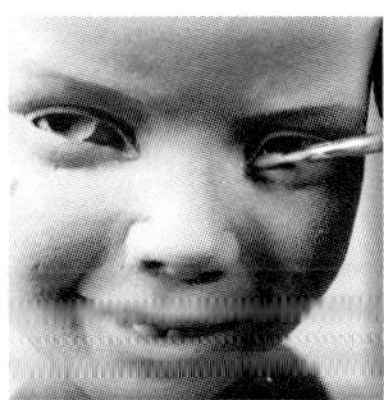

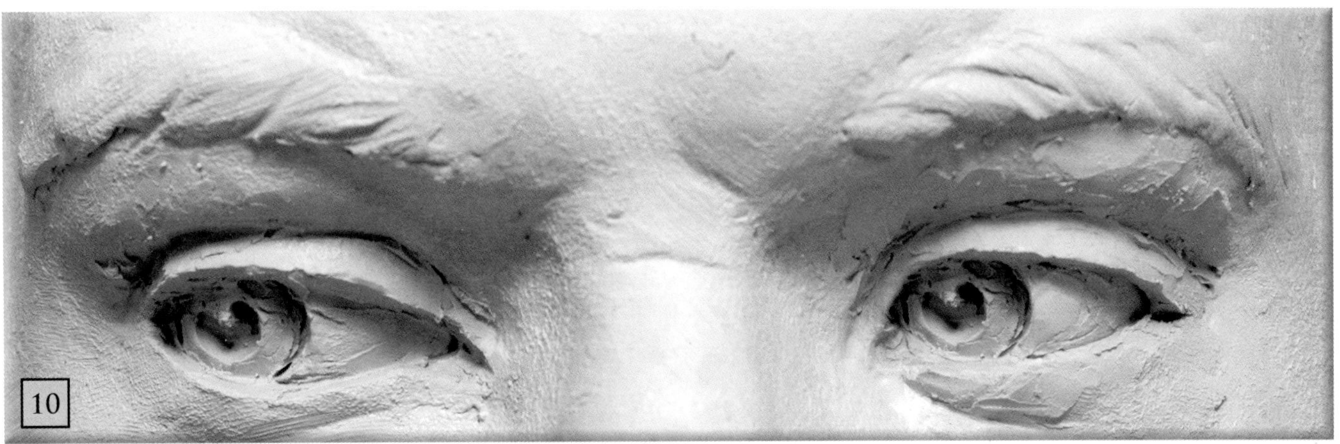


**10.** Notice the effect that the volume of the cornea has on the shape of the eyelid.

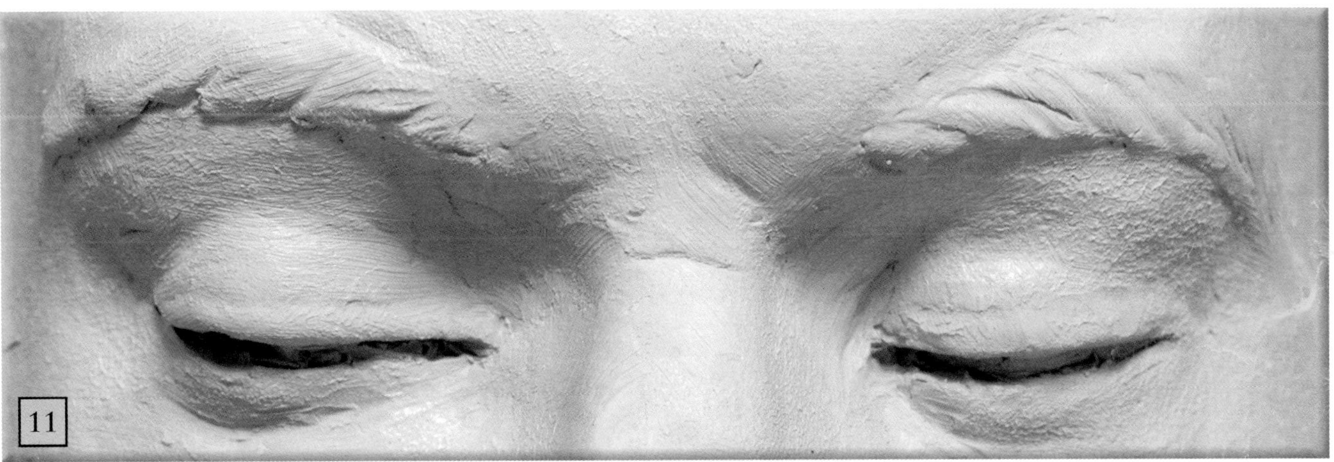


**11.** Even with the eyes closed, the volume of the cornea under the eyelid is visible, indicating the direction the eyes are turned.

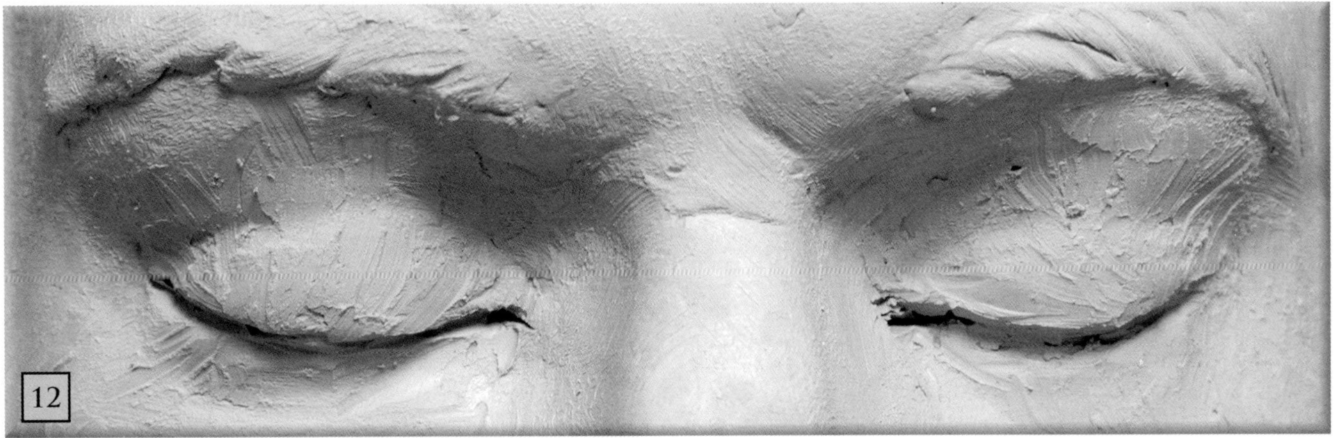


**12.** When we are asleep the upper eyelid entirely covers the eyeball. The volume of the cornea shows at the bottom edge of the upper eyelid, and the lower eyelid is completely relaxed.

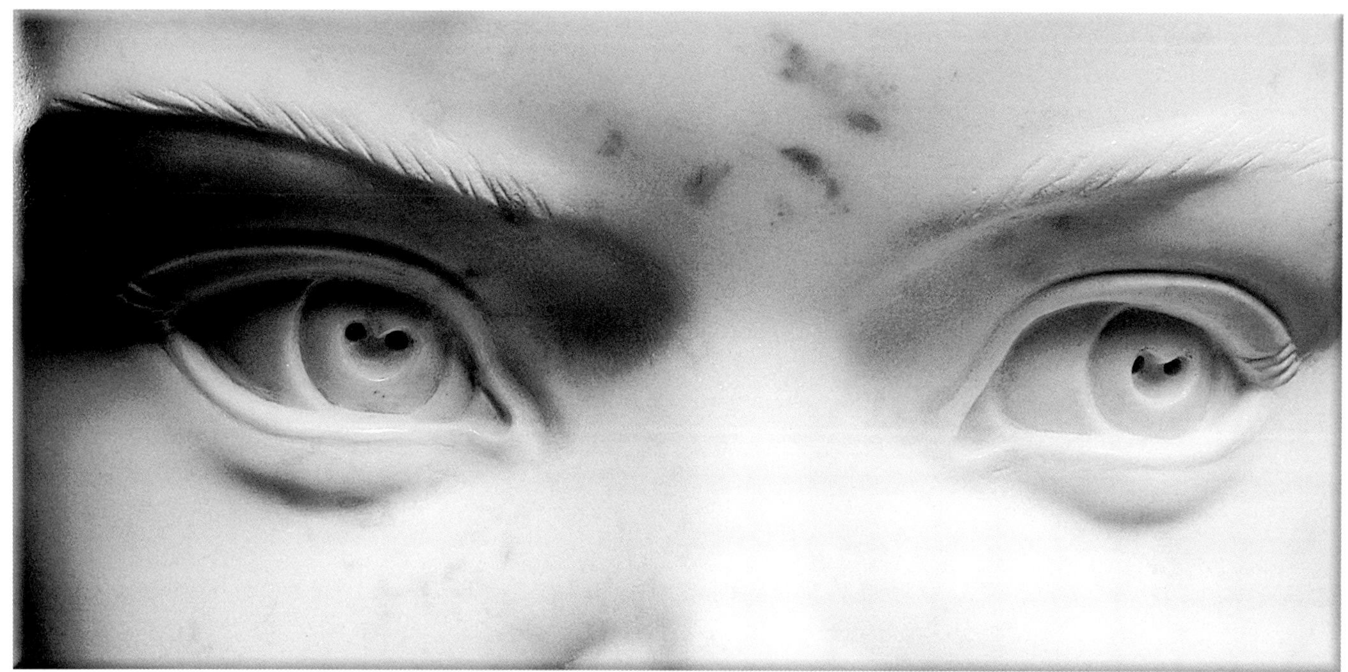

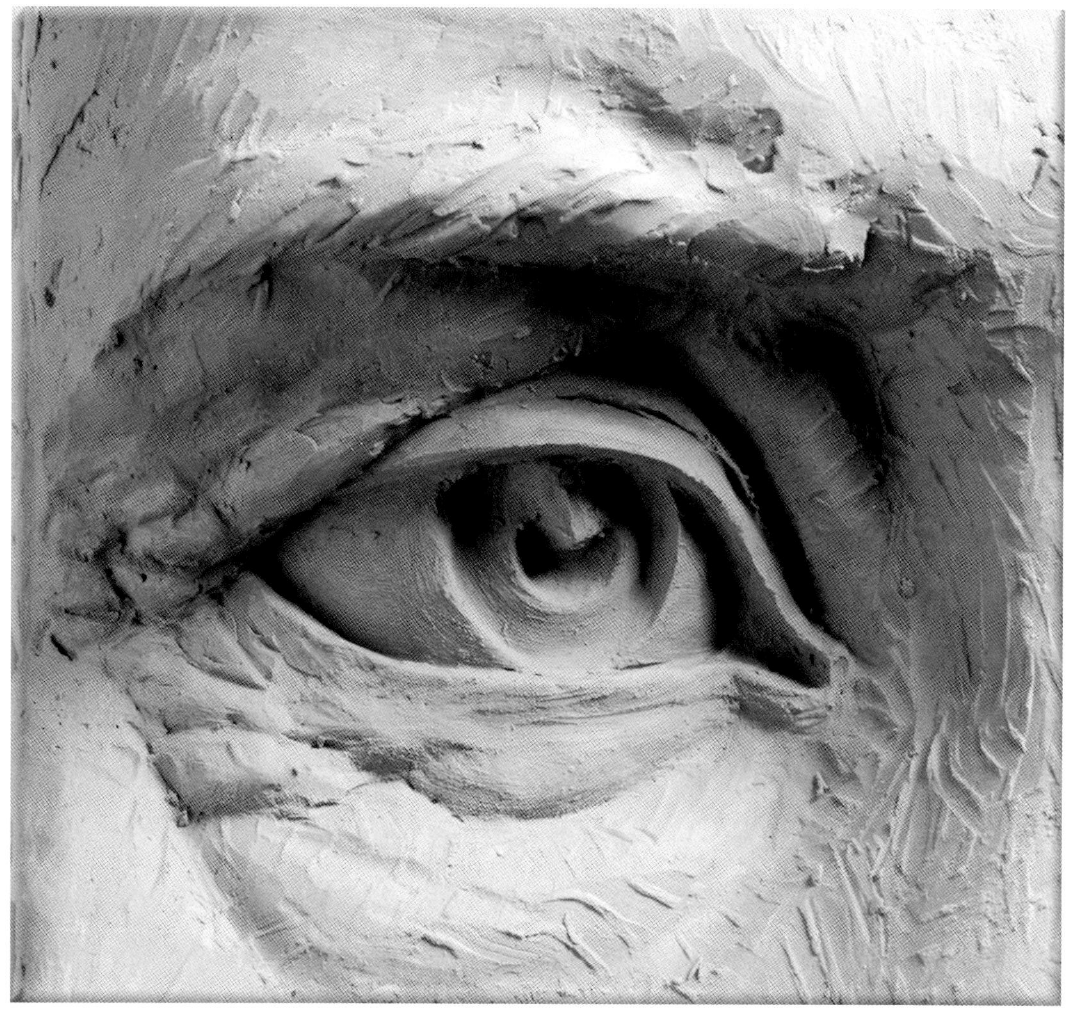

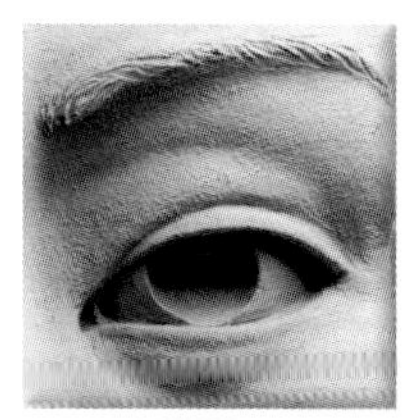
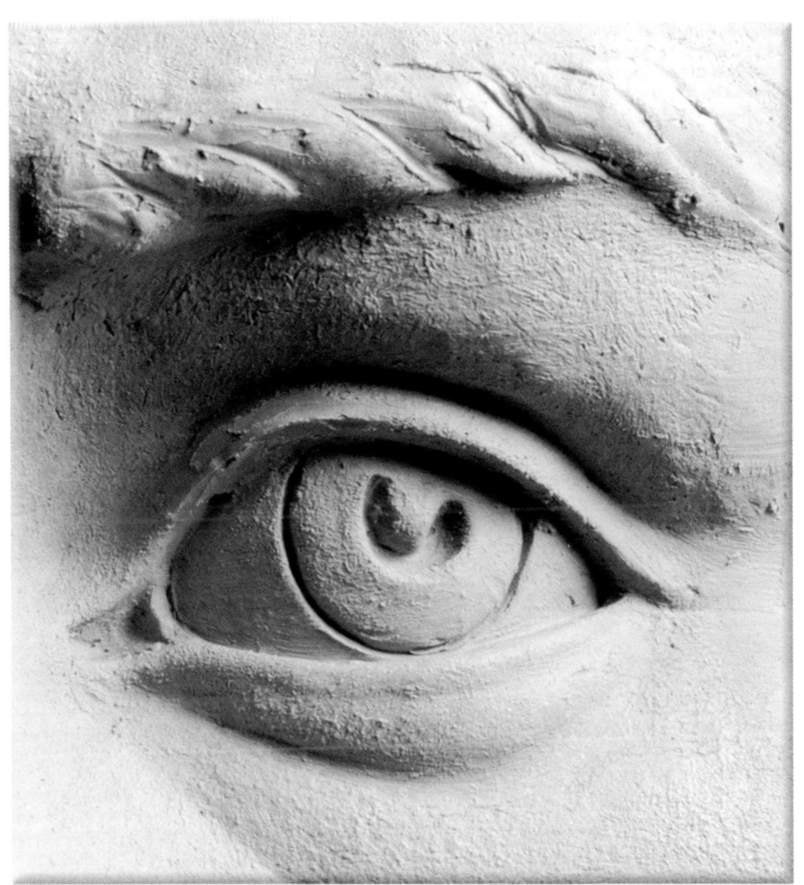
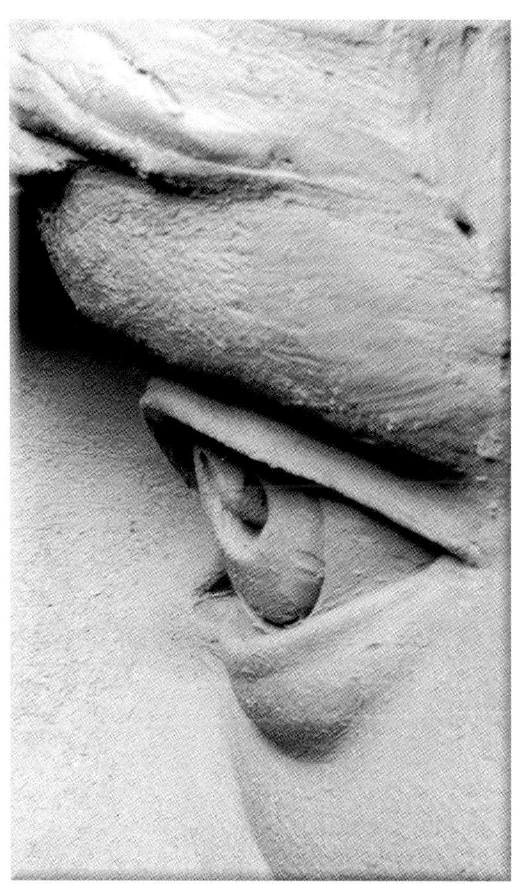
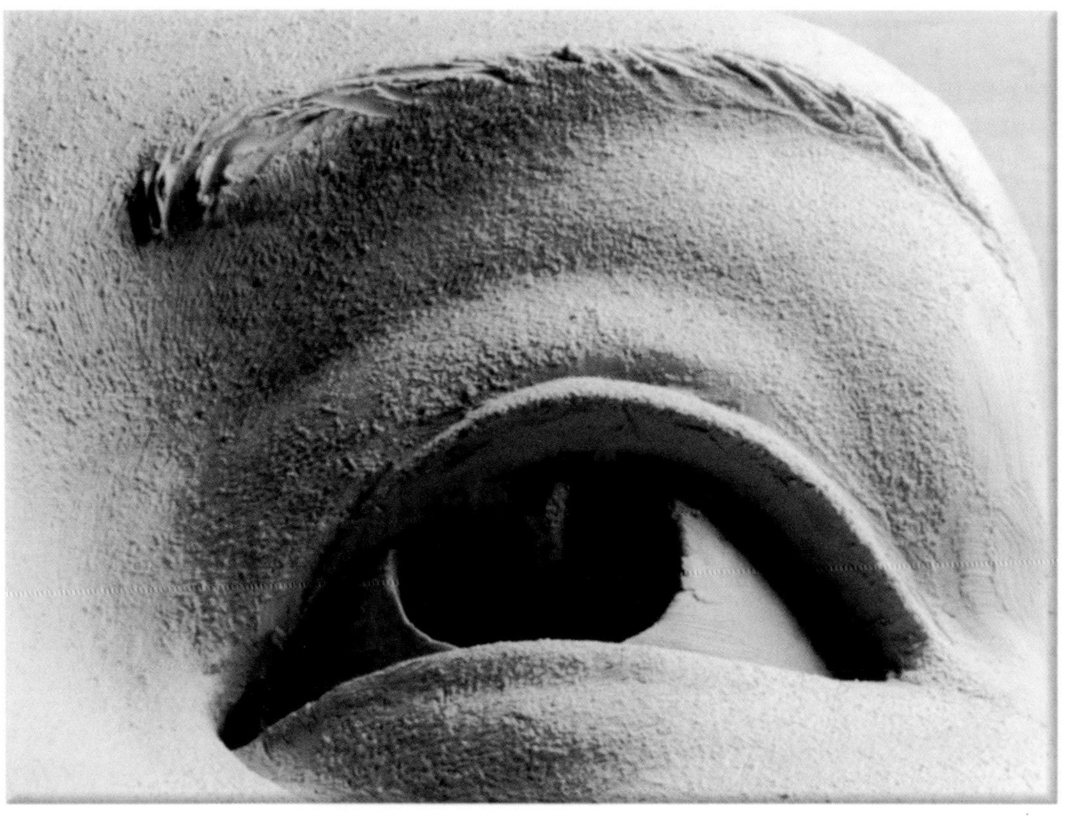

## The Mouth

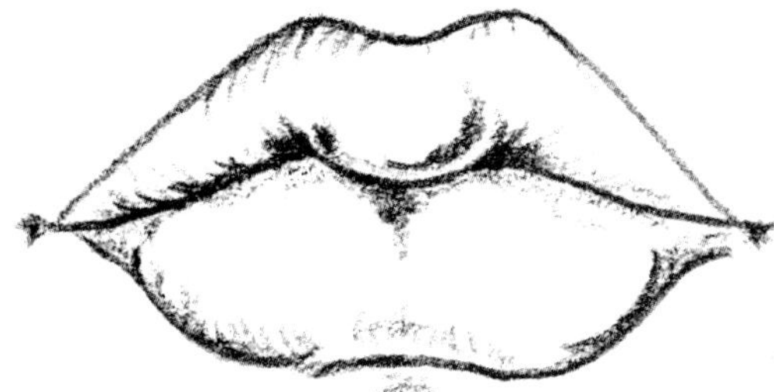

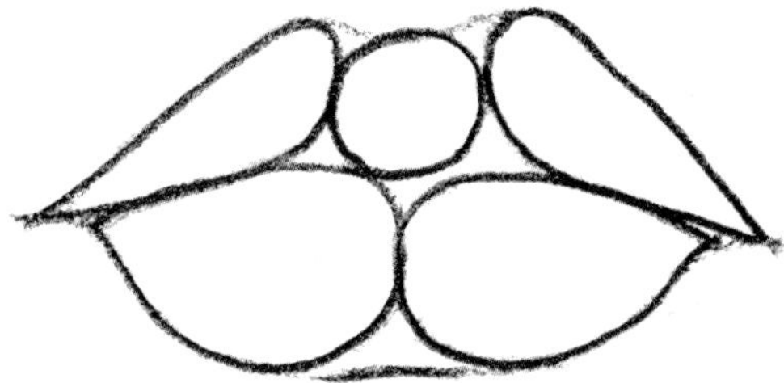

THE MOUTH

The nose and eyes are built around and anchored to the bones of the skull. The mouth differs in that it is more floating. It is the most mobile part of the face and an important feature in conveying the mood of the individual. Once again, knowledge of the underlying bone structure facilitates the three-dimensional visualization of the general structure of the mouth. The maxilla, mandible and the teeth determine the shape of the "barrel" of the mouth as seen in the photo below showing a skull viewed from underneath. A shallow groove underneath the nose, the philtrum, is centered between two planes that are separated from the cheeks by the nasolabial furrow. The lower lip is separated from the chin by a depression called the mentolabial groove. The upper lip is made of three principle volumes and the lower lip of two. The upper lip is flatter in its planes and generally more prominent than the lower lip. A ridge outlining the edge of the lips where the thinner skin of the lips meets the facial skin is often visible.

There are so many muscles involved in the motion of the mouth that a serious study of their action is necessary. However, the following demonstrations are focused on the mouth in repose.

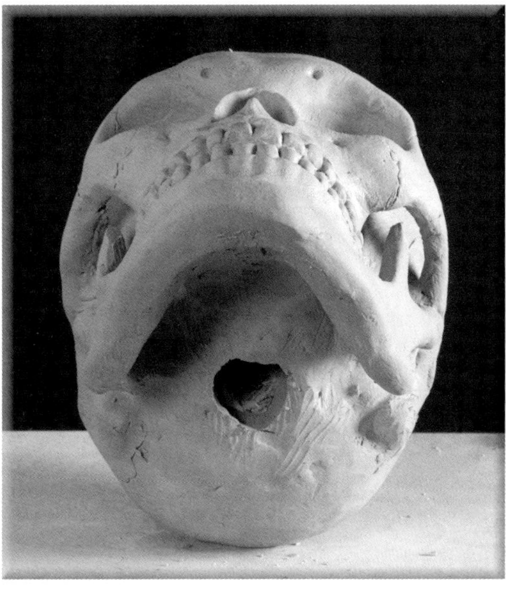

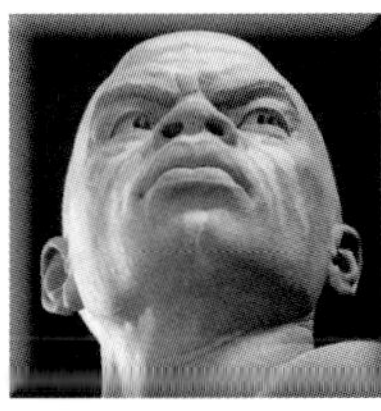

## Demonstration 6: Modeling a Child's Mouth

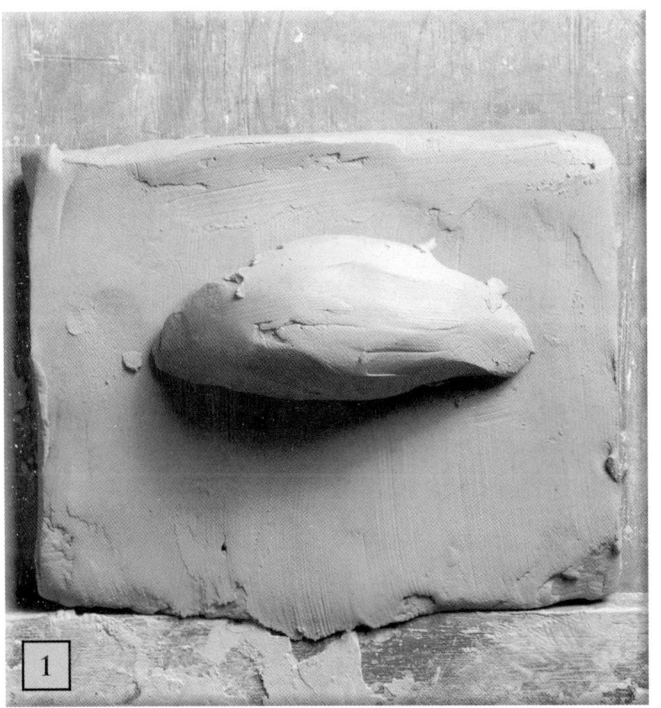

1. A short coil of clay is applied to the base.

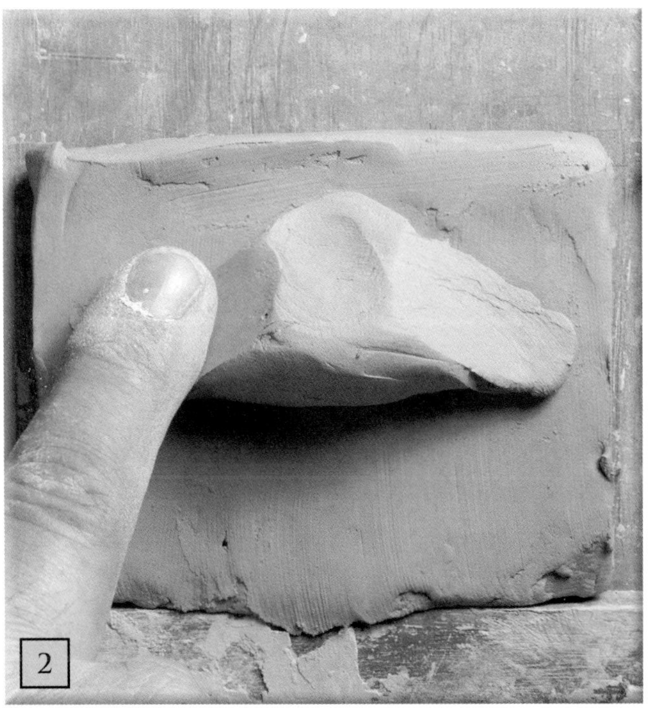

2. The two lateral planes of the upper part of the mouth, as well as the philtrum, are shaped with the finger.

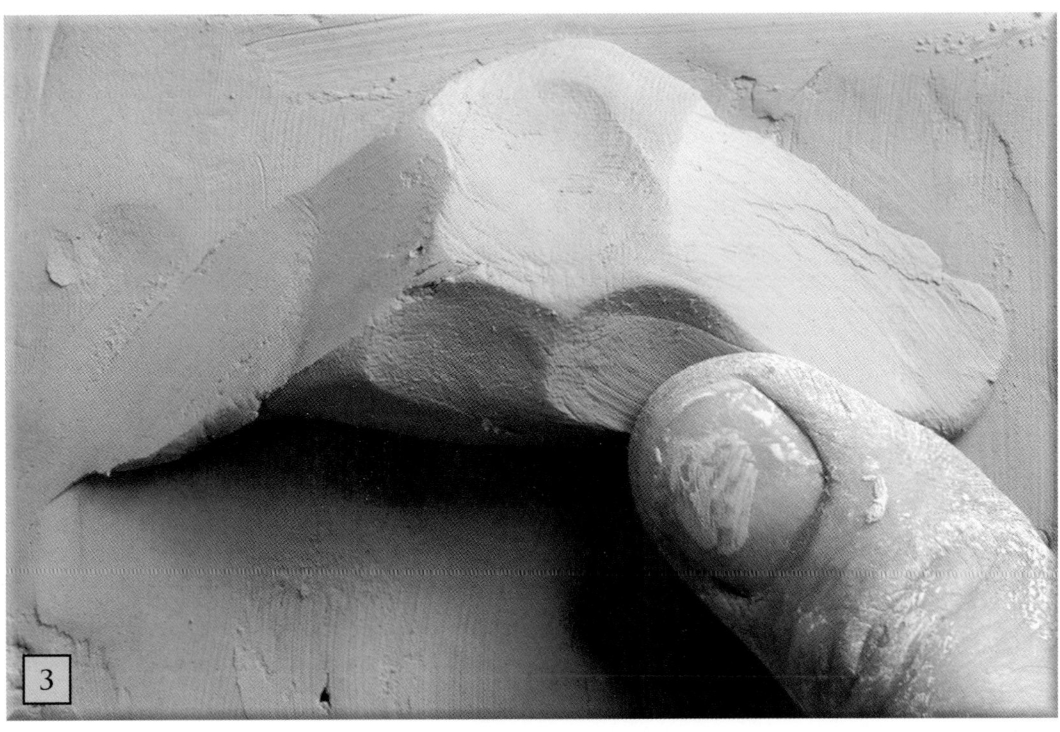

3. The ridge of the upper lip is defined with the thumb.

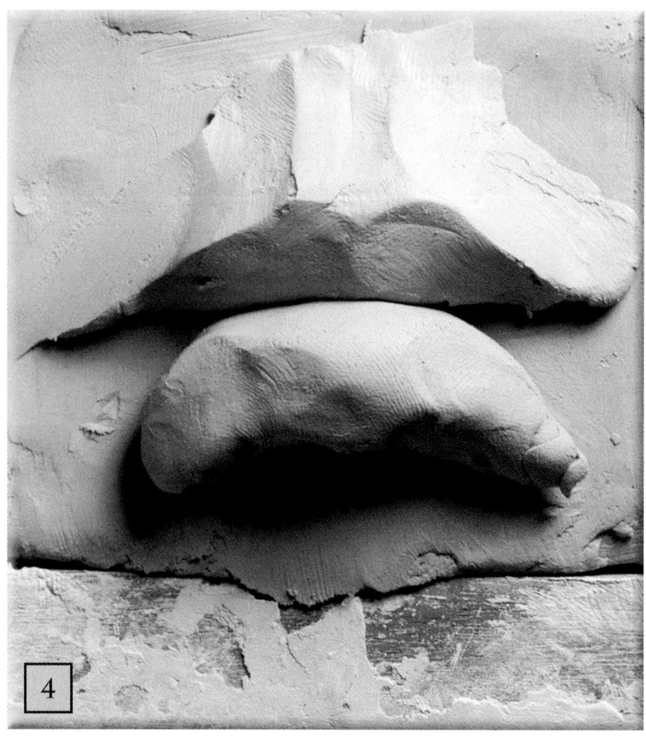

4. A somewhat smaller coil, bent at the extremities, is applied.

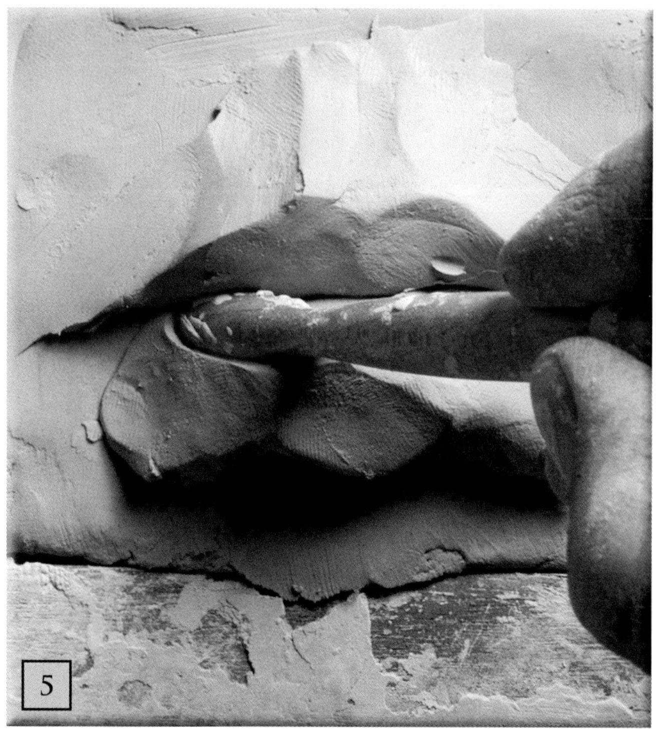

5. A spoon-shaped tool is used to push in the corners of the mouth and to form the ridge of the lower lip.

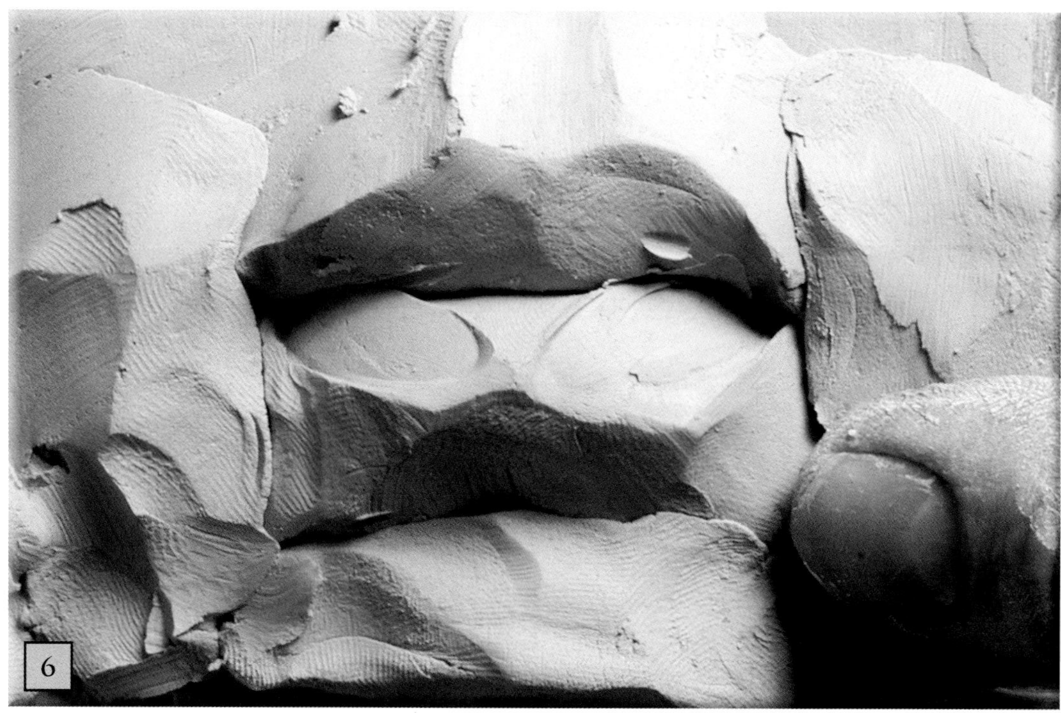

6. Volumes are added on each side and folded in toward the corners.

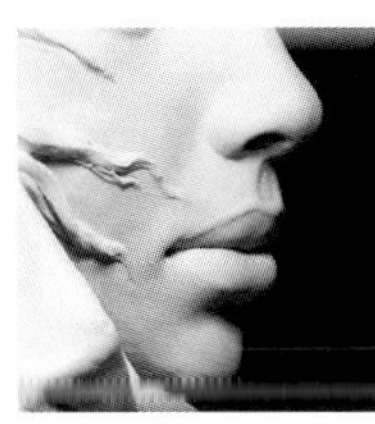

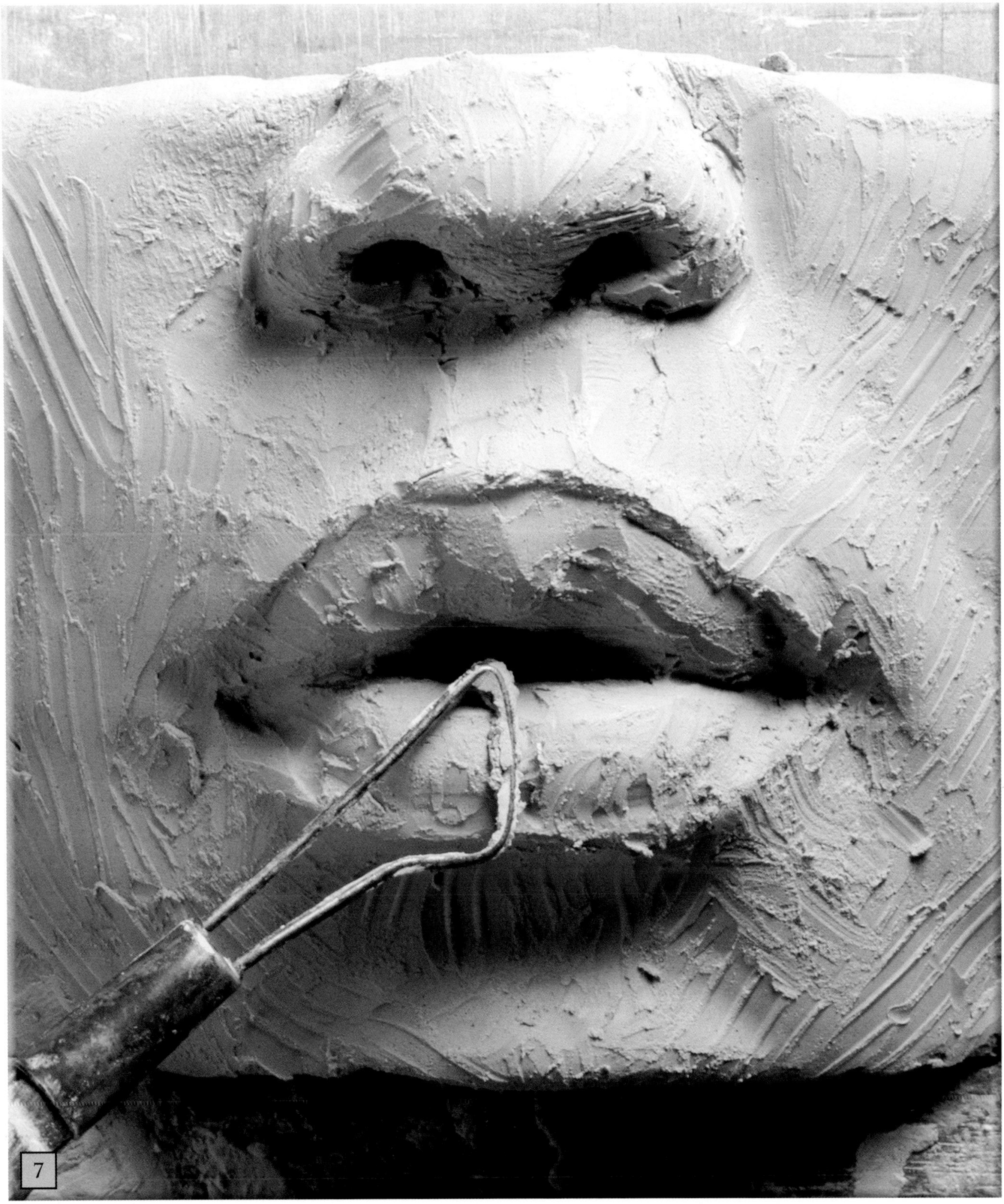

7. The base of the nose can be added as a reference point. Here, the lips are slightly parted and the volumes refined with a wire tool.

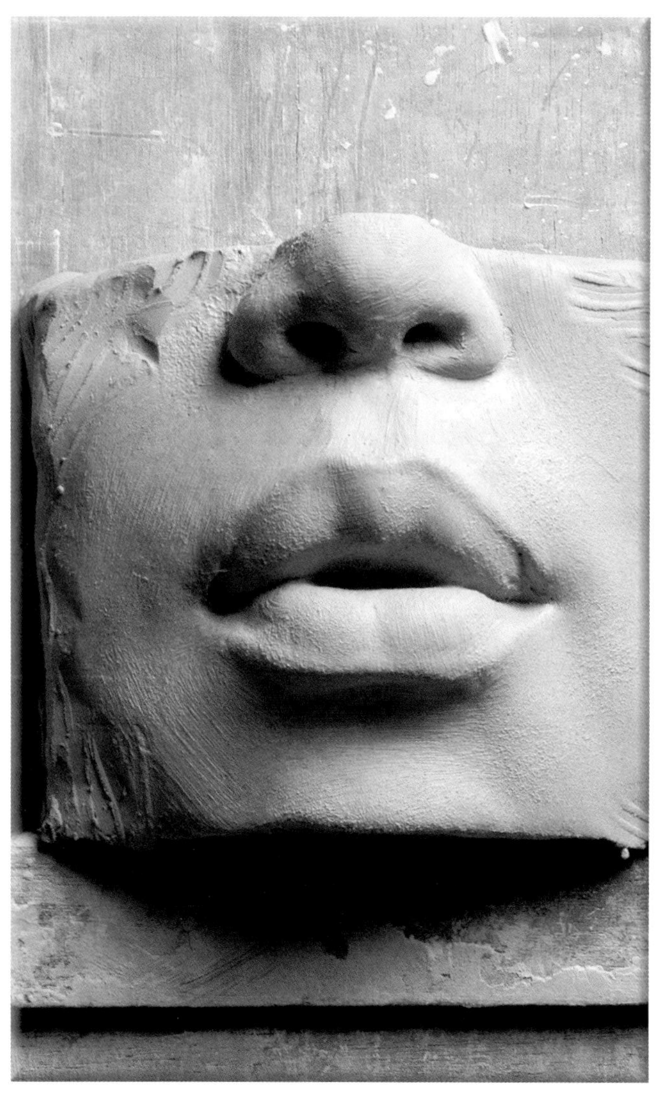

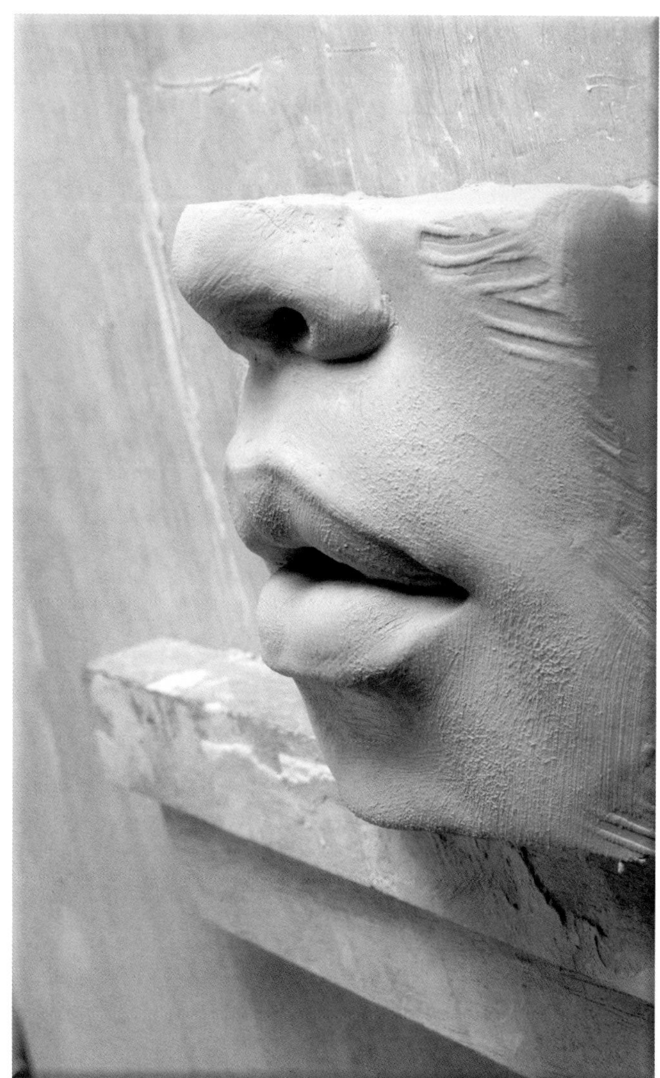

The above photos provide a comparison between a child's mouth and an adult woman's mouth.

In general, a young child's mouth is pouty and more round than an adult's.

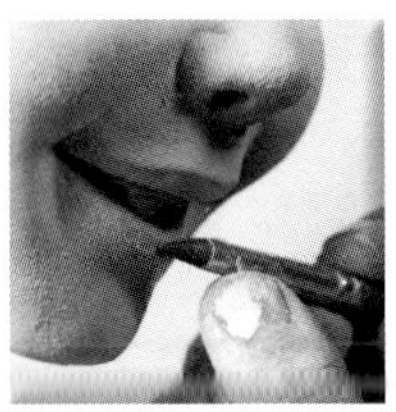

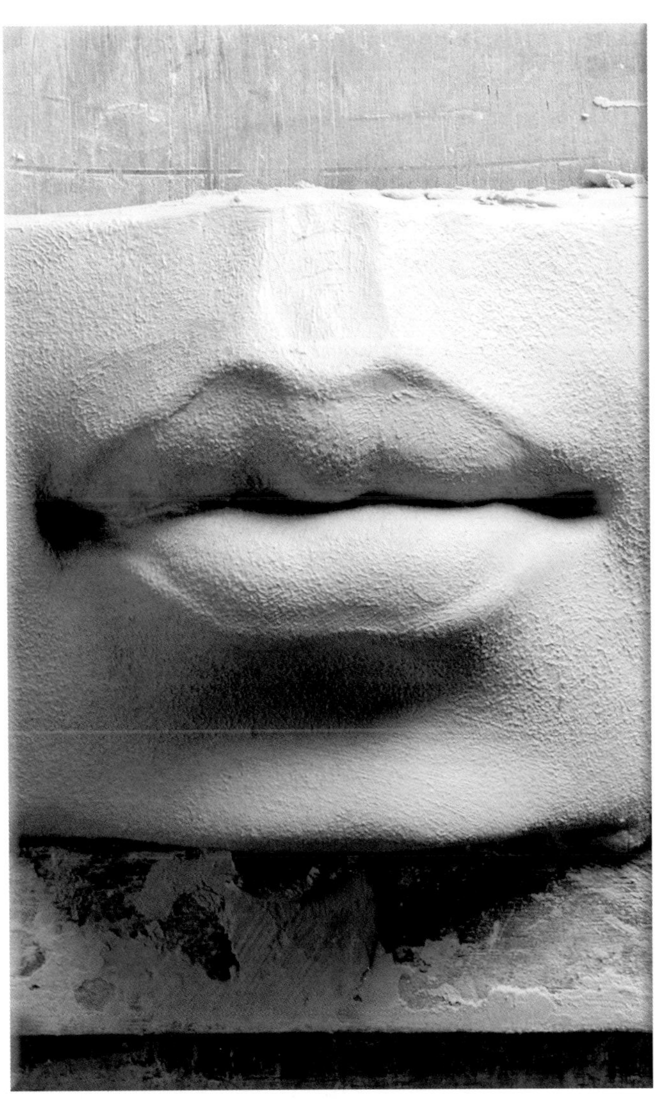

In the adult, the mouth is proportionally wider and the lips thinner. This can vary greatly from person to person.

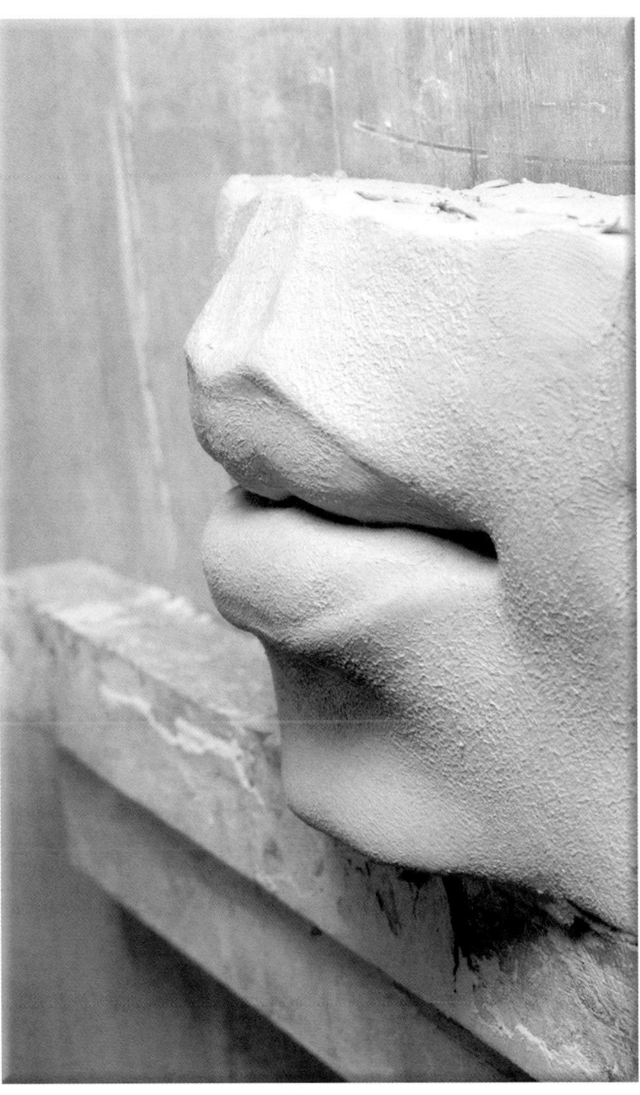

Notice the volumes on each side and under the lower lip. These are always visible, though not always as pronounced.

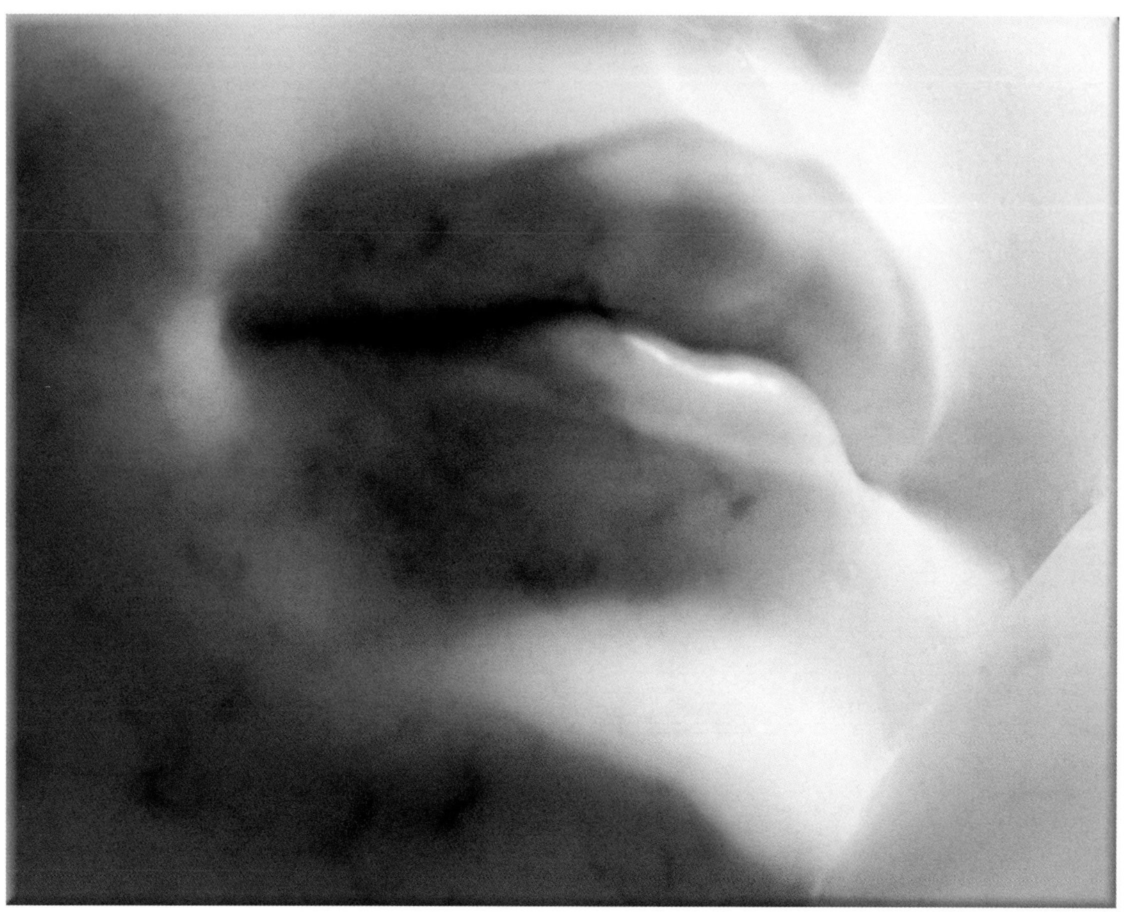

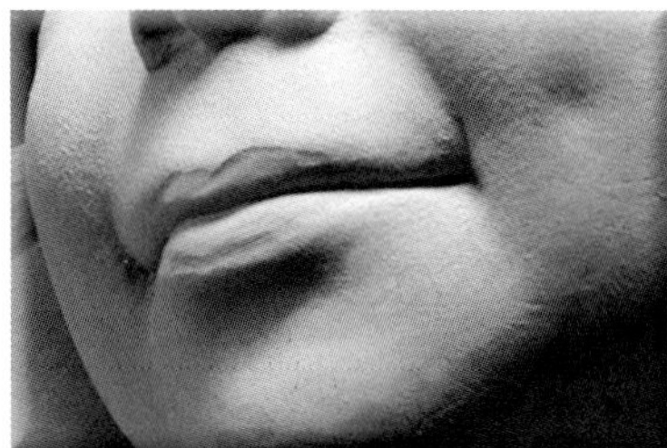

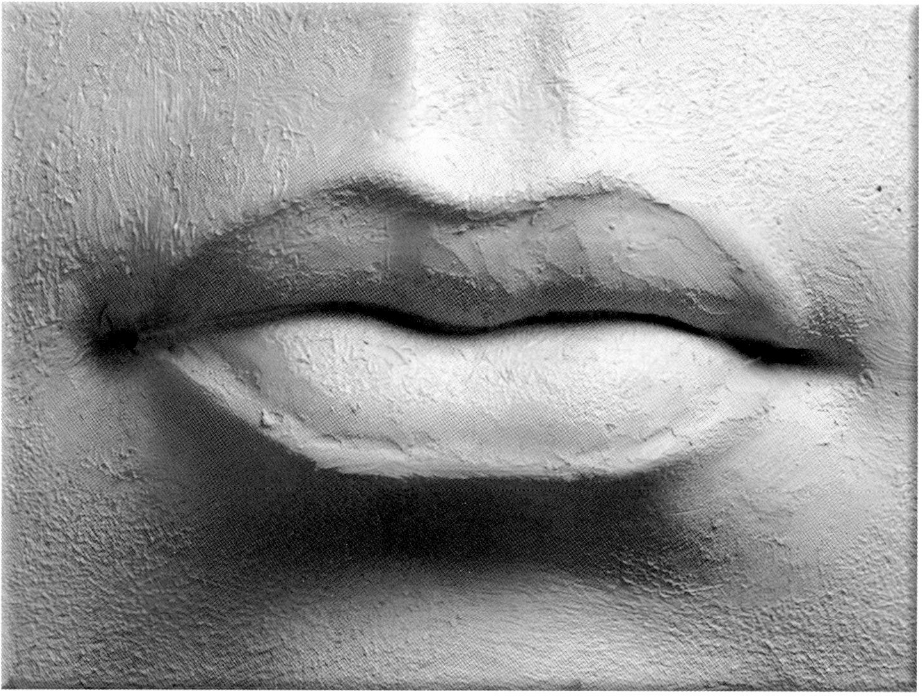

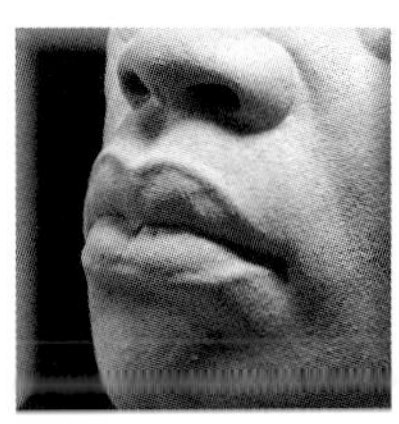

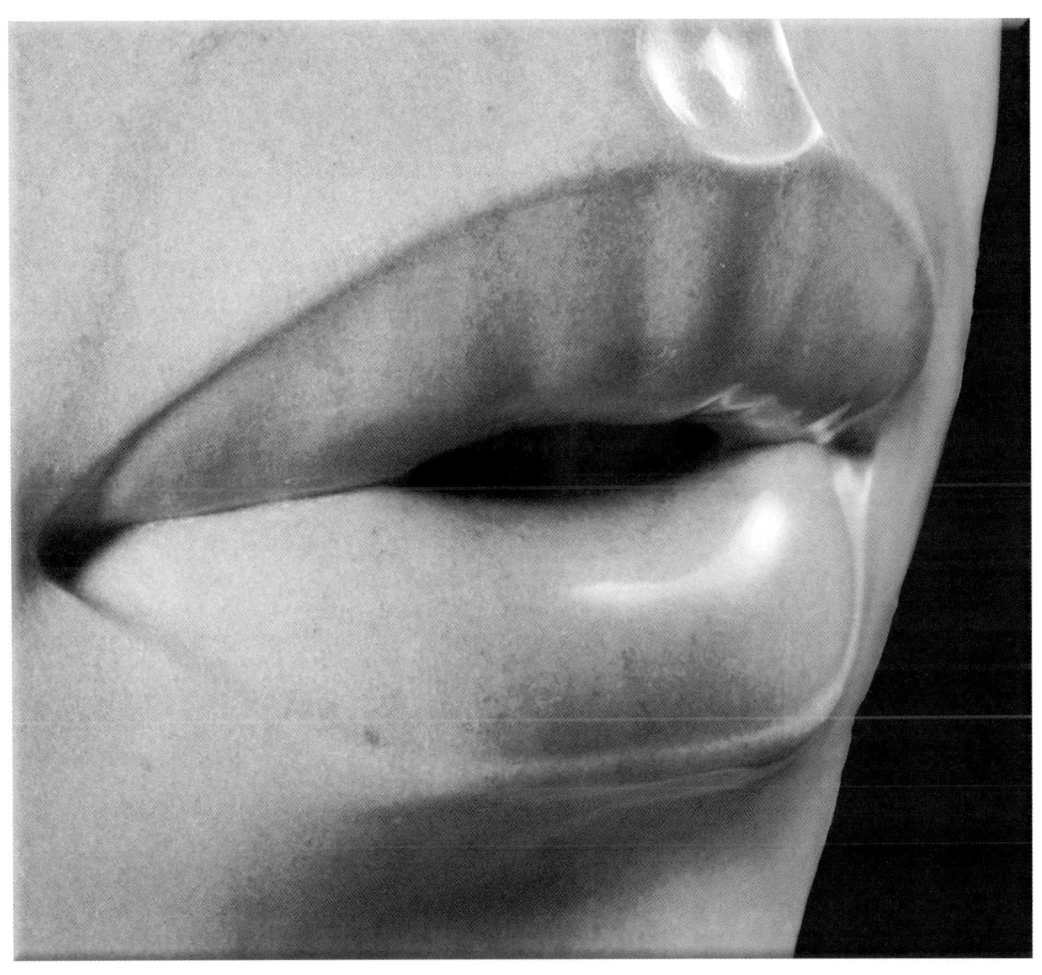

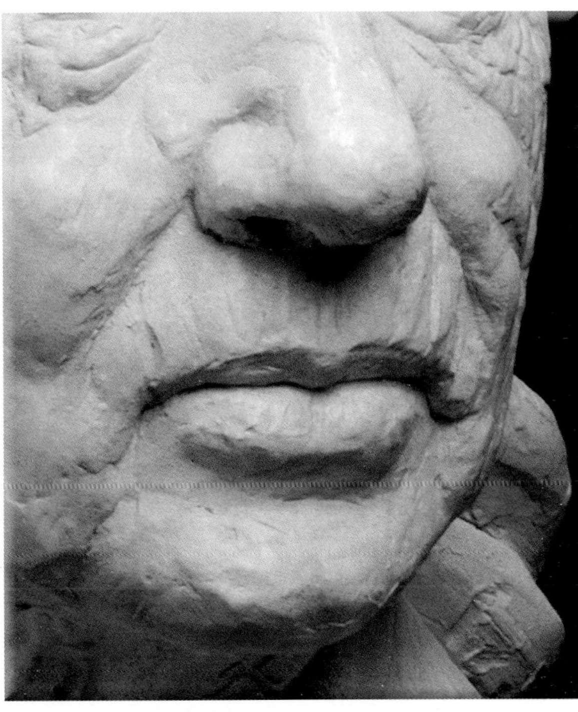

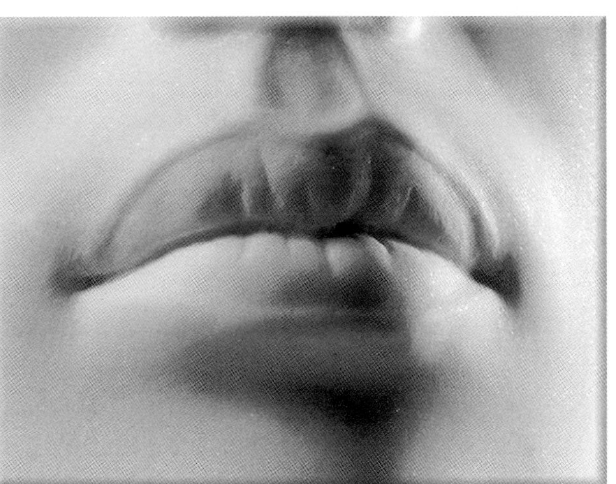

## The Ears

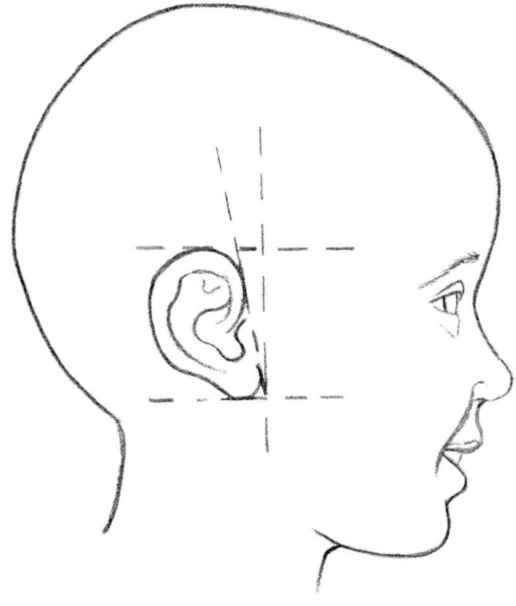

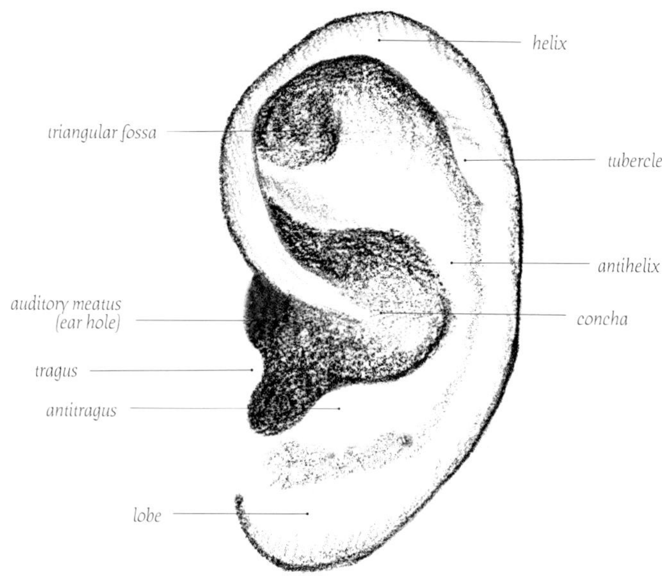


THE EAR

The upper portion of the ear is elastic cartilage covered by a thin layer of skin and the lower portion, the lobe, is fibrous, fatty tissue. The ear lies behind the joint of the jaw and is tilted slightly backward. It can differ greatly in size and shape from person to person and must be measured and studied carefully. The placement of the ears has a great impact on the accuracy of the likeness and should not be rushed or neglected. The ear has five main volumes: the helix, antihelix, concha, lobe and tragus. Additional features to study are the triangular fossa, the antitragus, the tubercle, which is more or less visible from person to person, and the position of the external auditory meatus.

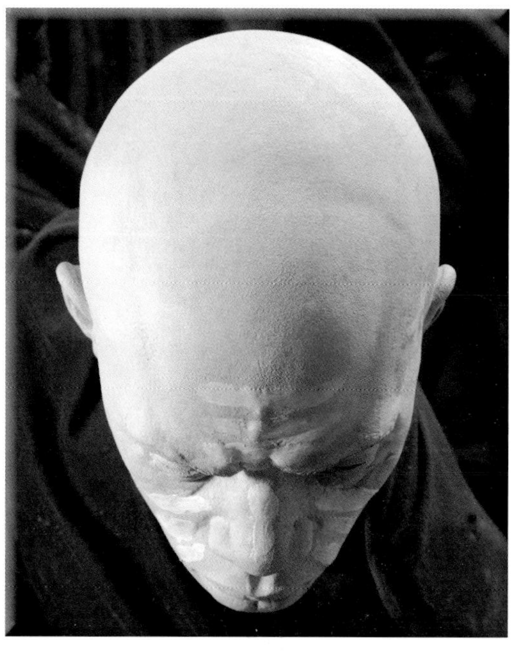

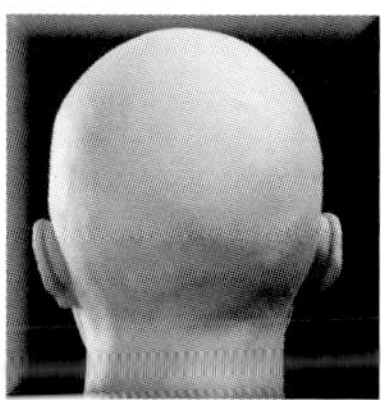

## Demonstration 7: Modeling the Ears

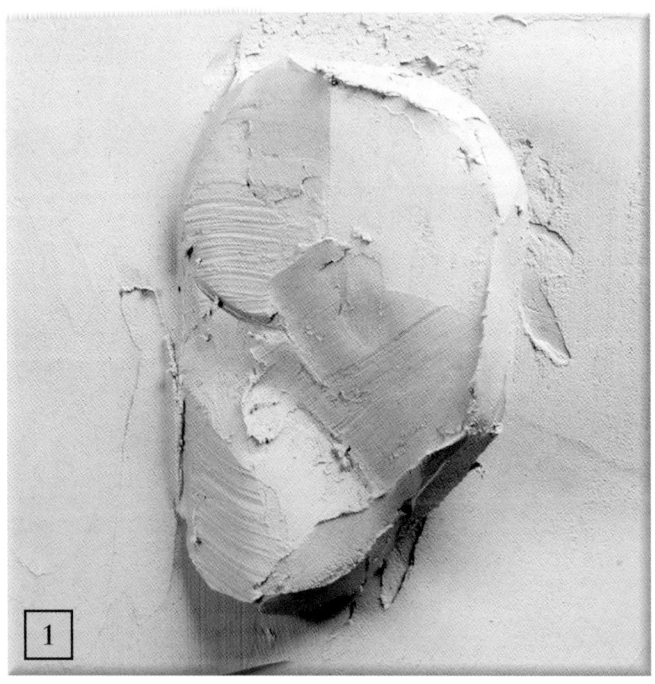


1. A piece of clay, in the form of a wedge, is applied to the base. Once the basic shape of the ear is formed, the planes are then defined.

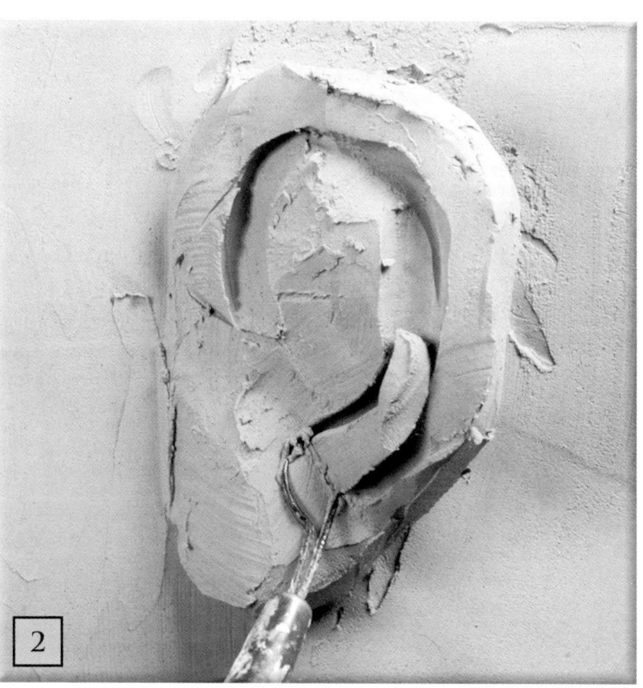


2. A coil of clay paralleling the outer edge of the ear is removed with a wire tool. This separates the helix from the antihelix and stops at the top of the ear lobe.

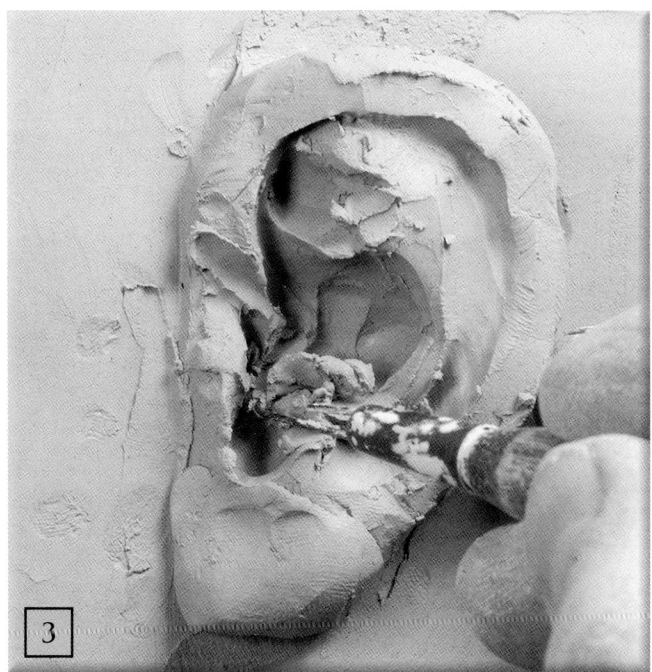


3. The wire tool is used to remove clay from the center to form the concha and from the upper part of the antihelix to form the triangular fossa.

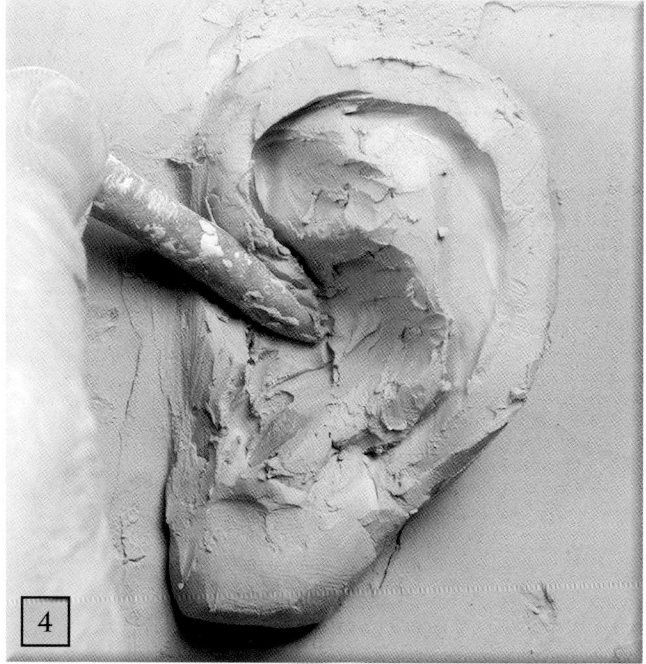


4. The helix emerges from the floor of the concha. It must be remembered that the helix is a three-dimensional structure that follows the perimeter of the ear and blends into the lobe.

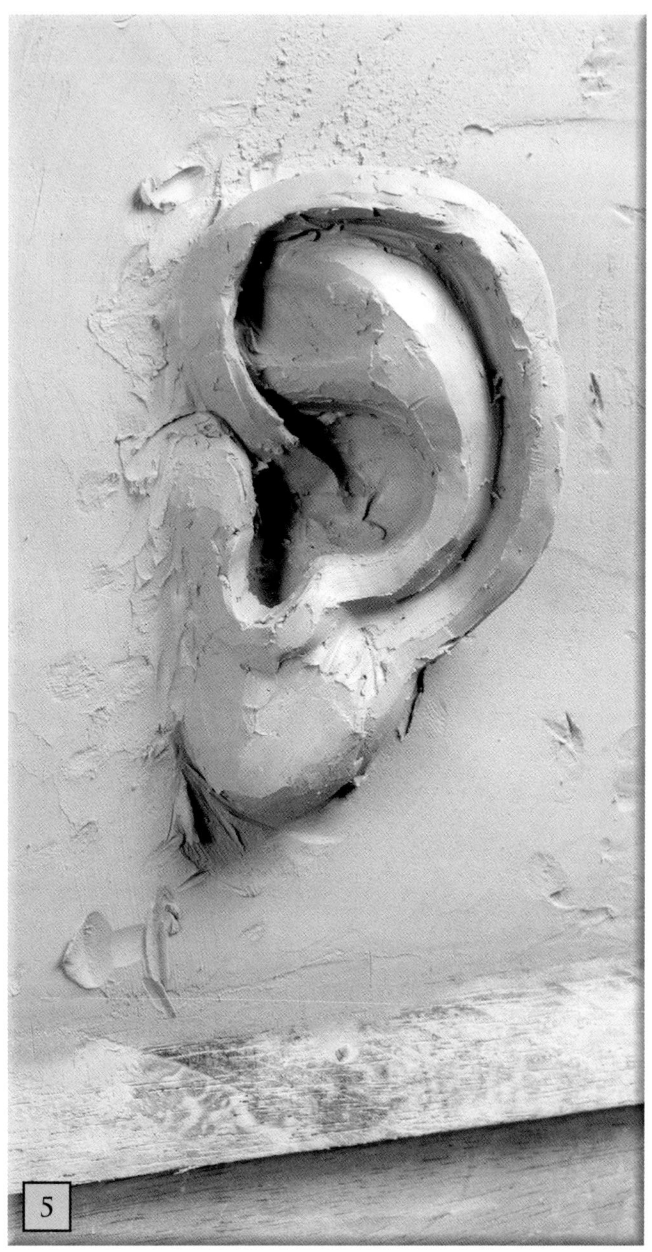


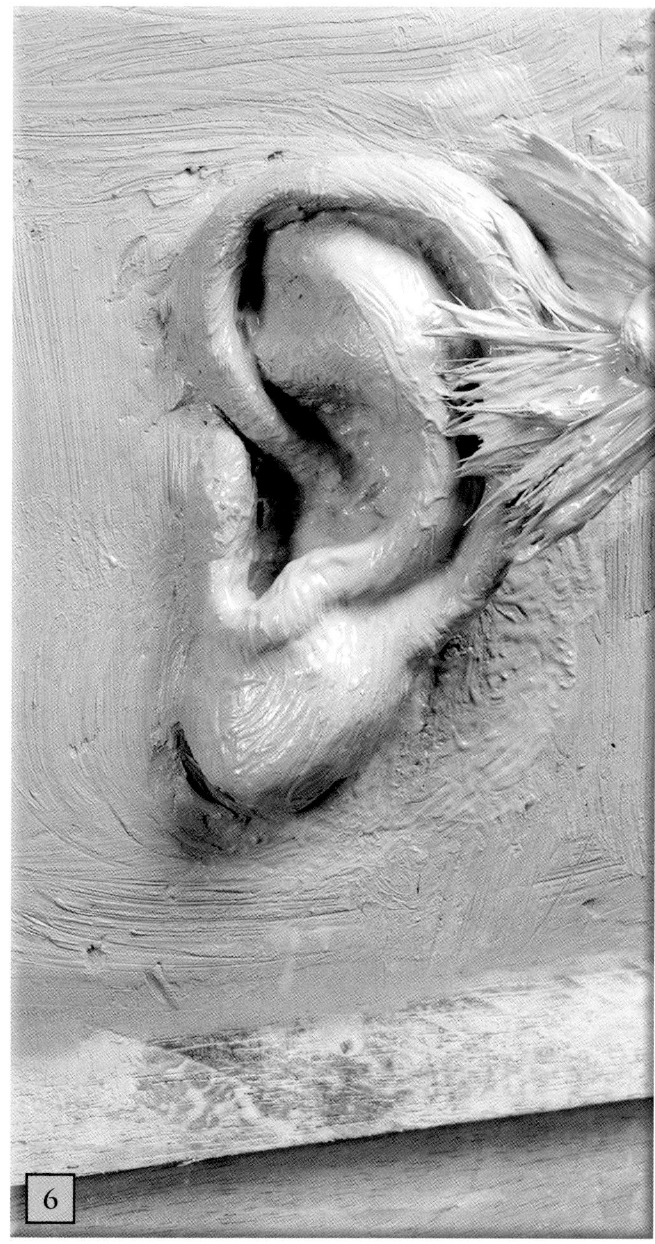


**5.** Finding the planes helps define the correct volumes.

**6.** The surface is smoothed with a wet brush. The final texture is achieved with a soft sponge.

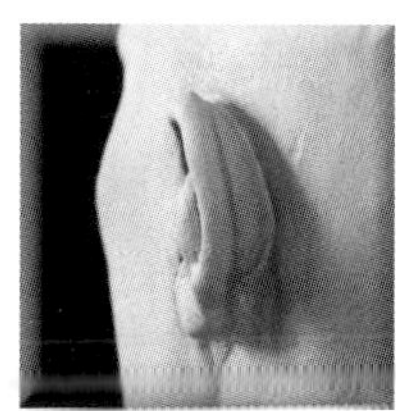

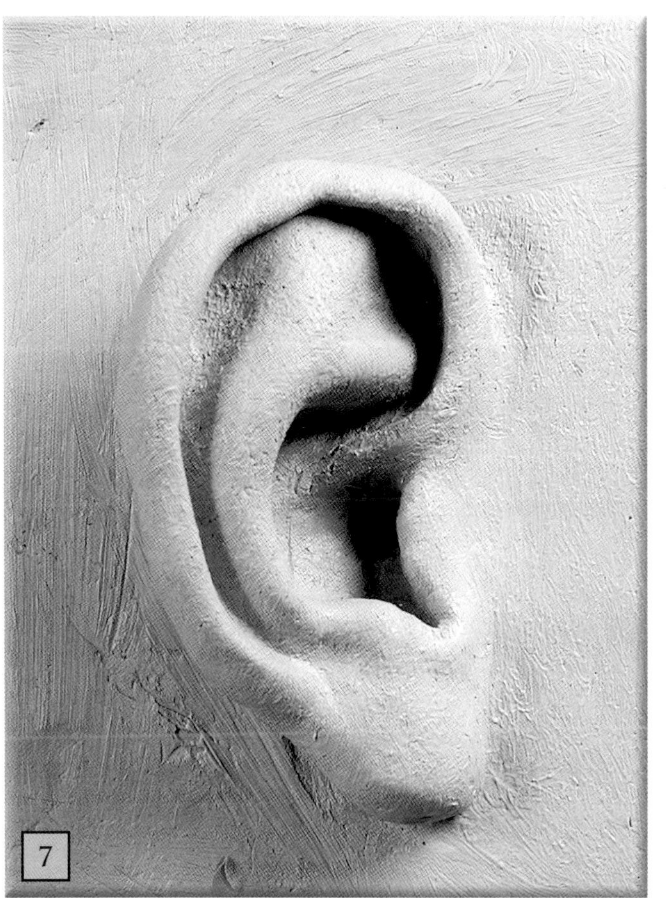


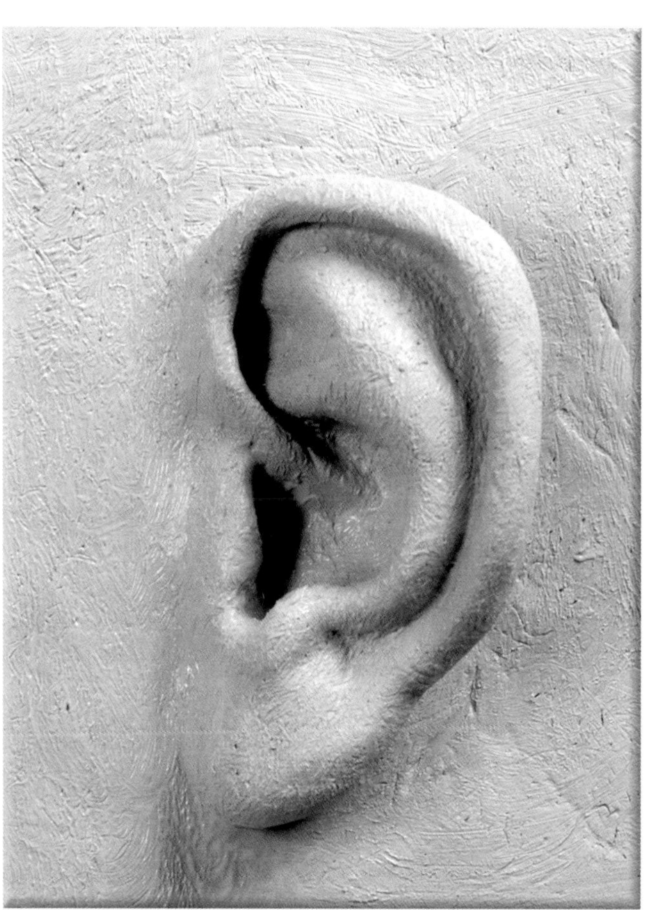

7. The finished work must be observed from many different angles in order to correct the volumes.

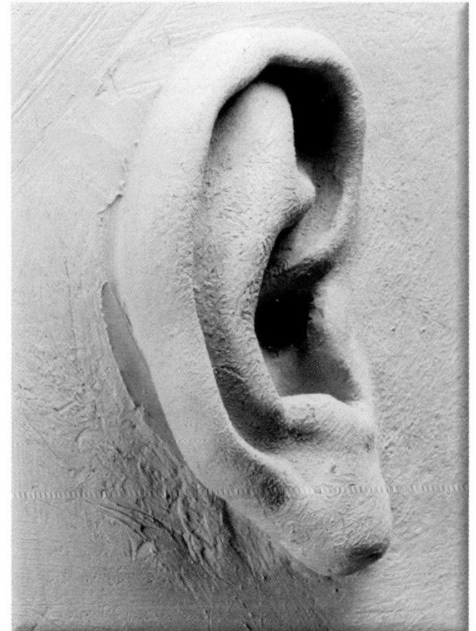

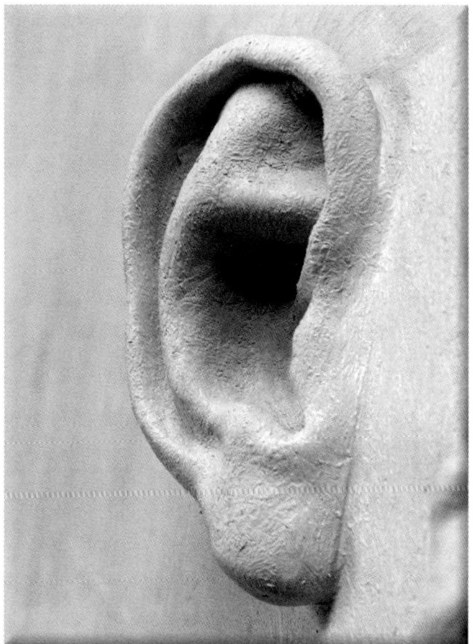

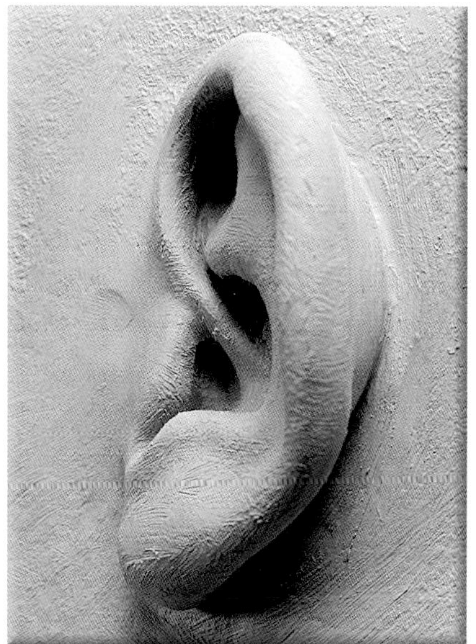

The shape of the helix determines the outline of the ear when viewed from the front, but is more easily analyzed when viewed from the back.

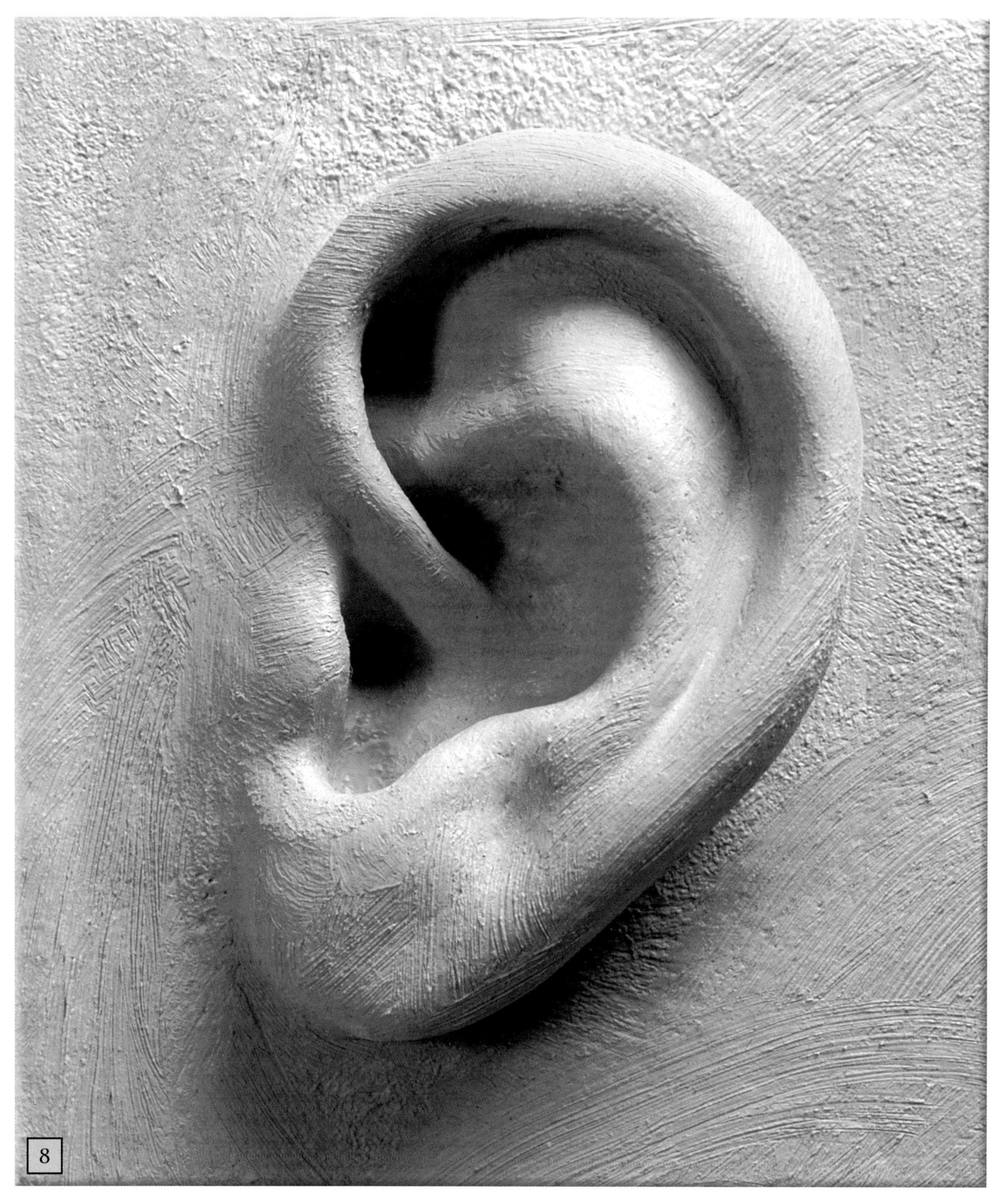


8. A baby's ear is round overall and has soft curves.

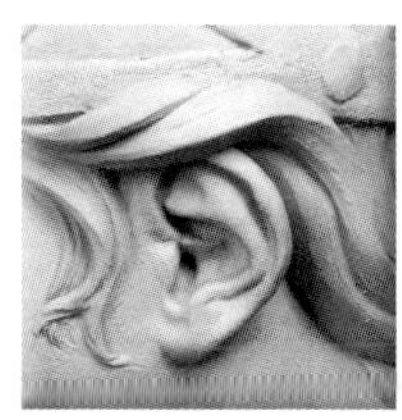

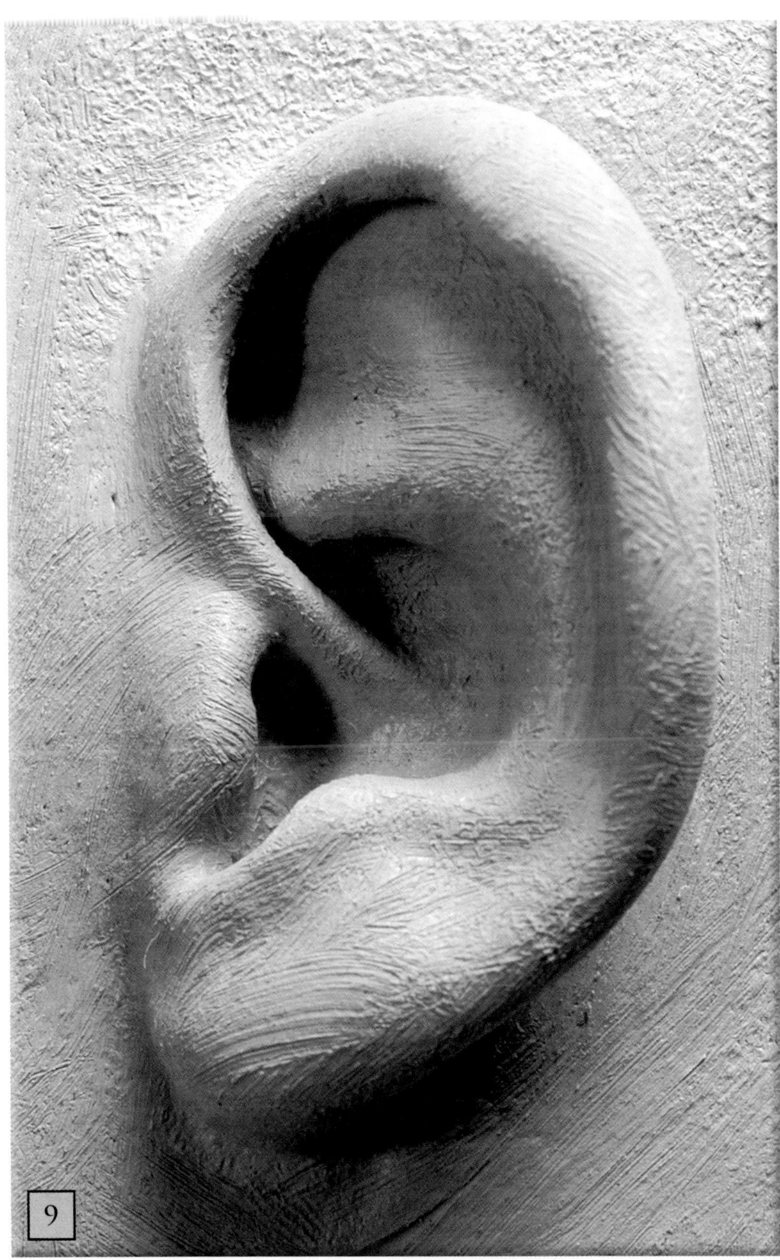


**9.** By the age of four, the ear is already beginning to elongate.

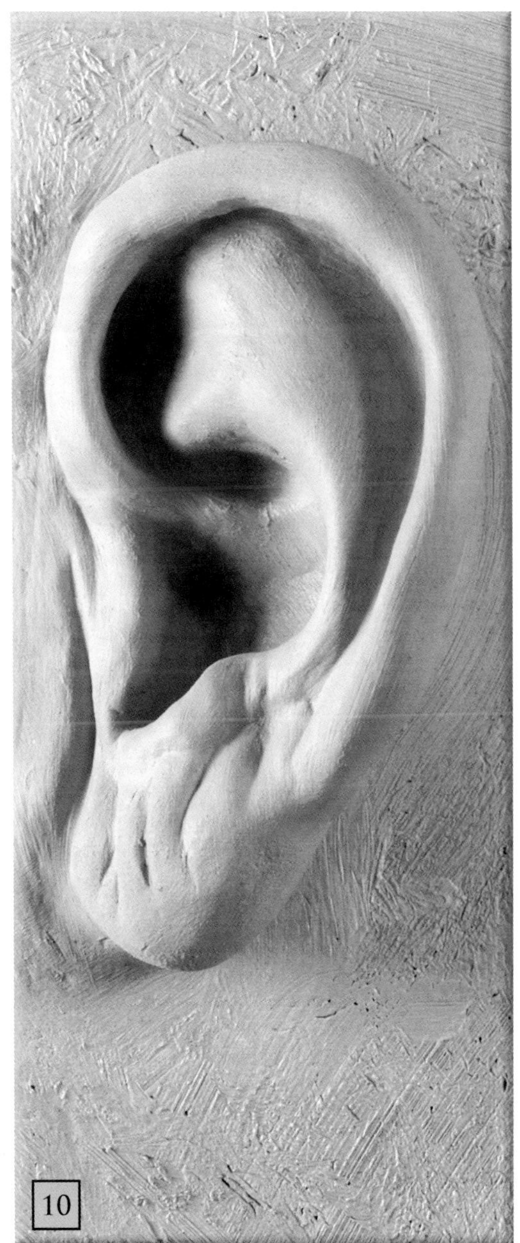


**10.** A pattern of vertical wrinkles on the lobe and in front of the tragus appears in an older person.

## The Hair

In order to successfully model hair, it is necessary to observe how it grows around the face, specifically the origin of each mass, its planes, its general direction and the way it curves. It is only after these volumes are in place that the details are added.

The roots of the hair around the face and on the neck must be blended with the flesh in a subtle transition to prevent a wig-like effect. Hair on the sides of the head grows back away from the temples. This is especially visible in men's sideburns. The hair on the top of the head grows in all directions around a central point called the crown of the cranium.

Hair is pliable and fibrous by nature and the masses of clay representing hair should flow in continuous curves, even in short or straight hair. It should be noted that, technically, a single hair is never straight. It is particularly important when rendering a short haircut to give some curvature to the directional lines of the surface texture.

Separate strands of hair can cross over and under one another. Their curves can be tight or long, but they should never be broken (see example in step 3). They should also make sense, i.e., have a beginning, a point of attachment; middle, usually showing more volume; and, an end. Specifically, a particular strand should not arbitrarily be lost in the whole nor appear out of nowhere without a logical, if not always visible, point of attachment. It is important to become familiar with the ways hair behaves in real life before attempting to interpret or abstractly render it in clay.

The very dynamic style of hair in the following demonstration provides a clear visualization of the above principles.

## Demonstration 8: Modeling the Hair

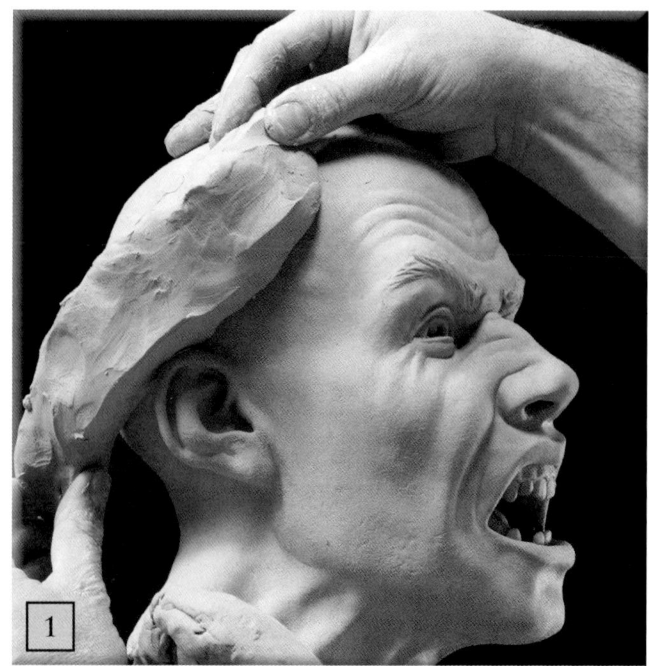


**1.** The hair is applied in slabs growing out of the scalp and curving toward the back of the head. It is pressed firmly, especially at the root.

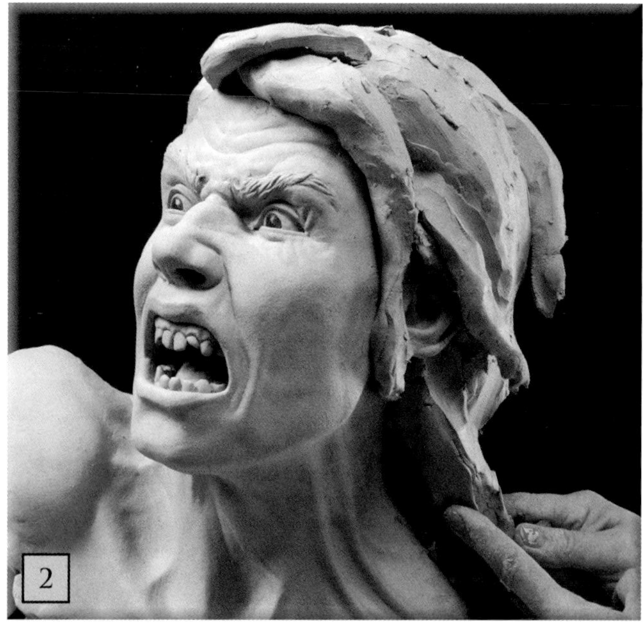


**2.** Smaller coils of clay are applied, always starting from the root and following the general direction of the particular hairstyle. Generally, each strand develops more volume as it extends from the root, and then reduces again at the end.

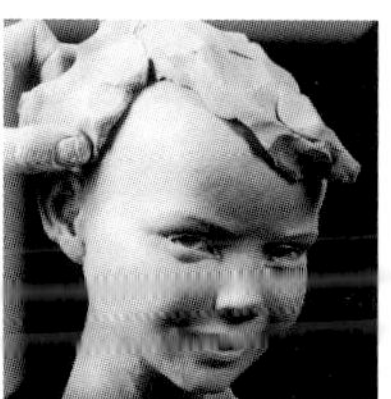

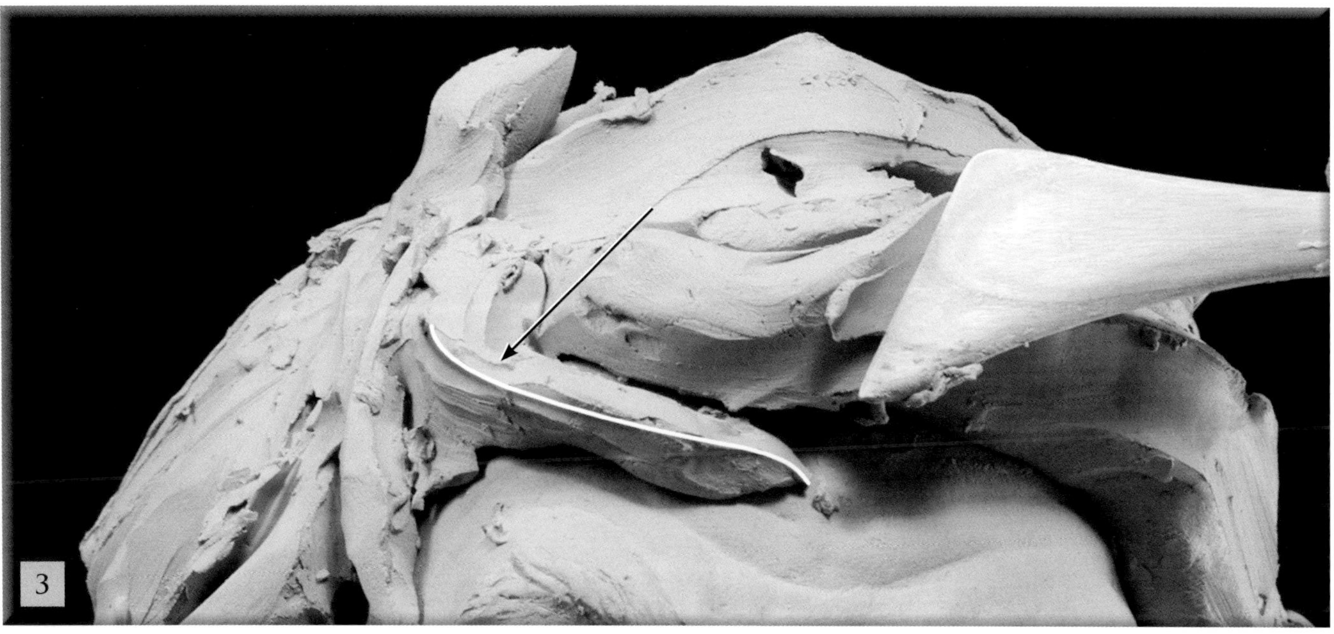


**3.** The planes of each mass of hair are defined with a wooden tool. The arrow points to a typical example of a broken curve, and the way it should be.

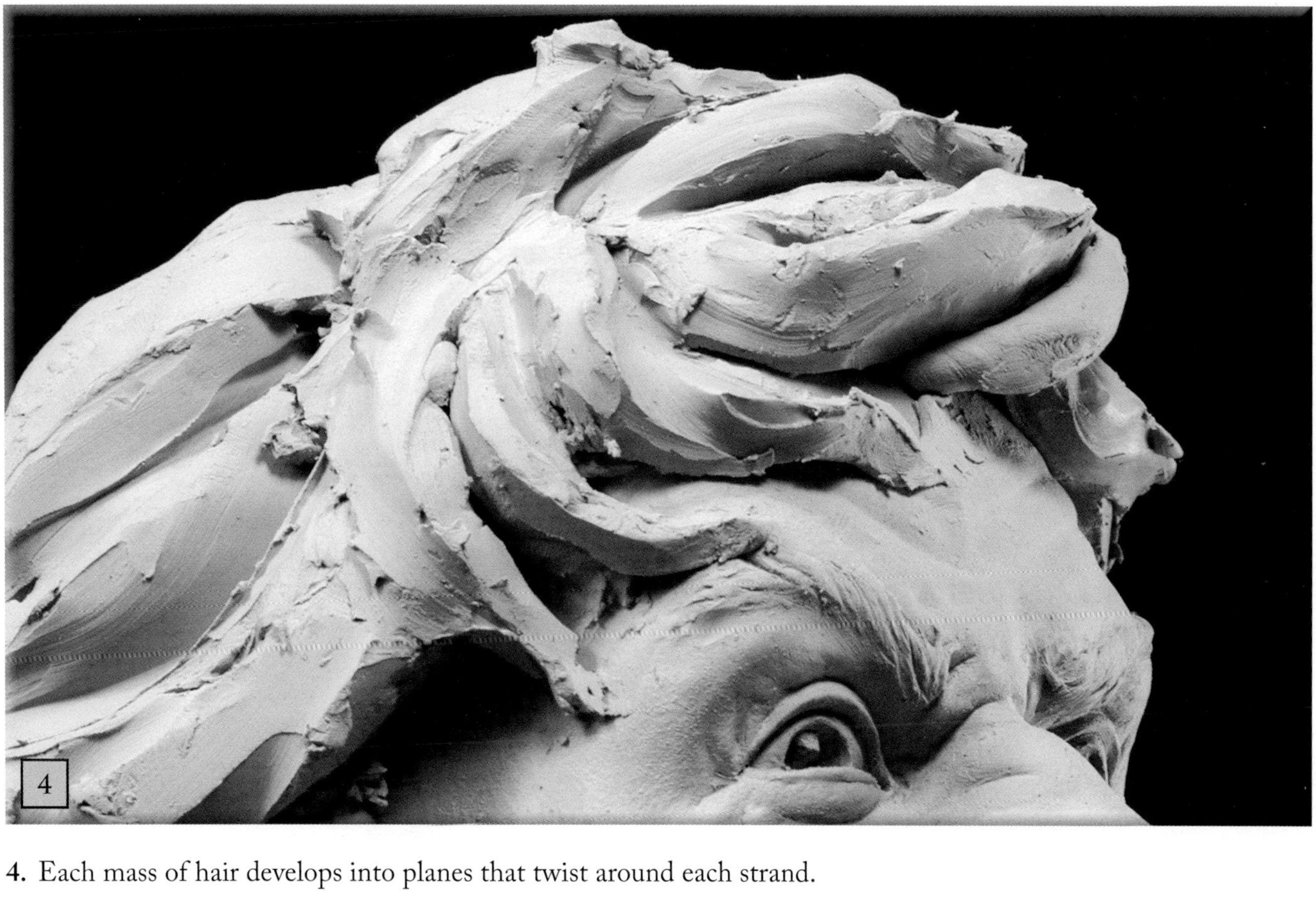

**4.** Each mass of hair develops into planes that twist around each strand.

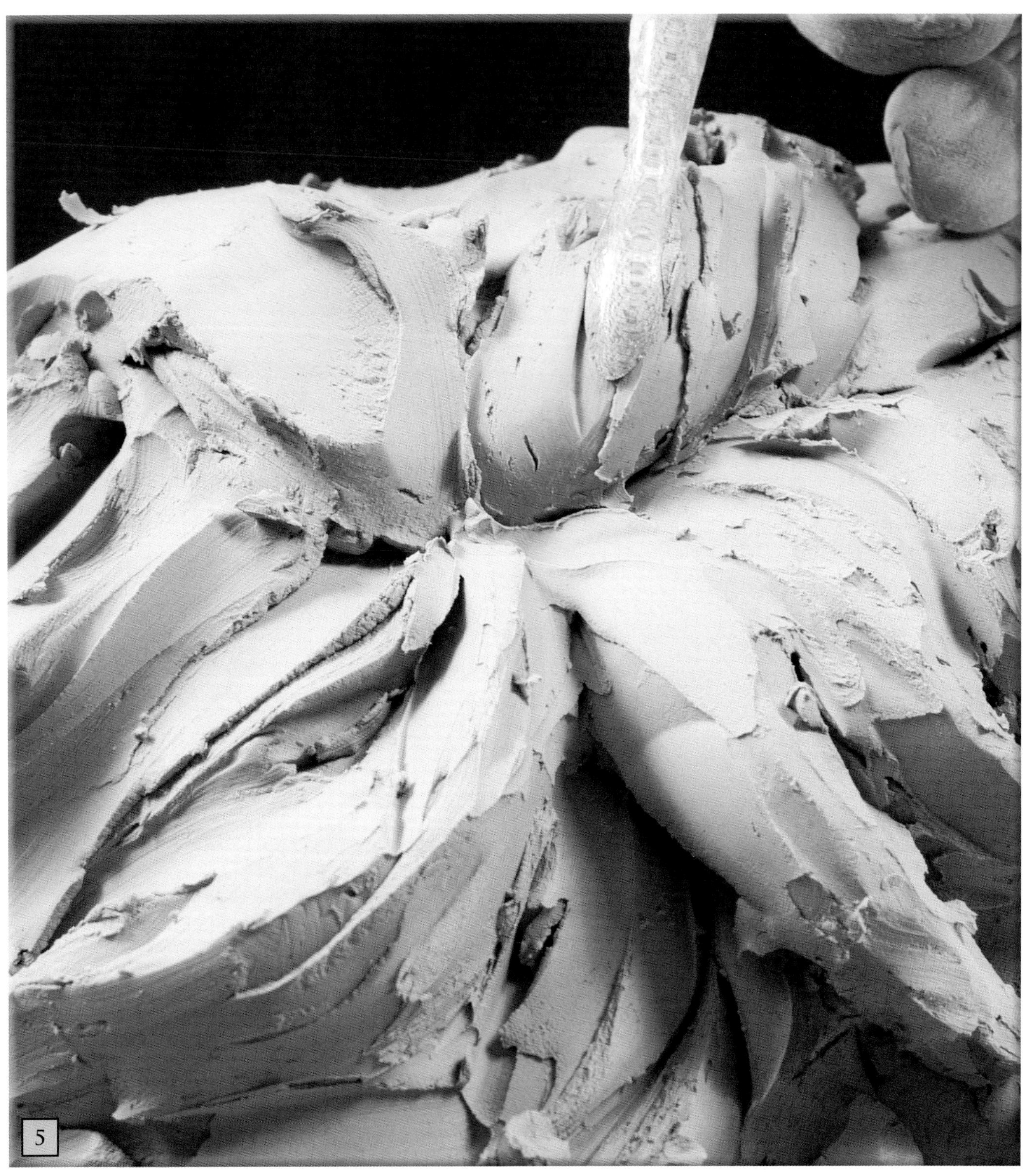


5. At the root, each volume springs in individual clusters and radiates from the crown of the cranium. The points of attachment are reinforced with a wooden tool.

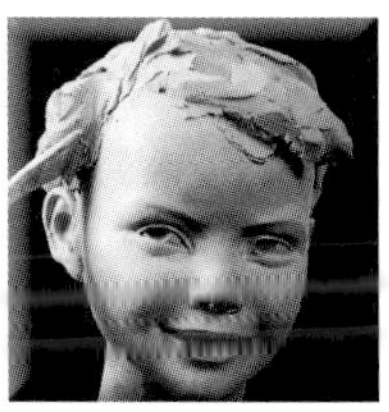

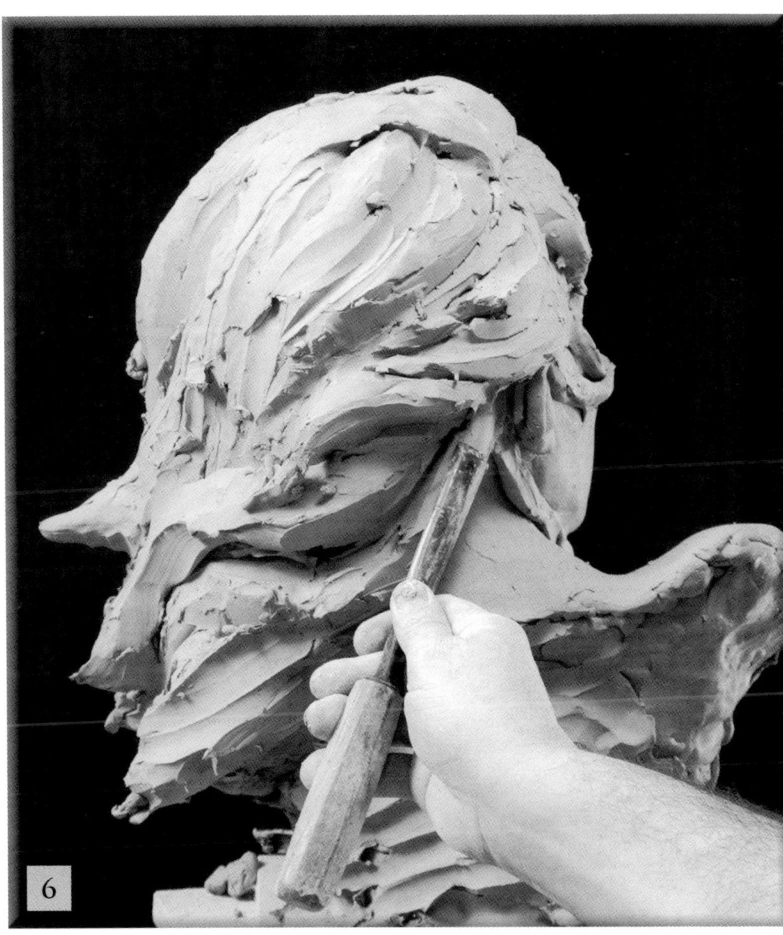


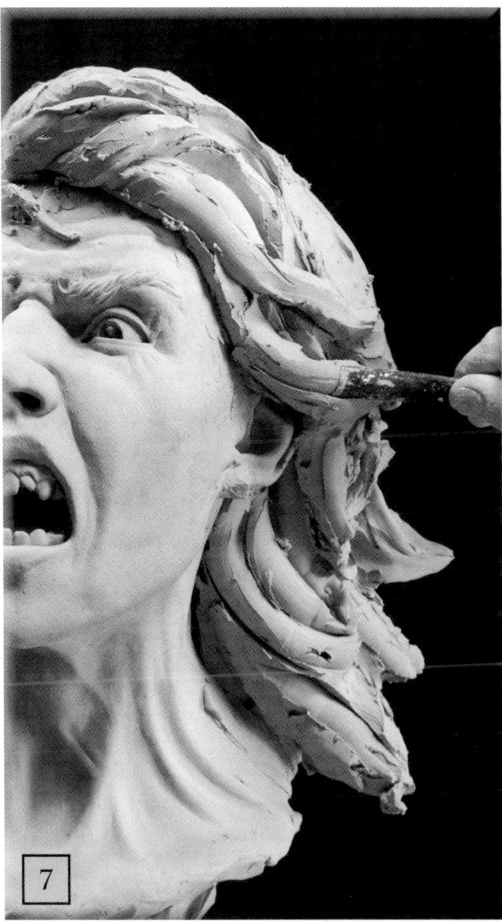


6, 7. A woodcarving gouge is used to pull, shape and separate the different strands of hair.

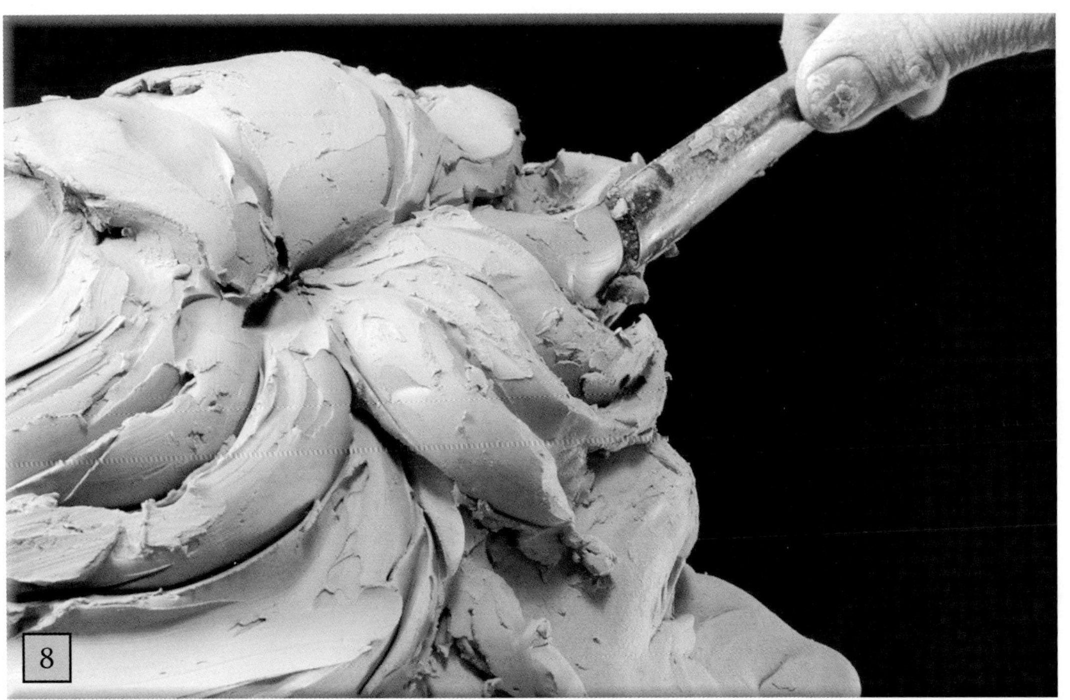


8. The gouge is pushed firmly against the clay, then pulled to form fluid curves. The outside, as well as the inside of the gouge, is used to create both concave and convex shapes.

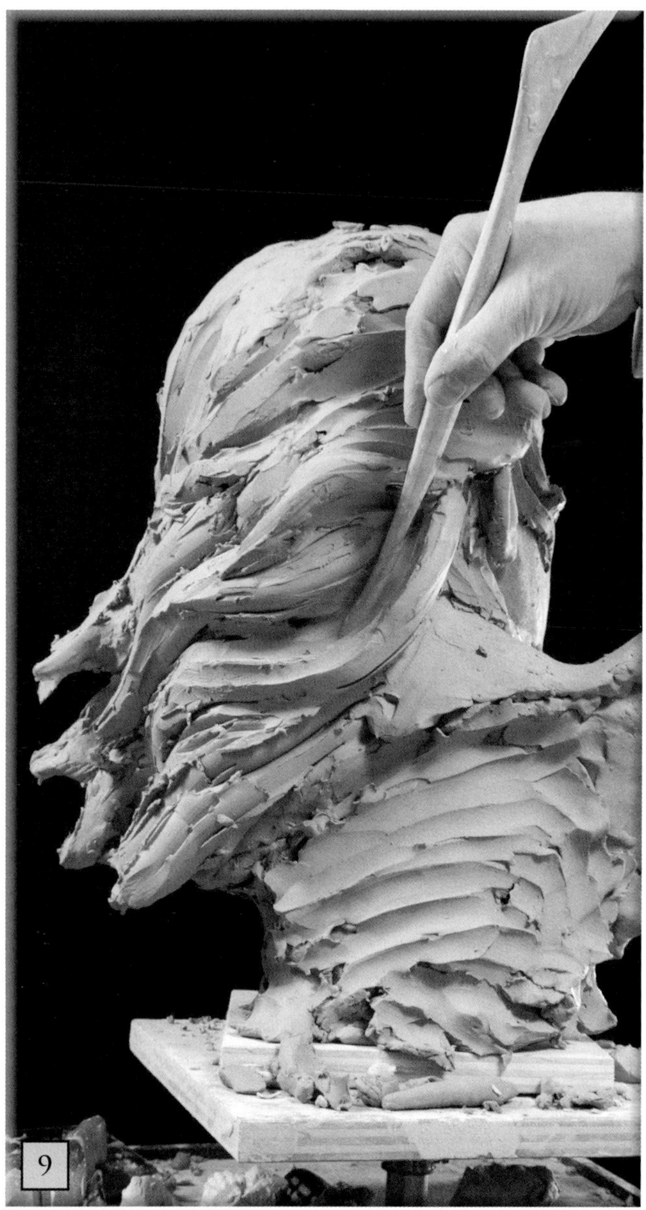


**9.** The deeper grooves are defined with a rounded, wooden tool.

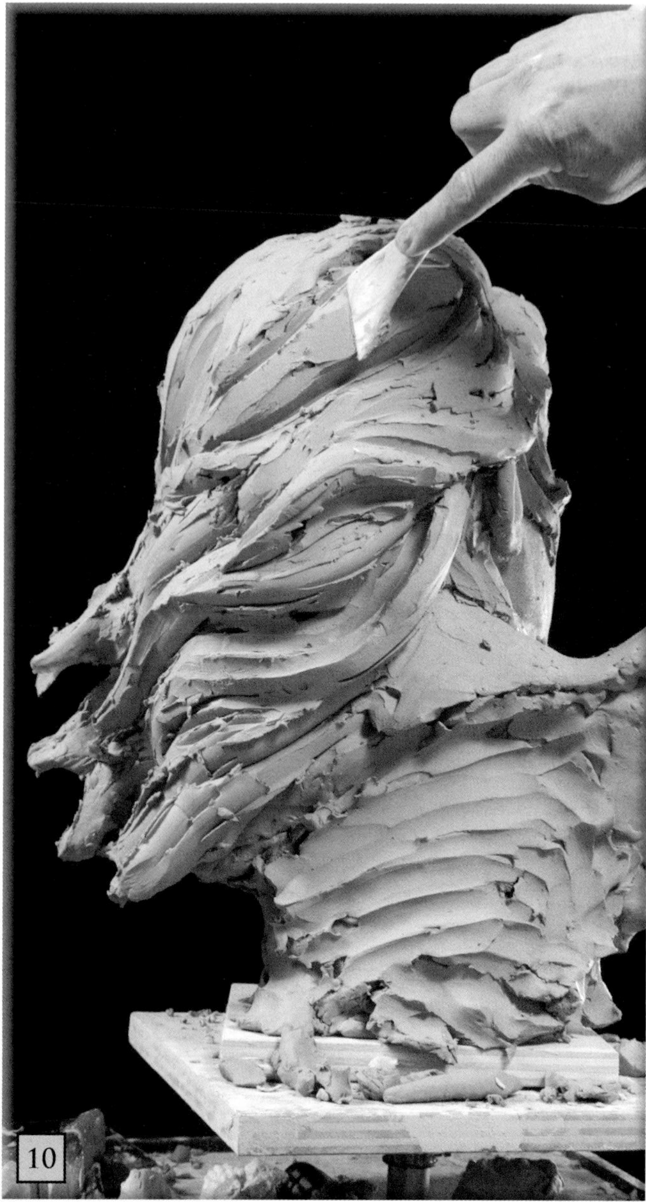


**10.** Finding the main planes of each strand helps to organize the general flow of the hair.

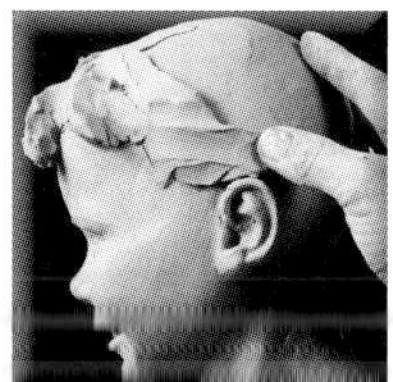

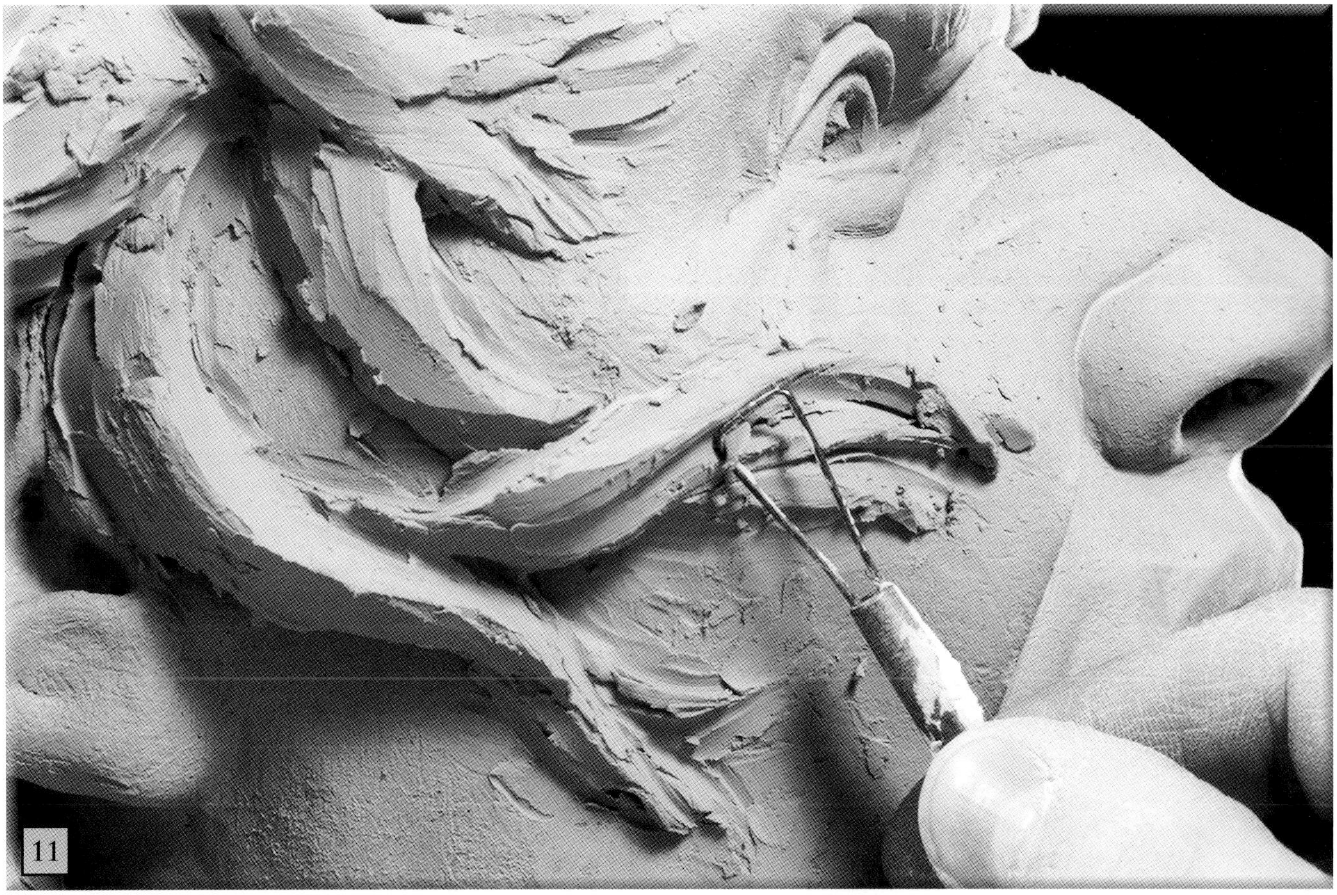

11. The tips of the hair are refined with wire tools.

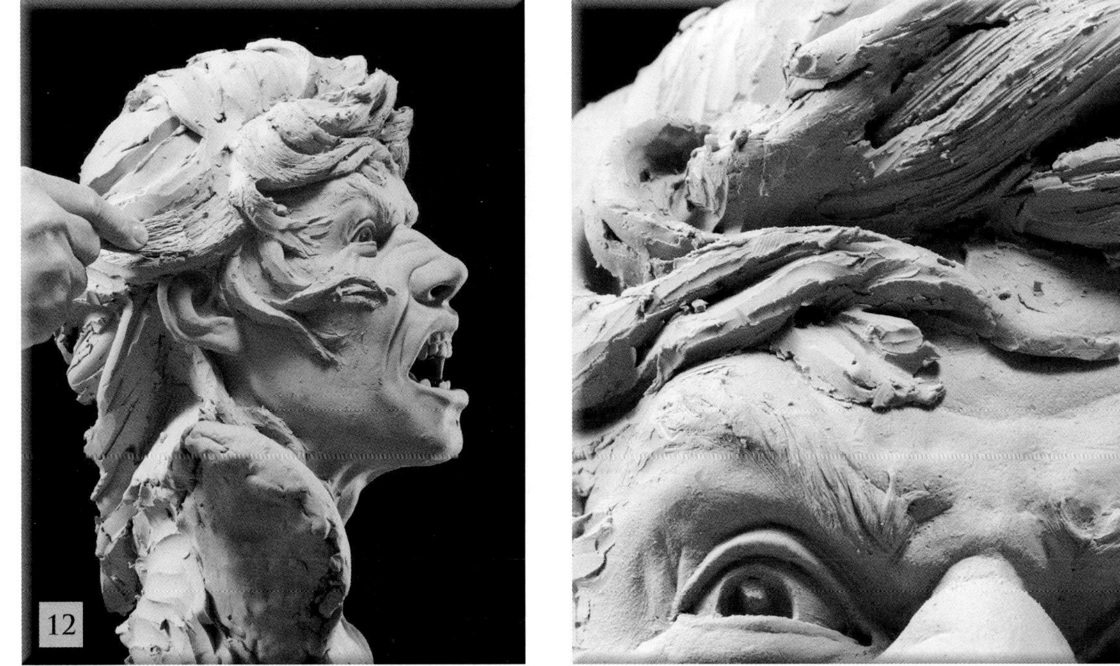

12. A bristle brush is dragged in the direction of the hair, not to add texture but to shape the clay into continuous curves.

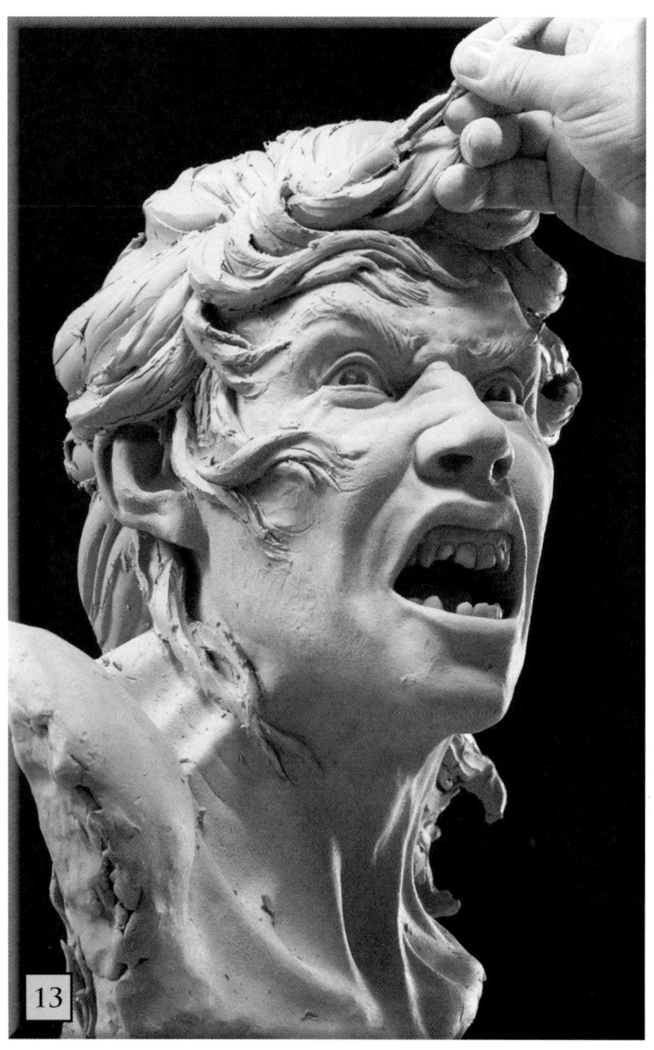

13. Clusters are further divided with a smaller gouge or cuticle pusher.

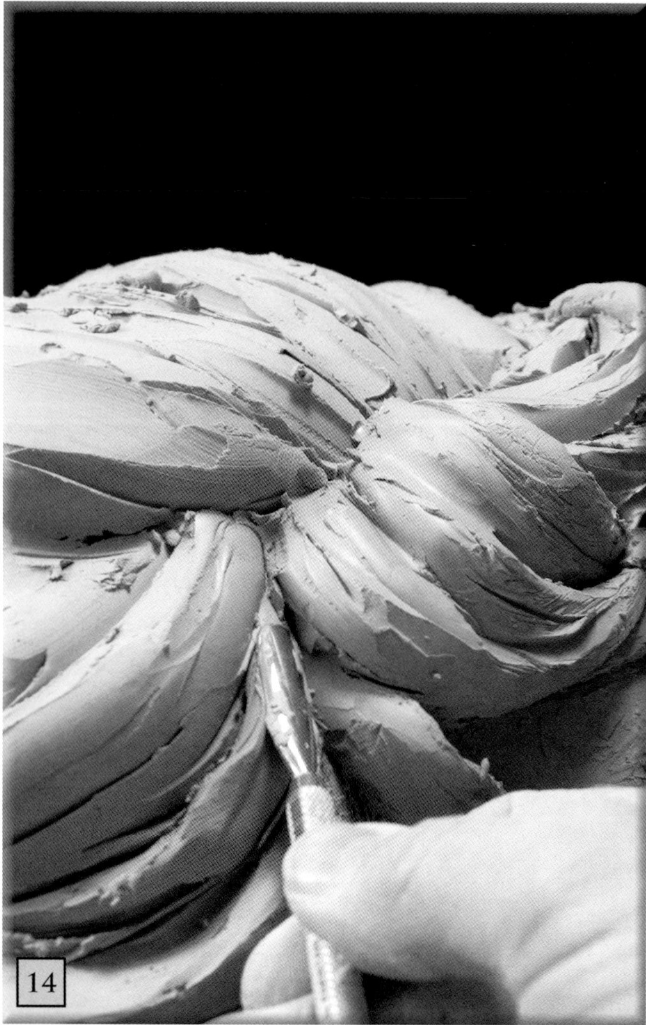

14. The root of each strand must be well defined, keeping in mind that they start at scalp level.

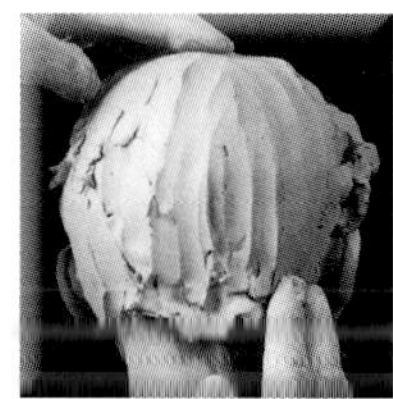

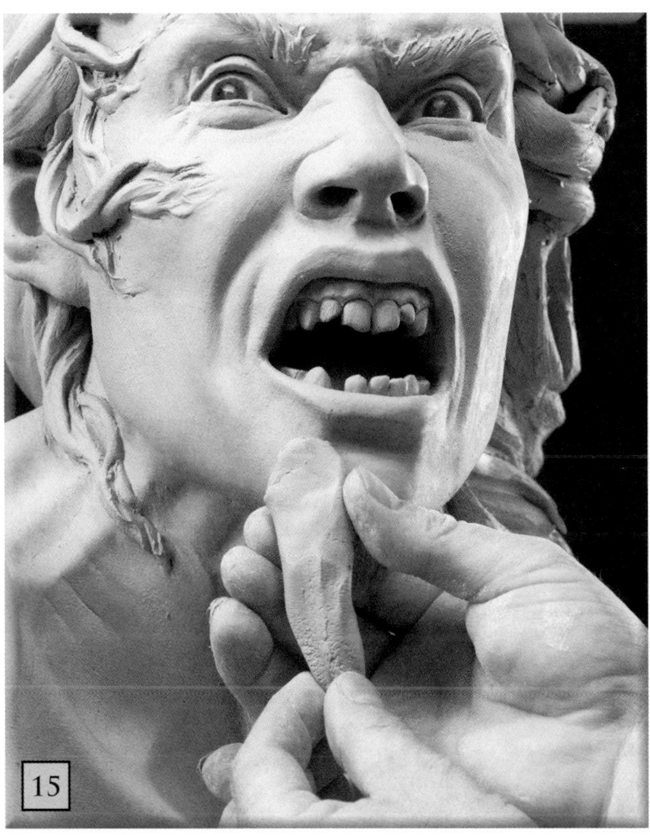

15. Facial hair is constructed in the same manner. Independent coils are firmly rooted to the chin.

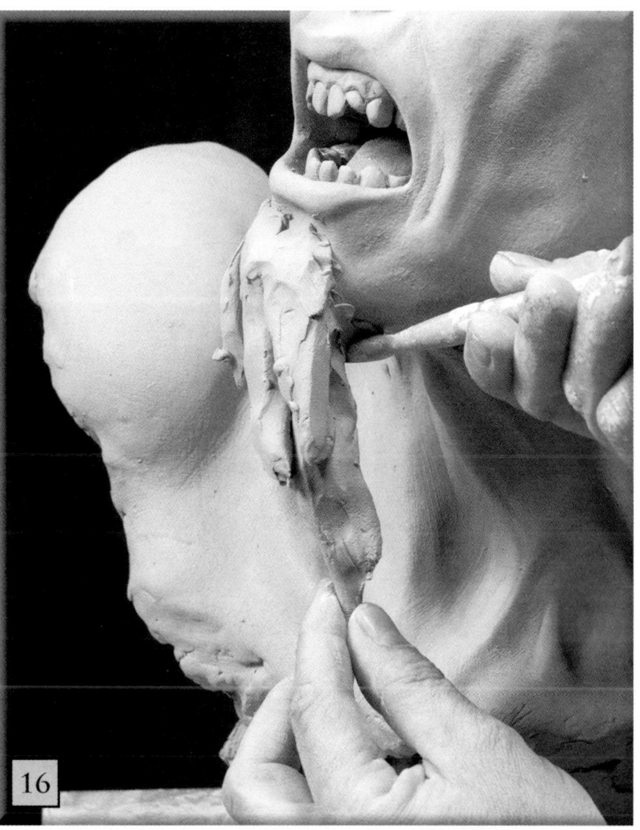

16. The coils of clay are secured in the back as well as the front.

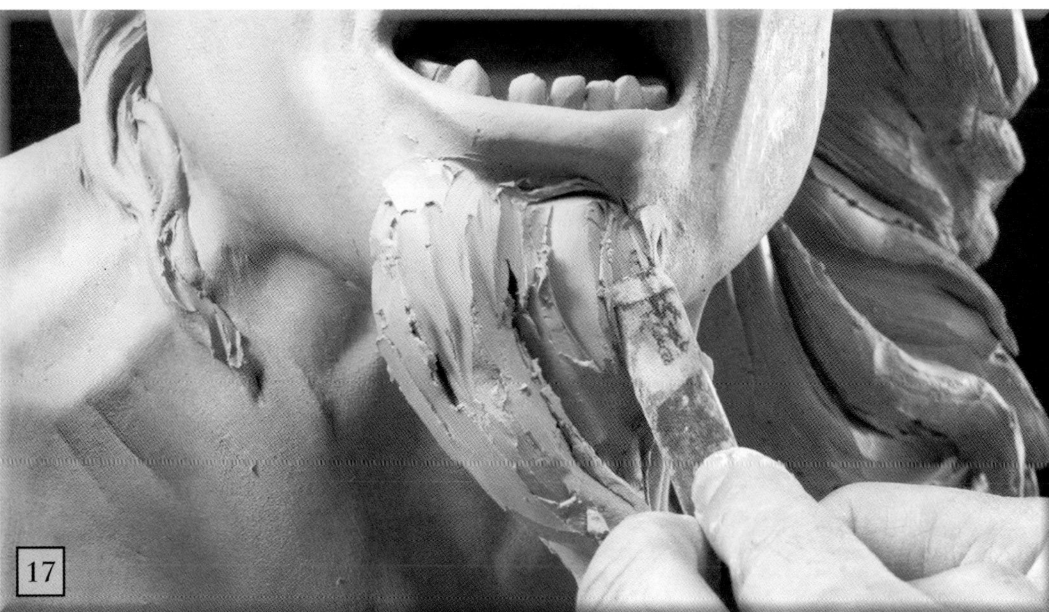

17. The planes of each cluster are defined with a woodcarving gouge.

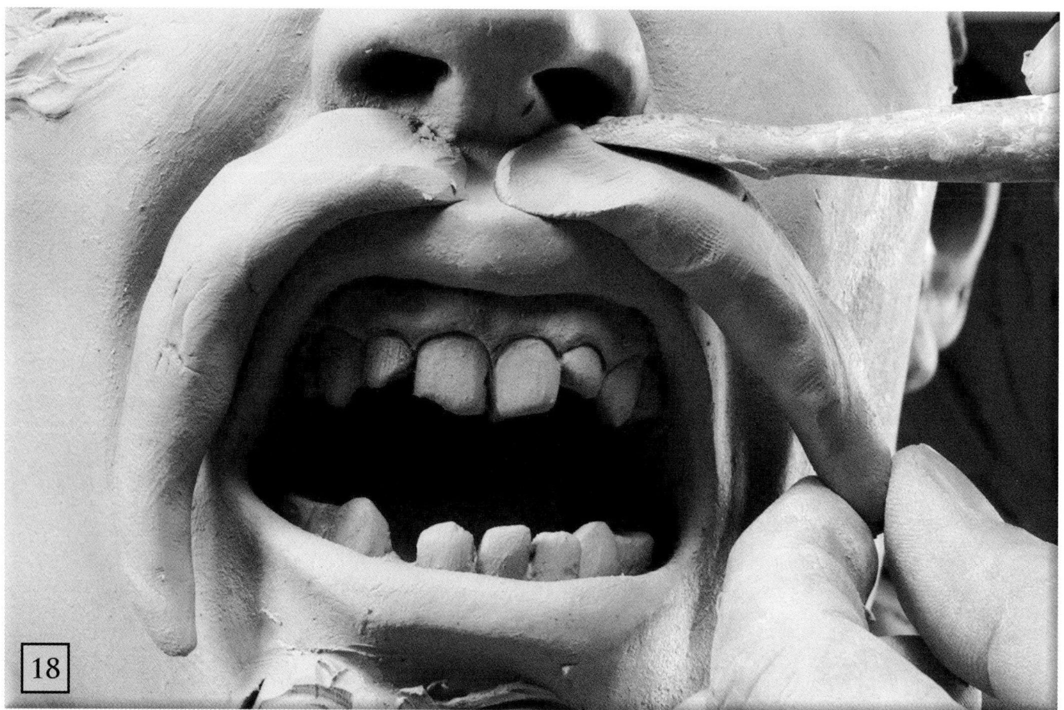


**18, 19.** Each side of the moustache is applied in one piece with the different strands of hair defined with a small gouge and wooden tool.

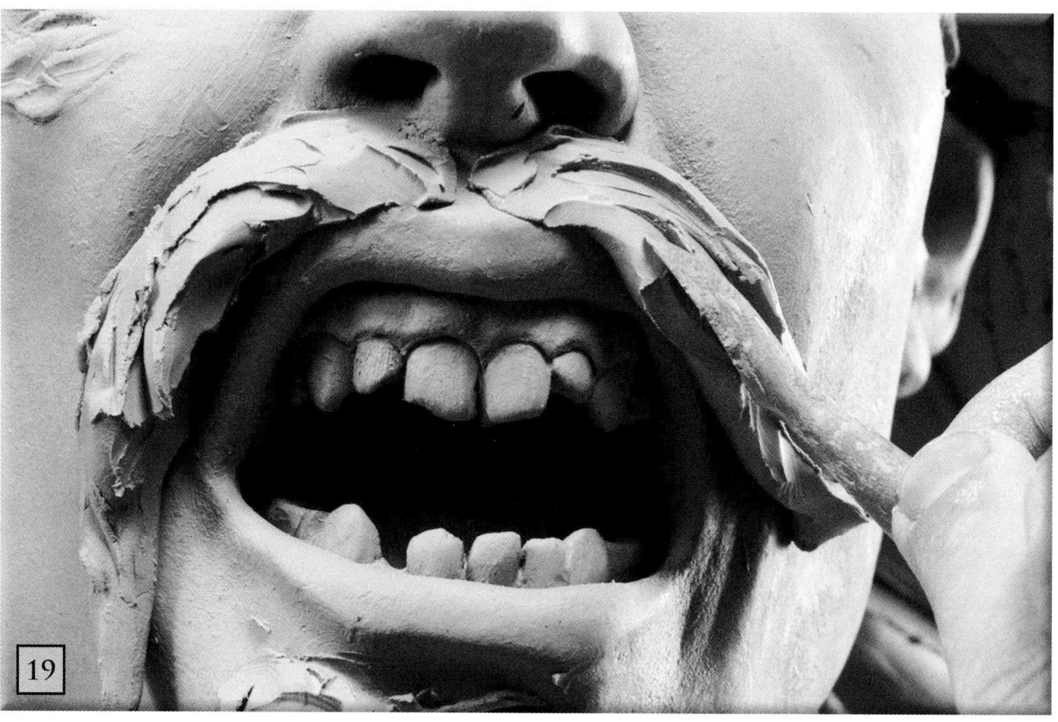

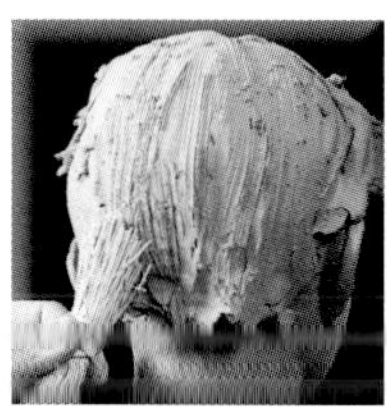

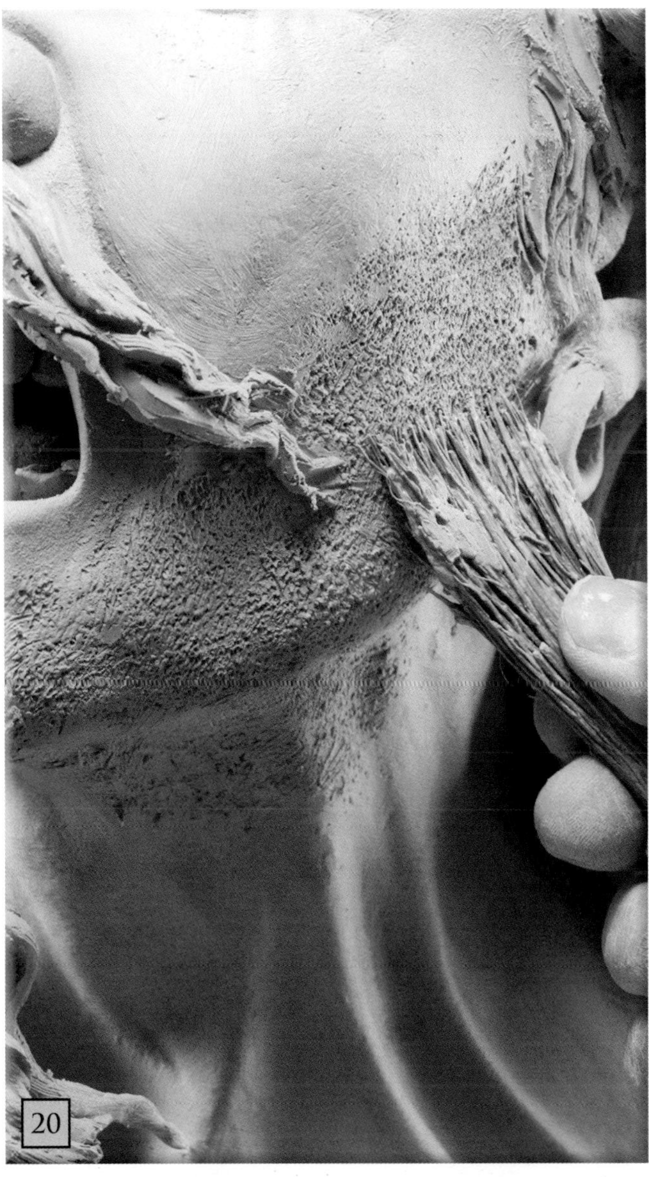


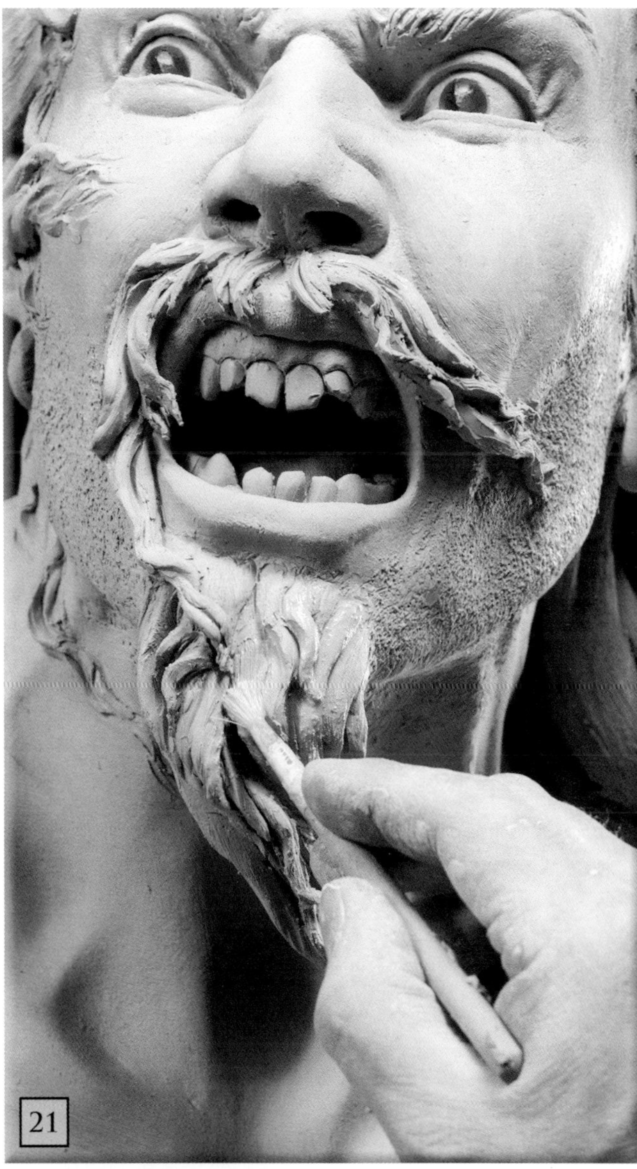


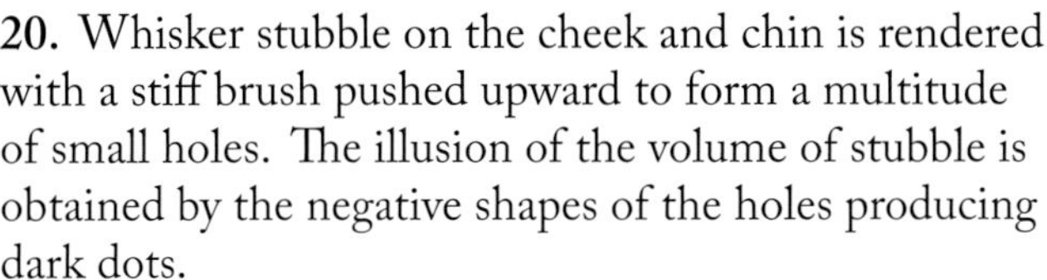
**20.** Whisker stubble on the cheek and chin is rendered with a stiff brush pushed upward to form a multitude of small holes. The illusion of the volume of stubble is obtained by the negative shapes of the holes producing dark dots.

**21.** The final texture is refined with a short-haired brush. It is better not to overdo the linear texture produced by the brush. It would result in a rope-like effect, especially in this type of hair.

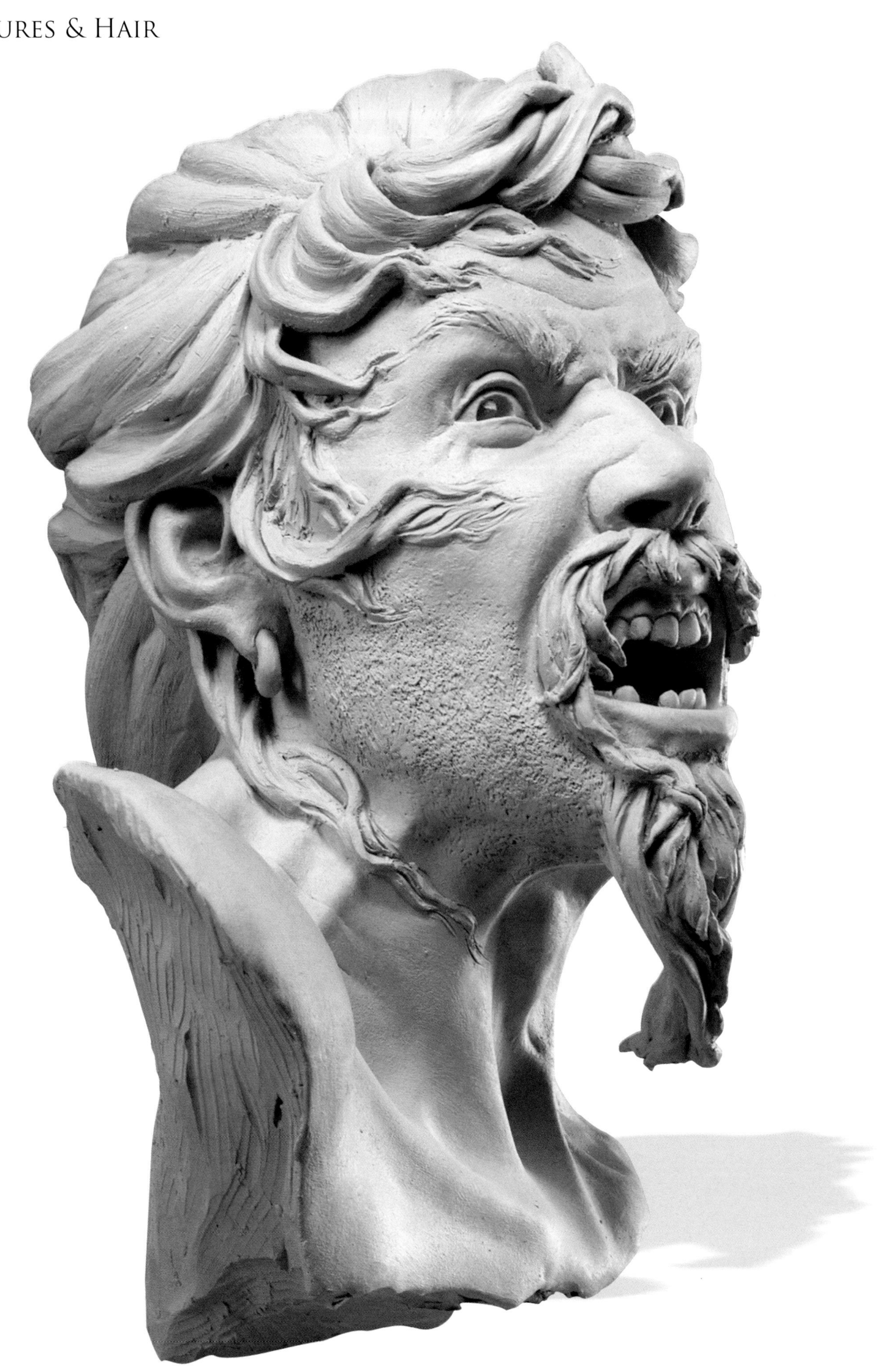

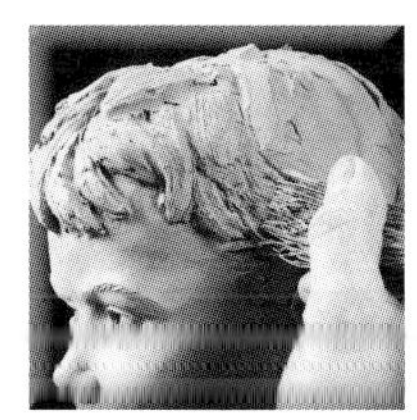

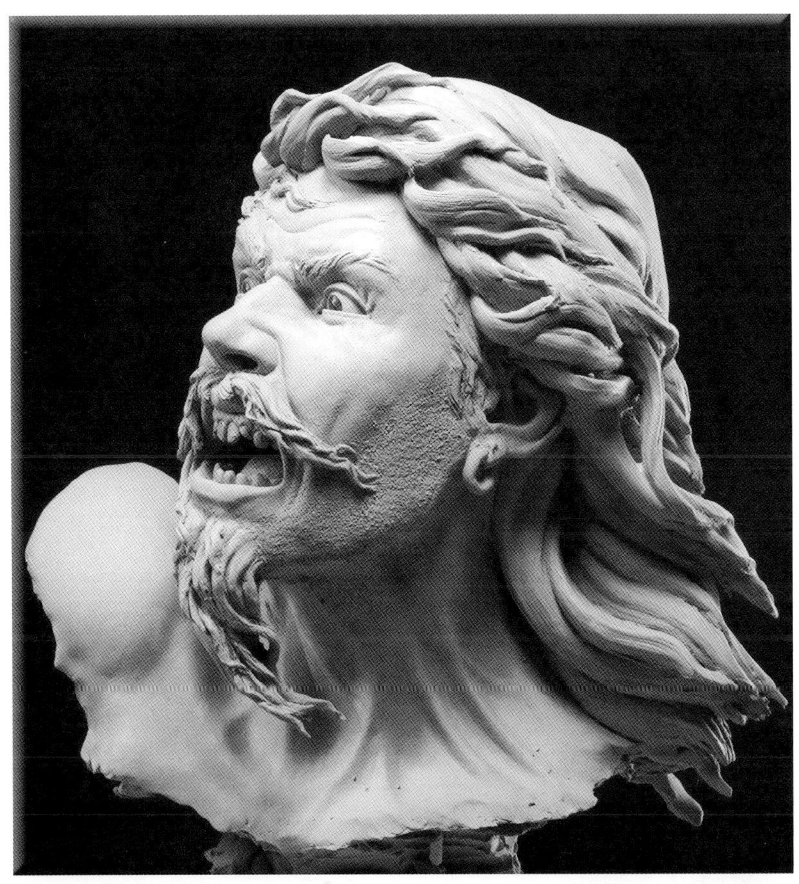

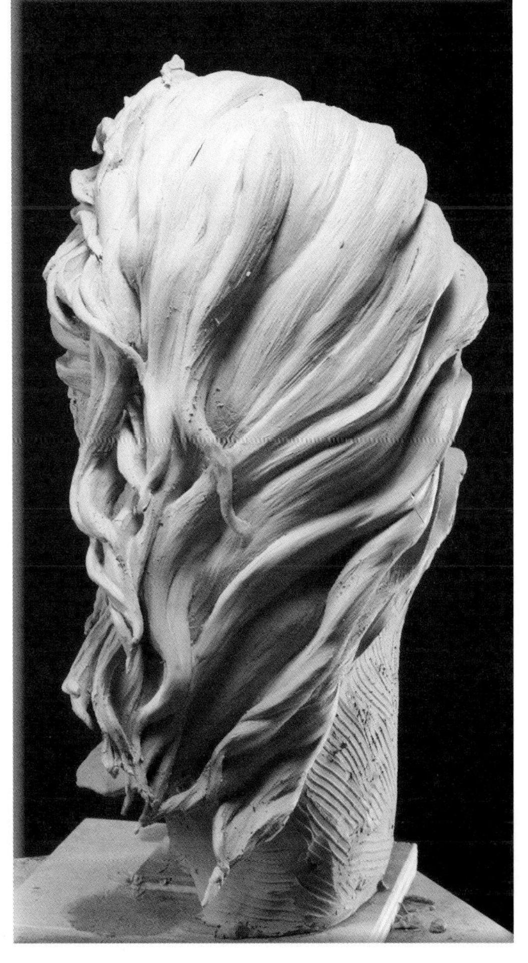

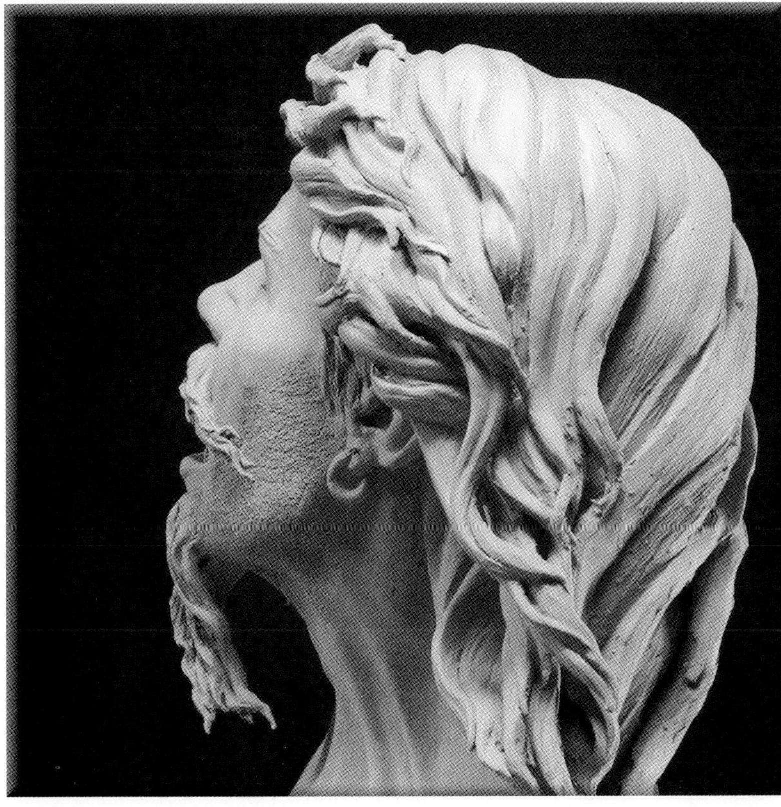

Once the structures of the features and hair are understood, experimentation with stylization can produce interesting effects.

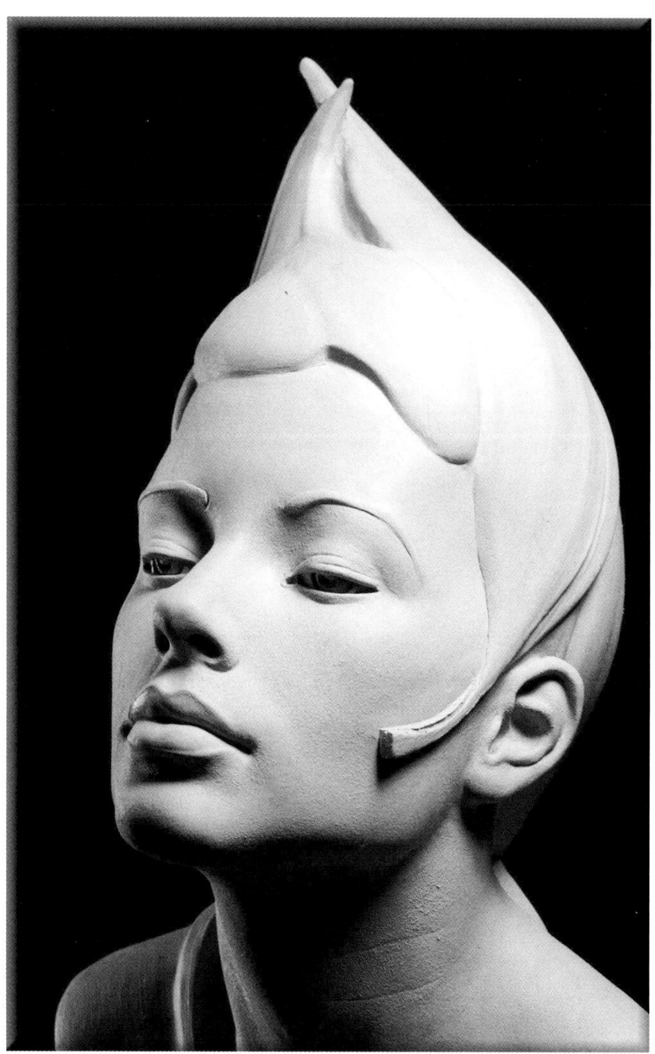

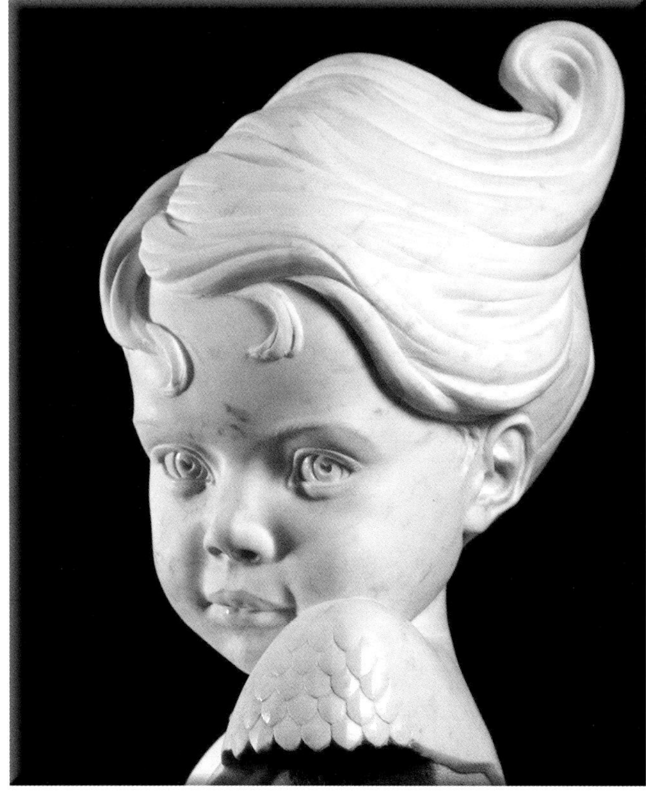

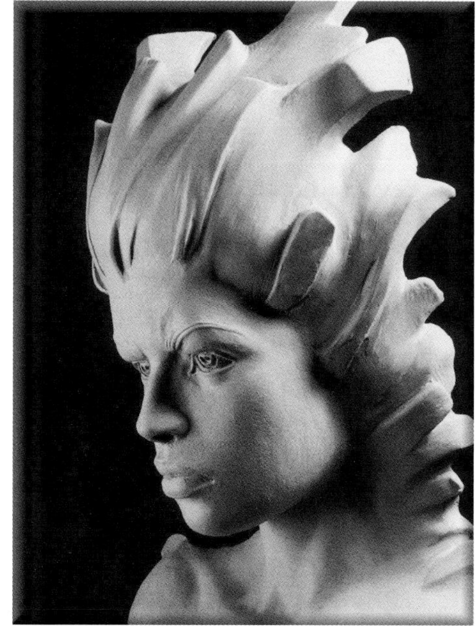

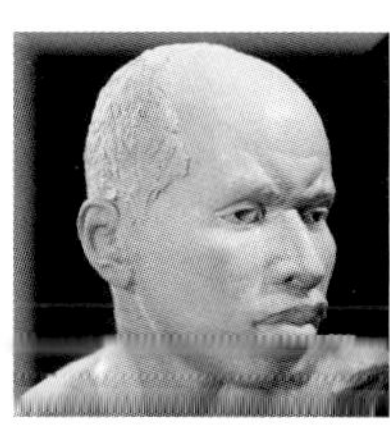

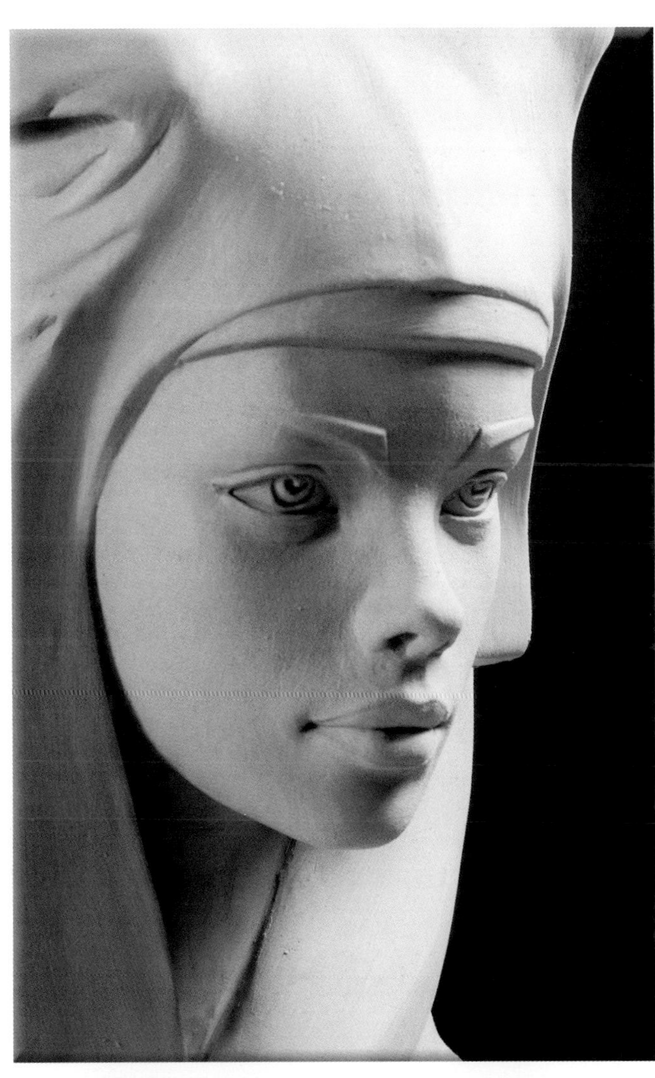

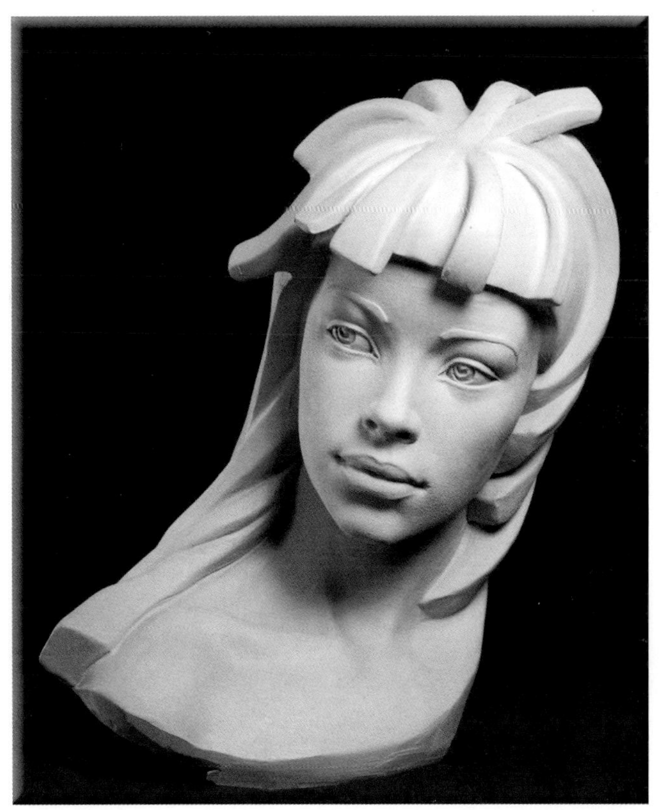

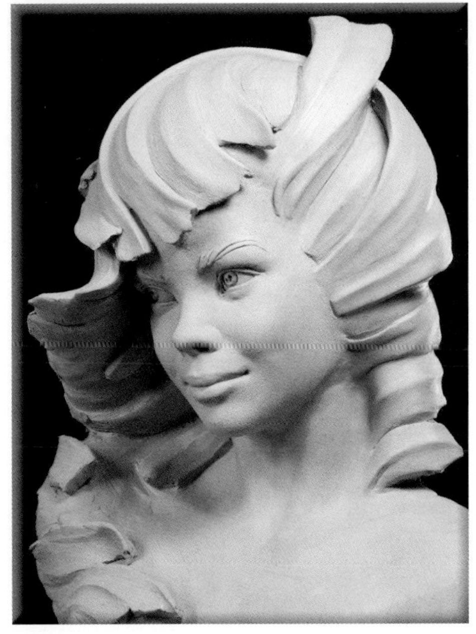

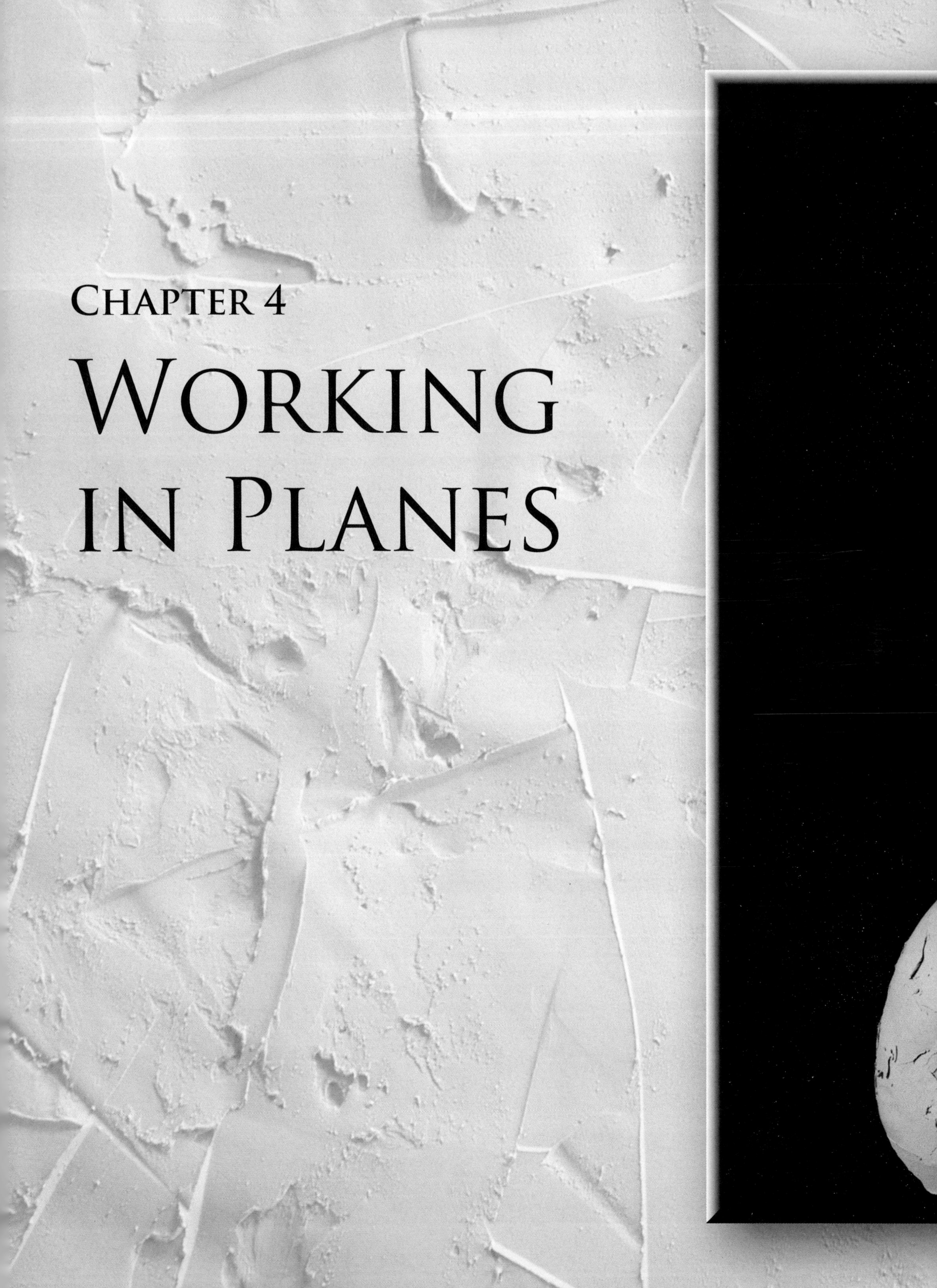

# Chapter 4
# Working in Planes

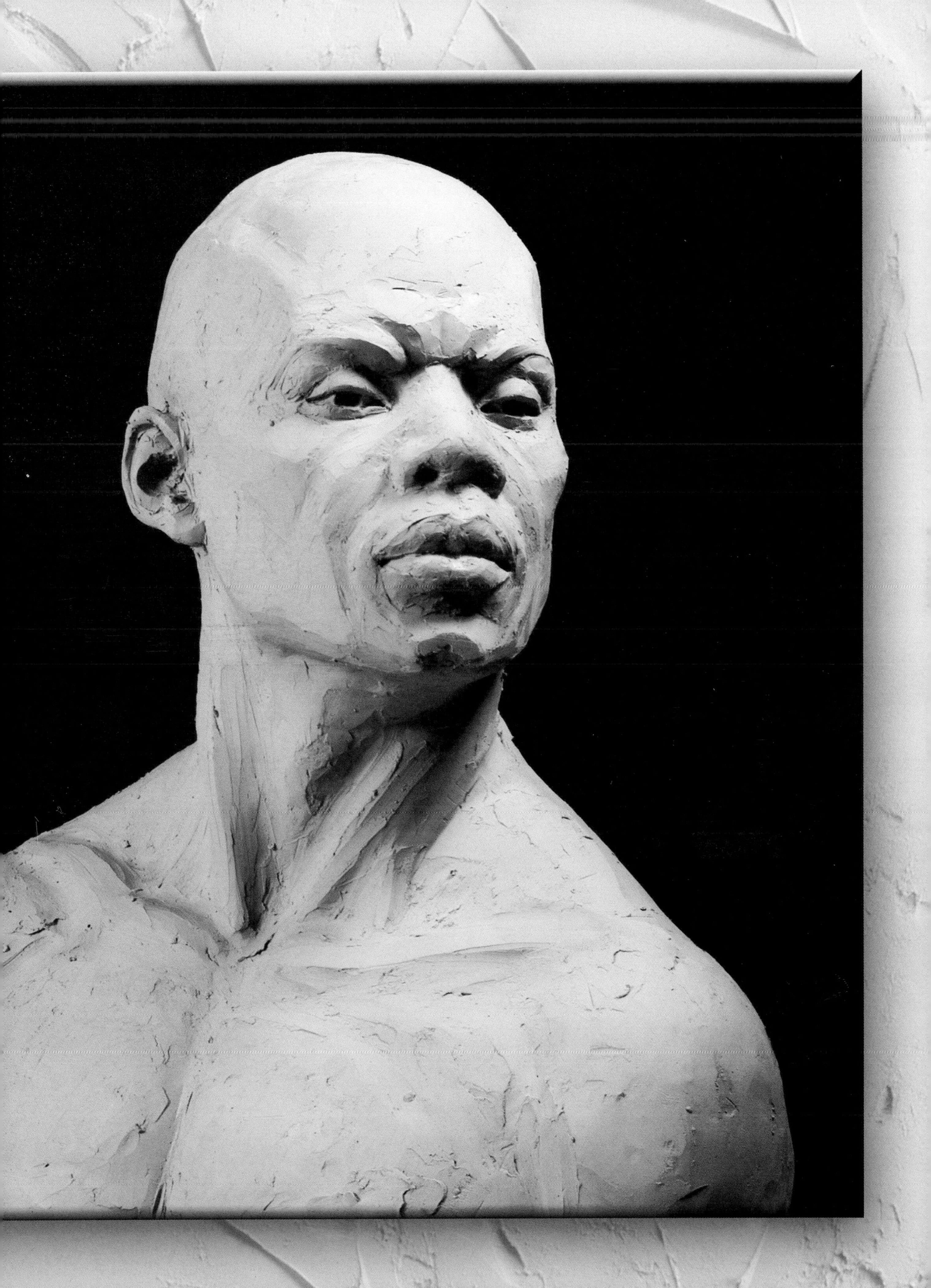

## Understanding Planes

The volumes of the human face can be simplified by dividing them into a number of curvilinear planes comprising each facial feature. The previous demonstrations on modeling the nose and ear show that every volume can be divided into planes and that it is important to recognize, analyze and then develop these planes. When the planes are developed, they form lines and ridges that define their shapes. These shapes help to better define and control the symmetry of the sculpture (or lack thereof) by comparing their similarities from one side of the face to the other. An experienced sculptor can easily render the likeness of a person with only a few simple planes developed from the general bone structure and particular features. The photos shown here illustrate this concept.

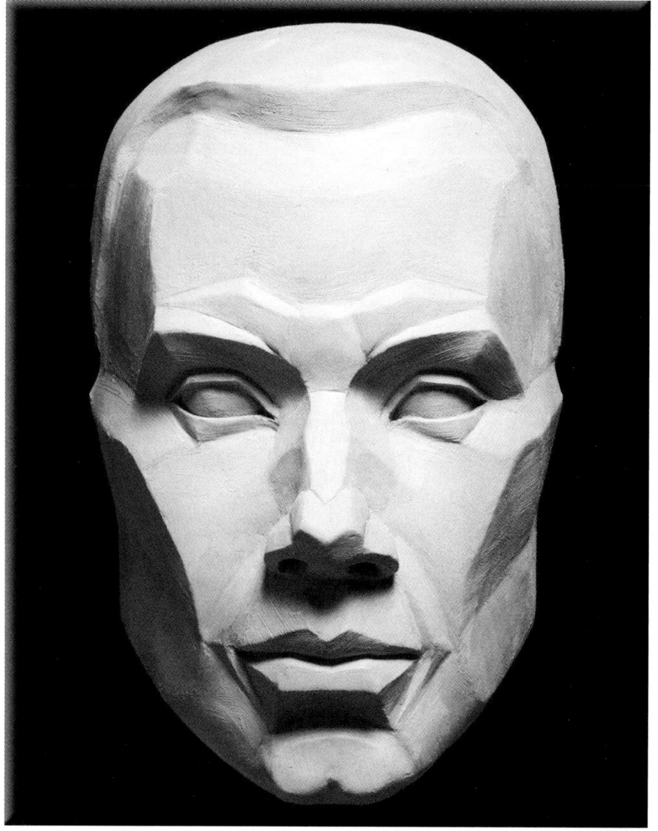

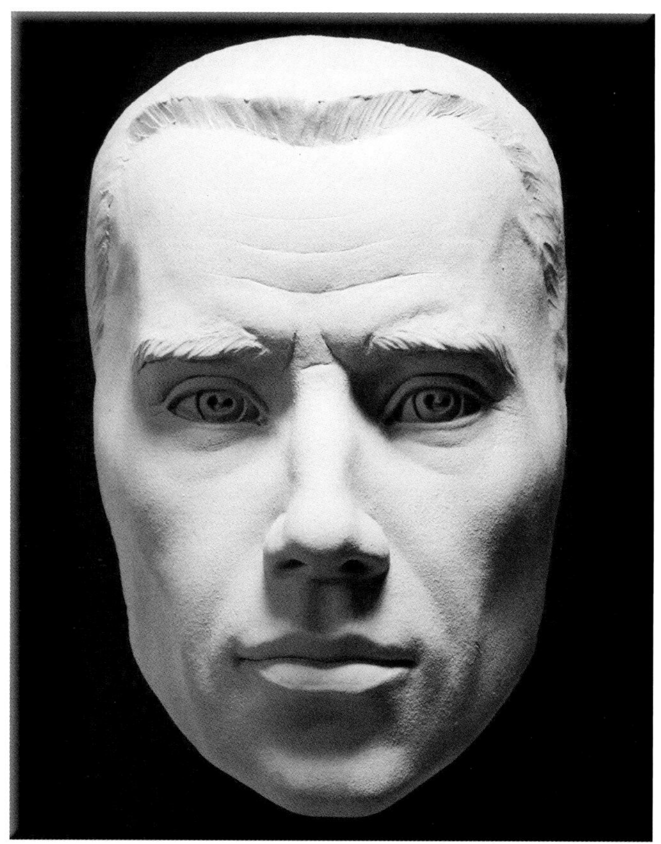

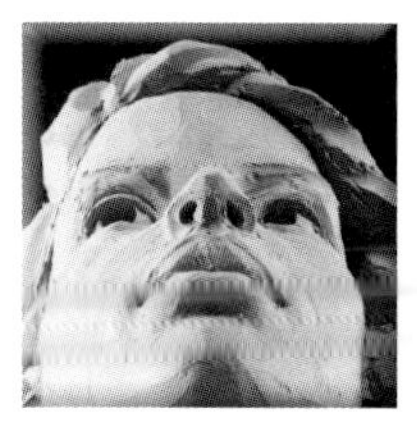

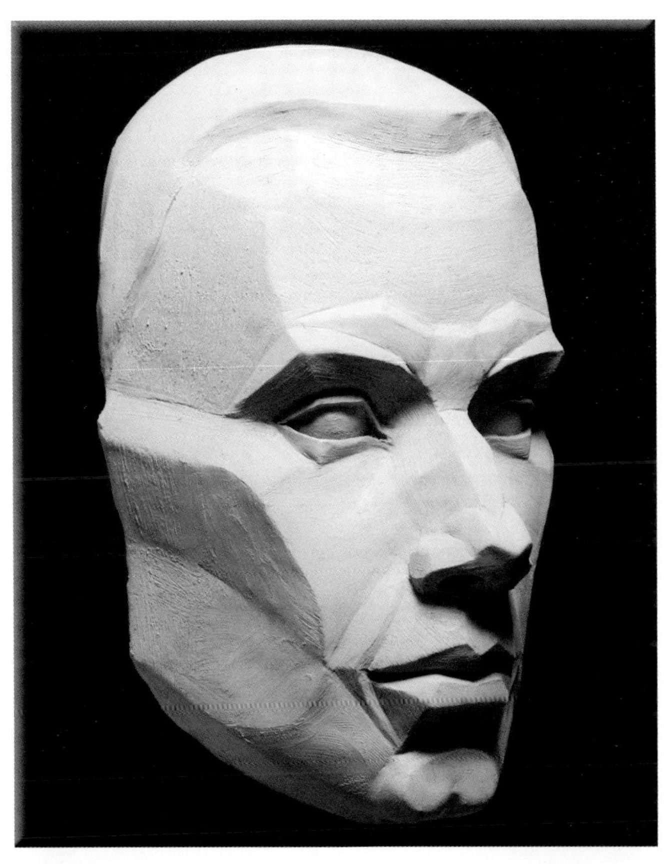

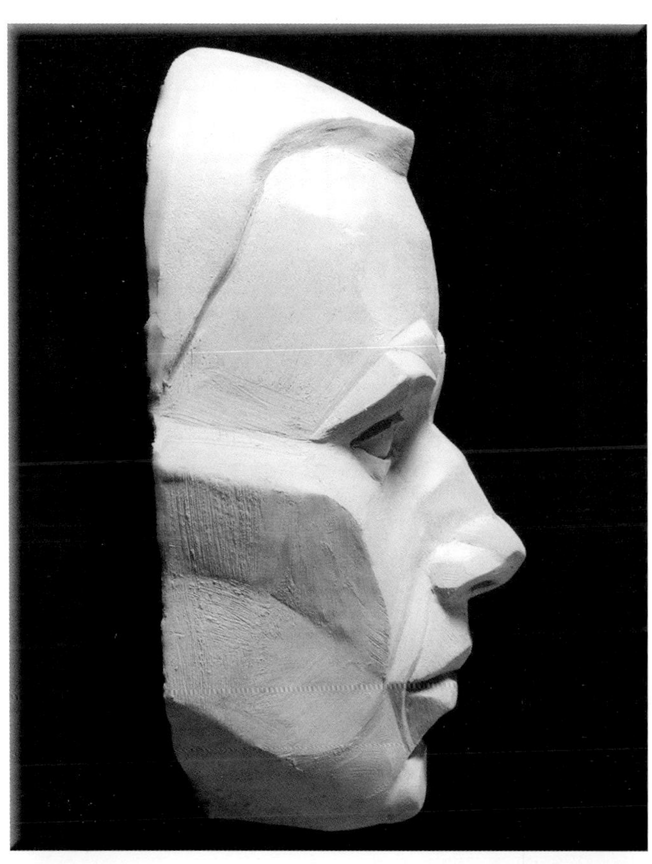

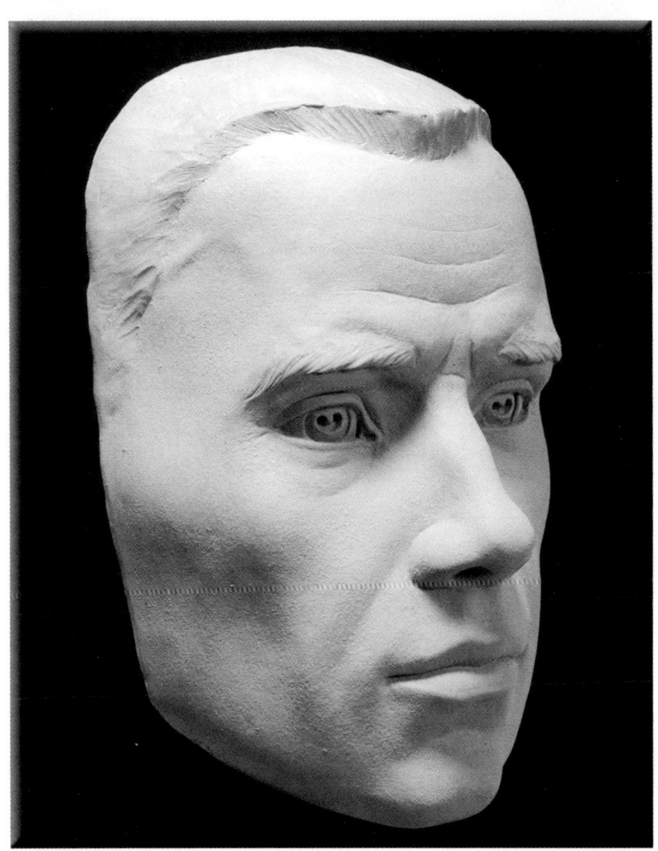

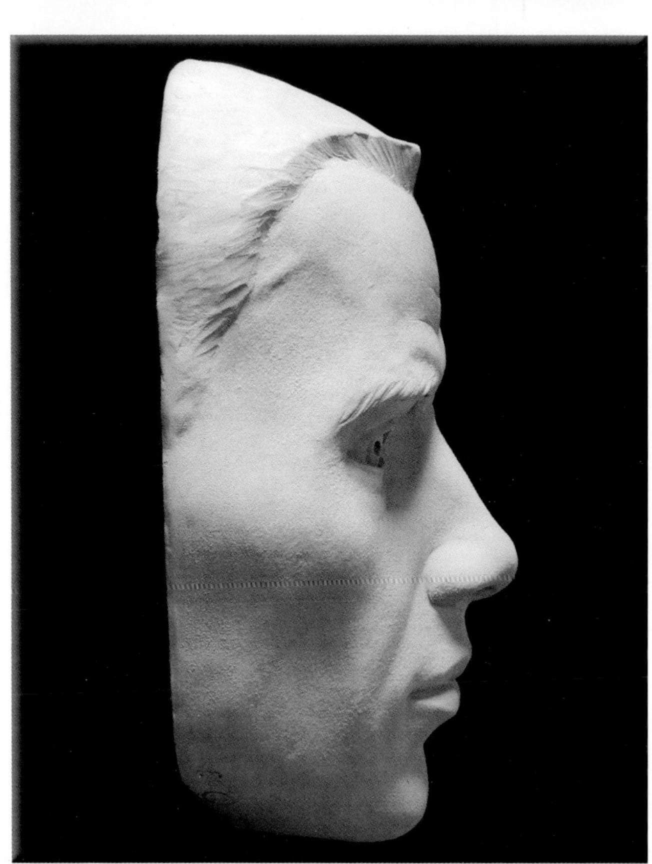

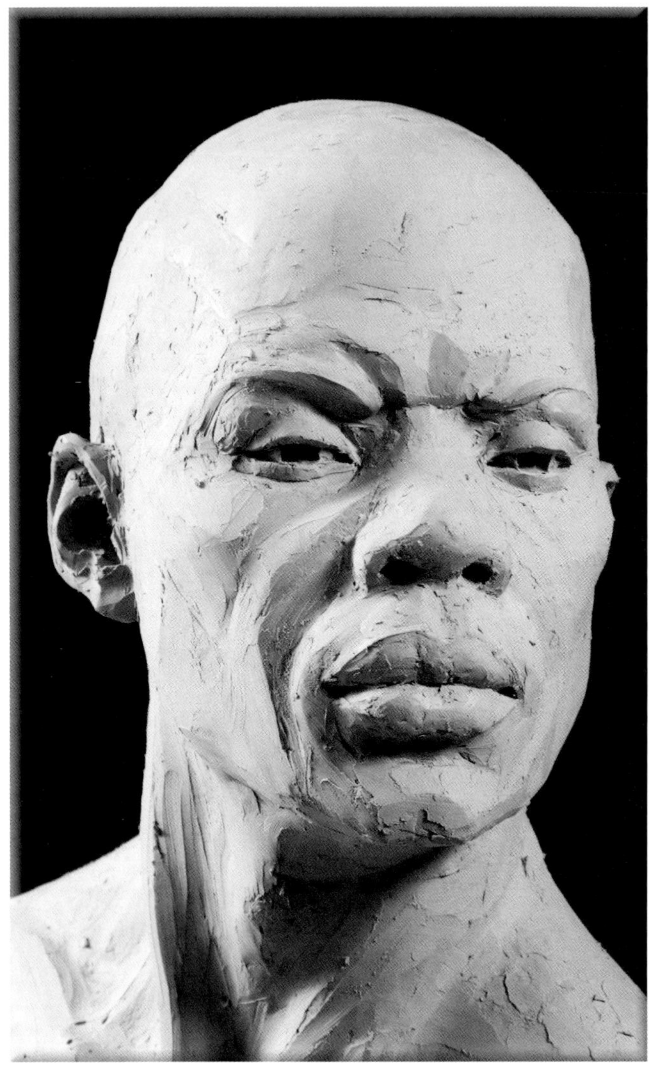

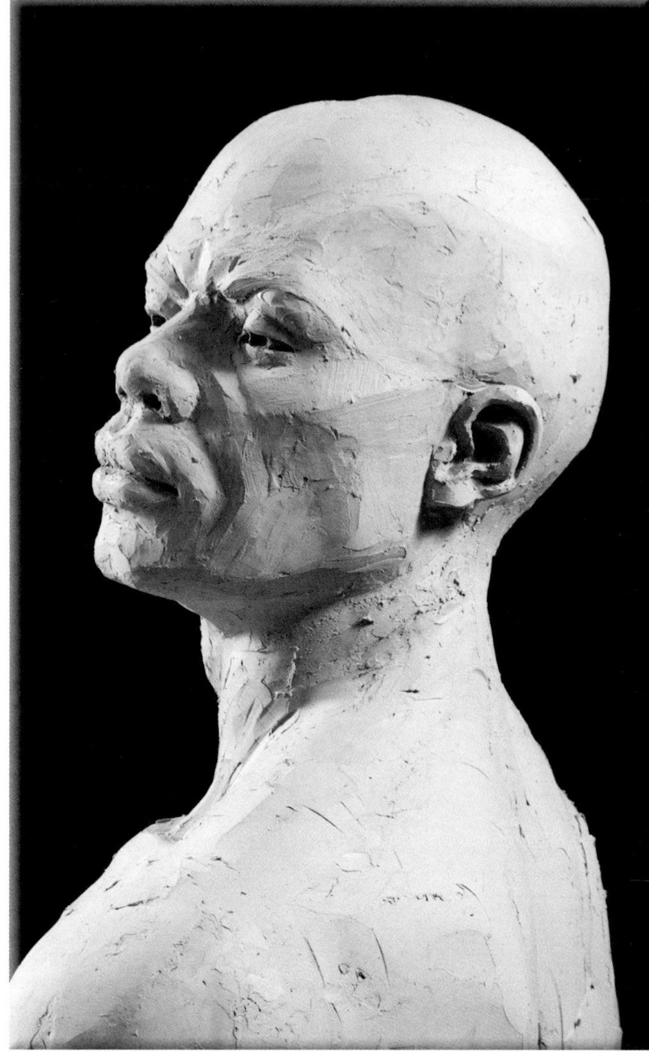

It is good practice to find even small planes (seen here in the chin, brow ridge, and neck, in addition to the general shape) before refining. Here the planes are shown more integrated into the sculpture, but they are still visible. The use of strong side lighting results in the creation of a great variety of shades and well-defined lines. If the work is lit from the front, these lines become more difficult to visualize.

The following exercise demonstrates the modeling of a portrait starting with well-defined planes. The base is constructed very rapidly and can be thought of as a three-dimensional sketch. This method has the advantage of forcing the student to focus mainly on the overall shape, rather than on particular features.

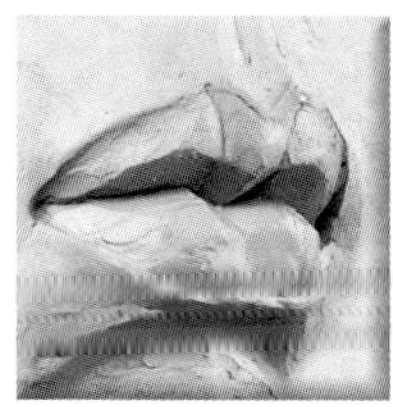

## Demonstration 9: Modeling Planes

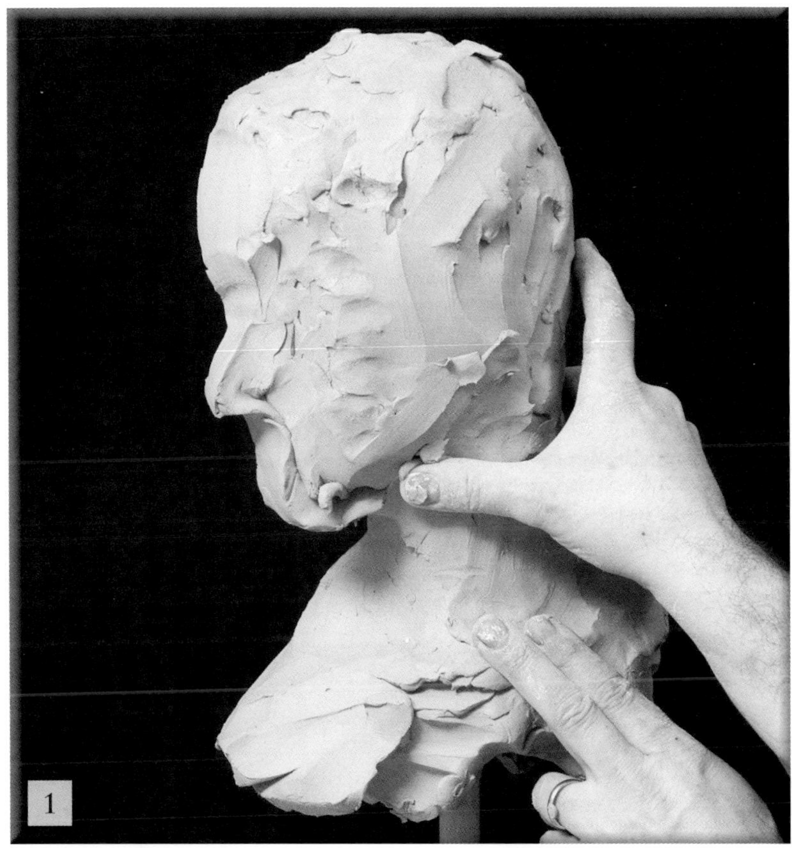


1. In this case, the attitude of the head and shoulders is decided from the beginning and the profile is defined as the base line.

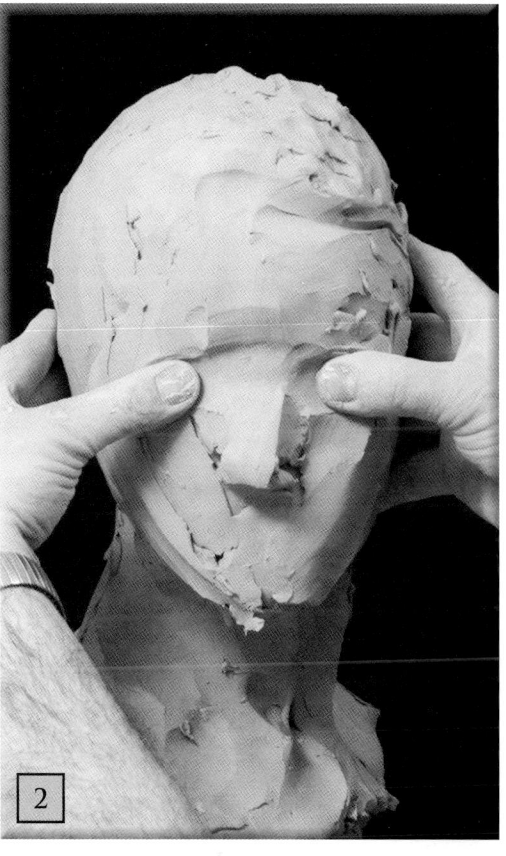


2. As soon as the profile is in place, the width of the face is decided and the orbital cavities are lightly indicated.

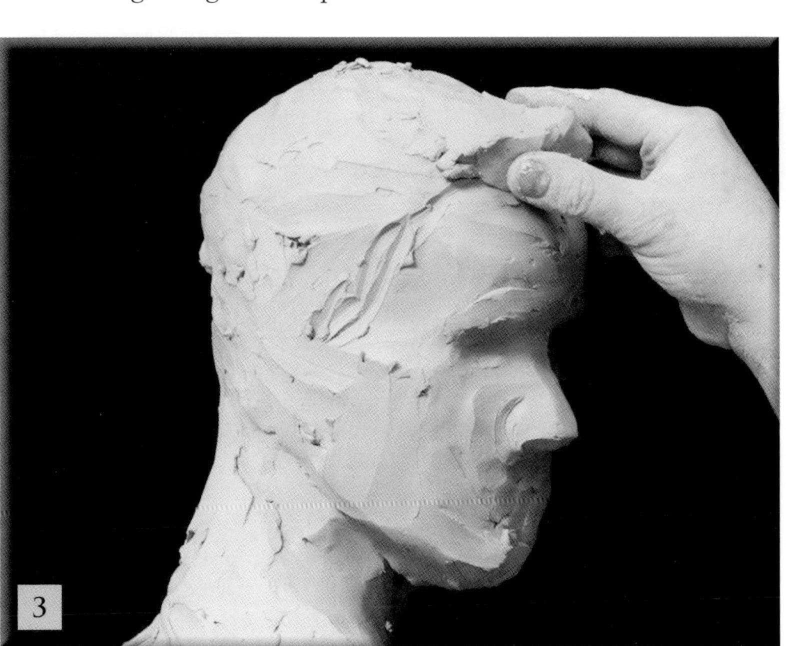


3. The hairline is traced around the face and the planes of the hair masses are built.

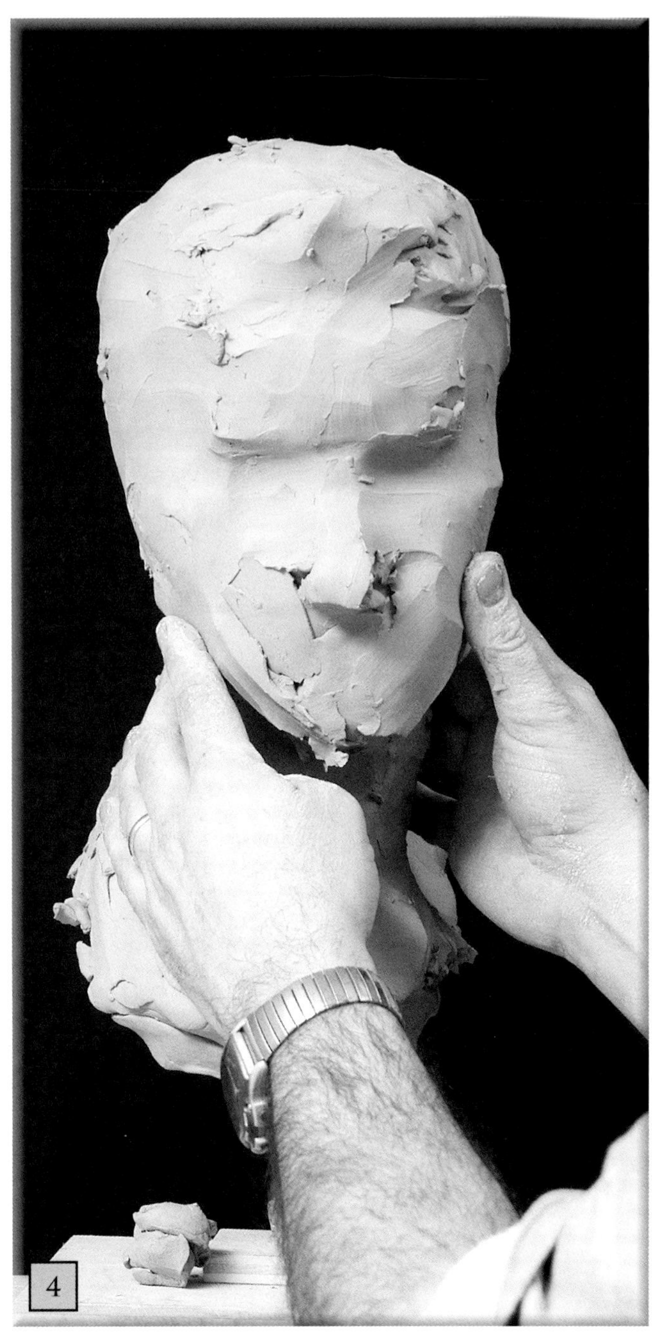


4. The volumes of the jaw are added.

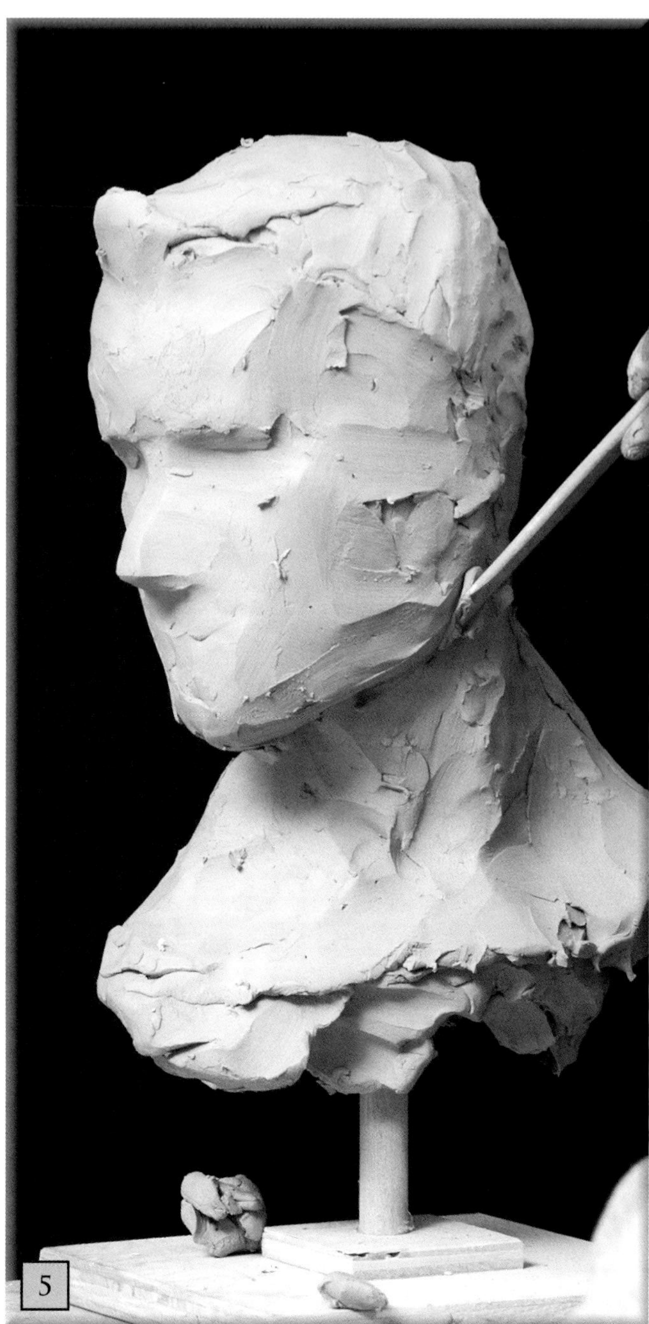


5. The bottom edges of the jaw are defined with a wooden tool.

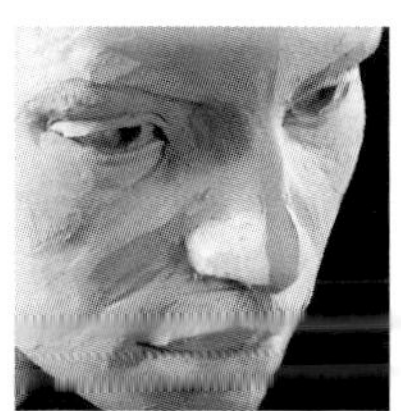

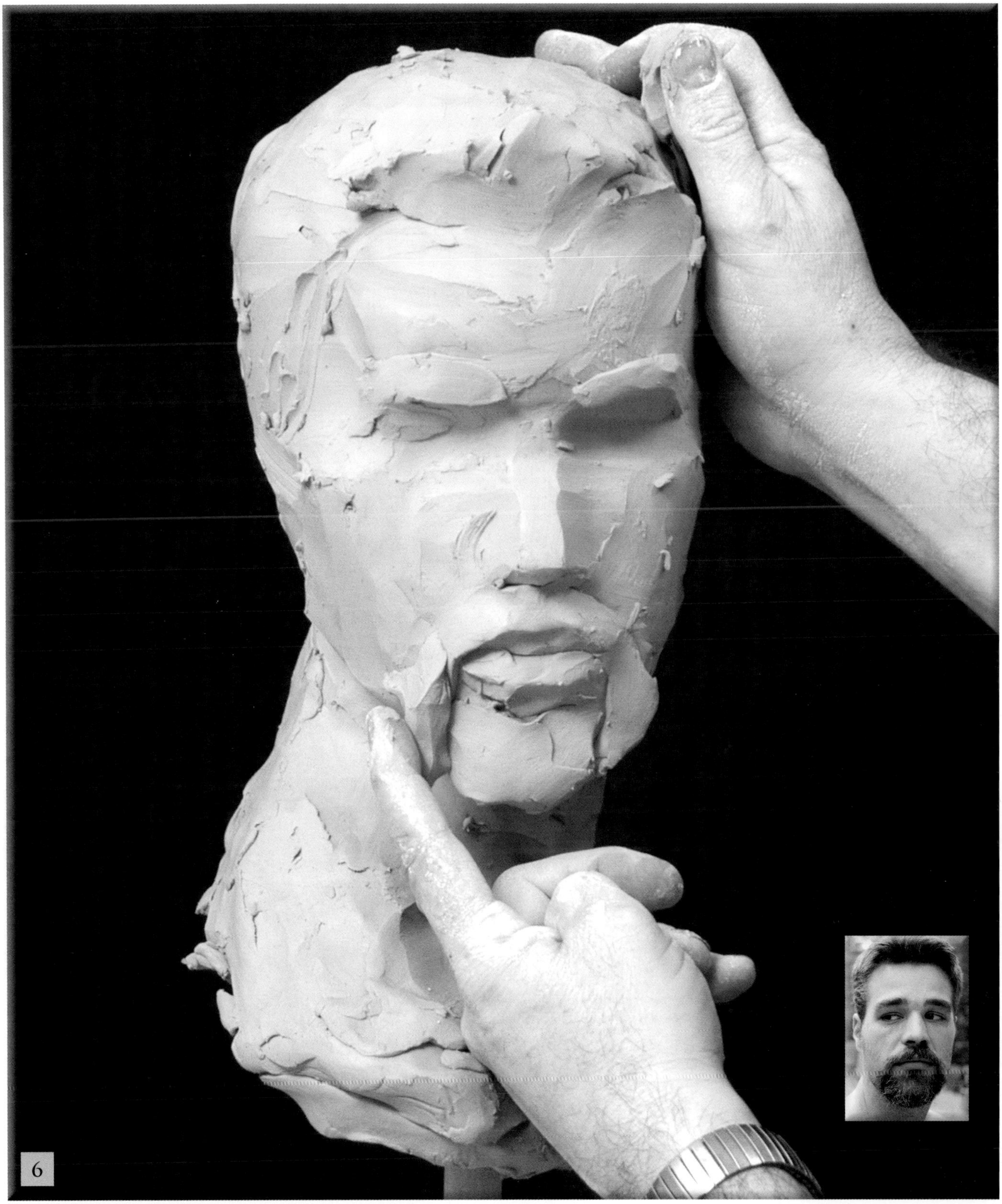

6

**6.** Here the volumes of the moustache and the beard are added, in addition to the eyebrows. At this point a basic likeness to the model should already be apparent.

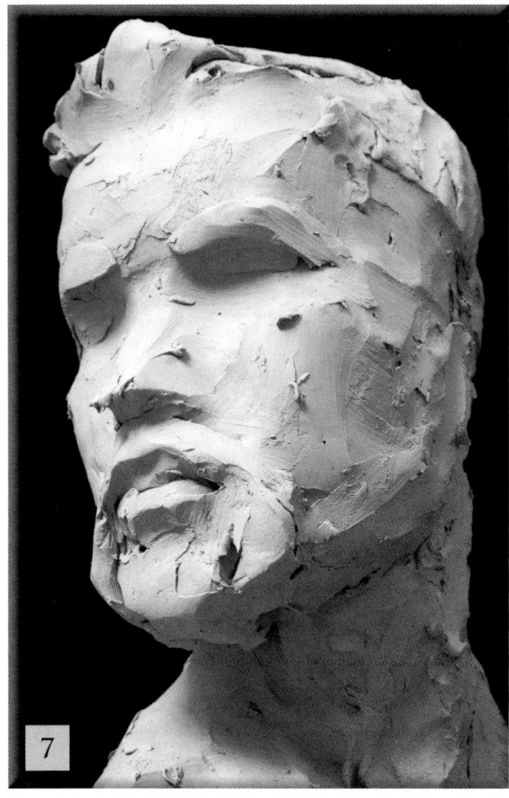


7. Until the main volumes are in place, the work is accomplished at a very fast pace. When working rapidly, a rhythm gets established. It feels somewhat like a dance. The artist applies some clay, then steps back to look at the model, applies some more and steps back again, and so on. Only a few measurements, such as height and width, are taken in order to prevent the breaking of this rhythm.

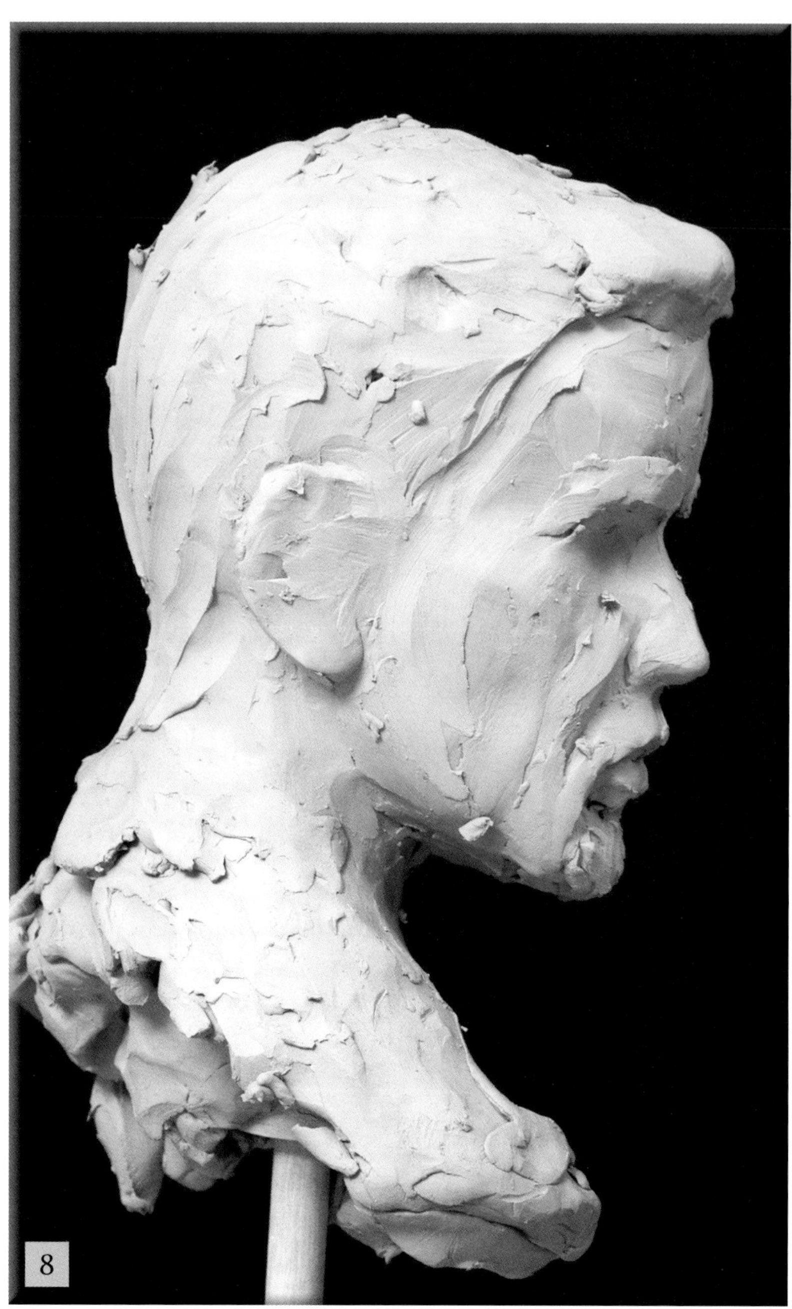


8. When the structure is established, the volumes are checked with calipers and adjusted if need be. Then the ears are positioned.

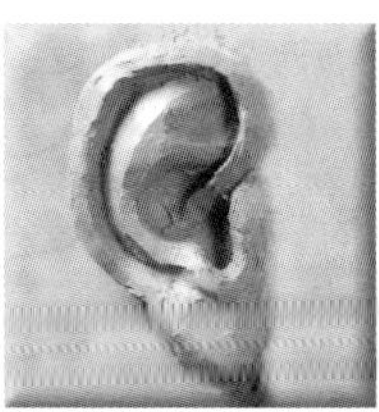

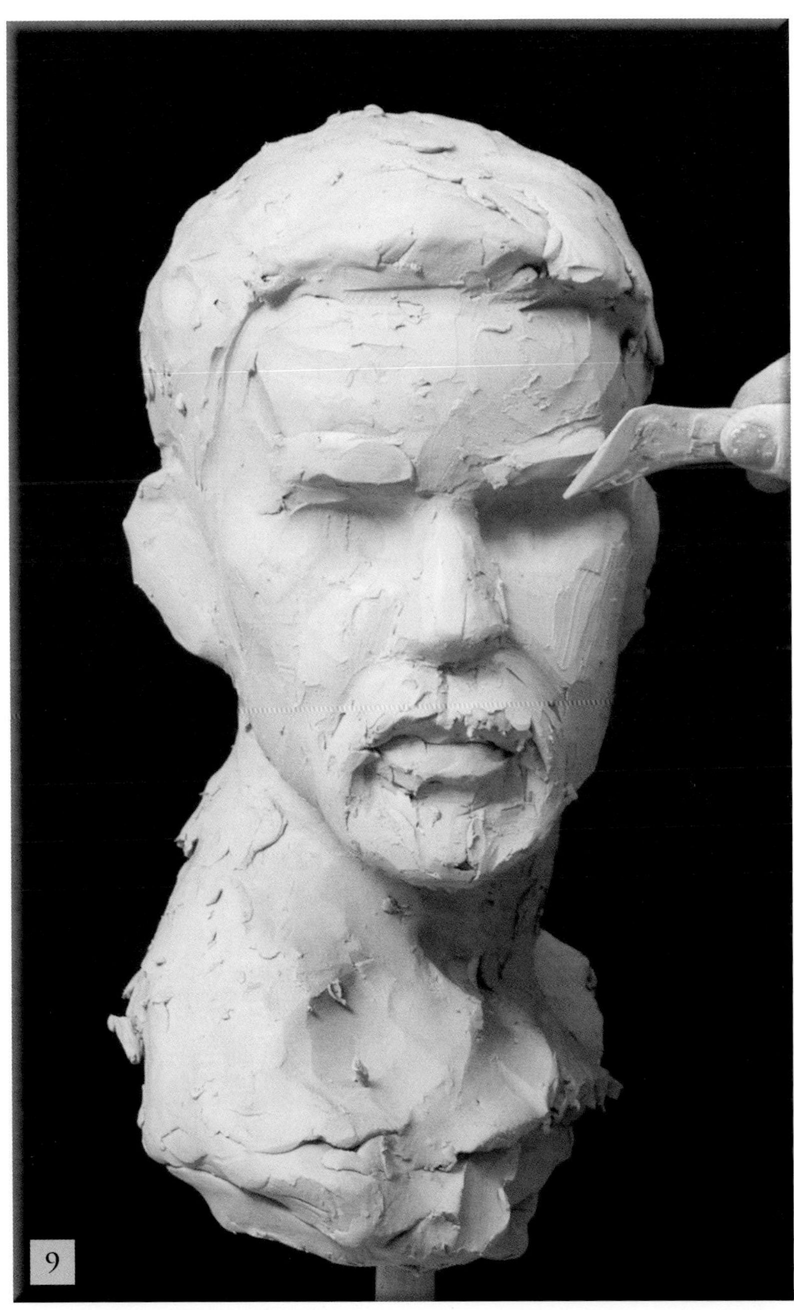


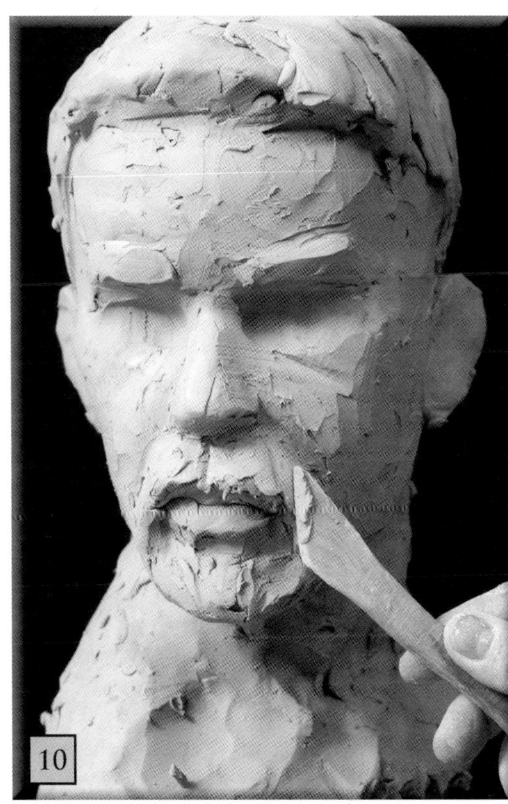


**10.** Any corrections to the general volumes should be done before proceeding.

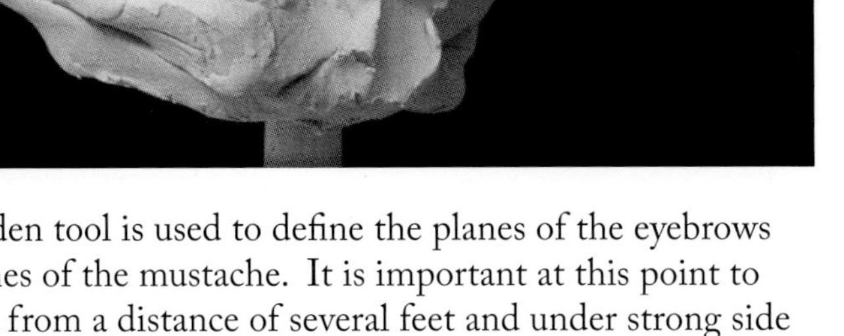

**9.** A flat wooden tool is used to define the planes of the eyebrows and the volumes of the mustache. It is important at this point to view the work from a distance of several feet and under strong side light.

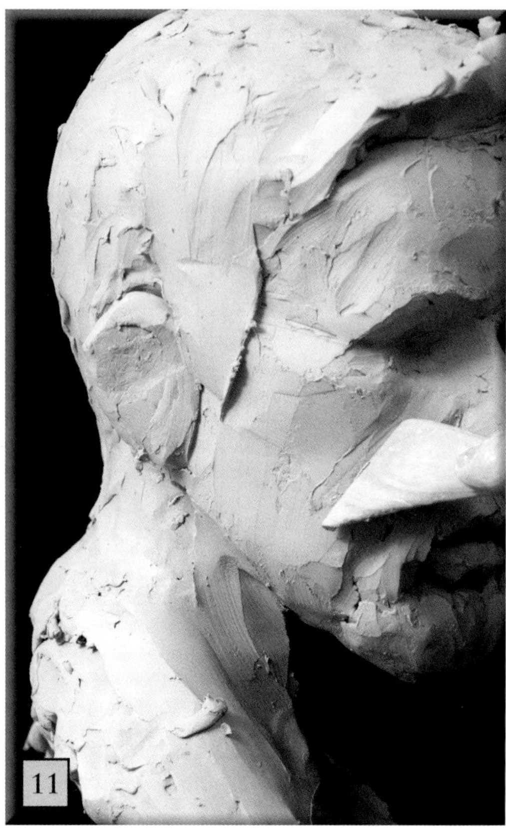


**11.** Further work is done on the face with flat wooden tools.

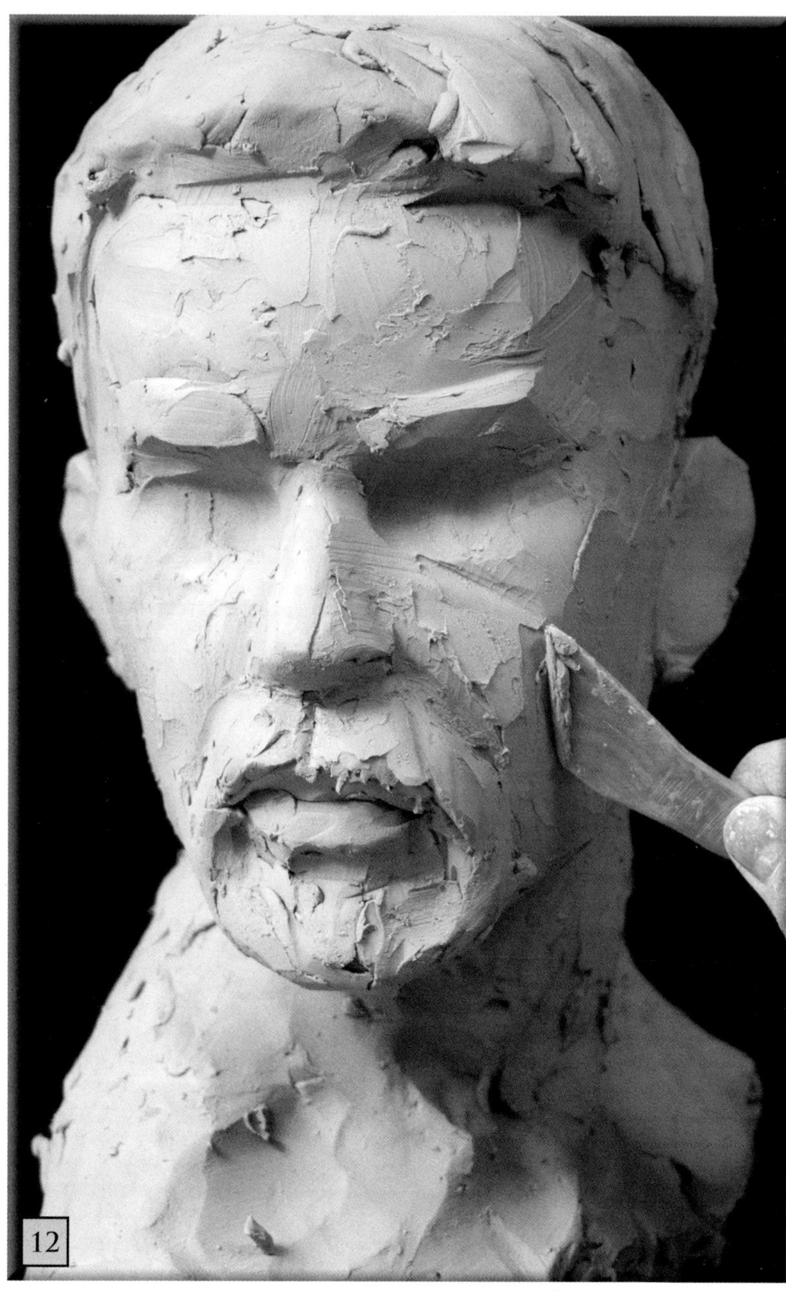


**12.** The clay is still very soft. To prevent any distortions of the main volumes, the planes are defined by light scraping motions.

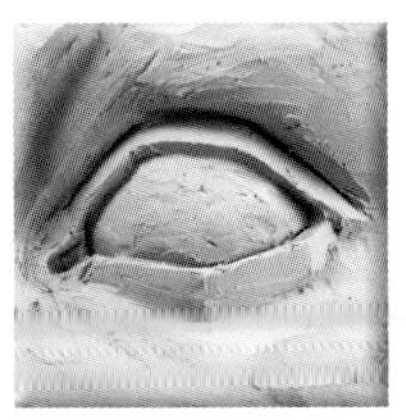

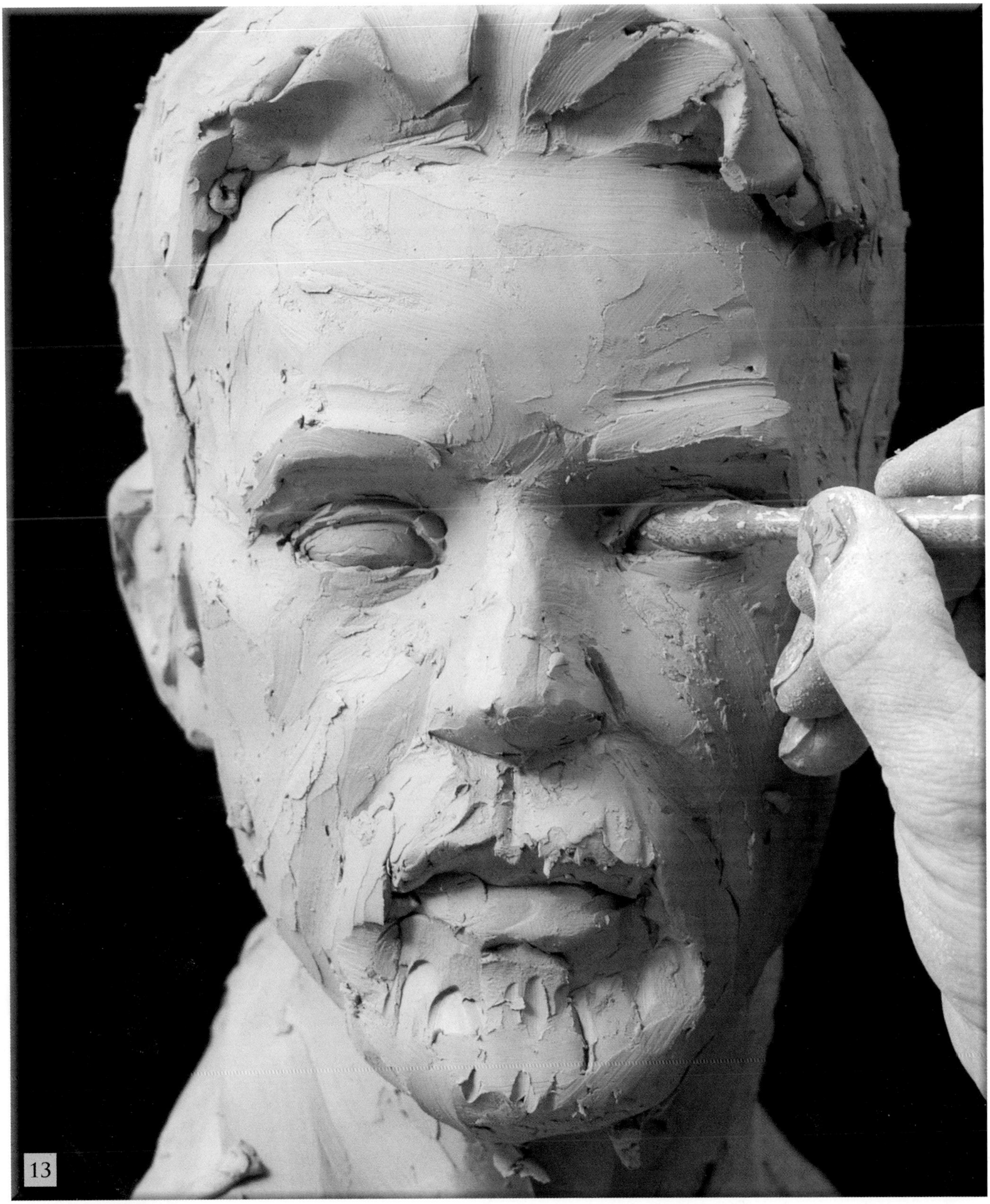

13

**13.** The eyes can also be brought into planes. The eyeball should be perfectly spherical, and the edges of the eyelids made of a series of strait lines. This is apparent in the corner photo in the upper right.

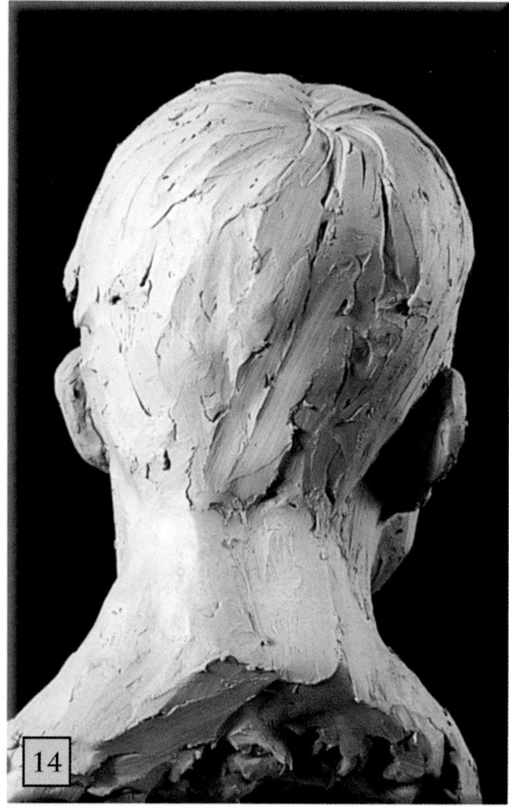



**14.** On the back of the neck, the trapezius muscles are developed in four distinctive planes.

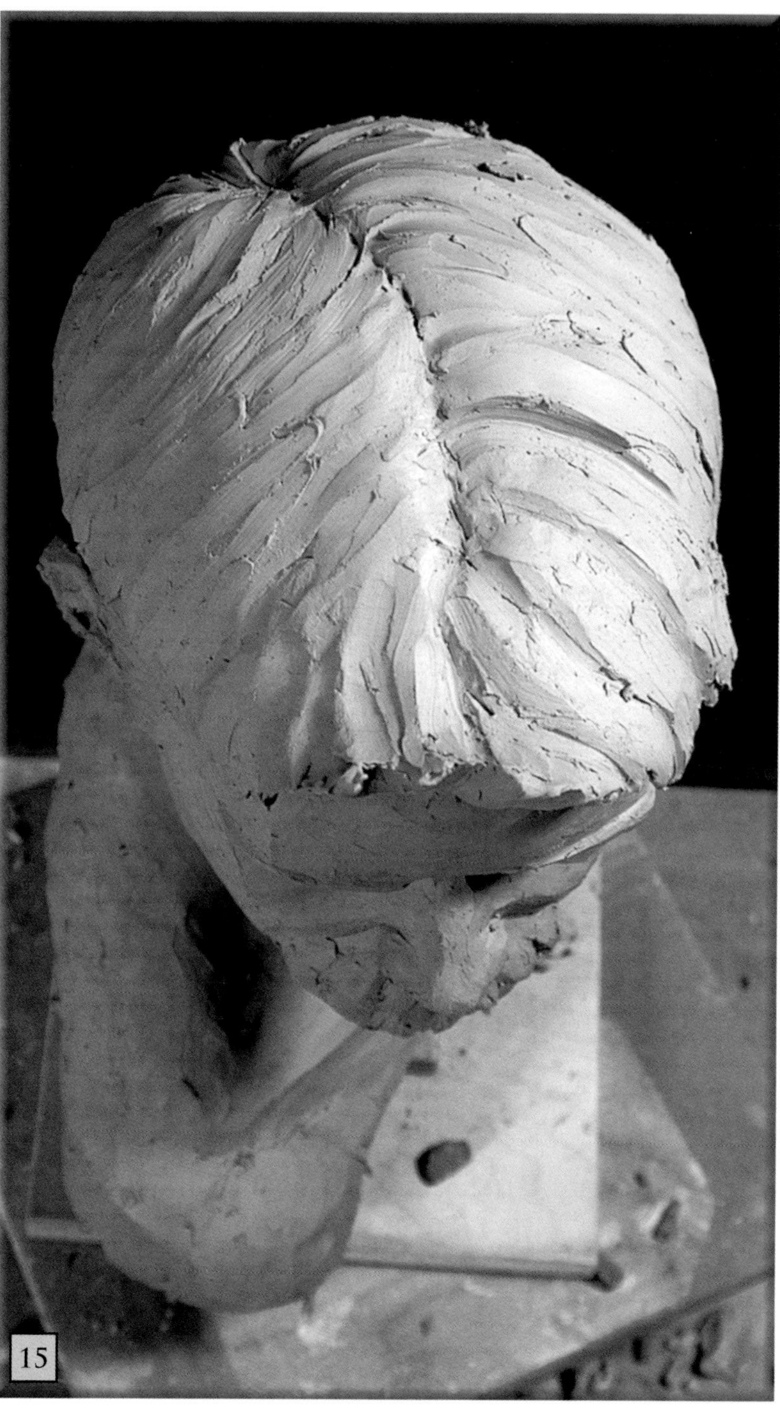



**15.** The planes of the hair are defined starting from the crown of the cranium. The work must be seen from above in order to control the symmetry of the hair mass.

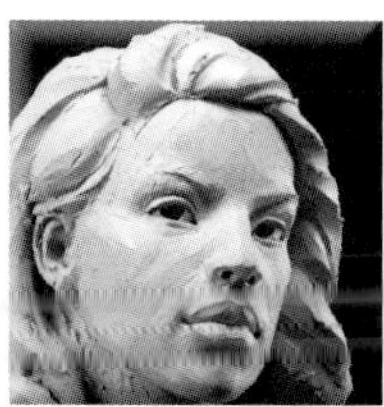

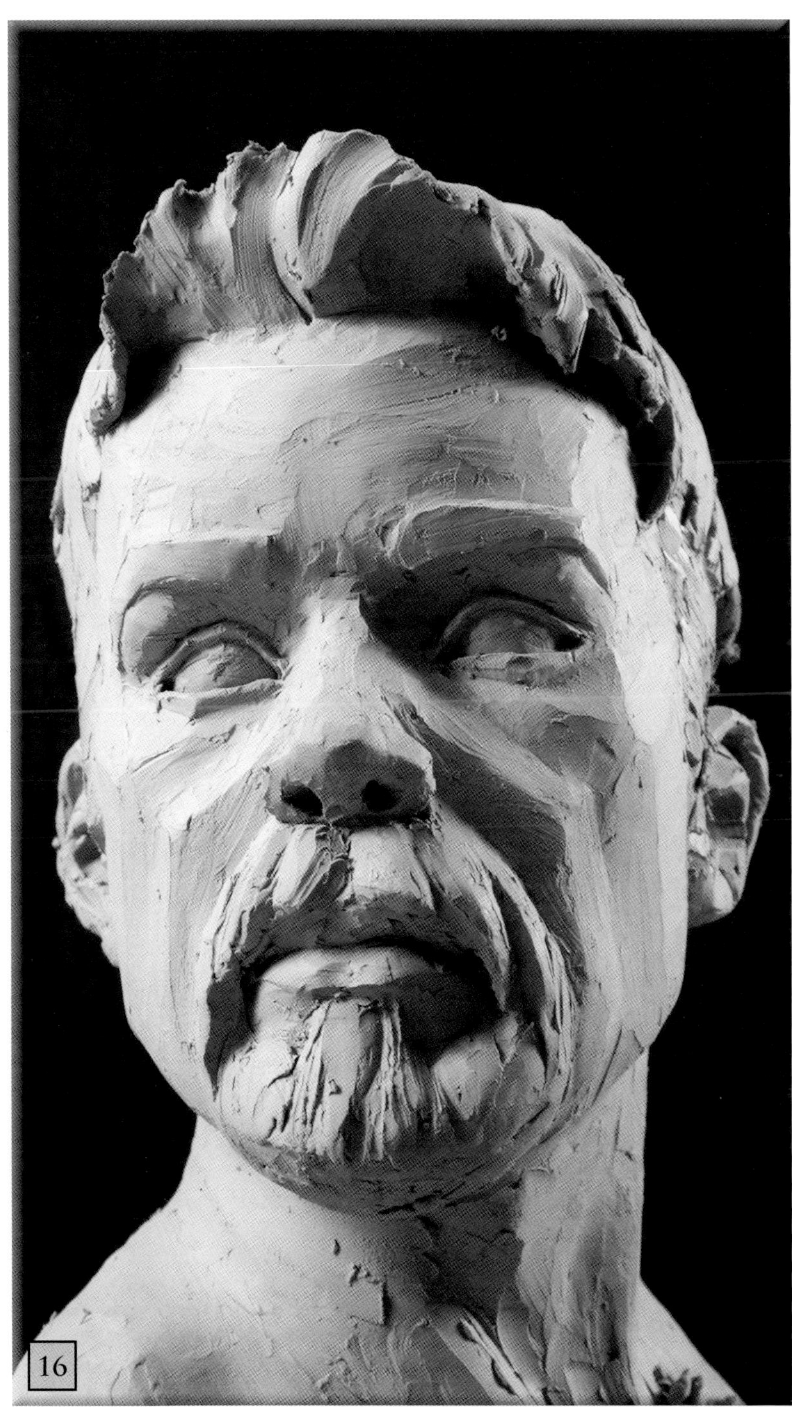

16. A full mustache is composed of three distinctive volumes on each side of the center line as shown here. The planes of the temples, forehead, cheeks, jaw and nose are clearly defined.

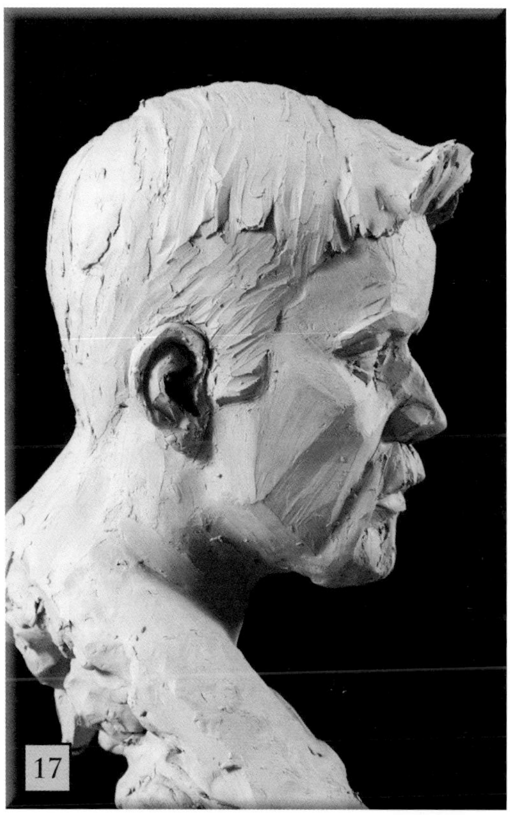

17. The bust, as well as the model, must be rotated slowly under strong side lighting in order to verify the accuracy of the planes. At this point the sculpture is ready for final smoothing.

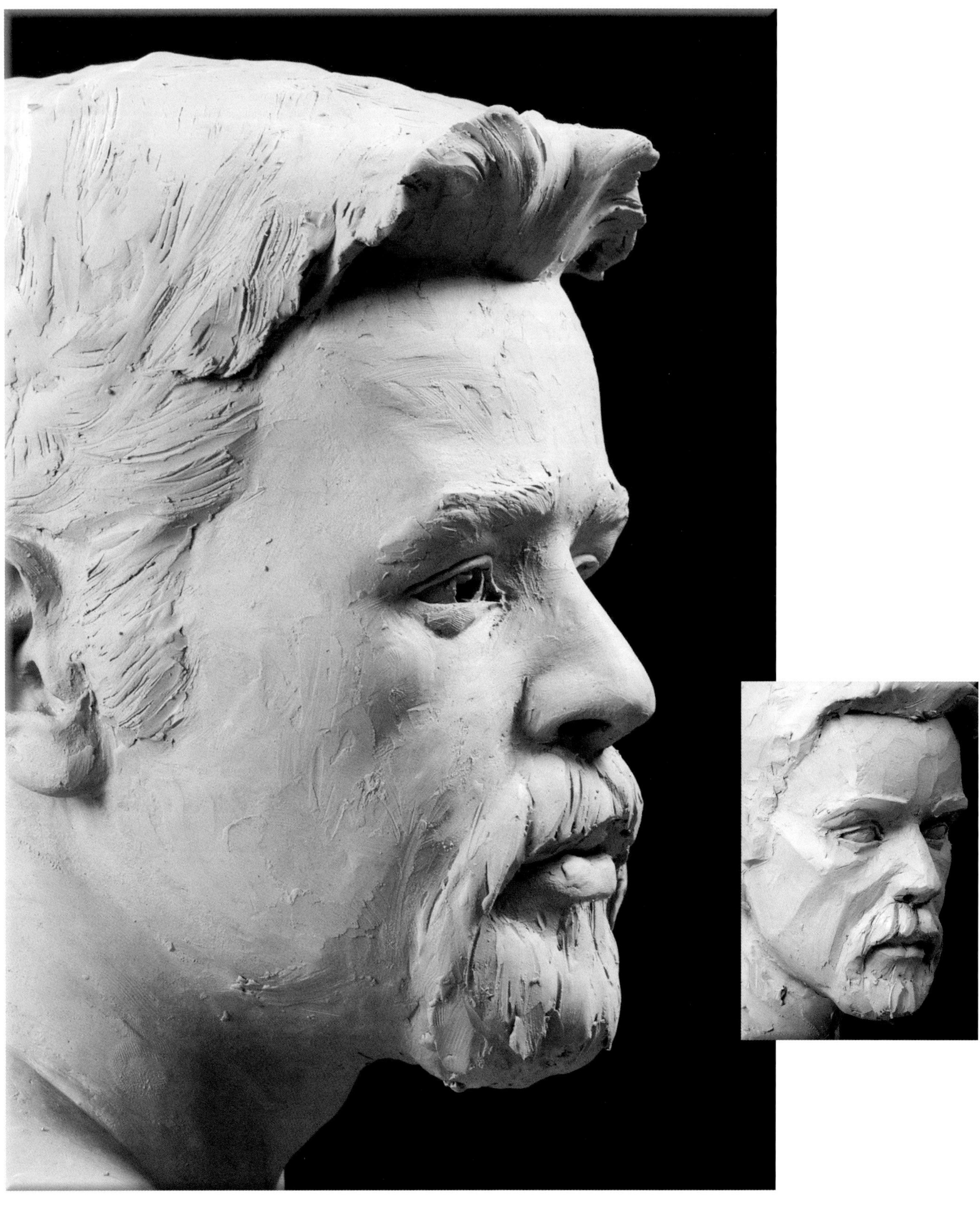

In this case, the edges of the planes are simply blended using only the tip of the fingers, leaving the surface texture somewhat rough.

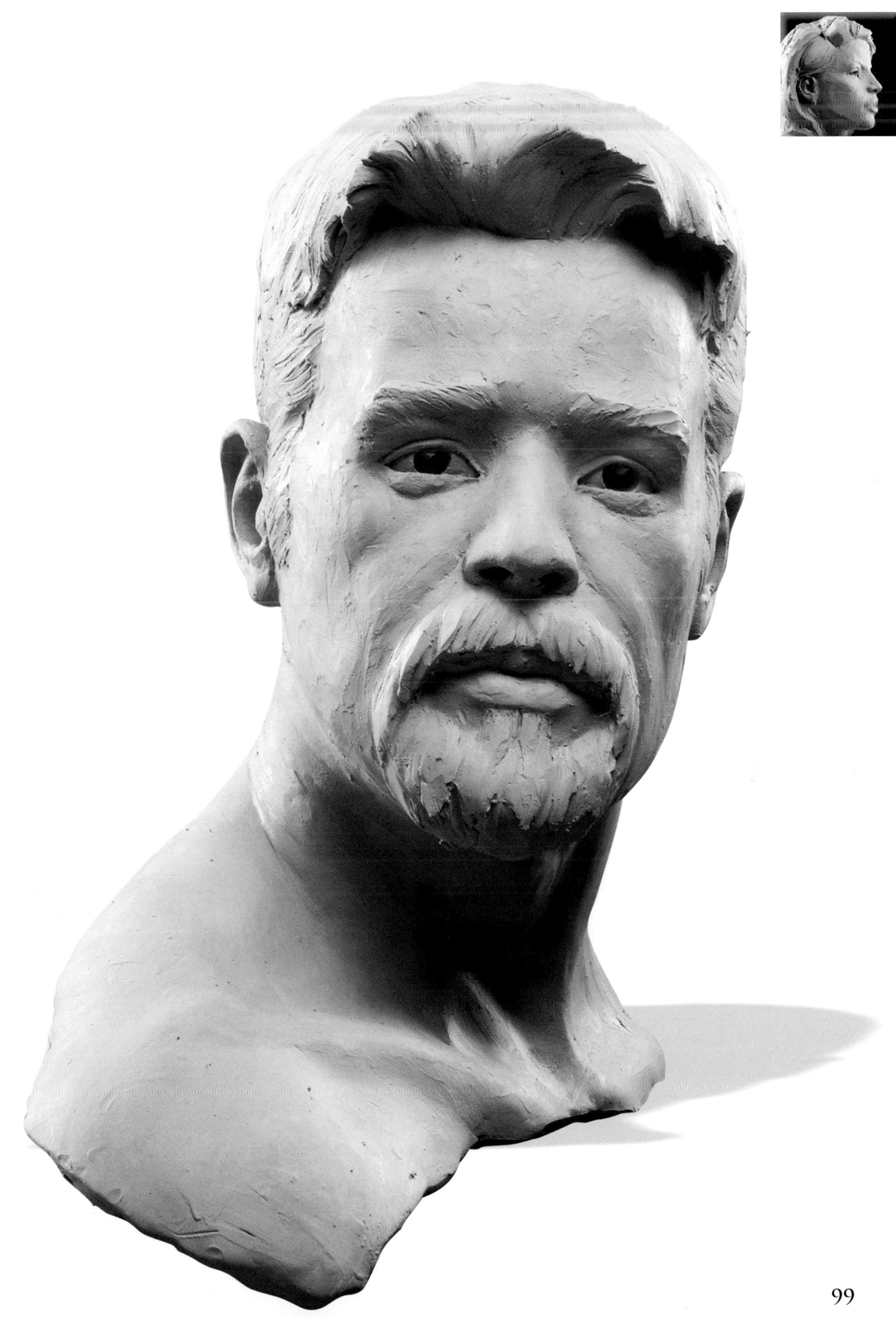

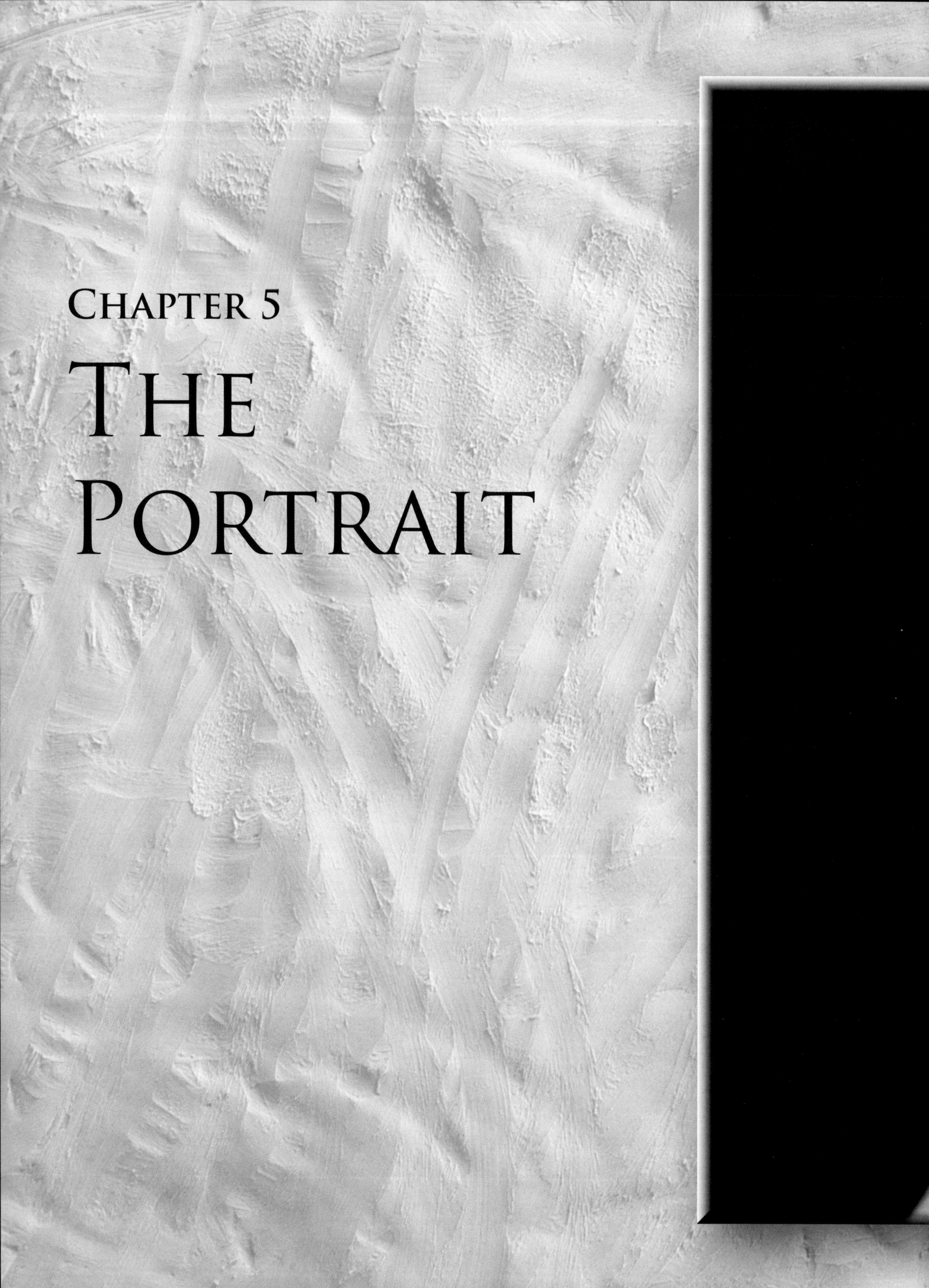

# Chapter 5
# The Portrait

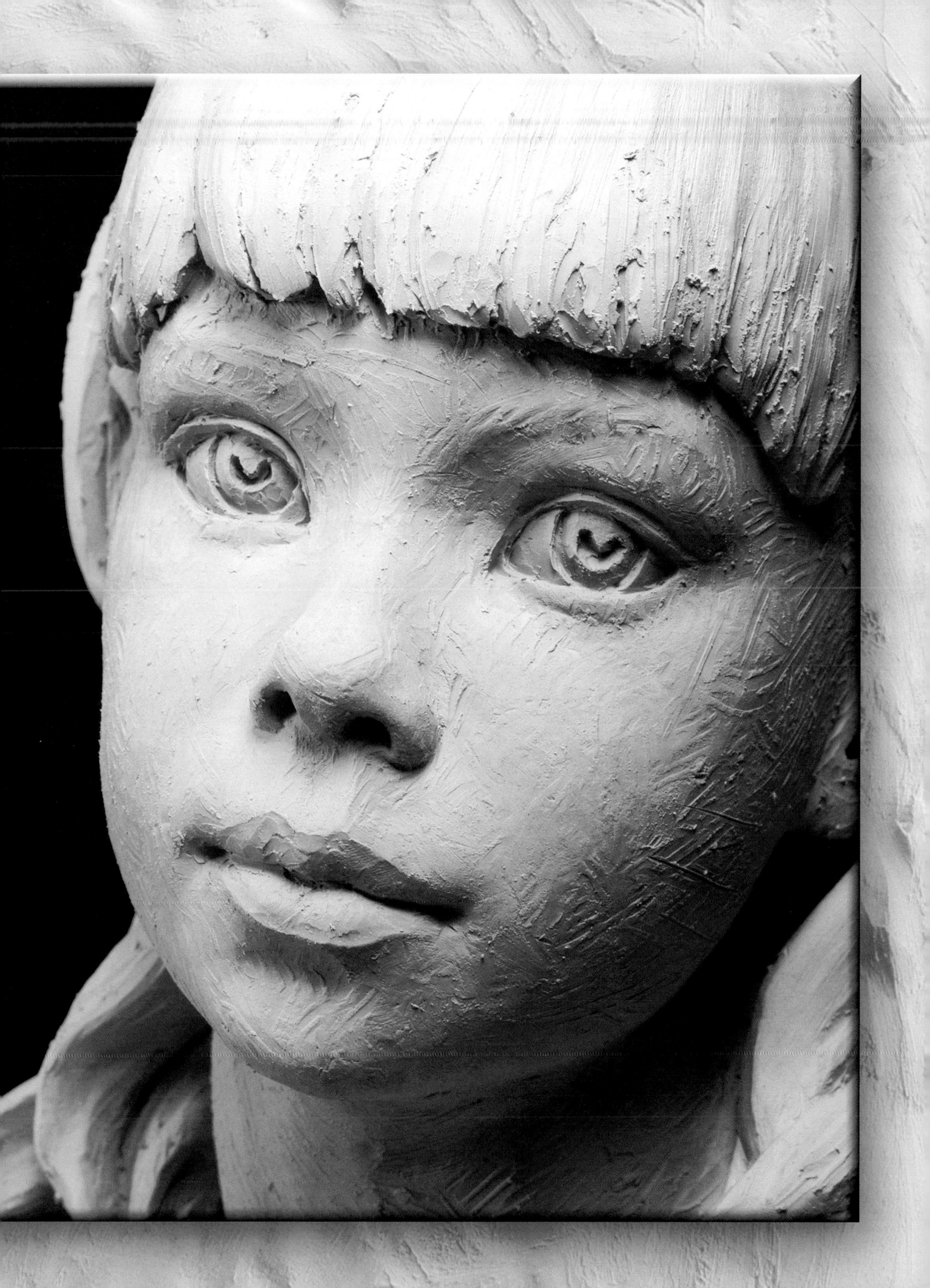

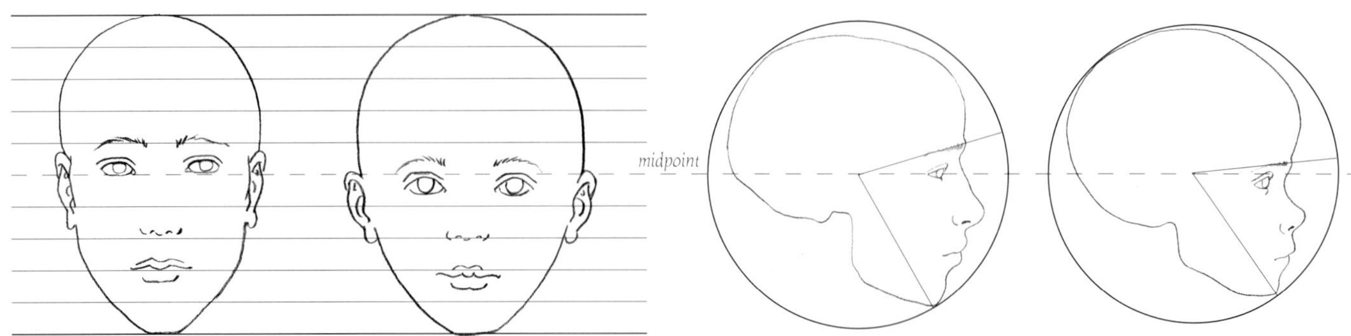


**Feature Placement Comparison**

**Facial & Cranial Mass Comparison**

The potential success of using the following approach for modeling a portrait depends on two factors that are more easily understood when considered separately. The first is the ability to model each feature independently of the rest of the face; the second is the understanding of the general volumes of the face when seen as planes.

In the following demonstration the planes are subtle due to the young age of the model, but they still need to be developed correctly. If the underlying structure has not been accurately constructed, even carefully rendered features by themselves will not result in an accurate portrait.

This unusual approach to figurative modeling enables the student to learn a methodical and systematic progression, rather than an empirical approach. Even though this technique may seem mechanical, it has proven to be an effective way to develop basic skills.

The placement of the features on a child's face differs from that of an adult mainly in that the eyes appear lower. Furthermore, a child's cranial mass is proportionally larger. The diagrams above can be used as a basic guide, keeping in mind that there can be variations from one model to another.

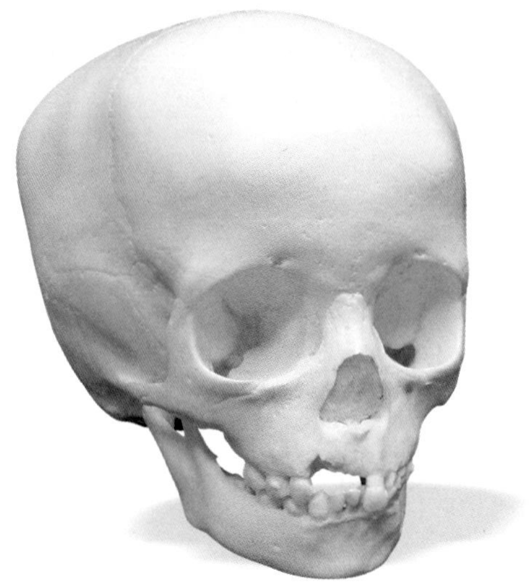

**Skull of a Five-year-old Child**

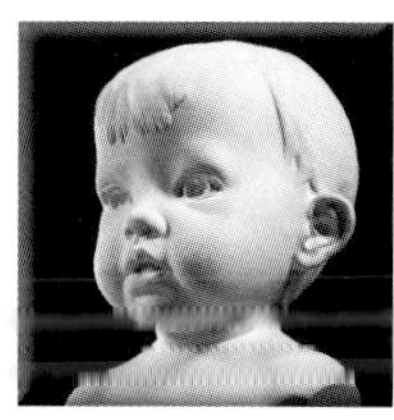

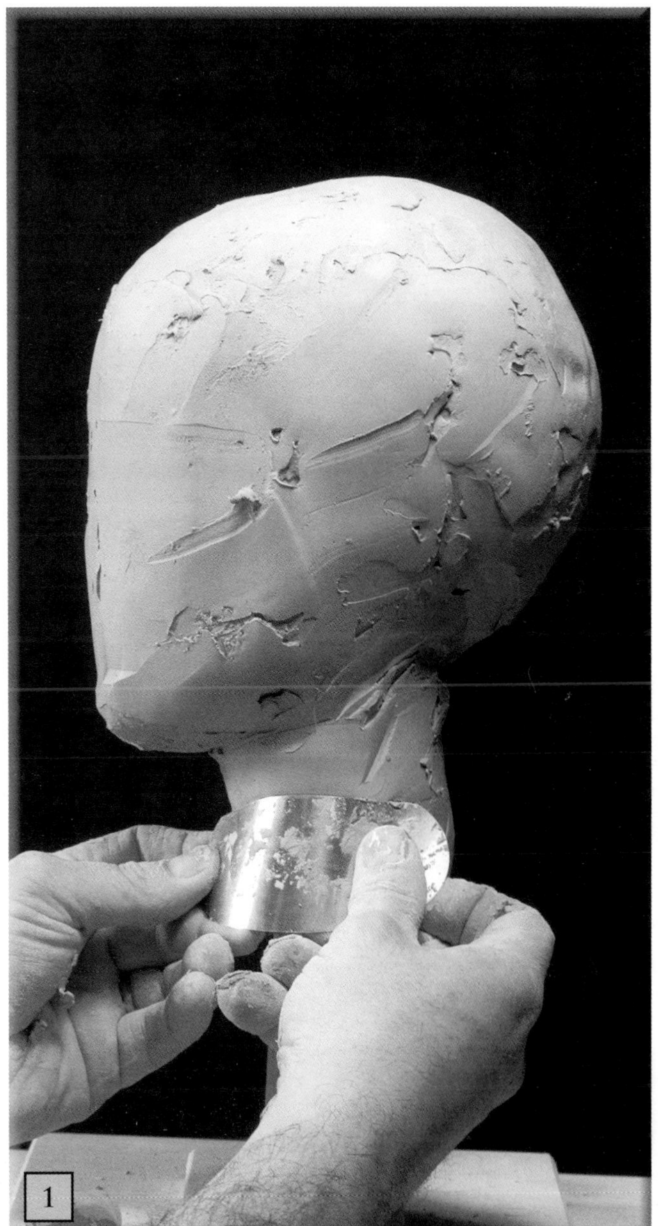

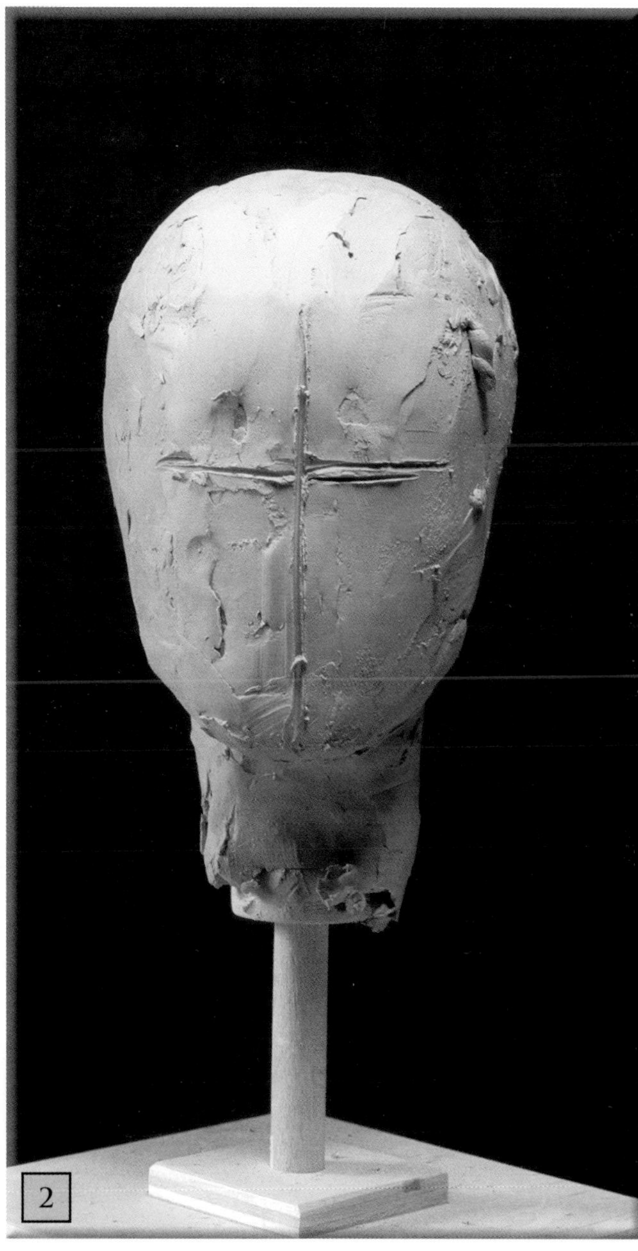

**1, 2.** While observing the model and following the steps for forming the skull, the volumes of the bone structure are built. The neck is added, resting on the adjustable ring of the armature, providing support to the mass of the head. This extra support is especially important when working with very soft clay.

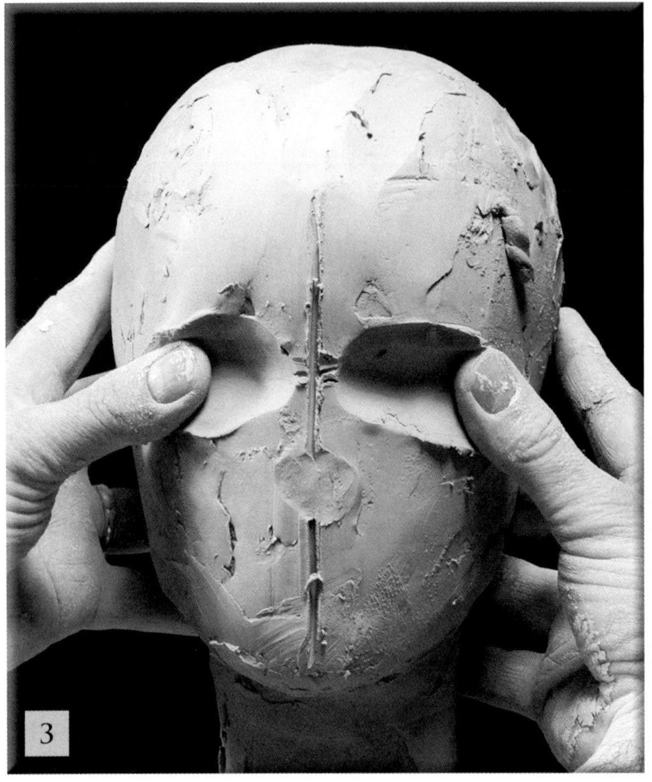


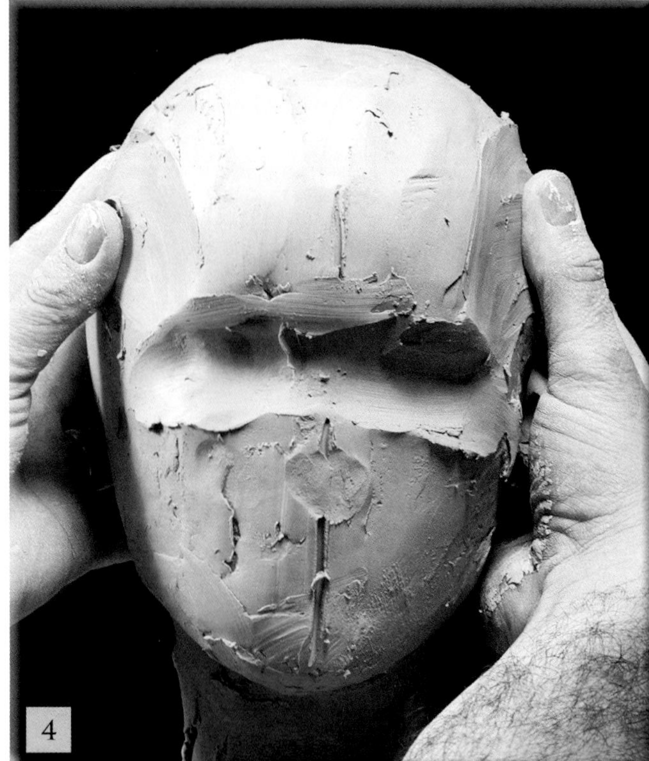


3. The location of the orbital cavity is one of the most important features in defining age. If placed too high, the portrait will invariably look too old. It is not necessary to dig the orbits as deep as they are in reality since they will need to be filled in for the construction of the eyeball. It is important however, to determine with precision the shape of the edges of the orbit formed by the superciliary arch, the zygomatic bone, and the nasal bone.

4. The temporal lines mark the transition between the frontal and temporal bones. These lines are defined by a change of plane visible in this picture.

5. Once established, the planes are blended together to form the general structure of the head. The nasal cavity and the barrel of the mouth are slightly indicated.

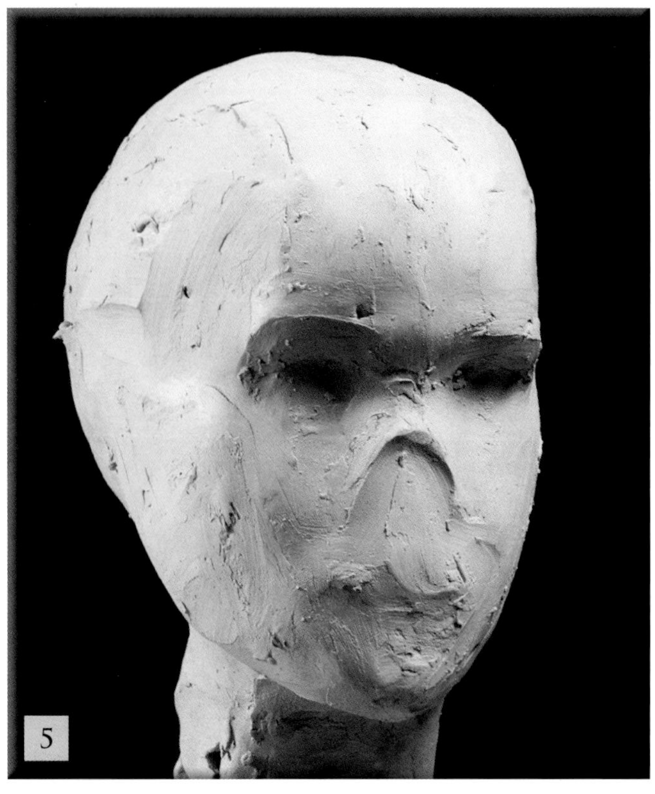

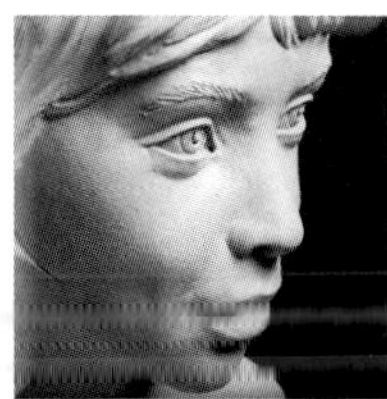

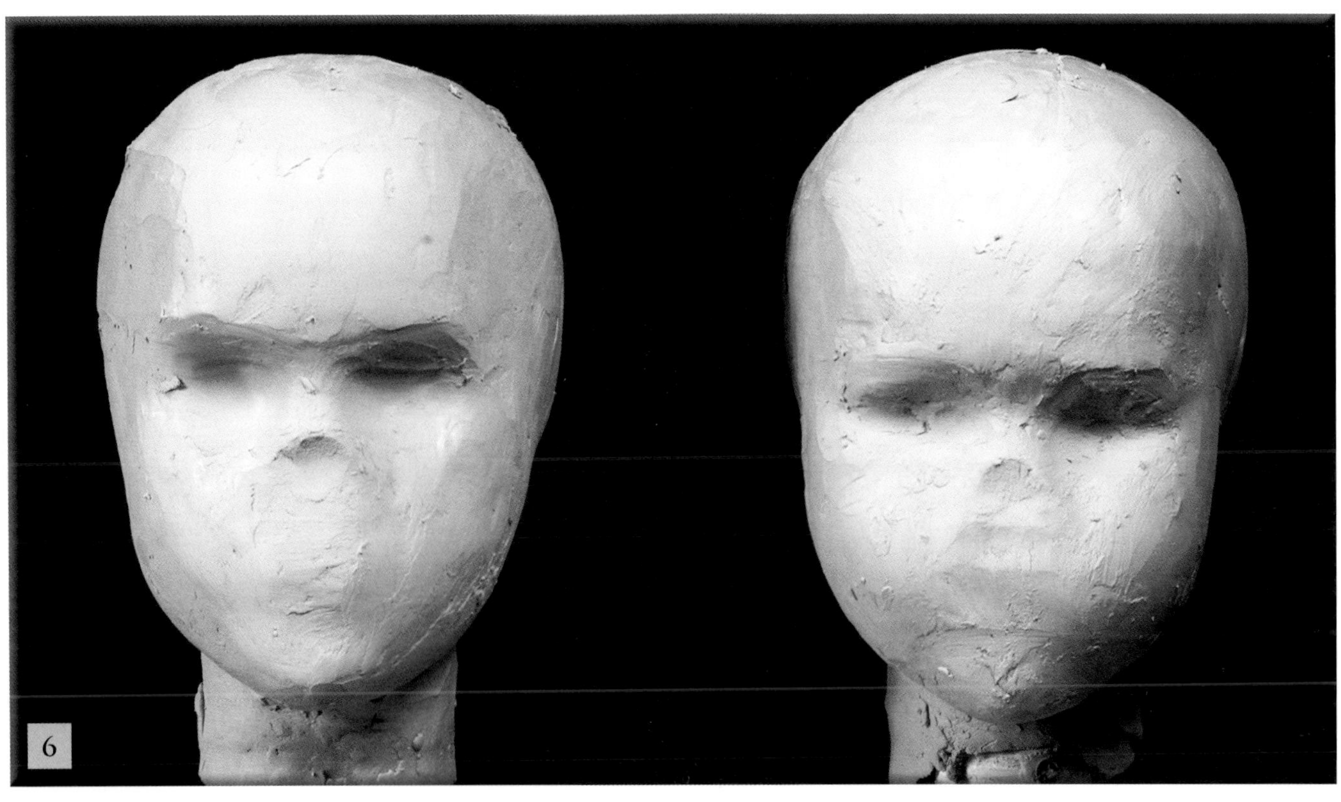

**6, 7.** These photos illustrate the differences in the planes between a six-year-old (on the left) and a three-year-old child (on the right).

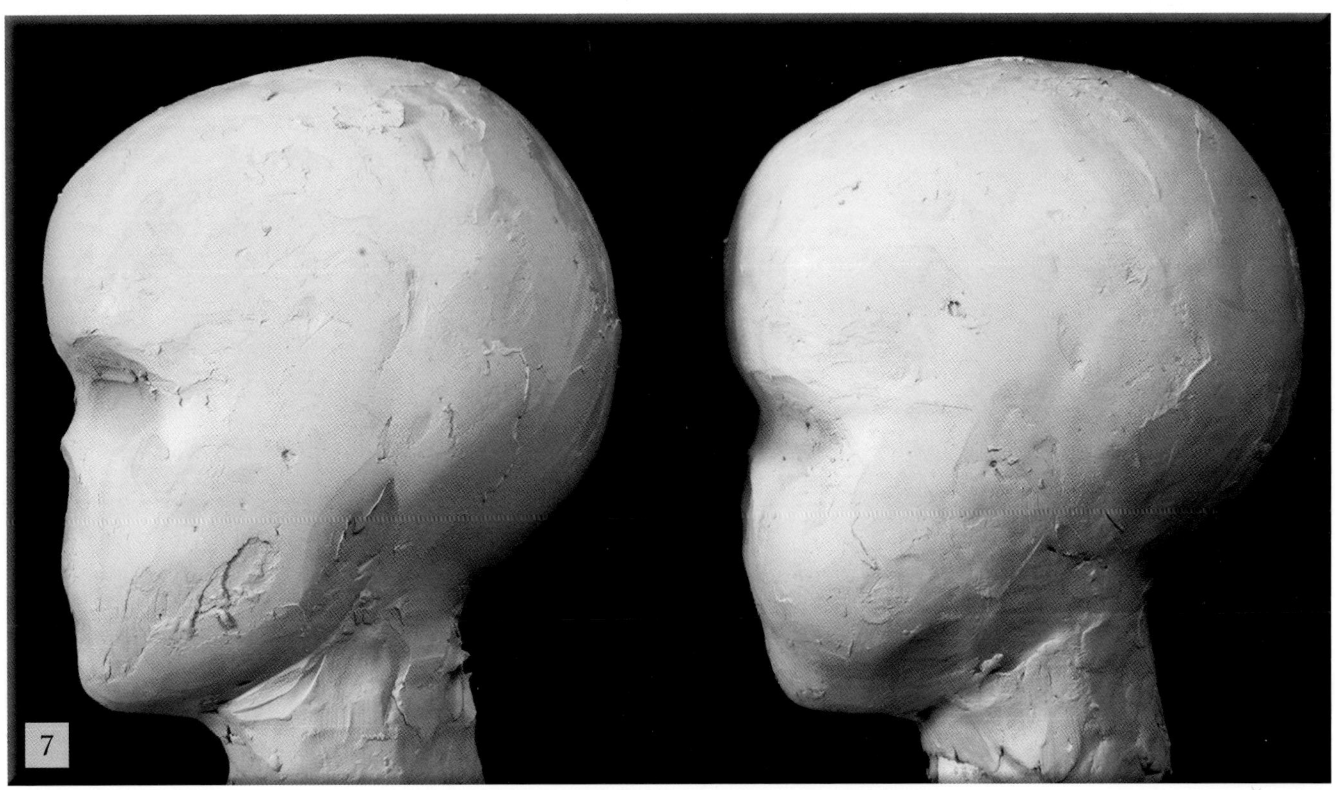

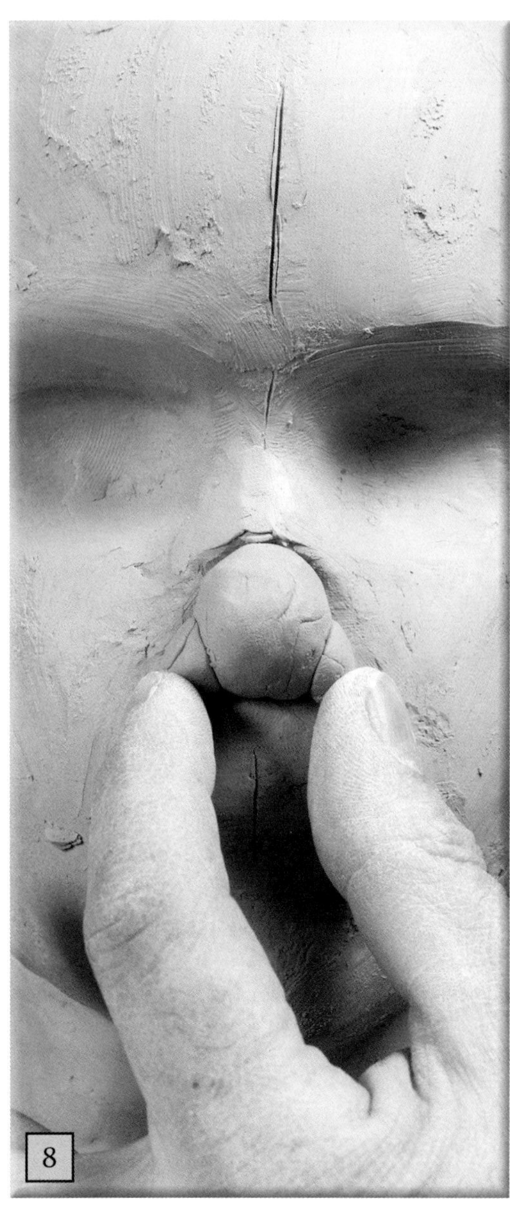

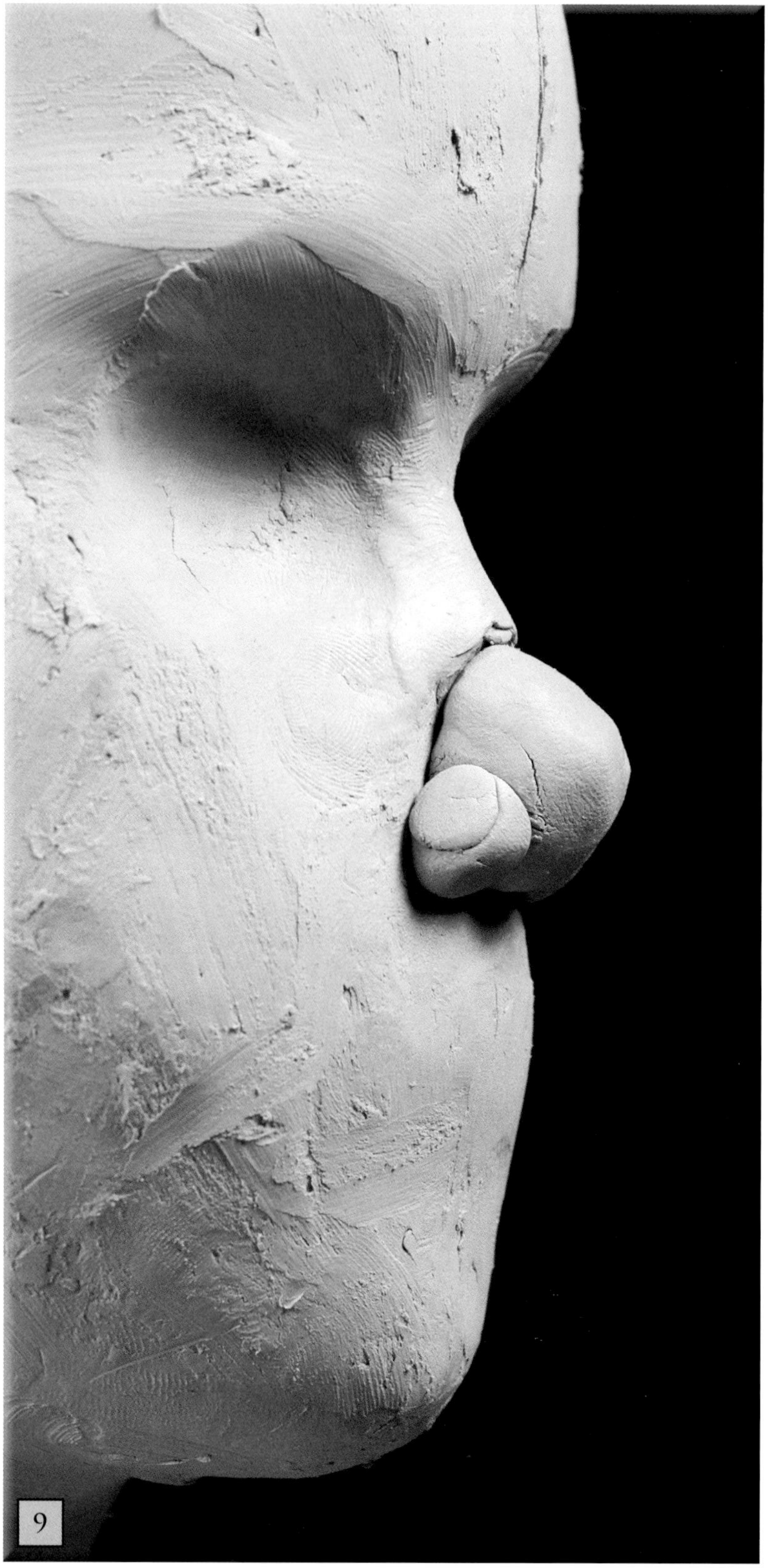

8, 9. The nose is constructed as shown in Chapter 3. The three balls are applied to form a triangle at the base of the nasal bone. It is necessary at this point to look at the work from the profile to make sure that the volumes of the nose are correct.

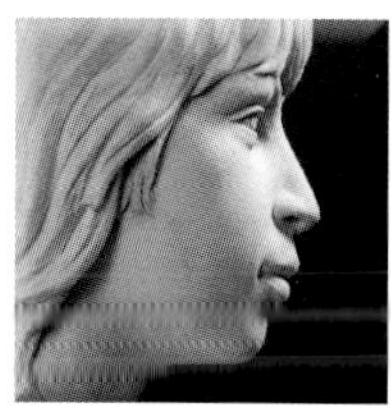

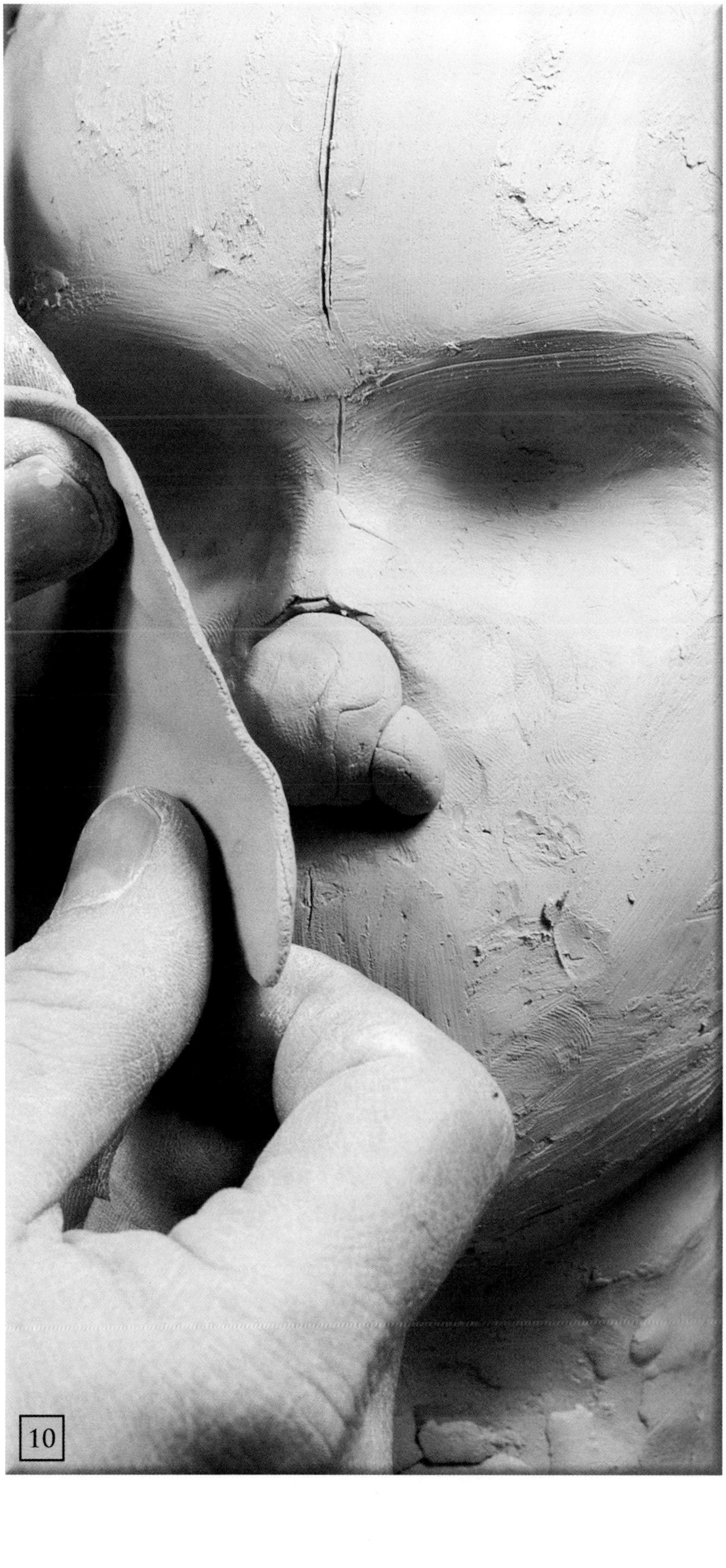

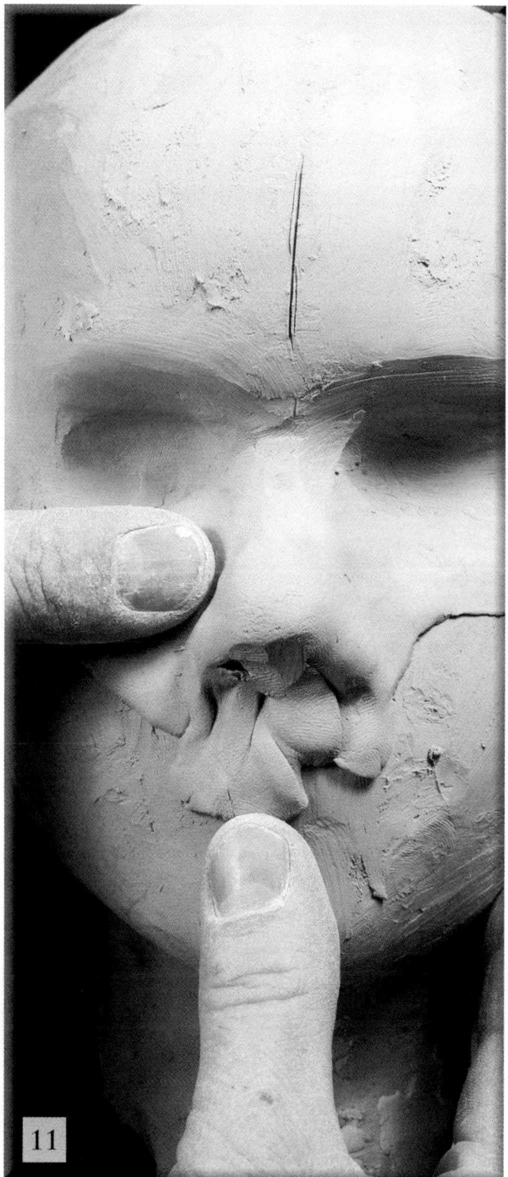


**10, 11.** The thin layer of clay applied over the three balls needs to be shaped rapidly between the thumb and the forefinger. If it is flattened using the palms of the hands, it has a tendency to dry out and develop small cracks on its surface when applied. The clay is pressed gently to follow the shape underneath. The excess is blended into the surface of the face.

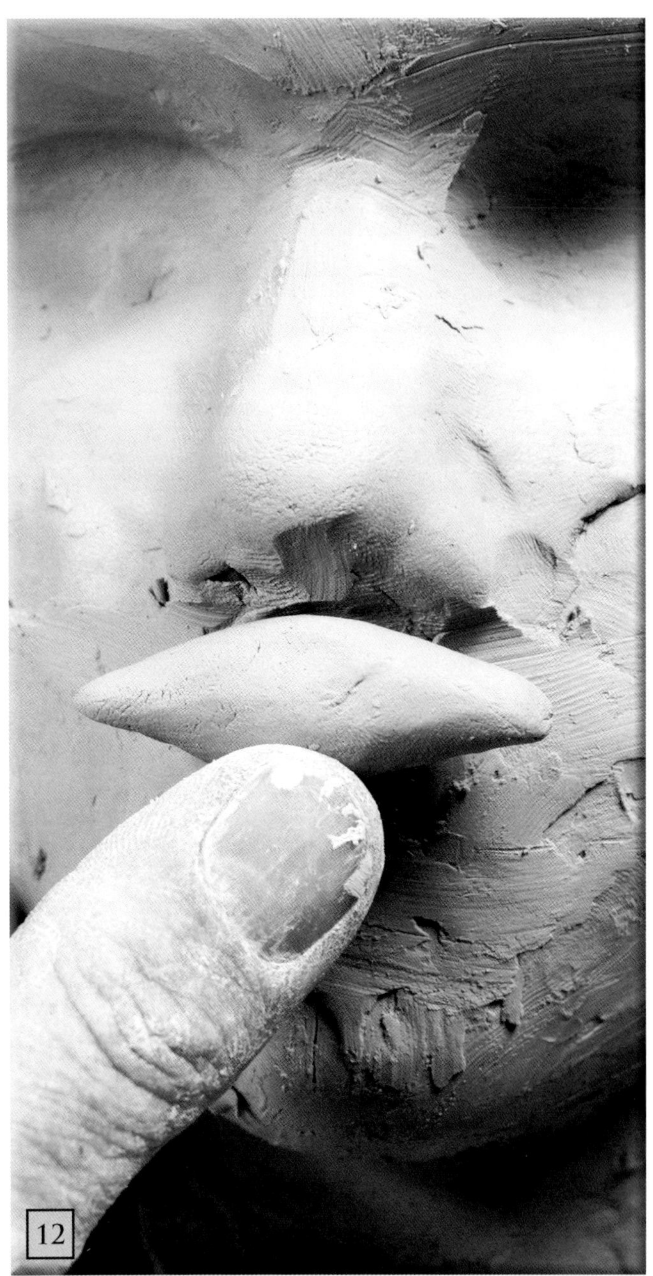


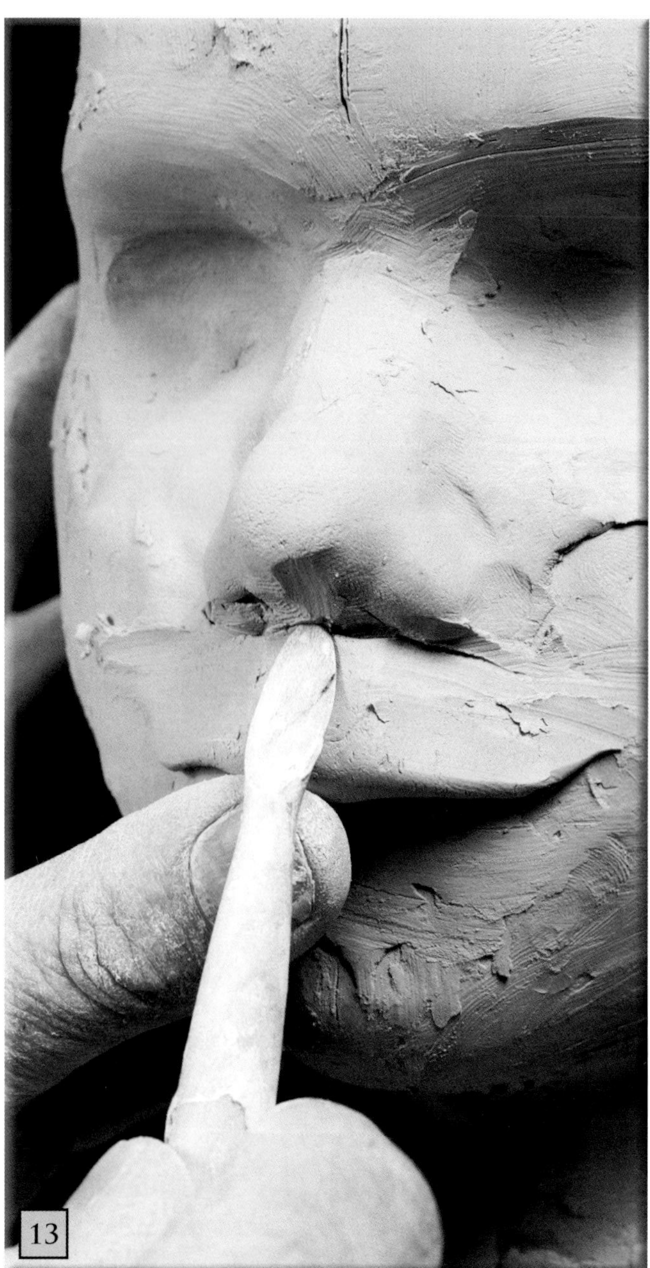


**12.** The volume of the upper lip depends on the model and must be checked from the profile as soon as it is in place.

**13.** In most people the philtrum, when seen in profile, is not vertical. It slopes back and upward toward the nose as shown above by the angle of the tool.

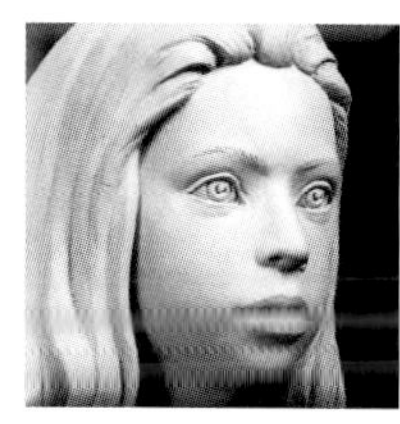

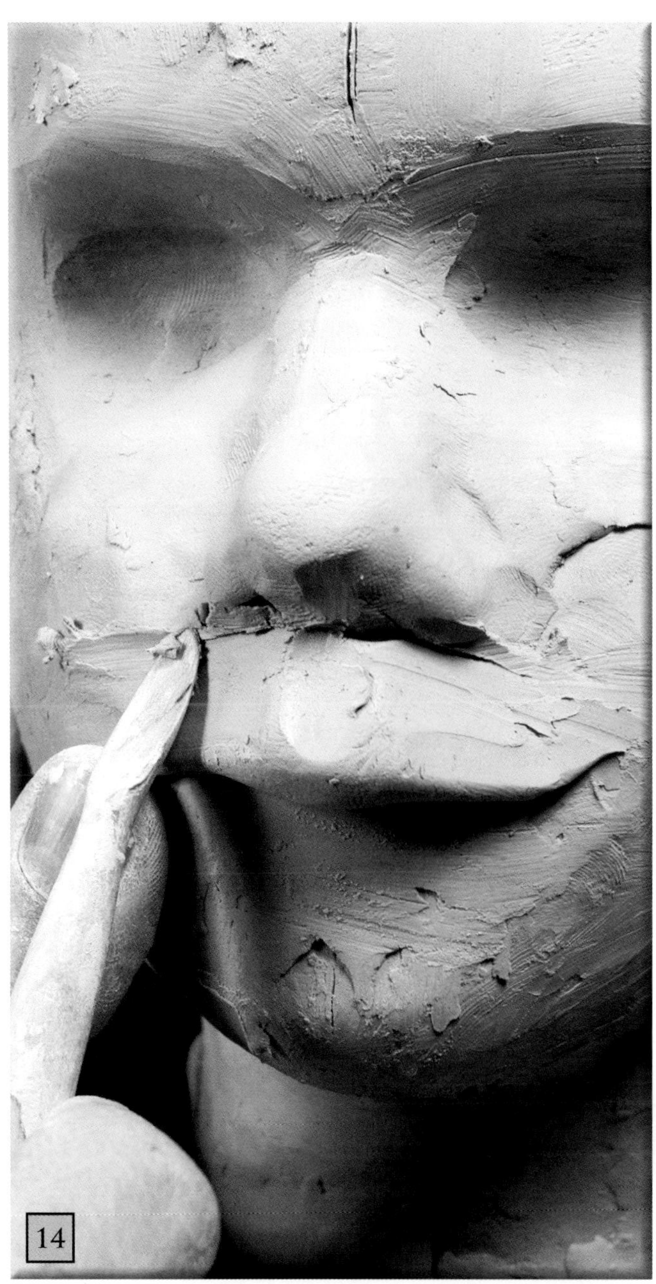

14. The two lateral planes of the upper lip slope back toward the nostrils and the cheeks.

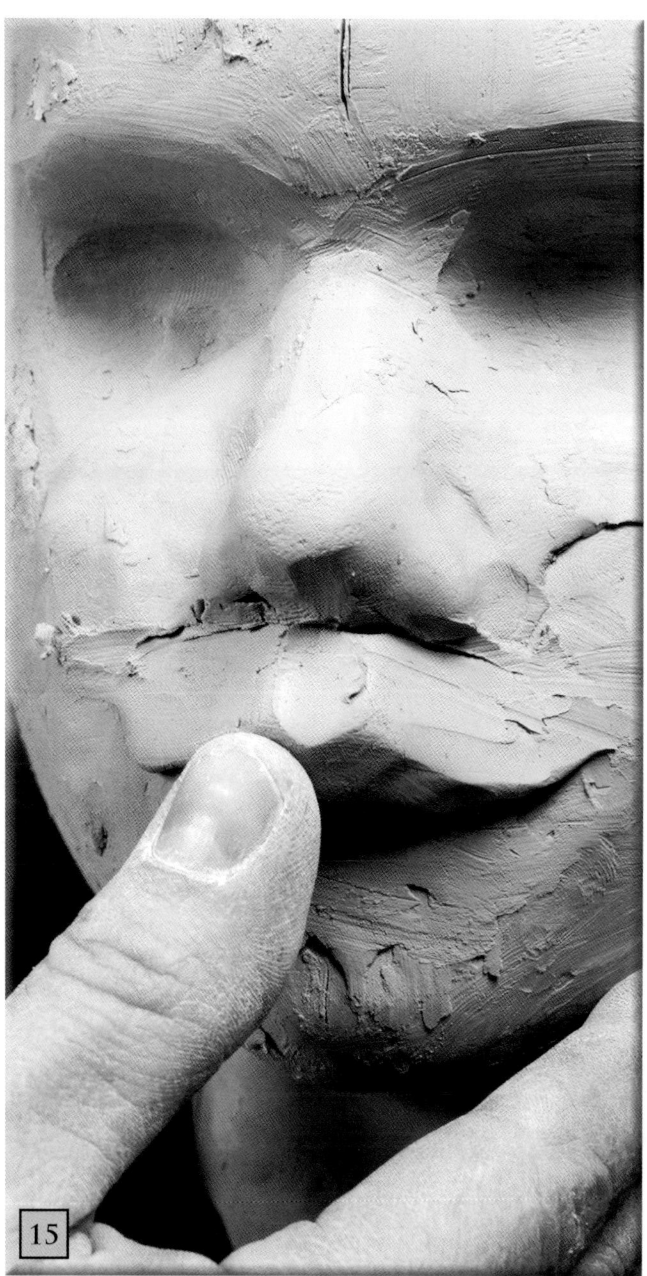

15. The ridge defining the shape of the upper lip is formed by the transition between the different planes.

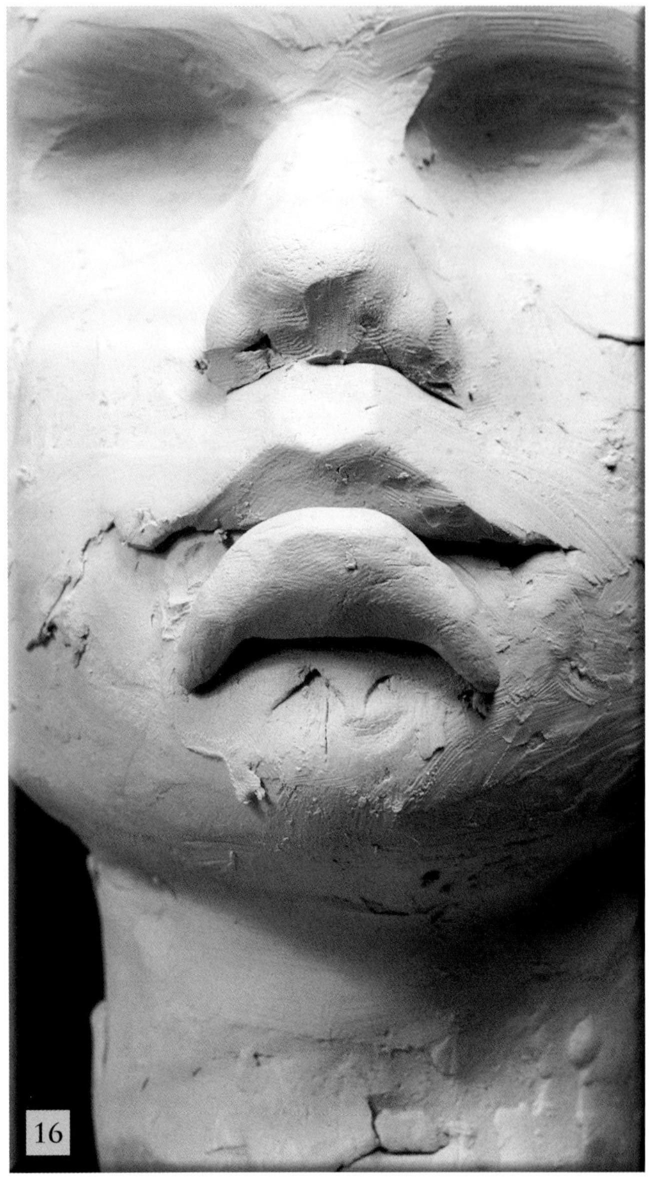

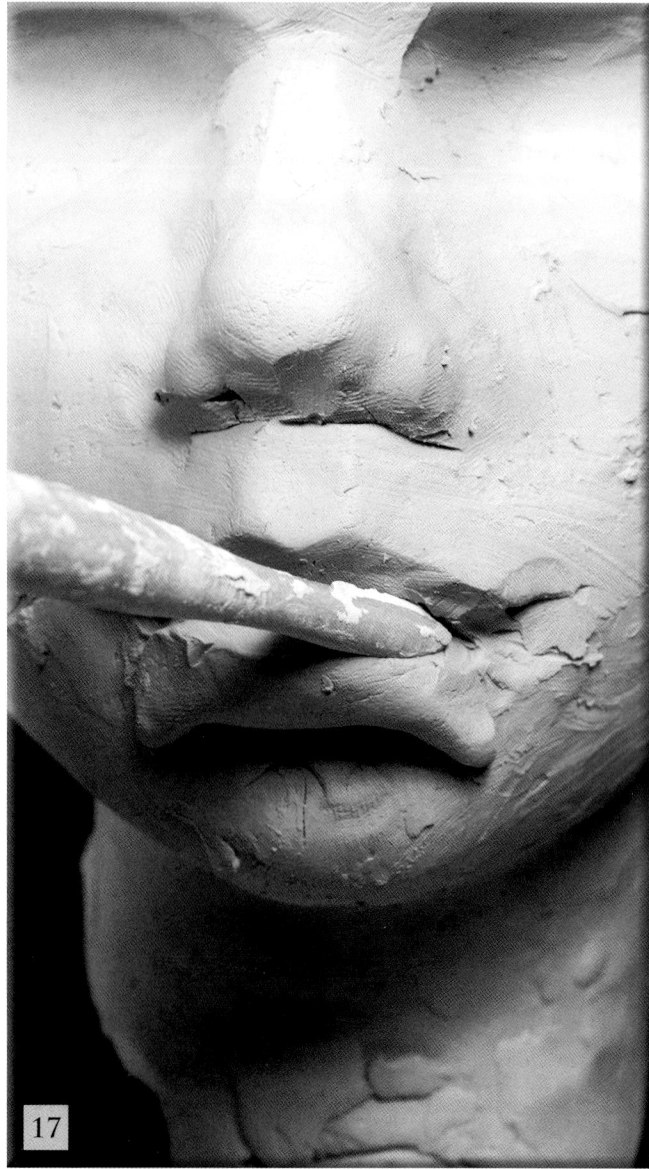

**16.** Once the volume of the lower lip is in place it also needs to be checked from the profile and compared with the model.

**17.** The planes of the lip are defined with the concave side of the wooden tool. Where the interior planes of the lower lip meet with those of the upper lip, a line is created. This line is the parting of the mouth and needs to be identical to the one on the model. Its shape can vary greatly depending on the expression.

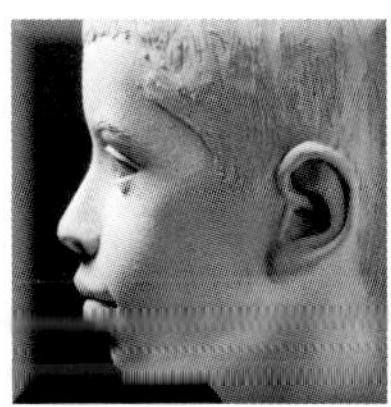

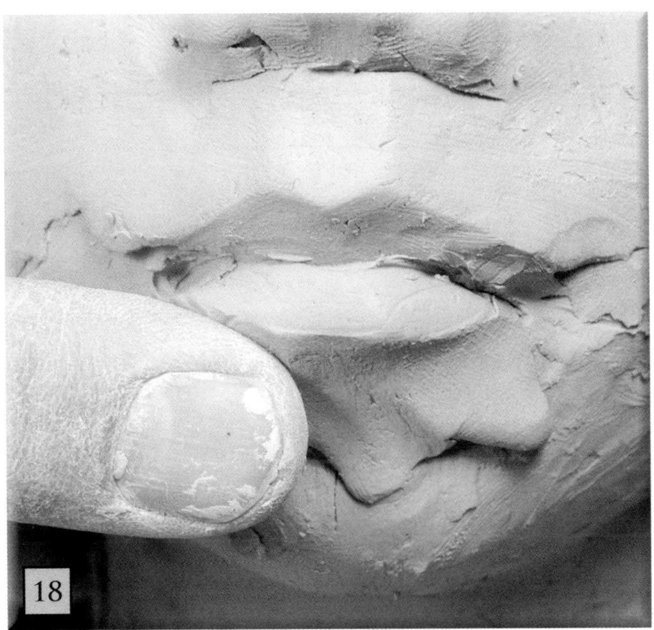


18. The ridge formed by the transition between the upper and lower planes determines the shape of the lower lip.

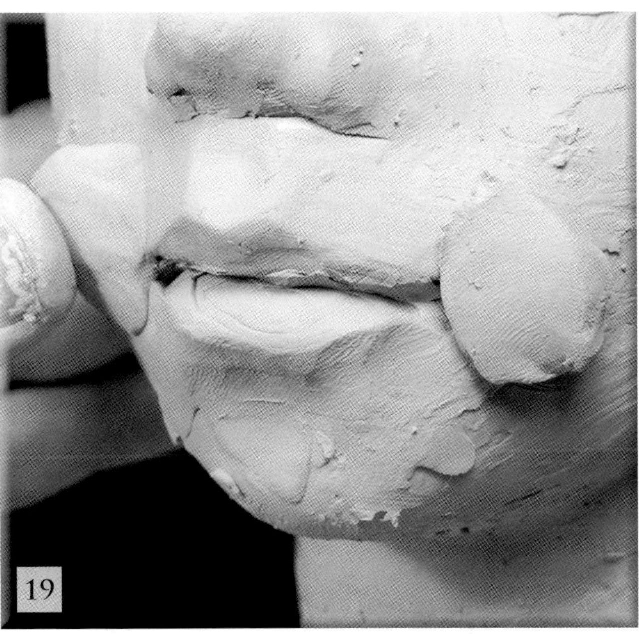


19. A small amount of clay is added on each side to accentuate the depth of the corners of the mouth.

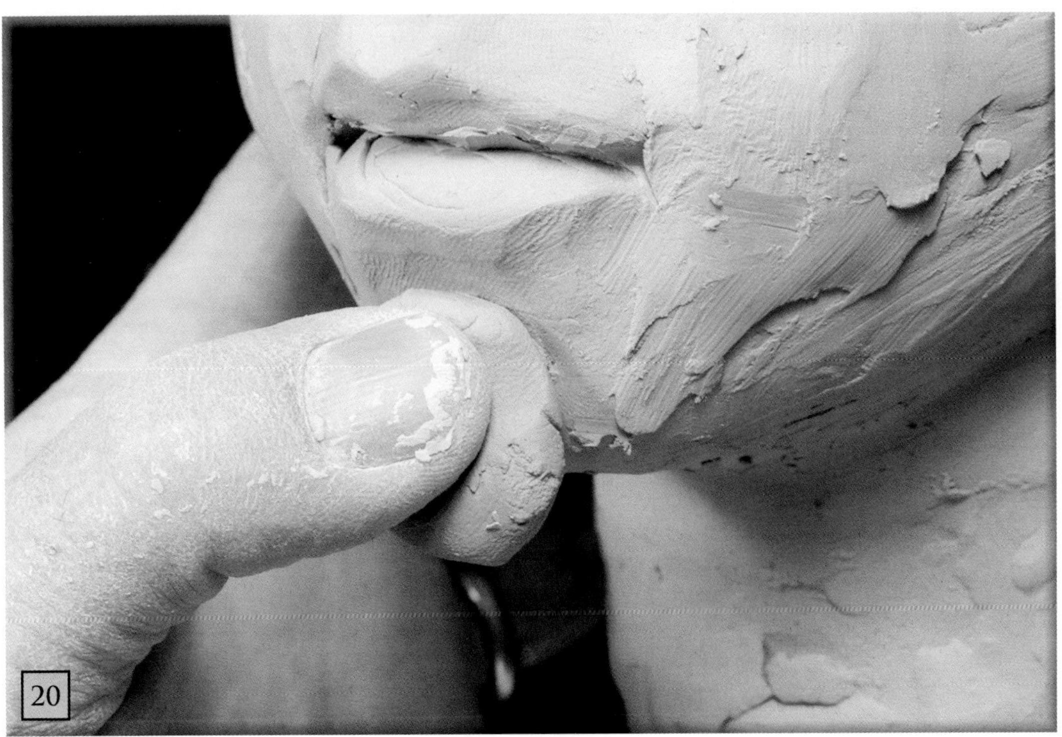


20. The protrusion of the chin can only be determined by studying the profile of the model.

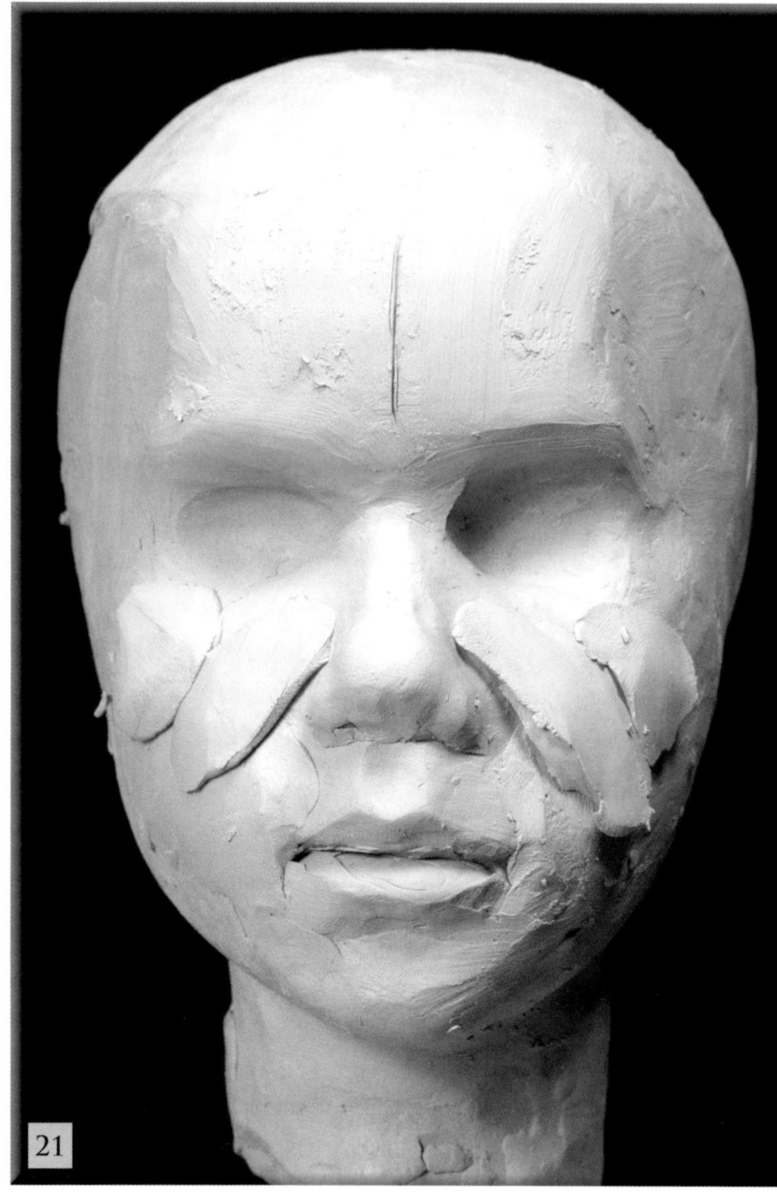


**21.** Coils of clay are added on both sides of the nose to create a rounded bridge between the nasal bone and the cheeks. Two smaller pieces are also applied on the cheekbone to create the fatty fold seen in most children.

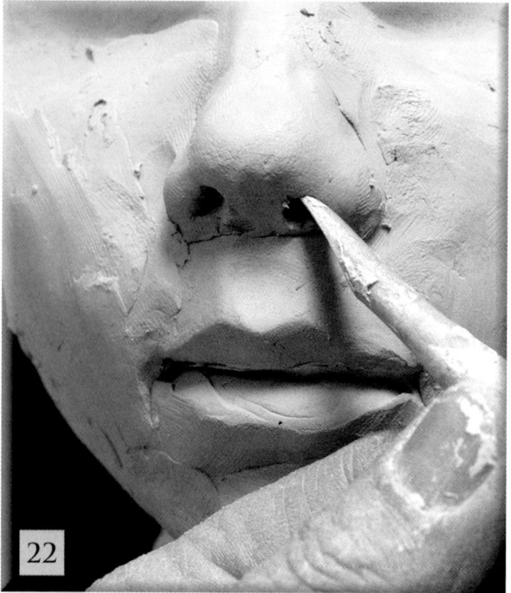


**22.** The inside of the nostrils is shaped with a wooden tool.

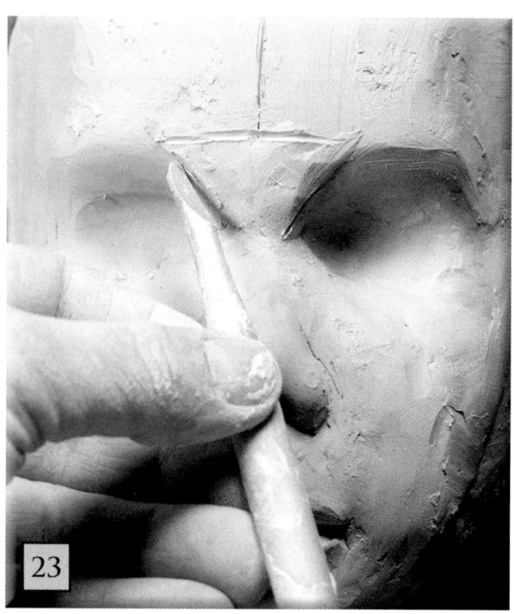


**23.** In this model, as well as in the majority of people, there is a small plane in the form of a triangle that can be traced from the beginning of the eyebrows to the center of the deepest part of the nasal bone.

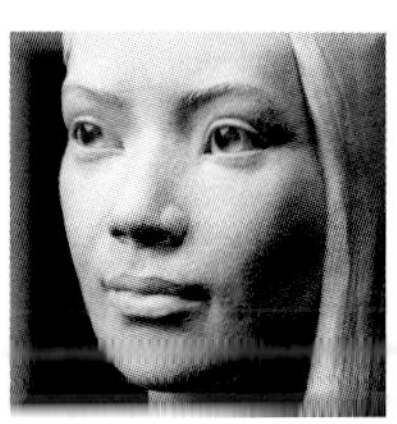

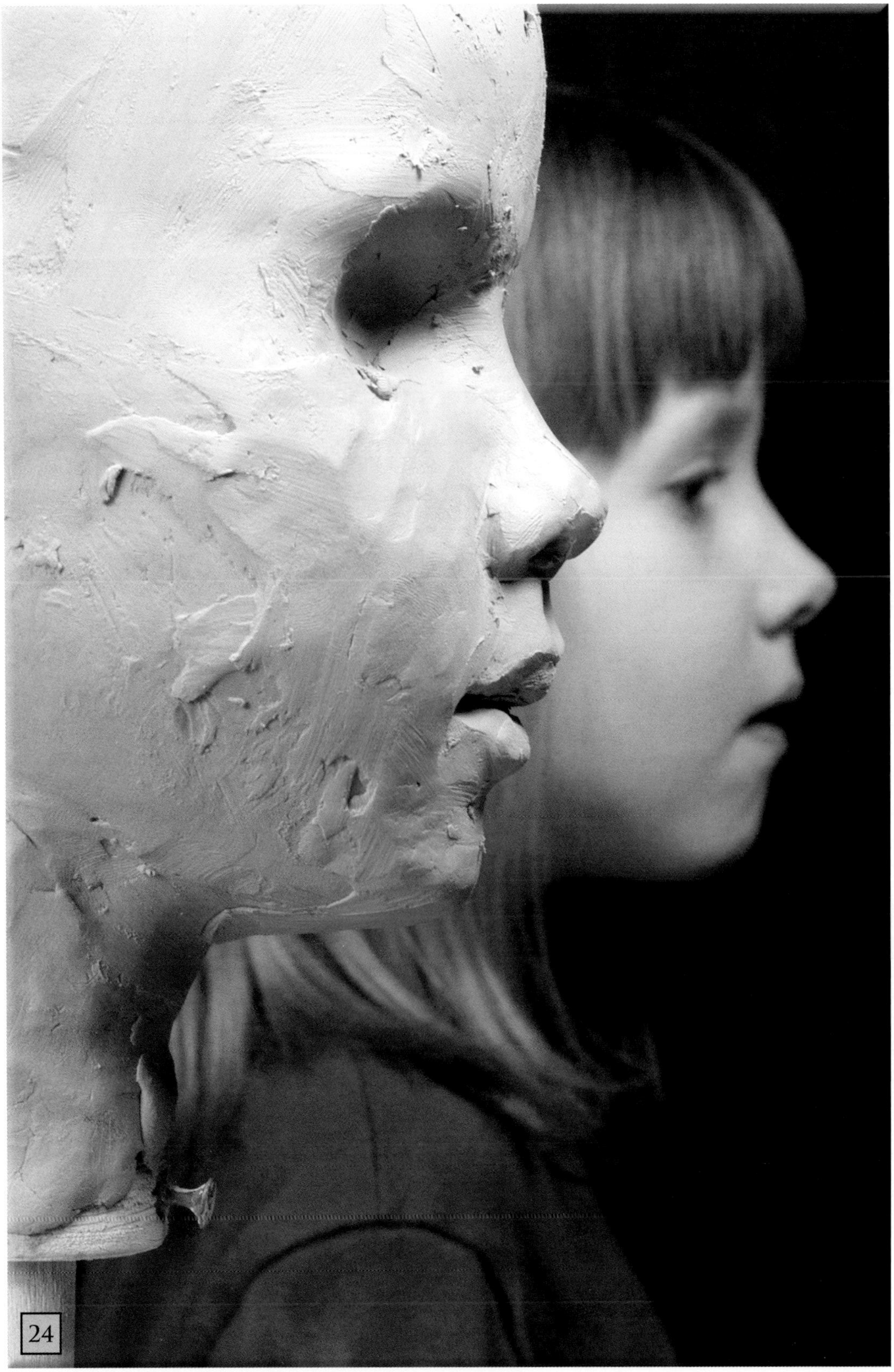

**24.** The accuracy of the profile is checked periodically.

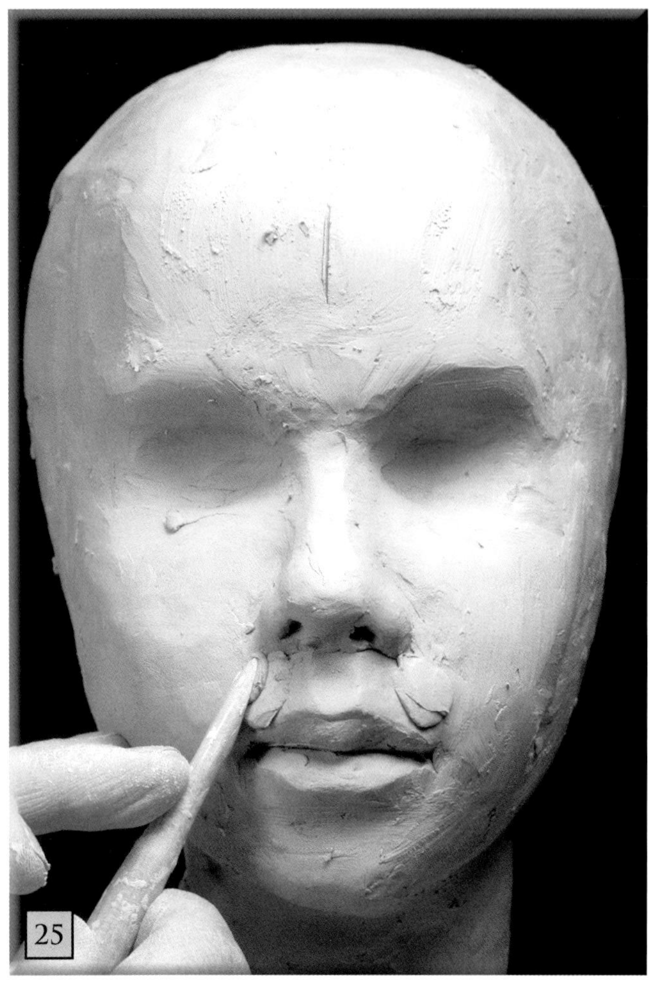

**25.** Smaller volumes are built on both sides of the upper lip. It is important to add volumes to both sides of the face at the same time to ensure facial symmetry.

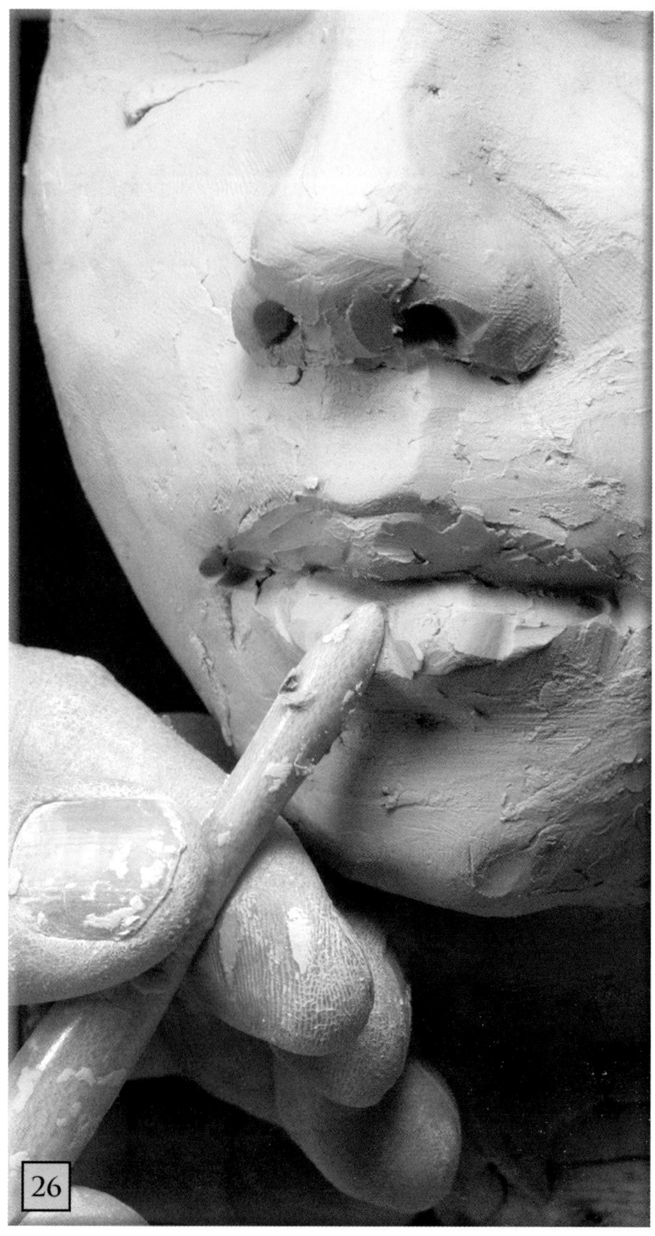

**26.** A small amount of clay is added to both the upper and lower lips to define the five main volumes of the mouth (see diagram of the mouth, page 56).

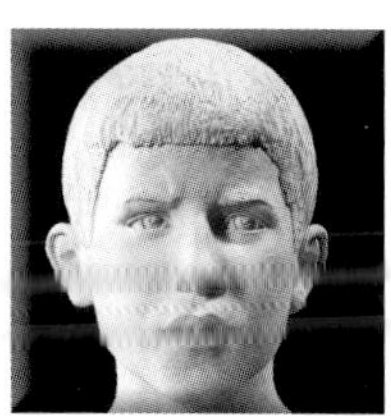

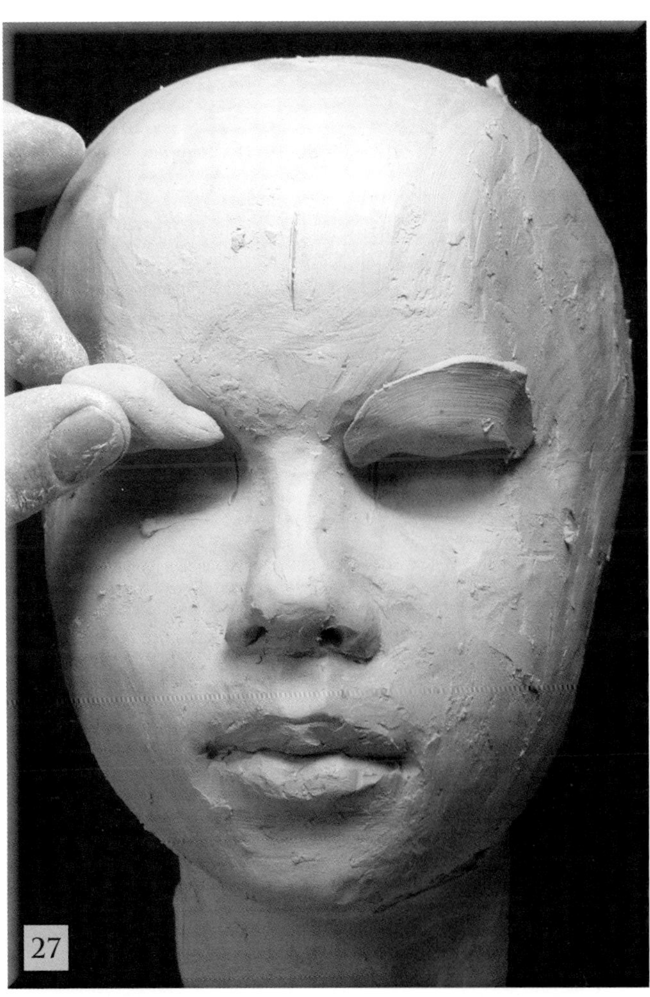

27. The volumes of the upper eyelids are applied to both sides at the same time.

28. The transition between the planes of the forehead and those of the upper eyelids define the shape of the eyebrows. It must be clearly indicated.

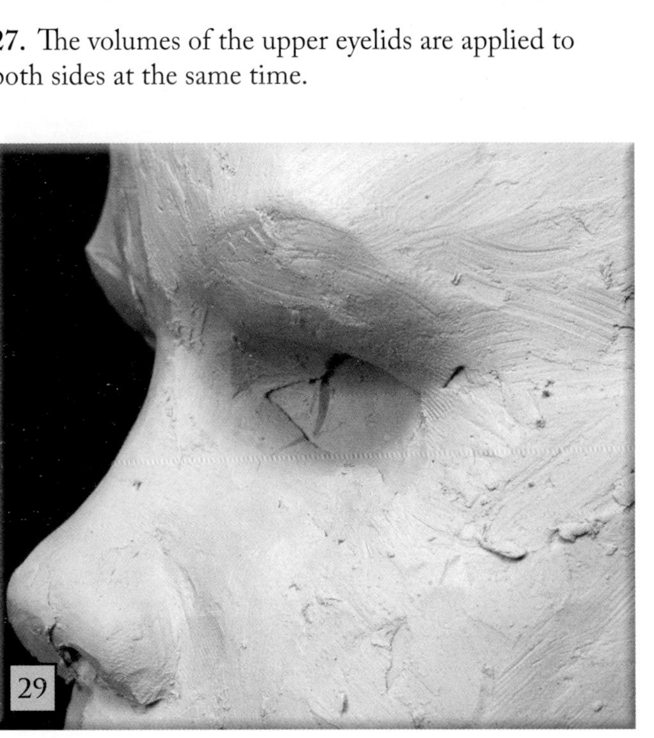

29. The volumes created on the inside and the upper part of the eye socket must remain rounded. The tendency is to flatten them (see pages 134-135).

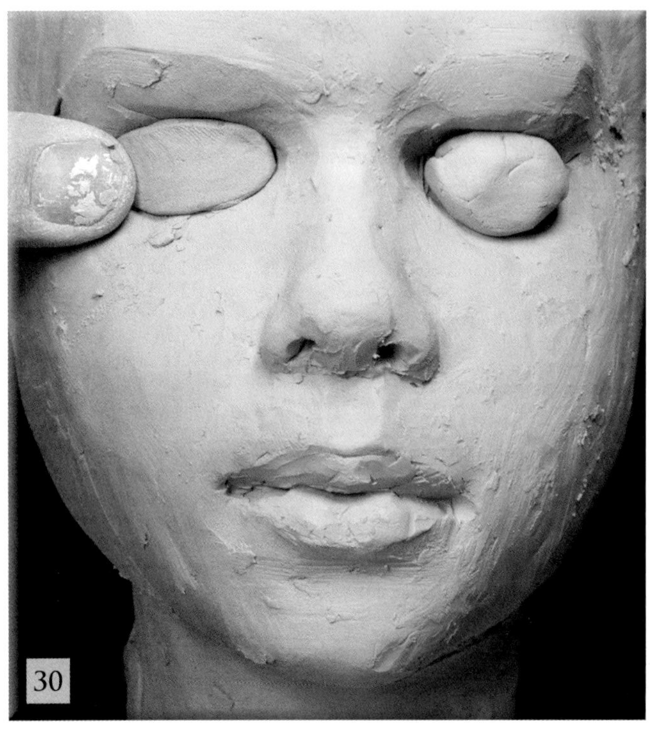

30. As mentioned earlier, the placement of the eyes is critical to achieve a likeness. If the bone structure is accurate, the eyeballs are simply centered in the orbital cavity. The depth of the eye is more difficult to determine. It can only be judged from the profile by careful study of the model, and should be the first concern.

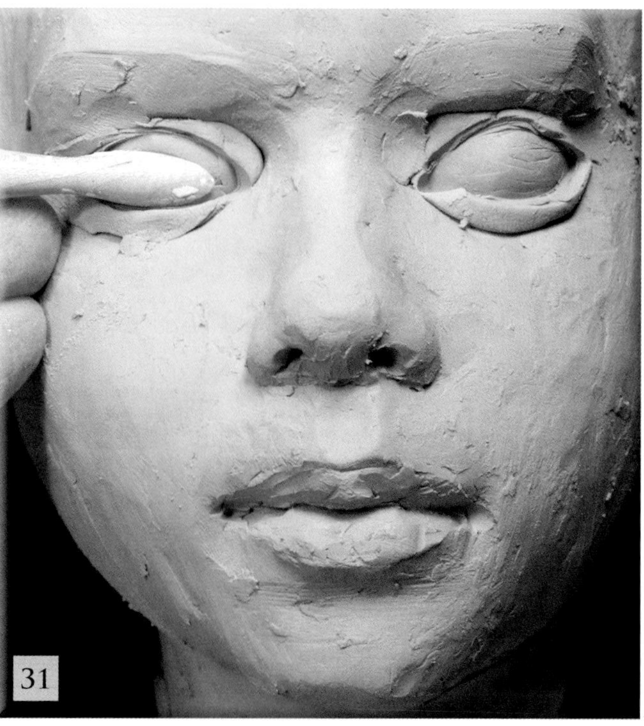

31. Using calipers, the height of the eyes can be checked by measuring the distance between the corner of the mouth and the center of the lower eyelid. The distance between the eyes also needs to be checked.

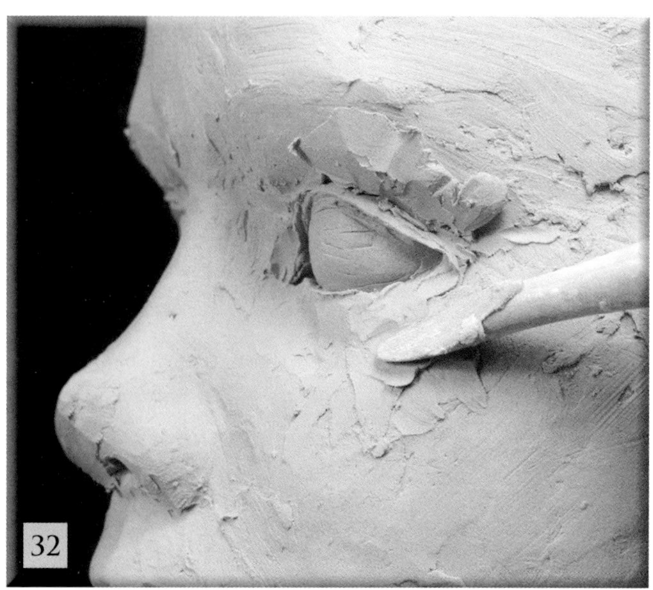

32. After refining the eyelids, more clay is added over the cheekbone to adjust the volume of fat often seen in children.

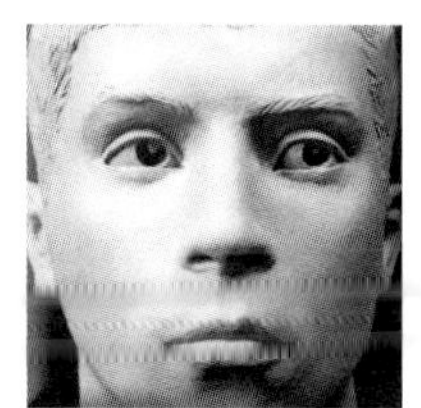

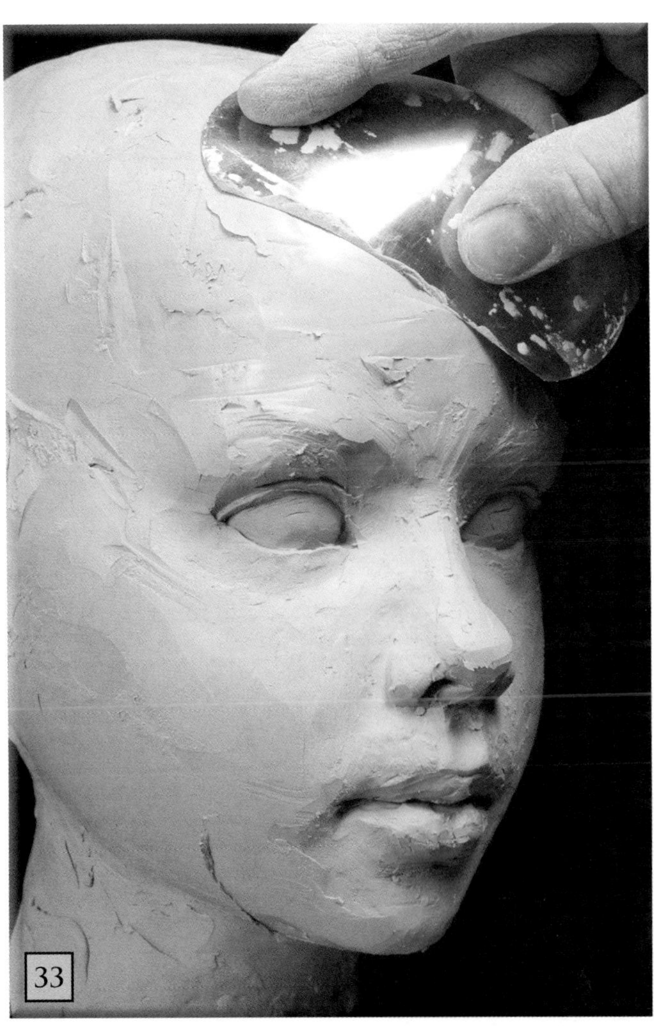


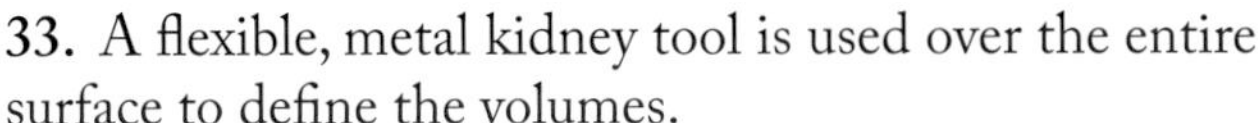
**33.** A flexible, metal kidney tool is used over the entire surface to define the volumes.

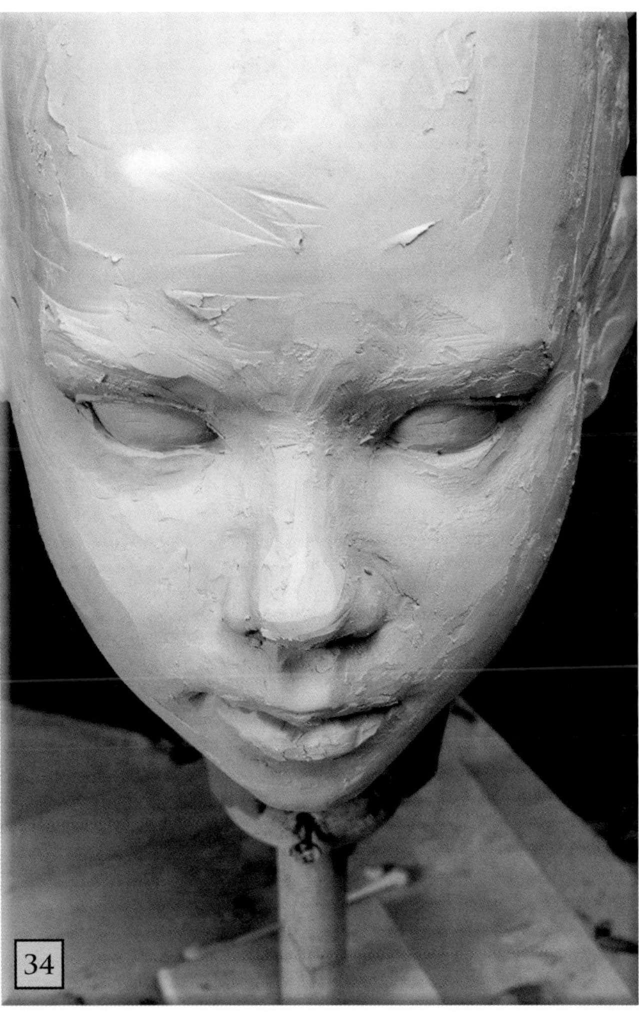


**34.** As shown in this picture, it is important to view the work from every angle to detect potential symmetry problems and fix them as the work progresses. Note the difference in volumes from one side of the jaw to the other.

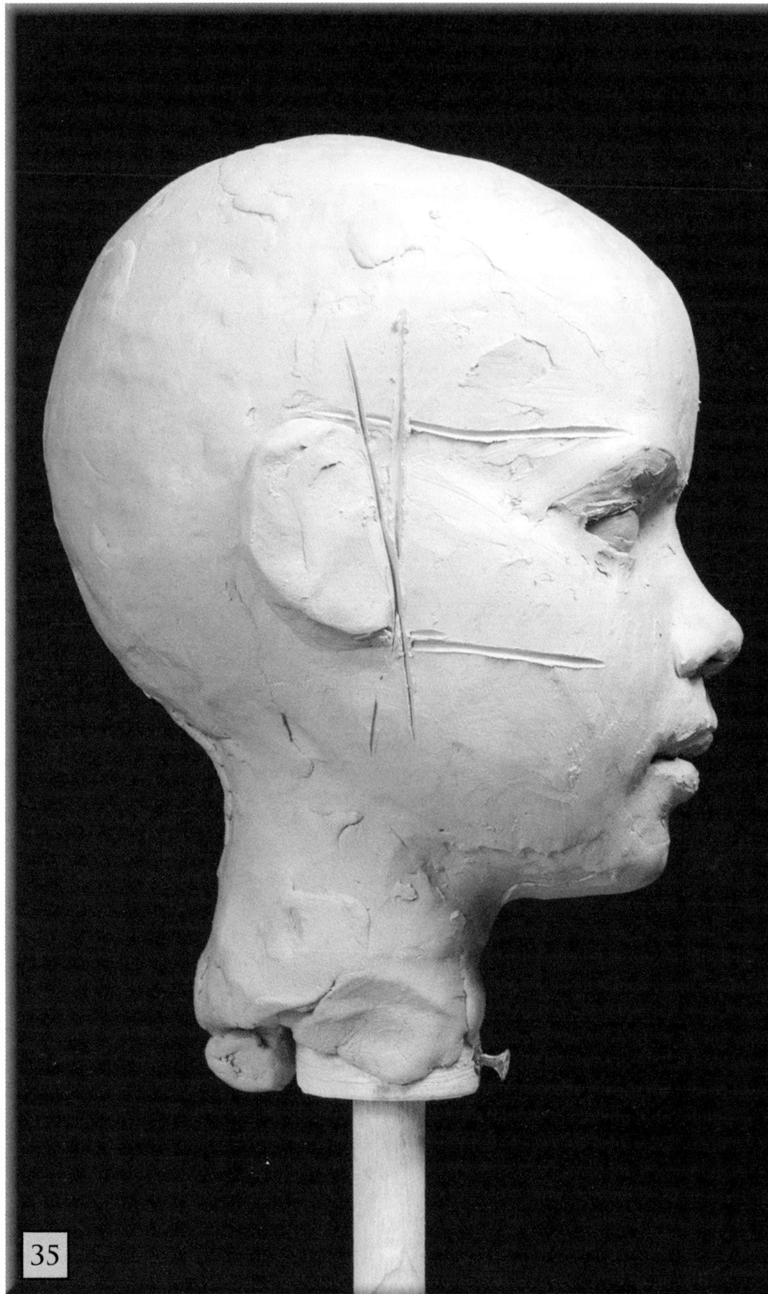

35. The ear is placed just behind the mid-point between the tip of the nose and the back of the head at a slight angle. The height of the ear is usually projected from the top of the eyebrow and the bottom of the nose. It is necessary, however, to measure the specific model with calipers.

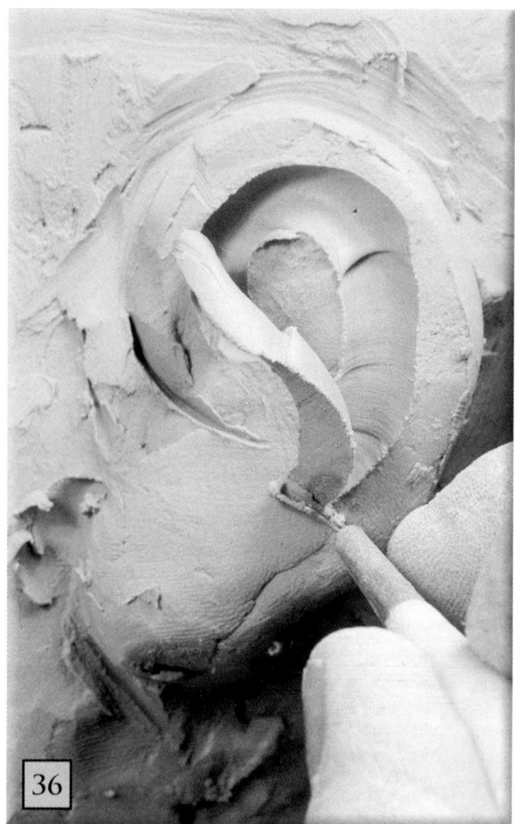

36. The interior shape of the ear is defined with a wire tool.

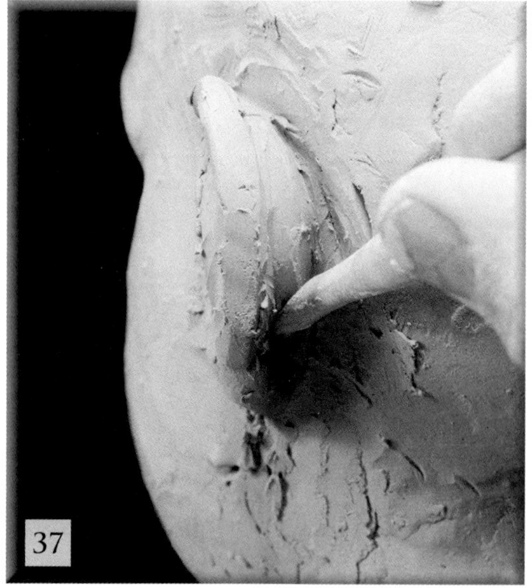

37. The back of the ear needs to be shaped at this time, because it will be difficult to reach once the hair is in place.

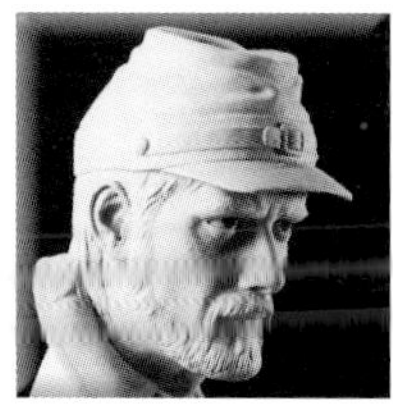

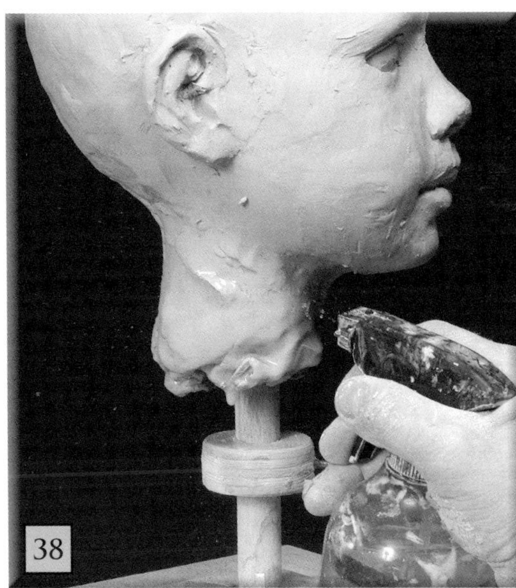

38. Using a spray bottle, the neck area is moistened before adding the volumes of the sternocleidomastoid, trapezius muscles and clavicles.

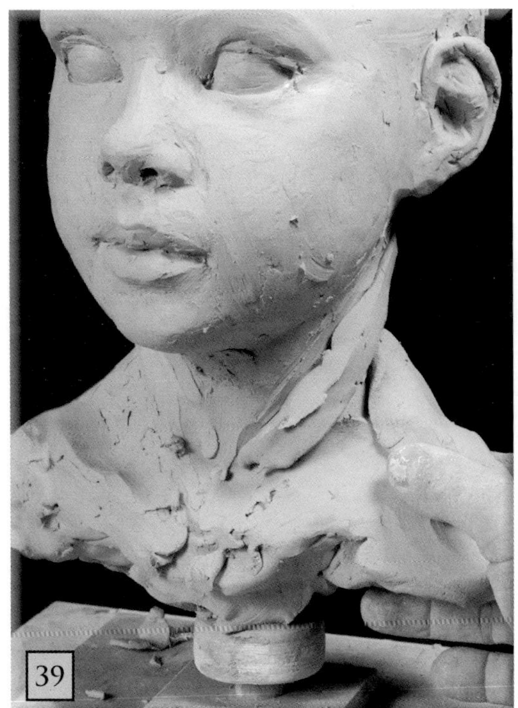

39. Notice that the support ring has been lowered to prevent it from becoming embedded into the sculpture.

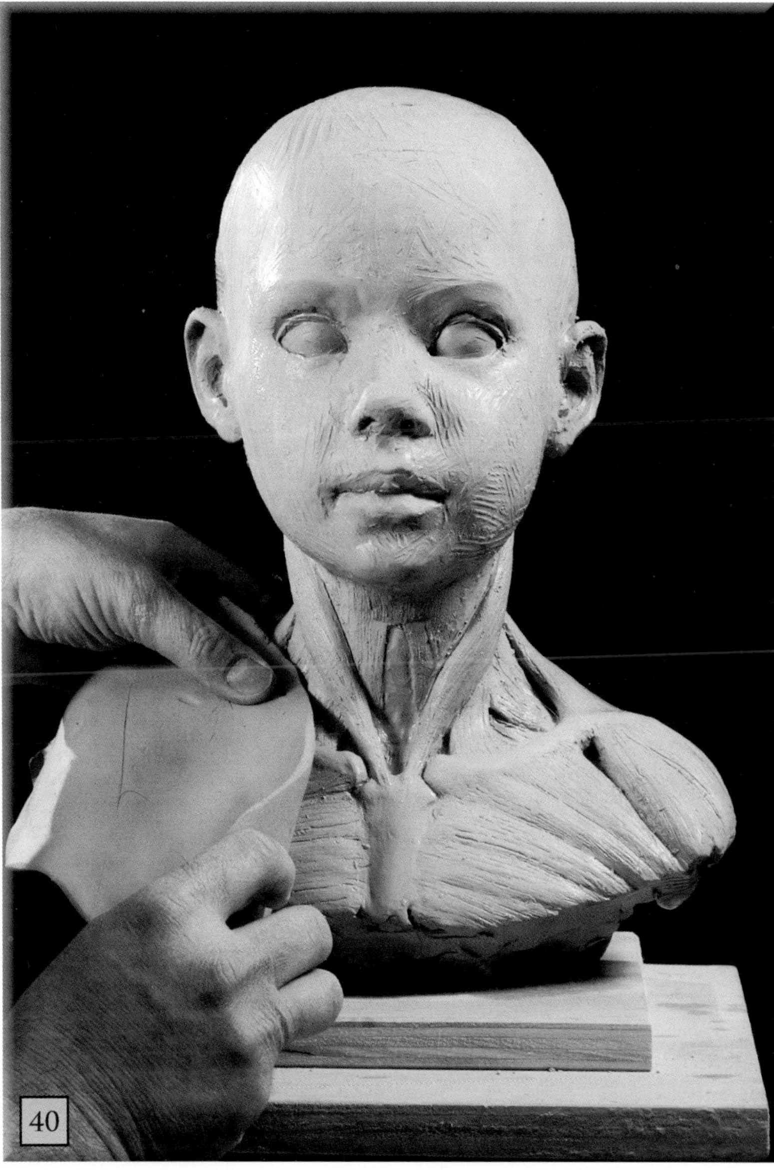

40. Even though it is good practice, under normal circumstances it would not be necessary to render all of the underlying musculature. In this case it was done for the previous discussions in Chapter 2; therefore, adding a thin layer of clay over the entire surface is all that is required to achieve the proper volumes.

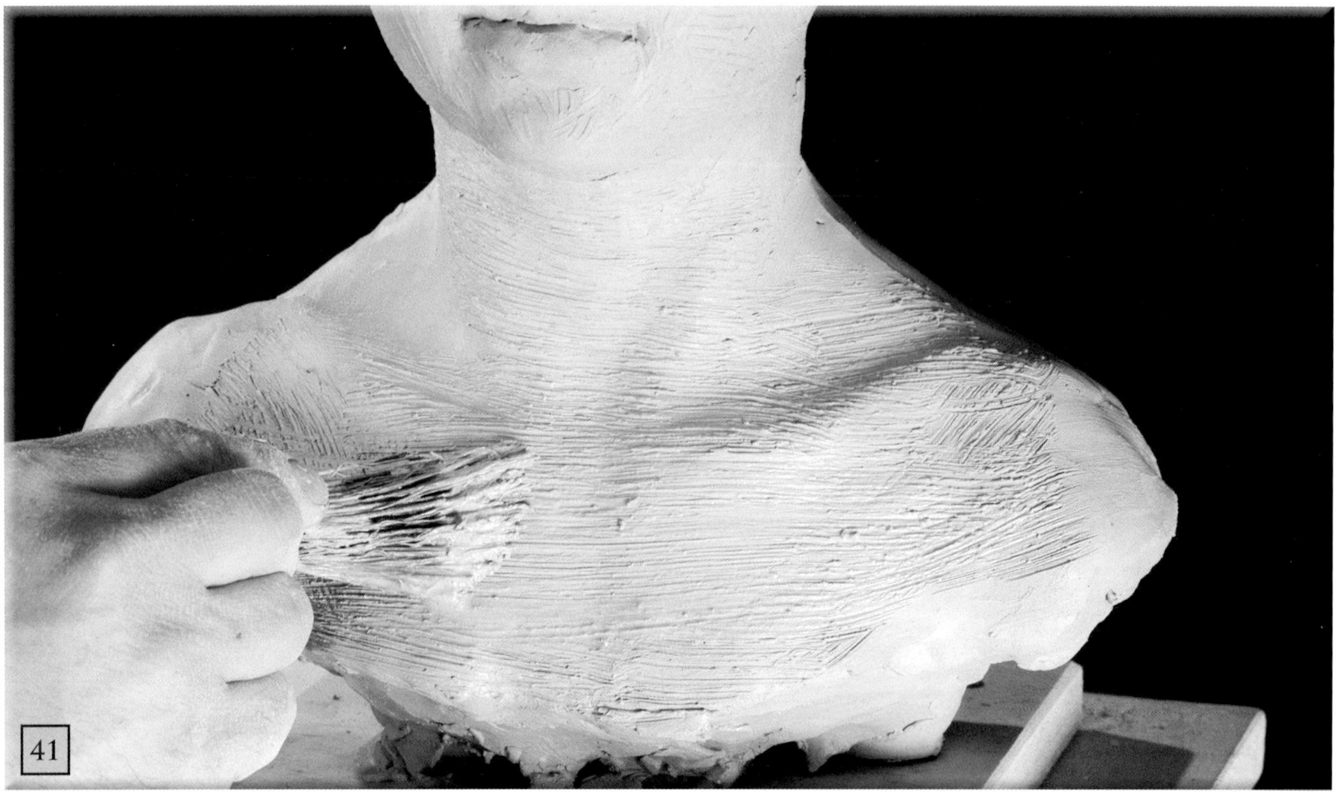

**41, 42.** After building the volumes of the neck and shoulders, a wet bristle brush is used to get rid of any unwanted surface bumps. Then, with a rough sponge, the surface is further refined.

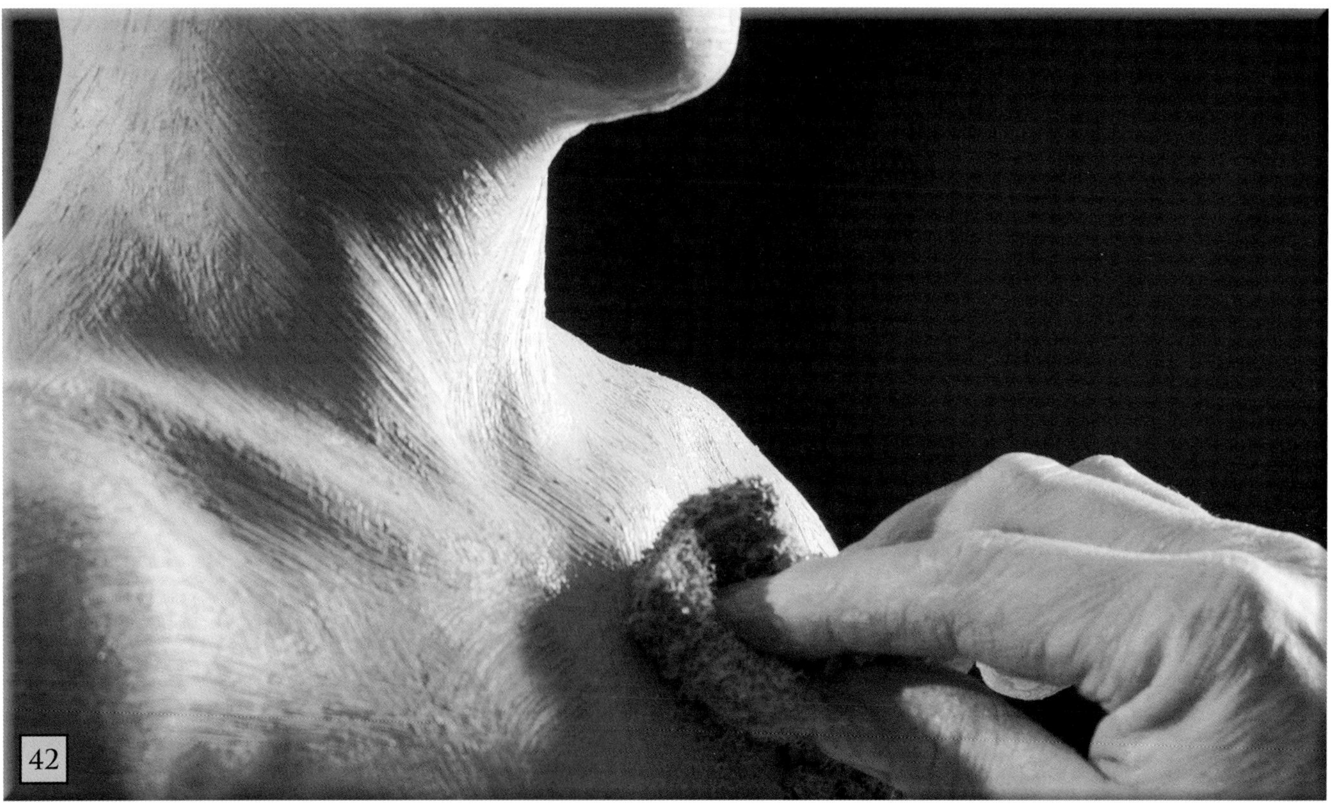

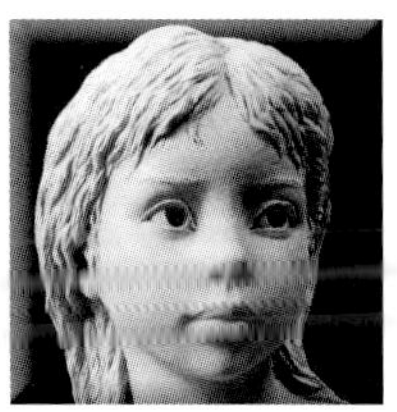

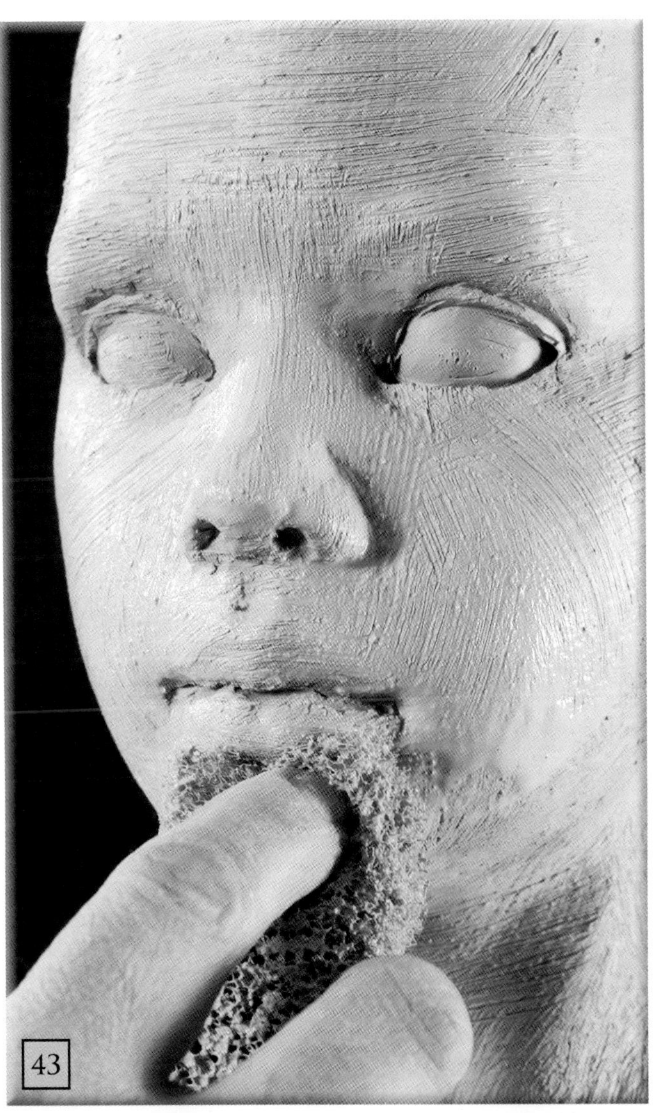

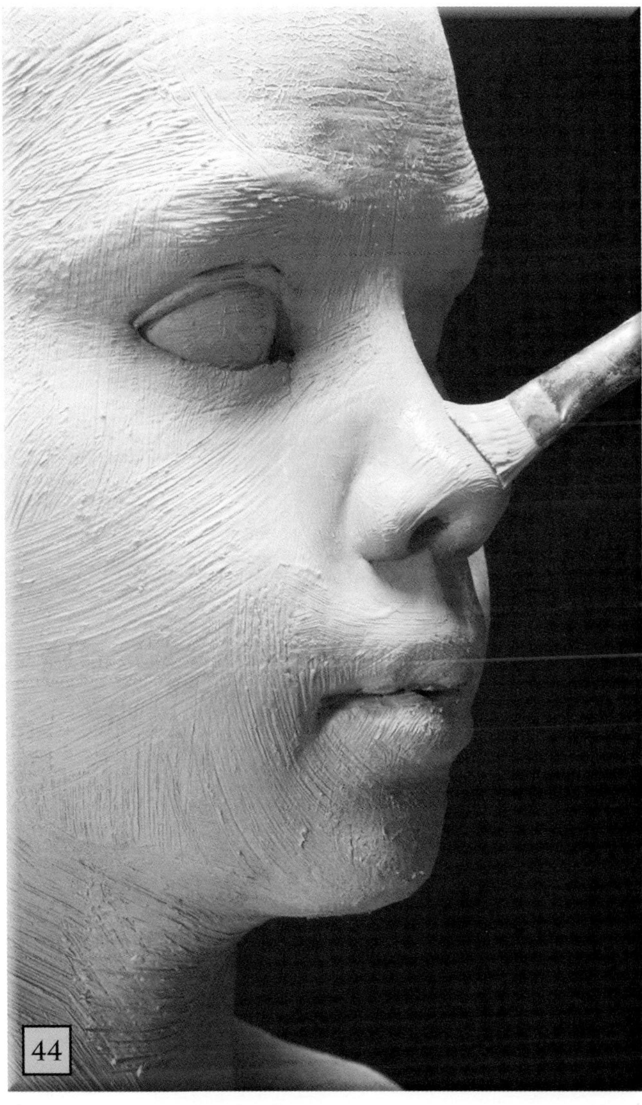

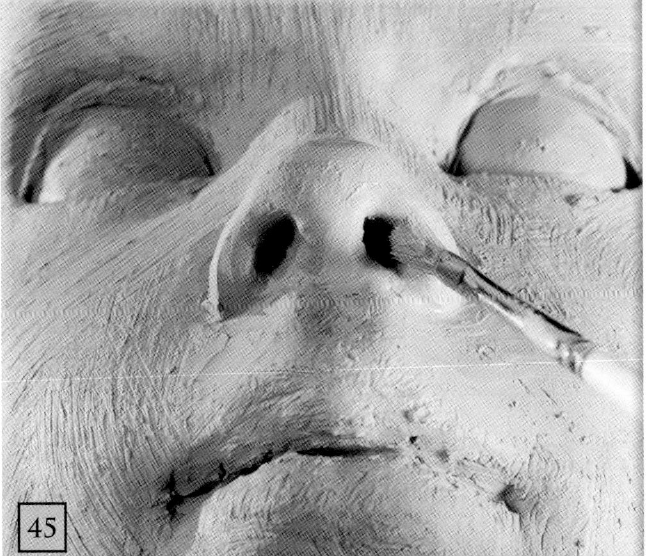

**43.** The rough sponge is also used on the face. Like the bristle brush, it helps to remove surface imperfections, but less aggressively.

**44, 45.** A soft brush is used to refine the surface. It is important to understand that the goal here is not to create the final texture. Sometimes the volumes need to be smooth in order to check their accuracy. This is especially necessary in the case of small complex areas such as the nose, mouth and eyes. The final texture can be achieved later.

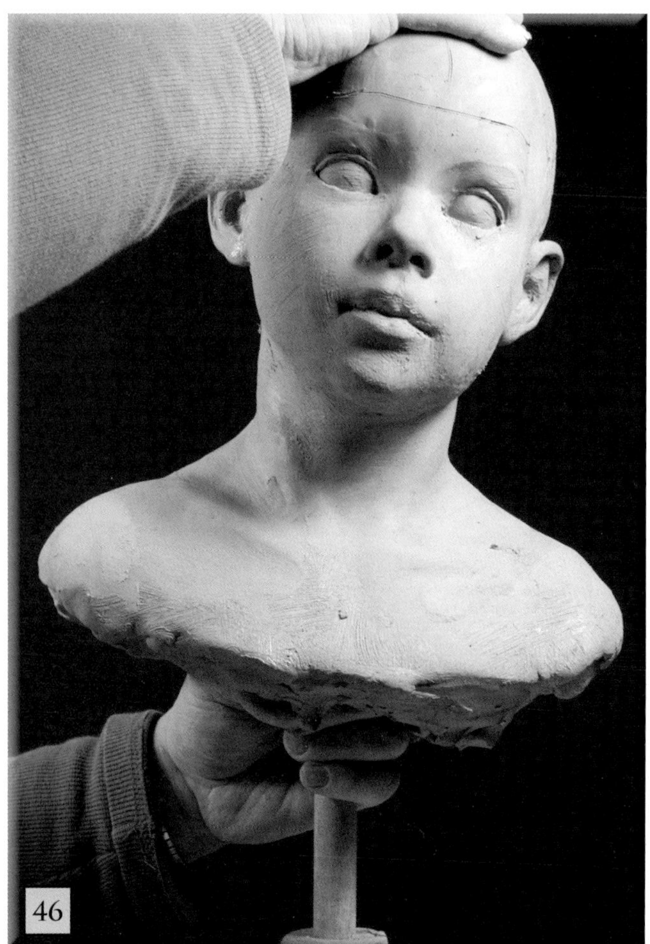

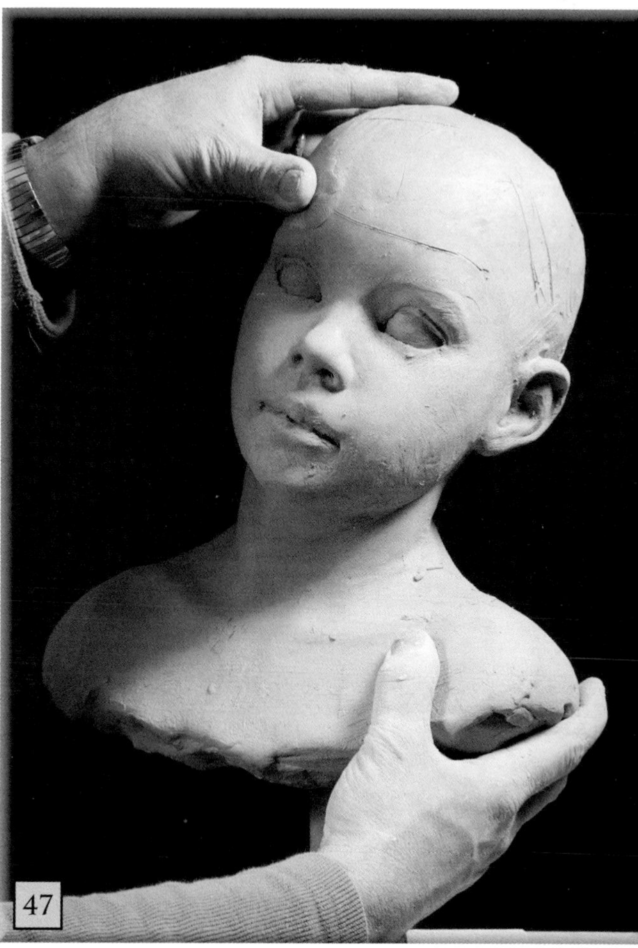

**46, 47.** The bust is raised on the sculpting armature and the head position is changed.

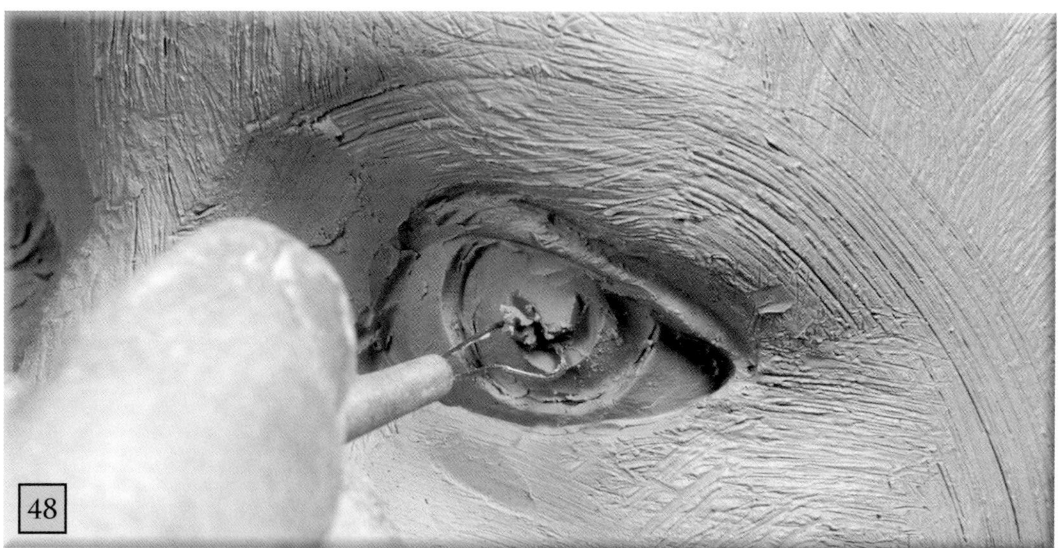

**48.** The iris and pupil are indicated with a small wire tool. In this case, the shallow iris is used to represent clear eyes.

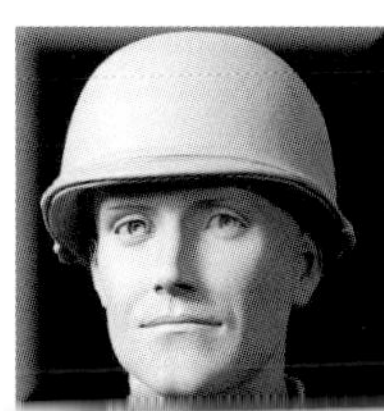

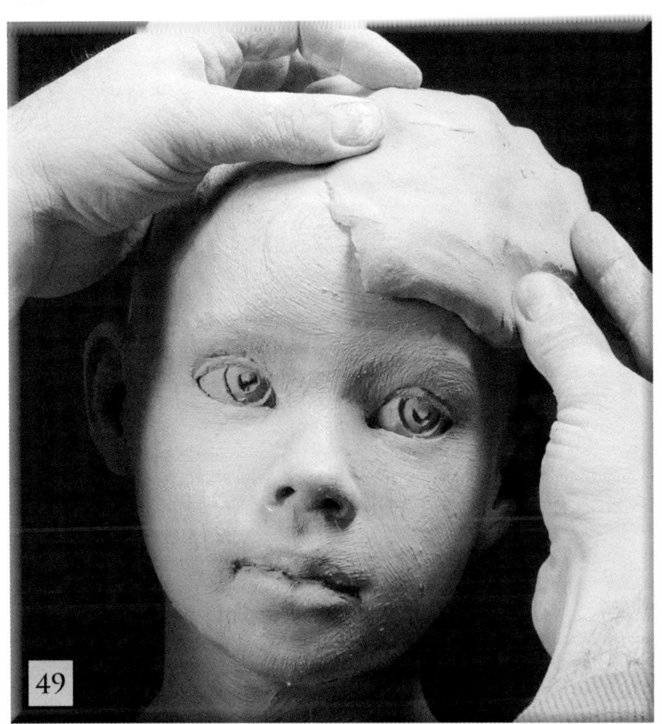

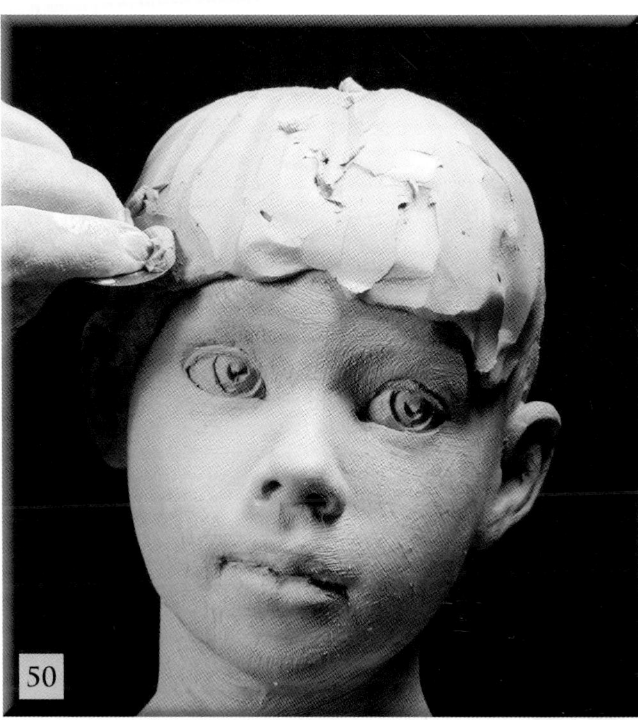

**49, 50.** The hair is applied as distinctive masses, then shaped with a flexible metal tool.

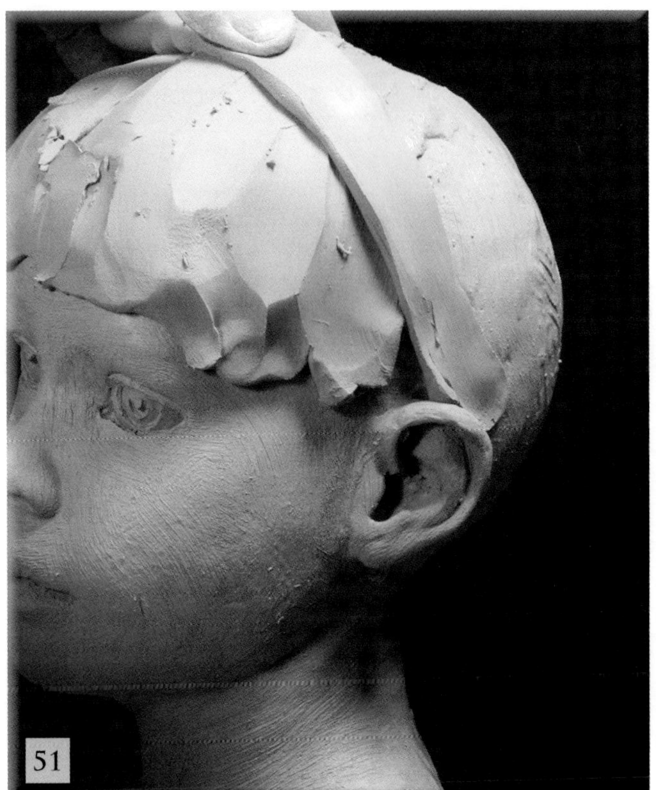

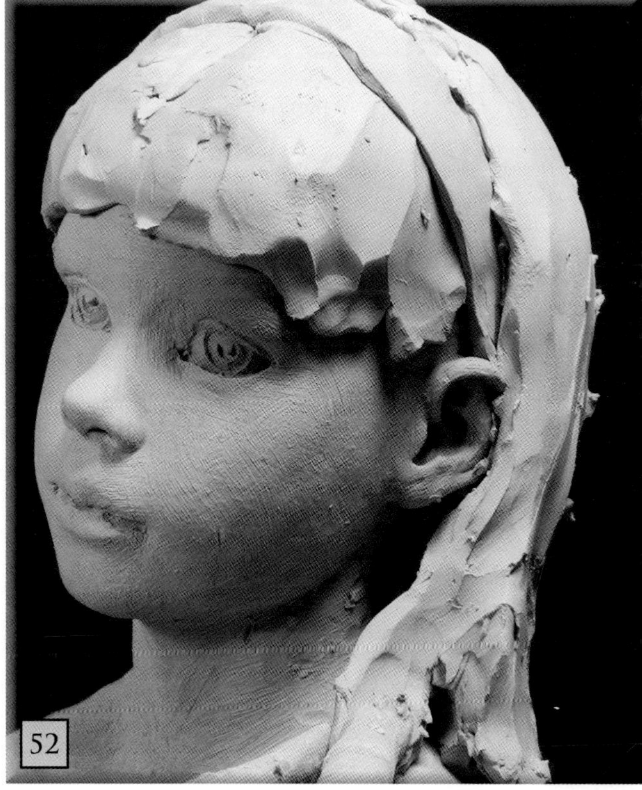

**51, 52.** A hair band is made of a flattened coil of clay pressed firmly from ear to ear. More hair mass is then applied.

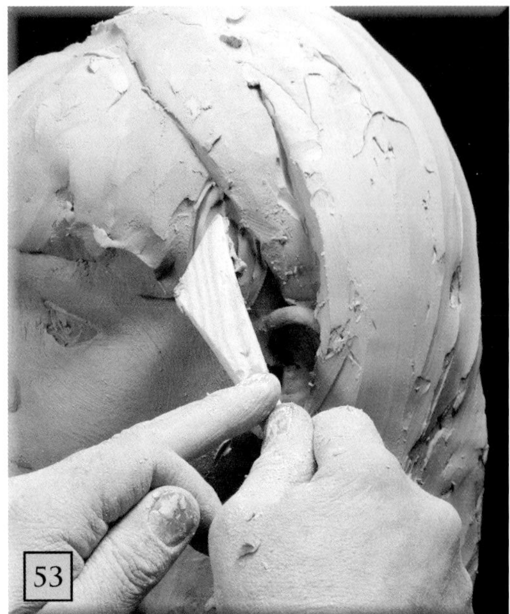


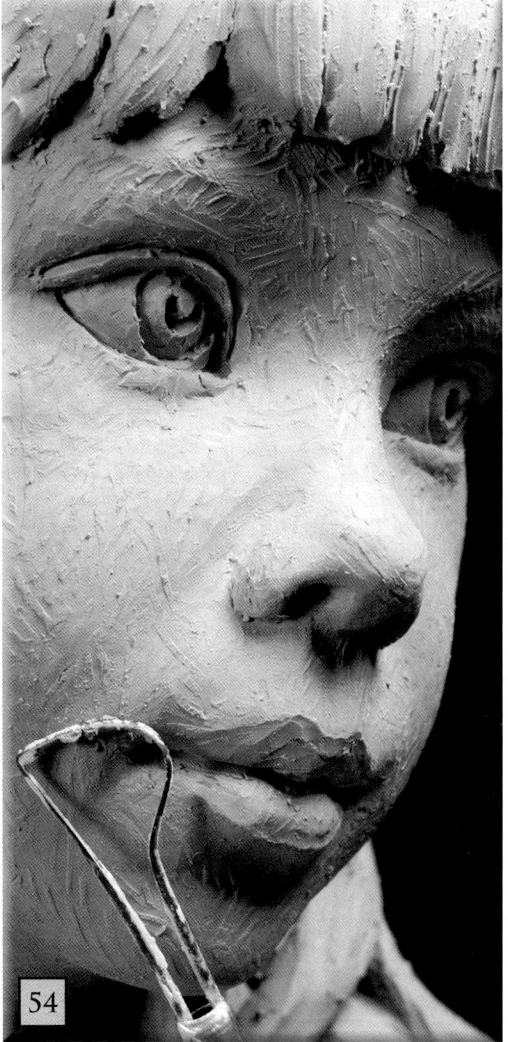


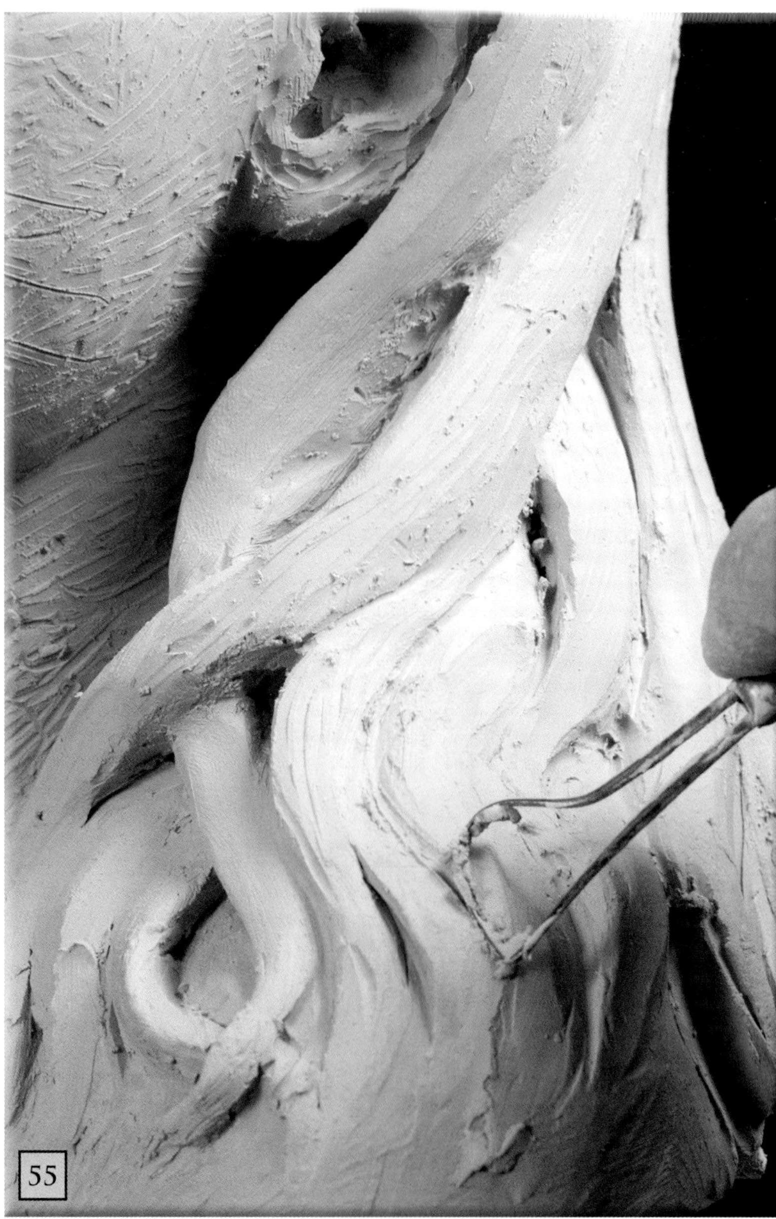


53, 54, 55. Many different tools can be used to refine and texture the hair and skin surfaces. Prior to refining further, it is beneficial to leave the piece covered and out of sight for several days. A fresh eye may reveal structural weaknesses previously unnoticed. If the sculpture were completely finished at this point, one might hesitate to modify these imperfections, which almost always become more noticeable over time.

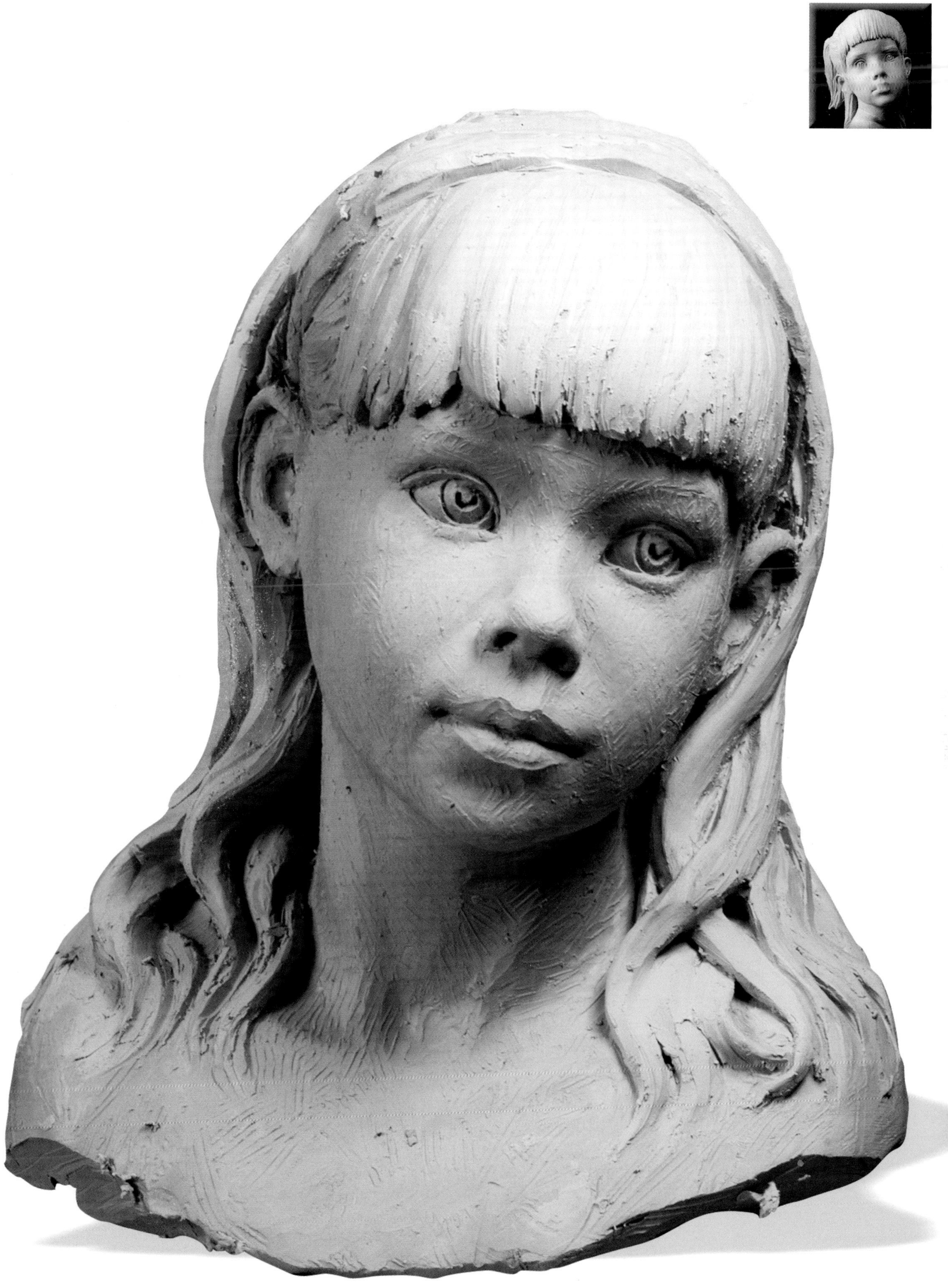

## The Oversized Portrait

Sculpting an oversized portrait presents particular challenges and requires a different approach depending on the degree of enlargement. Up to approximately twice life-size, it can be done by direct measurements from the model using proportional calipers. Any work that needs to be larger, requires first, the modeling of a life-size maquette and then the use of mechanical enlarging techniques such as a pantograph. The portrait shown on these pages is exactly twice life-size and was modeled using proportional calipers.

One of the difficulties when modeling an oversized portrait is to keep the features in proportion, because the closeness to the piece prevents an accurate judgement of the volumes. It is, more than ever, necessary to have good lighting, to work in a standing position and to have plenty of room to back up from the sculpture. There is a tendency when working oversized to make the features too small and to flatten the face. The use of proportional calipers to take precise measurements is a big help, but it is as important to work mainly in profile and three-quarter avoiding the front view as much as possible.

The same techniques used throughout Chapter 5 can be applied to a sculpture that is large. The following photos illustrate some of the precautions to be considered.

Water-based clay is very heavy. To lighten the weight of the sculpture, paper is wrapped around the dowel forming the entire core of the head and shoulders.

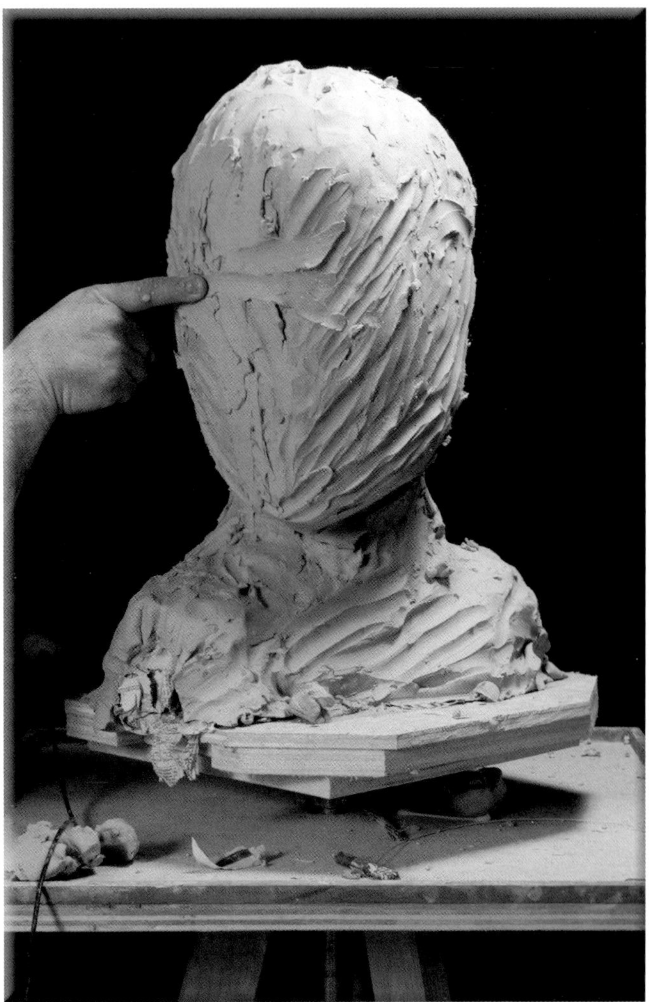

The basic volumes are built out of harder clay to prevent collapse. It can either be clay that is somewhat drier, or clay with grog, because it has more body.

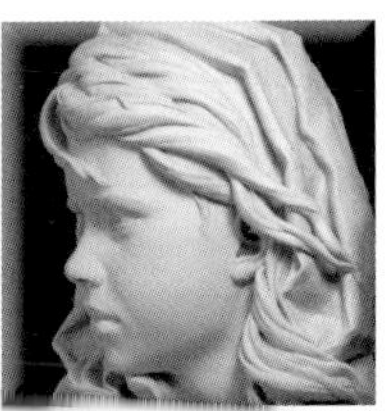

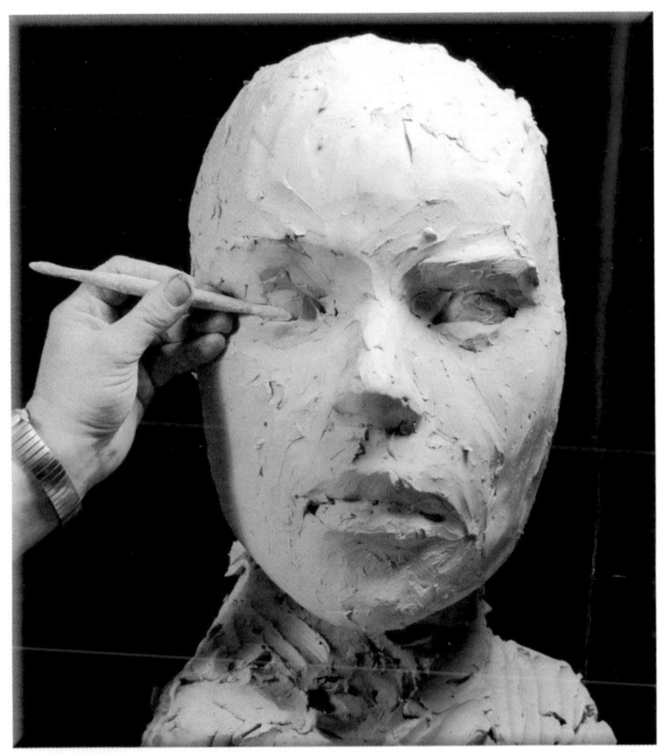

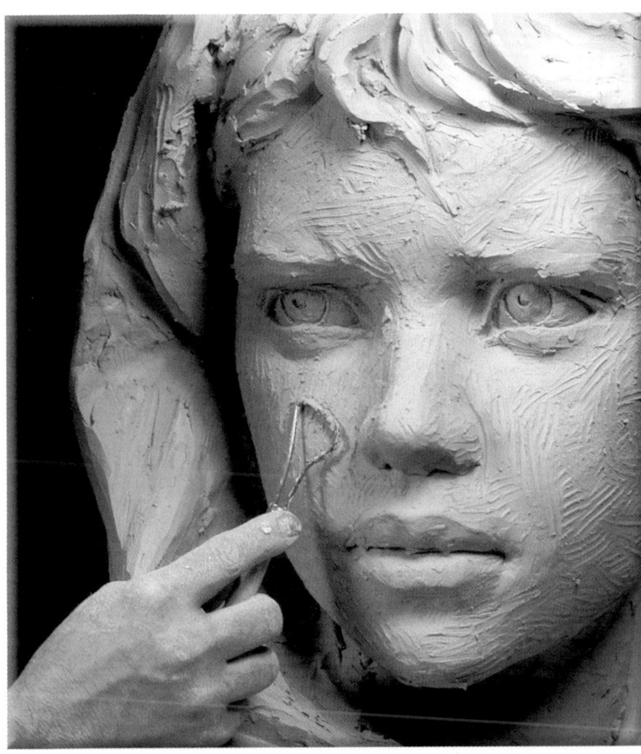

Most of the tools used are essentially the same; however, larger serrated loop tools are useful.

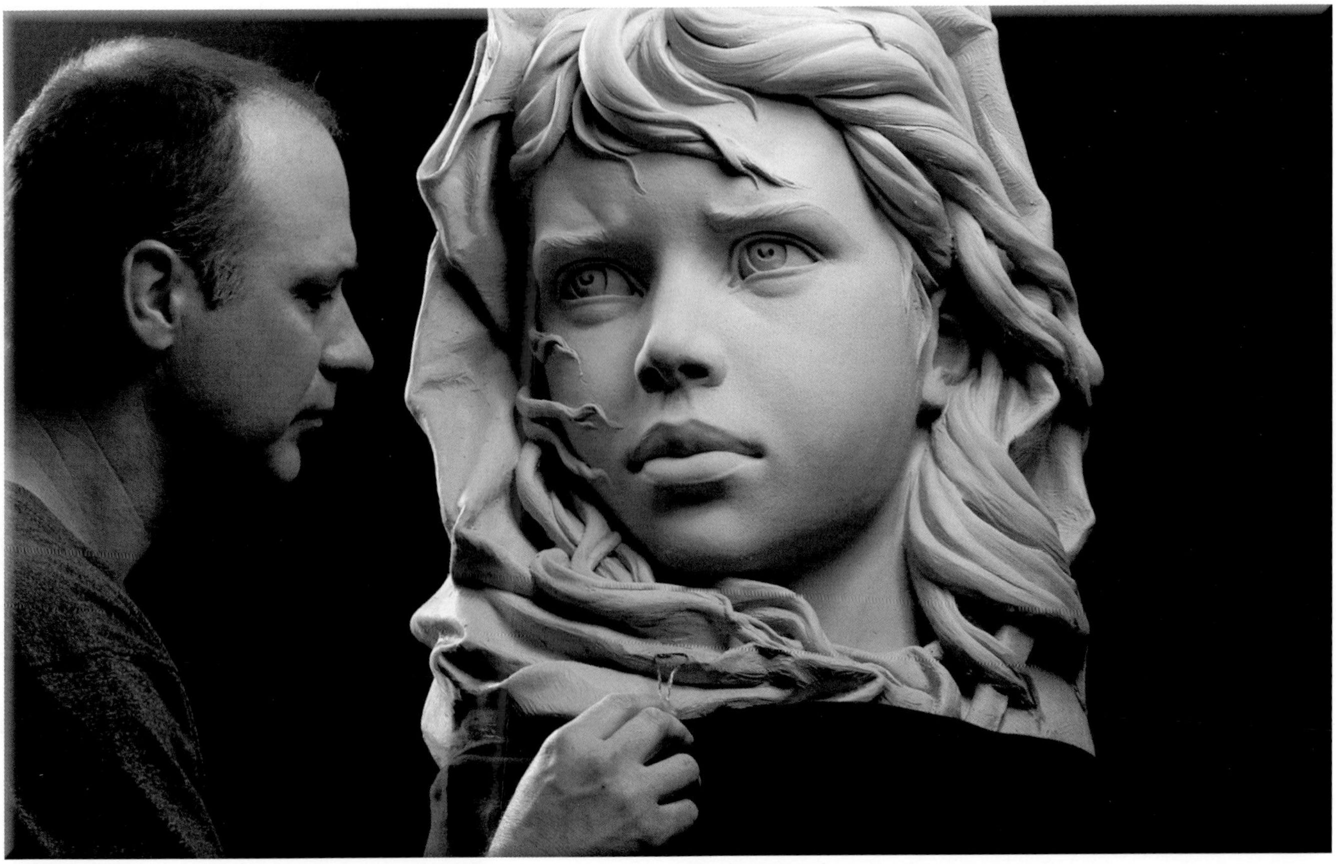

Chapter 6

# Common Mistakes

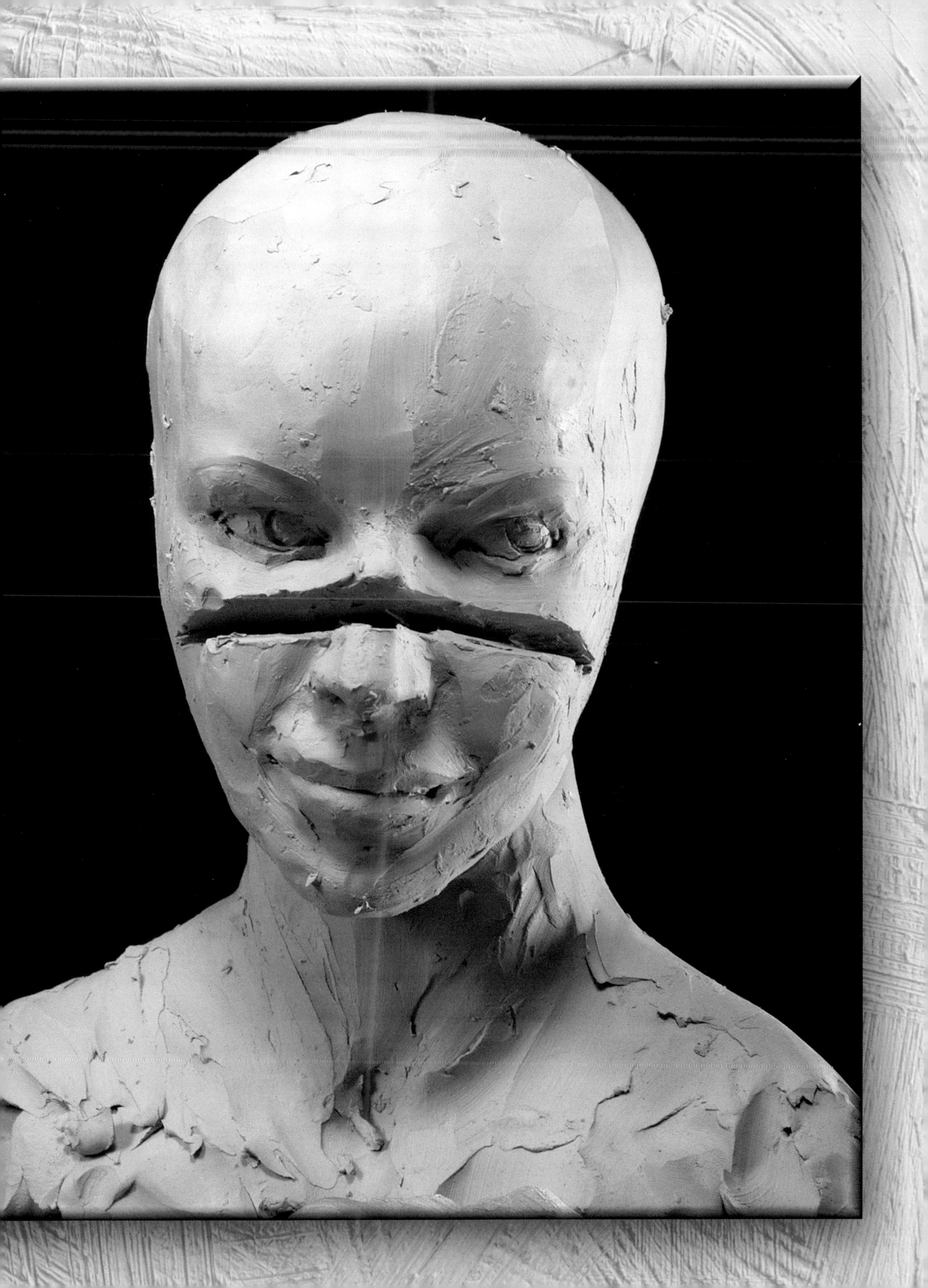

## Main Proportions

Misunderstood volumes can come from lack of experience, but is often due to not observing a methodical approach. Even though some of these problems could be avoided by the use of calipers or simple observation during the sculpting process, it seems that there is a recurring series of mistakes often made by beginners. The following chapter points out the most common of these mistakes and offers some simple solutions on how to correct them.

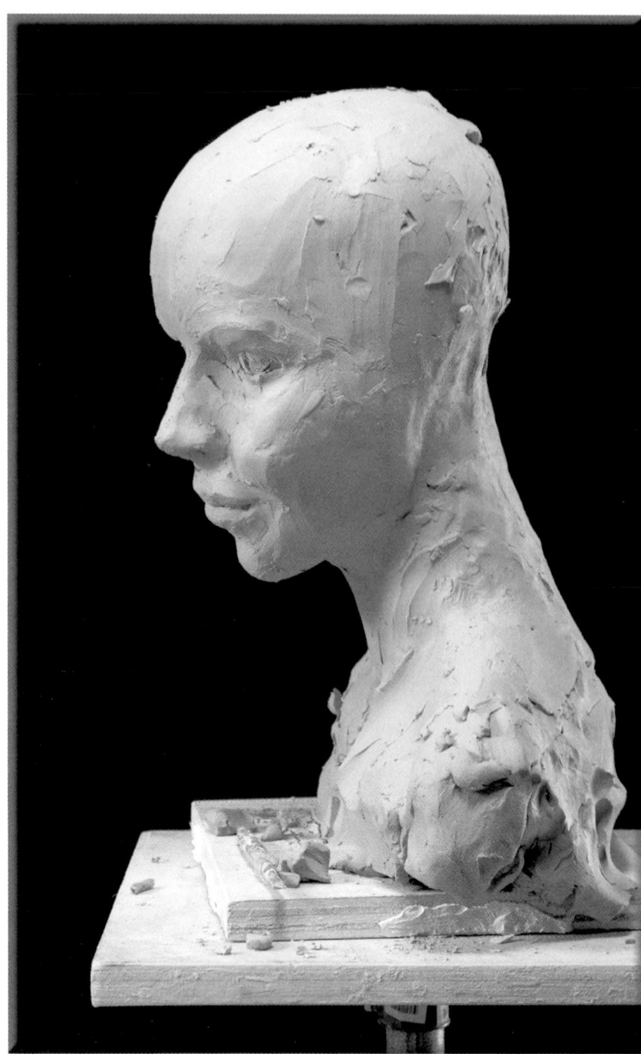

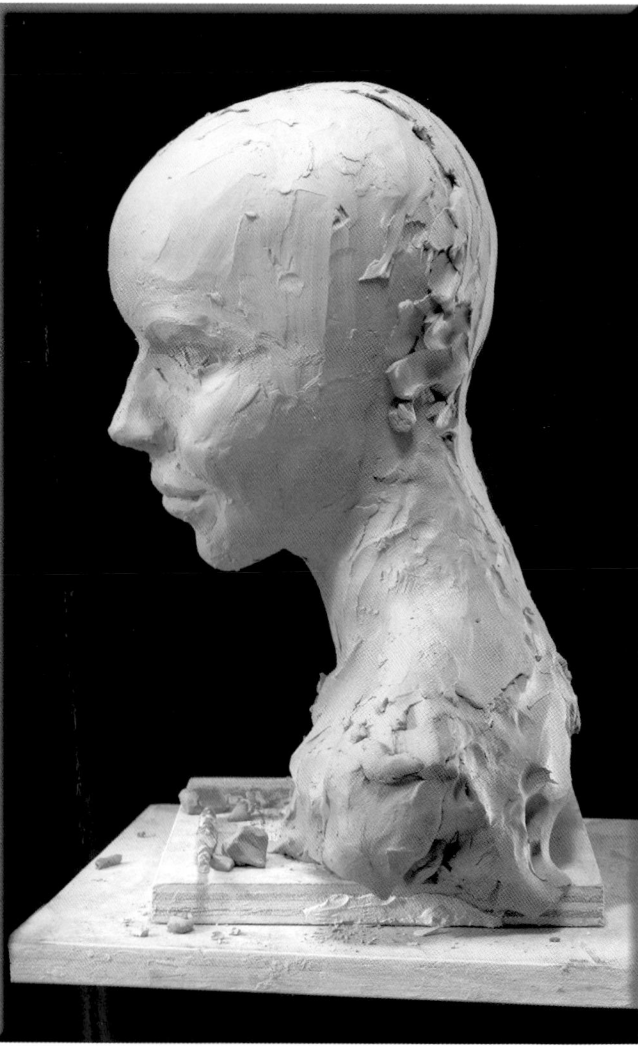

Students are often so focused on the face, that they neglect the surrounding volumes. This neglect almost always results in disproportion between the face and the cranium. Most often the face is sculpted larger than it should be. If the portrait has to be of a specific size, it may have to be resculpted from the start. However, if a larger final size is not critical, the problem can be easily fixed.

In this example, the cranium needs more volume. A coil of clay is first added along the center line to define the correct profile. Then the sides can be filled in with more clay. The best way to prevent this problem is to pay particular attention to the vertical placement of the eyes and to the size of each feature.

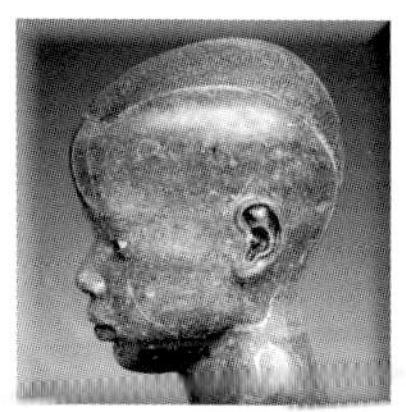

## Modification of the Profile

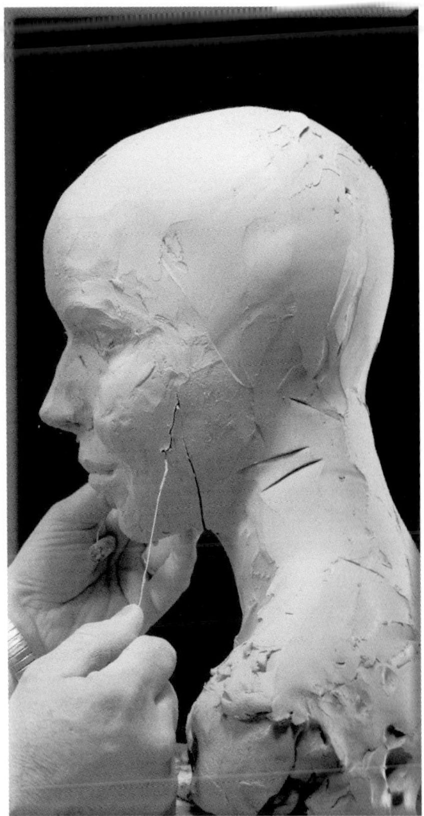

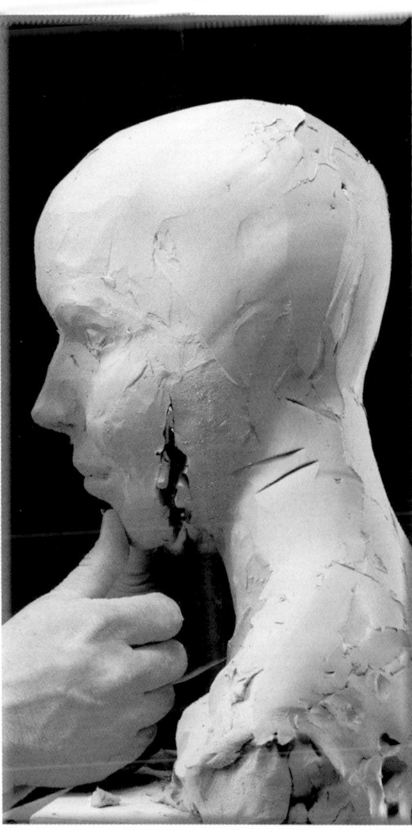

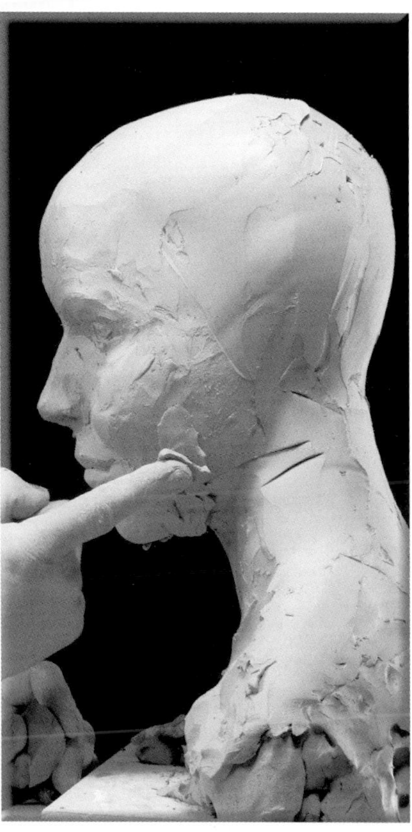

Sometimes the profile needs to be modified after the features are already in place. Removing a wedge of clay under the chin allows good control of the volumes without having to redo the nose and mouth. In this case, the base of the face is pushed backward then the remaining crack is repaired with soft clay. If the consistency of the clay forming the sculpture is already firm, some precaution must be taken. The inside of the crack should be moistened with a brush prior to fixing it to prevent reopening during the drying process. The same method can be used to bring the base of the face forward.

## Vertical Adjustments

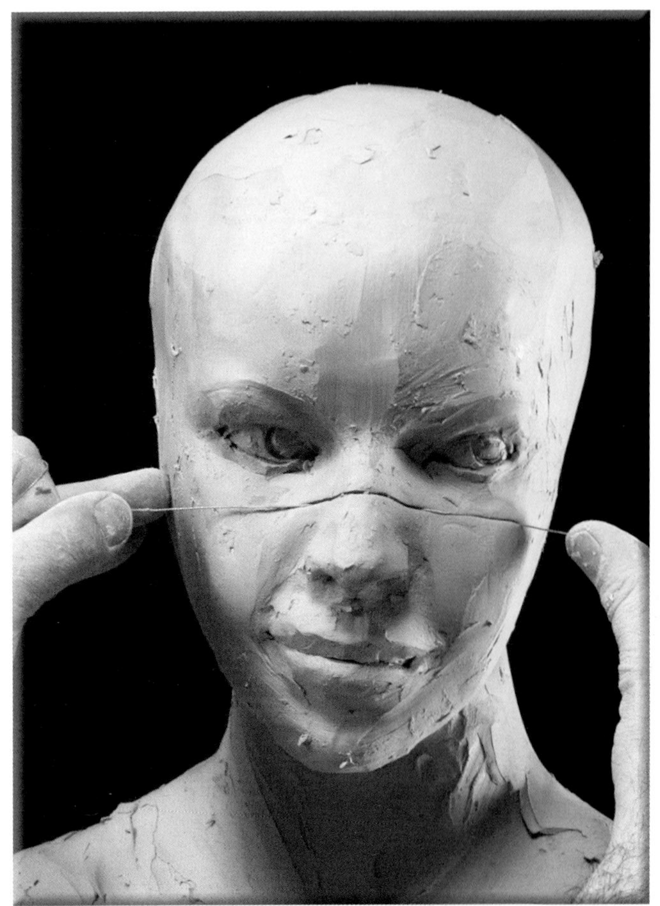

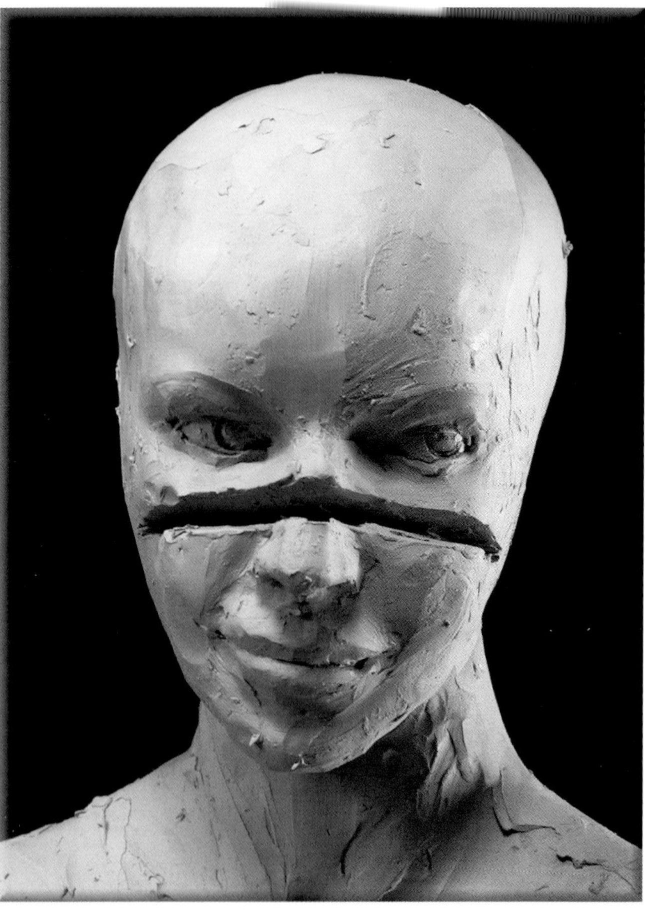

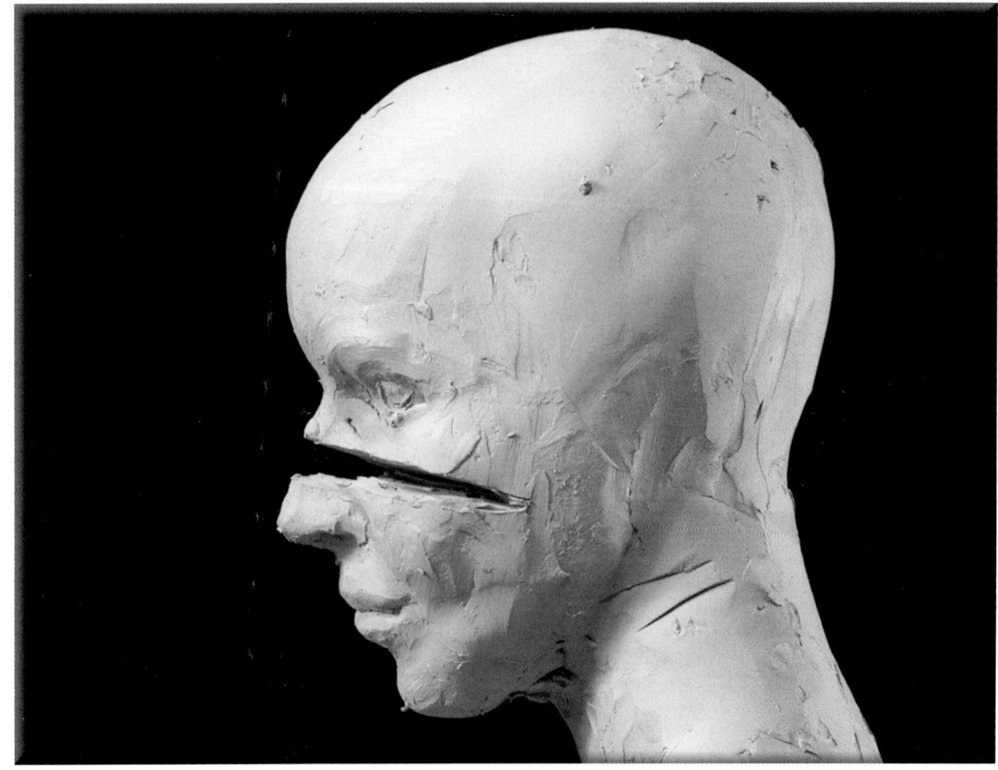

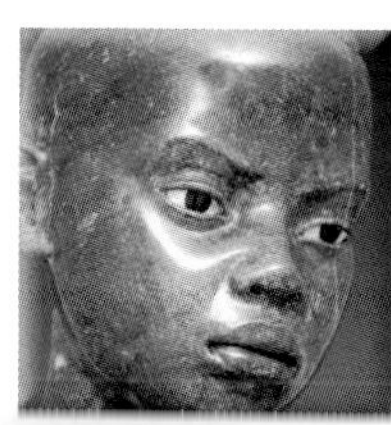

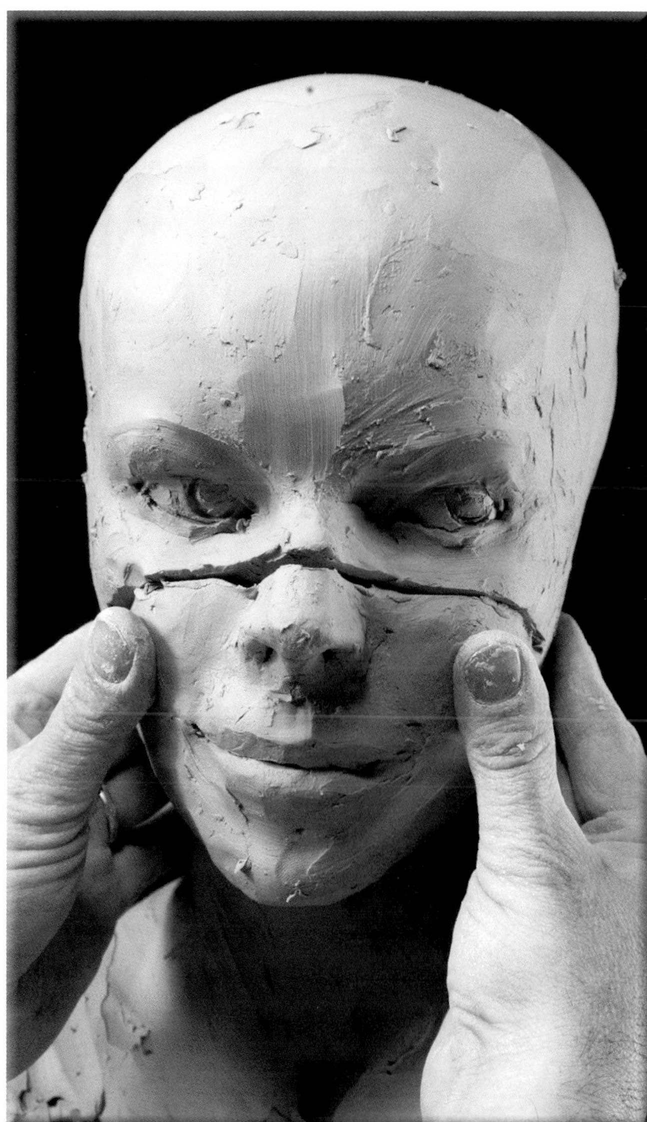

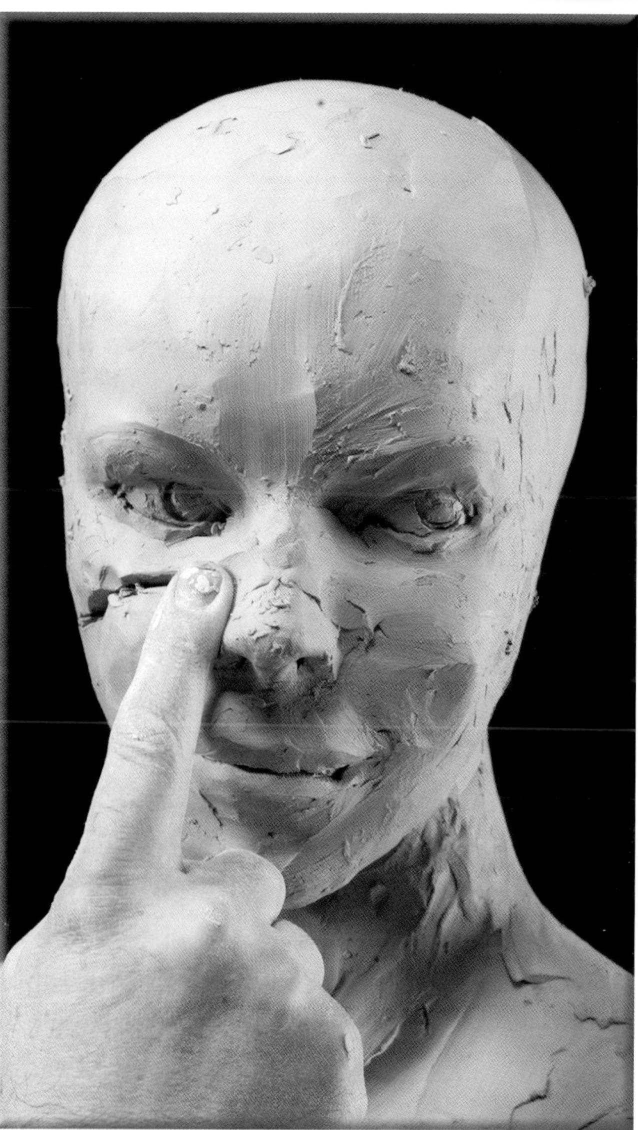

The same method can be applied to shorten or elongate the face. In this case, it is done to shorten the nose by pushing the face upward once the wedge has been removed. It could also be used in the same manner between the nose and the mouth. Even though this method might seem traumatic, it is an easy, fast, and safe way to fix small proportion problems. Notice that the slicing is made in areas simple to repair and that have little impact on the more complex features such as the nose, mouth, and eyes.

## Flat or Concave Upper Eyelid

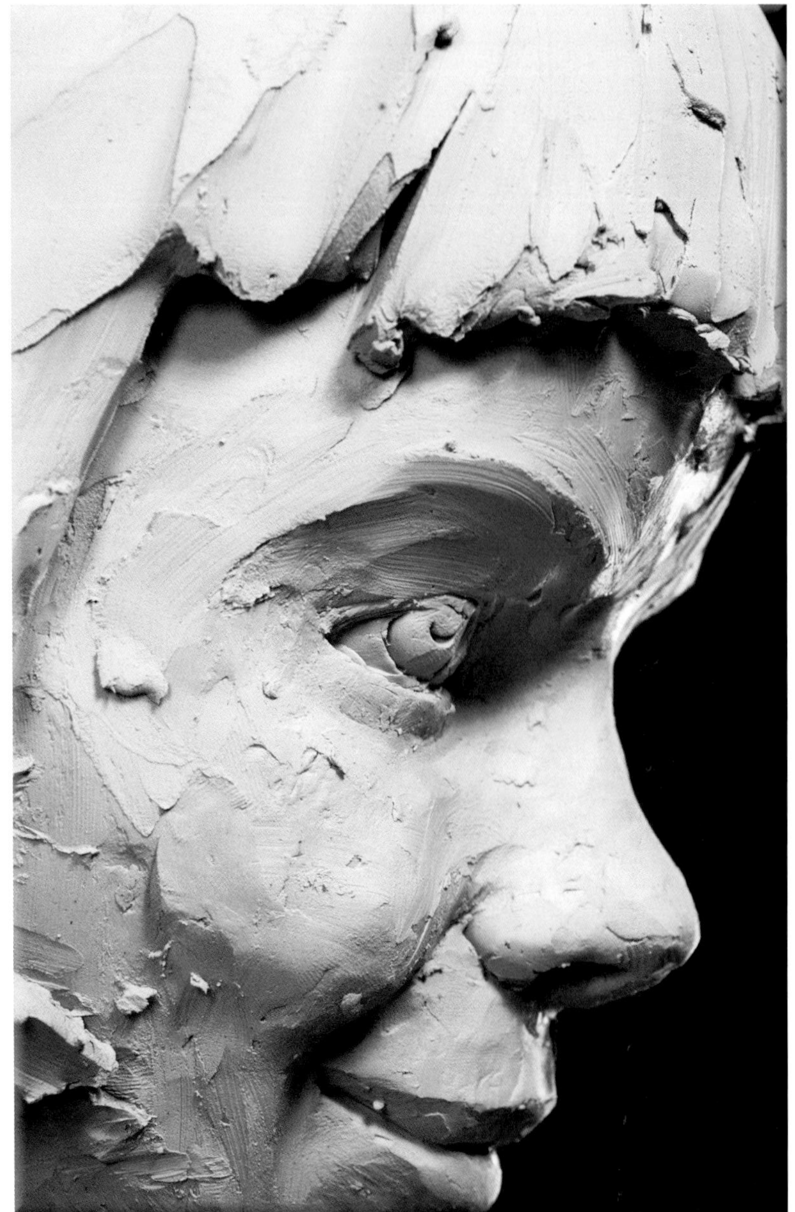

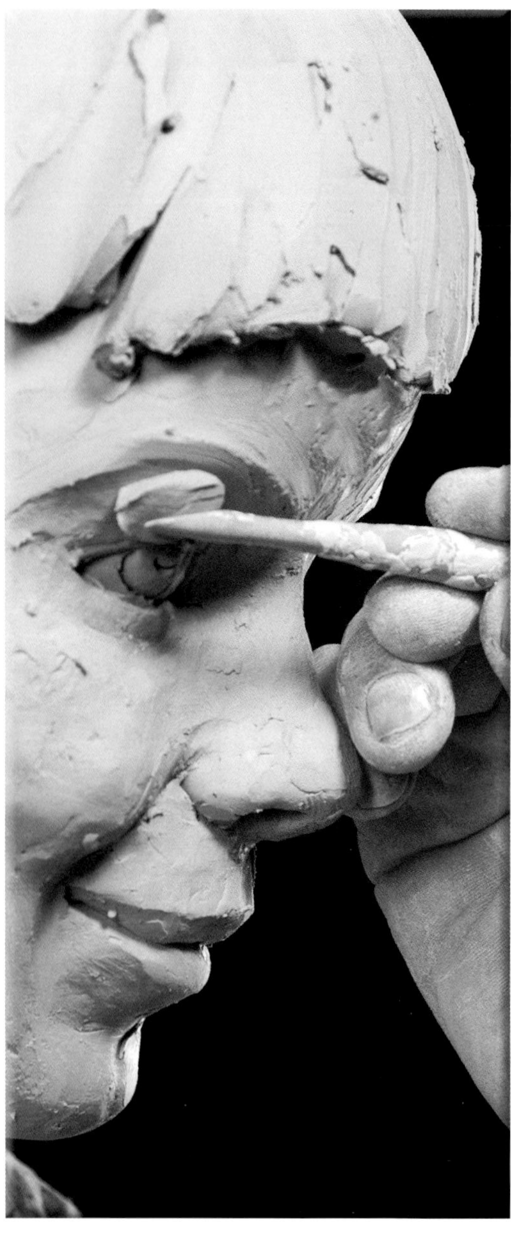

The volumes of the upper eyelid are often neglected by students, resulting in a flat, or even concave plane instead of a convex one. This phenomenon has the effect to give a surprised expression to the eyes even when none is intended. To fix this problem clay needs to be added under the eyebrow and rounded.

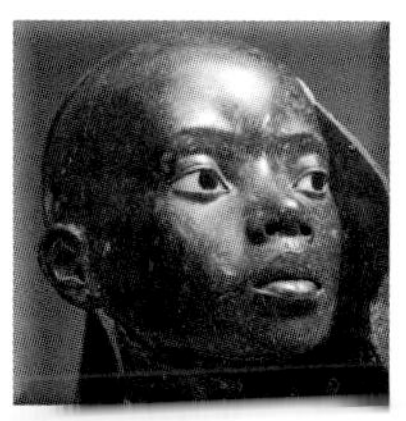

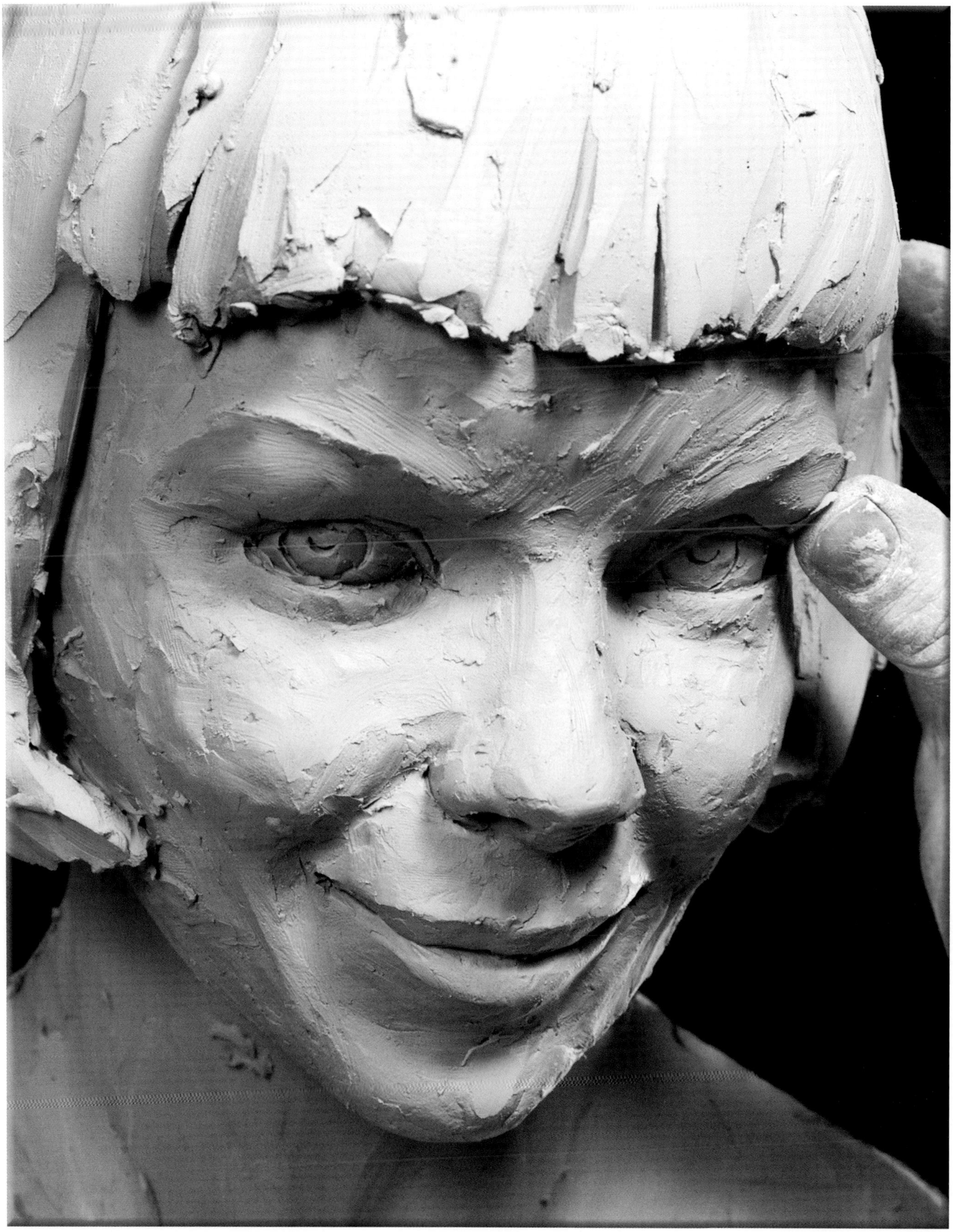

## Corner of the Mouth

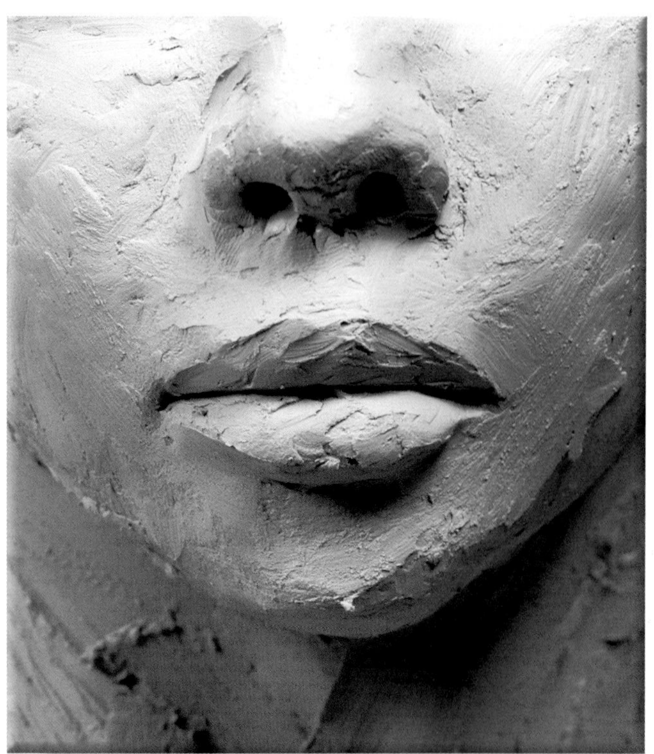
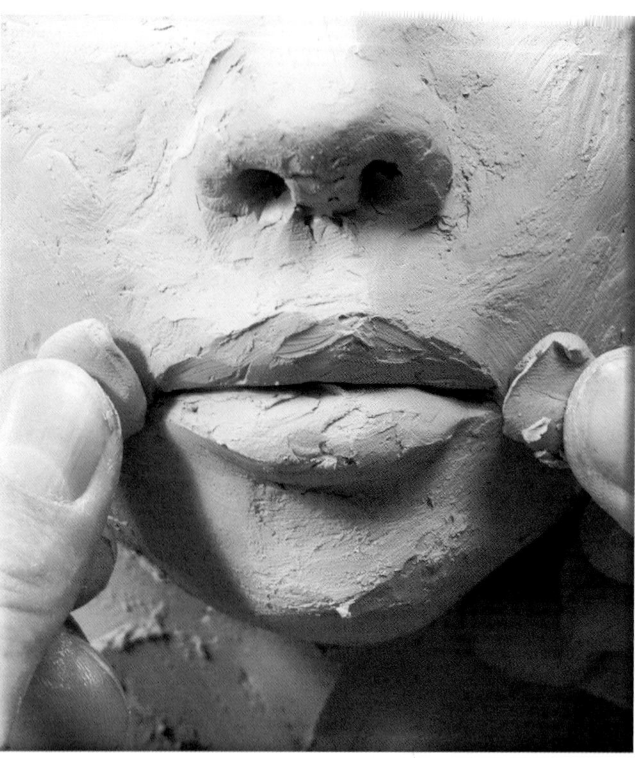

The corners of the mouth should be deeper than the surrounding facial tissues. There is also a bulging of the flesh on each side of the mouth produced by the intricate connection of several muscles underneath. These volumes are often neglected resulting in a flat and angry looking mouth.

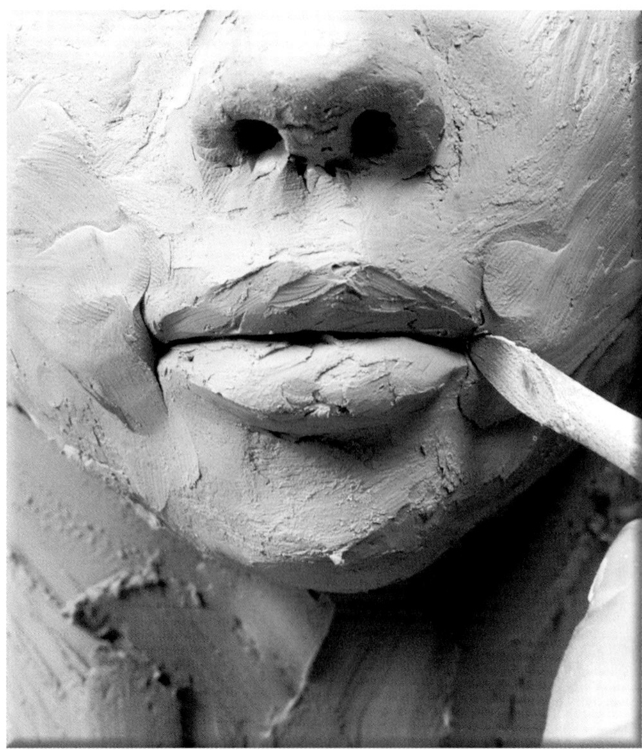
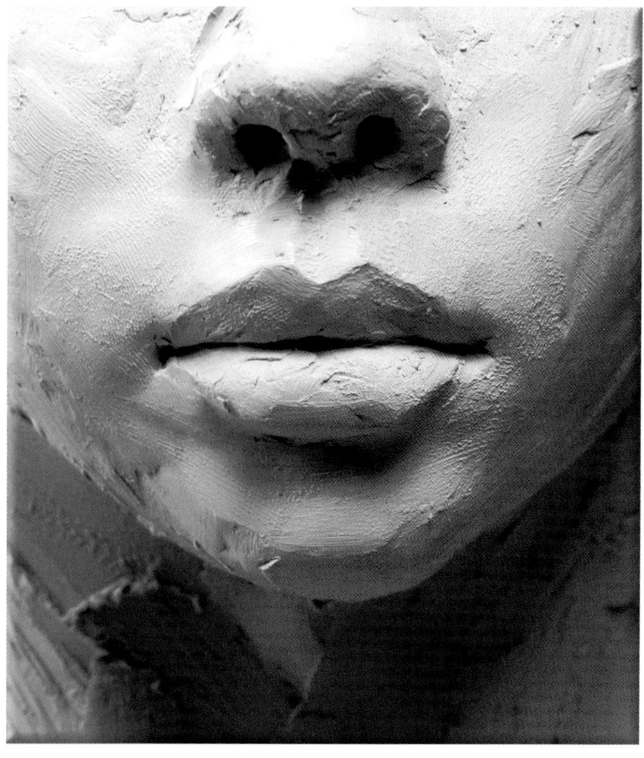

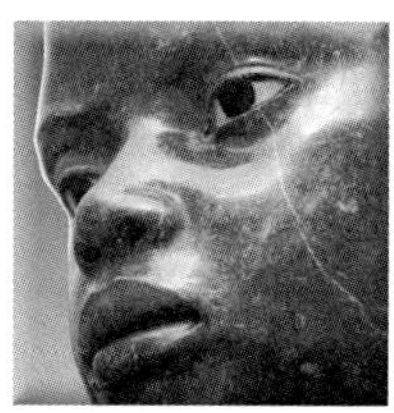

## Plane of the Philtrum

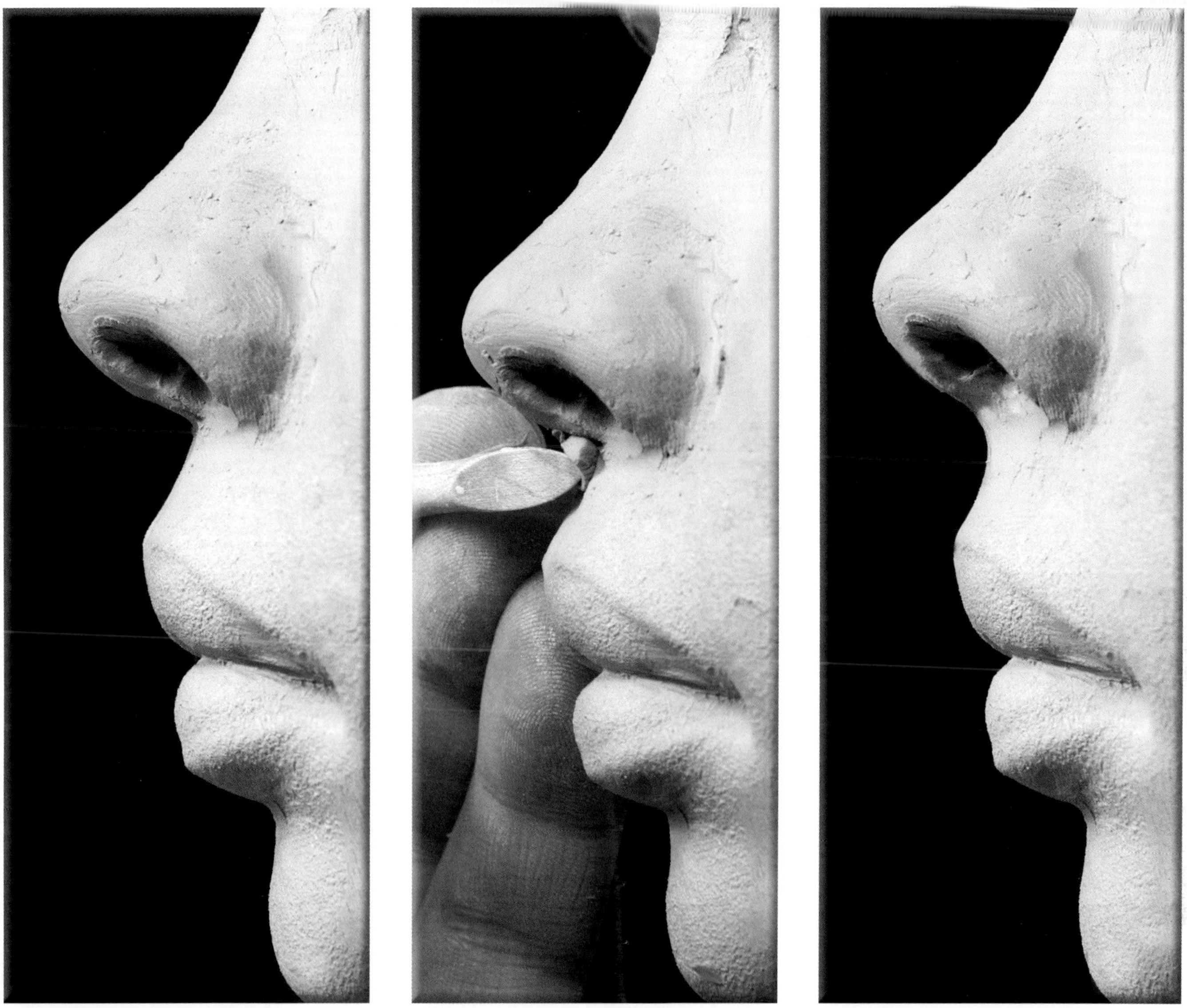

The nose does not meet the upper lip at a sharp angle. A plane, or soft curve marks the transition between the two. This is particularly noticeable in the outline of the profile. Refer back to the explanation on page 38.

## Angle of the Eye

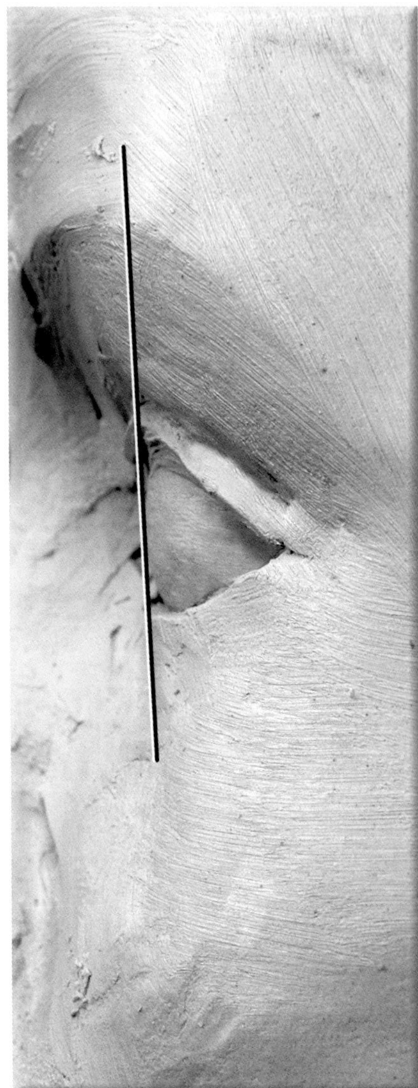

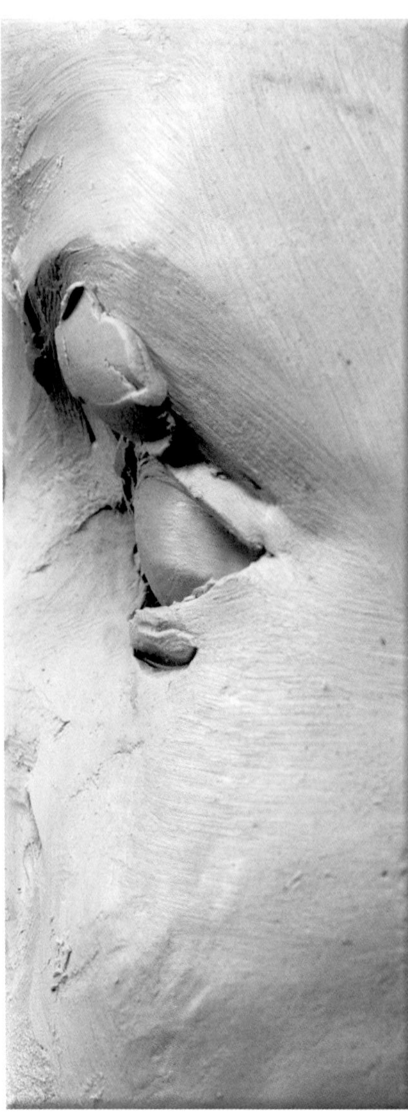

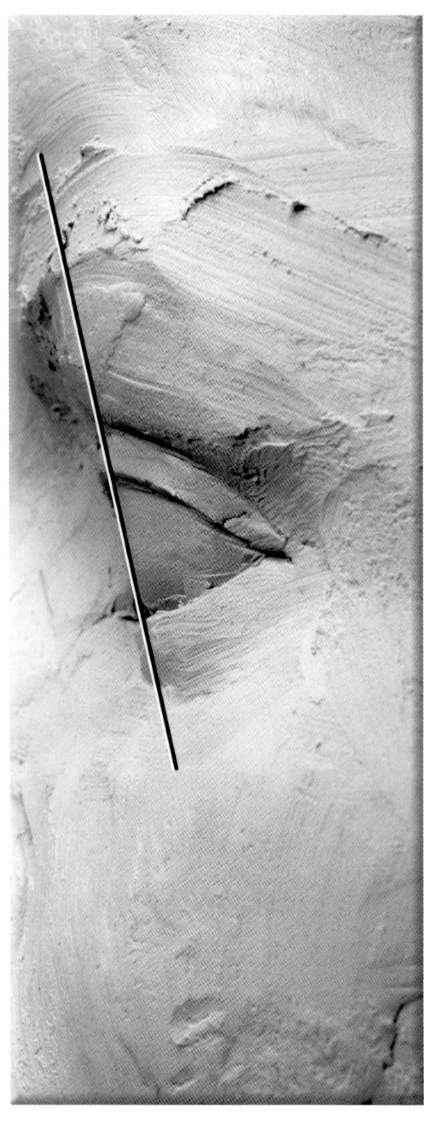

Perhaps the most common mistake made when modeling the eye is the lack of protrusion of the upper lid in relation to the lower lid (see diagram, page 48). This has the effect of flattening the face. Once again this is more noticeable when viewed in profile. In the example above, volume is added to the upper eyelid but sometimes it is the lower eyelid that needs to be recessed. In that case, the concave side of the wooden tool is used to push the lower part of the eyeball. Then the thickness of the eyelid is readjusted to follow the curvature of the eyeball.

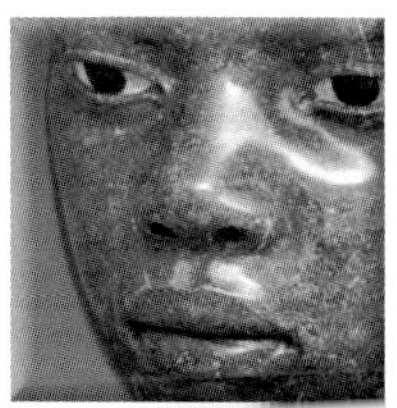

## Planes of the Lips

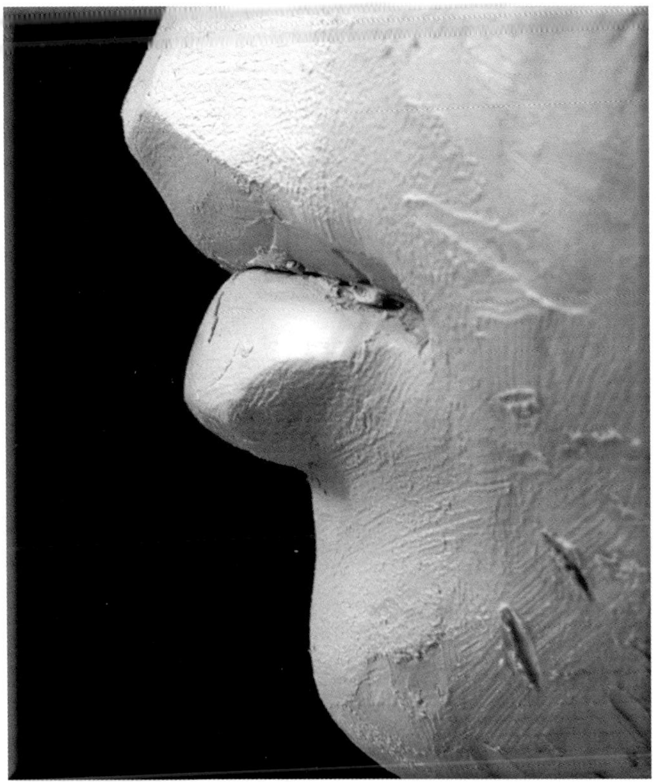

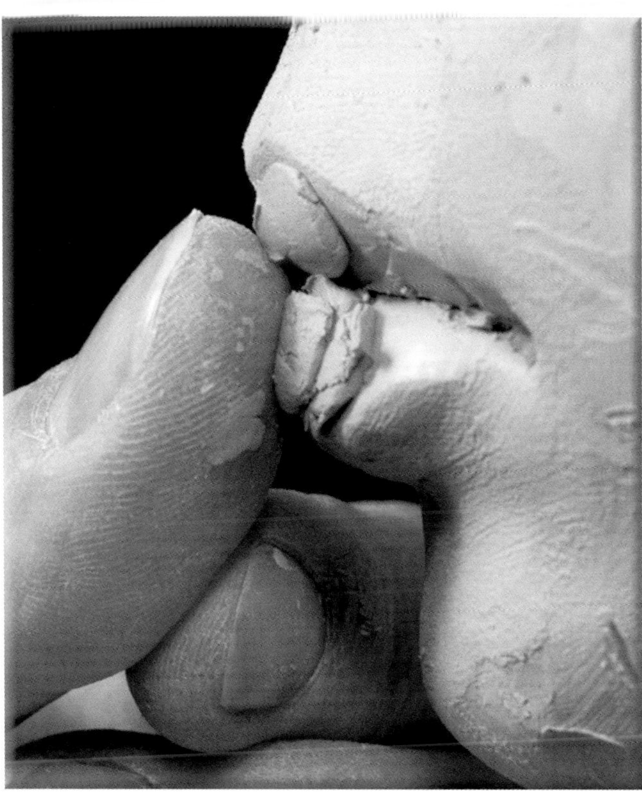

The roundness of the lips is easier to assess when viewed from profile. The lips are often too flat and need to be built up with respect to their particular shapes.

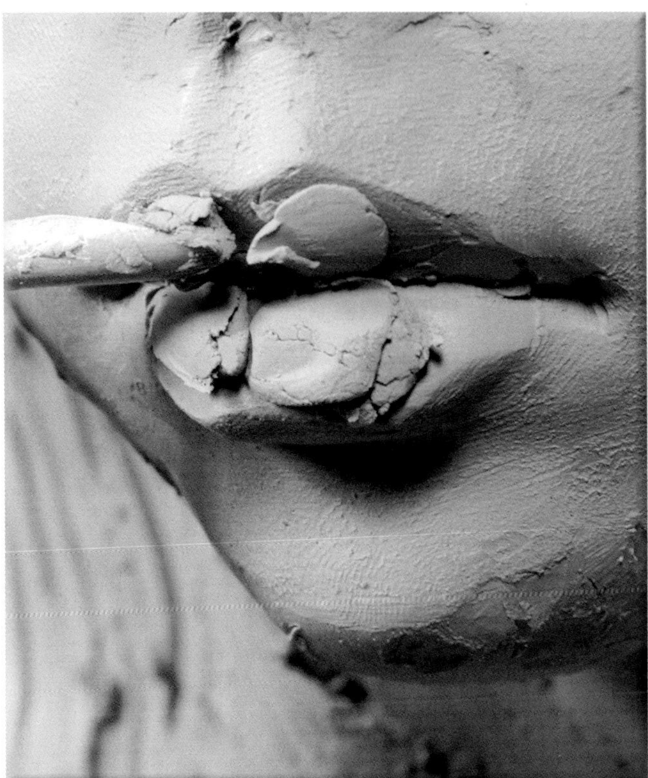

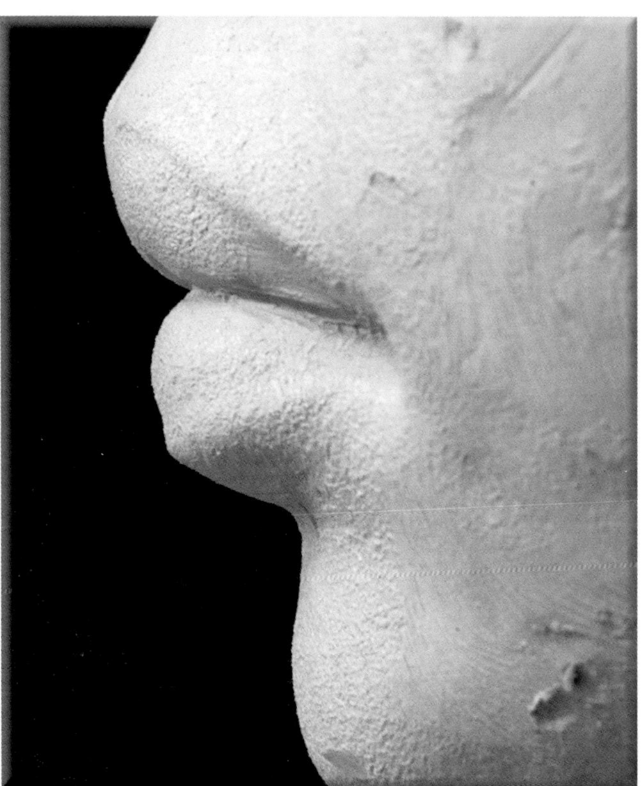

## Medial Corner of the Eye

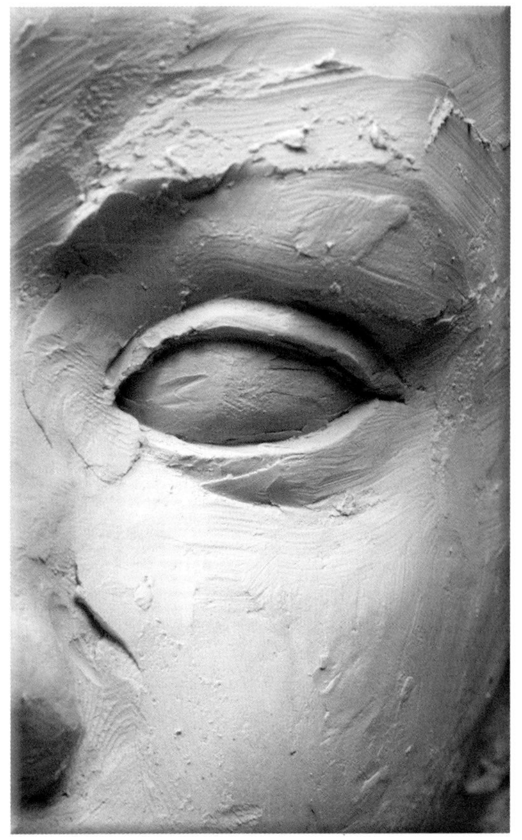

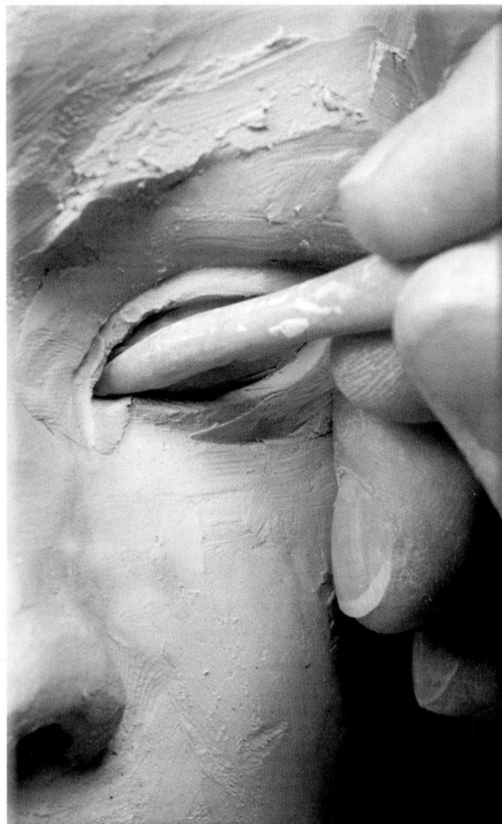

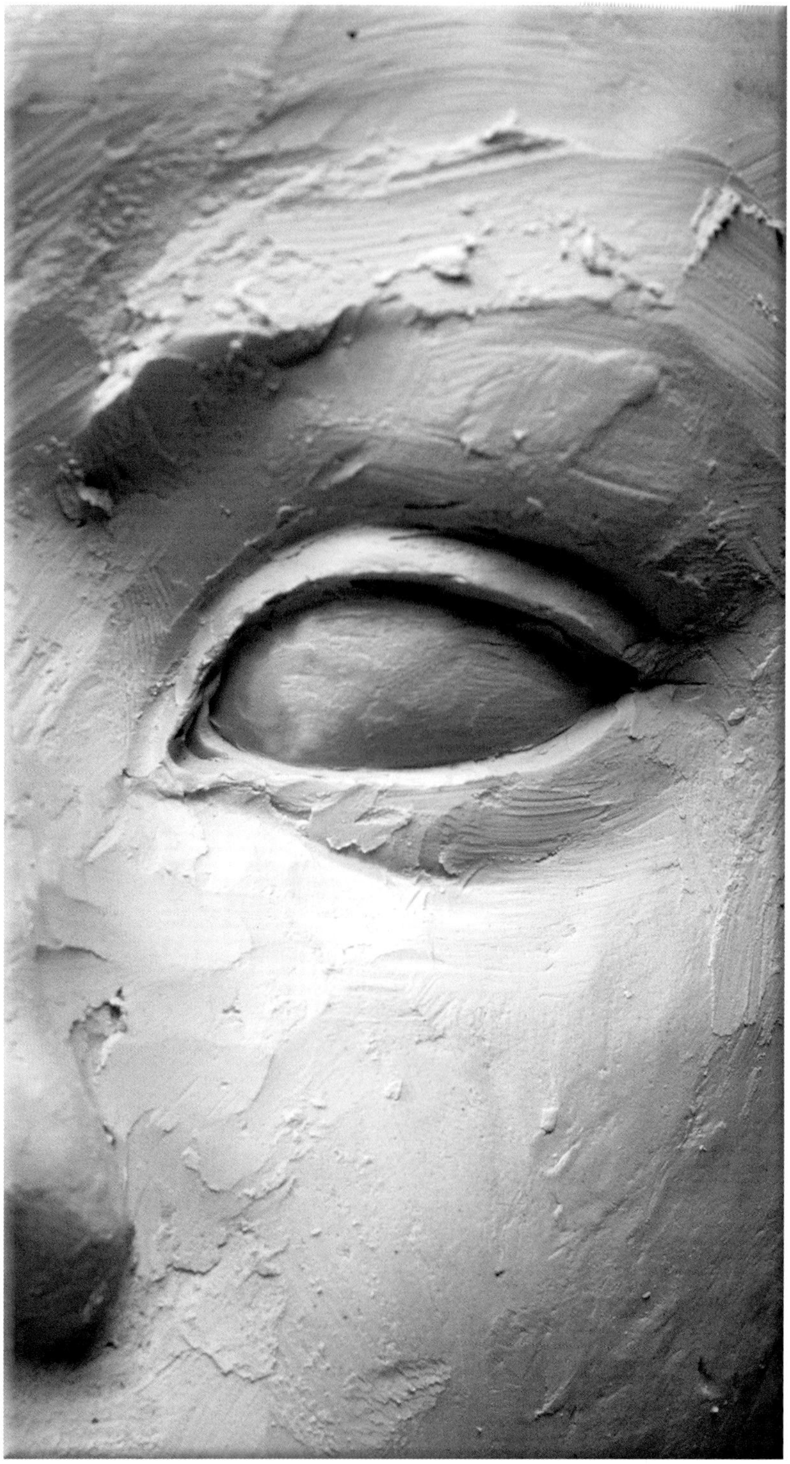

The shape of the eye is not an oval. Particular attention should be given to the level of the inside corner of the eye. It is always lower than the outer corner.

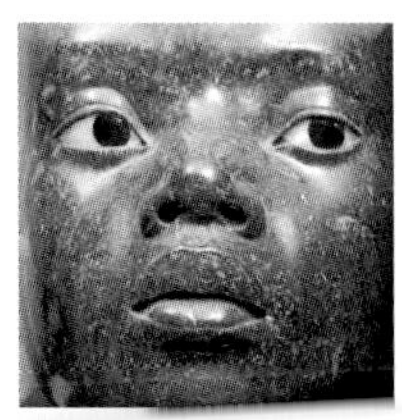

## Modifications from Inside

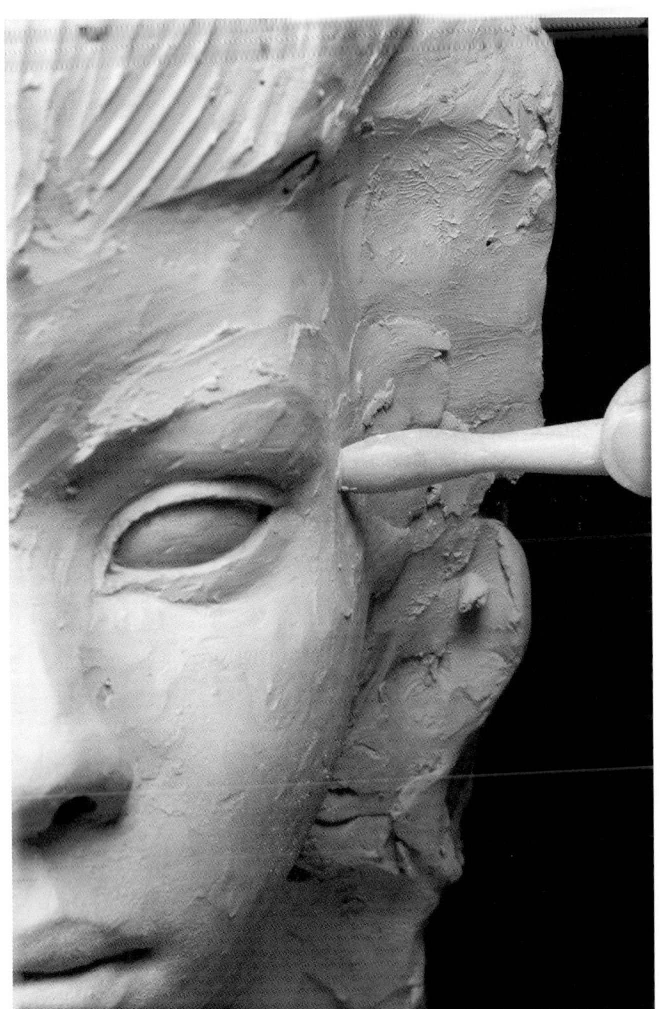

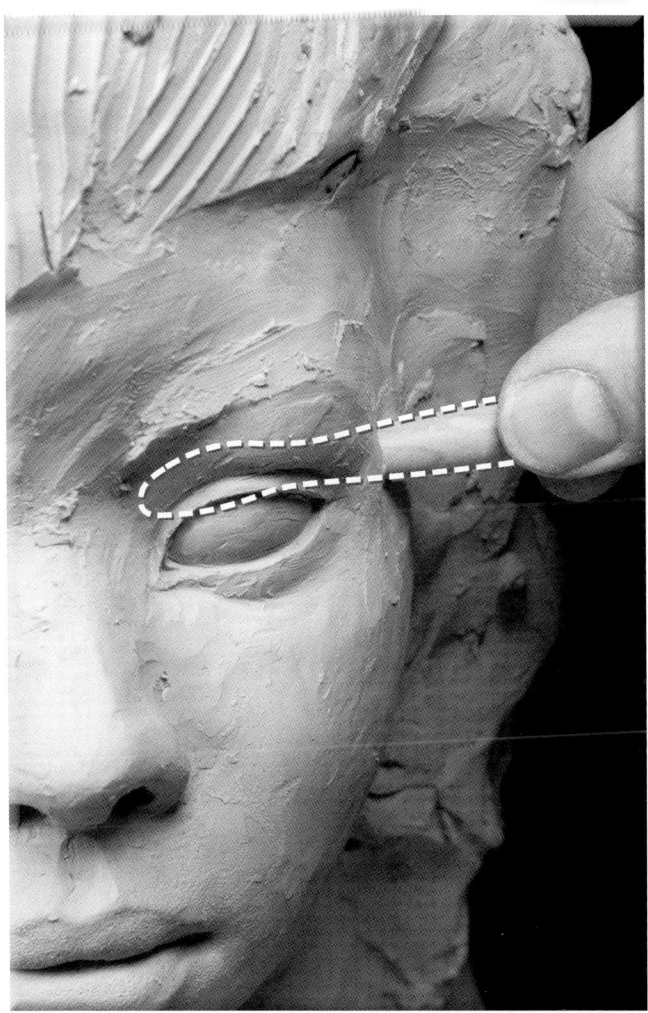

Sometimes one of the features such as the corner of an eye is too deep on the face. Instead of building on it, a wooden tool can be inserted inside the sculpture and used as a lever to push out the corner of the eye. This method can also be used if the nose, or the mouth, need to be pulled forward. This method has the advantage of controlling the depth of the features with minimal damage to work already done. Once the adjustment is done, the hole created by the tool is simply plugged with soft clay.

# Chapter 7
# Expression

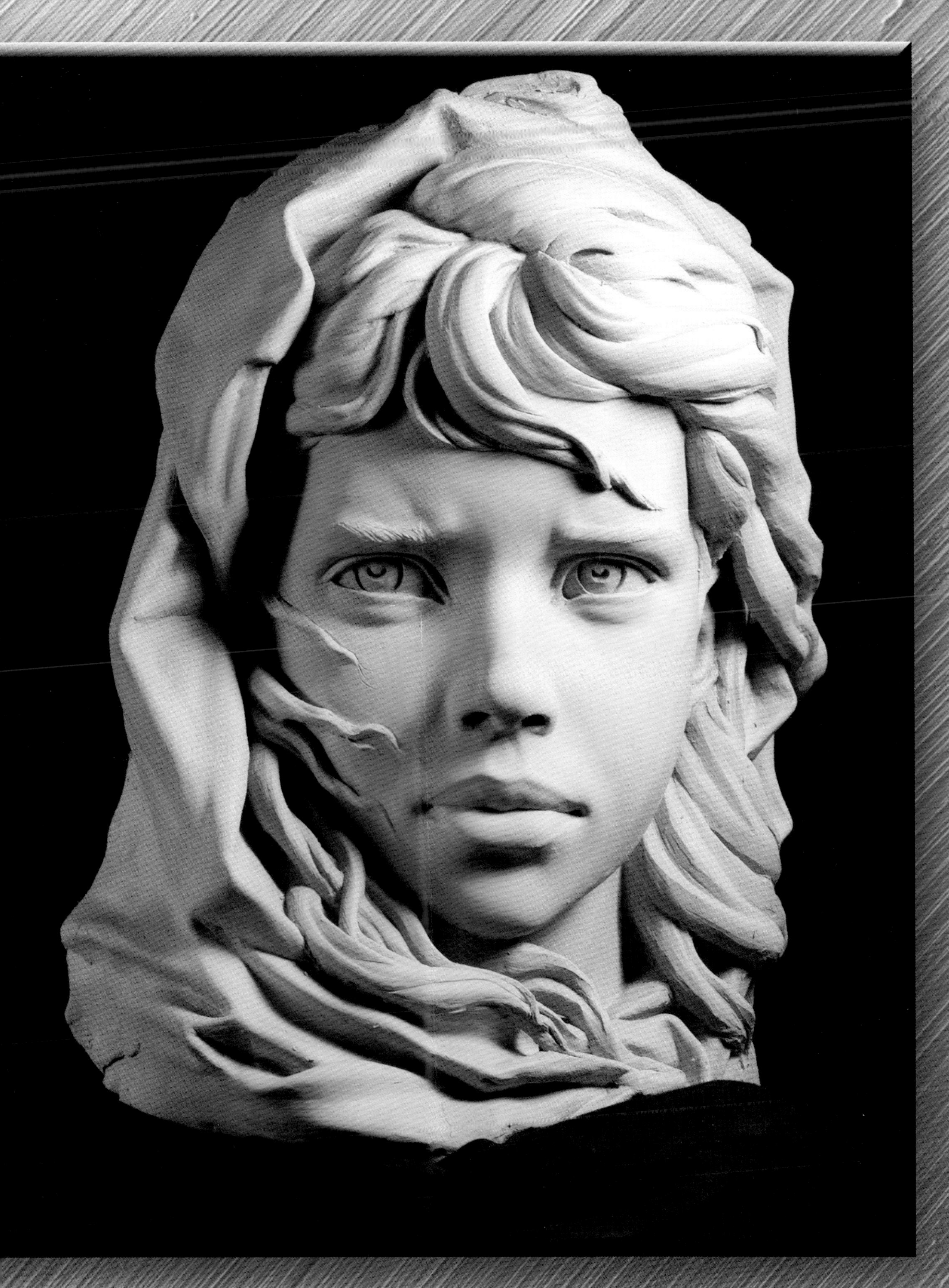

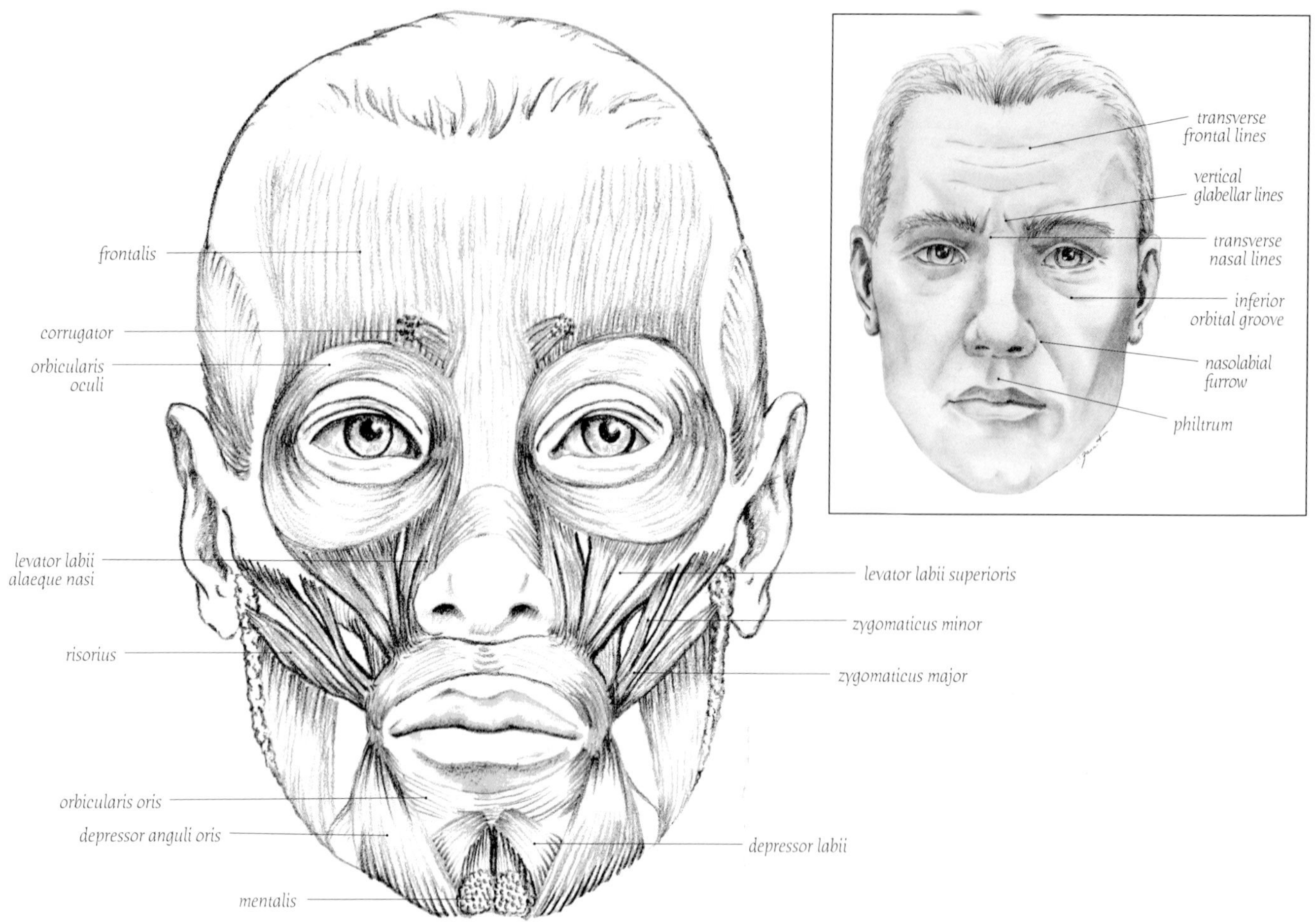


## FACIAL MUSCLES & LANDMARKS OF EXPRESSION

Facial expressions are a powerful mode of communicating our feelings to one another on a deep and immediate level. Physical changes on the face combined with body language are often even more powerful than words. Beneath the skin, muscles lying over one another form a matrix of moving tissues that cover our face. When these muscles contract or relax they move the face, forming expressions.

Some muscles are very small, but their subtle effects on the face can be as powerful in depicting emotion as larger muscle masses. For example, the contraction of the small mentalis muscle has the indirect effect of pushing up the lower lip, that if not itself contracted, will project out resulting in a pouting expression (see photo on page 7). A slight contraction of the corrugator will create a frown, and the smallest pull on the levator labii superior will produce a sneer.

When sculpting a portrait, a great deal of attention must be focused on the physical action of the facial muscles in order to communicate the mood of the piece. By studying and understanding the muscles of the face we stand a greater chance of not only depicting the chosen expression, but also of achieving a better likeness of the model.

The following photos are a brief study of a few expressions. The possibilities are endless and students are encouraged to practice on different models. The studies shown here were modeled on a near vertical board and focus only on the face. During these exercises, as during any sculpting session, it is important to view the work from every angle including profile, three quarter view, and from above and below. Working in a standing position facilitates this task and also allows the artist to step back and see the work from a distance. Once again, light is critical and either the light source or the work must be moved constantly to ensure that the desired expression remains constant regardless of the angle from which the piece is viewed.

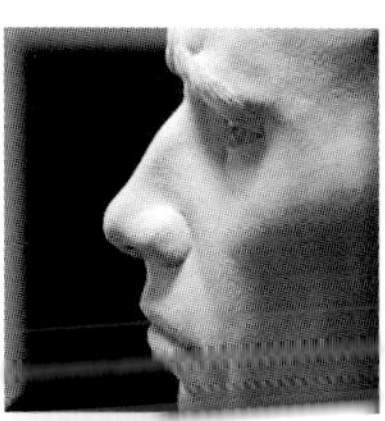

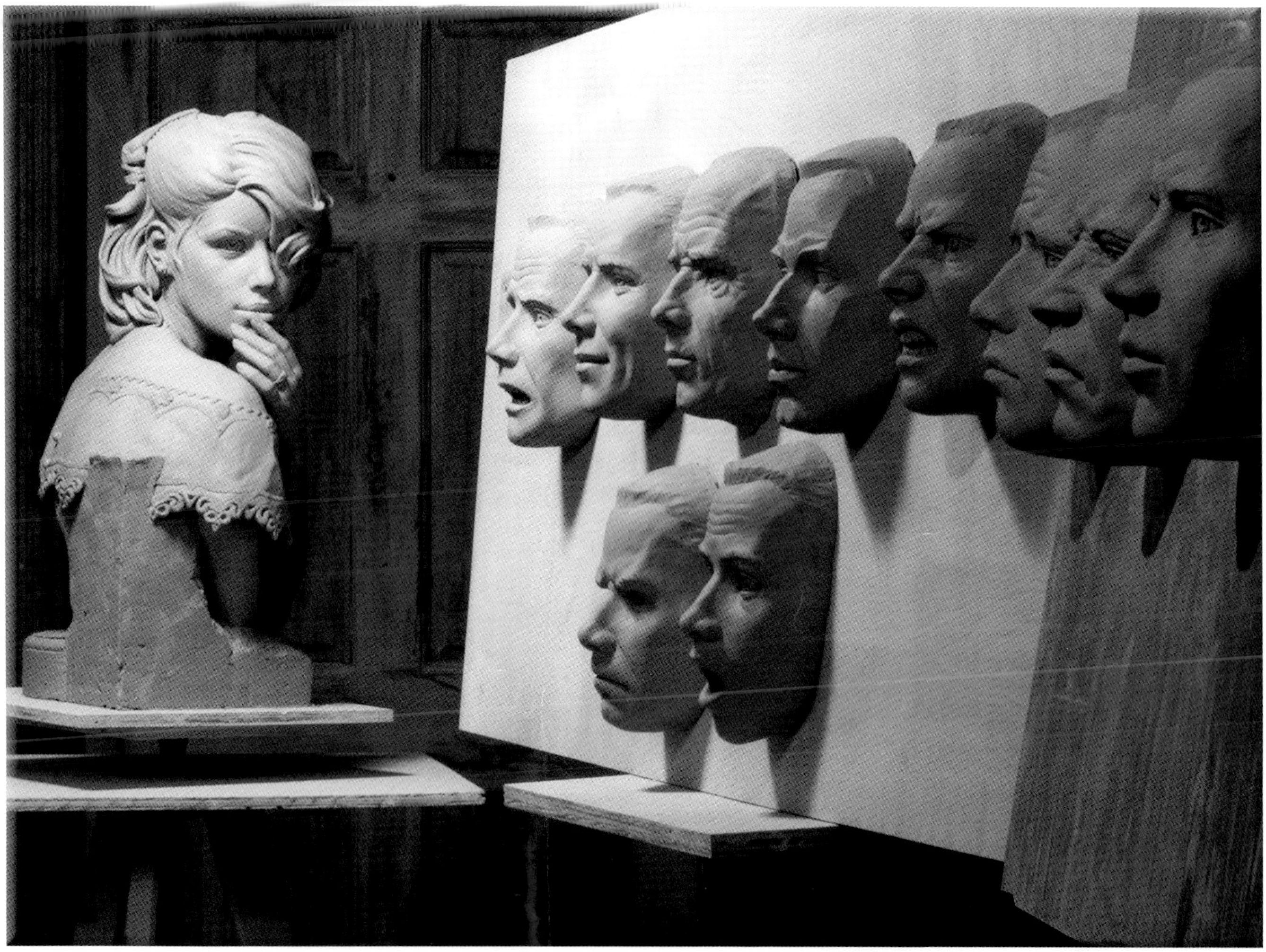

Expression is not only created by certain physical particularities of the face, but also body language and surrounding environmental factors. The sculpture shown above was originally intended to display an introspective, thoughtful expression. Once placed near the grouping of masks, she seemed to take on a look of quiet amusement.

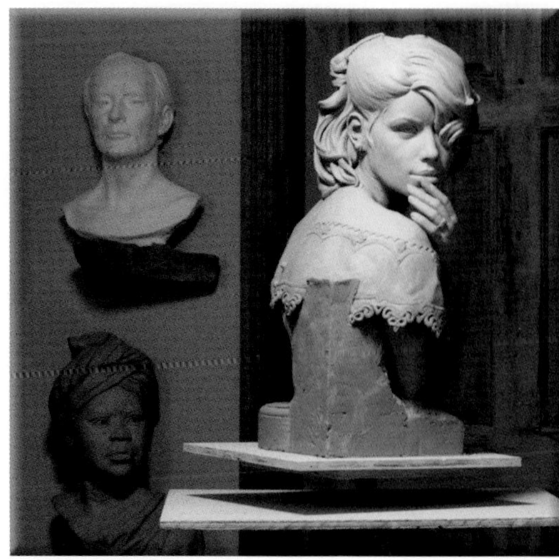

The same portrait shown in conjunction with pieces having different expressions gives the impression that the subject is contemplating something suspicious.

## Repose

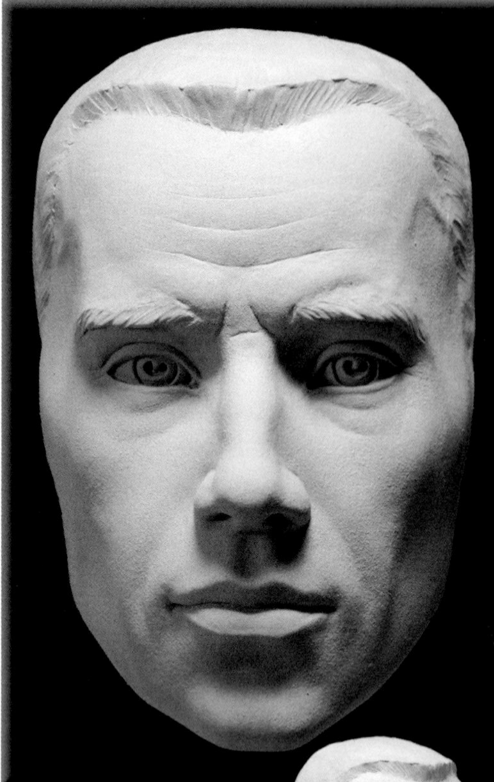

The face in repose is modeled first to serve as the reference piece for all other expressions. Since this sculpture must be kept intact, a second piece, identical to the reference piece, is sculpted and used to create the different expressions.

## Rage

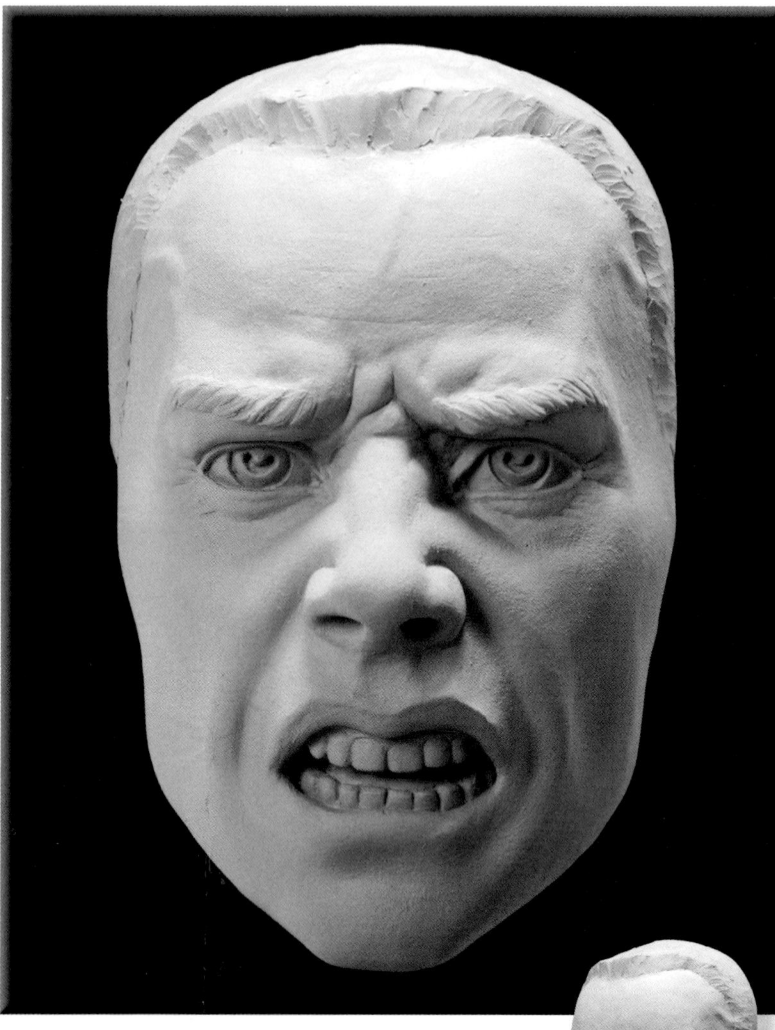

The corrugators pull the inner corners of the eyebrows toward the center of the face. The contraction of the corrugators also pulls a horizontal fold across the upper eyelids. The lower edge of the eyebrow drops below the level of the upper eyelid. This action also deepens the vertical glabellar lines. The action of the levator labii alaeque nasi also deepens the transverse nasal lines. The contraction of the orbicularis oculi creates the wrinkles in the outer corner of the eye and puffiness in the lower eyelid. In some people the veins on the forehead and the temples become visible. The pull of the levator labii deepens the nasolabial furrow and the inferior orbital groove while also creating the folds on each side of the nose. The nostrils flare and pull upward. The upper lips tense and lift upward, above the upper teeth. The orbicularis oris contracts and straightens the lower lip while the depressor labii inferioris pulls it down into a U-shape to expose the lower teeth. The risorius muscles pull the corners of the mouth to create the vertical folds on the lower cheeks.

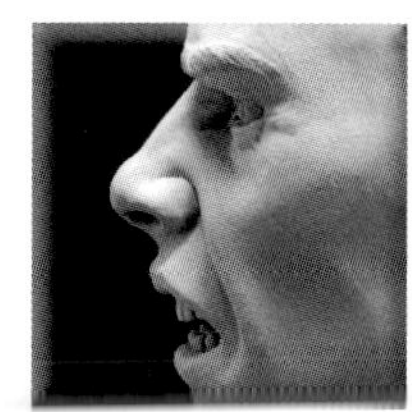

## Anger

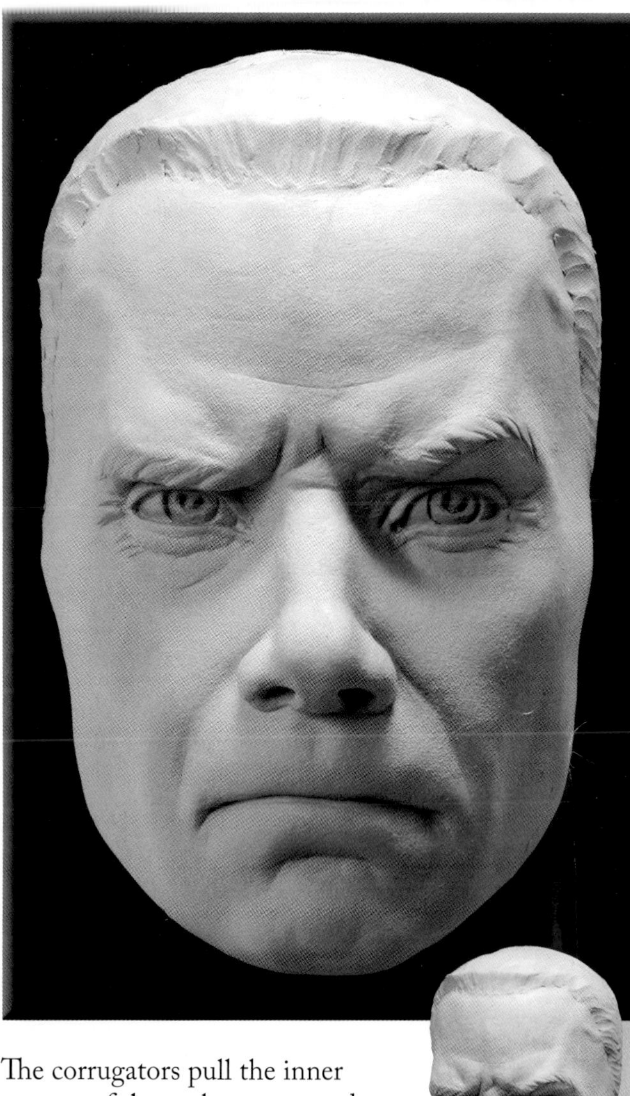

The corrugators pull the inner corners of the eyebrows toward the center of the face. The lower edge of the eyebrow drops below the level of the upper eyelid. The vertical glabellar lines deepen. The contraction of the orbicularis oculi creates wrinkles on the outer corner of the eye and puffiness in the lower eyelid. The lips compress making them almost disappear. The mentalis contracts, roughening the chin and creates bulges above and below the mouth.

## Smile

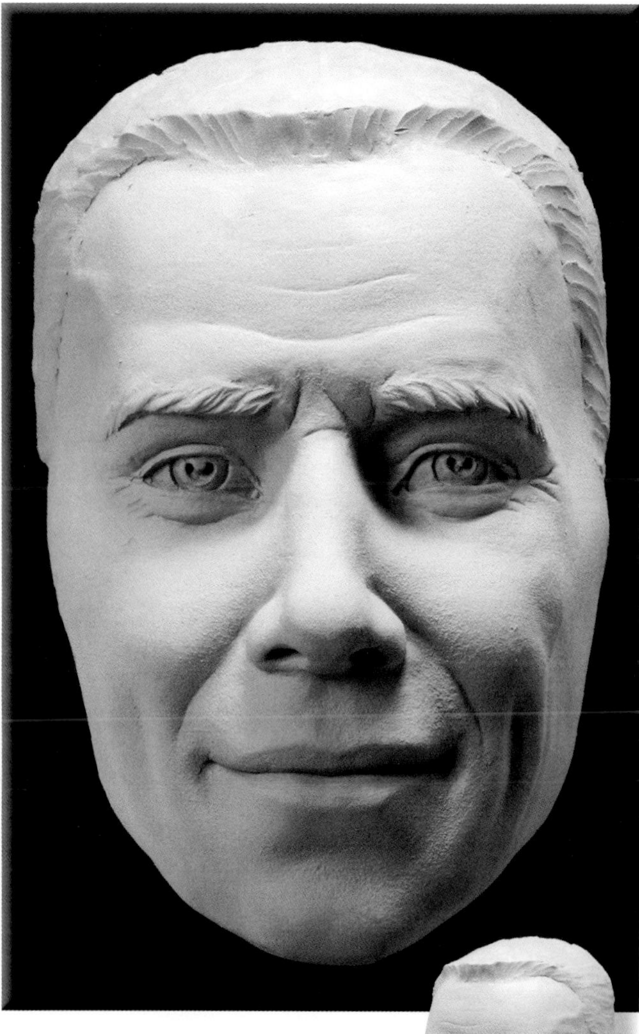

The first hint of a smile on any face is produced by the simultaneous contraction of the orbicularis oculi, which narrows the eye and causes wrinkles to radiate from its outer corner, and the zygomaticus major, which pulls the corner of the mouth upward and back towards the ear. The lower lid shortens slightly and bulges covering part of the iris. Fine winkles appear between the upper cheek and the lower lid. The cheek rises, creating a bulge of tissue (the "apple" of the cheek) level with the wing of the nose and the nasolabial furrow deepens slightly. The lips stretch against the teeth and become thinner and straighter because the zygomaticus major tightens the orbicularis oris against the skull. The philtrum becomes shallower and vertical folds appear on the lower cheeks.

## Surprise

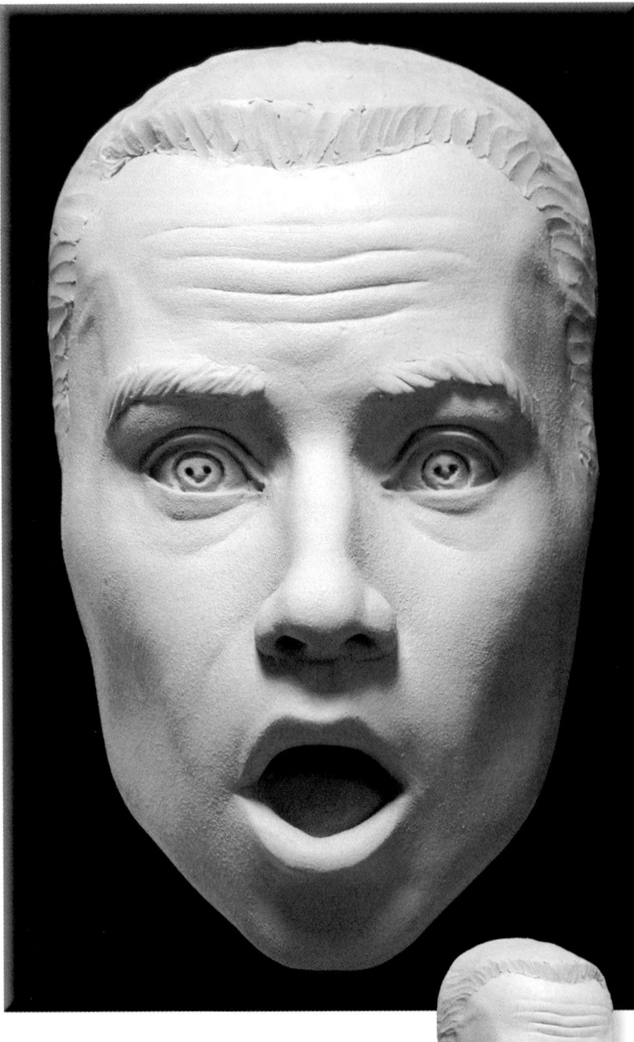

In a look of surprise, the mouth can be contracted into an O-shape. The frontalis lifts the eyebrow and creates folds on the forehead. The eyes open wide and the lower lids are relaxed. The mouth drops open and the orbicularis oris and surrounding muscles are relaxed. The face appears elongated due to the drop of the mandible and the hollowing of the cheeks. In the pleasantly surprised look, which includes a faint smile the zygomaticus muscles pull the lips back making the mouth tense and the "apple" part of the cheeks bulge slightly.

## Sadness

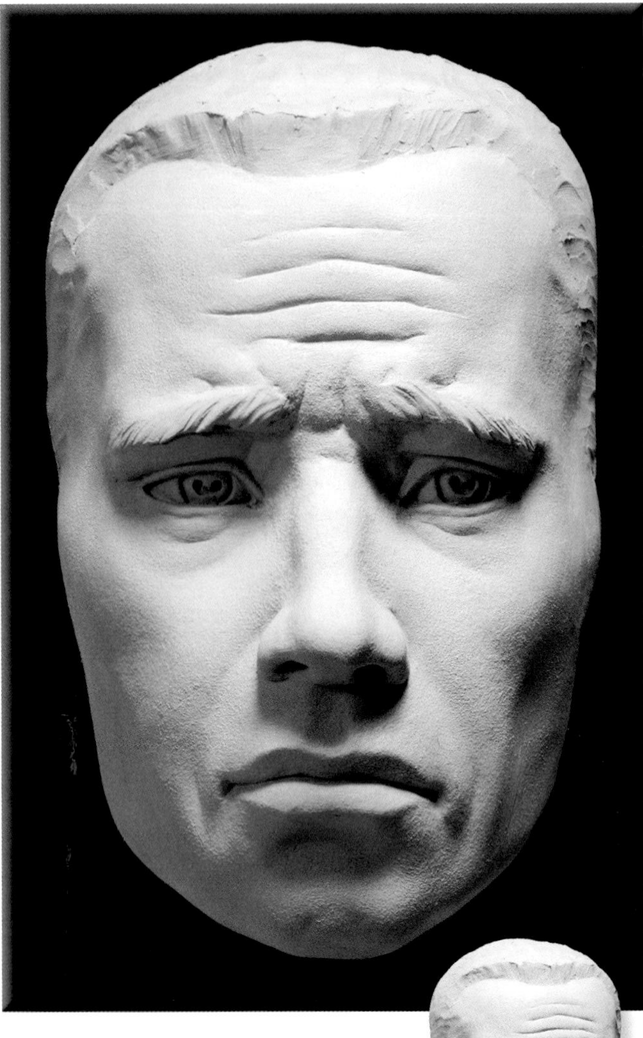

The upward twist of the medial third of the eyebrows is the strongest indication of the sad face. The inner eyebrow end is bunched up by the corrugator and pulled upward by the frontalis. The action of the frontalis sometimes deepens the transverse frontal lines. The lower portion of the orbicularis oculi partly contracts provoking a slight bulging of the lower eyelid. The upper eyelid becomes partly covered by a fold of skin pulled across by the lift of the brow which accentuates the downward slant toward the outer corner of the eye. The corners of the mouth are pulled down by the depressor anguli oris. The action of the depressor anguli oris is also responsible for the formation of the curved folds on the lower corners of the mouth. The mentalis contracts creating a roughening of the chin.

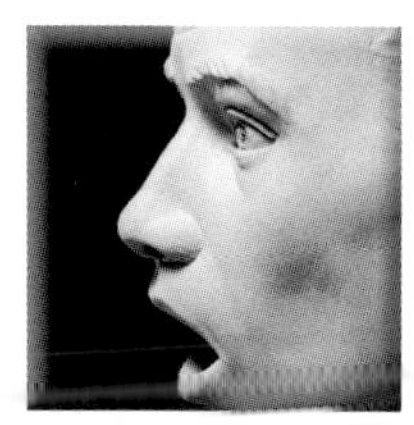

## Disgust

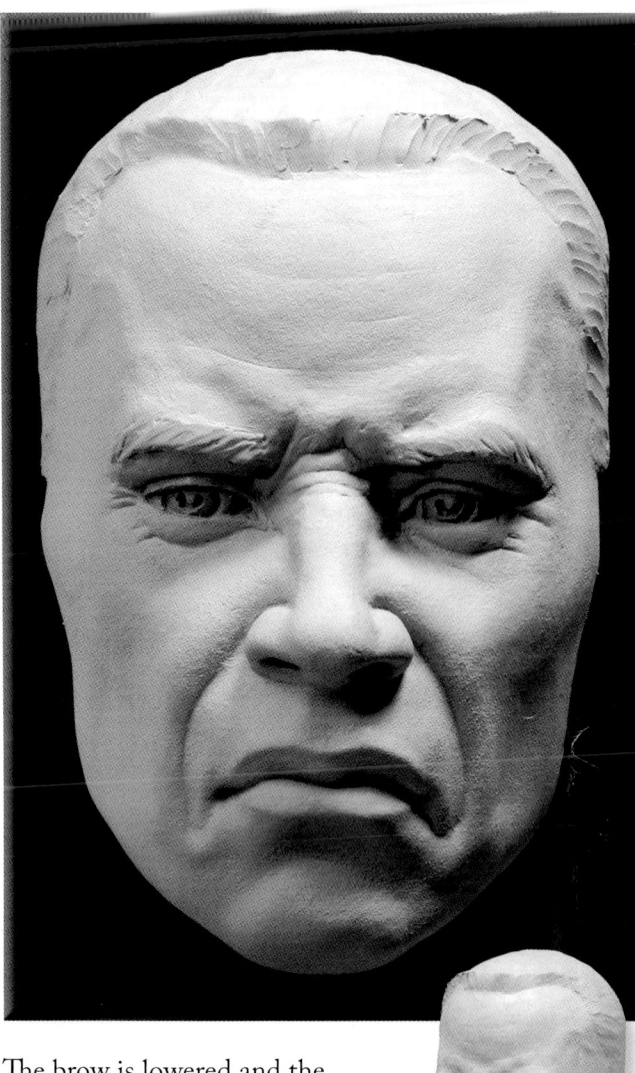

The brow is lowered and the transverse frontal lines are diminished by the action of the corrugator. The orbicularis oculi contracts, causing the eyes to squint and form wrinkles on the outer corner. The levator labii alaeque nasi raises the skin on the side of the nose, in addition to the wings themselves, which, combined with the action of the corrugator, accentuates the transverse nasal lines and the vertical glabellar lines. Levator labii superioris squares off the upper lip, puffs the cheeks and deepens the upper corner of the nasolabial furrow. The action of the mentalis pushes up the lower lip while the depressor anguli oris pulls the corners down giving the mouth a square look.

## Fear

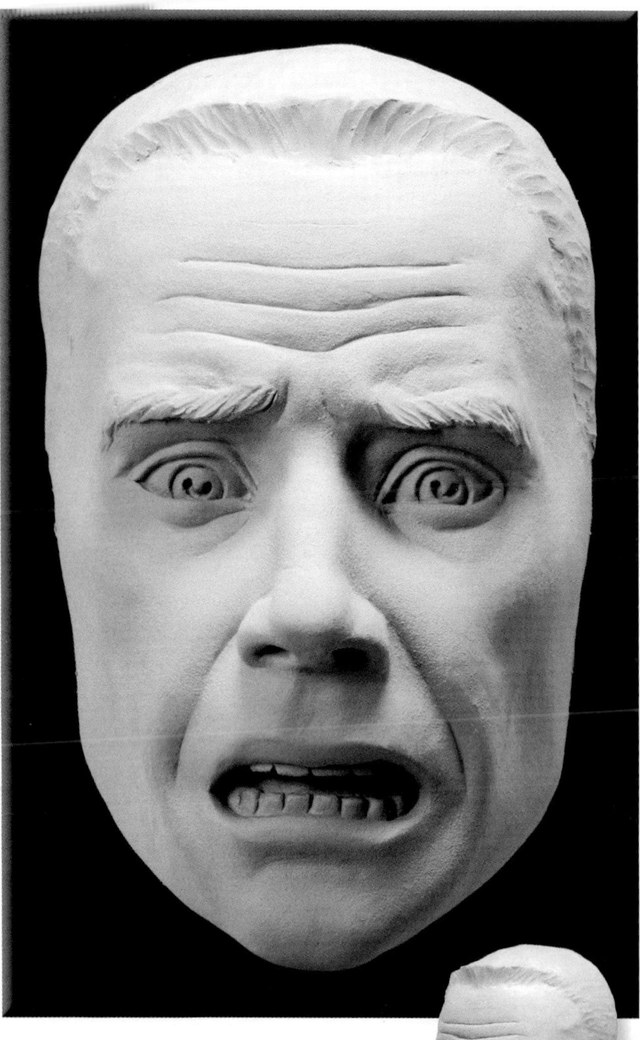

The brow is lifted by the frontalis, but unlike in the look of surprise, the corrugators also pull the medial part of the eyebrows inward and downward. The transverse frontal lines, as well as the vertical glabellar lines, deepen. In the look of fear the eyes always widen and in most case the lower eyelids tense. The mouth opens and is stretched to the sides by the actions of the risorius and platysma combined. The lower lip is strait across, displaying the lower teeth, but the upper lip is relaxed. The nasolabial furrow deepens and the nostrils widen slightly.

## Demonstration 11: Experimenting with Expressions

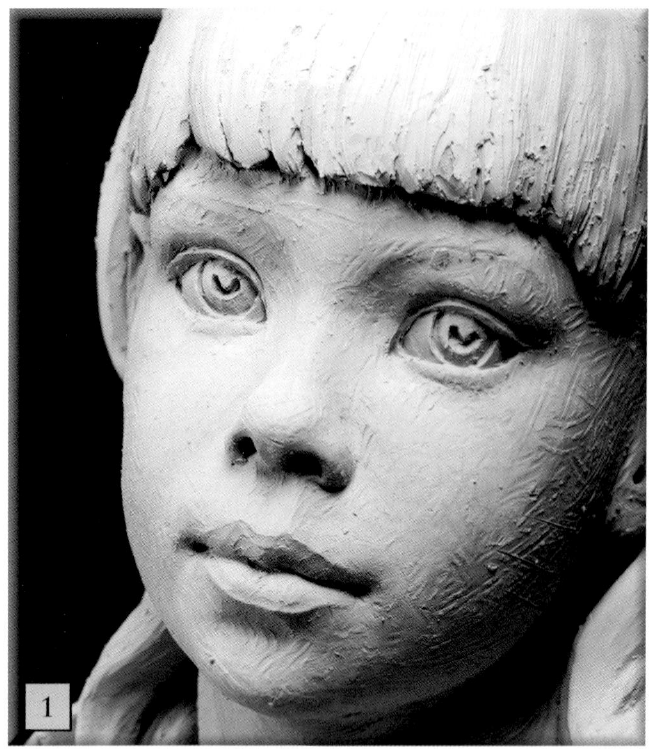

Practice the following demonstrations at a fast pace in order to keep the focus on the main planes rather than the details. The age and gender are not important but the clay must be soft and pliable so the volumes can be moved easily.

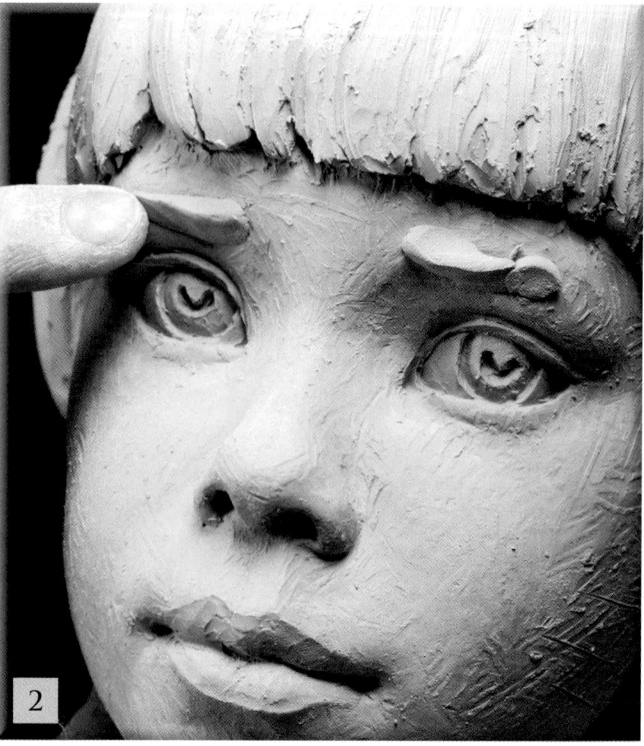

**1, 2.** A small piece of clay is added to the eyebrow to lift the inner side and lower the outer side.

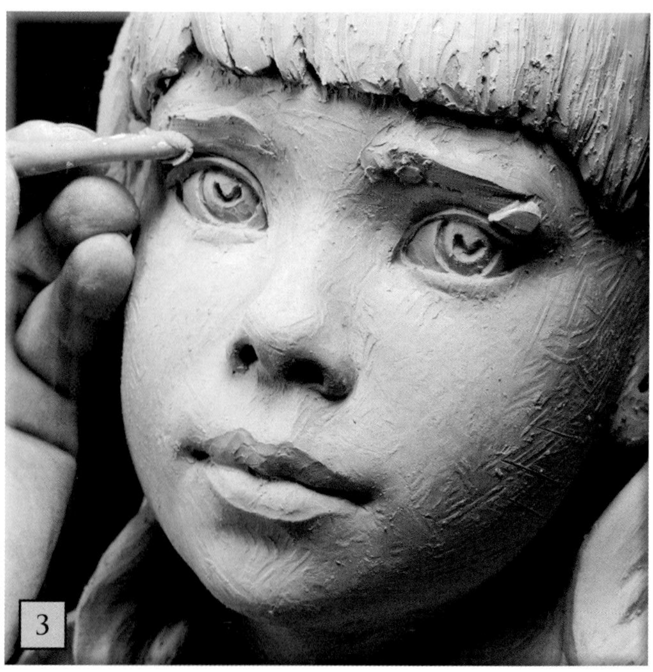

**3.** Lowering the outer corners of the eyebrows forces the skin above the eyelid to bulge slightly more than usual. Volumes are added with the wooden tool.

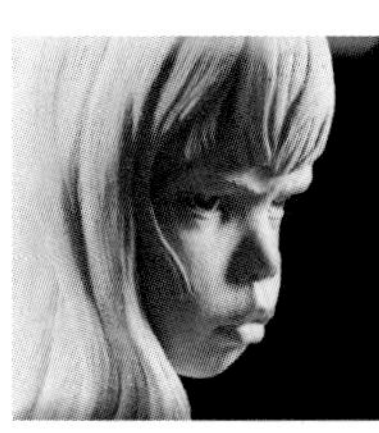

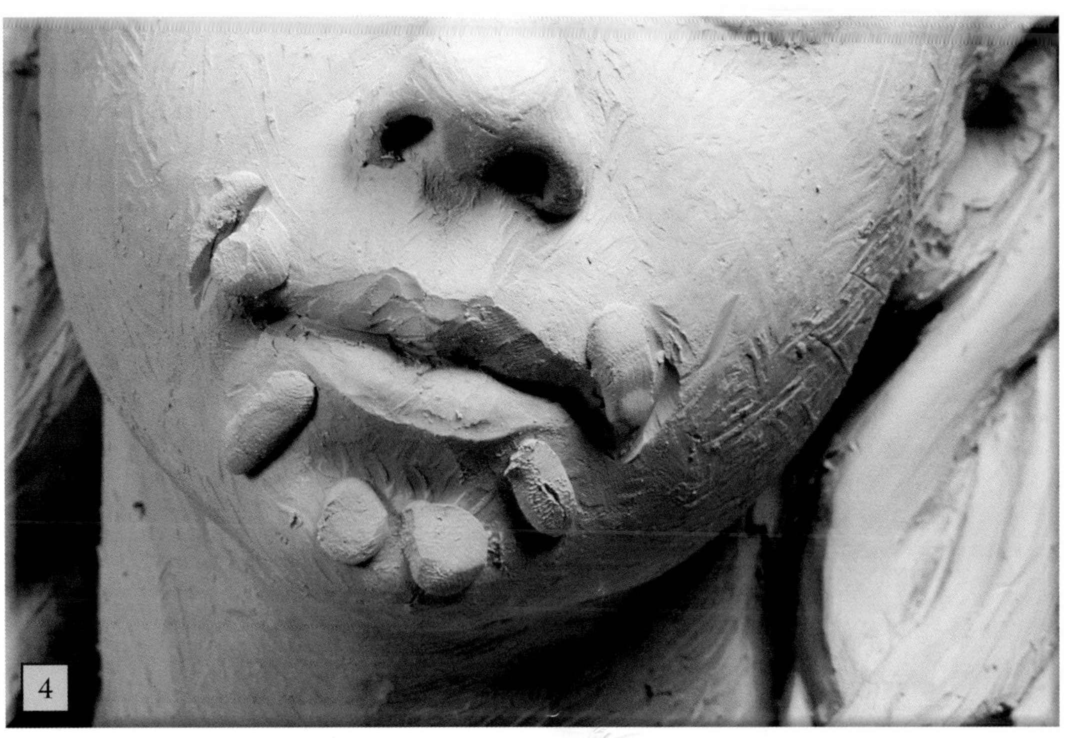


**4.** The bulging of the volumes shown in this picture is the direct result of the contraction of the mentalis muscles.

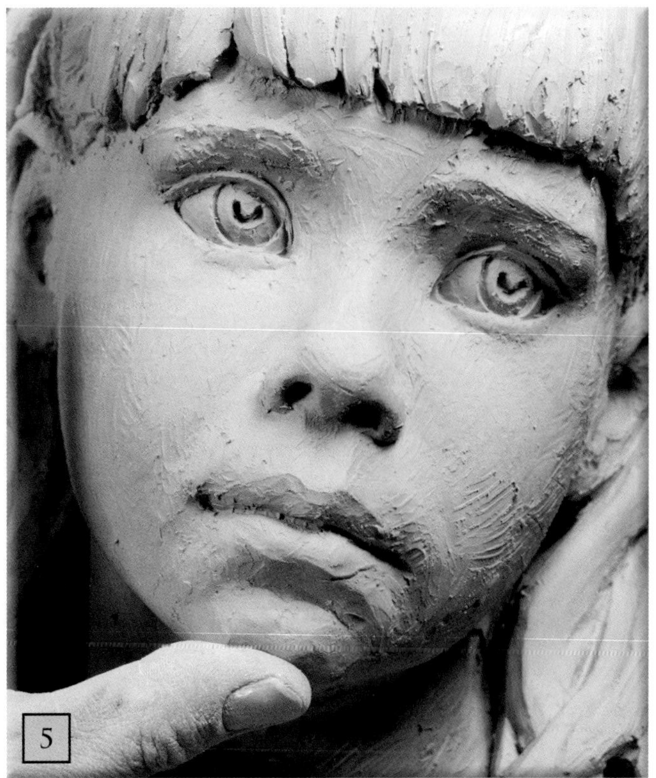


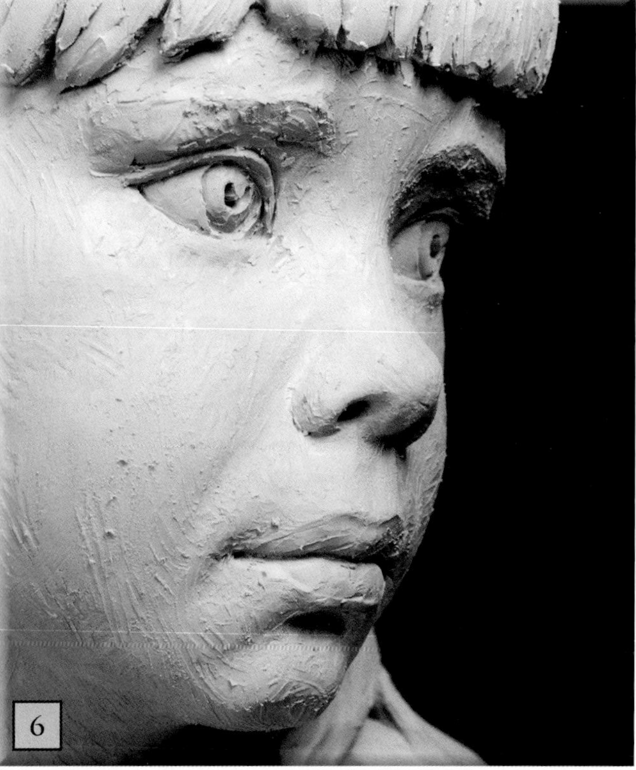


**5, 6.** The chin is slightly lifted and the lower lip pushed out for the pout. The nasolabial furrow is deeper.

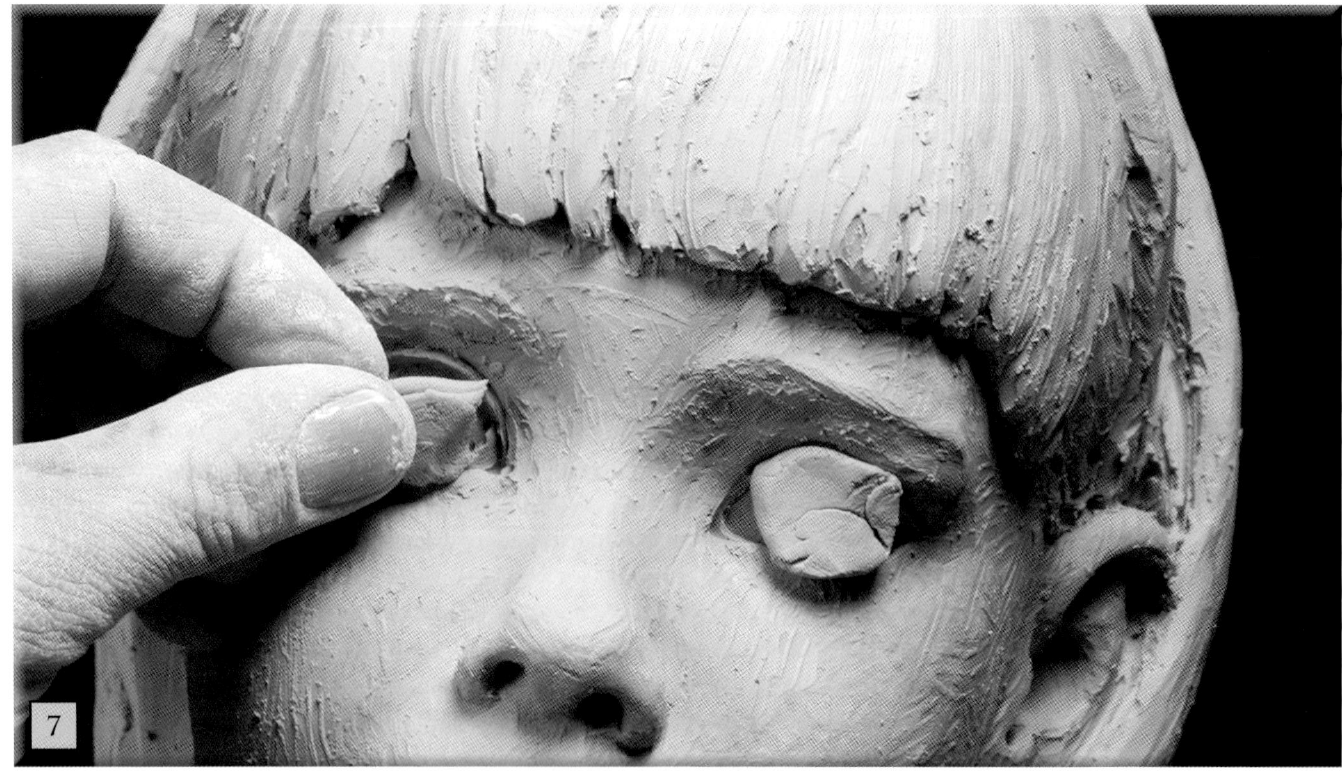

7. To close the eye, it is easier to add a small piece of clay over its entire surface and then cut the shape of the edge of the upper eyelid.

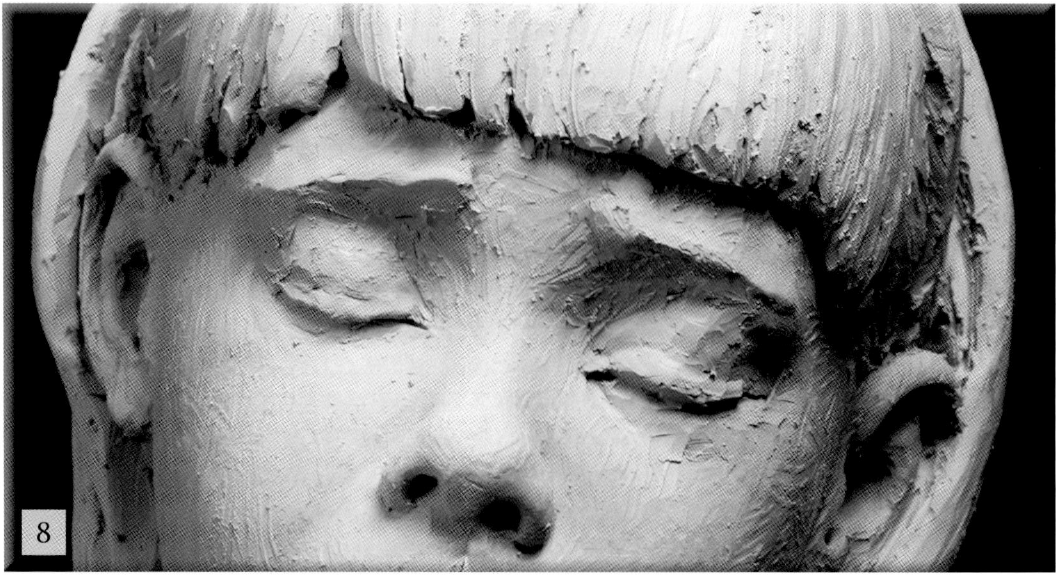

8. The inner eyebrows are pulled upward by the frontalis and bunched up by the corrugators. When the eyes are closed, the edges of the upper eyelids form an S-shape.

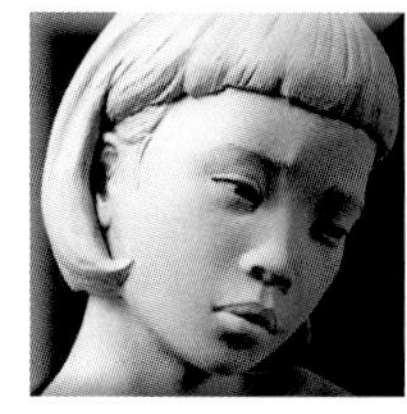

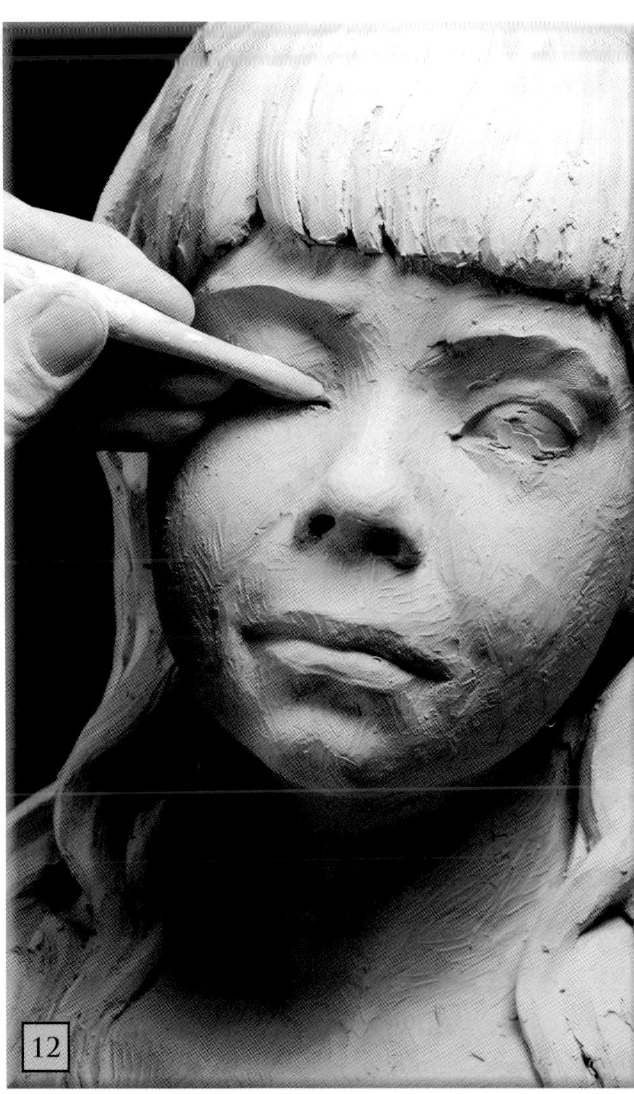


**11, 12.** Still working rapidly, the eye is reopened simply by pushing the wooden tool to imprint the shape. At this point, the lower eyelid retains the same shape and remains in the same position. Only the upper lid is modified.

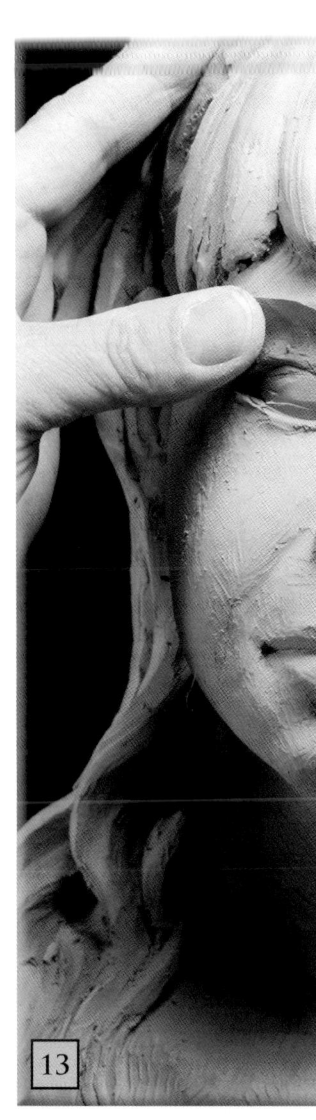


**13.** The medial end of the e
while the center is lifted to f

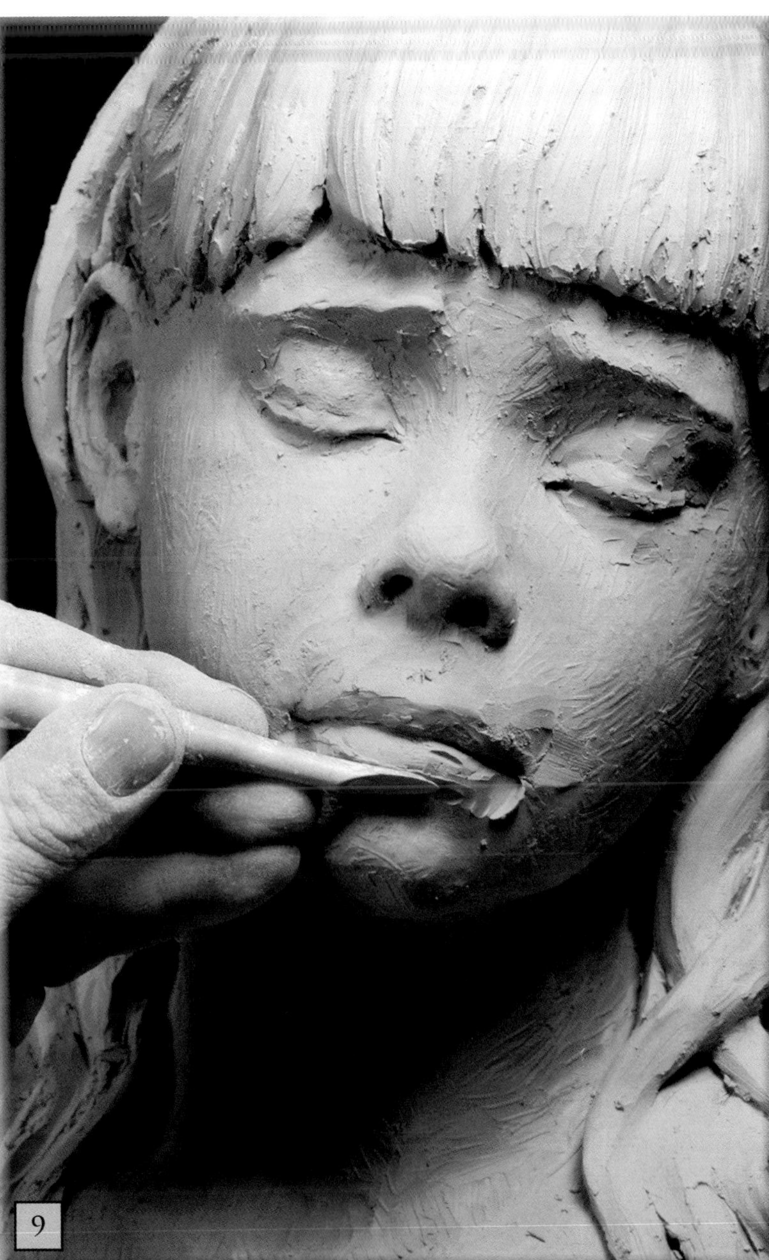


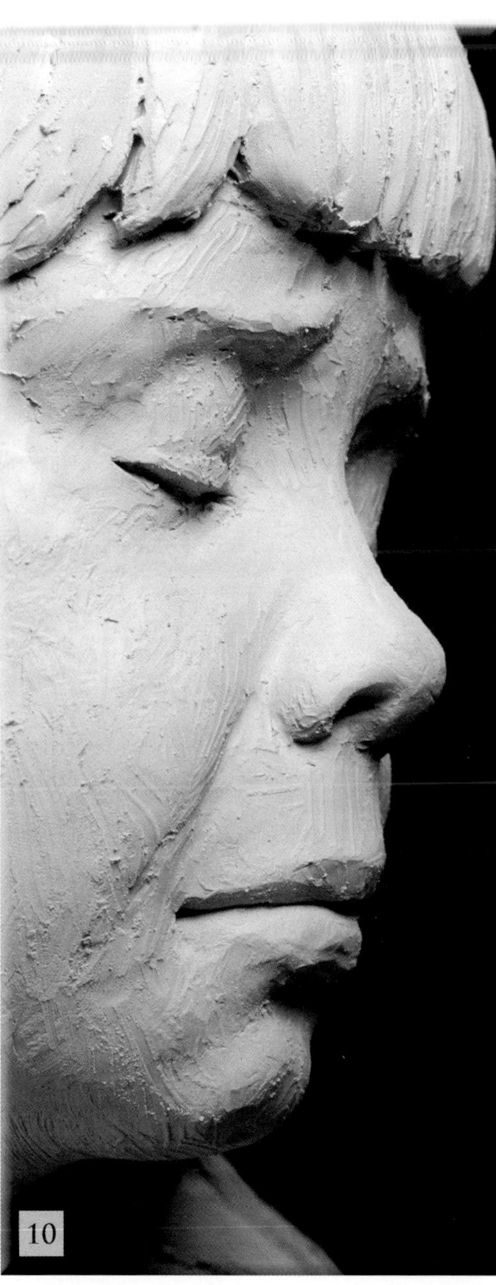


**9, 10.** The center of the lower lip is lifted further, the corners lowered and pushed backward. The center of the lower lip is lifted further by the action of the mentalis and the corners are pulled down by the depressor anguli oris. This has the effect of pressing the lips together, making them appear thinner. Contraction of the mentalis also creates a roughening of the chin. Note the bulge of the eyeball visible through the upper lid.

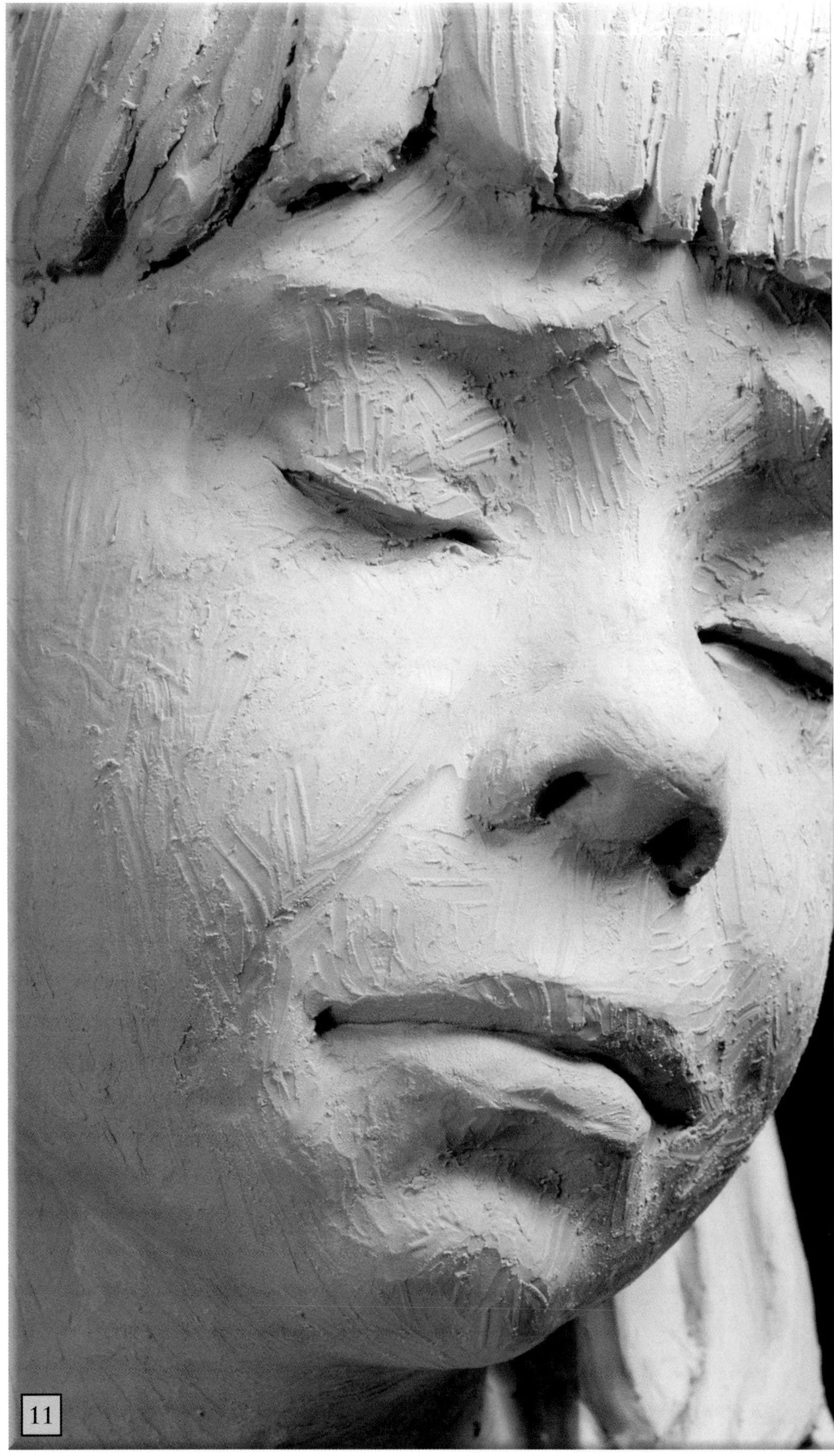





**14.** Under the action of the zygomaticus major the cheeks swell and the corners of the mouth are pulled up and backwards. A fair amount of clay needs to be added and centered at the level of the nose wings.

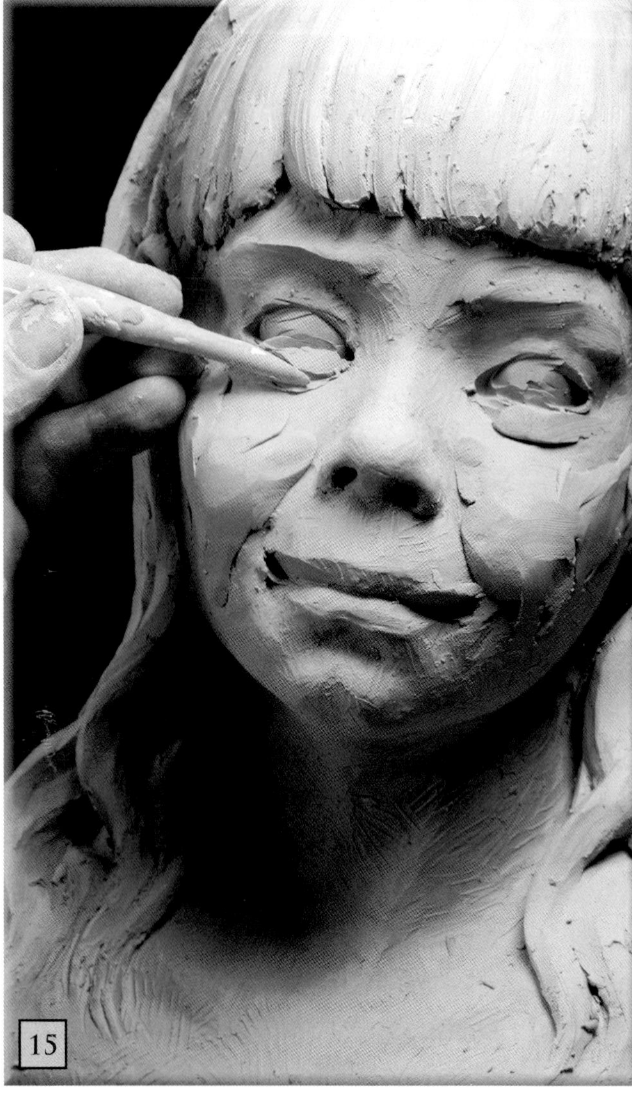

**15.** Clay must be added under the eye to form the bulging created by the tightening of the lower lid. This is a very important feature of the expression of joy. Notice that all the changes made are left rough since no time should be wasted refining the surface until all the volumes are in place.

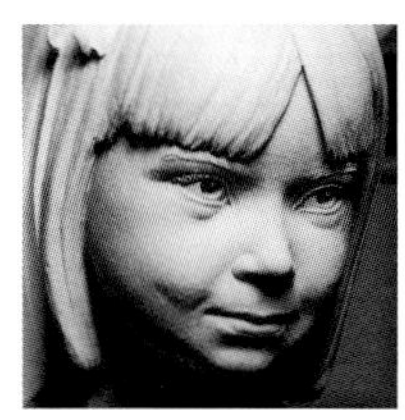

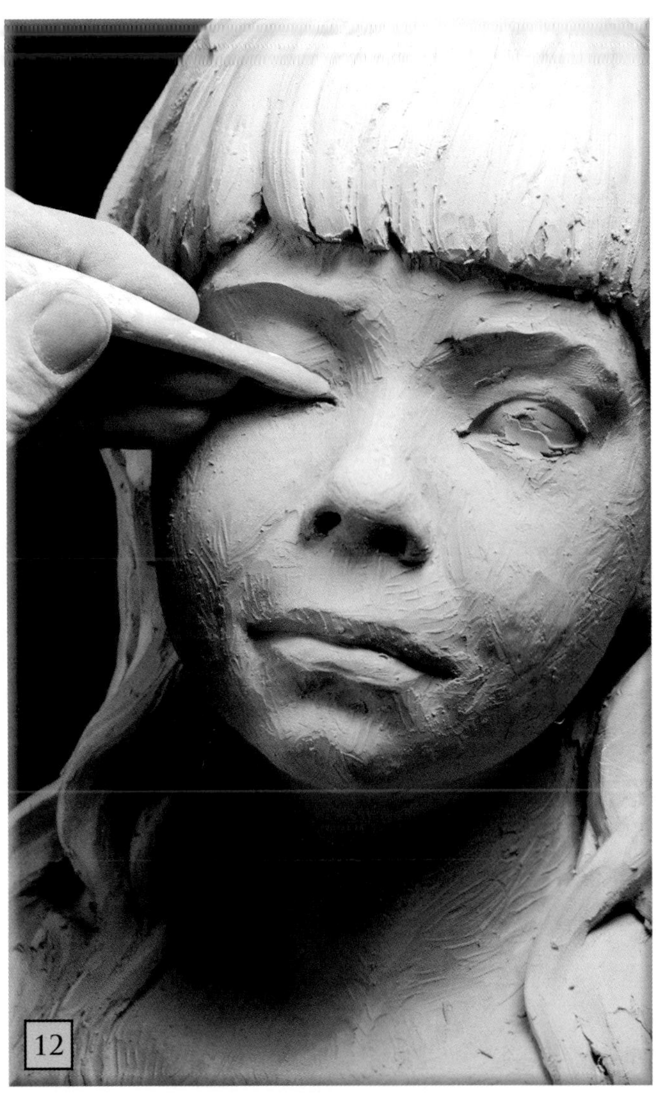


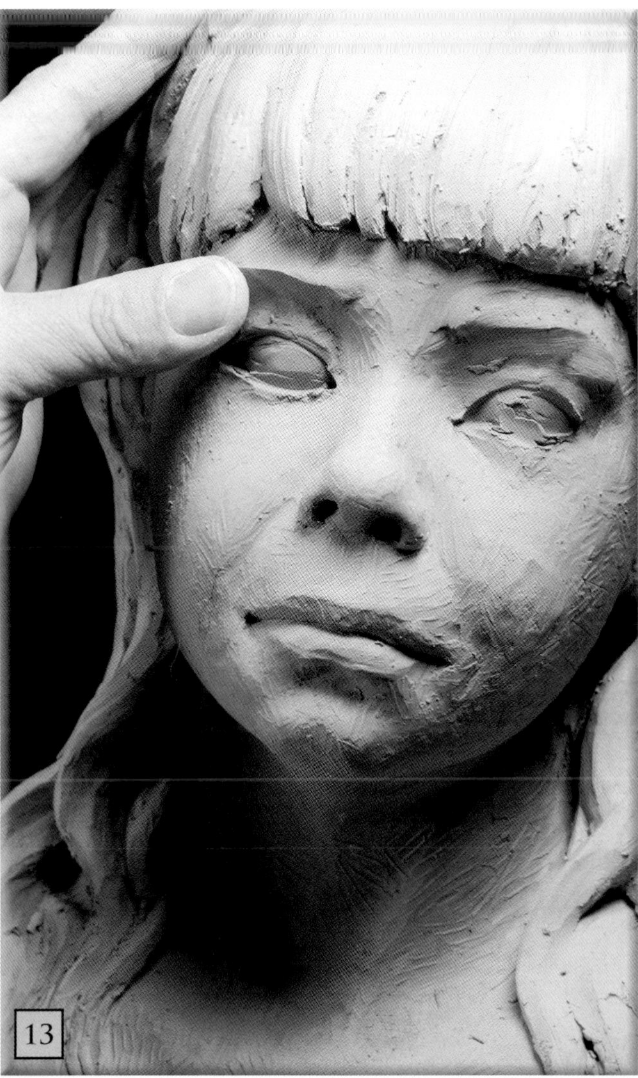


**11, 12.** Still working rapidly, the eye is reopened simply by pushing the wooden tool to imprint the shape. At this point, the lower eyelid retains the same shape and remains in the same position. Only the upper lid is modified.

**13.** The medial end of the eyebrow is lowered slightly while the center is lifted to form an arch.

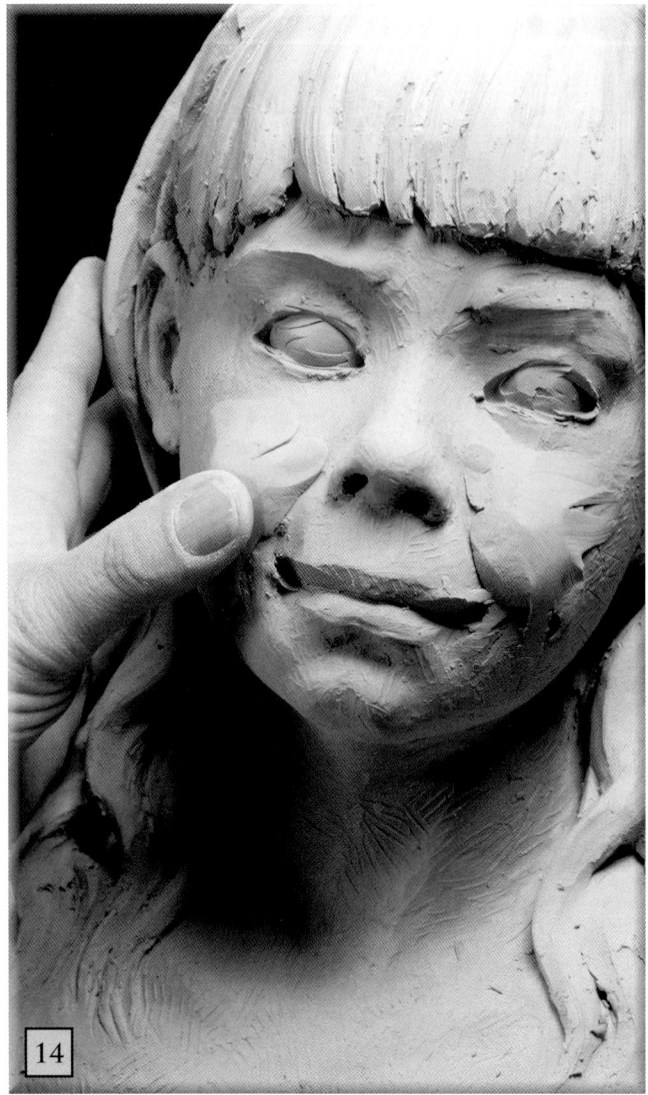


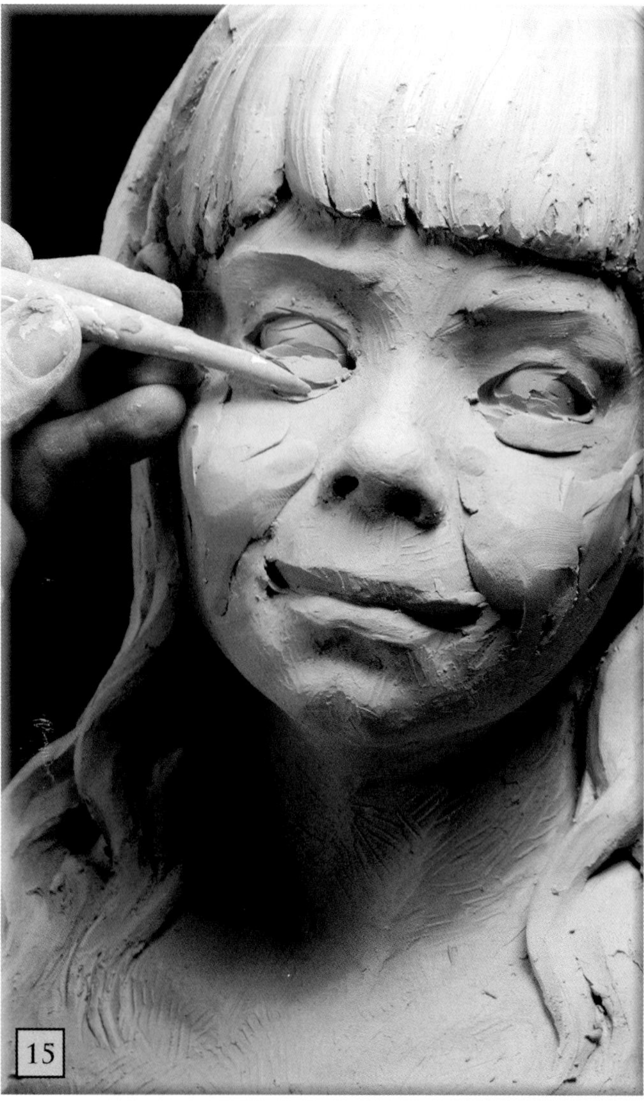


**14.** Under the action of the zygomaticus major the cheeks swell and the corners of the mouth are pulled up and backwards. A fair amount of clay needs to be added and centered at the level of the nose wings.

**15.** Clay must be added under the eye to form the bulging created by the tightening of the lower lid. This is a very important feature of the expression of joy. Notice that all the changes made are left rough since no time should be wasted refining the surface until all the volumes are in place.

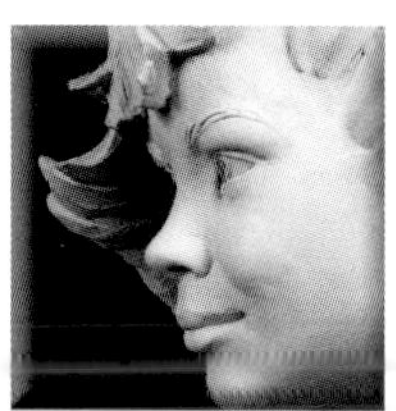

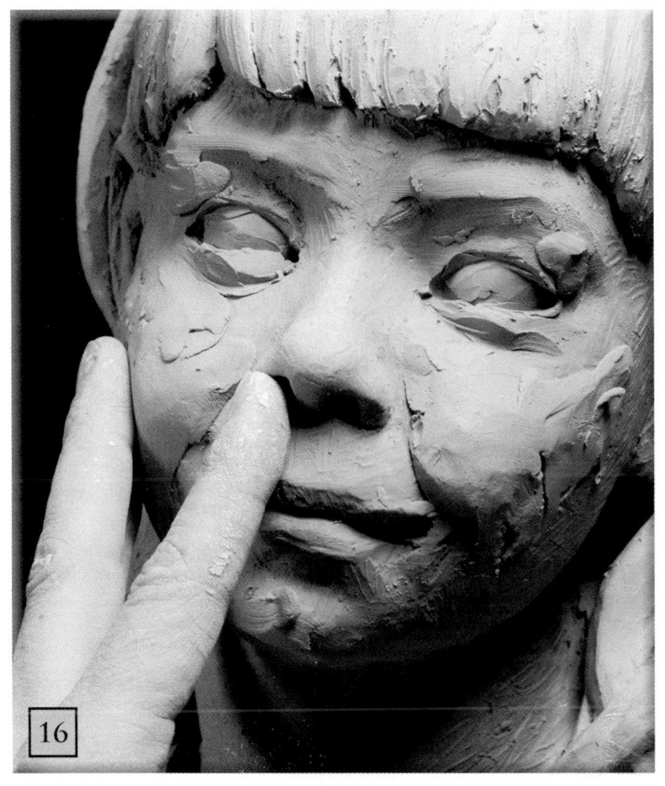

16. The wings of the nose are lifted slightly.

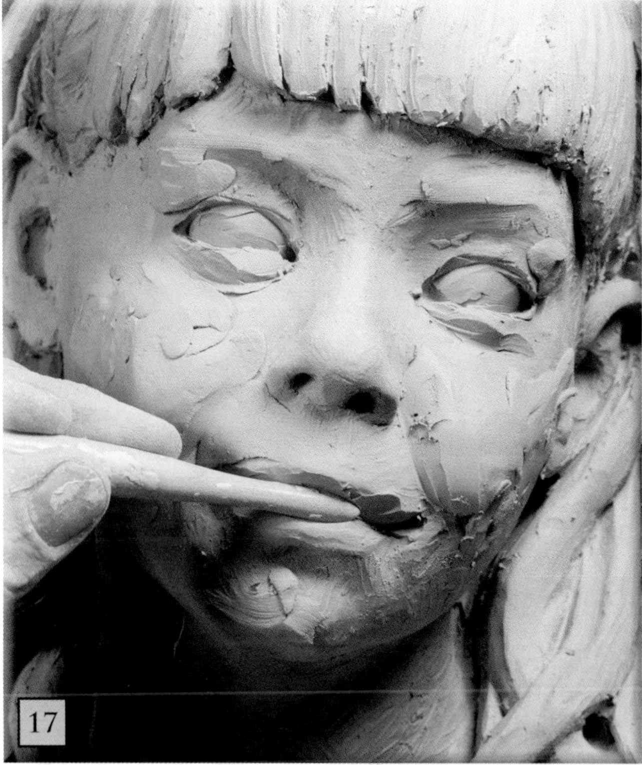

17. The lips are parted with the wooden tool.

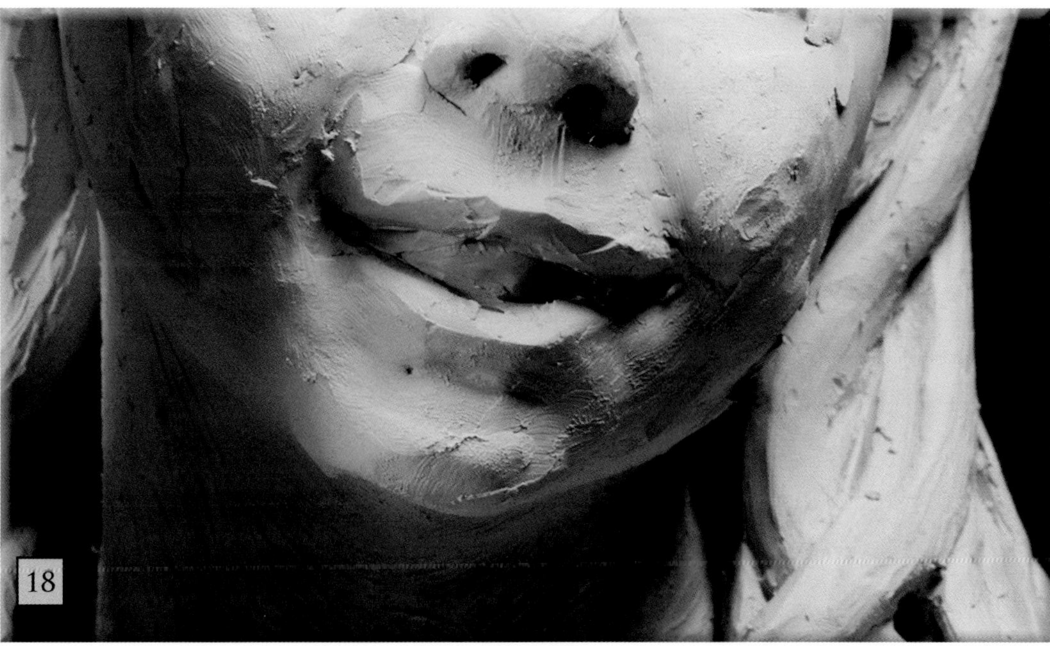

18. The general shape of the teeth is modeled. The planes of the teeth should be recessed enough to allow the appropriate thickness of the lips, keeping in mind that the lips are thinner due to the pull of the zygomaticus on the orbicularis oris.

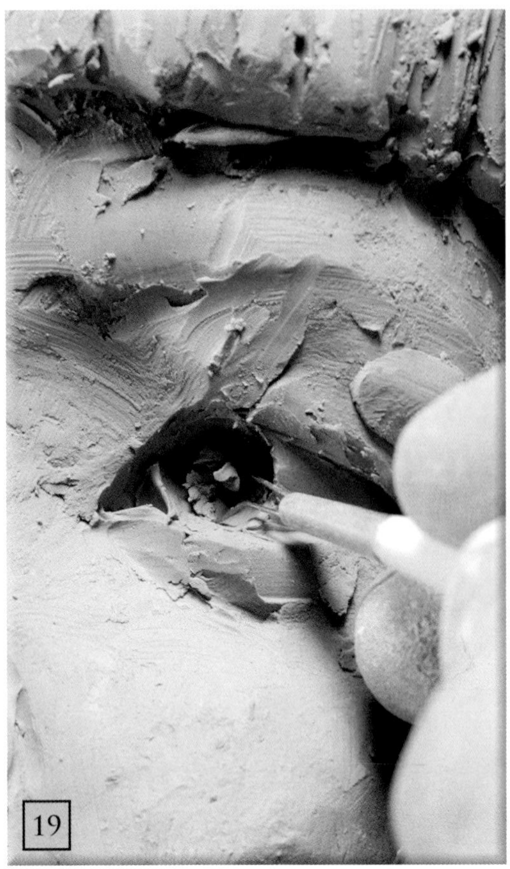

**19.** In this case the iris is deepened to create the illusion of darker eyes. This is done by creating a bowl-shaped hollow with a small loop tool. When indicating the iris, the tendency is to set the position of the eyes in such a way that the sculpture seems to be looking at you. The problem is that you are standing only a foot or two from it and when you step back it will stare at a point in space unnaturally close. To prevent the risk of creating a cross-eyed look, the artist must step back at least six to eight feet from the work to verify the position of the stare.

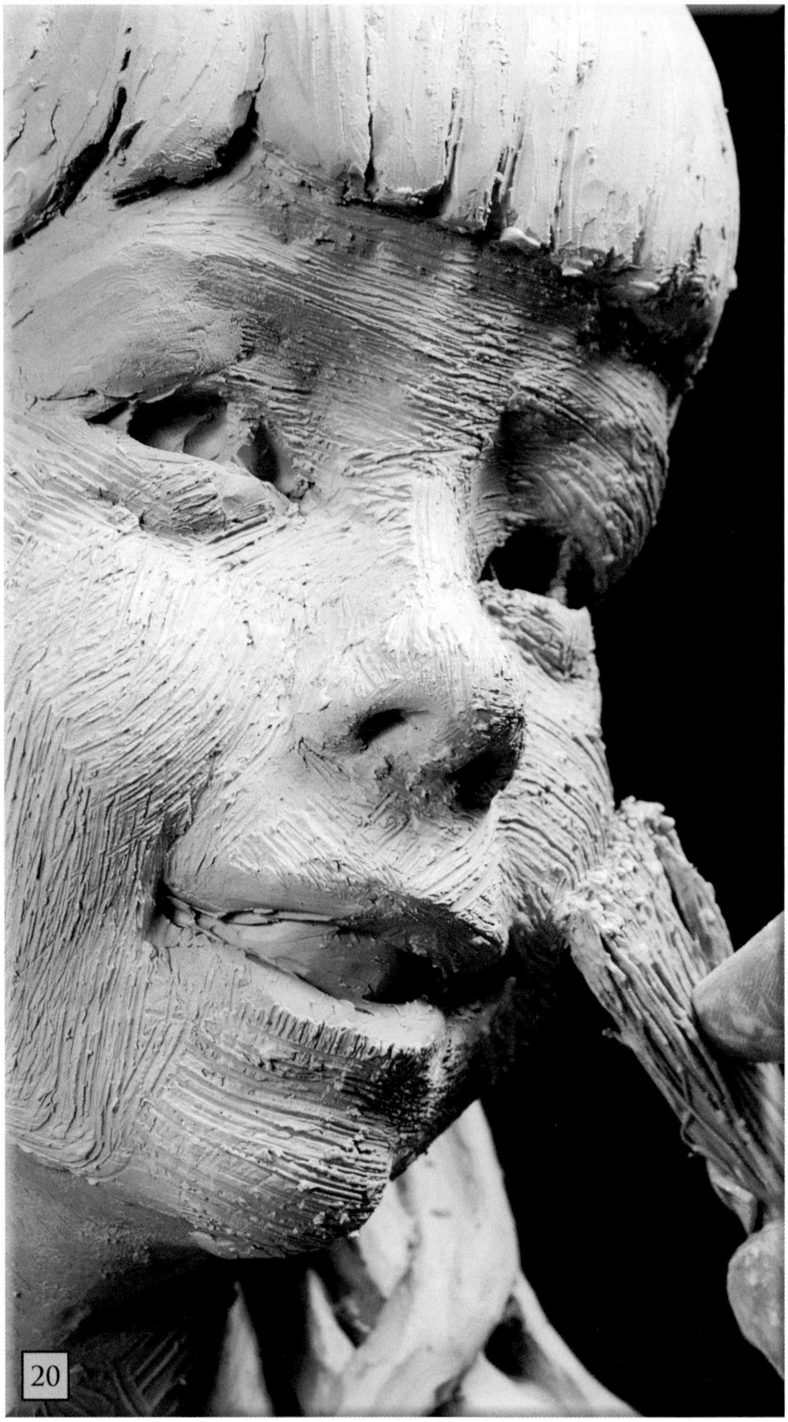

**20.** Once all the volumes are in place, a stiff bristle brush is used to blend them together. Finer brushes can be used to soften the surface.

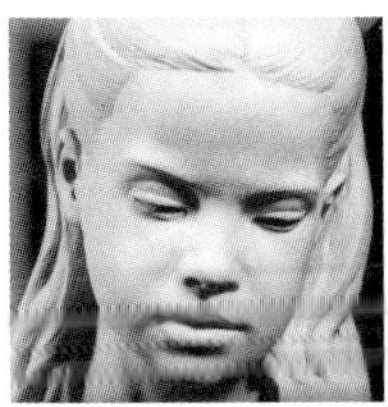

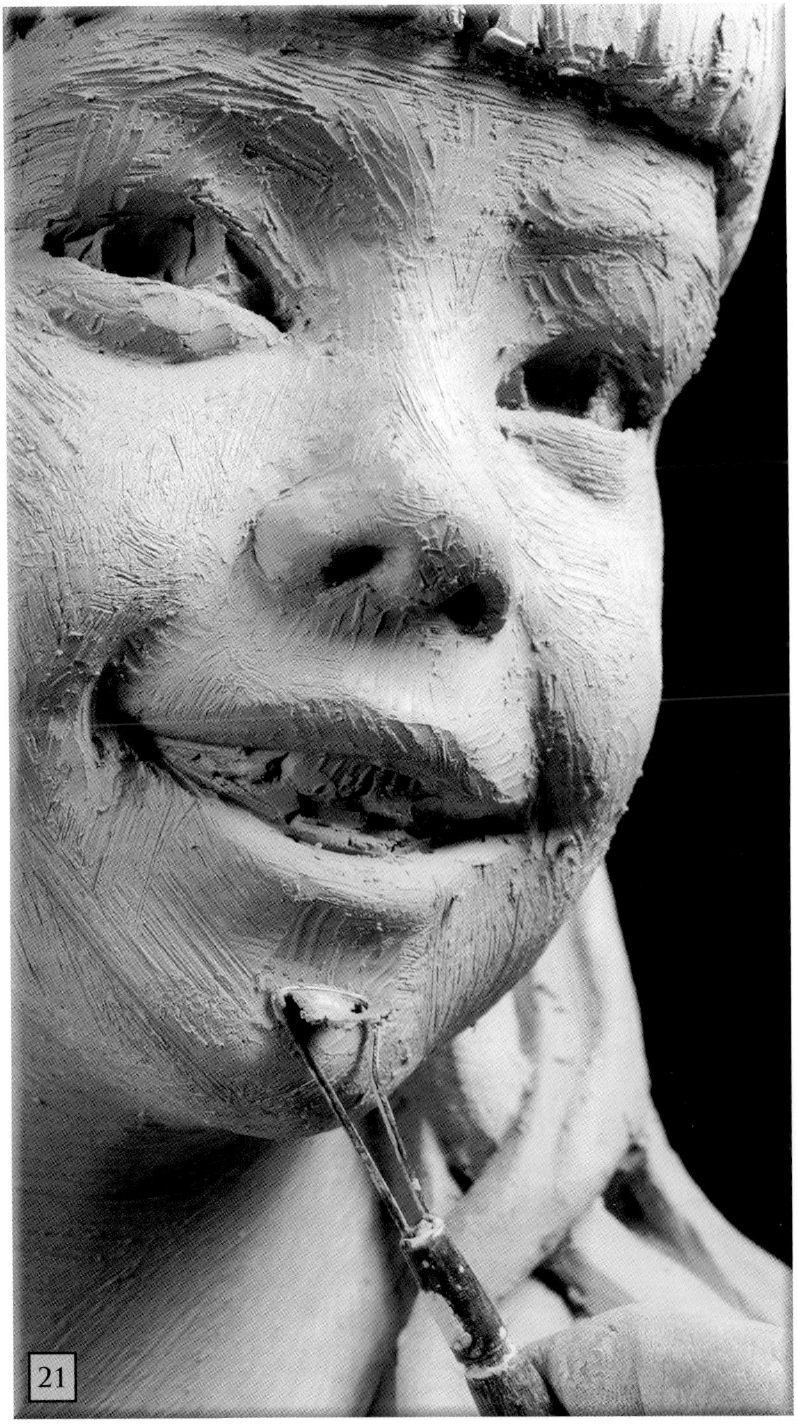

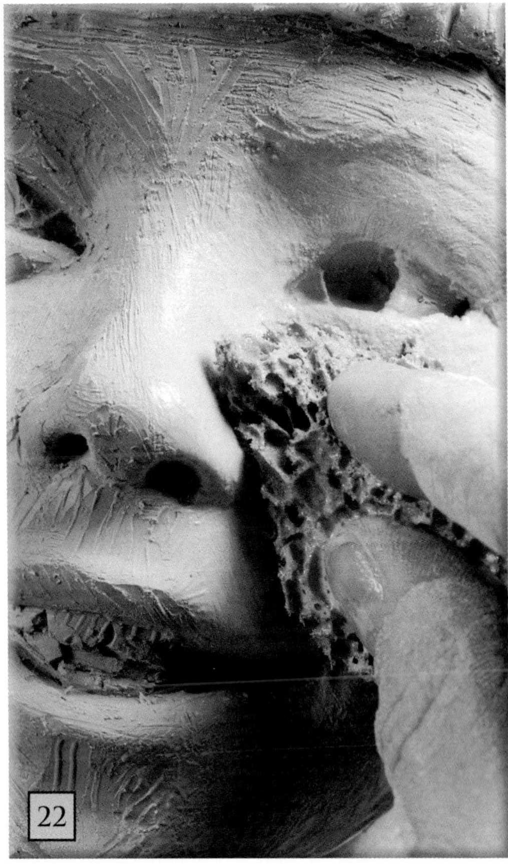

**22.** A wet, rough sponge is used to erase the tool marks. Care should be taken to not use too much water as it would soften the surface and make it difficult to work on small details. However, if need be, a heat gun can be used with caution to dry the surface of the clay in order to refine details. Never use a heating device other than for the purpose of drying small areas, and to a consistency no harder than leather. *Note: in no case should it be used to accelerate the final drying process of the sculpture.*

**21.** The shape of the individual teeth is modeled and the volumes of the face refined with a serrated tool.

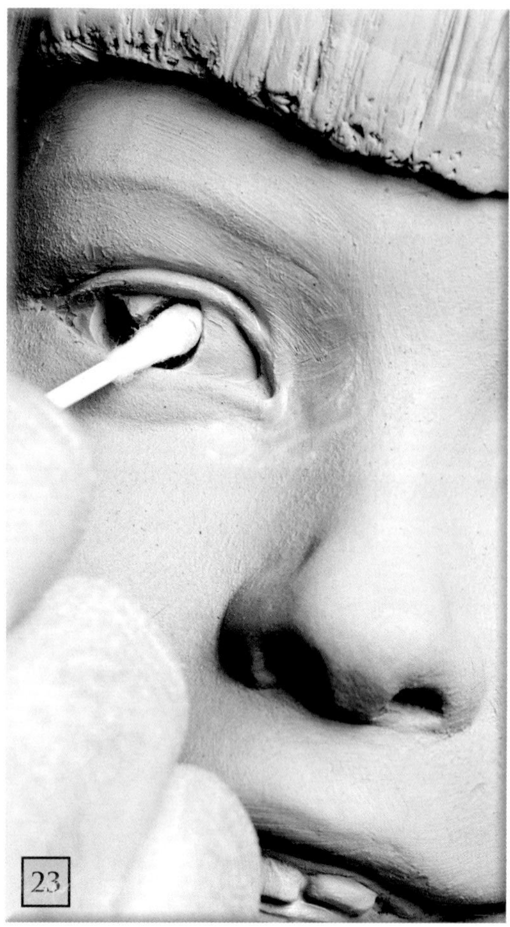

23. Small triangles of clay are added to the inside top of the iris to create highlights. When these highlights are positioned to the bottom of the iris they give a somewhat passive look to the eyes. When placed at the top, a more dynamic look is achieved. Cotton swabs are used to refine the interior of the iris.

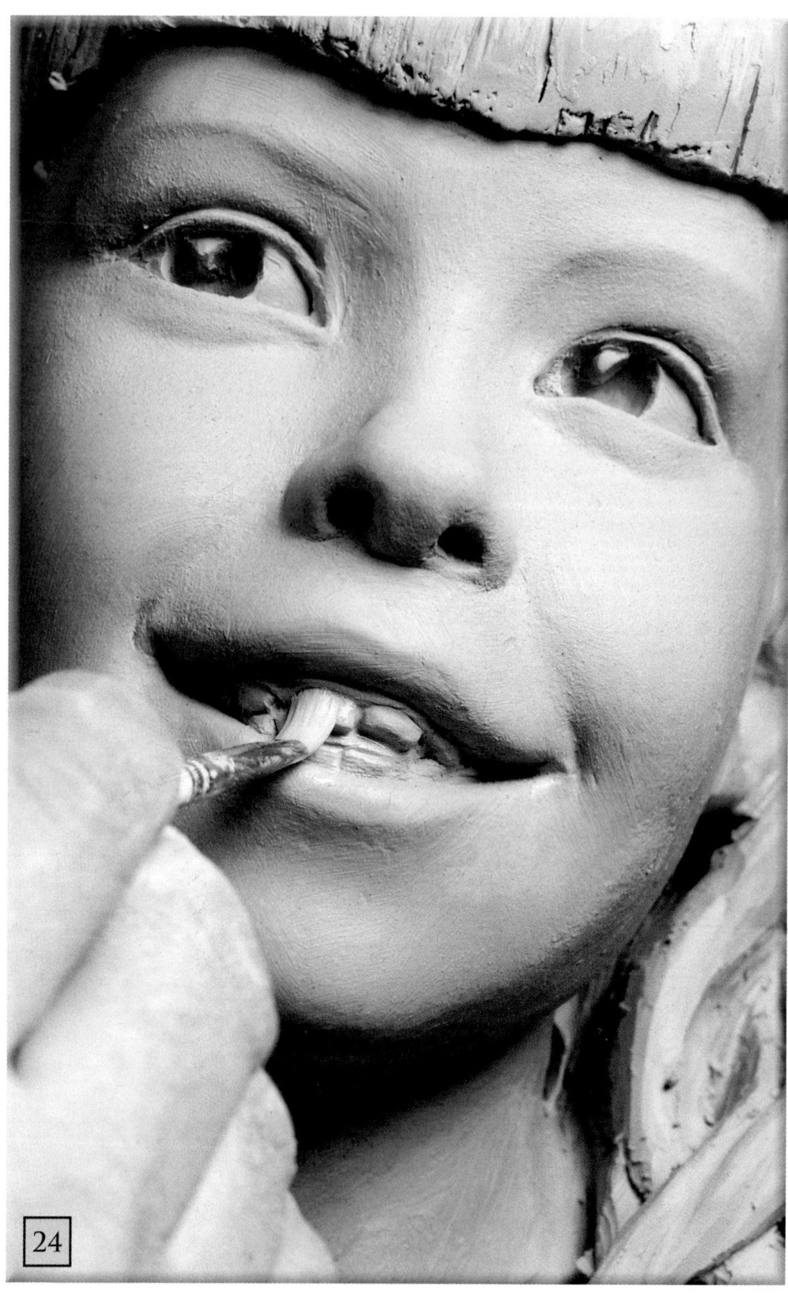

24. Soft brushes are used to refine hard to reach areas such as the teeth, the nostrils and the eyelids.

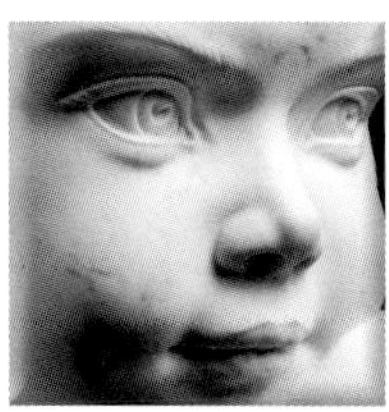

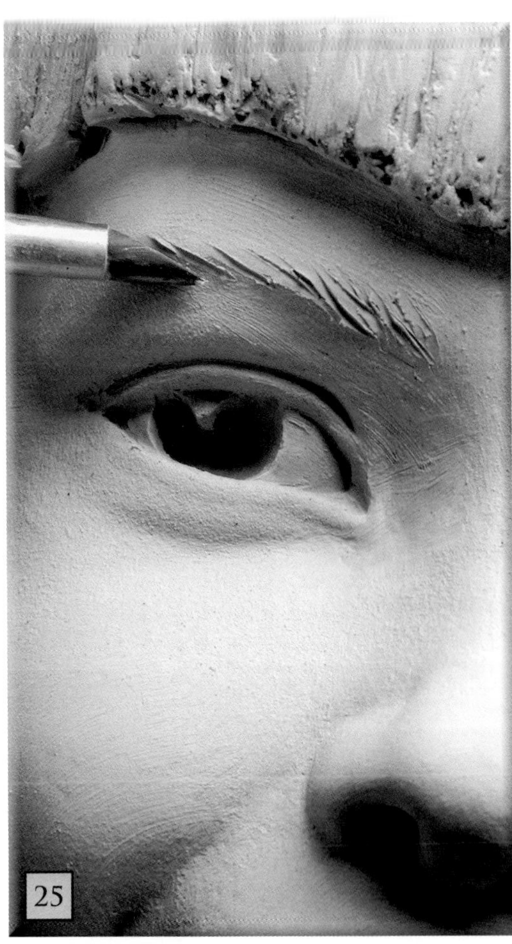

**25.** Notice that the edge of the brow ridge is built slightly thicker than it should be. This is the thickness necessary for the volume of the brow hairs. They are defined with a rubber tipped tool.

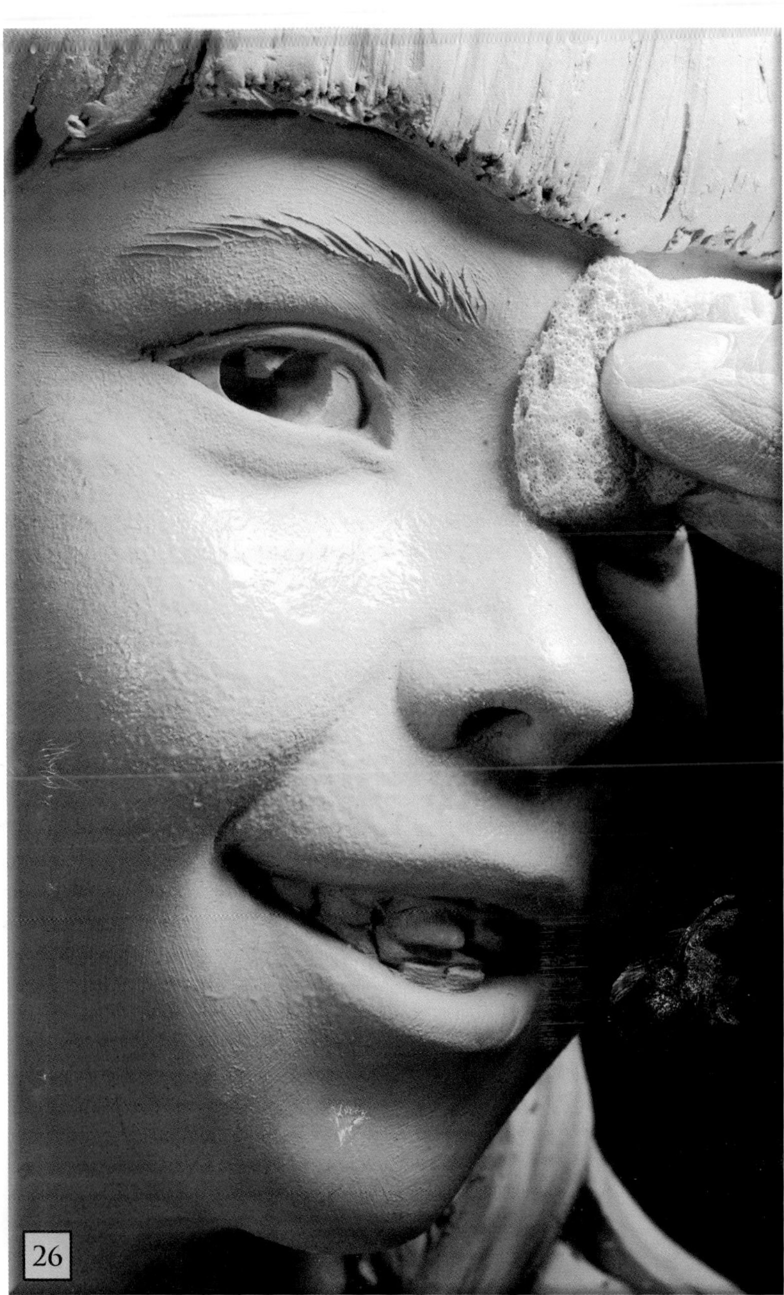

**26.** In this case, the final texture is achieved by dabbing a soft sponge to the surface of the clay. Care should be taken not to wash away the details of the features. Here too, a heat gun can be useful to control the consistency of the clay.

27. As long as the clay is pliable, modifications and additions can be performed easily. Here, the left shoulder was lifted slightly, and a second portrait added to the sculpture. When sculpting fabric, a three dimensional sample is necessary. Due to the fidgety nature of the models, a silk bow was tied to a plaster head to serve as reference.

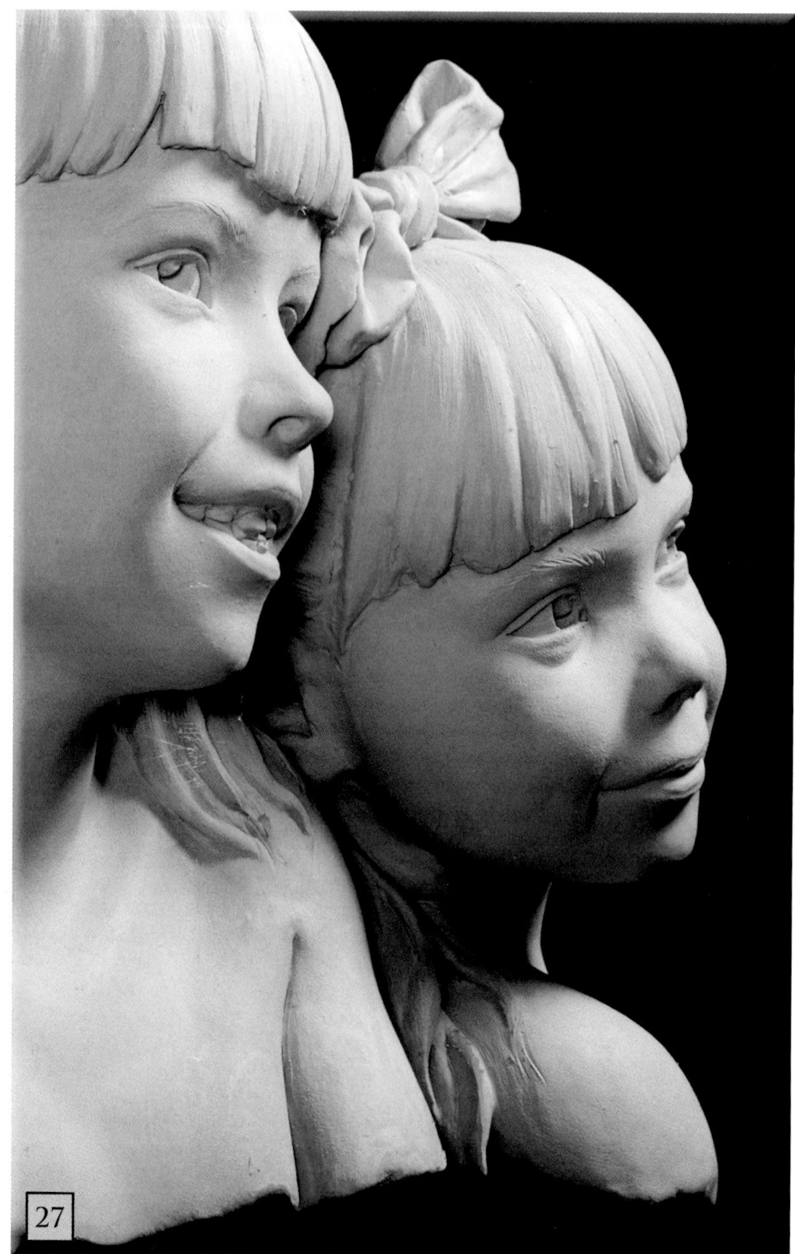


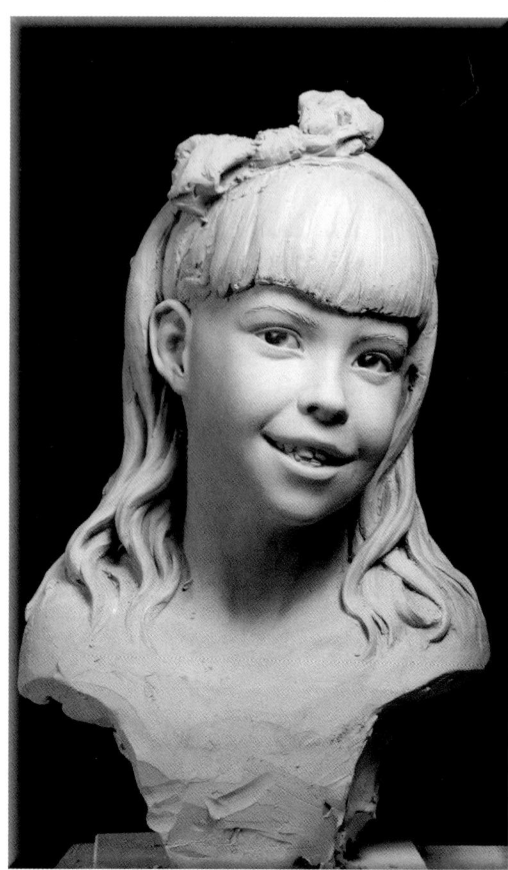

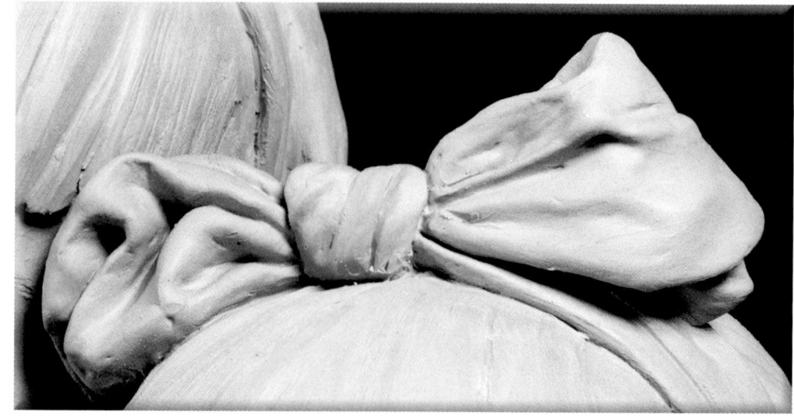

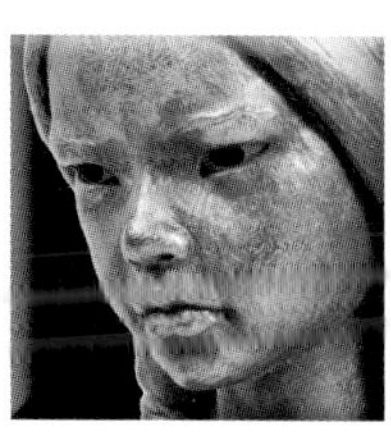

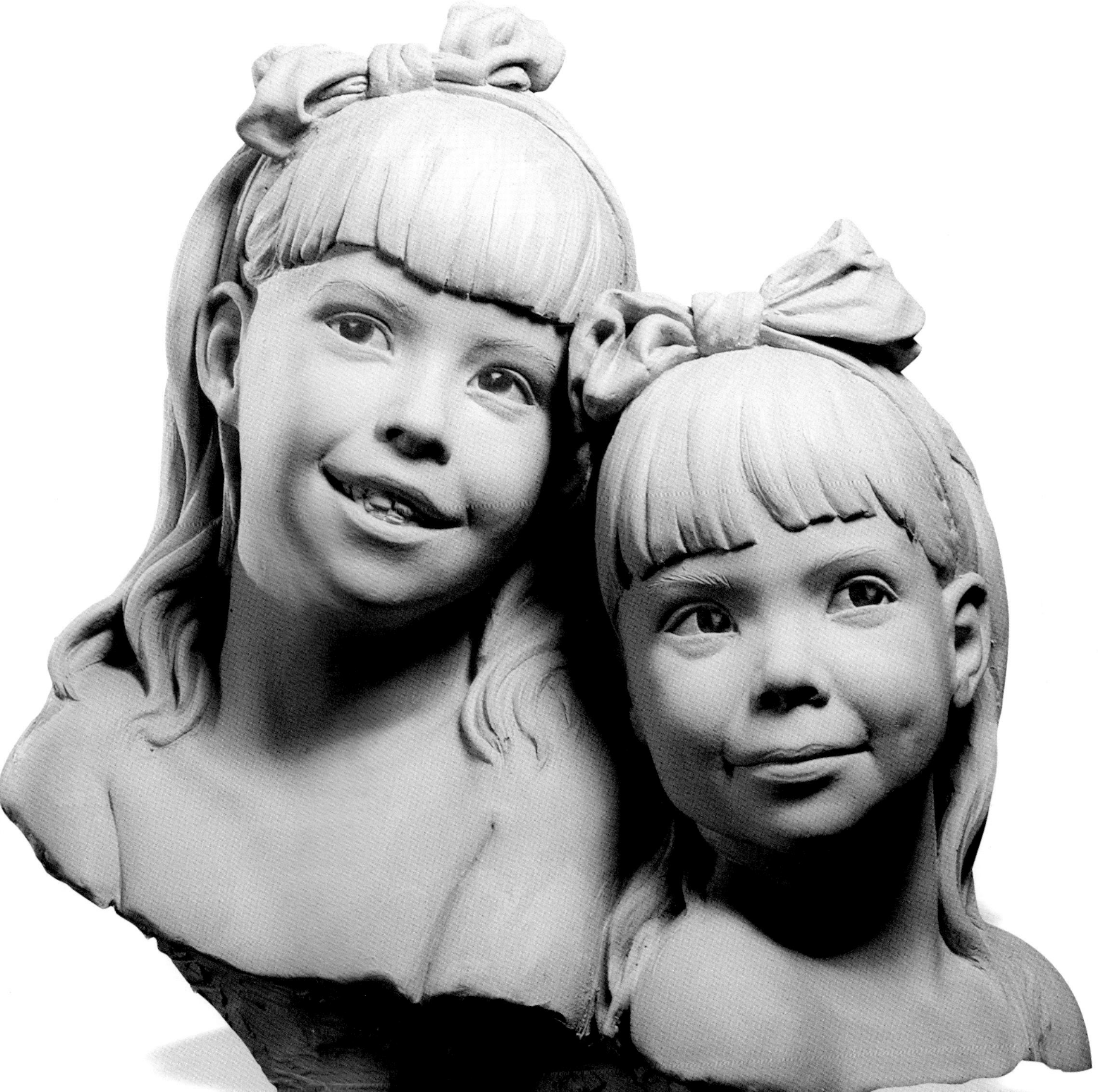

In any sculpted portrait, it is important that the expression remain constant when viewed from all angles. This can only be obtained by a constant review of the work during the sculpting process. Rotating the sculpture under proper lighting is the key to mastering expression.

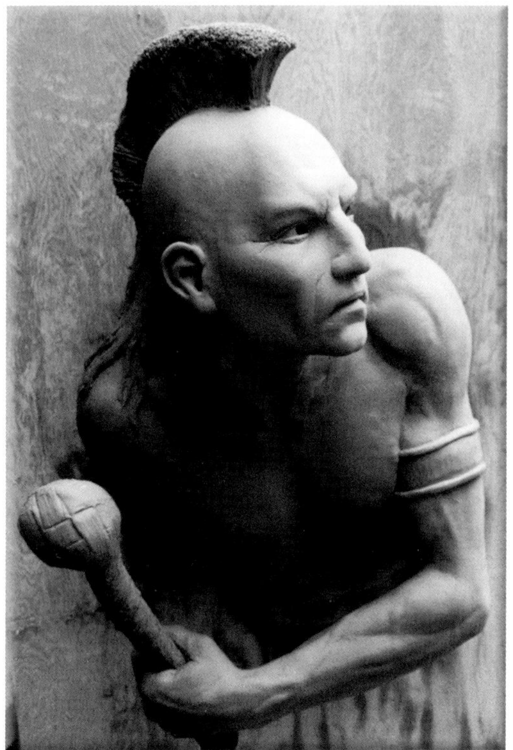

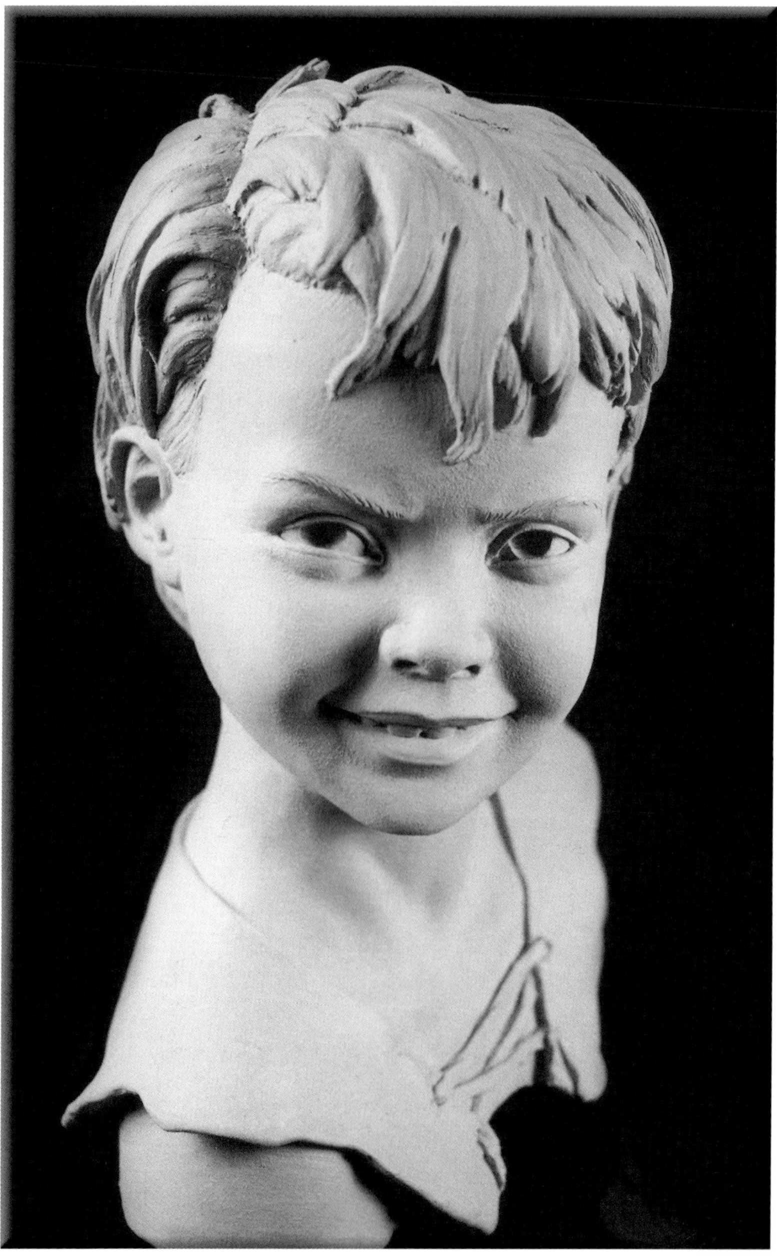

A mischievous expression is achieved with the combination of a smile while the corrugators are contracted raising one eyebrow more than the other. The eyes are turned toward the side of the lifted brow and slightly upward.

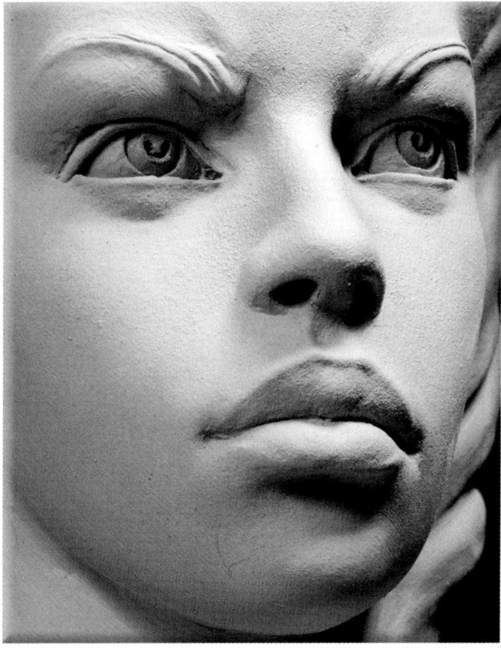

The direction of the stare is critical to convey an expression.

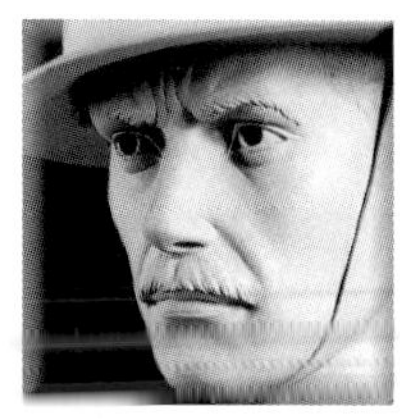

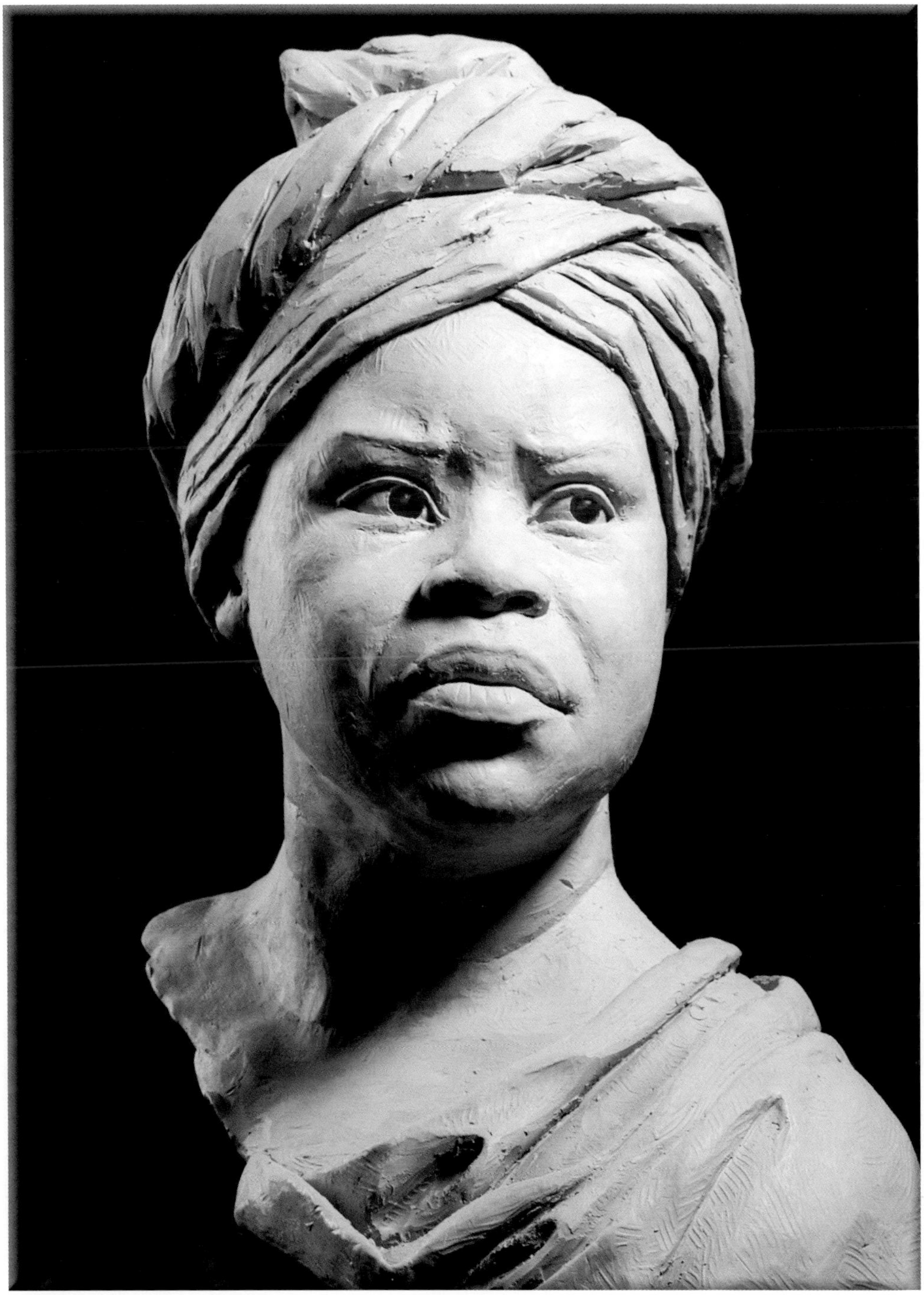

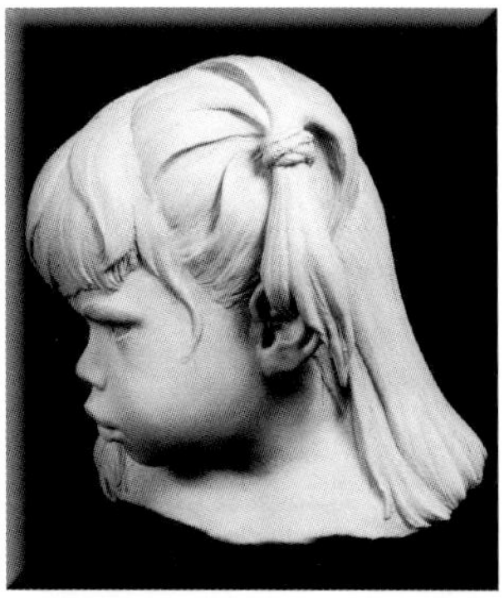

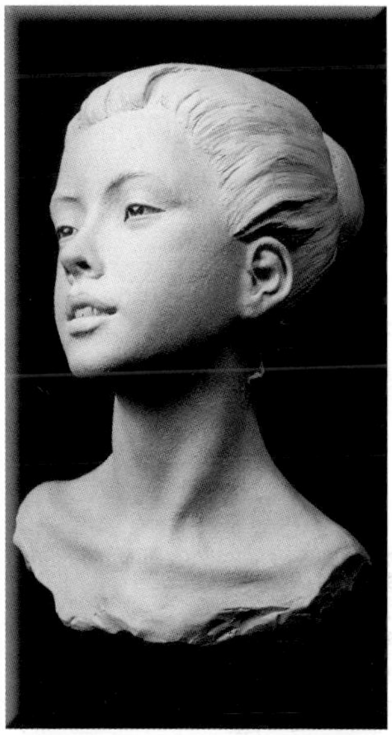

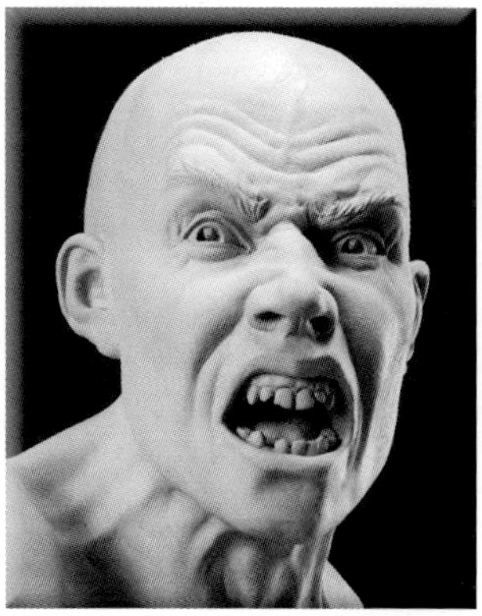

When the mentalis muscles contract, the skin of the chin is roughened, and if the lower lip is relaxed, it is pushed out forming a pout as seen in the photo of the young girl in the upper right corner.

The gesture of the head and shoulders has a profound effect on expression.

Chapter 8

# Finishing Techniques

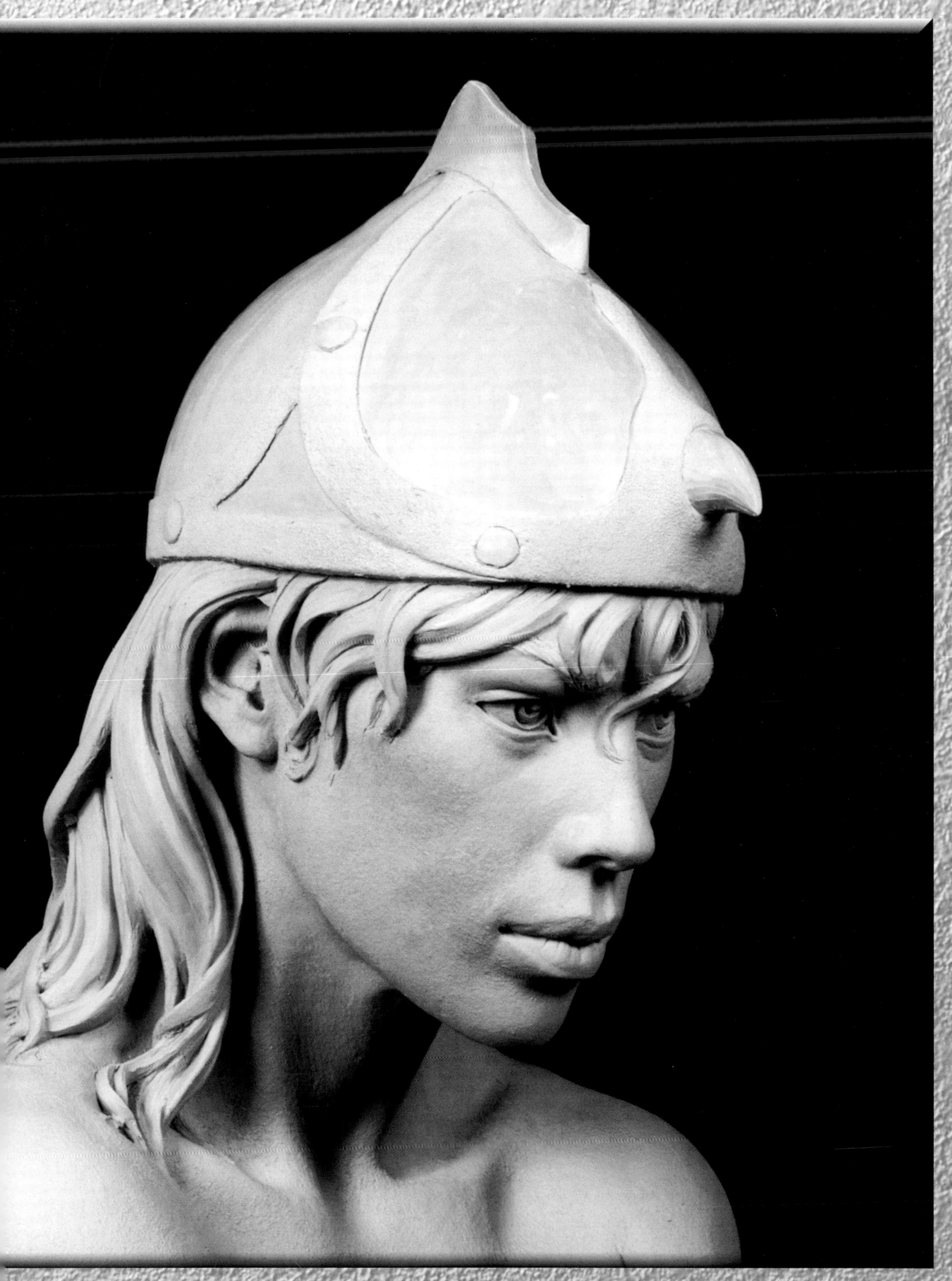

## Textures

One of the advantages of water-based clay is that it lends itself to infinite possibilities of surface textures. From very wet clay to completely dry, each stage of consistency can be used to achieve a variety of finishes. The following examples are only a few of the many possible options.

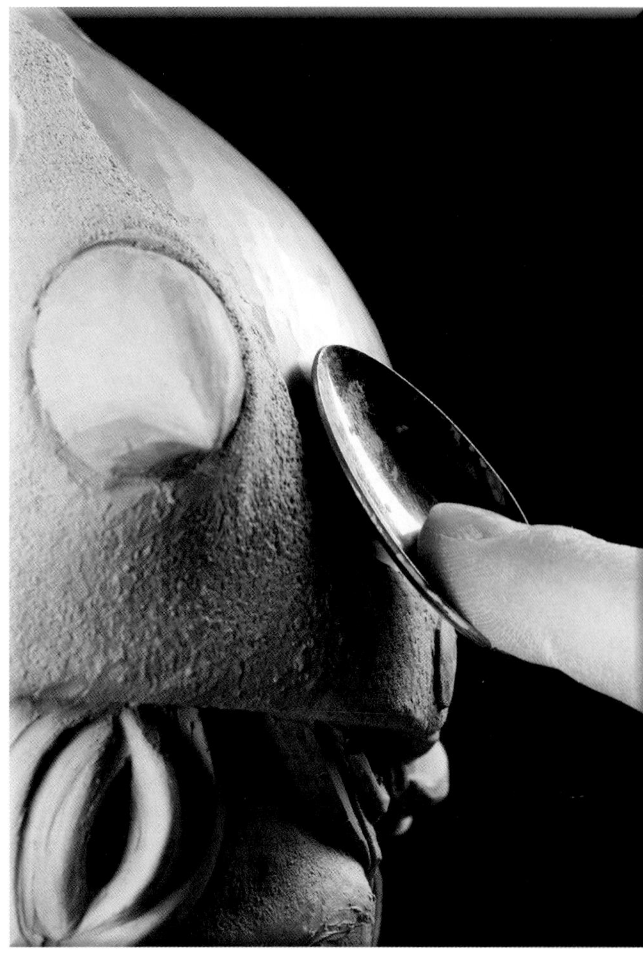

To achieve the texture of hammered metal, a spoon is used to burnish the surface of the clay when it is leather-hard. The remaining surface of the goddess' helmet was created with a wet, rough sponge.

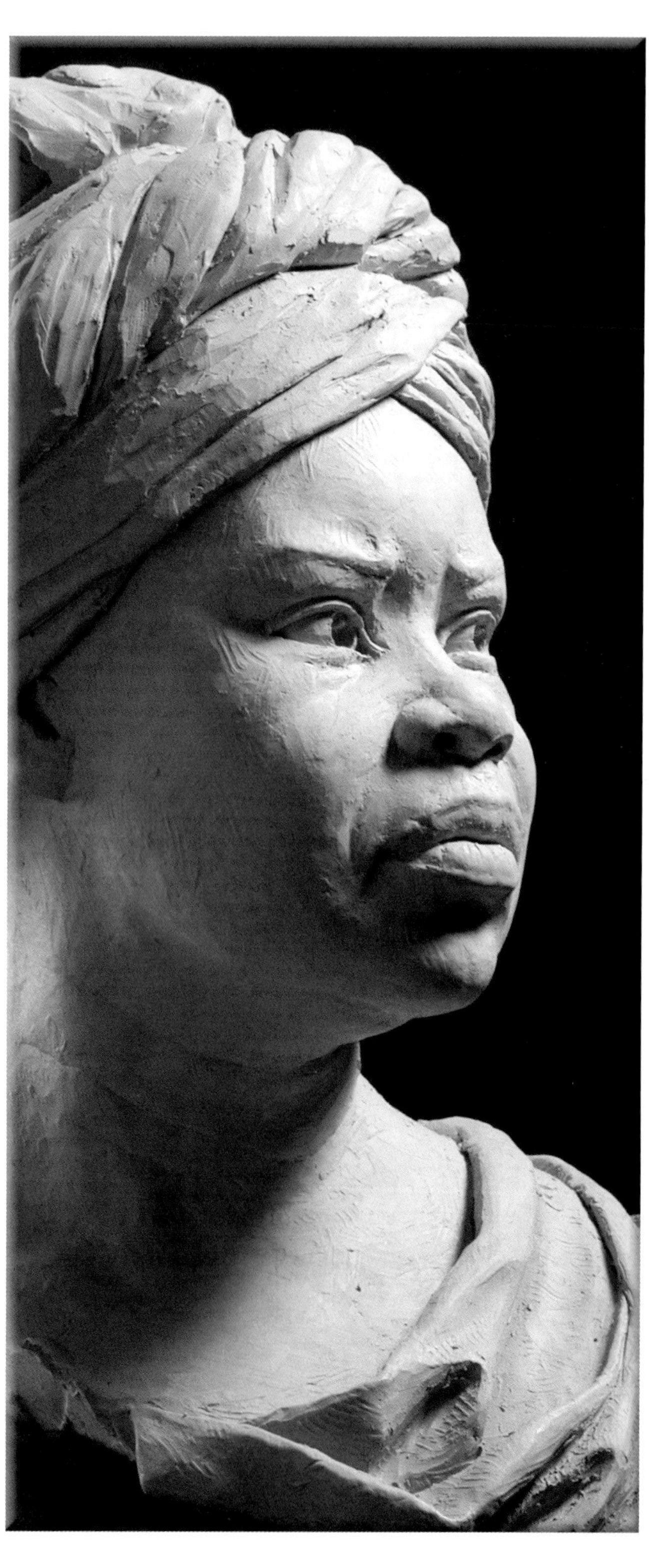

After the planes were developed on the sculpture above, they were blended together with a flat wooden tool and the tip of the fingers. Then, a serrated tool was used to roughen the entire surface. Note that trying to hide mistakes with a rough texture always fails to fool the viewer.

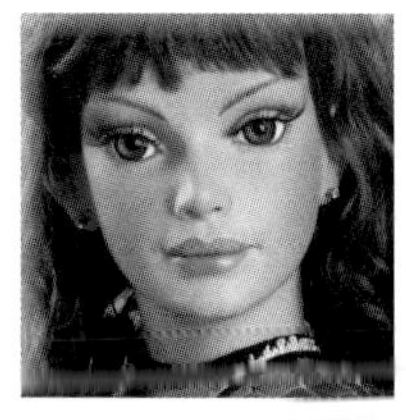

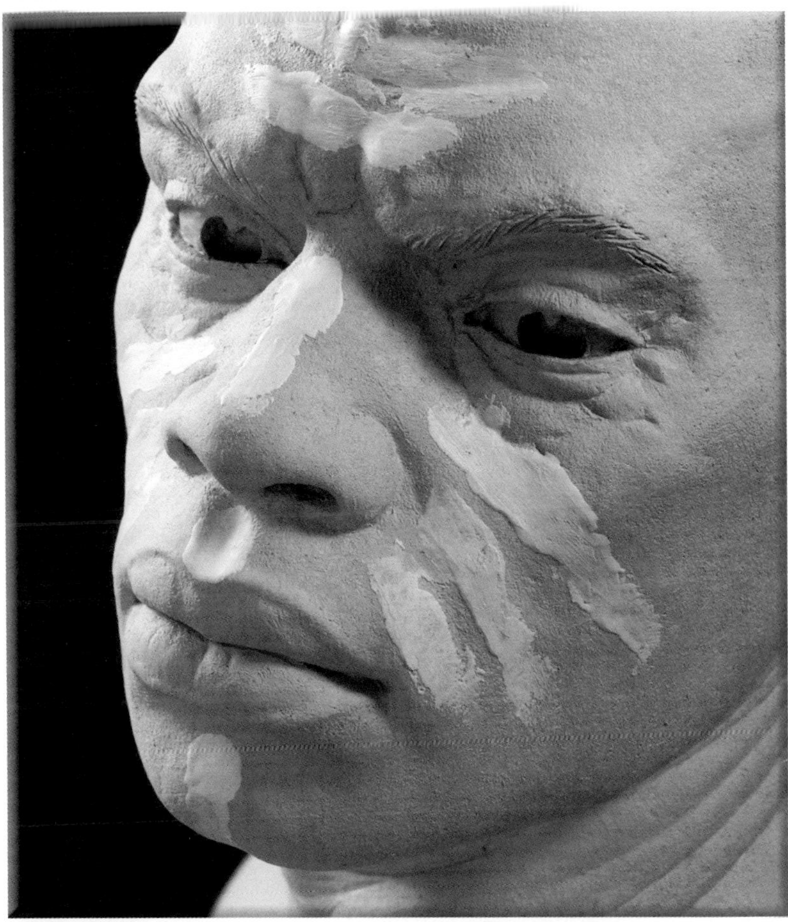

The final texture on the portrait to the left, was accomplished by dabbing a fan brush over the surface. The war paint was made with porcelain slip that will remain white after firing.

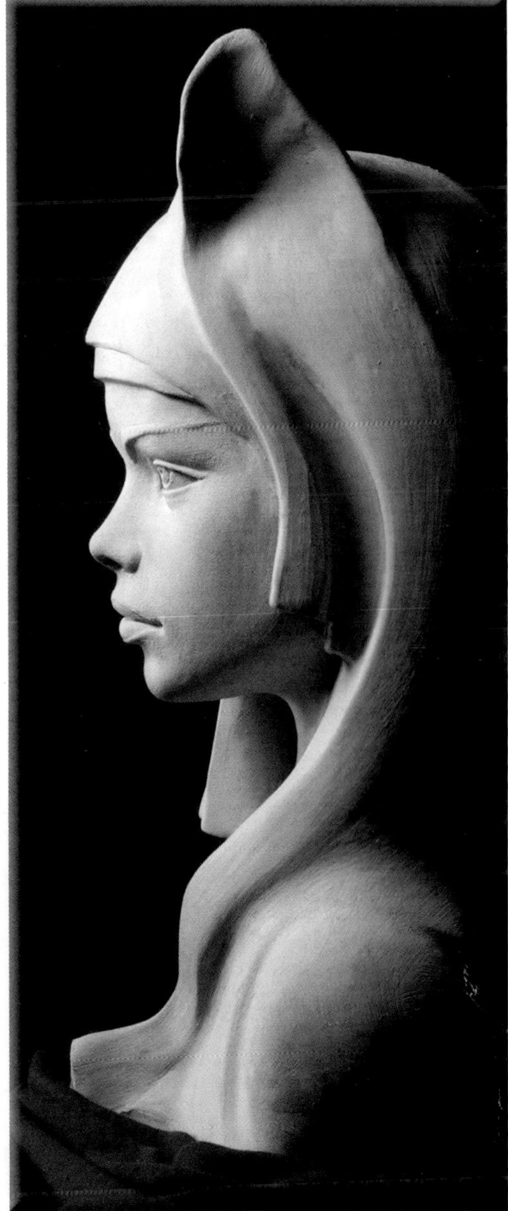

To render a silky finish, the clay is first smoothed as much as possible with a soft sponge, then water is "painted" over the surface with a very soft, flat brush.

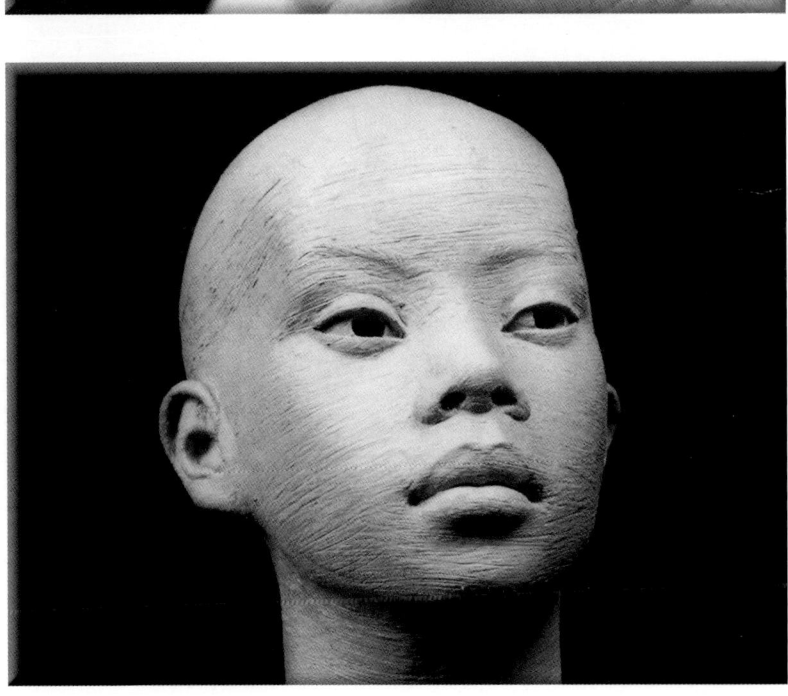

A stiff bristle brush was run horizontally over this entire sculpture when the clay was leather-hard. Then the surface was coated with a light slurry.

## The Firing Process

There are several ways to preserve a sculpture made of water-based clay. The most economical is to fire it in a high-fire kiln. It is important to understand the complex changes occurring in clay during firing in order to avoid unpleasant surprises.

During firing, the atmospheric water still present at room temperature begins to leave the clay at approximately 400°F. At 900°F, some of the water that is chemically combined with the clay begins to leave and by 1300°F (red heat) all such water has left the clay. Shortly after this, the organic matter in the clay burns out and the first appreciable shrinkage of the clay occurs. The impurities contained in the clay in the form of carbonates or sulfates of calcium, magnesium and iron decompose giving off a gas in the form of carbon dioxide or sulfur dioxide. Iron and other low-melting compounds begin to combine with silica found in various clay minerals and form a glassy bond. Between 1750°F and 1850°F, silica combines with alumina to form the interlocking crystals called mullite.

The maturing temperature of earthenware is between 1840°-2000°F (cone 04-07). The clay used throughout this book fires to approximately 1873°F (cone 06). After firing, earthenware is still quite porous and more fragile than stoneware that matures between 2300°-2500°F (cone 6-13) resulting in complete vitrification.

Prior to firing, the piece should be allowed to dry slowly over a period of several weeks to eliminate as much moisture as possible. Once bone dry (no longer cool to the touch), the sculpture is placed in the kiln. A preliminary heating is necessary to remove the remaining moisture always present in "dry" clay at room temperature. This initial heating period should be at least three hours with the kiln lid open to allow the temperature to rise slowly. Heating raw clay too rapidly causes the trapped water vapor to turn to steam. The resulting expansion will cause the thickest parts of the sculpture to explode. For the remainder of the firing, the kiln lid is closed and the rise in temperature should be gradual, over a period of eight hours for medium sized pieces (life-sized busts) and up to twelve hours for larger pieces. The cooling off time should also be gradual (at least as long as the firing time). The kiln should never be opened until the temperature drops to 300°F.

## Demonstration 12: Hollowing a Sculpture

In order to reduce the risk of damage during firing, the sculpture must be hollowed out while the clay is still workable. If the sculpture needs to be sliced open in order to proceed, the clay must be at just the correct consistency. If too wet, it would be difficult to manipulate. The clay being soft would get distorted easily and run the risk of collapsing once hollowed. If too dry, it would be difficult to slice, and could even crack. Thus, it is important to monitor the drying of the clay until its surface feels firm, yet still pliable.

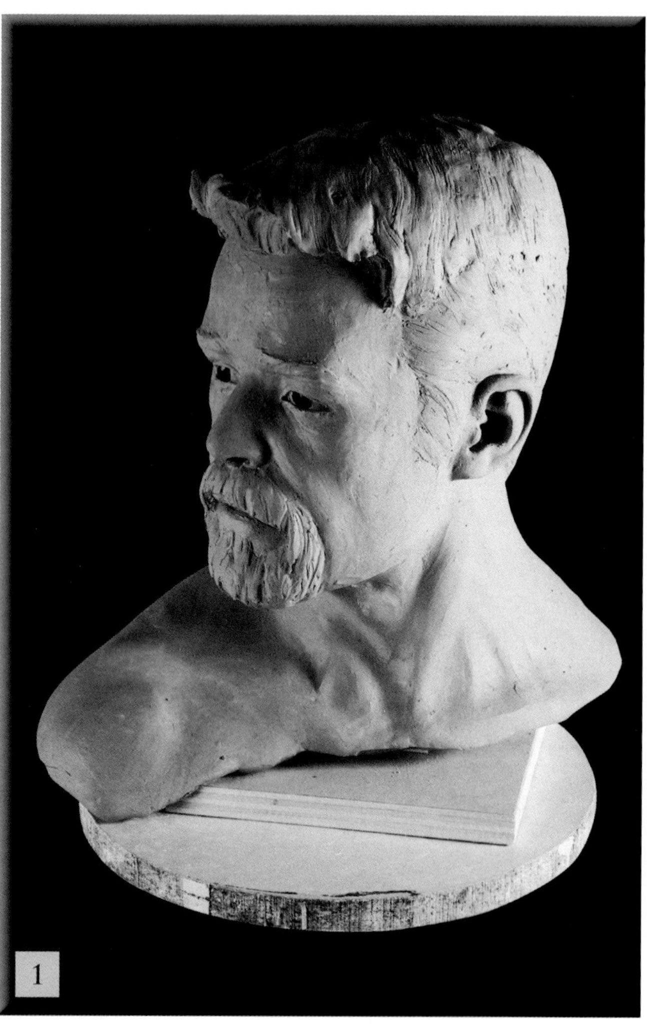


**1.** The sculpture is placed on a turntable and carefully studied from various angles to evaluate the most unobtrusive placement for the slicing line.

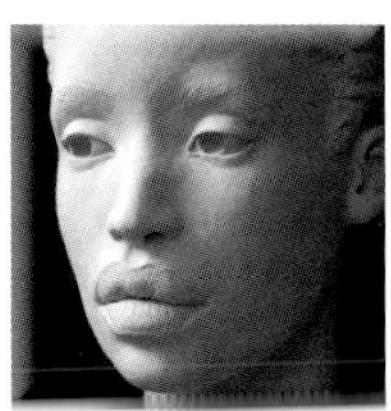

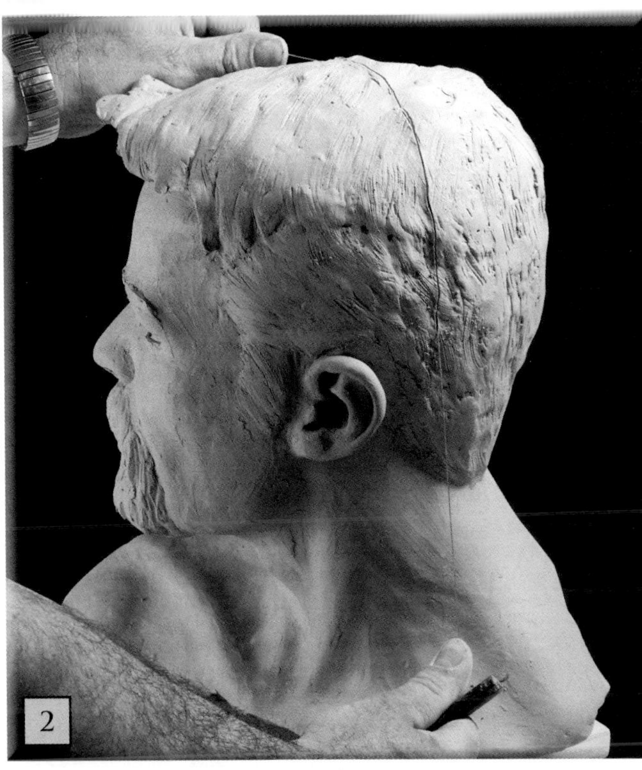


2, 3. In this case, the bust is sliced vertically into two approximately equal parts with a clay cutting wire. The slicing line runs on one side in front of the right ear, and on the other side in back of the left ear.

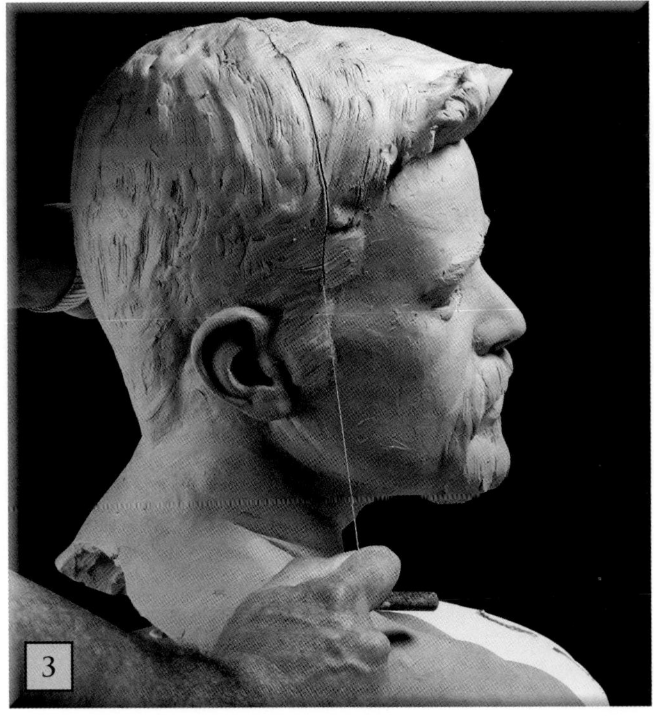


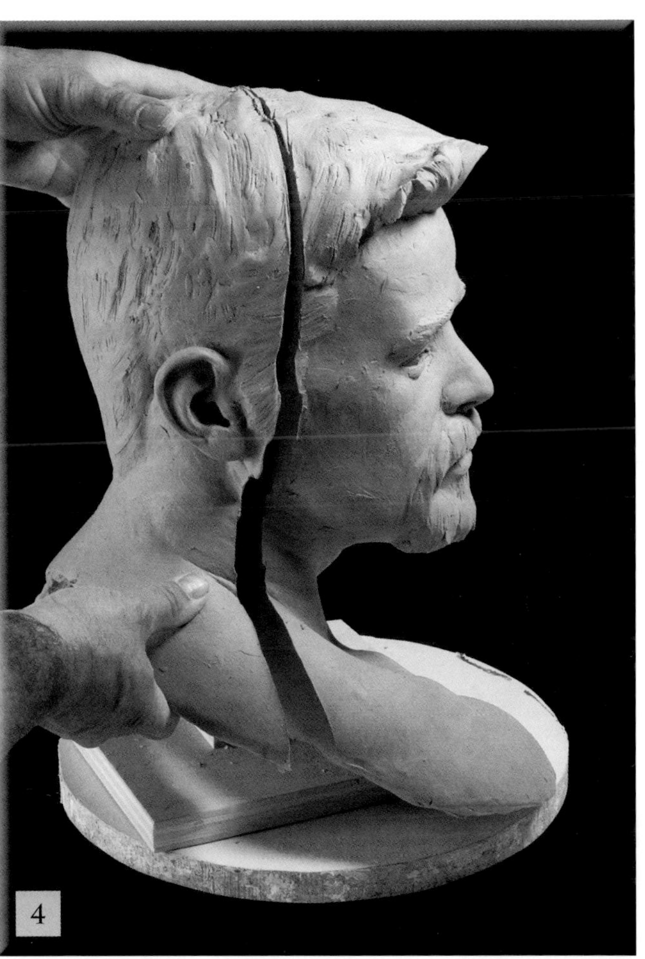


4. The two halves are pried apart.

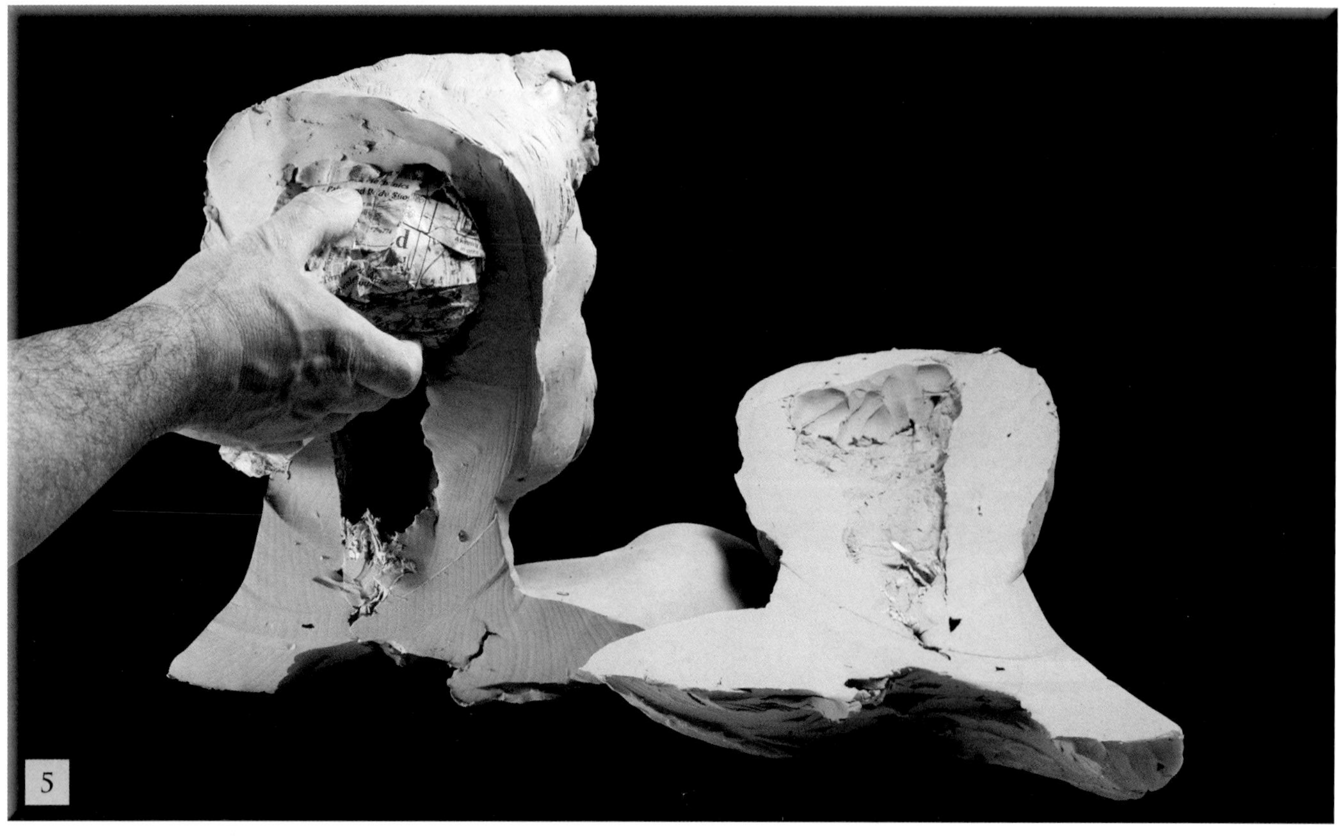

5. The paper core is carefully removed.

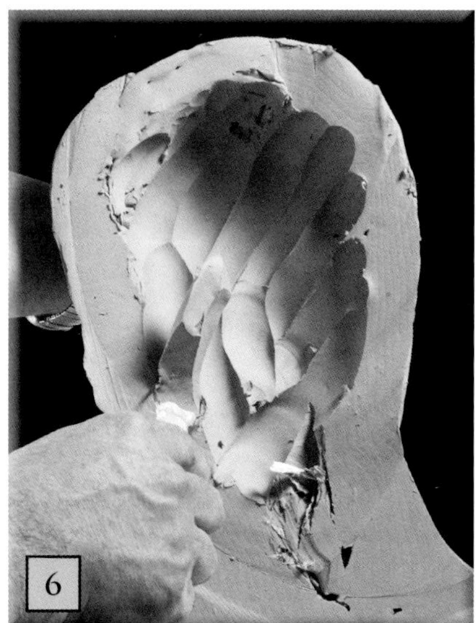

6. The back half is scooped out to a consistent thickness of approximately $^{3}/_{4}$".

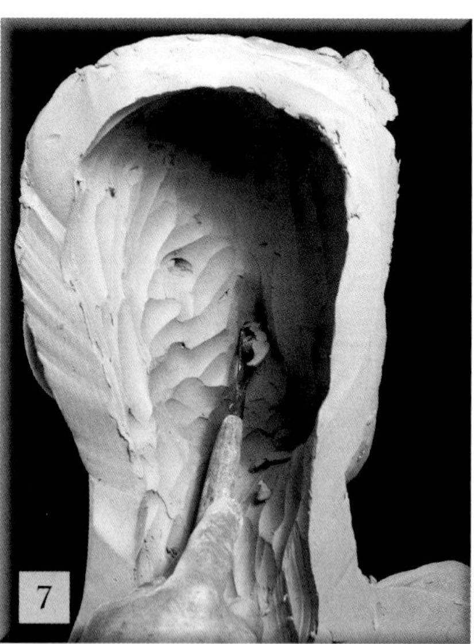

7. On the face side, particular attention should be paid to the nose and chin area. It is very common to leave these areas too thick for fear of going through them.

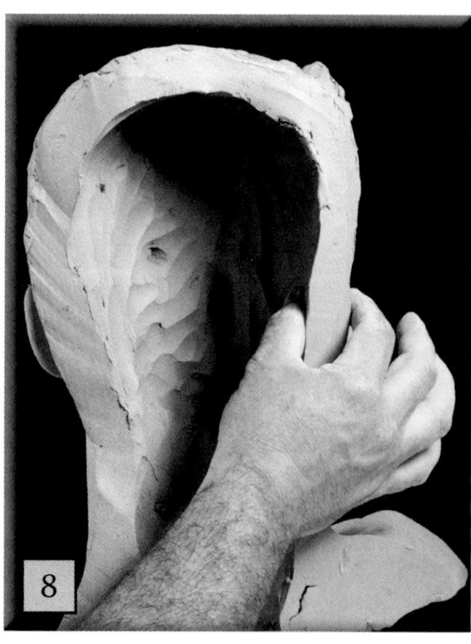

8. The consistency of the thickness can be felt by hand around the edges.

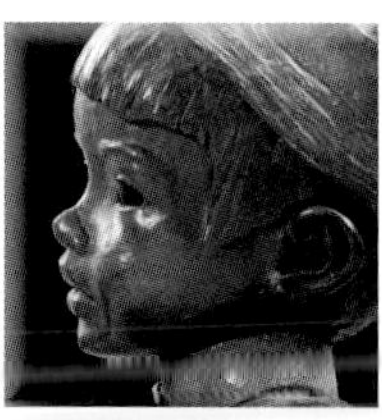

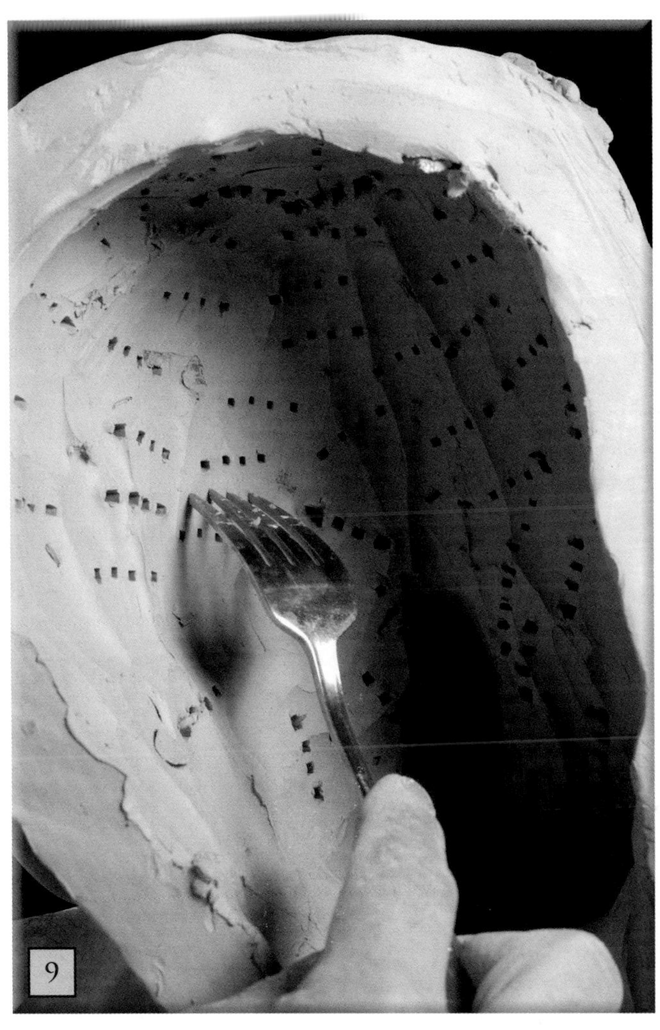

**9.** A series of holes 1/2" deep on the inside of the sculpture facilitates the evacuation of steam and gases during firing.

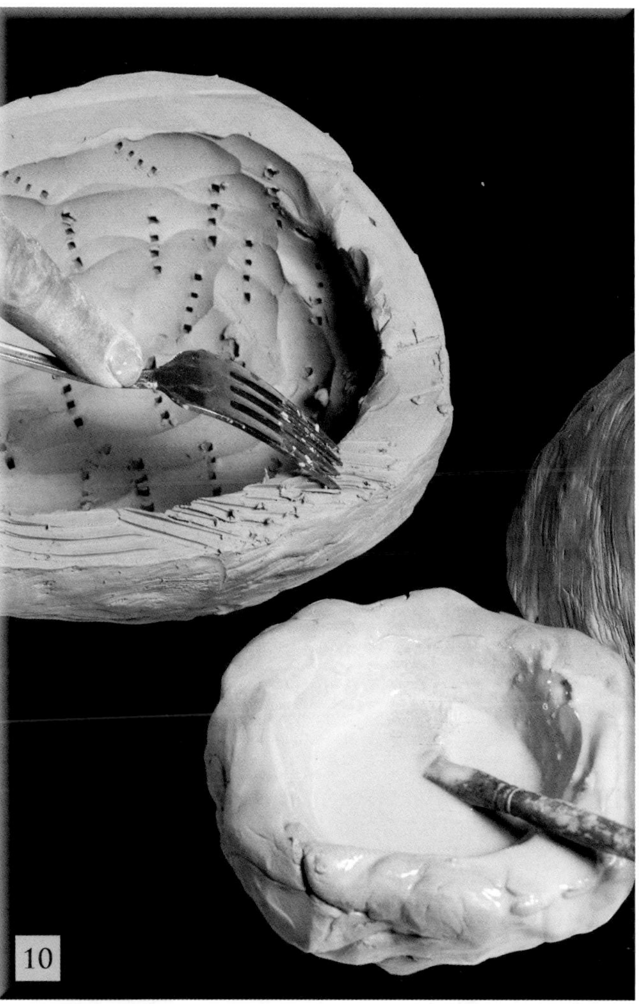

**10.** The surface of the edges are scored with a fork. A small bowl shaped out of fresh clay is filled with water to form a slurry.

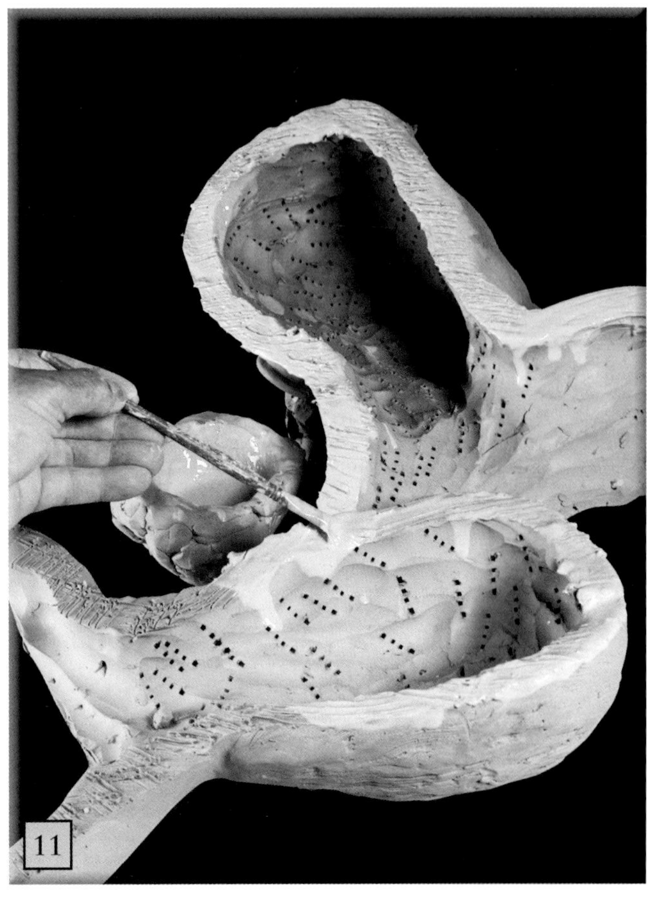

11. With a soft brush, the slurry is applied on both the back and front edges of the piece.

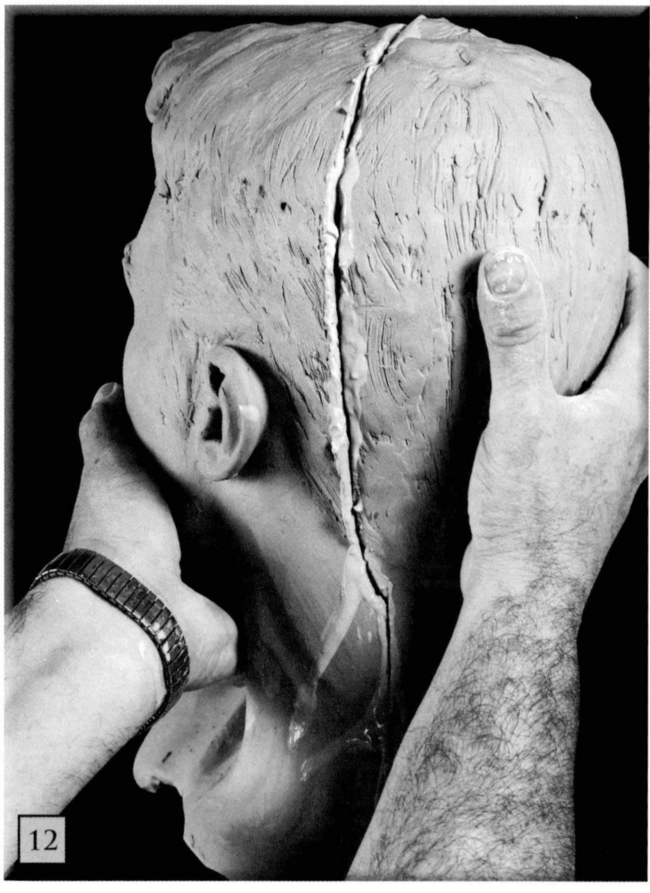

12, 13. The two parts are reassembled and pressure is applied all along the seam to close any gap and ensure a strong bond.

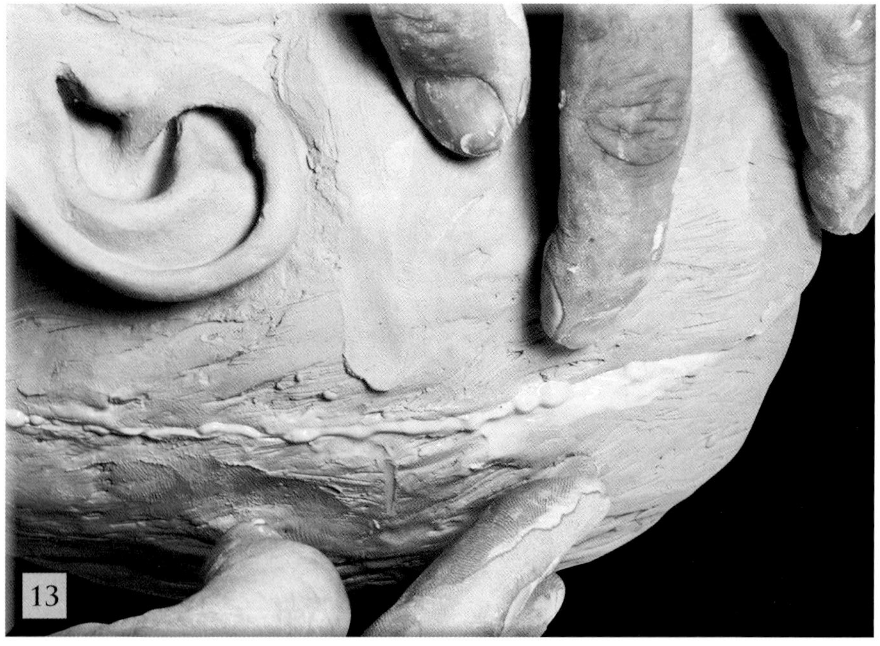

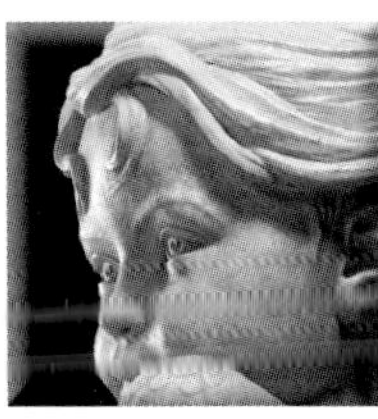

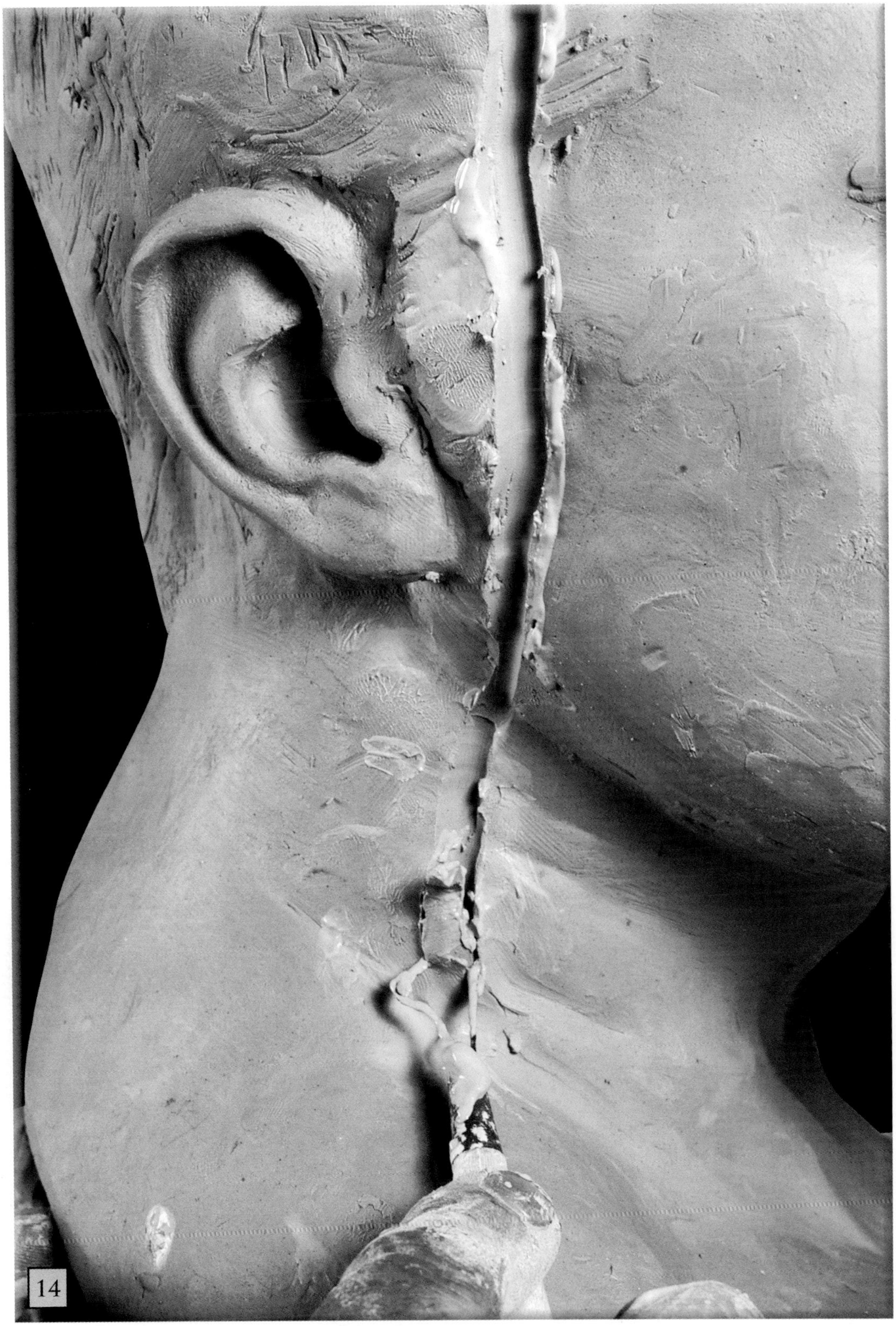

**14.** Next, the piece is placed back on the armature for support. To reinforce the bond between the two halves, a $^{1}/_{4}$" groove is first dug along the entire seam.

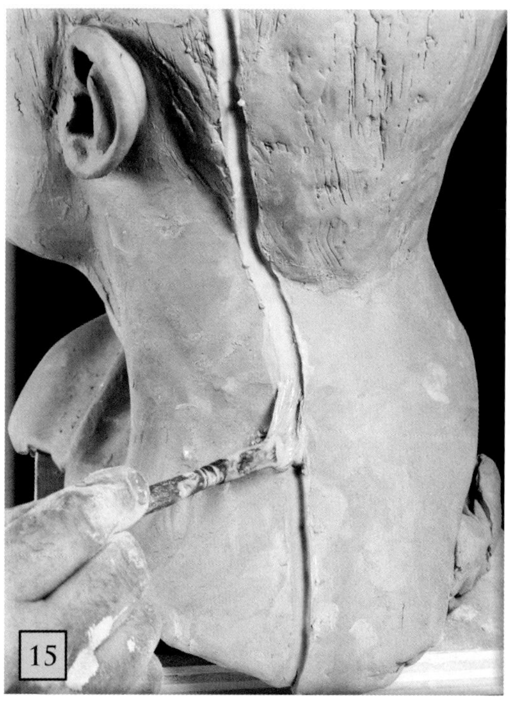

15. The groove is moistened with slurry.

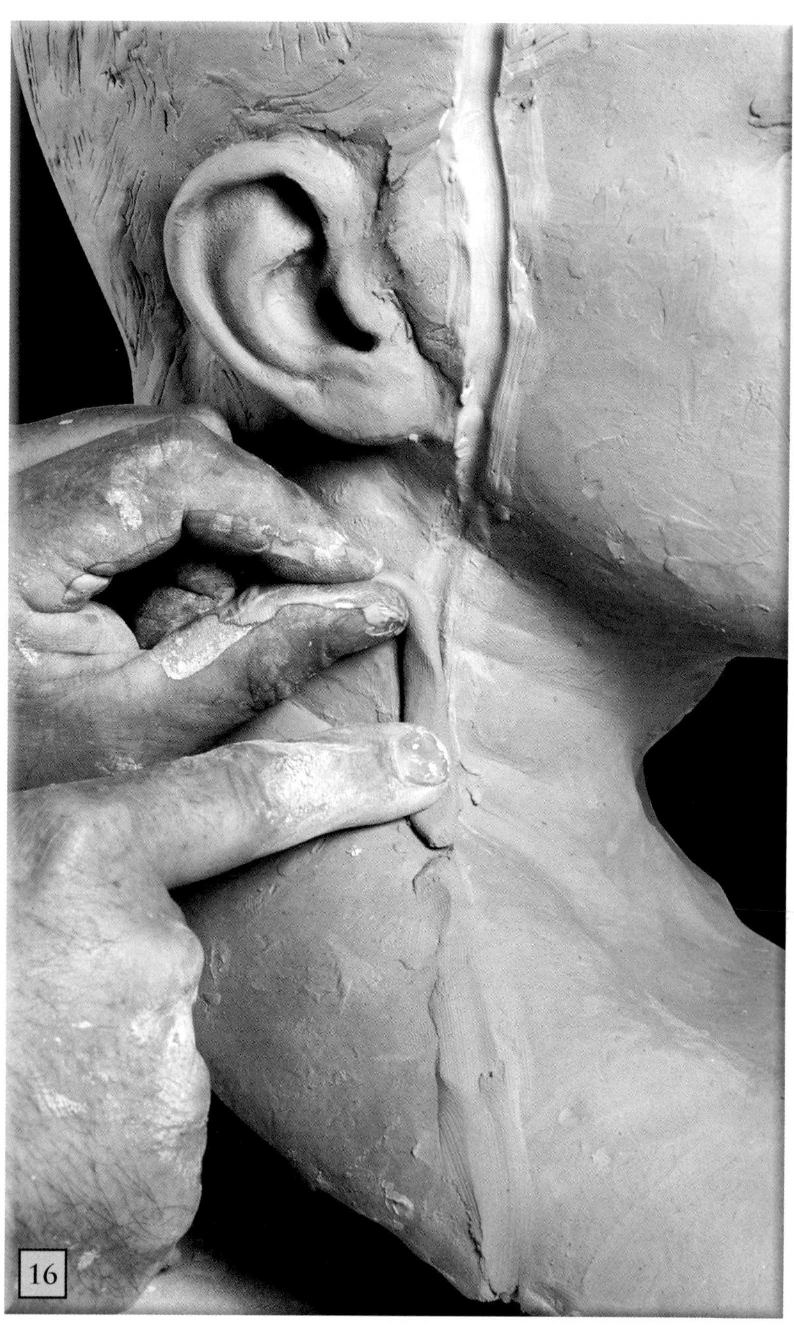

16. Then the groove is refilled with clay. It is better to use clay that has already somewhat hardened. Fresh, wet clay will shrink more than the surrounding surface, creating a depression visible when dry.

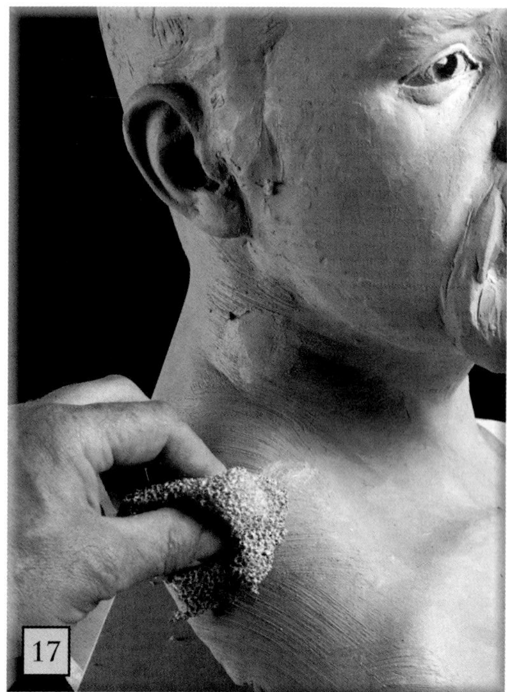

17. All traces of the seam are erased with a rough sponge. Now, the final texture of the sculpture can be achieved and the final drying process can begin.

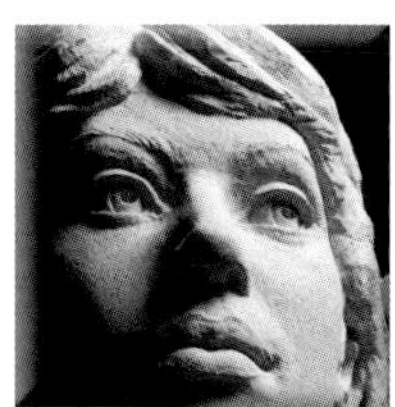

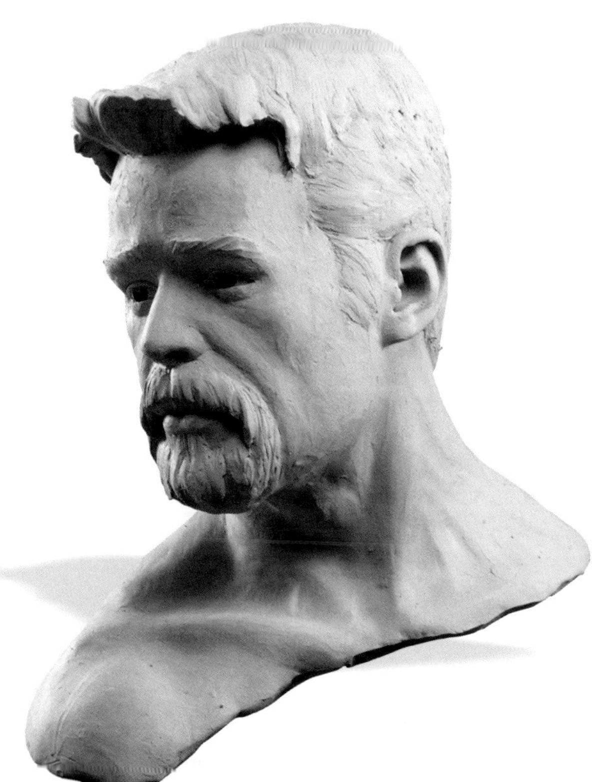

**18.** It is better to leave the piece under a plastic bag for a week to equalize the moisture within it before allowing it to dry completely. The sculpture is ready to be fired when bone dry.

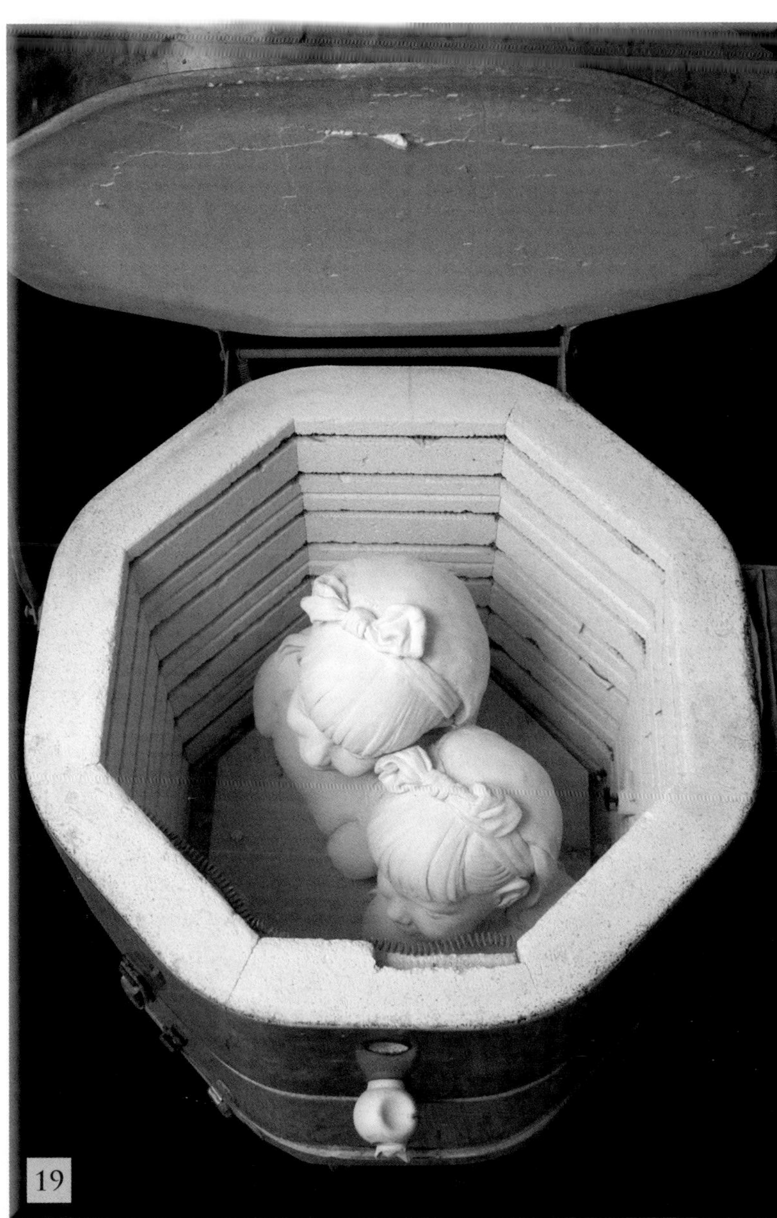

**19.** If space and time allow, it is often a great help with intricate or delicate pieces to place them in the kiln while still damp and leave them to dry for several weeks. This avoids the risk of damaging the piece while loading it once it has become even more brittle.

## Demonstration 13: Repairing a Broken Sculpture

Sometimes, small cracks appear during firing that can easily be repaired with spackling putty. However, if the kiln temperature is raised too rapidly, the piece may explode with devastating results. The following segment demonstrates that even a very damaged sculpture can be successfully repaired. In this case, four busts were fired together and the temperature was accidentally set on high. Fortunately, all the faces had been turned toward the center of the kiln, protecting them from flying shards. When attempting this type of repair, it is critical to have all materials on hand prior to beginning. Plaster sets up very quickly. Steps 8-17 took only twenty minutes.

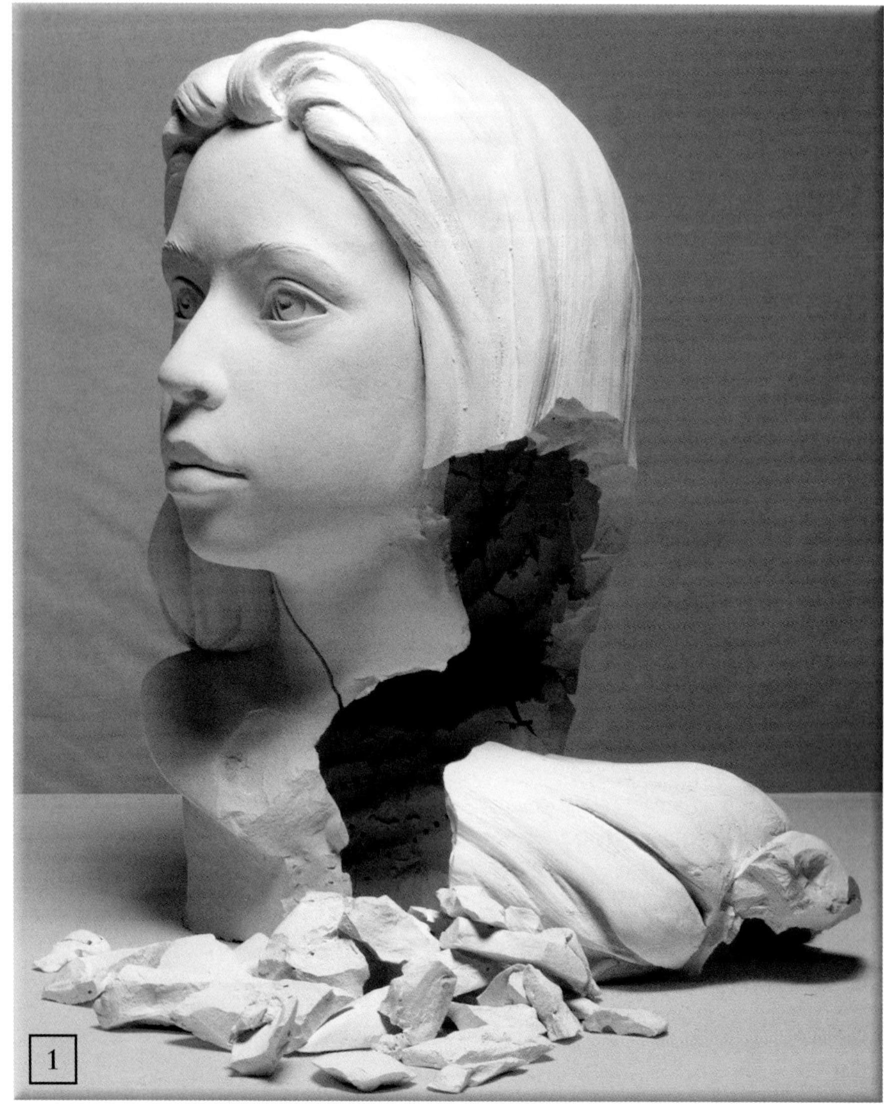

1

**Materials List:**

| | |
|---|---|
| Super Glue™ | Disposable Brushes |
| Cab-O-Sil® | Cardboard |
| Epoxy Glue | Scissors |
| Hydrocal® | Rubber Scraper |
| Plastic Cups | Metal Scraper |
| Mixing Sticks | Files |
| Plastic Bowls | Pot Scrubbers |
| Water | Sponges |

**1.** The pieces are collected. The smallest ones, which will be replaced by Hydrocal®, are ignored. Hydrocal® is a US Gypsum type of plaster with very high compressive strength and a low absorption rate. These properties make it a more suitable product than #1 pottery plaster that is usually used for waste and slip casting molds. Throughout the following demonstration the term plaster refers to Hydrocal®.

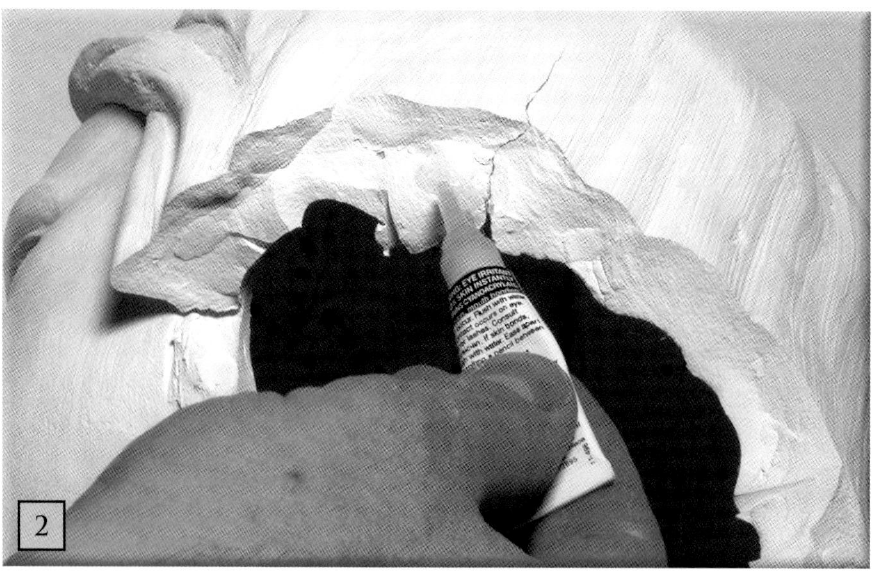

2

**2.** A small quantity of Super Glue™ is used to create a preliminary bond between the broken pieces.

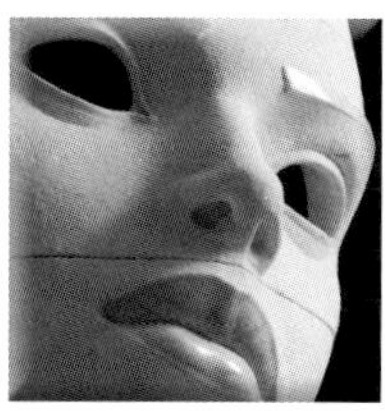

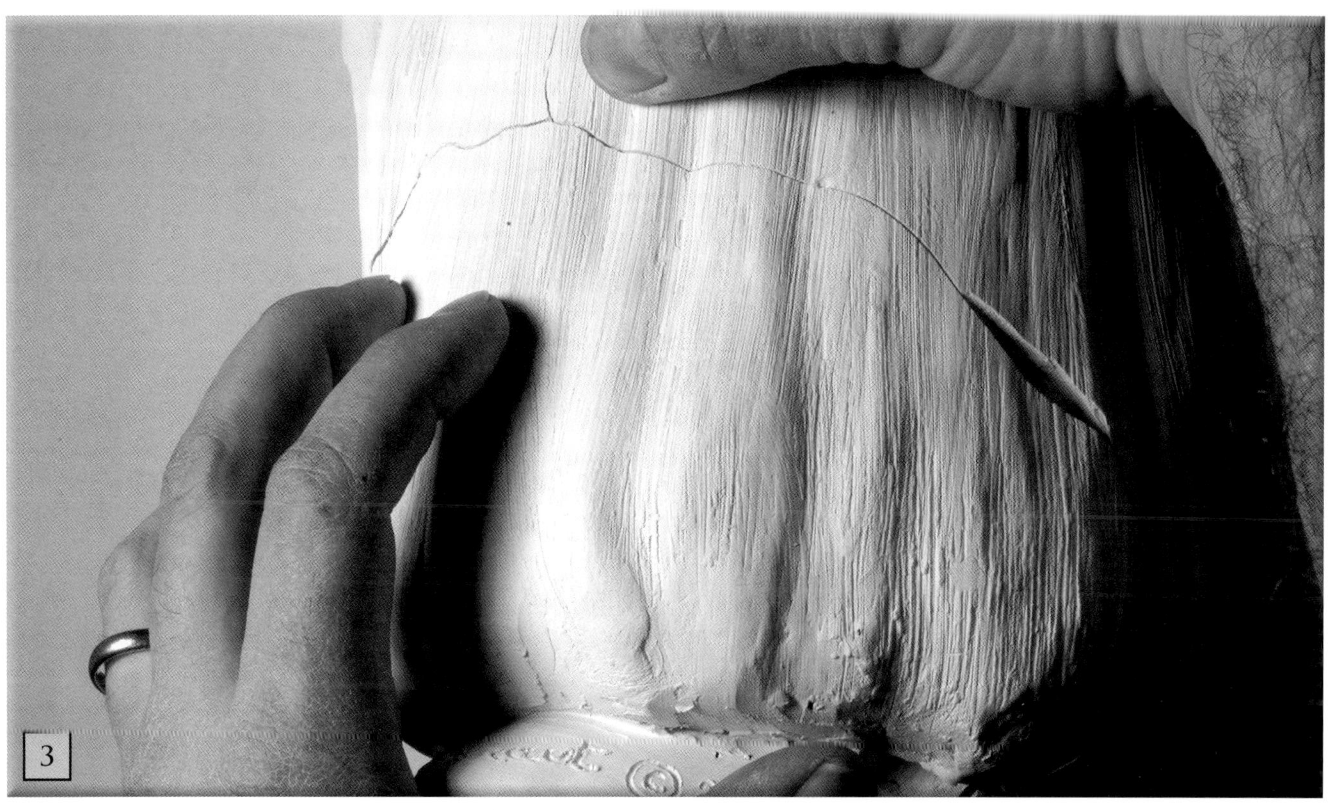

**3.** Super Glue™ requires only a few seconds of pressure to create a bond.

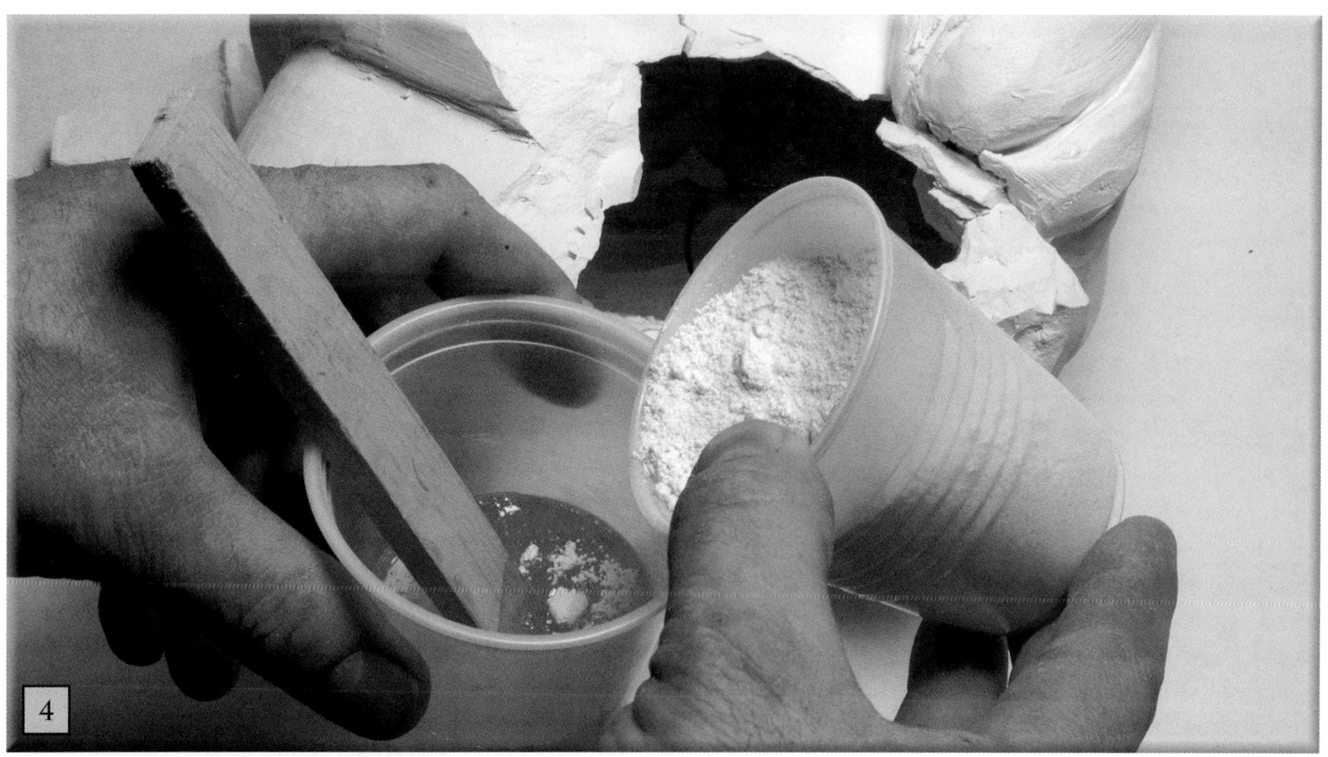

**4.** Two-part epoxy glue is mixed with Cab-O-Sil®, a thickening powder, to form a paste.

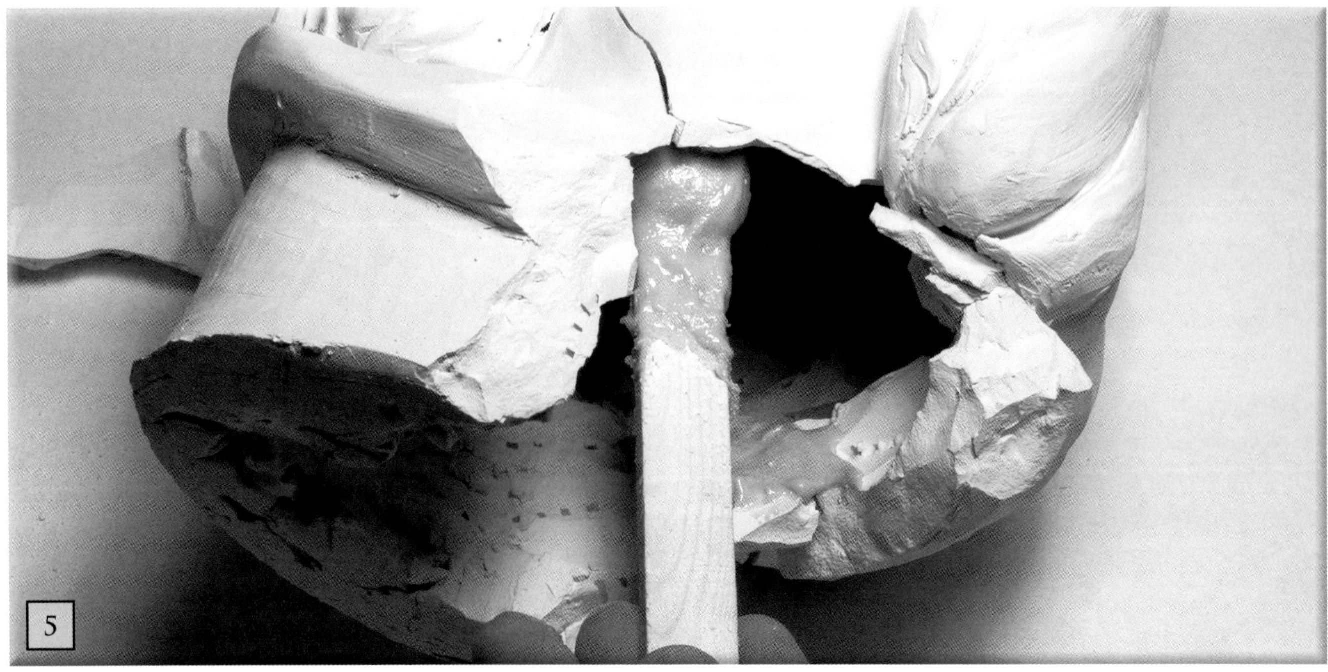

5. The paste is applied from the inside along any cracks to reinforce the assemblage.

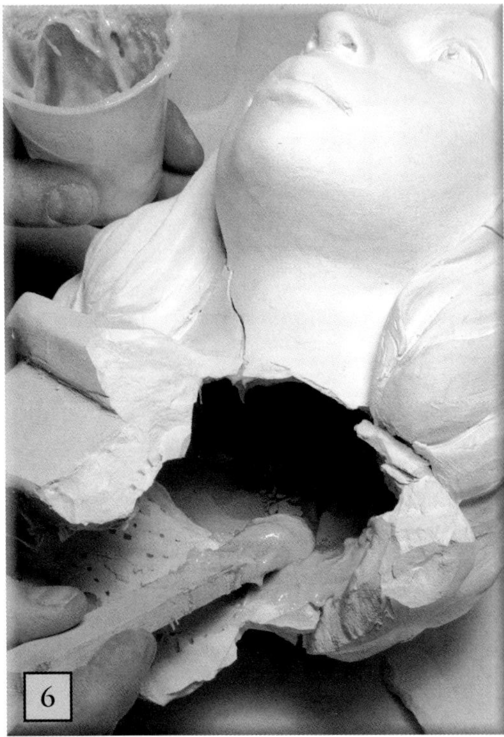

6. It is important to prevent the epoxy glue from seeping through the cracks to the exterior surface. These cracks will be repaired with plaster, which is easier to sand than epoxy.

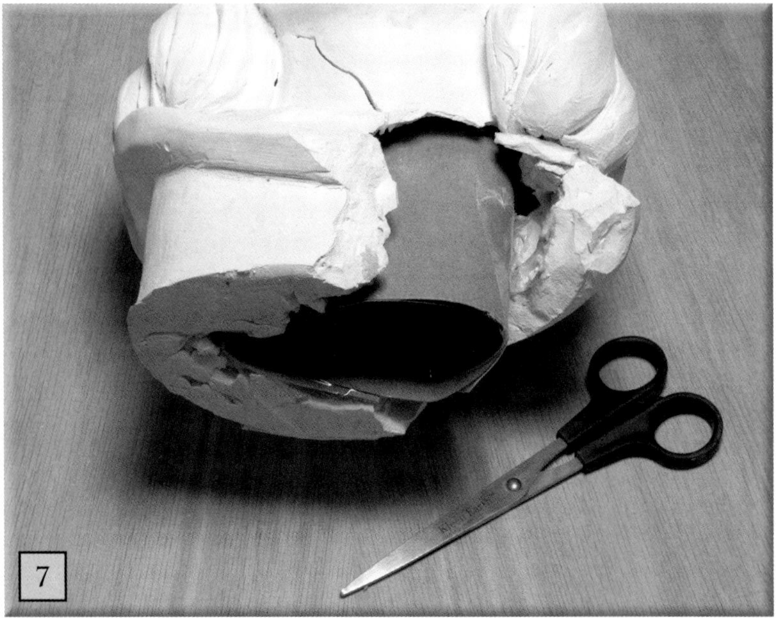

7. The large area still missing needs to be rebuilt with plaster. To prevent filling the entire head with plaster, a tube of light-weight cardboard is inserted into the neck area. This technique is used to control the thickness of the repair so that it is consistent with the thickness of the original clay.

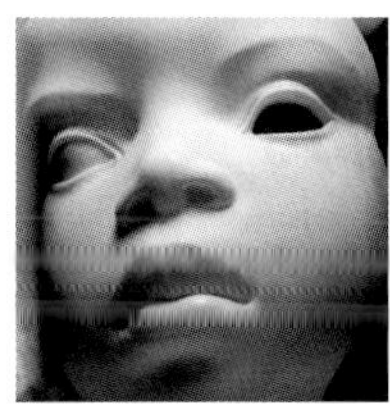

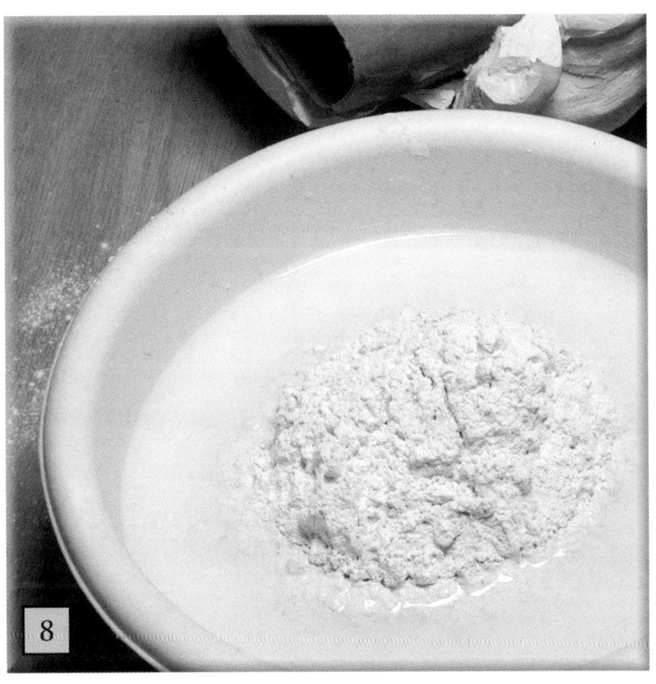

8. The plaster is sifted into a bowl of tepid water. The best ratio for this purpose is 1:2 by weight, e.g., 8 oz. of water to 16 oz. plaster. It is left to soak for 2 minutes, and then stirred with a rubber scraper.

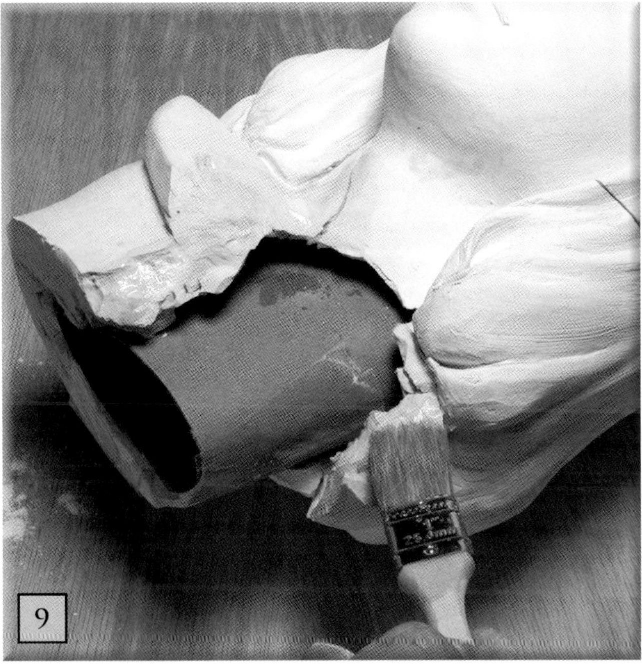

9. While the plaster is soaking, the terracotta is moistened with a brush and water.

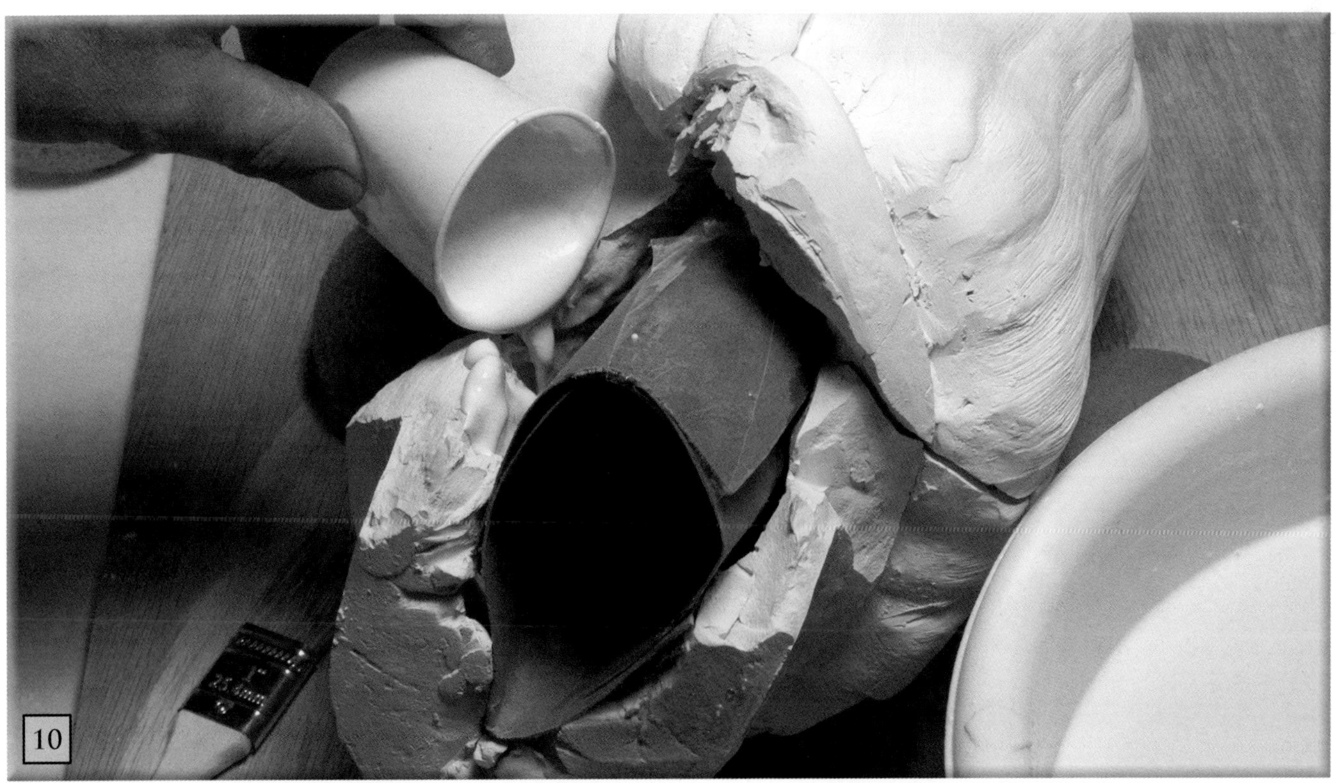

10. While the plaster is still liquid, it is poured between the cardboard and the terracotta.

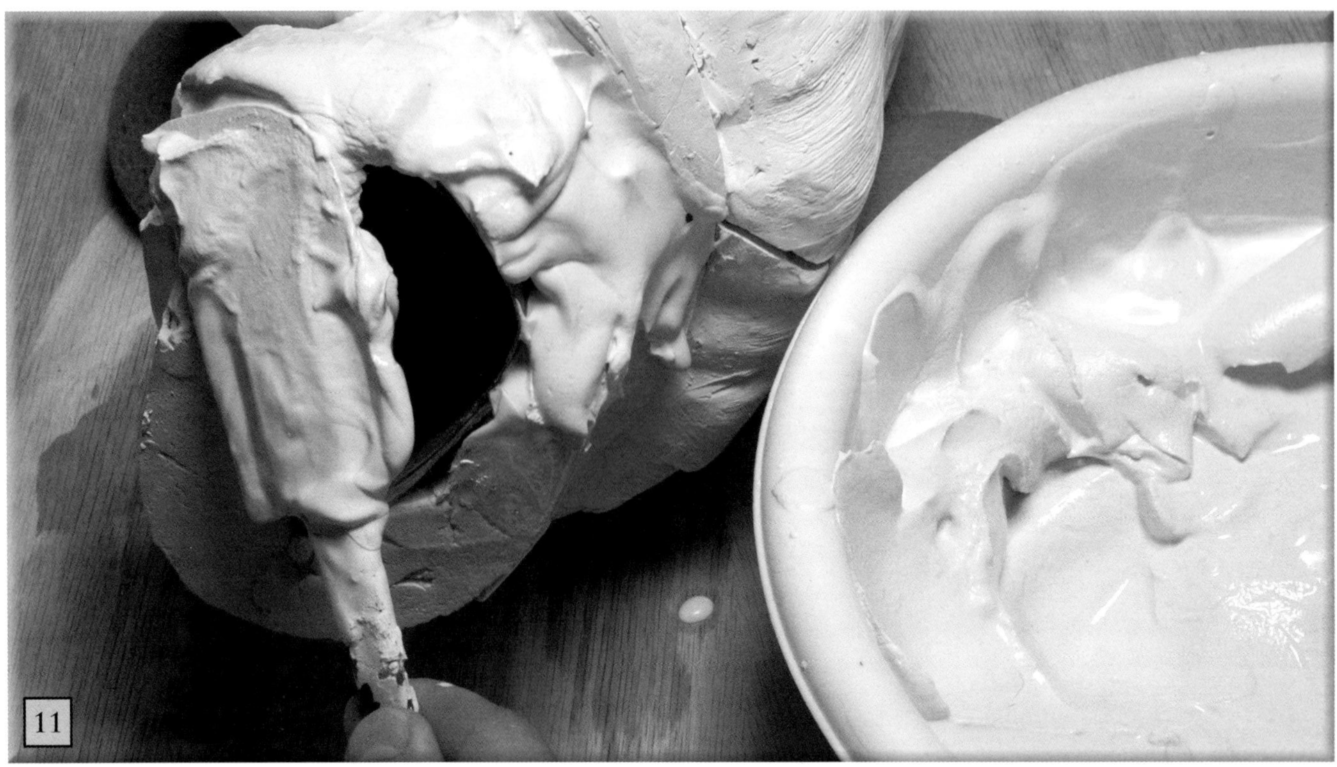


**11.** As the plaster thickens, a rubber scraper is used to build up the missing volumes.

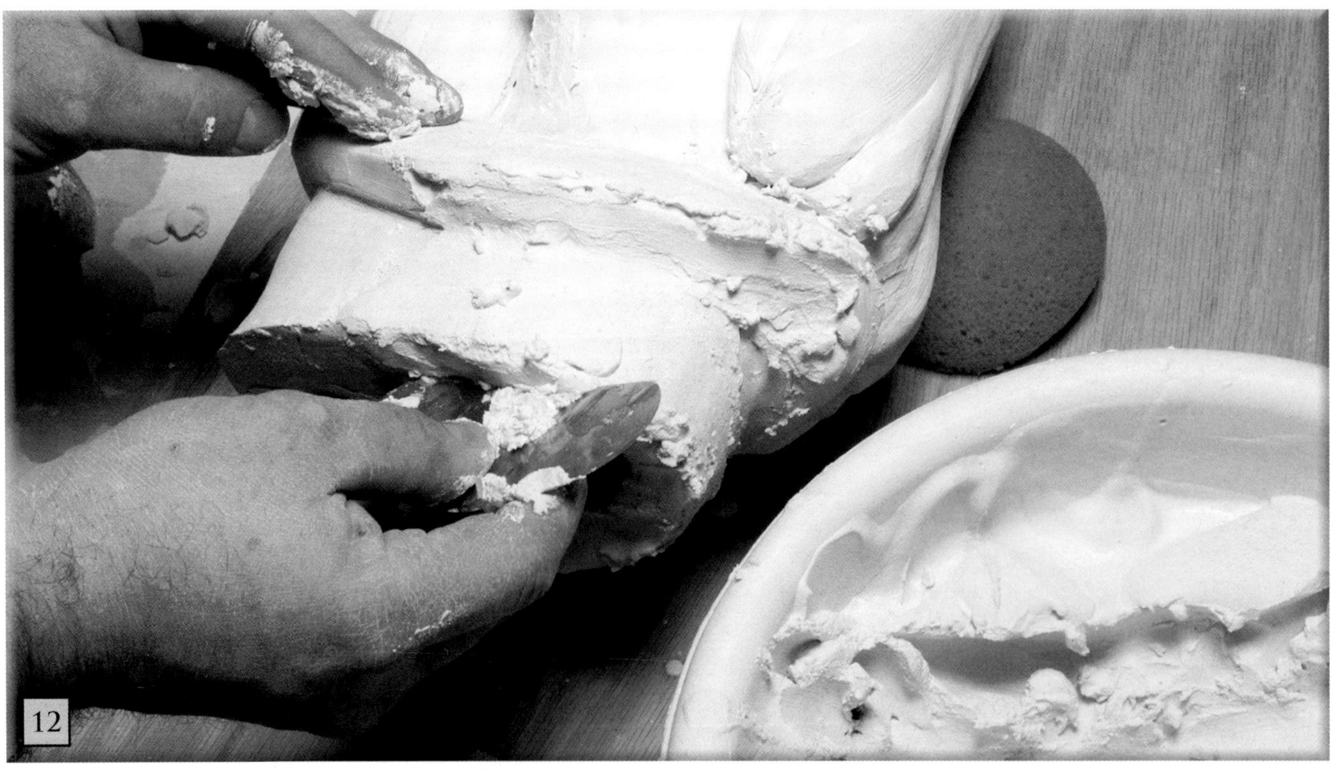


**12.** The plaster rapidly reaches the ideal consistency to re-sculpt the lost portion of the piece.

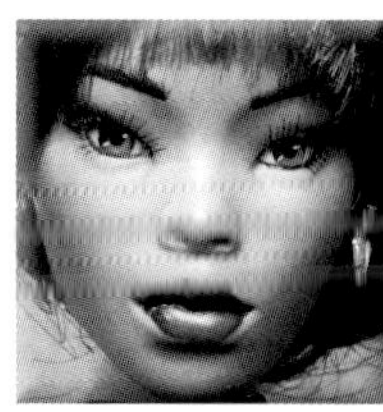

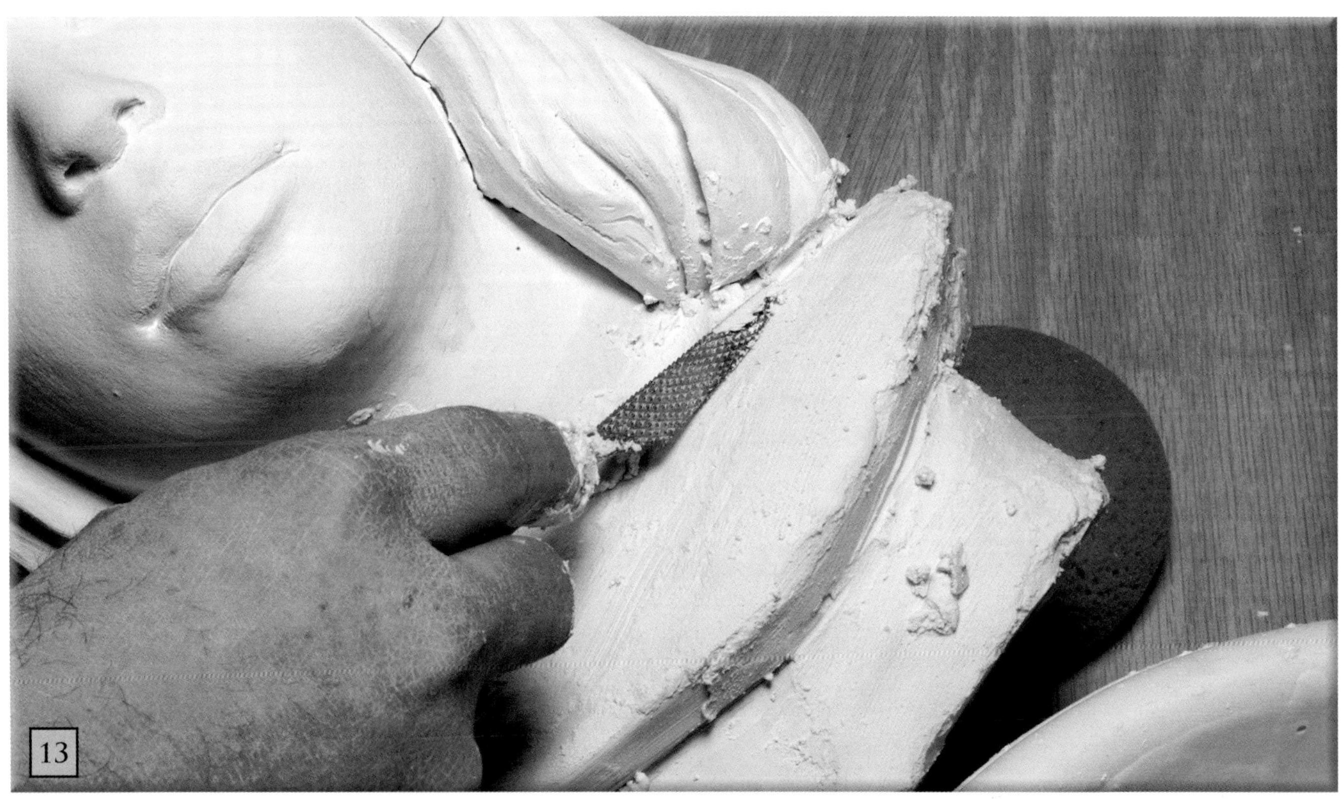


**13.** The surface is shaped with a curved file and the remaining cracks are filled.

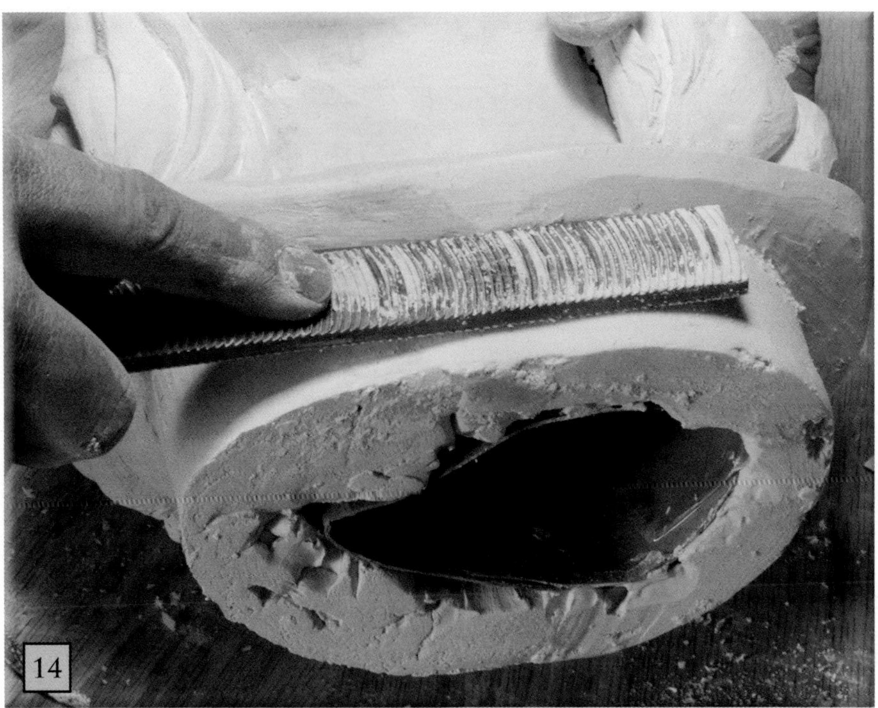


**14.** At this point the plaster has hardened and can be refined with a flat file.

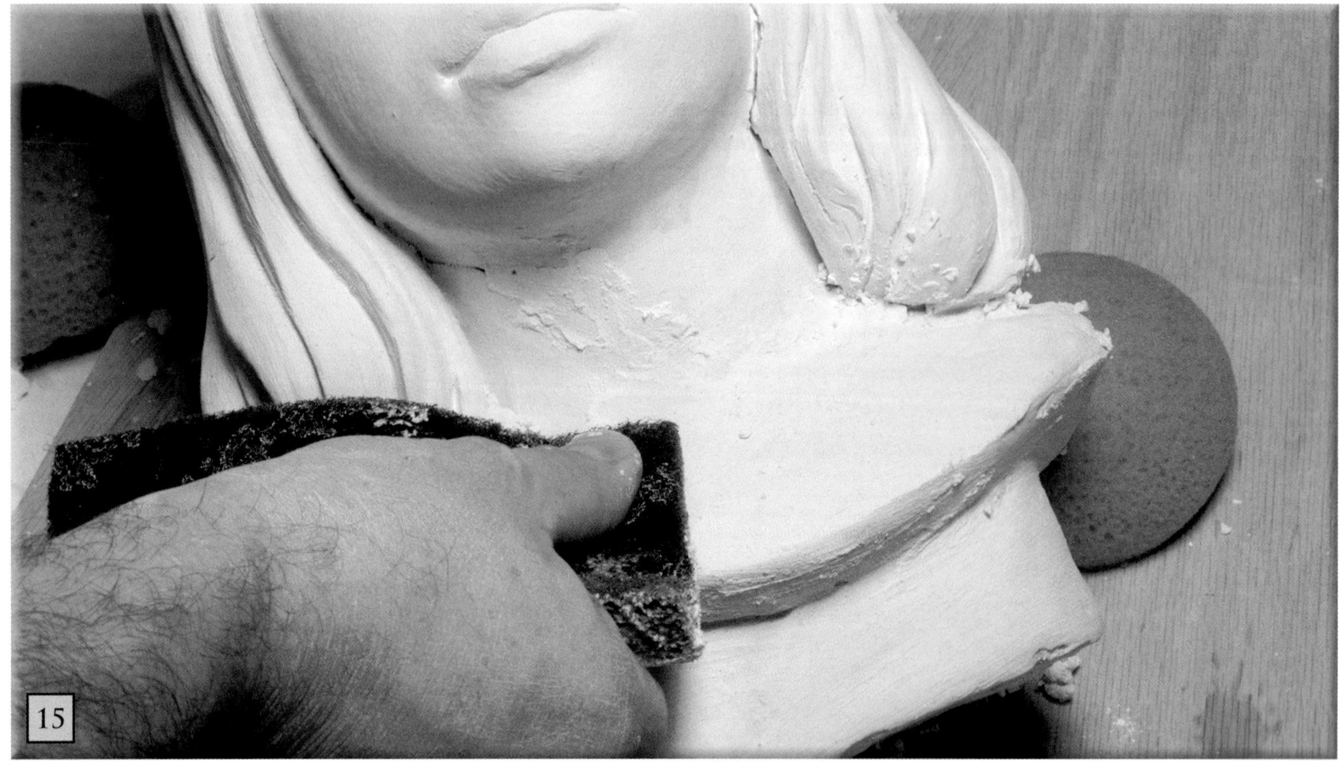

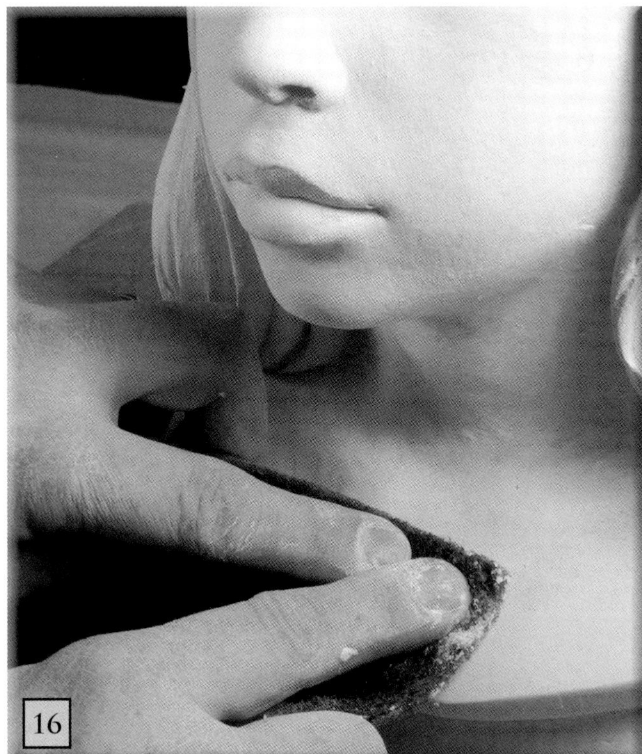

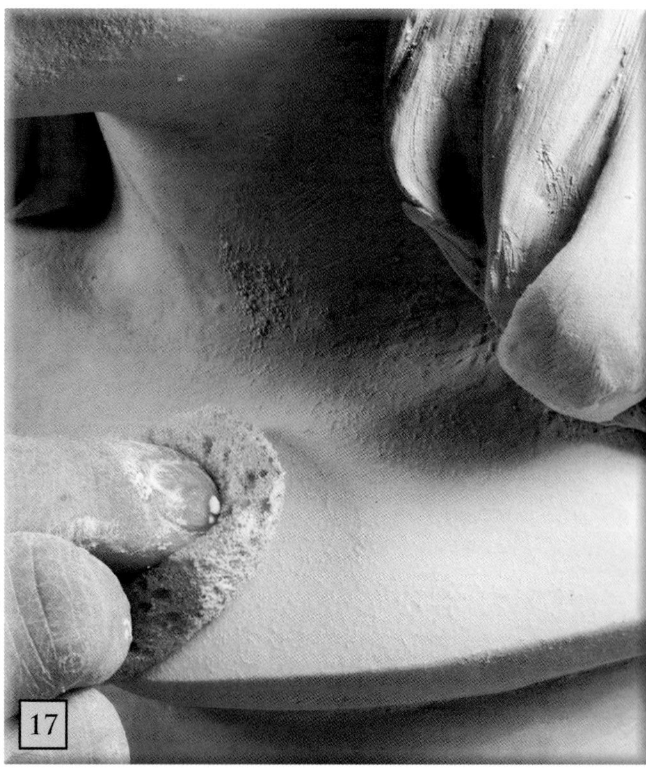

**15, 16.** A damp pot scrubber works best to sand surface imperfections.

**17.** To achieve the same texture as the rest of the piece, more plaster is mixed and applied with a sponge to the surface of the repaired area.

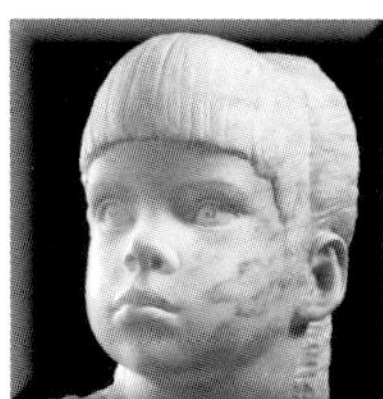

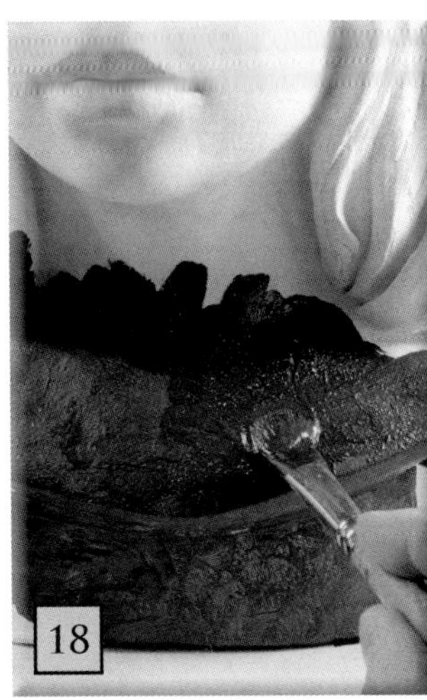


**18.** The piece needs to dry completely (several days) before applying the final patina. Commercially prepared patinas are available in hobby stores in various finishes such as aged bronze, metal, stone, etc. A piece can also be stained with wood finishing products, shoe polish, water-based stain, waxes or any combination.

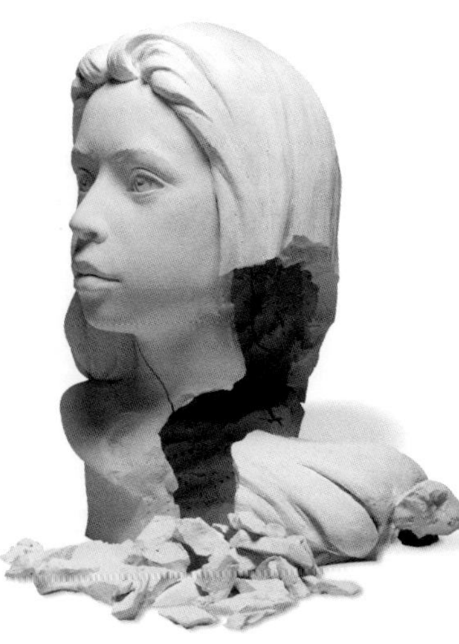

**19.** The final repair is invisible and permanent.

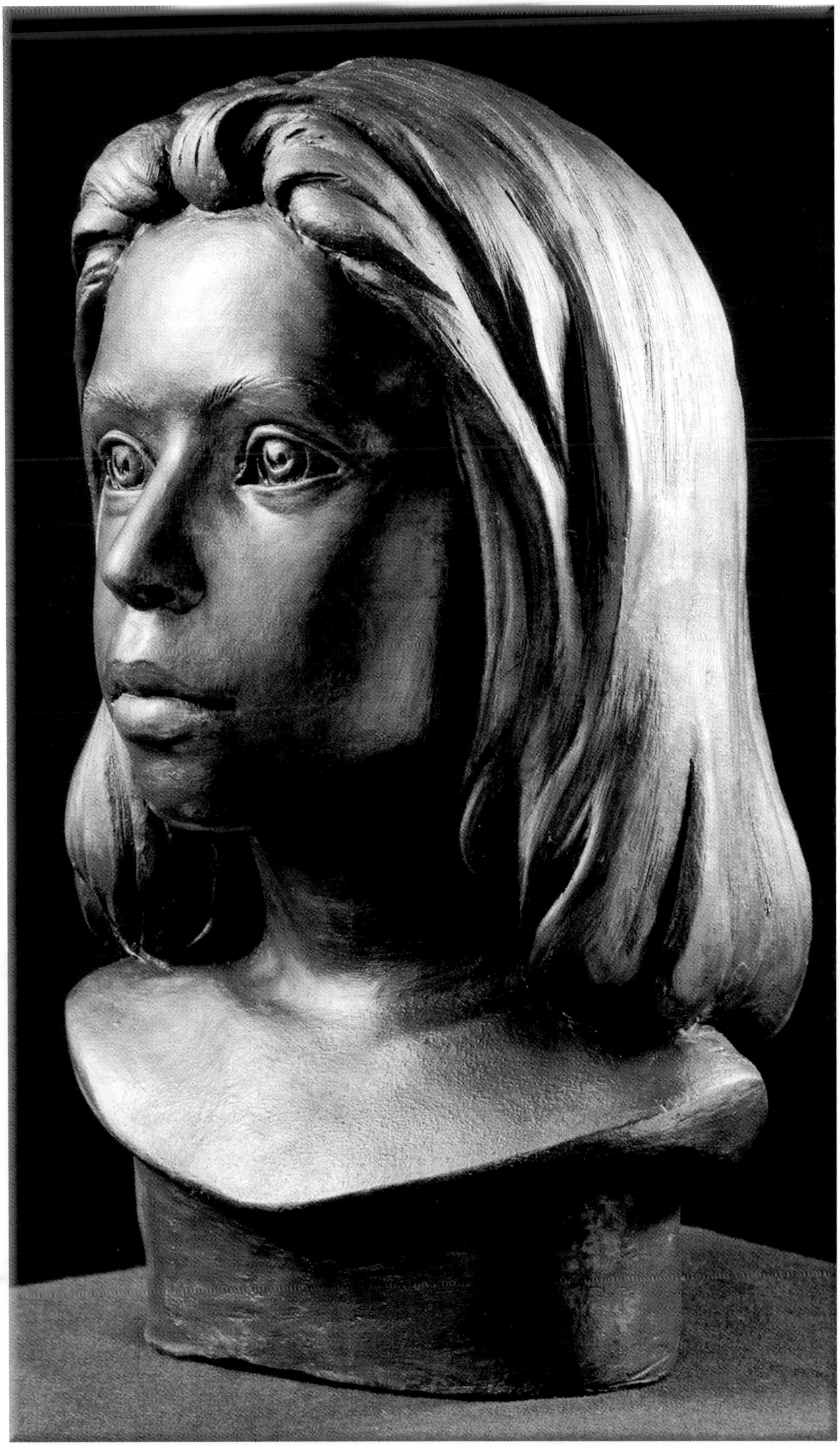

## Demonstration 14: Making a Rubber Mold

While firing water-based clay is the easiest way to preserve an original work, it is sometimes necessary to create a mold in order to duplicate the piece. A flexible rubber mold is the current industry standard used in bronze production. The most commonly used type of mold for a portrait consists of a two-part flexible rubber mold contained within a two-part rigid mother mold. The following method is not the only one that can be used to make a flexible mold, but it is one that will give good results. While it may appear to be complex, a good quality mold with an invisible seam can be achieved with a little bit of practice and a methodical approach. The products used in this demonstration are manufactured by Smooth-On, but a number of other companies offer similar brushable rubber compounds.

Brush-On™ 40 is soft and very flexible with a good abrasion resistance and high tear strength. Mixing with a ratio of 1 to 1 by volume is easy and provides a smooth consistency.

**No matter what type of products are chosen to make a mold, the instruction and safety sheets provided by the manufacturer must be read carefully. Most of these materials are toxic! The use of gloves and adequate ventilation are priorities.**

In order to make this chapter as useful as possible, each step is illustrated in chronological order. Before trying to follow the procedure the whole process must be read, each phase understood, and all of the products and materials ready for use.

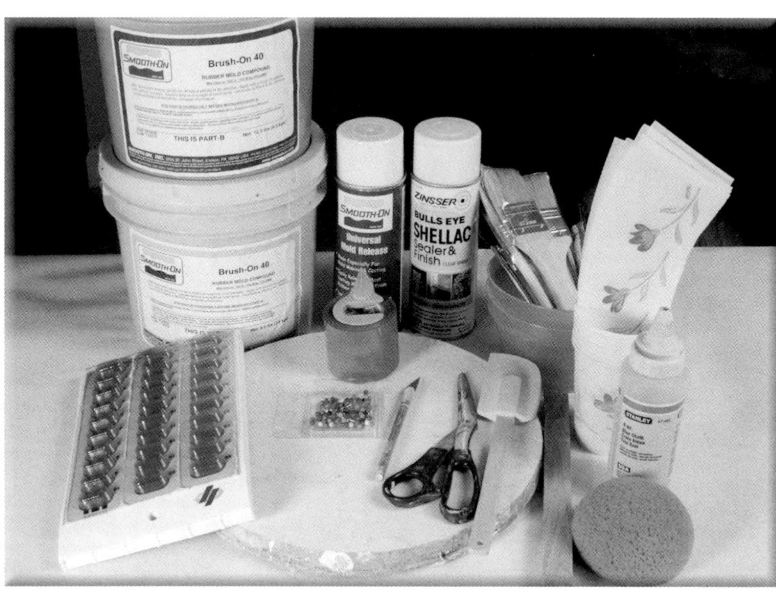


**Materials List**

Shellac
Universal Mold Release
Brush-On™ 40
Waxed Paper Cups
Plastic Pill Forms
Hemp Fiber
Straight Pins
#1 Pottery Plaster
Pigmented Powdered Chalk
Disposable Flat Brushes
Scissors
Craft Knife
Plastic Cups
Disposable Gloves
Plastic Bowls
Turn Table
Sponges
Rubber Scraper
Stirring Sticks
Thin Tape

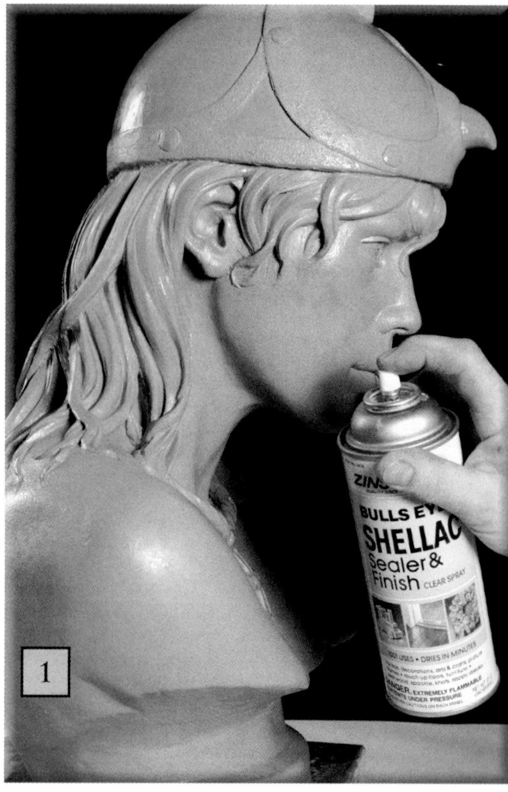


1\. Installing the sculpture on a turntable is not entirely necessary but it makes the process much easier. The surface of the sculpture needs too be somewhat dry. If need be, the piece can be exposed to ambient air for a few hours prior to beginning. Two thin coats of shellac are applied to the entire surface to seal in the moisture.

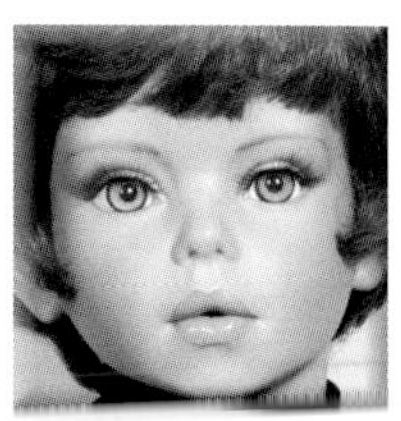

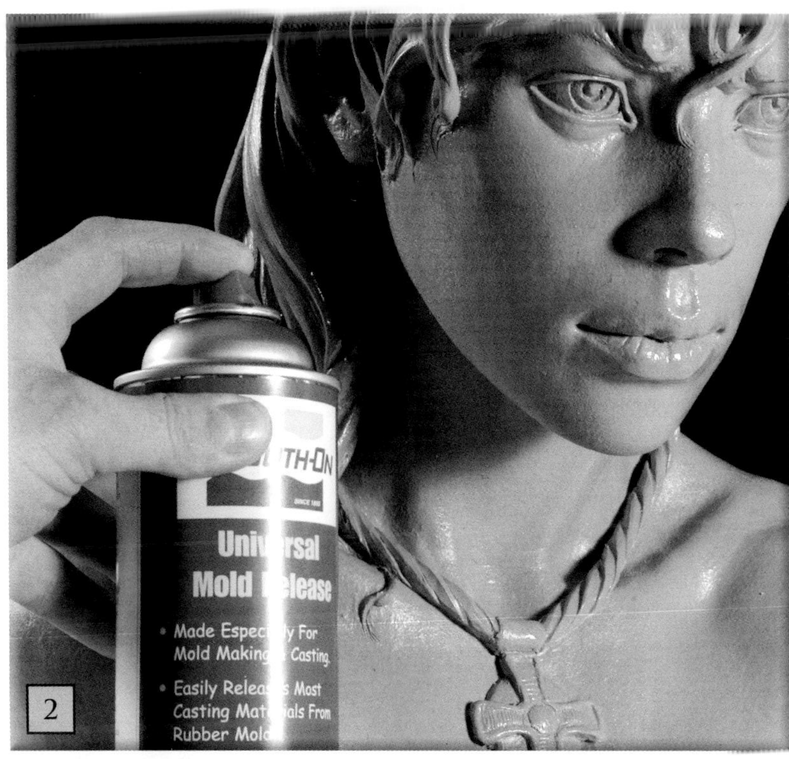


2. The shellac must be completely dry prior to adding the release agent. Two hours is usually the time required. Working in an environment with a temperature above 65°F is best.

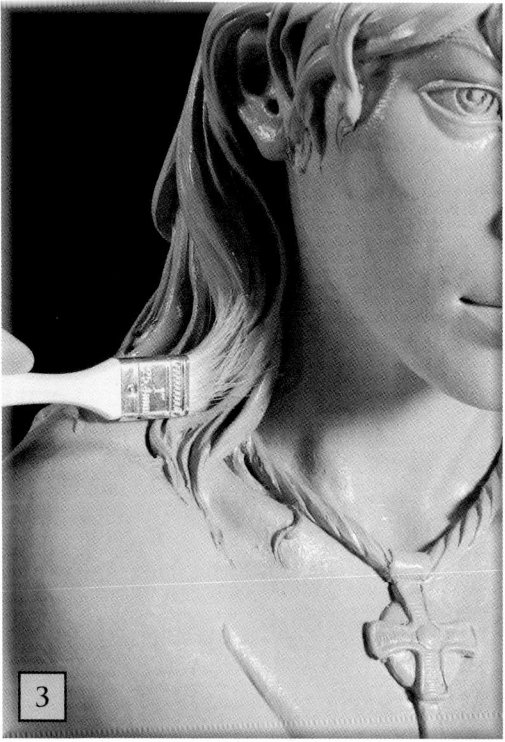

3. The release agent is sprayed on the sculpture then brushed over all surfaces to ensure thorough coverage. A final thin mist is applied and left to dry for at least twenty minutes.

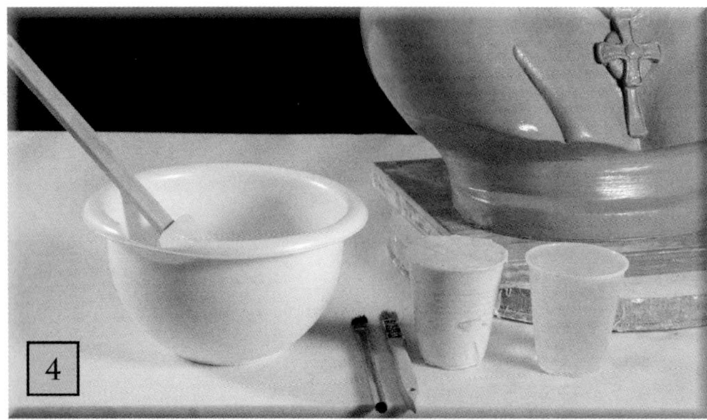

4. It is a good idea to apply a mist of mold release on the inside and outside of the mixing containers in order to be able to peel off the remaining rubber when dry. Keeping a set of four or five ready for use prevents having to stop in mid-process to clean out the containers.

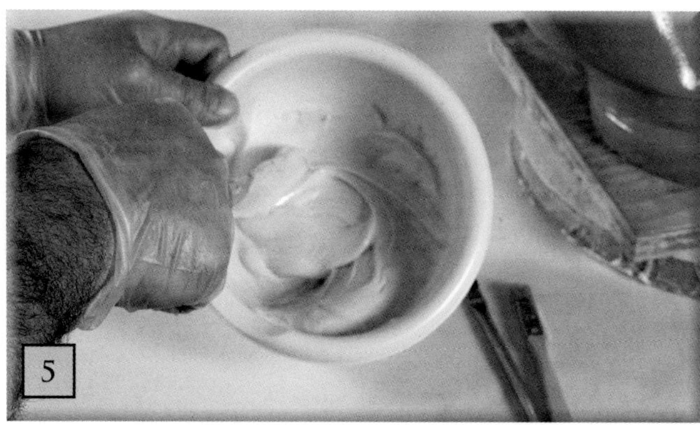

5. A 4 oz. plastic cup is filled to the top with Part B, which is a paste, making sure to eliminate any large voids. The top is leveled and then emptied into a larger container. Next a clean cup of the same size is filled with part A and emptied into the mixing container. It is better to start with small quantities of mix to learn what amount can be handled comfortably. The mix is stirred thoroughly for three minutes making sure that the sides and bottom of the mixing container are scraped several times.

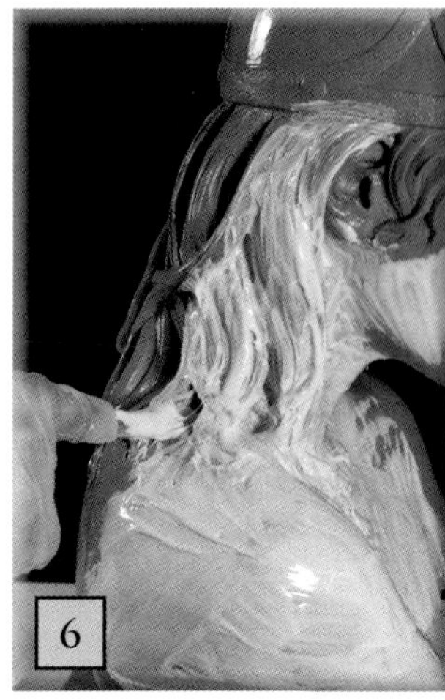

6. The first coat of rubber is applied in a thin layer using dabbing stokes with a brush to capture the details and reduce entrapped air. If the brush is too soft, the bristles can be cut shorter to make it stiffer. As many batches as necessary are mixed to cover the entire surface of the sculpture with the first coat and then the brush is discarded as it is not worth trying to save. The rubber is then left to set at room temperature for thirty or forty minutes. Do not at any point during the mold process allow the rubber to fully cure between layers.

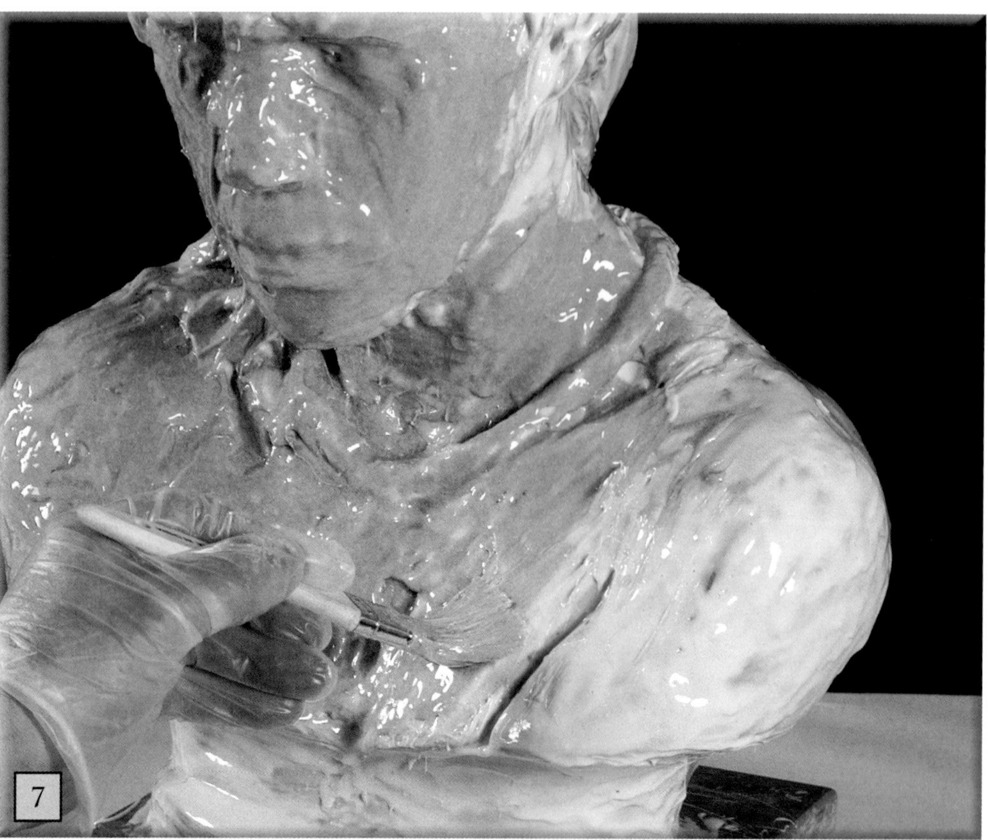

7. A second layer is applied. When the rubber is mixed for the second coat, although not necessary, a small amount of colored powder is added to the mix to distinguish the different layers.

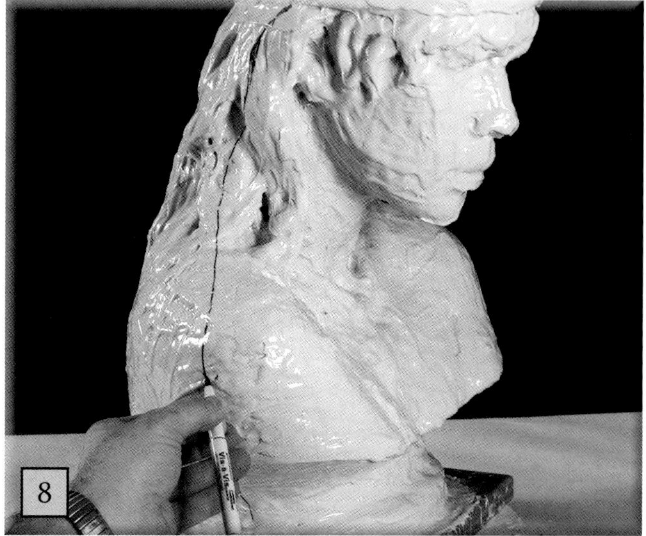

8. The rubber is left to set for two hours, then a fine line is traced to divide the sculpture into two halves following the outer most edge to avoid deep undercuts. This line will become the parting line of the mold.

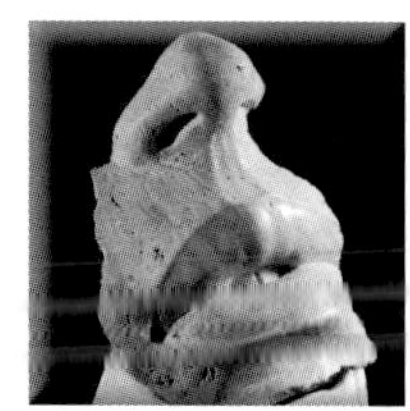

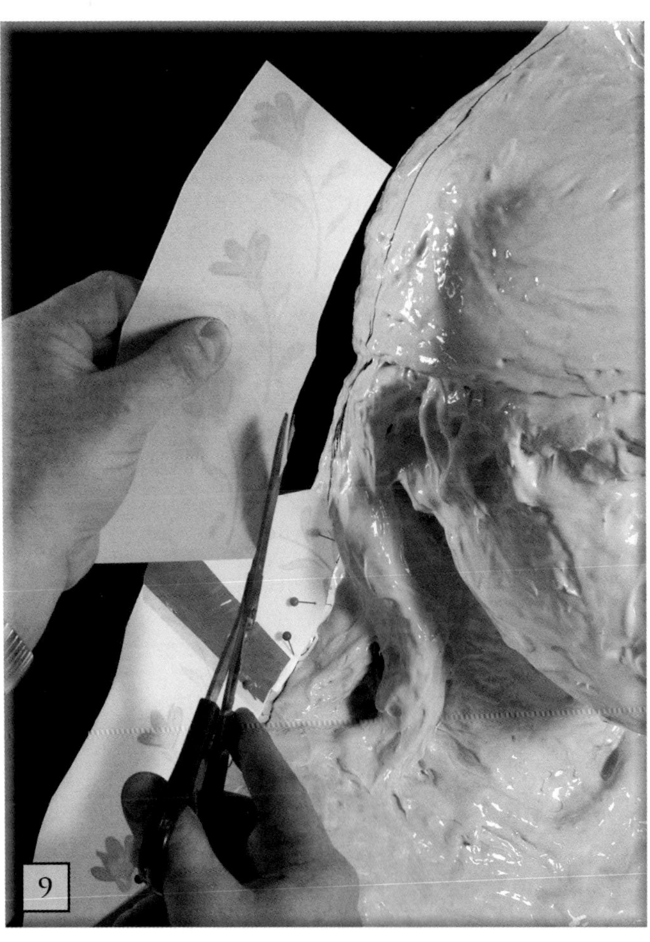


9. Paper shims are cut from wax-coated paper cups, following the shape of the sculpture.

10. The shims are created in order to provide a surface into which keys will be inserted. They are attached to the sculpture along each side of the parting line with dressmaker pins.

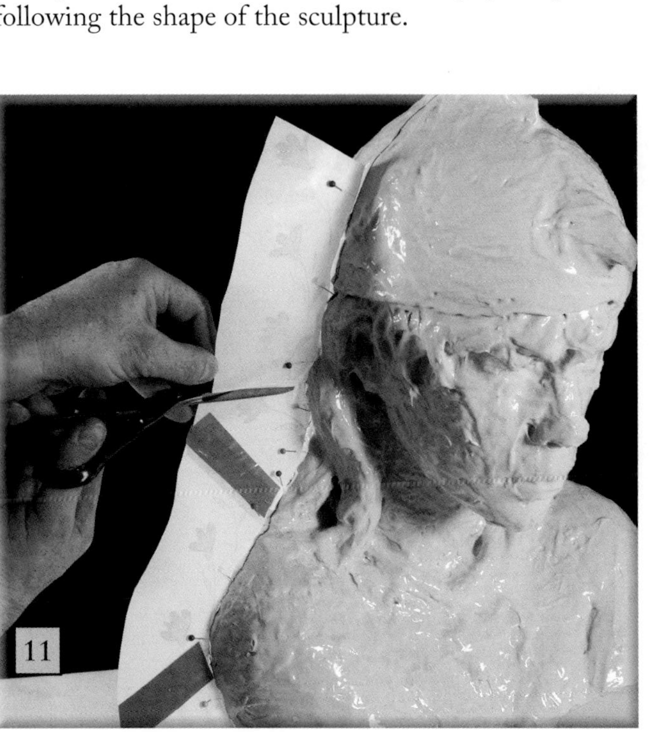


11. Each section overlaps the previous one by one inch and is then cut through the two layers to make a clean connection.

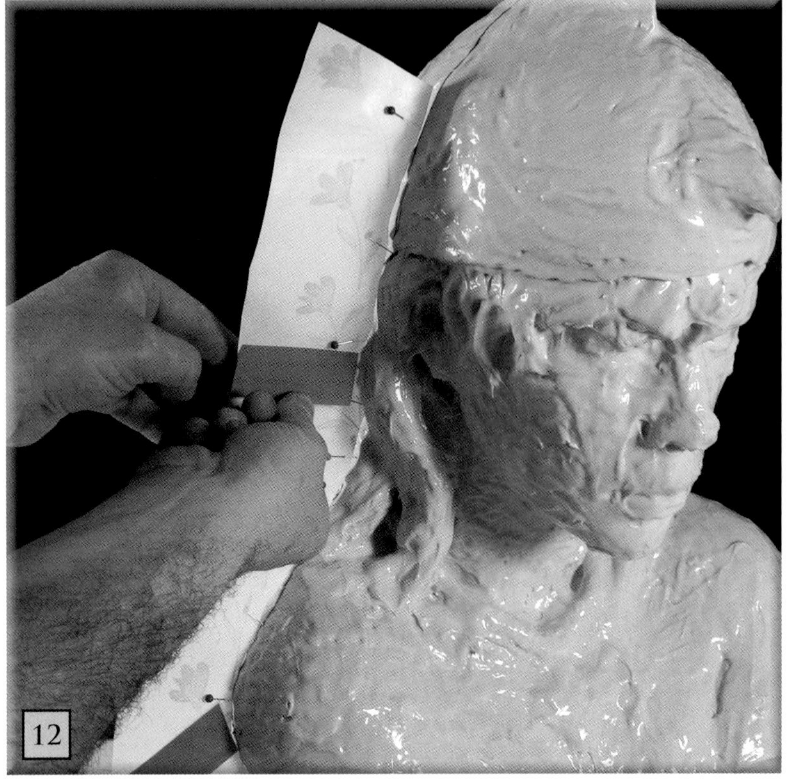


**12.** Each section is taped to the other on both sides.

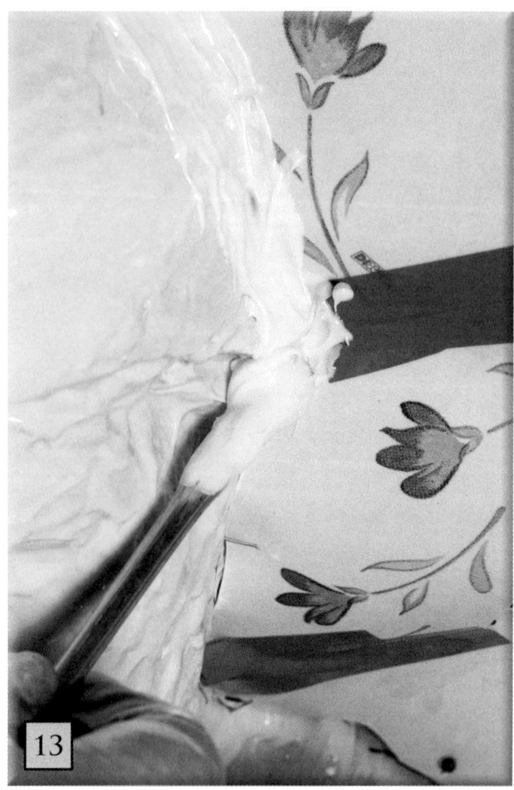


**13.** A bead of rubber is applied along the base of the shim on both sides to anchor it to the sculpture. It is left to harden for about two hours before proceeding to the next step.

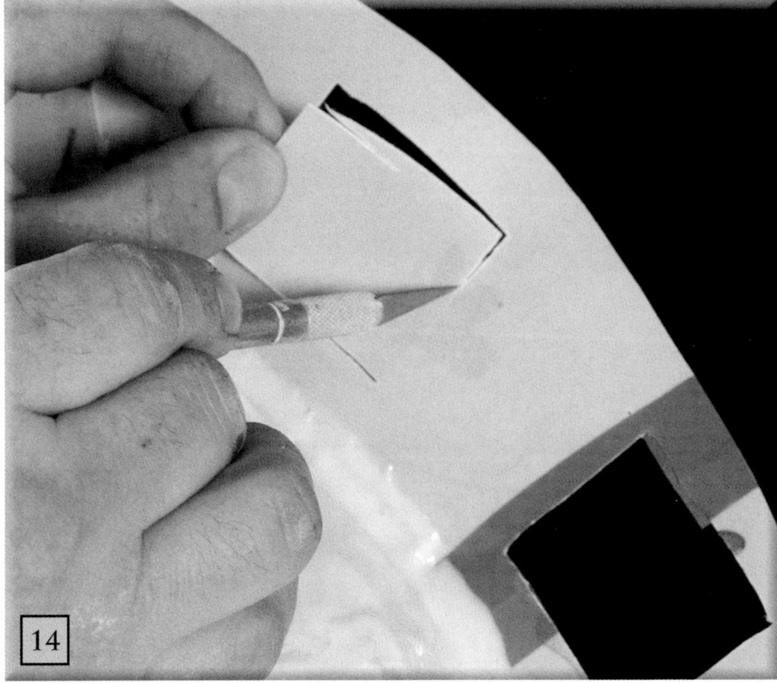


**14.** The pins are removed and then square openings are cut into the shim using a sharp craft knife.

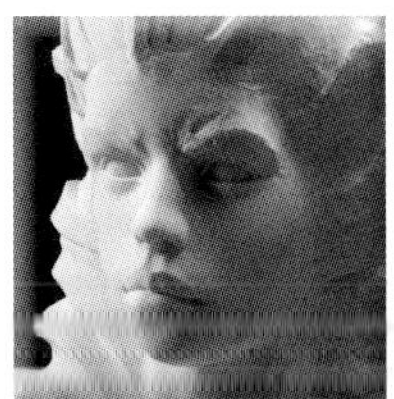

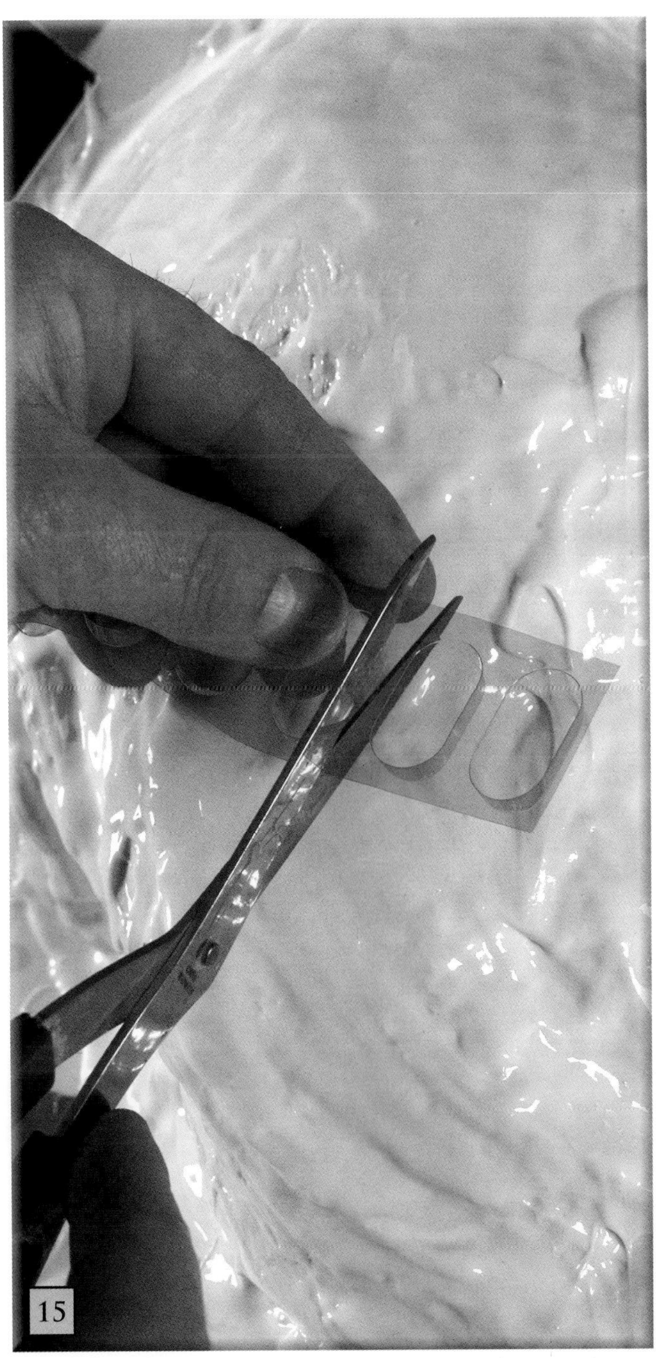

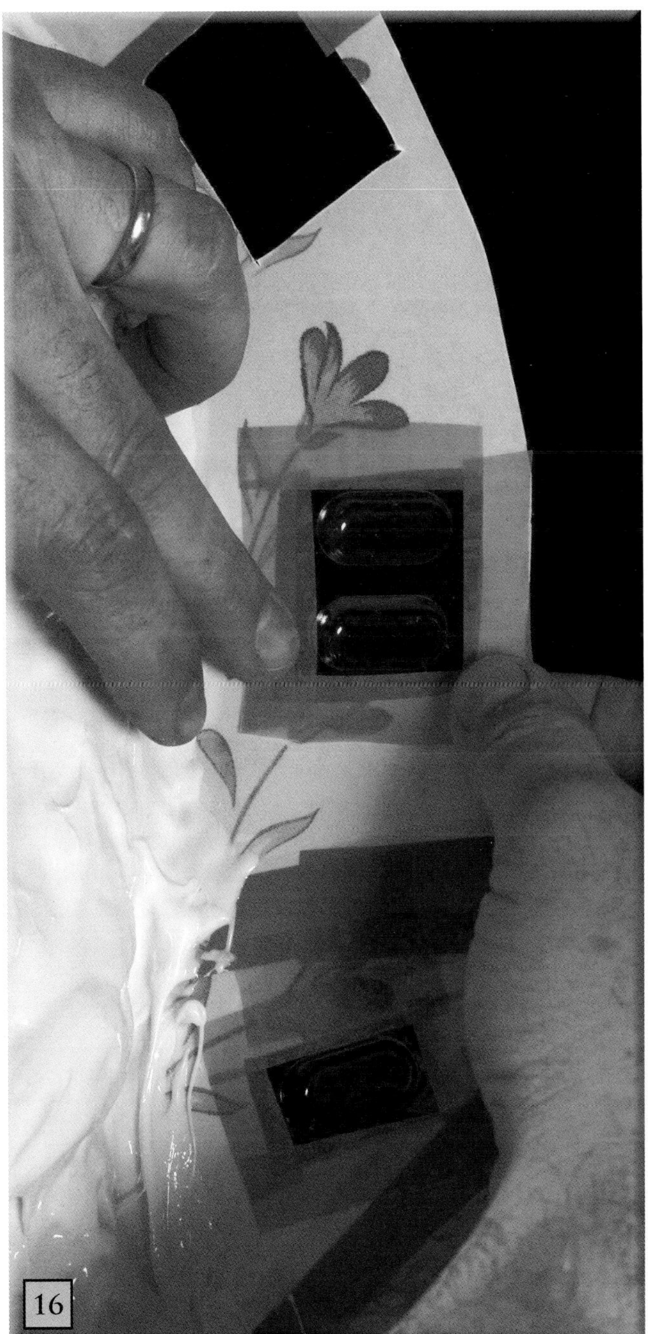

**15.** The openings need to be large enough to accommodate one or two pill forms (available by order from any pharmacy). These pill forms are used to create keys to ensure that the two parts align perfectly once the sculpture has been removed and the mold is hollow.

**16.** The pill form is fitted into the hole and attached on both sides with tape.

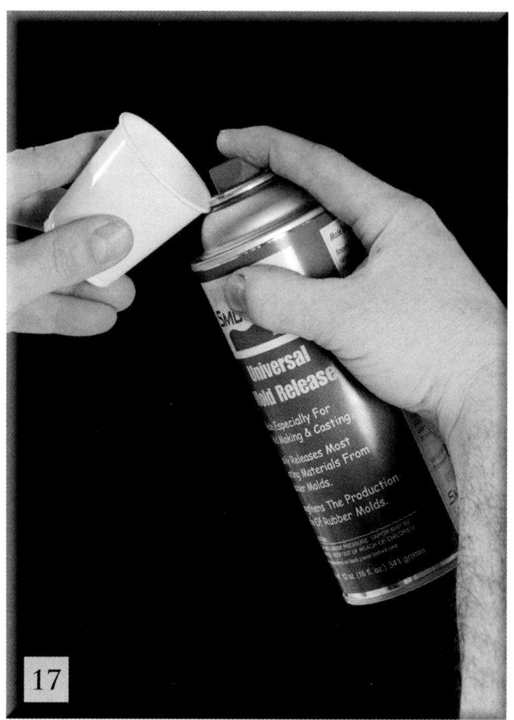


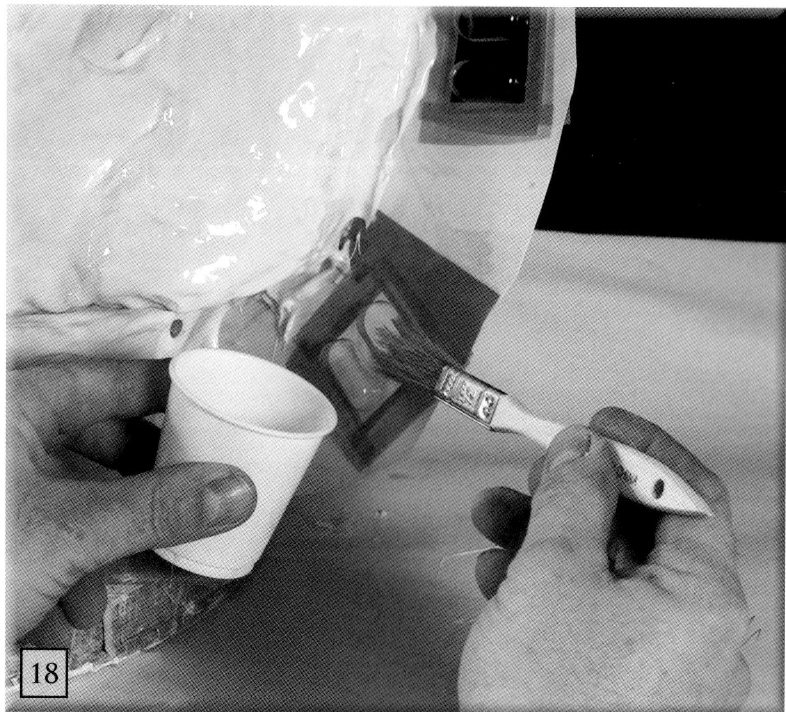

**17, 18.** In order to prevent the rubber from sticking to the pill containers, mold release must be applied to them while making certain that none of the release agent comes in contact with rubber already on the sculpture as delamination may result. *Note: to prevent this problem, a small quantity of mold release is sprayed into a cup and then brushed onto the pill containers. This must be done outside of the work area to avoid over spray and contamination of the rubber already on the piece.* No mold release is necessary on the waxed shims. Wash any mold release from your hands before touching the rubber.

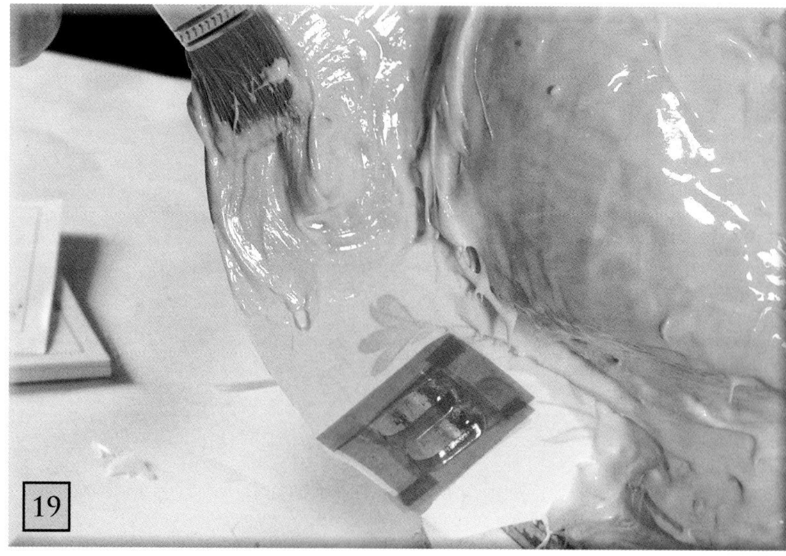

**19.** Two more coats of rubber are applied to the entire surface (including shims) alternating pigmented layers every other mix.

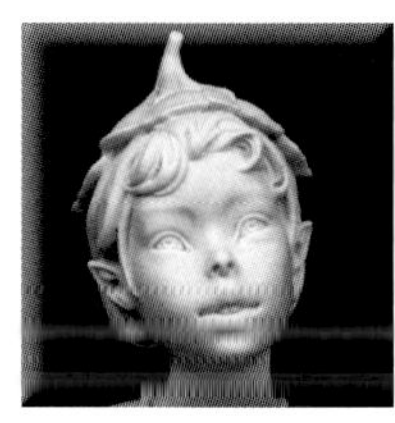

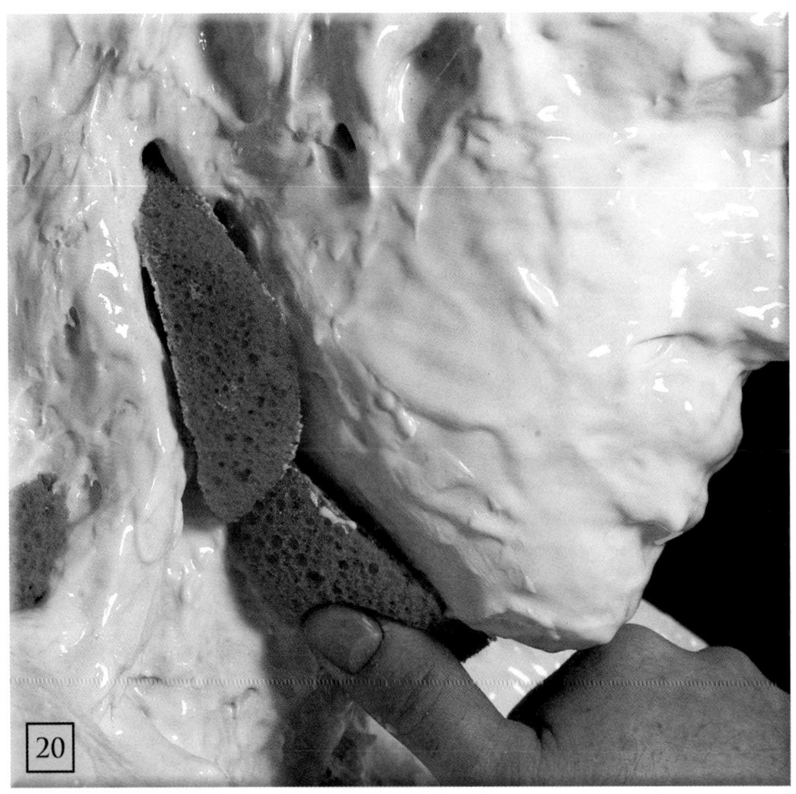

20. If deep undercuts are present, which would prevent the rigid mother mold from releasing, sponges can be embedded into the rubber at critical points to fill up the undercuts and still provide enough flexibility for the mother mold to be removed. The sponge pieces will adhere better if first both they and the sculpture are brushed with rubber and allowed to become tacky (usually 20-30 minutes).

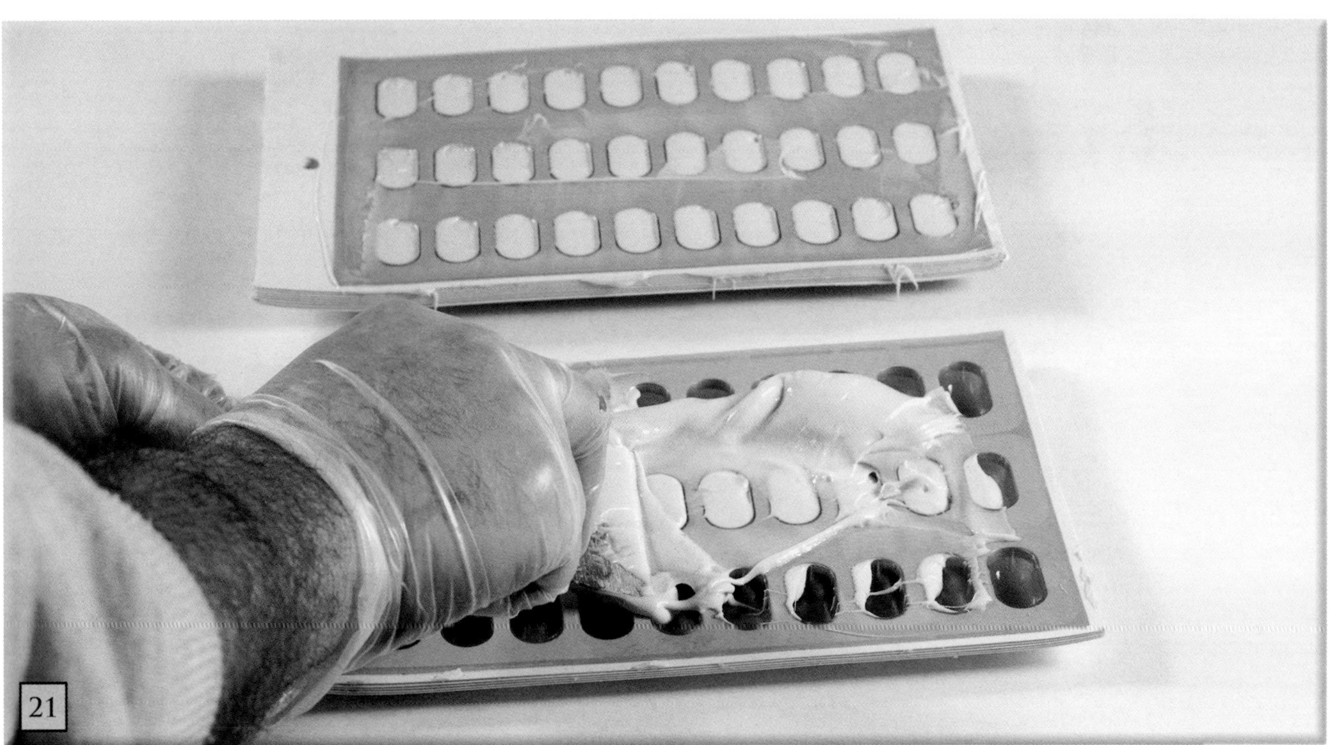

21. At this point, rubber keys are prepared that will be attached to the mold after the last coat. These keys provide points for later alignment of the rubber mold to the mother mold. Pill container trays are sprayed with mold release (outside the room), filled with rubber, then put aside to cure.

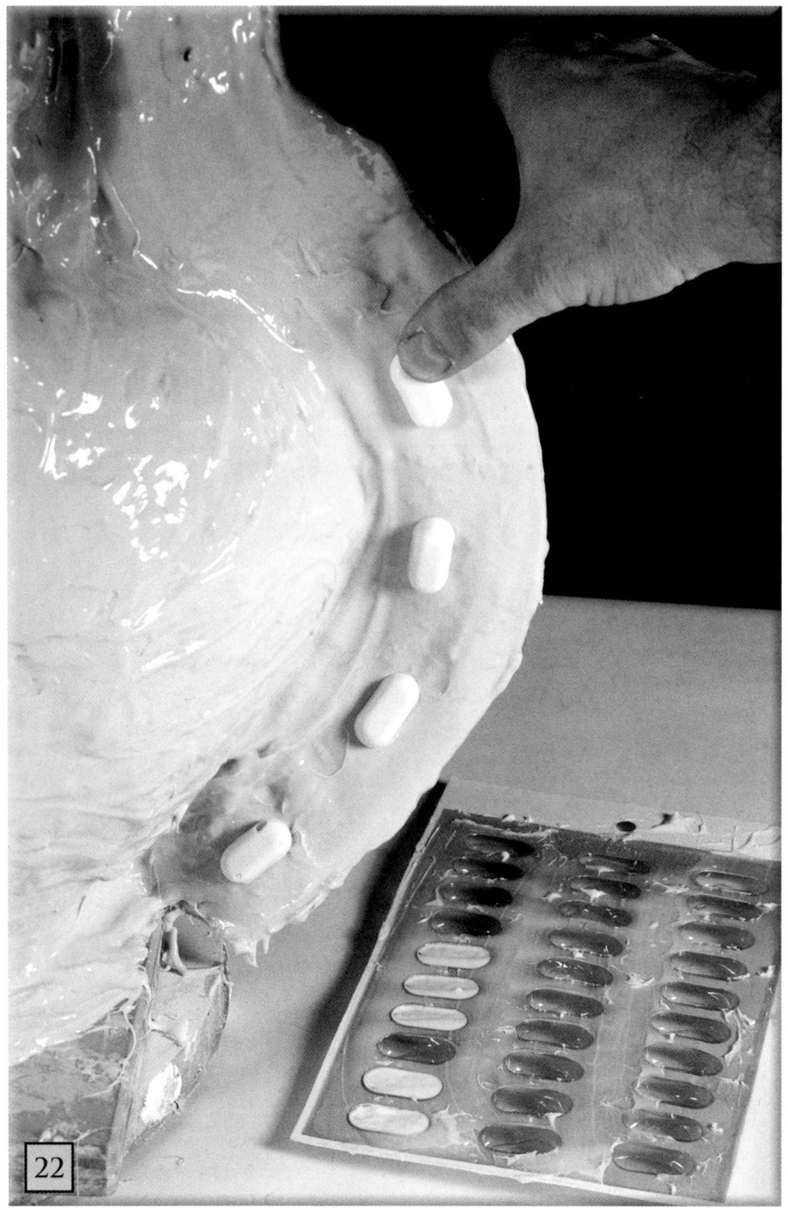

22. Two more coats of rubber are applied to the entire mold, including the shims and sponges. According to the manufacturer, the final thickness should be 3/8". While the last coat is still tacky, the rubber keys are removed from the tray and stuck onto the shims around the piece on both sides, as well as a few places on the outer most parts of the sculpture. These keys will prevent the flexible mold from shifting inside the mother mold. Be careful not to create undercuts by placing keys on the sides or underneath the face.

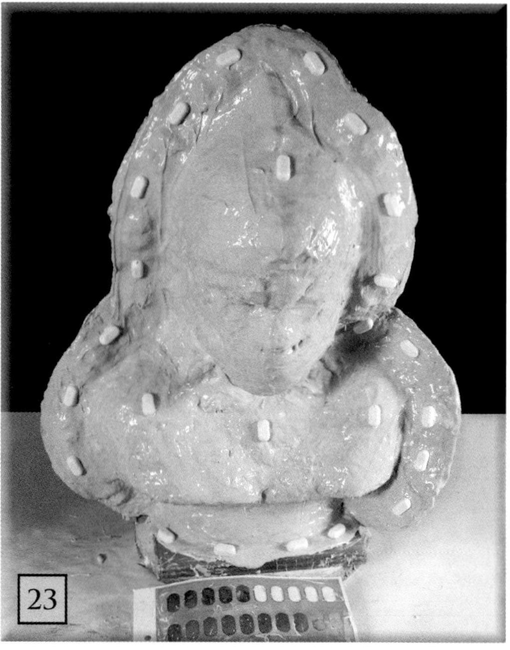

23. The mold is allowed to cure overnight at room temperature.

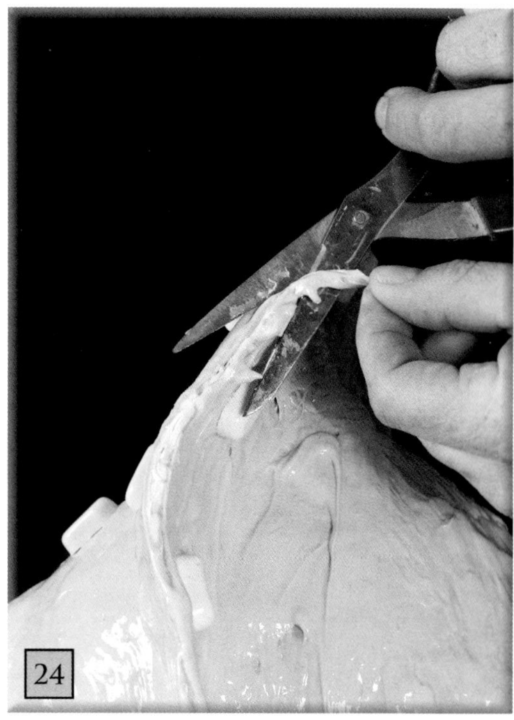

24. The edges of the rubber-coated shims are trimmed with scissors to obtain a clean edge.

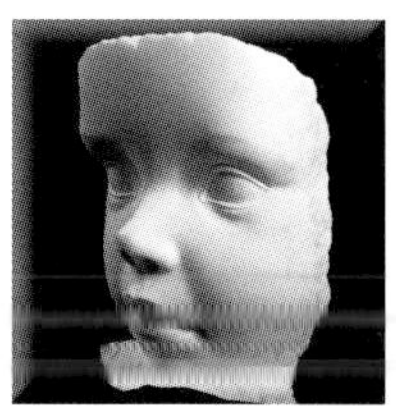

## Making the Mother Mold

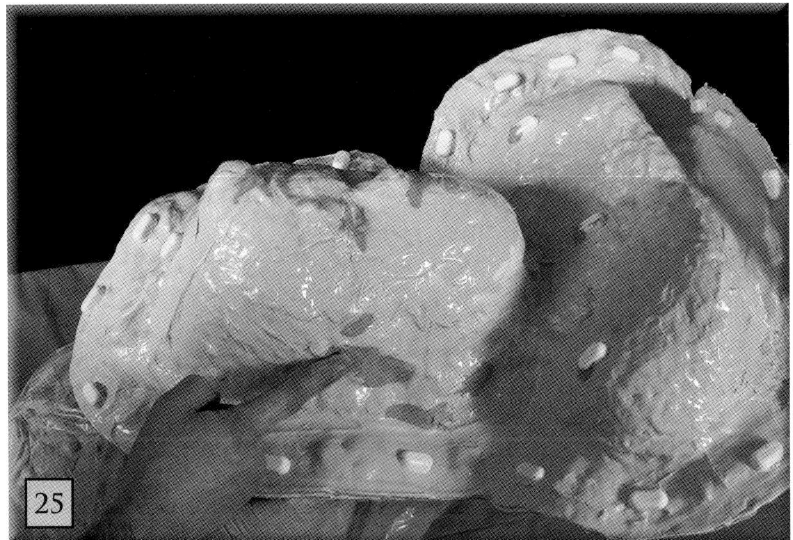
25

**25.** A rigid outer shell called a mother mold needs to be built around the flexible mold to prevent its distortion during the casting process. Mold release is applied over the entire surface of the rubber and then any small undercuts filled with water-based clay to prevent the mother mold from catching.

26. It is easier to build the mother mold on one side at a time. Hemp fibers are soaked in water for about 15 minutes, removed and then left to drip while preparing the plaster. Dry plaster is sifted into a container of water until a mound is visible above the surface. After the mound has sunk into the water, the plaster is stirred for about two minutes. The wet hemp is dipped into the plaster and applied to the rubber, forming an even layer.

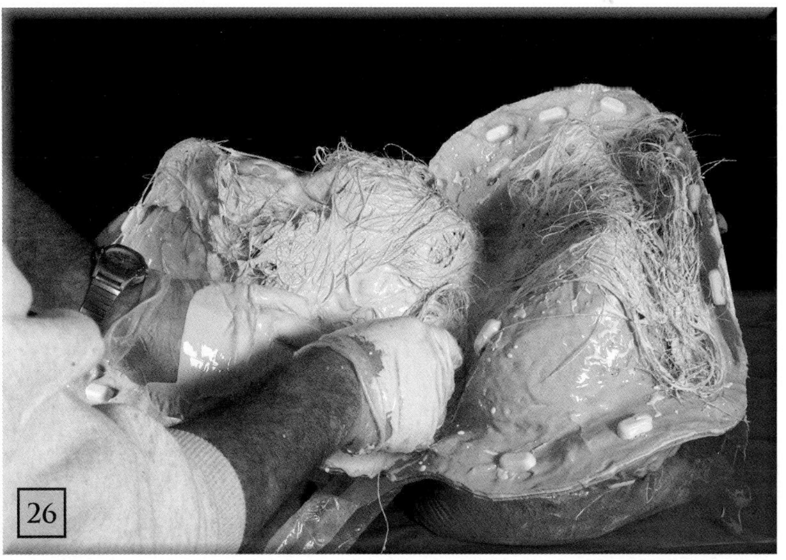
26

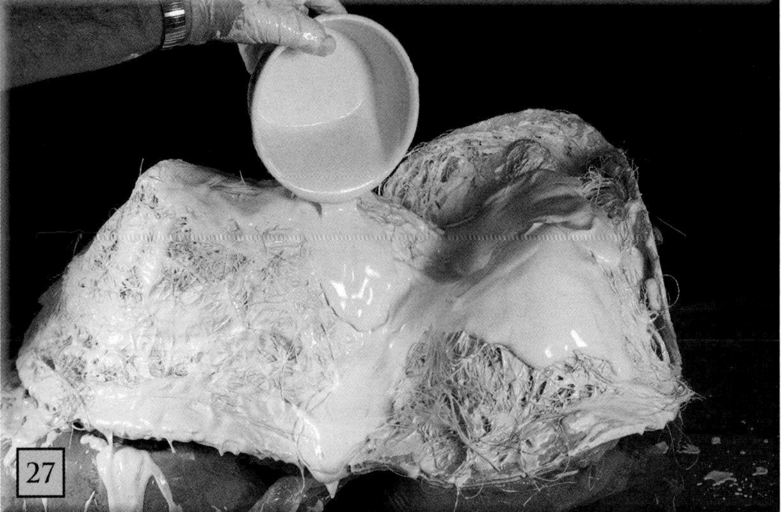
27

**27.** More plaster is added to fill any voids. It is not always possible to set the sculpture horizontally; in such cases add a bit more plaster to the water to obtain a thicker consistency and apply it vertically. Using warmer water will also accelerate the setting of the plaster.

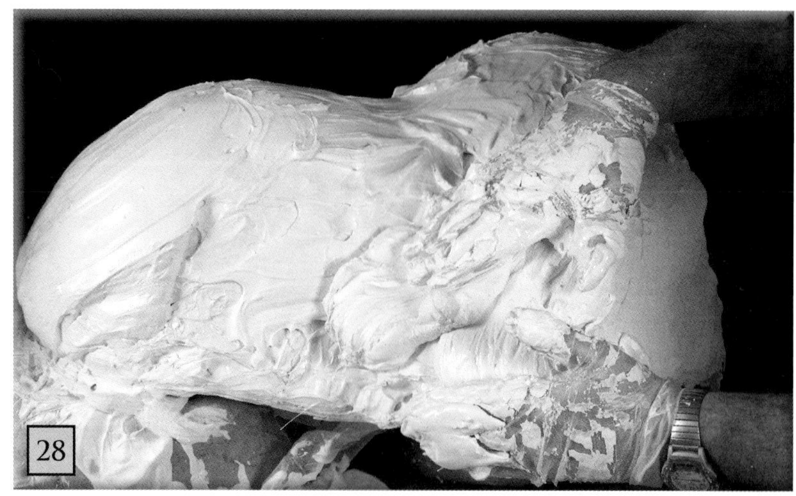

28. As the plaster begins to set, a layer of about one inch is built over the entire surface including the shims.

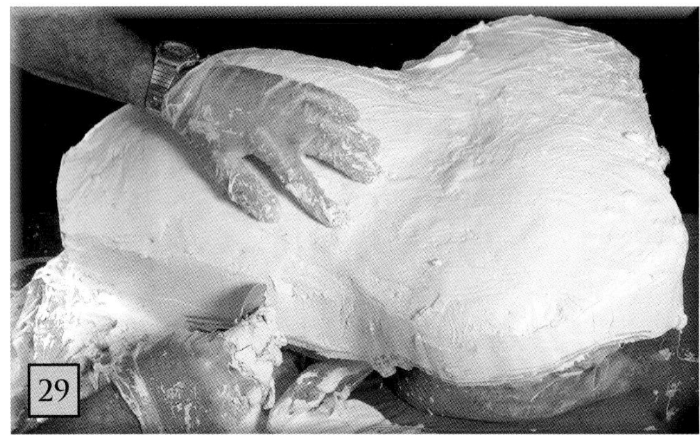

29. The sides are scraped to make sure that the edges of the rubber-coated shims are visible.

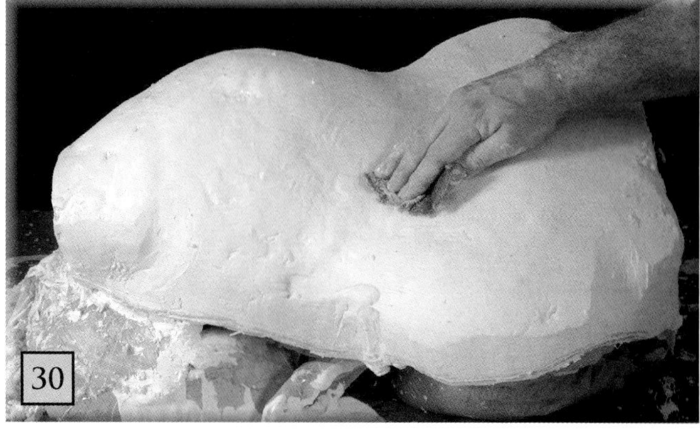

30. The plaster needs to be smoothed to facilitate handling. Once it has set (about 30 minutes), the piece can be turned over and the operation repeated on the other side.

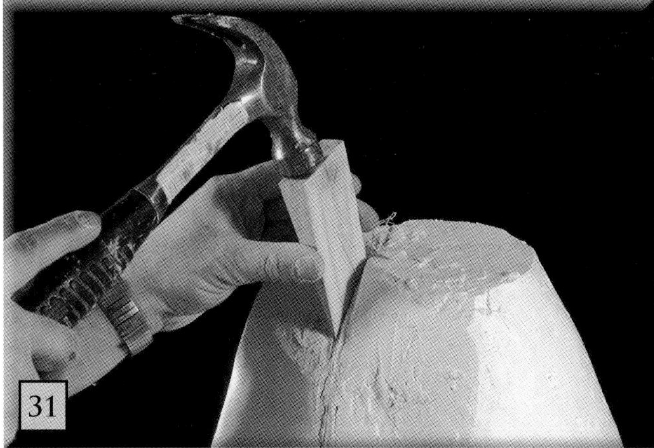

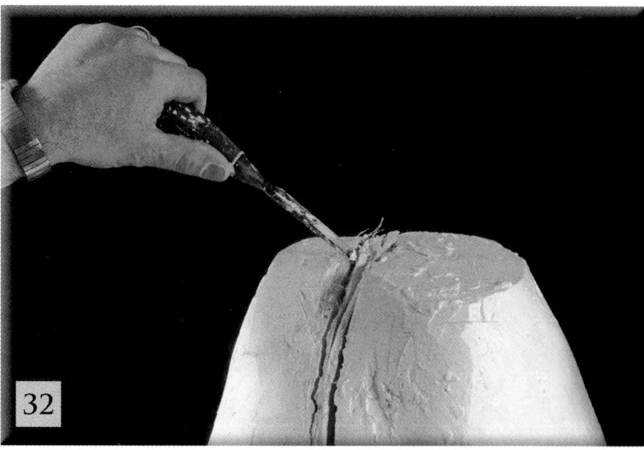

31, 32. Wooden wedges and some chisels are used to very gently pry open the mother mold.

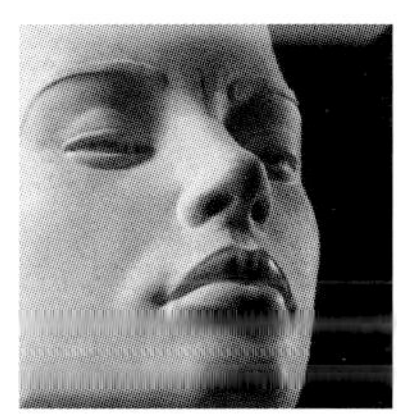

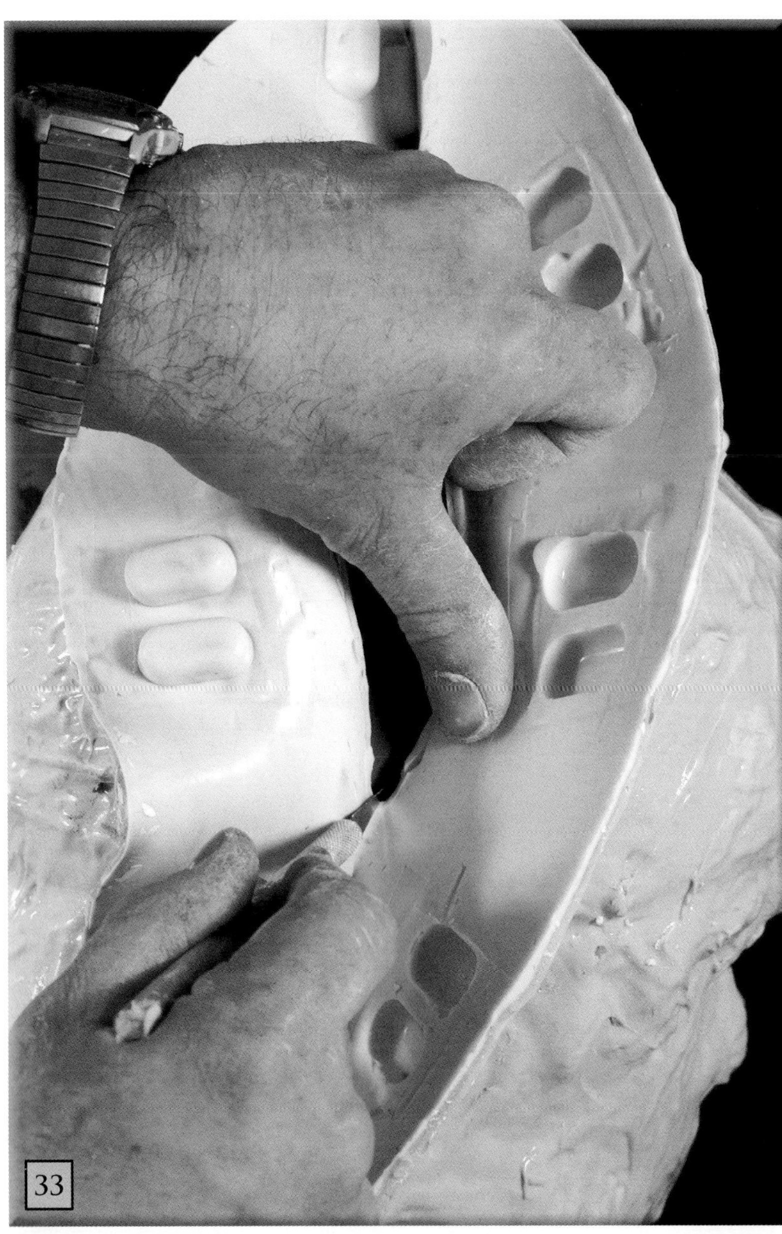


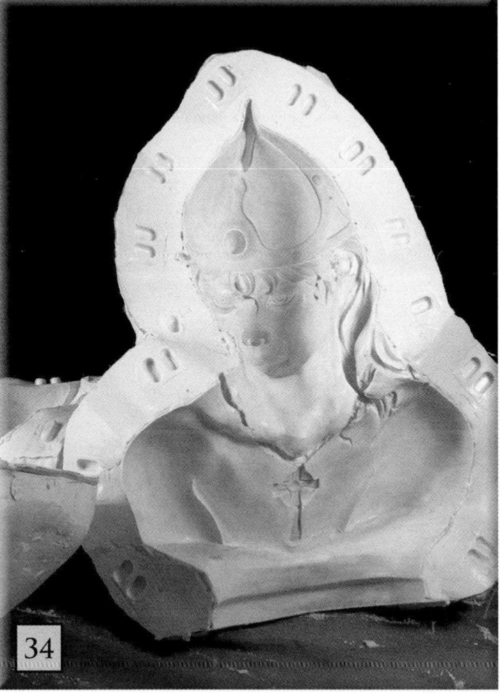


**34, 35.** All of the mold pieces should be washed with soap and any remaining clay removed. The mold is reassembled and secured with rubber bands or packing plastic wrap available through shipping suppliers. It is important to keep the mold sealed during storage to prevent warping. It is now ready to be used to cast plaster, resin, wax or a variety of other materials.

**33.** Once the paper and pill containers have been removed, the rubber is pried open on each side of the shim. The thin film of rubber remaining against the clay is cut with a knife. The above photo shows the keys and key holes that ensure proper alignment of the two halves of the mold.

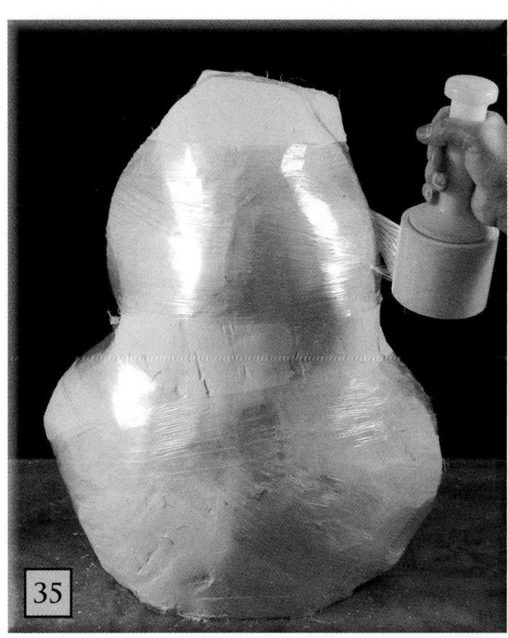

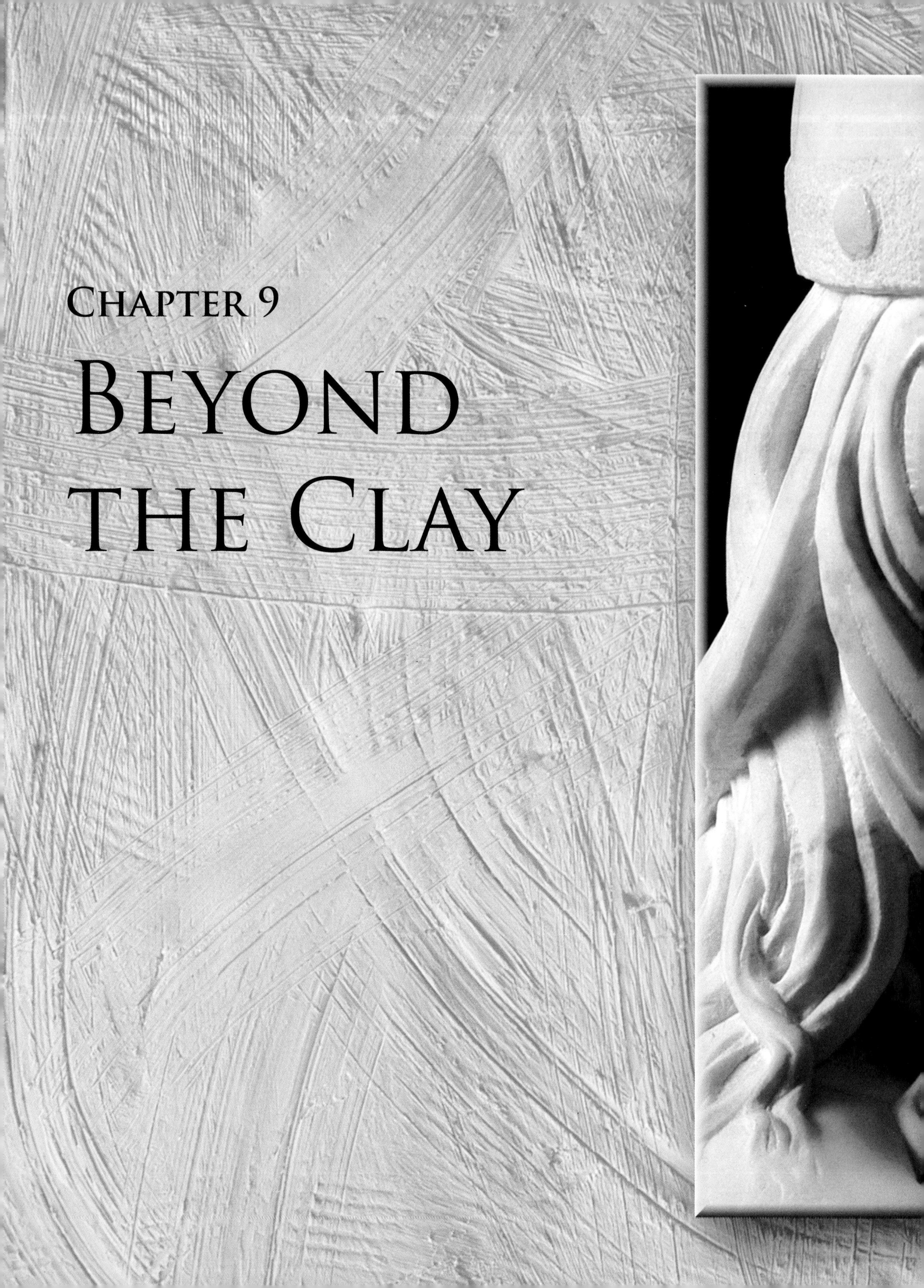

# CHAPTER 9

# BEYOND THE CLAY

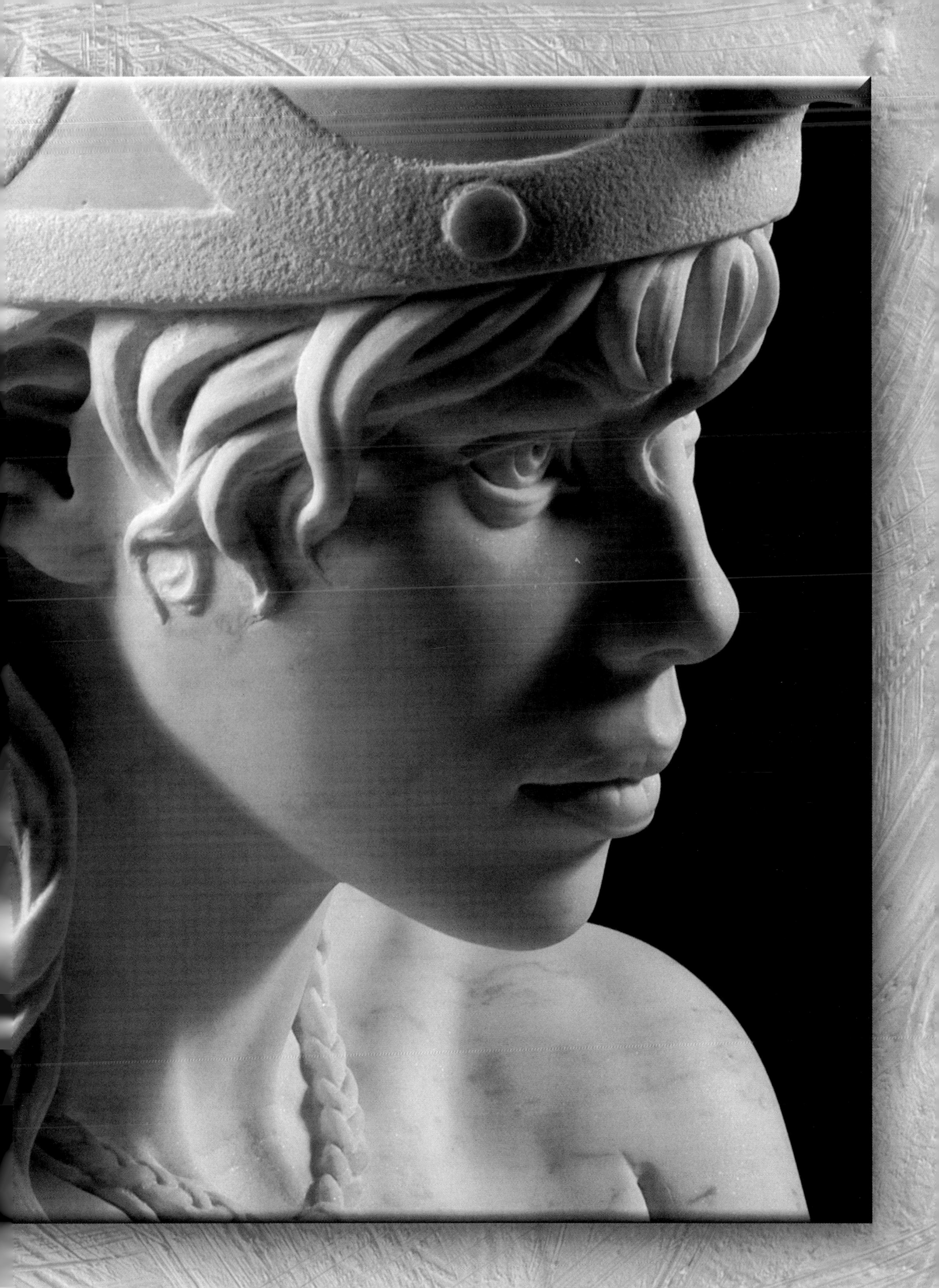

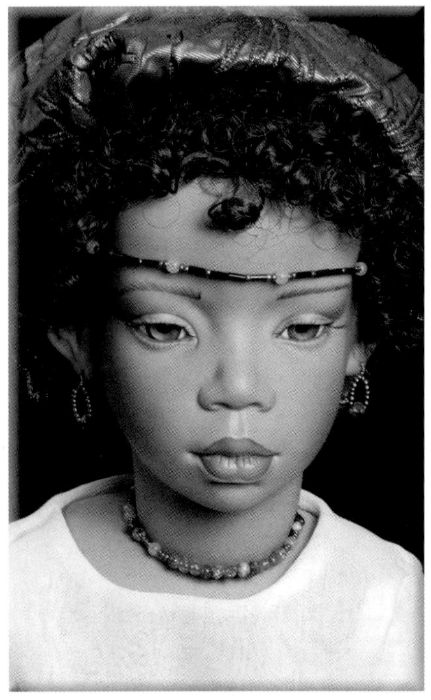

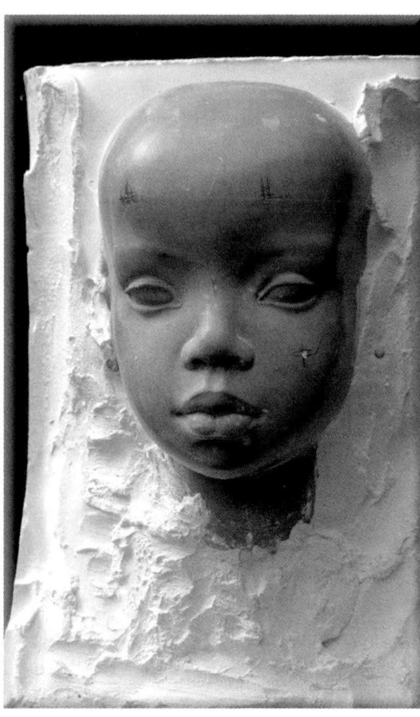

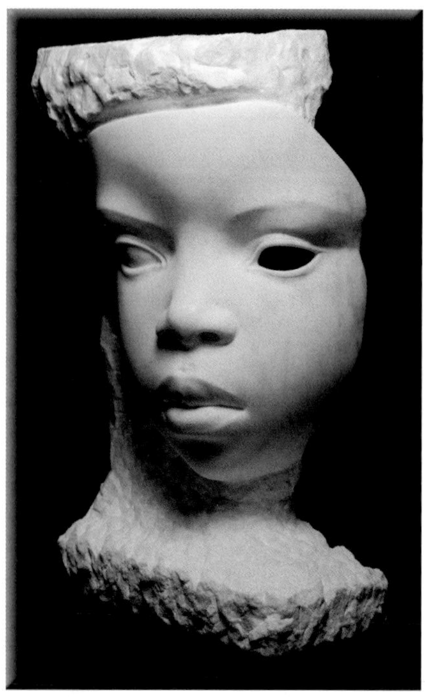

Water-based clay is the easiest and most practical medium for modeling the portrait. Beside the advantages it offers during the modeling process, such as plasticity and a wide range of consistencies, it can also be fired to an extremely hard material called terracotta. Finishing can then be done in a variety of patinas. This is a very fast and economical way to preserve a sculpture and has been used for thousands of years. It allows the artist to practice and build a body of work at a minimum expense of both time and money.

However, there are other options available to preserve, or even transform a sculpture made of clay. The most common method involves making a mold, either rigid or flexible, in which a liquid casting material is poured and left to solidify. The materials of choice include plaster, wax, resin, porcelain, etc.

The clay model can also be used as a maquette (meaning working model) from which the sculpture can be carved in a solid material such as marble or wood. A maquette is also often used as reference to enlarge a sculpture to monumental scale.

The three photos above show several different uses of an original model. The piece in the center was modeled in water-based clay, fired, refined, then primed with a sanding sealer to serve as a prototype. A plaster mold was made, from which a porcelain cast was produced (left photo). Later the piece was secured in plaster and used as a maquette to carve a marble sculpture that is three times larger than the original (right photo).

Each of the two sculptures on the facing page was first modeled in water-based clay. The piece shown in the inset was then carved oversized in Tennessee marble. The smaller sculpture was cast in resin as a model for the toy industry.

Regardless of the size and material of the final sculpture, the original model determines the quality of the finished product. The techniques demonstrated in this book can be applied for sculpting the face for a variety of applications from portraits to figurines and action figures to dolls and monuments, in such fields as the collectible industry, the toy industry, film and theater, fine art, architecture, forensics, fashion, etc.

The chart on pages 202-203 illustrates some of the options possible for the use of a portrait sculpted in water-based clay.

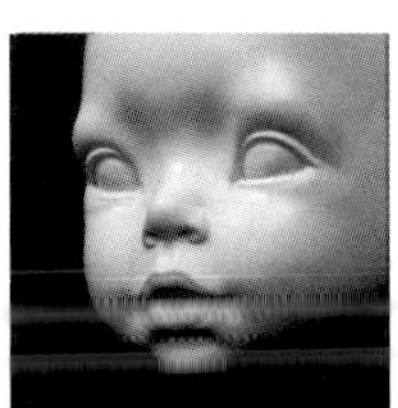

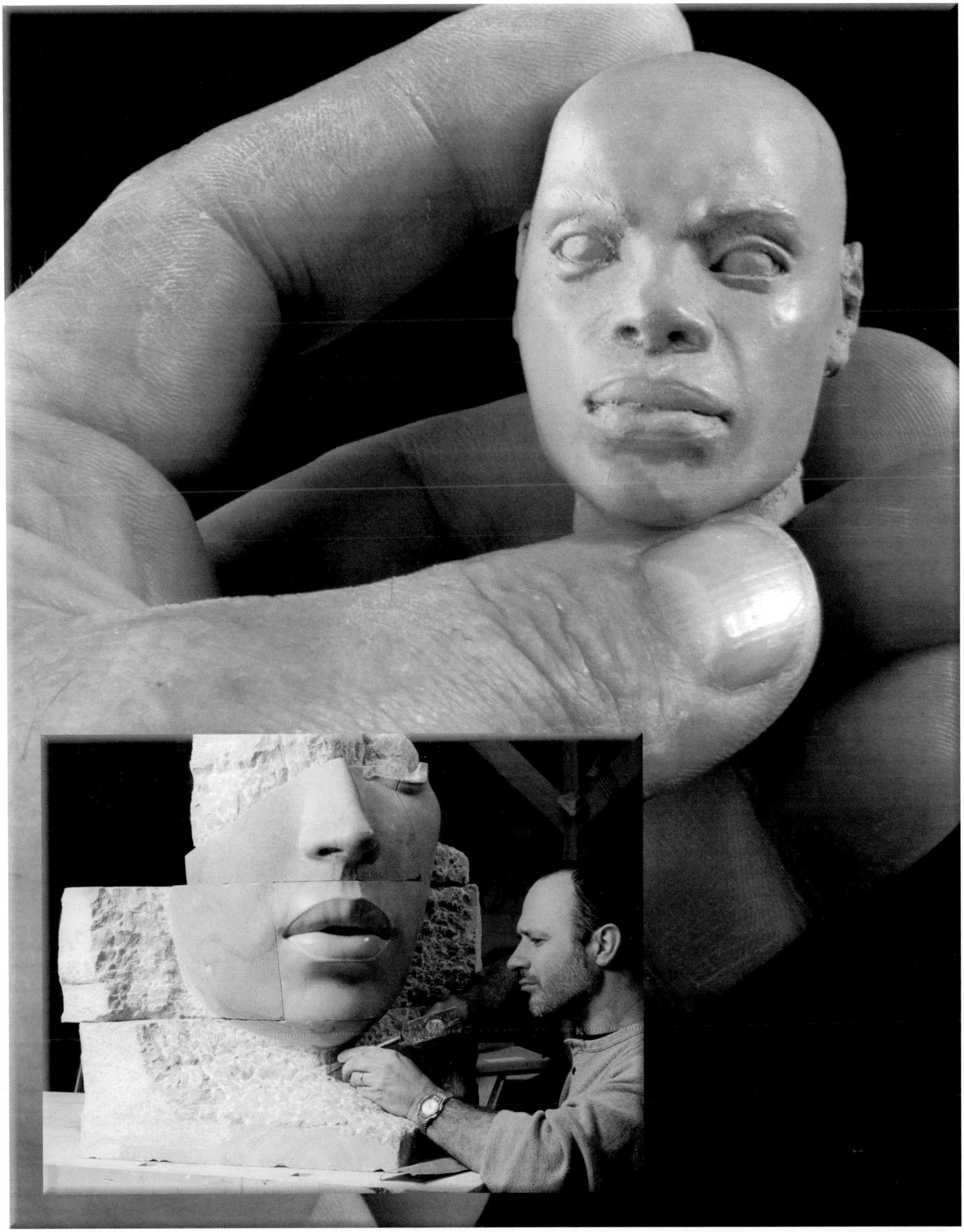

## CHRONOLOGY OF OPTIONAL MEDIA

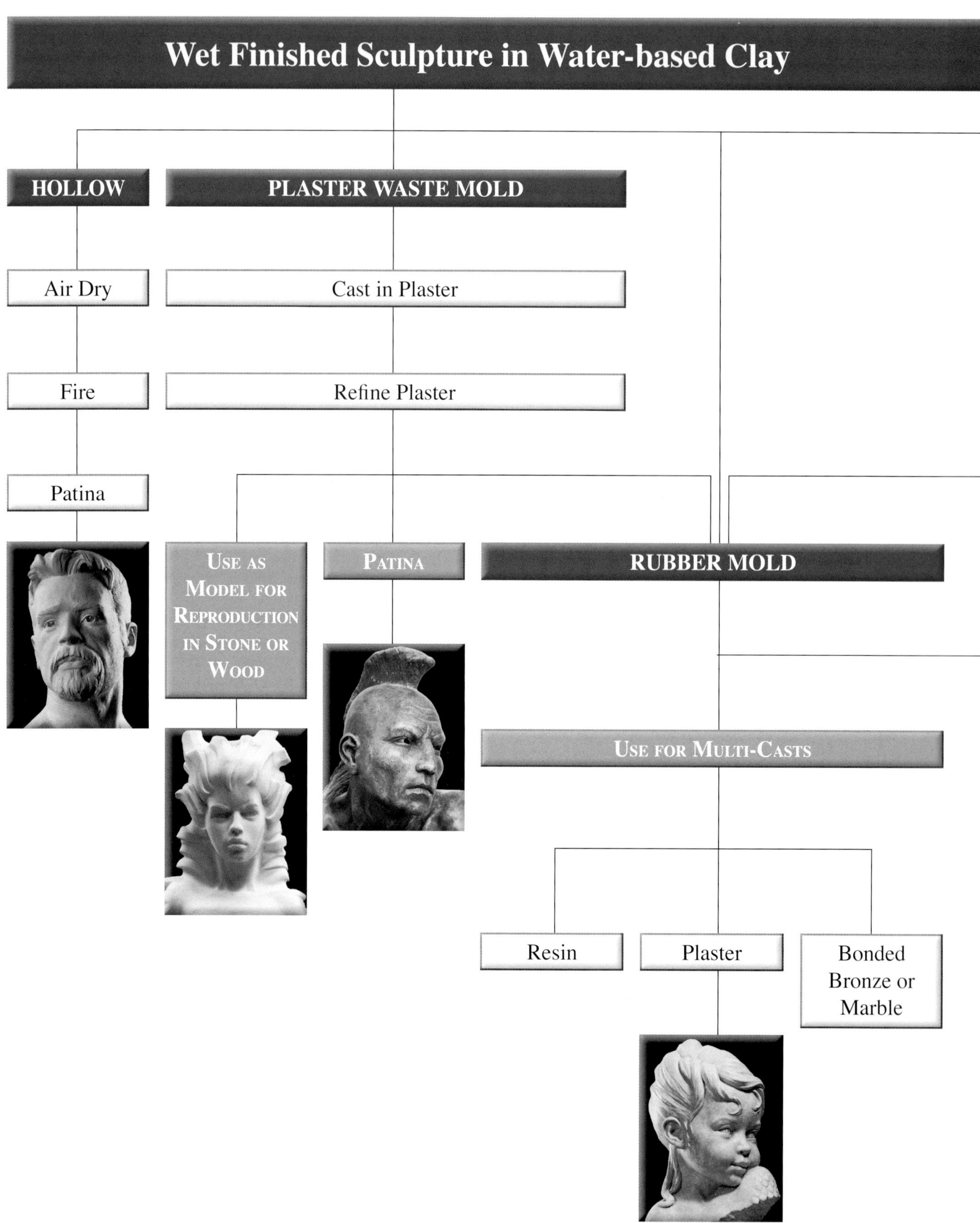

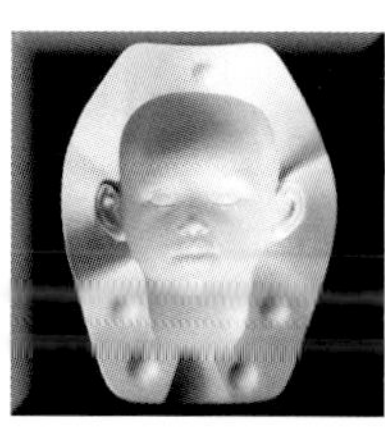

**ROUGH PLASTER MULTIPLE PART MOLD USED FOR REFINING**

Cast in
• *Hydrocal®* • *Wax* • *Ceramic* • *Porcelain*

Refine

**METAL MOLD FOR TOY PRODUCTION**

Vinyl or Plastic

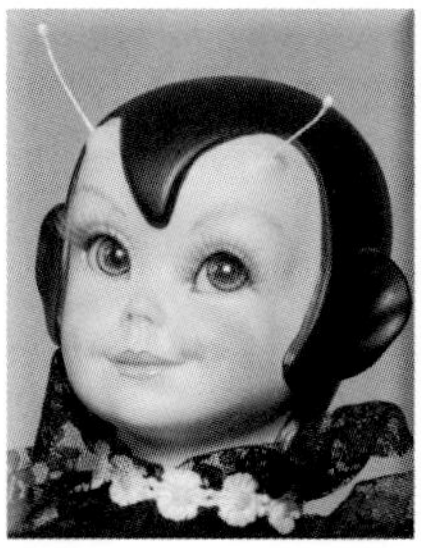

**PLASTER PRODUCTION MOLD**

Multiple Slip Cast

**Porcelain** — Fire — China Paint

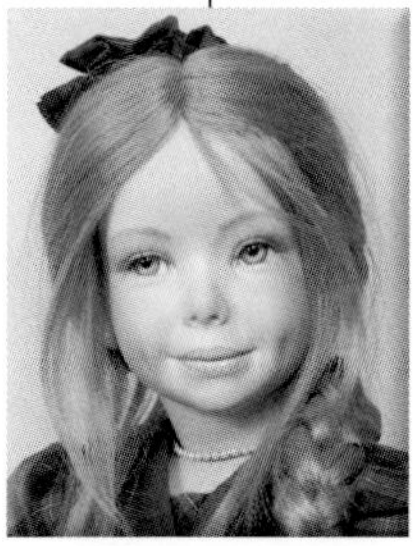

**Ceramic** — Fire — Glaze

**Composition** — Air Dry — Paint

**CAST IN FOUNDRY WAX**

Ceramic Shell

Bronze Casting

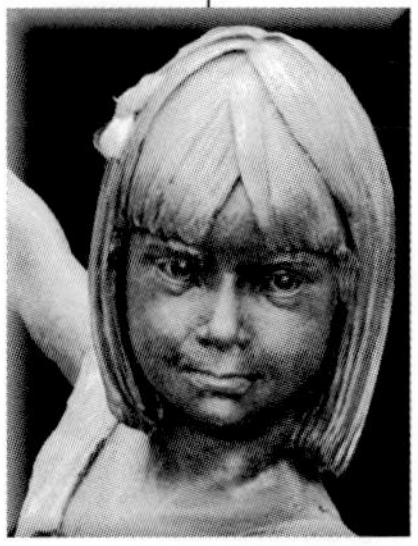

# ABOUT THE AUTHORS

Philippe Faraut received his degree in woodcarving and the construction of French fine furniture from Germain Sommeillier in Annecy, France, his boyhood home. An avid traveler, Philippe's destinations have allowed him the opportunity to study the cultures of many countries in Europe, Asia, Africa and the Caribbean, thus influencing his work in portraiture. After establishing residence in the Chesapeake Bay area of Virginia, he developed an interest in modeling the head in clay. Soon, thereafter, he began to teach sculpting, and it was at his first formal class that he met his future wife.

Charisse Scott Faraut born in Ithaca, New York graduated magna cum laude with a BFA from Syracuse University, majoring in illustration. Her photography and articles on porcelain designs have appeared in numerous trade magazines.

PCF Studios, Inc. was created in 1994 through which the couple combined their skills to develop sculpted prototypes for various industries, specialized sculpting tools, three-dimensional reference materials and an instructional sculpting video series.

Philippe and Charisse have created numerous original works ranging from six-inch porcelain figurines to monuments in both stone and bronze. Philippe has exhibited his sculptures in various galleries and national competitions including several of the National Sculpture Society's Annual Exhibitions shown in New York City and Brookgreen Gardens, South Carolina, as well as the American Portrait Society's Annual Exhibit in New York City. In addition, he has studied forensic reconstruction with internationally recognized expert Betty Pat Gatliff.

The couple has traveled throughout the United States and Canada, teaching sculptors and aspiring sculptors how to render portraits in clay at private studios and institutions such as the Longview Museum of Fine Art in Texas. Their Upstate New York studio, offering classes in portraiture and figure sculpting, was expanded in 2004 to accommodate Philippe's stone carving seminars.

---

## *Acknowledgements*

*Thank you to all the students who have attended Philippe's seminars since 1992. Volumes of insight have been gained by exploring your questions and searching for clear explanations.*

*Our gratitude to Richard McDermott Miller for allowing us the opportunity to reprint "Is it Genetic?", his essay on figurative sculpture.*

*Special thanks to Shaun Congdon, Clifford Leonard and John and Jeanine Scott for their contributions, and to our daughters Alexis and Madison for their hours of modeling.*

*To Kat Nichols and Charles Burdick, thank you for all of your technical assistance and for believing this project was a worthy endeavor.*

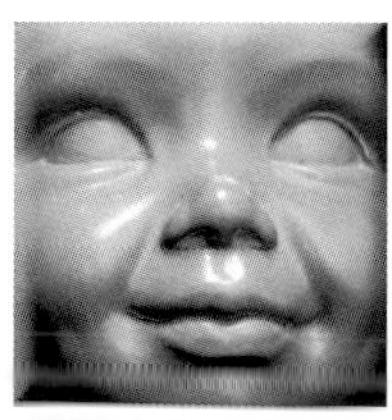

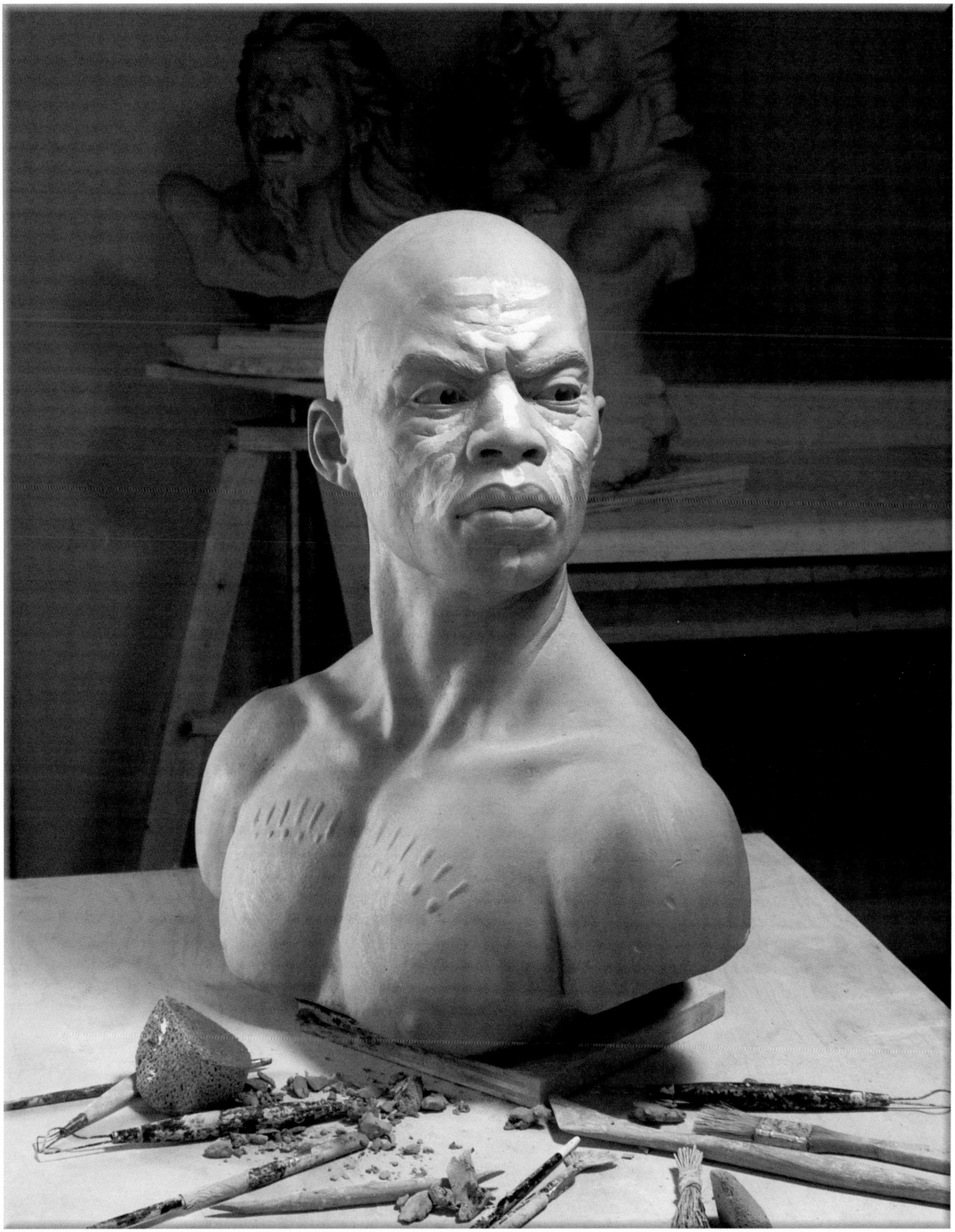

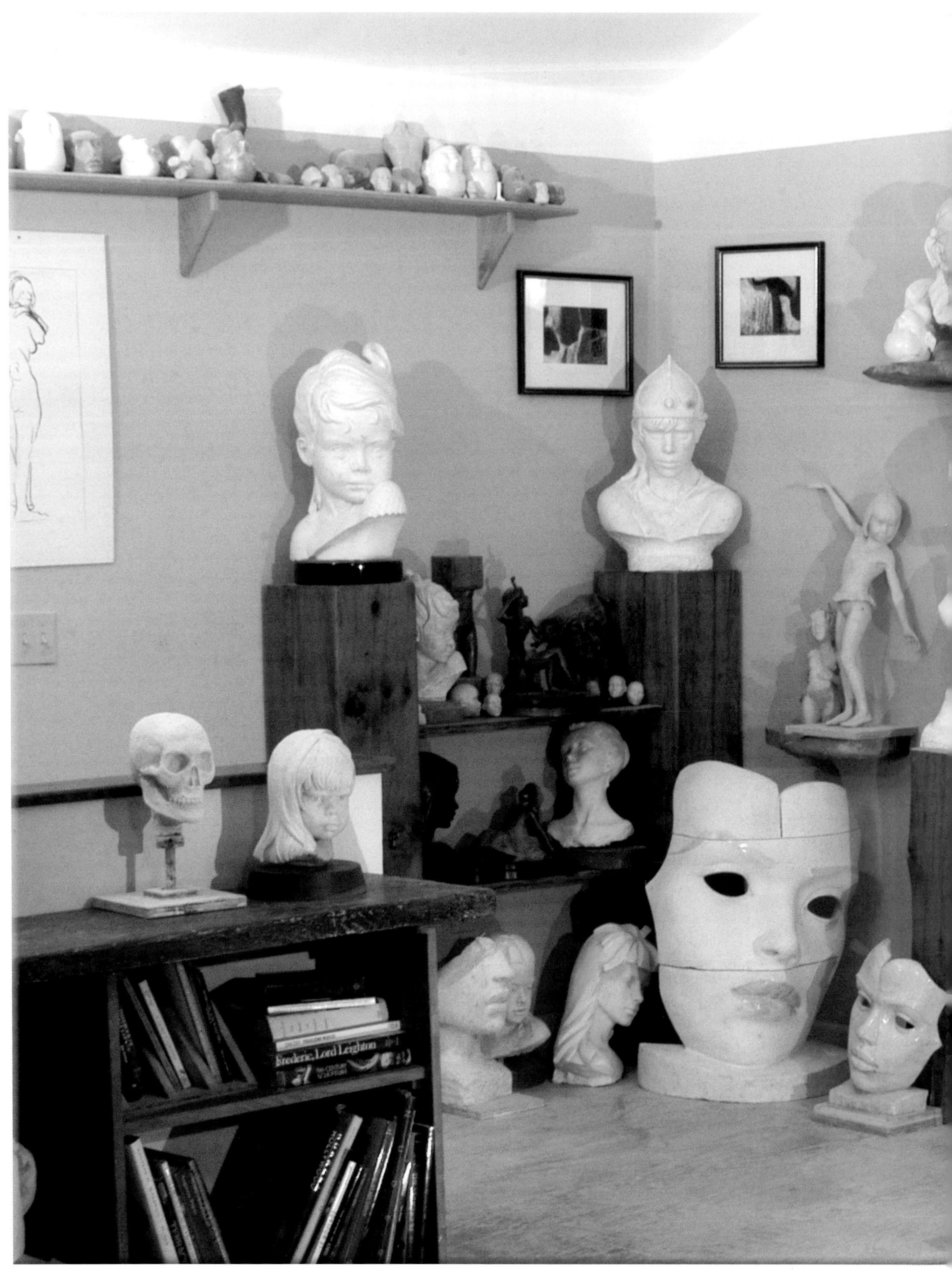
Frederic, Lord Leighton

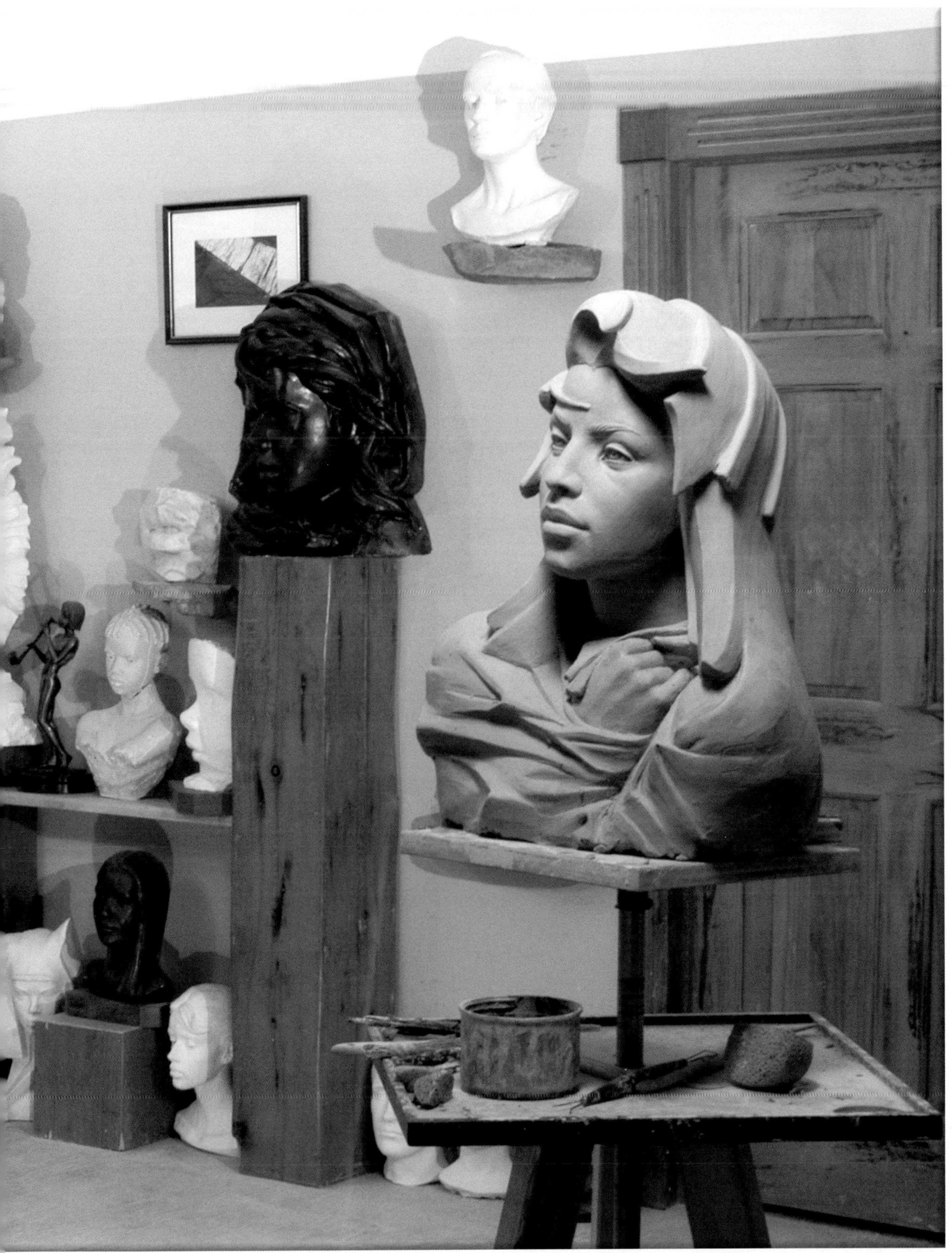

# Appendix A: Corner Photo Index

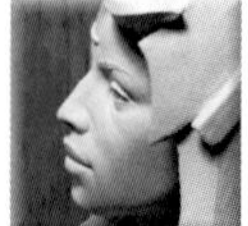
Page III
*Until Then*, detail, clay

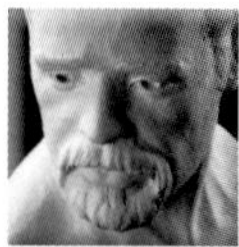
Page V
*Tim*, terracotta

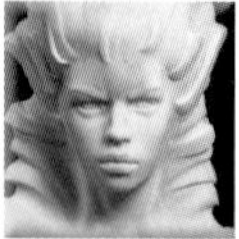
Page VII
*Winter Storm*, detail, marble

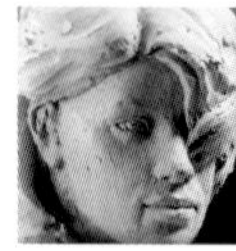
Page 3
*Wife and Other*, detail, clay

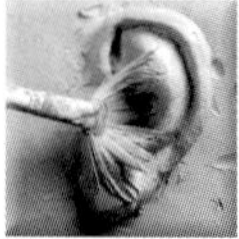
Page 5
*Ear*, clay

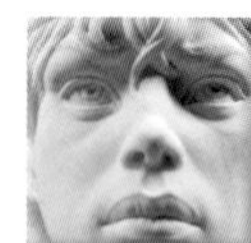
Page 7
*La Nuit des Temps*, detail, marble

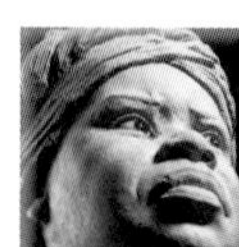
Page 9
*Connie*, detail, clay

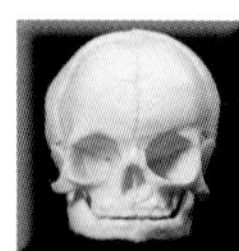
Page 13
*Fetal Skull*, resin by Anatomical Chart Co.

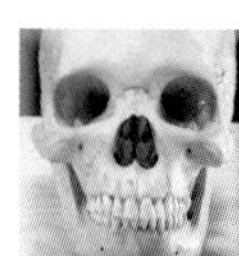
Page 15
*Female Skull*, bone

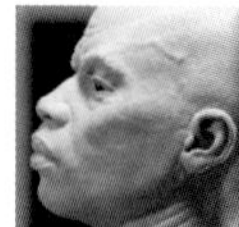
Page 17
*Study for Zimbabwe*, detail, clay

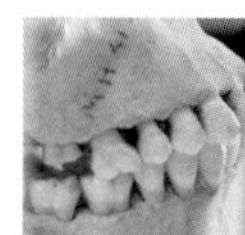
Page 19
*Profile of Teeth*, detail, bone

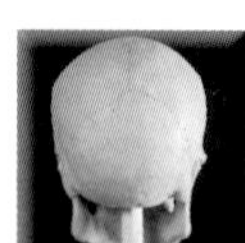
Page 21
*Skull from Back*, clay

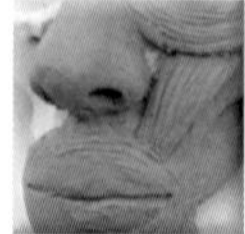
Page 23
*Forensic Reconstruction*, detail, clay

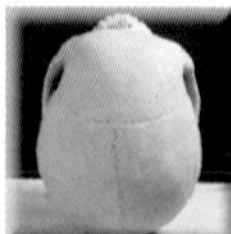
Page 25
*Skull from Above*, clay

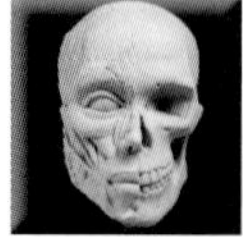
Page 27
*Skull with Muscles*, clay

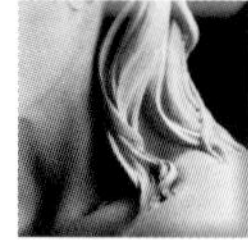
Page 29
*La Nuit des Temps*, detail, clay

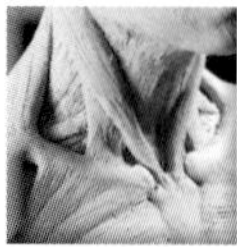
Page 31
*Neck Muscles of a Child*, detail, clay

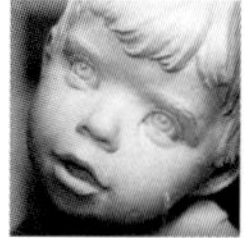
Page 33
*Waiting for Daddy*, detail, clay

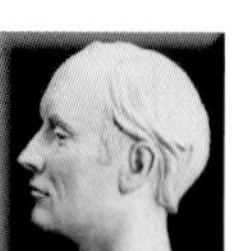
Page 35
*Jean François*, clay

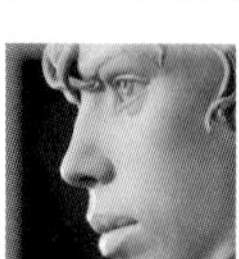
Page 39
*La Nuit des Temps*, detail, clay

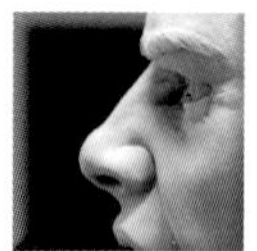
Page 41
*Mask of Rage*, detail, clay

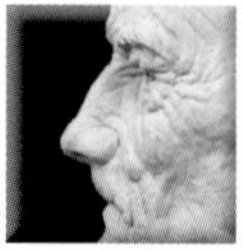
Page 43
*Mask of Antiquity*, detail, clay

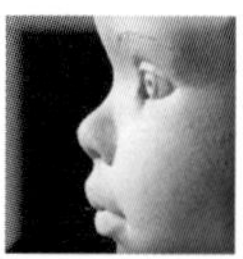
Page 45
*Mask of Infancy*, detail, clay

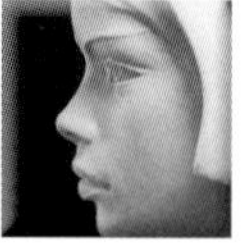
Page 47
*The Guardian*, detail, clay

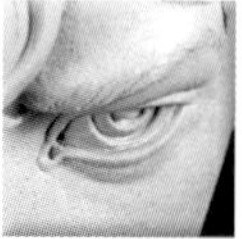
Page 49
*La Nuit des Temps*, detail, clay

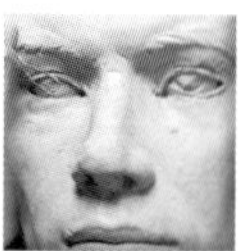
Page 51
*Detailing the Iris*, clay

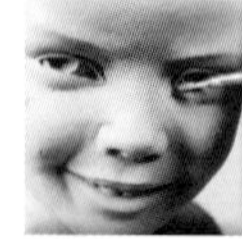
Page 53
*Neverland*, detailing the eye, clay

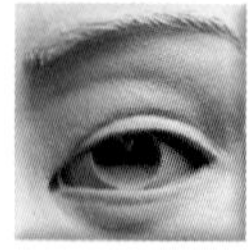
Page 55
*Asian Eye*, clay

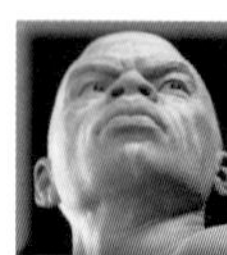
Page 57
*Zimbabwe*, detail, clay

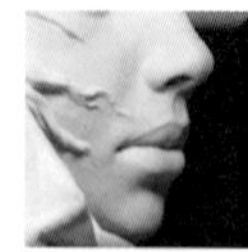
Page 59
*The Fisherman's Daughter*, detail, clay

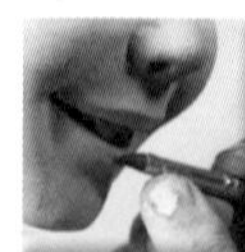
Page 61
*Neverland*, detailing the mouth, clay

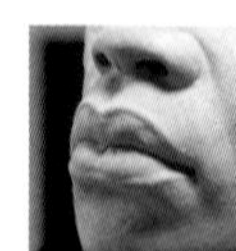
Page 63
*Zimbabwe*, detail, clay

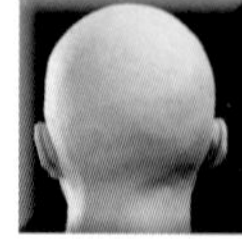
Page 65
*Zimbabwe*, detail, clay

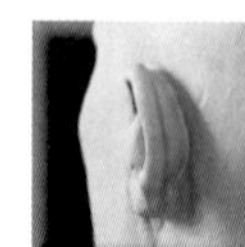
Page 67
*Zimbabwe*, detail, clay

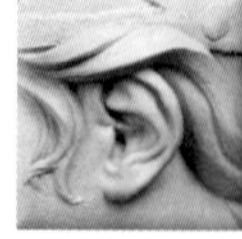
Page 69
*La Nuit des Temps*, detail, clay

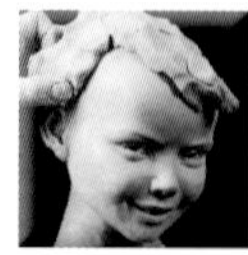
Page 71
*Neverland*, detailing the hair, clay

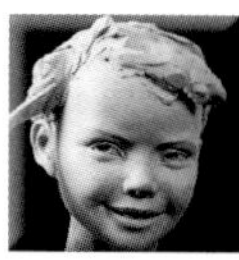
Page 73
*Neverland*, detailing the hair, clay

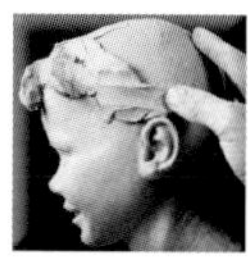
Page 75
*Neverland*, detailing the hair, clay

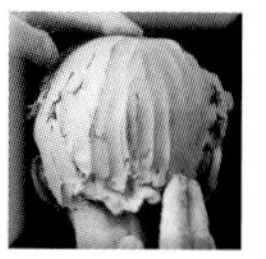
Page 77
*Neverland*, detailing the hair, clay

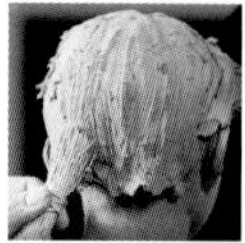
Page 79
*Neverland*, detailing the hair, clay

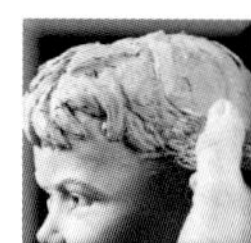
Page 81
*Neverland*, detailing the hair, clay

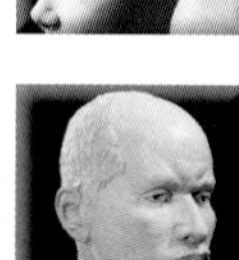
Page 83
*Leo*, detail, clay

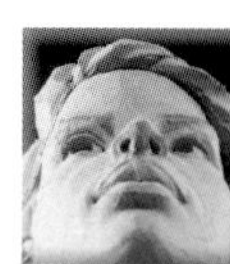
Page 87
*Study*, detail, clay

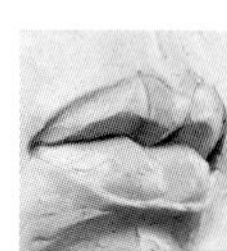
Page 89
*Planes of the Mouth*, clay

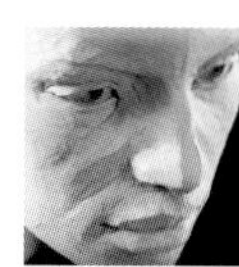
Page 91
*Study*, detail, clay

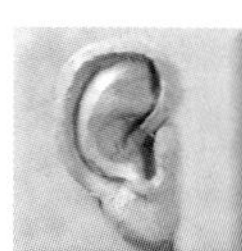
Page 93
*Planes of the Ear*, clay

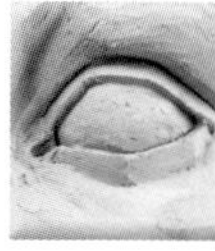
Page 95
*Planes of the Eye*, clay

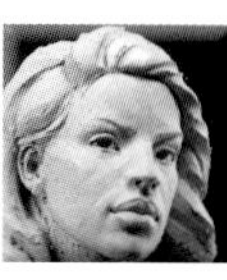
Page 97
*Study*, detail, clay

# Appendix B: Additional Titles

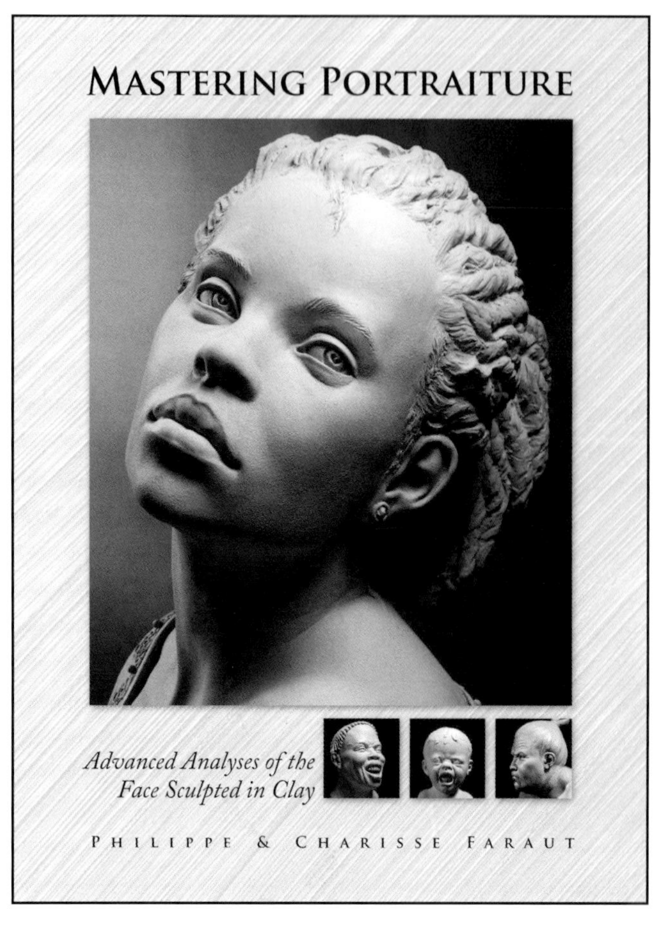


Hardcover book, 230 pages with 600 photographs.

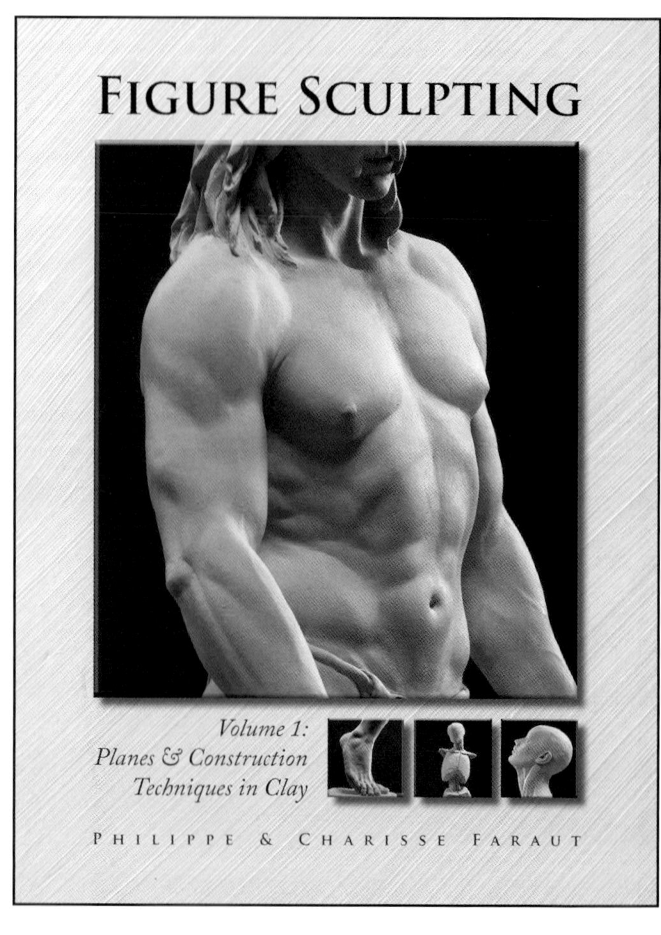


Hardcover book, 230 pages with 700 photographs.

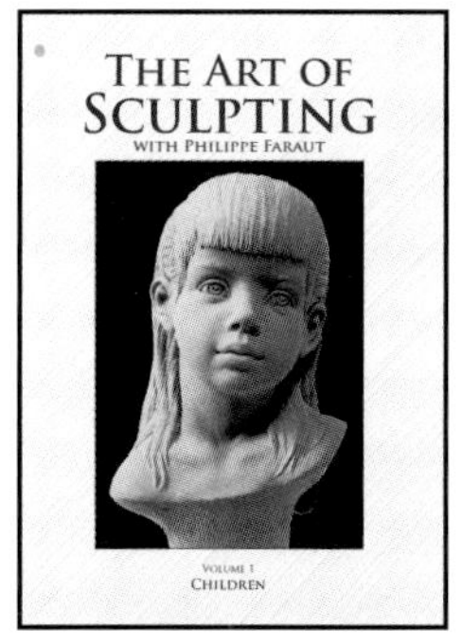


DVD, 89 minutes.

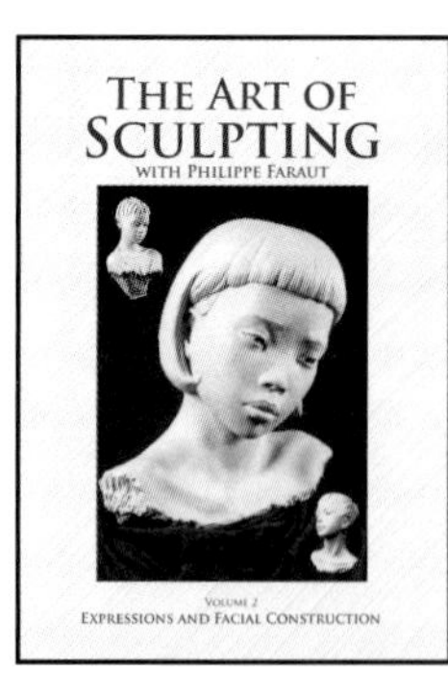


DVD, 110 minutes.

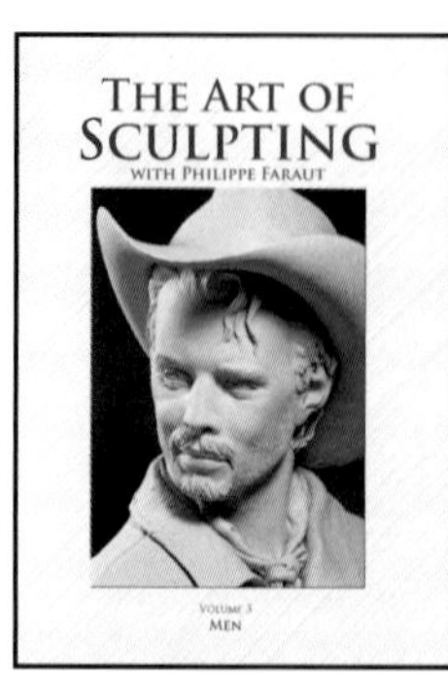


DVD, 111 minutes.

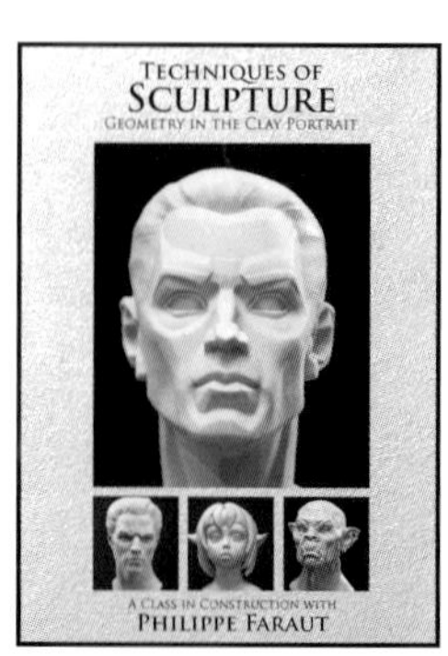


DVD, 83 minutes.

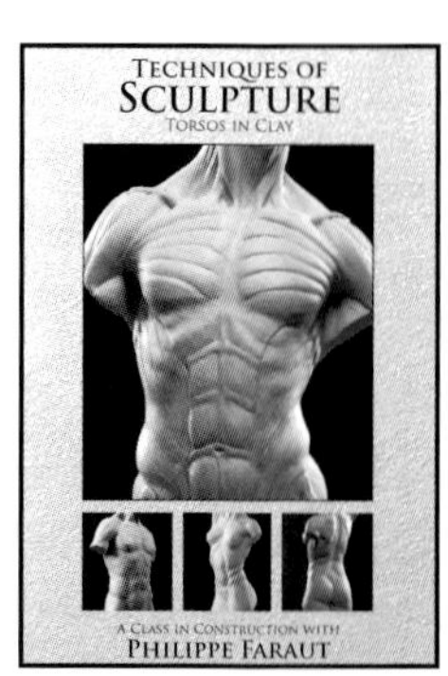


DVD, 89 minutes.

# Bibliography & Recommended Reading


Bates, Brian & John Cleese. *The Human Face.* Butler & Tanner Limited, London: 2001. ISBN: 0-7894-7836-6.

Baudry, Marie-Thérèse. *Sculpture: Méthode et Vocabulaire.* Editions du Patrimoine, Paris: 2000. ISBN: 2-85822-459-5.

Faigin, Gary. *The Artist's Complete Guide to Facial Expression.* Watson-Guptill Publications, New York: 1990. ISBN: 0-8230-1628-5.

Frith, Donald E. *Mold Making for Ceramics.* Chilton Book Company, Radnor, PA: 1985. ISBN: 0-8019-7359-7.

Goldfinger, Eliot. *Human Anatomy for Artists: The Elements of Form.* Oxford Univerity Press, New York: 1991. ISBN: 0-19-505260-4.

Gordon, Louise. *How to Draw the Human Head: Techniques and Anatomy.* Penguin Books, New York: 1983. ISBN: 014046560X.

Grubbs, Daisy. *Modeling a Likeness in Clay.* Watson-Guptill Publications, New York: 1982. ISBN: 0-8230-3094-6.

Hamm, Jack. *Drawing the Head and Figure.* Perigee, New York: 1983. ISBN: 0-399-50791-4

Hogarth, Burne. *Drawing the Human Head.* Watson-Guptill Publications, New York: 1989. ISBN: 0-8230-1376-6.

Langland, Tuck. *From Clay to Bronze: a studios guide to figurative sculpture.* Watson-Guptill Publications, New York: 1999. ISBN: 0-8230-0638-7.

Lanteri, Edouard. *Modelling and Sculpting the Human Figure.* Dover Publications, Inc., New York: 1985. ISBN: 0 486-25006-7.

Lucchesi, Bruno & Margit Malmstrom. *Modeling the Head in Clay.* Watson-Guptill Publications, New York: 1996. ISBN: 0-8230-3099-7.

Peck, Stephen Rogers. *Atlas of Human Anatomy for the Artist.* Oxford University Press, Inc., New York: 1982. ISBN: 0-19-503095-8.

Rich, Jack C. *The Materials and Methods of Sculpture.* Dover Publications, Inc., New York: 1988. ISBN: 0-486-25742-8.

Rubins, David K. *The Human Figure: An Antaomy for Artists.* Penguin Books, New York: 1976. ISBN: 0 14 11 4243 1.

Simblet, Sarah & John Davis. *Anatomy for the Artist.* DK Publishing, Inc., New York: 2001. ISBN: 0-7894-8045-X.

Taylor, Karen T. *Forensic Art and Illustration.* CRC Press, LLC., Boca Raton, FL: 2001. ISBN: 0-8493-8118-5.

Wittkower, Rudolf. *Bernini: The Sculptor of the Roman Baroque.* Phaidon Press Limited, London: 1997. ISBN: 0-7148-3715-6.

**Periodicals:**

*Sculptural Pursuit.* Hammer & Pen Productions, LLC., PO Box 262283, Highlands Ranch, CO 80163-2283. Tel: 303-738-9892. www.sculpturalpursuit.com. ISSN: 1541-7514.

*Sculpture Review.* National Sculpture Society, Inc., 237 Park Ave., New York, NY 10017. Tel: 212-764-5645. Fax: 212-764-5651. www.sculpturereview.com. ISSN: 0747-5284.

# Glossary

**air dry:** leaving a sculpture to dry naturally

**armature:** a frame or rod used by sculptors to support work being modeled in clay

**barrel of the mouth:** rounded volume between the nose and chin caused by the curvature of the maxilla and mandible

**bone dry:** very dry

**bronze:** an alloy of copper and tin

**calipers:** an instrument consisting of two jaws used to measure the distance between two points

**carving:** work produced by an engraver or sculptor

**cast:** an impression taken from a mold

**casting:** reproducing from a mold

**china painting:** painting on porcelain that requires firing to become permanent

**concave:** hollow as the inside of a bowl

**convex:** curved like the exterior of a sphere

**earthenware clay:** clay that when fired at low heat remains slightly porous

**foundry:** an establishment that casts artwork in metal

**grog:** fired clay that has been crushed and added to raw clay to reduce shrinkage during firing

**hemp:** fibers from hemp available through rope manufacturers

**Hydrocal®:** a US Gypsum type of plaster with high compressive strength

**keys:** locking devices used on the joining surfaces of a mold to ensure correct alignment

**kiln:** a oven used to fire clay or ceramic

**lateral:** away from the middle, extending toward the side

**leather hard:** having the consistency of leather

**maquette:** from the French word meaning small model

**medial:** toward the middle

**modeling:** shaping out of a material such as clay

**mold:** a cavity in which a substance is shaped

**mother mold:** a shell created out of rigid material to prevent distortion that houses a flexible mold

**multicast:** refers to a number of castings pulled from the same mold

**oil-based clay:** a modeling compound consisting of clay, oil and wax that never dries

**ossification:** formation of bone

**pantograph:** an instrument used for copying to a specific scale

**parting line:** the line created at the separation of two parts of a mold

**patina:** the final coloring of a sculpture

**pegmatite rock:** a coarse type of granite found in veins

**planes, curvilinear:** surfaces where all points lie in the same plane bounded by curved lines

**plaster:** a powdery substance composed of calcium sulfate

**porcelain clay:** a highly refined and very plastic modeling material that is white when fired

**pottery plaster:** plaster used primarily in the production of molds

**raw clay:** unfired clay

**resin:** a liquid casting material that hardens by chemical reaction

**sculpting:** the act of carving or modeling

**sculpture:** a three dimensional piece of art

**shims:** temporary, thin walls created between various parts of a mold during the mold making process

**slip:** liquid clay

**slip casting:** the process of pouring slip into a plaster mold and draining, leaving only a thin layer

**slurry:** a suspension of clay in water

**stoneware:** clay that vitrifies when fired at high heat

**terracotta:** fired clay

**undercut:** any overhanging portion of a sculpture that prevents the mold from pulling off

**vitrification:** the process of converting to a glassy substance by heat and fusion

**waste mold:** a plaster mold, used only once, that needs to be destroyed in order to free a cast

**water-based clay:** a modeling compound consisting of clay and water

# Index

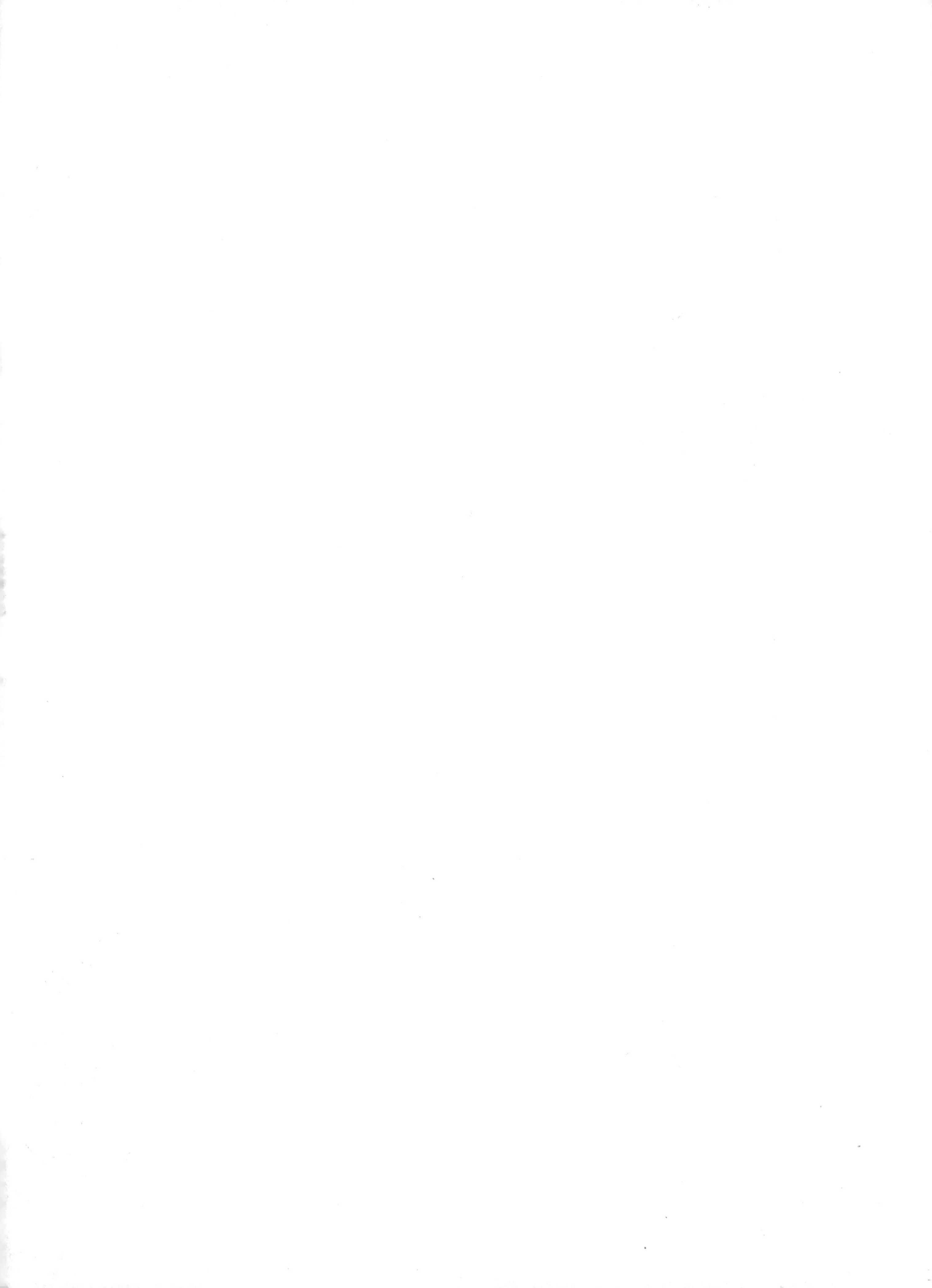